CRIMINAL JUSTICE POLICY:
ORIGINS AND EFFECTIVENESS

CRIMINAL JUSTICE POLICY

ORIGINS AND EFFECTIVENESS

Jacinta M. Gau

UNIVERSITY OF CENTRAL FLORIDA

NEW YORK   OXFORD

OXFORD UNIVERSITY PRESS

Oxford University Press is a department of the University of Oxford.
It furthers the University's objective of excellence in research, scholarship,
and education by publishing worldwide. Oxford is a registered trade mark of
Oxford University Press in the UK and certain other countries.

Published in the United States of America by Oxford University Press
198 Madison Avenue, New York, NY 10016, United States of America.

Library of Congress Cataloging-in-Publication Data

Names: Gau, Jacinta M., 1982– author.
Title: Criminal justice policy: origins and effectiveness / Jacinta Gau,
    University of Central Florida.
Description: First Edition. | New York: Oxford University Press, [2018]
Identifiers: LCCN 2017036140 (print) | LCCN 2017037980 (ebook) |
    ISBN 9780190859442 (ebook) | ISBN 9780190210939 (pbk.) |
    ISBN 9780190859718 (looseleaf)
Subjects: LCSH: Criminal justice, Administration of. | Crime. | Criminal law.
Classification: LCC HV7419 (ebook) | LCC HV7419 .G38 2018 (print) |
    DDC 364—dc23
LC record available at https://lccn.loc.gov/2017036140

9 8 7 6 5 4 3 2 1
Printed by Sheridan Books, Inc., United States of America.

BRIEF CONTENTS

CHAPTER 1:   Introduction   *1*

CHAPTER 2:   Deterrence and Incapacitation   *8*

CHAPTER 3:   Drug Policy   *18*

CHAPTER 4:   Sex-Offender Policy   *39*

CHAPTER 5:   Gang Policy   *57*

CHAPTER 6:   Juvenile Justice   *75*

CHAPTER 7:   Gun Policy   *96*

CHAPTER 8:   Mass Incarceration   *114*

CHAPTER 9:   The Death Penalty   *130*

CHAPTER 10:   Intermediate Sanctions   *148*

CHAPTER 11:   White-Collar Offending   *167*

CHAPTER 12:   Human Trafficking   *186*

CHAPTER 13:   Police Policy   *205*

CHAPTER 14:   Correctional Treatment and Rehabilitation   *224*

CHAPTER 15:   New Horizons: The Promise of Community-Based Crime Control   *242*

CONTENTS

PREFACE *xiii*

ACKNOWLEDGMENTS *xv*

CHAPTER 1   **Introduction**   *1*

Analytical Lens   *3*

Premise: Crime and Criminal-Justice Policy Are Driven by Political, Social, and Economic Factors   *5*

Premise: Policies Should Be Critically Analyzed on the Basis of Logic and Theory   *5*

Premise: Empirical Evidence Is the Best Policy Guide   *6*

CHAPTER 2   **Deterrence and Incapacitation**   *8*

Introduction   *8*

Retribution and Rehabilitation   *9*

Assumptions and Empirical Tests of Deterrence Theory   *10*

Assumptions and Empirical Tests of Incapacitation Theory   *13*

Policy Implications   *16*

Conclusion   *16*

Discussion Questions   *17*

CHAPTER 3   **Drug Policy**   *18*

Introduction   *18*

A Brief History of Drug Trends   *19*

Legal and Political Origins of Federal Drug Laws and Policies   *20*

Drug Laws and Policies   *21*

Before the War on Drugs: Early Laws   *21*

The War on Drugs   *24*

Drug Courts   *25*

Decriminalization and Legalization   *26*

Prescription Drugs   *27*

Examining the Rationales   *28*

Deterrence   *28*

Incapacitation   *30*

Prevention and Treatment   *31*

The Empirical Status of Drug Policy   *32*

The War on Drugs   *32*

Drug Courts   *34*

Prevention Programs   *35*

Efforts to Reduce Prescription-Pill Abuse   *36*

Conclusion   *36*

Discussion Questions   *37*

CHAPTER **4**   **Sex-Offender Policy**   *39*

Introduction   *39*

History of Sex-Offender Laws and Policies   *40*

Examining the Rationales   *42*

The Assumption that Sex Offenders Are "Sick"   *43*

The Assumption that Sex Offenders Will Reoffend   *43*

The Assumption that the Sex-Offender Label Is Accurate   *44*

Shaming and Deterrence (SORN)   *46*

Geographic Proximity (Residency Restrictions)   *47*

Treatment and Incapacitation (Civil Commitment)   *48*

The Empirical Status of Sex-Offender Policies   *49*

Registration and Notification   *49*

Residency Restrictions   *50*

Civil Commitment   *51*

Collateral Consequences   *52*

Alternative SO Policies   *53*

Conclusion   *54*

Discussion Questions   *55*

CHAPTER **5**   **Gang Policy**   *57*

Introduction   *57*

Theoretical Explanations for Gang Membership and Activity   *58*

Individual-Level Predictors of Gang Involvement and Desistance   *58*

Macrolevel and Microlevel Explanations for Gang Behavior   *59*

Enhancement: The Criminogenic Properties of Gangs   *60*

The Roles of Violence and Drugs in Gang Operations   *61*

Gang Structure, Organization, and Rivalries   *62*

Gang Policies   *63*

Examining the Rationales   *65*

Prevention   *65*

Intervention   *66*

Suppression   *68*

The Empirical Status of Modern Gang Policy   *70*

Conclusion   *73*

Discussion Questions   *74*

CHAPTER **6**   **Juvenile Justice**   *75*

Introduction   *75*

History and Origins of the Juvenile System   *76*

Definitions and Overview of Juvenile-Court Procedures   *79*

Disproportionate Minority Contact   *80*

Juvenile-Justice Policies   *81*

Curfews   *82*

Diversion   *82*

Waivers   *83*

Teen Courts and Status-Offender Programs   *84*

Out-of-Home Placement   *85*

Examining the Rationales   *86*

Curfews: Prevention   *86*

Treatment and Rehabilitation   *87*

Status Offenses: Child Saving   *88*

The Empirical Status of Juvenile-Justice Policies   *89*

Curfews   *89*

Diversion   *89*

Waivers   *90*

Teen Courts and Status-Offender Programs   *91*

Out-of-Home Placement   *93*

Conclusion   *93*

Discussion Questions   *94*

CHAPTER **7**   **Gun Policy**   *96*

Introduction   *96*

Gun Policy and the Constitution   *97*

Primary and Secondary Gun Markets *98*

Gun Policies *98*

Efforts to Make Guns Unavailable to High-Risk Individuals *99*

Assault Weapons Bans *101*

Firearm Sentence Enhancements *102*

Concealed Carry and Gun Buybacks *102*

Examining the Rationales *103*

Efforts to Make Guns Unavailable to High-Risk Individuals *103*

Assault Weapons Bans *105*

Firearm Sentence Enhancements *106*

Concealed Carry and Gun Buybacks *107*

The Empirical Status of Modern Gun Policy *108*

Efforts to Make Guns Unavailable to High-Risk Individuals *108*

Assault Weapons Bans *110*

Firearm Sentence Enhancements *110*

Concealed Carry and Gun Buybacks *111*

Conclusion *112*

Discussion Questions *112*

CHAPTER **8**   **Mass Incarceration**   *114*

Introduction *114*

Historical Trends in Incarceration *115*

Contemporary Incarceration Trends *118*

Examining the Rationales *121*

Deterrence *121*

Incapacitation *123*

Rehabilitation *125*

The Empirical Status of Mass Incarceration *125*

Conclusion *128*

Discussion Questions *129*

CHAPTER **9**   **The Death Penalty**   *130*

Introduction *130*

History and Origins of the Death Penalty *131*

Historical Trends in Capital Punishment in the West *131*

The Death Penalty in the United States *132*

The Legal Development of Capital Punishment in the United States *133*

Controversies in Death-Penalty Policy *134*

Racial and Gender Disparities *135*

Wrongful Convictions *136*

Judicial Elections   *138*

The Brutalization Hypothesis   *139*

Examining the Rationales   *139*

Deterrence   *139*

Public Opinion   *142*

The Empirical Status of the Death Penalty   *143*

Conclusion   *145*

Discussion Questions   *146*

CHAPTER 10   **Intermediate Sanctions**   *148*

Introduction   *148*

Origins and Types of Intermediate Sanctions   *149*

Politics and Public Opinion   *153*

Examining the Rationales   *154*

Cost-Effectiveness   *155*

Interchangeability and the Principle of
Rough Equivalence   *157*

The Empirical Status of Intermediate Sanctions   *158*

Conclusion   *165*

Discussion Questions   *165*

CHAPTER 11   **White-Collar Offending**   *167*

Introduction   *167*

What Is White-Collar Offending?   *169*

History of White-Collar Offending Laws and Policies   *170*

Examining the Rationales   *174*

Compliance   *175*

Deterrence   *176*

**Theories of White-Collar Offending: Implications for Law and
Policy**   *179*

Conclusion   *183*

Discussion Questions   *184*

CHAPTER 12   **Human Trafficking**   *186*

Introduction   *186*

Defining Human Trafficking and the Role of Consent   *187*

Trafficking Prevalence and Victims   *188*

Is Human Trafficking a Form of Organized Crime?   *189*

Human-Trafficking Policies and Their Origins *190*

Examining the Rationales *193*

The Criminal-Justice Response: Punishing the Traffickers *194*

The Human-Rights Response: Preventing Trafficking *195*

Unilateral Sanctions versus International Collaboration *196*

The Empirical Status of Human-Trafficking Policies *197*

The TVPA and the U.S. Role in International Policies *198*

Domestic Policies in the United States *198*

Future Directions for Human-Trafficking Policies *199*

Improving Labor-Migration and Human-Rights Laws *199*

Smart Use of Economic Sanctions *201*

Domestic Law-Enforcement Activities *201*

Conclusion *202*

Discussion Questions *203*

CHAPTER **13** **Police Policy** *205*

Introduction *205*

A Brief History of Policing in the United States *205*

Contemporary Police Policies and Their Origins *209*

Order-Maintenance Policing *209*

Problem-Oriented Policing *210*

Community Policing *211*

Data-Driven Policing *212*

Examining the Rationales *215*

Offender-Based Deterrence *215*

The Broken Windows Thesis *215*

Place-Based and Problem-Based Prevention *216*

Citizen and Community Involvement *218*

The Empirical Status of Police Policies *218*

Order-Maintenance Policing *219*

Problem-Oriented Policing *219*

Community Policing *220*

Data-Driven Policing *221*

Conclusion *222*

Discussion Questions *223*

CHAPTER **14** **Correctional Treatment and Rehabilitation** *224*

Introduction *224*

Mental Illness and Substance Abuse Among Criminal Offenders *225*

History of Correctional Treatment and Rehabilitation *227*

Current Trends in Correctional Treatment and Rehabilitation *228*

Rehabilitation Techniques and Programs *229*

Examining the Rationale *233*

    Rehabilitation and Ethical Justifications for Criminal Punishment *233*

    The Principles of Effective Correctional Rehabilitation *234*

The Empirical Status of Correctional Treatment and Rehabilitation *235*

Conclusion *240*

Discussion Questions *241*

CHAPTER **15** **New Horizons:**
The Promise of Community-Based
Crime Control *242*

Introduction *242*

Hard Lessons: How the Punishment-Oriented System Is Backfiring *243*

The Theoretical Origins of Community-Based Control *244*

The Theoretical Origins of Place-Based Crime Prevention *245*

Tying It together: Communities as Places *246*

Reducing Fear of Crime *248*

Promoting Cohesion, Informal Control, and Quality of Life *249*

Police–Community Collaboration *250*

Community Courts *252*

Restorative Justice and Victim-Centered Approaches *252*

Enlisting Local Leaders, Groups, and Nonprofits *254*

Adjusting the Ideology: Applications from Public Health *255*

Conclusion *256*

Discussion Questions *257*

REFERENCES *259*
INDEX *310*

PREFACE

The inspiration for this book arose from my deepening frustration with pervasive misunderstandings about the criminal-justice system and the multitude of policies that combine to form that system. In particular, there is a widespread misconception that the policies and institutions created to prevent, reduce, and control crime flow directly (and logically) from crime. Popular support for existing policies rests partially on a presumption that state and federal laws, agency rules, and organizational goals are products of accurate information about crime and the people who commit it.

This turns out to be an overly simple view, and one that instills a perilous complacency in its adherents. "Perilous" because current policies contain flaws (some of them severe) that limit their effectiveness at protecting the public and can even increase victimization risks and the probability that people who have committed crime in the past will reoffend. Policies also frequently run afoul of principles of social justice. If the criminal-justice system cannot always be expected to make people's lives better, at a minimum it should not make them worse. In this, too, present policies prove inadequate.

The criminal-justice system and its constituent policies are largely the province of politicians and practitioners. Scholarly research and the academics who produce it are consulted little, if at all, in the development and implementation of new laws and policies. Although signs point optimistically toward a greater collaboration between scholars and practitioners in localized endeavors, the divide remains strongly ingrained, especially at the legislative level. Partisan and electoral politics cloud the legislative process. Intellectuals are all too often mocked rather than deferred to. Reasoned deliberation gives way to rhetoric, and complex social problems are stripped down to vacuous catchphrases. The democratic process is undermined. This intellectually compromised approach to public policy is all too evident in the criminal-justice system, where fear and emotion eclipse rational dialogue and preclude the development of evidence-based policies and practices.

My goal in this book is twofold. First, I intend to demonstrate the contextual nature of criminal-justice and crime policies. To accomplish this, I situate policies intended to control crime and punish wrongdoers within their histories. No policy sprang from nothing;

each has an origin. Each policy covered in this book is traced back to its source (or sources) and described as an outgrowth of its subtext. Second, I endeavor to provide a comprehensive depiction of the empirical status of each policy. For this, I evaluate policies' effectiveness using the best available evidence. At times, the evidence is strong. At other times, it is modest, weak, or virtually nonexistent. A few chapters dispense with the evaluation effort entirely and instead pursue a discourse in promising policy options that merit attention.

I did not set out to write a book critiquing the system. My initial plan was to simply summarize the evidence. As I dug deeper into each policy, however, I realized than an antiseptic summary would not suffice. Many modern policies have controversial origins. Most have weaknesses, and a few are deeply problematic. Although some empirical evaluations reveal support for existing policies, on balance the evidence is discouraging.

The theoretical, historical, and empirical literature led me to the conviction that a "neutral" approach would inevitably constitute a fictionalized one. There is no way to be neutral when confronted with such profound, influential subject matter as the criminal-justice system. I dabbled in journalism in college, and as I wrote this book the wise words of my former professor sounded in my mind: "You do not have to be objective. You just have to be fair." Objectivity commonly requires artificially elevating the weaker side of a debate in order to generate the illusion of empirical, logical, or moral equivalence with the stronger side. Fairness, by contrast, allows the evaluator to admit that one side wins out over the other or that there is no clear winner at all. Fairness is the process of allotting each side its due consideration and then making an honest assessment after the evidence has been tallied.

This book represents a fair assessment of each policy. I do not ignore evidence that contradicts some preconceived vantage point, nor do I defend any perspective that lacks empirical or theoretical substance. I hope this book both informs readers and incites them to think critically about current policies and promising alternatives. An informed public is powerful and will be the force taking the criminal-justice system into a brighter future.

Jacinta M. Gau, Ph.D.
November 2017

ACKNOWLEDGMENTS

The writing and production of this book was a team effort and I owe debts of gratitude. Steve Helba and Larissa Albright of Oxford University Press provided stellar editorial guidance. Several people offered insightful feedback that significantly improved the quality of many chapters. My colleagues Drs. William Moreto, Eugene Paoline, Kristina Childs, and Jennifer Peck graciously agreed to examine some chapters. I would like to thank the following reviewers for their feedback throughout the development of the manuscript: Robert Bing, University of Texas at Arlington; Sriram Chintakrindi, California State University, Stanislaus; James Dunn, Bucks New University; David M. Jones, University of Wisconsin, Oshkosh; Marcus-Antonio Galeste, Arizona State University; Tim Goddard, Florida International University; Lori Guevara, Fayetteville State University; Jeremy Olson, Seton Hill University; Kent H. Schafer, Ohio State University; SaRita Stewart, Cedar Valley College; Christine Tartaro, The Richard Stockton College of New Jersey; Mark Winton, University of Central Florida; Jennifer Wynn, CUNY: LaGuardia Community College/John Jay College of Criminal Justice; Yue Zhuo, St. John's University. Finally, I received important research assistance from students Lucas Alward, Devin Cowan, Frances Abderhalden, and Sherah Basham. All these individuals helped make this book happen. Any errors, of course, remain my own.

CHAPTER 1

INTRODUCTION

Policy can be hard to define with precision. The *Oxford English Dictionary* (OED) states that policy is "a course or principle of action adopted or proposed by a government, party, business, or individual." With respect to *public policy*, the OED offers "the principles, often unwritten, upon which social laws are based." Policy is a convergence of legislation, constitutional law, administrative goals and needs, and the organizational factors that shape the discretionary decision making of line-level personnel.

Policy is not the same as law, although the two can often be difficult to disentangle when discussing governmental actions and both are intertwined throughout this book. Law typically forms the basis for policy, but requires interpretation and implementation. Legislatures enact statutes detailing the actions they want public agencies and actors to start (or stop) doing, but statutes are merely words on paper until the people running these agencies breathe life into them by translating them into action. Legislation is the *what*, but it lacks a *how* element. Legislation is often vague in places, sometimes out of legislative error and sometimes because of intent; lawmakers know they must leave room for discretion in the implementation or application of laws. Legislators cannot anticipate all the questions and challenges that will arise during the process of turning written words into policy. Because law is a blunt instrument, agency personnel must make decisions about how to act in ambiguous circumstances. They must try to interpret the intent of the law. Additionally, they have to figure out how to make the law compatible with their organizational structure, function, capability, and needs.

Courts also make law and shape policy. State courts strike down, uphold, or reinterpret statutes enacted by their respective state legislatures, and federal courts do the same with laws passed by Congress. The United States Supreme Court, in particular, possesses immense power to invalidate state and federal legislation that, in the justices' eyes, run afoul of the U.S. Constitution or its amendments. Courts are passive agents, in that they cannot issue rulings about the constitutionality of any law until a case challenging it comes before them; once such a challenge has been brought, though, courts can be forces for sweeping change.

Upon issuance of law or a court ruling with significant implications for public policy, agency actors come into play. While this book does not include a discussion of how agencies shape policy implementation—that is a subject upon which entire books are devoted—readers should be aware of the bureaucracy and discretionary decision making that exist behind the scenes. Public agencies are arranged bureaucratically, which means higher-ranking authorities develop rules and procedures governing lower-ranking employees' job duties. These lower-ranking employees are the public face of the agency; they have the least amount of formal authority, but they often possess a great degree of discretionary latitude. Police officers, parole and probation officers, social workers, and others who work in the field directly interfacing with members of the public are frequently placed in situations in which they can choose from multiple courses of action.

Often, these situations are of a low-visibility nature. A police officer who encounters a juvenile out after curfew or a probation officer who learns that a client has missed a required counseling session, for instance, can opt to make an arrest or issue a warning. These officers" choices may have tremendous consequences for that youth or probationer. Street-level discretion arises from the nature of public-service bureaucracies. Similar to the ways in which laws say *what* but not *how*, bureaucratic rules and regulations tell employees what to do and not to do, but these rules and regulations cannot proactively tell them what (not) to do in the multitude of situations they will face as they carry out their jobs. There are also actors in the justice system, such as prosecutors, who are explicitly vested with broad decision-making power. The purpose of this latitude is to ensure that the application of the criminal law is fair and comports with abstract principles of justice.

Every socially beneficial use of discretion carries the potential for misuse and abuse. The same authority permitting officers and prosecutors to decline to take formal action against minor lawbreaking out of compassion for people who make small mistakes likewise allows them to afford preferential treatment to certain groups (such as whites or those of the middle and upper classes) and to distribute disproportionately punitive responses to others (such as people of color and those in the lower classes). Discretionary decision making is referenced in several chapters, but even where it is not, the reader should recognize that it is frequently happening in the background and may materially impact policy outcomes.

The objects of analysis in this book are *crime policy* and *criminal-justice policy.* Crime policy focuses on proposed methods for reducing certain types of crimes. Gun policy and efforts to curtail recidivism among sex offenders are examples of crime policies. Criminal-justice policy pertains to the workings of the justice system and its constituent agencies. Juvenile-justice policies, mass incarceration, and intermediate sanctions are three of the criminal-justice policies that will be discussed in this book. The line between crime policy and criminal-justice policy is blurry and imprecise, and there is much overlap. Generally, for the sake of clarity, the term *crime policy* will be used when there is a specific crime category at issue (gun crime, sex offenses, and so on), while *criminal-justice policy* will refer to the approaches taken to reduce or prevent crime in a broader sense (such as mass incarceration, which affects wide swaths of offenders).

ANALYTICAL LENS

There are many different ways in which crime and criminal-justice policies can be carved up for analysis, and many lenses through which they can be interpreted. In this book, crime and criminal-justice policies are seen as flowing from legislation that is either substantive or symbolic. Substantive laws are crafted on the basis of a careful, informed study of a genuine problem, and they offer a sensible solution. Symbolic laws, by contrast, are hollow. In creating them, legislators construct a distorted or fictionalized version of a problem, exaggerate its magnitude to incite fear and anger, and then build a solution around the fiction they have created. Of course, since the problem was misconstrued at the beginning, the solution is senseless. Symbolic laws are a staple of partisan politics in which individual elected officials endeavor to earn and retain their seats and parties struggle for power over state and federal governments. Elected policymakers are frequently accused of "playing politics" by turning real public problems into symbols they can exploit for their own gain. When social and public ills are transformed into political footballs, symbolic laws' non-solutions are unhelpful, at best, and at worst may produce devastating collateral damage. This book critically examines the political uses—and manipulations—of crime and criminal justice, and discusses whether certain policies exist because they produce tangible benefits or, instead, serve some groups' political interests.

Public opinion is frequently invoked as a rationale for policy and as a justification for continuing to employ controversial crime-control measures (such as the death penalty). With substantial assistance from many unscrupulous media outlets' devotion to the doctrine of "if it bleeds, it leads," politicians and interest groups are able to generate and mold fear of crime and anger toward those who commit it. They then use that manufactured fear to justify implementing new policies or continuing old ones. In this formulation, of course, the public appears pawnlike, feebleminded, and easily duped. The more likely scenario is that the public often lacks the information necessary for making good policy decisions. Without a clear understanding of the empirical data, the citizenry is left with nothing but the claims put forth by elected officials and interest groups, possibly with some efforts by professional journalists and media outlets and reputable think tanks to either support or refute those claims.

Criminology and criminal-justice scholars bear part of the blame for this large-scale information void. They are often equally guilty of being uncritical of their own dogma—"publish or perish"—that prioritizes publication in peer-reviewed journals and trivializes or even discourages communication in other forms, such as publication in magazines aimed at practitioners like police chiefs and corrections officials. Academics have also traditionally shied away from the media and legislative spotlight. The reasons for this are diverse, but many spring from persistent self-doubt instilled through a misinterpretation of the scientific tenet that no single study proves (or disproves) anything. Every study, no matter how methodologically sound, has weaknesses and is specific to a particular context. Its results could be invalid or not generalizable. While it is correct to avoid leaping to rash conclusions about the effectiveness or ineffectiveness of a given policy on the basis of one—or even two or three—studies, scientists have gone astray in failing to put forth for public consideration the sum total of evidence available.

A rich body of empirical evidence pertaining to the causes of crime and effective policy responses has grown up since the advent of U.S. criminology in the 1930s and of the scholarly study of criminal justice in the 1960s. Scholars have evaluated most existing criminal-justice policies extensively and although gaps remain in this area of scientific inquiry, just as in any other, accumulated knowledge has reached a level sufficient to justify abandoning old, ineffective methods and adopting proven or promising new ones. Partnerships between academics and practitioners are cropping up nationwide, as are model programs promulgated by government agencies and think tanks that offer templates designed to be transportable across jurisdictions so that states and cities can implement evidence-based practices. The wealth of existing scientific information, and that which continues to issue from the academy, eliminates rational justification for bad policies and lays bare the purely political and opinion-based nature of many current crime and criminal-justice policies.

This book takes the optimistic position that obstacles to high-quality policy are surmountable with sufficient political willpower. A core theme of this book is that a greater reliance on science would inject rationality into crime and criminal-justice policy. Beyond that, though, is the necessity of adopting a willingness to be wrong. Politicians and other policymakers frequently dig in their heels and adamantly insist that their policies are good, even in the face of solid evidence to the contrary, because admitting error is one of the fastest forms of political suicide. Some promising policies have not yet amassed a large body of evidence supporting their efficacy, but initial results are sufficiently positive to make them worth trying. Innovation is key. At the same time, a policy that was given a legitimate trial run and is not accomplishing intended goals should be modified or abandoned. Policies should be treated as fluid and ever-changing, not rigid fixtures we are stuck with even though we know they are doing no good.

Along with a willingness to innovate and err should also come an emphasis on long-term results. Election cycles all too often foster an unhealthy obsession with short-term gratification. The lawmaker who votes in favor of a law that substantially increases the prison population has a number to point to when he or she runs for reelection, but the lawmaker who pushes for community-based policies to improve quality of life in distressed urban neighborhoods may not have a tangible outcome to offer the electorate. Achieving genuine crime control and fairness in the justice process requires playing the long game. Short-term "quick fixes" (which rarely fix anything) should be rejected in favor of reforms that may seem sluggish but which entail enduring, sustainable change that truly has an impact in the long run.

This book's line of inquiry begins with three premises that form the starting points of each chapter's discussion. They also serve as the organizing principles shaping and guiding each discussion as it flows outward from those starting points. These premises are described in the following pages so that readers fully understand the assumptions underlying each chapter's content and organization. The chapters' overarching goals are to demonstrate the validity of these claims. As with any starting assumptions, these premises are not set in stone and readers may find themselves skeptical of them. In such instances, critics are encouraged to identify the source of their dissatisfaction and proffer sound refutations. Even those who accept the premises and their supporting evidence as valid will benefit from formally stating a justification for their opinion. This book should facilitate critical-thinking exercises that challenge readers to examine their previously conceived notions about crime and criminal-justice policy.

PREMISE: CRIME AND CRIMINAL-JUSTICE POLICY ARE DRIVEN BY POLITICAL, SOCIAL, AND ECONOMIC FACTORS

The claim that crime policy is only tenuously related to crime will undoubtedly strike many people as extremely odd at first blush. What should crystalize over the course of reading this book is that crime and criminal-justice policy both result from a conglomeration of factors. High-profile murders, economic recessions and depressions, politicized rhetoric about immigrants, racial tensions and prejudices, and many other social, economic, and political issues provide the subtext for all crime and justice policies. These factors coalesce to form a web of policies that are removed, to a greater or lesser extent, from the problems they were intended to solve, as well as from the scientific evidence pertaining to their effectiveness—or ineffectiveness—at achieving stated goals.

The lawmaking process, too, widens the gap between policy and reality. The United States' tripartite system of government can bring legislative, executive, and judicial branches into conflict with one another, and even the legislative branch in conflict with itself (such as when the Senate and House of Representatives disagree on an issue). Federalism generates discord about the legitimate scope of federal control over states' approaches to crime control. The two-party system pits Republicans' and Democrats' traditional party platforms against one another and often squeezes out new ideas that do not fit in with established agendas. The structure and operation of the U.S. government (both at the federal and state levels) places several obstacles in the path of public policy.

PREMISE: POLICIES SHOULD BE CRITICALLY ANALYZED ON THE BASIS OF LOGIC AND THEORY

Crime policies are premised upon some foundational reason or logic, be it high-quality scientific evidence or so-called "commonsense" notions about how best to prevent people from engaging in criminal acts. In this book, each policy is analyzed in terms of its underlying premises and each premise, in turn, is critically examined for strengths and weaknesses. The goal is to determine whether the policy rests on solid ground or suffers from flaws that undermine its potential effectiveness.

In each chapter, the description of the policy under discussion and the summary of the empirical evidence pertaining to that policy's effectiveness are separated by a section parsing the policy's underlying logical rationale. The purpose of this organizational strategy is to pause briefly before delving into the obvious "Does it work?" question to first answer a less-obvious but equally important query: "Is there any good reason to believe it *would* work?" If a policy is grounded in poor logic or defective theory about the nature of criminal offending, then it is doomed for failure. (Unfortunately the reverse is not true; being logically sound is not a recipe for success absent a supporting action plan and effective implementation.) Each chapter's examination of the underlying rationales purported to justify the policy at hand segues into the summary of existing empirical research by setting the stage for a determination of *why* the policy works or does not work.

PREMISE: EMPIRICAL EVIDENCE IS THE BEST POLICY GUIDE

A central thesis of this book is that science should be the guiding factor shaping public policies. The method of analysis adopted here encourages readers to evaluate crime and criminal-justice policies in light of logic, theory, and (especially) empirical evidence. Politics, ideologies, and opinions are rejected as legitimate bases for laws and policies. None can be eliminated, since the government controls the criminal-justice system, but criminal justice need not be held hostage to partisanship and rhetoric. The United States' policy landscape would look radically different if policymakers paid more attention to scholarly empiricism and if the public regularly accessed academic knowledge about the causes of crime and the empirical standing of existing laws and policies.

Each chapter reviews the research pertaining to areas where the policy under examination has been effective, has not been effective, or has perhaps exerted unintended adverse consequences. The focus is on examining policies through a critical, social-scientific, empirical lens. Summaries of the best available evidence further the goal of informing the public and policymakers about what policies promote public safety, fairness, and justice, and which ones are symbolic or counterproductive. Questions about ethics and morality are generally set aside for present purposes, not because they lack relevance (they do not), but because they are outside the scope of the premise that policies should be driven, first and foremost, by evidence that they reduce crime, minimize costs, and do not exert collateral damage.

This three-pronged approach facilitates in-depth analysis of each policy discussed here. Since it is impossible for any book to include an exhaustive list of crime and criminal-justice policies, one of this text's major goals is to equip readers with an analytical framework they can bring to bear upon any crime, criminal-justice, or social policy. The first step is to trace a policy back to its historical origins and gain an understanding of the social, economic, and political factors that shaped the public's concern about, and policymakers' response to, a particular problem or ill. In so doing, the analyst should classify concerns and responses as being either substantive or symbolic. The analyst should also identify possible contributing factors that may seem unrelated on the surface but are hidden sources of dissatisfaction or fear.

The second step is to parse the underlying arguments put forward in favor of the policy. This exercise entails comparing and contrasting claims about the policy's purported efficacy against the empirical and theoretical knowledge regarding crime and crime control in general. In keeping with the outcome of the first step, the analyst should consider whether the policy is based upon a realistic understanding of the problem it is designed to correct or, instead, on a distorted or politicized version of it.

Lastly, the criminological and criminal-justice scientific literature should be consulted for an assessment of the policy's ability to reduce crime without generating collateral damage. This step can be onerous because, as described previously, scientific studies are often buried in journals not easily accessible to the public. Fortunately, many universities, think tanks, research organizations, private foundations, and governmental agencies produce publicly available reports based on primary data or systematic reviews of existing research. These reports are not good replacements for academic studies, but they can aid in developing an understanding of the empirical status of a given policy. Books, such as the present one, summarizing the available evidence are also helpful sources. As scholars move toward a greater appreciation of the need for stronger channels of communication with the public, access barriers should be gradually lifted, and, with luck, such barriers will soon be a relic of the past. Citizens should be skeptical consumers of policy, and to accomplish this they must possess the tools needed to critically evaluate logic and outcomes. It is hoped that this book will contribute to the advancement of this goal.

This book is structured to allow flexibility in chapter ordering. The chapters stand independently and need not be read in any particular sequence, with two exceptions. These caveats involve Chapters 2 and 15. Readers are encouraged to read Chapter 2 before moving on to the remaining chapters. Chapter 2 provides in-depth treatments of deterrence and incapacitation, the two primary guiding rationales policymakers and the public advance to justify tough crime-control measures. Familiarity with these theories and with the empirical evidence pertaining to how well policies grounded on one or both protect public safety will help readers identify strengths and weaknesses in the policies they encounter in subsequent chapters.

Chapter 15 is intended to be read last. It features promising approaches to crime control that entail substantial community involvement. The reader will notice while progressing through the book that many existing policies–particularly those emphasizing punishment and control—produce dismal outcomes. The material in Chapter 15 pertaining to community-oriented policies and programs brings the book to a close on a positive note. Punishment and control, by themselves, offer little in the way of crime prevention and justice, but there are alternatives. The reader is encouraged to view policies as a matter of choice, not fate. Ineffective policies can be eschewed in favor of proven or promising ones.

The writing and production of this book was a team effort and I owe debts of gratitude to several people. Steve Helba and Larissa Albright of Oxford University Press provided stellar editorial guidance. Several anonymous reviewers offered insightful feedback that significantly improved the quality of many chapters. My colleagues Drs. William Moreto, Eugene Paoline, Kristina Childs, and Jennifer Peck graciously examined some of the chapters. I received important research assistance from students Lucas Alward, Devin Cowan, Frances Abderhalden, and Sherah Basham, and several anonymous reviewers provided useful feedback. All these individuals helped make this book happen. Any errors, of course, remain my own.

CHAPTER 2

DETERRENCE AND INCAPACITATION

INTRODUCTION

All crime and criminal-justice policies are premised upon some underlying logic or rationale. Many, though not all, of these rationales spring from one of the major philosophies of punishment. It is important that policy be grounded in theory because theory offers a set of proposals for how the policy should be structured and enforced. Theory also provides a prediction about the likely impacts of the policy. Policymakers can use theory to propose ideas about what a policy seeks to accomplish, what it should look like in practice, and how it should be administered.

While a theoretical rationale is a necessary condition for any good policy, theory does not itself guarantee good policy. This is because many theories have flaws or weaknesses which, if not adequately accounted for, can compromise policies. A useful analogy is the construction of a house: A house build on concrete has a much better chance of staying upright and being an effective home than one built on soggy, uneven ground. This holds true irrespective of the quality of the house since even the strongest house will crack, crumble, or sink if set atop faulty terrain. Theory is the foundation, and a policy is only as good as the theory it is built on.

There are four main theories or philosophies of punishment intended to provide the logical foundation needed to create and justify crime and criminal-justice policy: retribution, rehabilitation, deterrence, and incapacitation (see, generally, Packer, 1968). This chapter briefly summarizes the key elements of the first two philosophies, and then delves into an in-depth analysis of the latter two. Because deterrence and incapacitation are the primary frameworks guiding crime and criminal-justice policy in the United States, and because they will crop up repeatedly in the chapters in this book, they are the theories given prominence in this chapter.

RETRIBUTION AND REHABILITATION

The retribution philosophy holds that criminal punishment is an end unto itself. Retributivists maintain that it is morally correct for a criminal act to invite punishment. This viewpoint is oriented to the past, meaning there is no concern for whether punishment alters an offender's likelihood of committing a new offense in the future. Retribution is frequently associated with phrases like "an eye for an eye" and, in common usage, is often couched as revenge.

Scholars would dispute, however, that retribution is interchangeable with revenge. Retribution's core precept is graduated punishment, whereby a sentence is determined by the severity of the offense. The proportionality principle (or just deserts, as it is often called) maintains that sentences should be uniformly applied to prevent disparities (hence the emphasis on the offense, not the offender) and that the amount of punishment and control levied upon an offender is closely matched to the offense to prevent over-punishment (von Hirsch & Ashworth, 2005). Scholars of the retributivist philosophy favor the use of alternatives to incarceration so that multiple punishment options exist and the goal of proportionality can reach fruition (von Hirsch, 1976). Support for retribution rests to some degree upon disillusion with rehabilitation's ability to effectively reform offenders and prevent recidivism, and on a skepticism about basing sentences on predictions about future behavior (von Hirsch, 1976, 1986). Retribution has no such lofty goals, and so may be seen as more strongly defensible on grounds of practicality and feasibility.

The rehabilitation philosophy advocates punishment as a means of identifying and seeking to improve offenders' underlying psychological and social needs. Correctional populations display high rates of mental illness and substance abuse (e.g., Bronson, Maruschak, & Berzofsky, 2015). Under a rehabilitative approach, punishment revolves around addressing these needs in order to help offenders make positive changes in their lives and move down a path away from criminal and other antisocial behaviors.

Rehabilitation suffered a severe setback in the 1970s with the publication of studies claiming to prove that nothing works in correctional treatment (e.g., Martinson, 1974). It rebounded, though, after more methodologically rigorous studies identified certain types of programs that do work and distilled the key principles of effective correctional rehabilitation: risk, need, and responsivity (Andrews et al., 1990). Programs that adhere to these three principles (the so-called "RNR model") produce noteworthy recidivism reductions compared to programs that deviate from the model or resort to simply warehousing offenders without any effort at treating them (e.g., Lipsey & Cullen, 2007).

The retribution and rehabilitation philosophies are woven throughout contemporary crime and criminal-justice policy. The just-deserts principle was the founding concept behind sentencing guidelines that give judges a limited range of punishment options based upon the severity of the offense and an offender's prior criminal history (von Hirsch, 2011). There is also widespread public support for rehabilitative approaches to juvenile justice (e.g., Moon, Sundt, Cullen, & Wright, 2000). Overall, though, these two philosophies appear less frequently than deterrence and incapacitation as the major justifications for crime and criminal-justice policies.

We turn now to deterrence and incapacitation. Each theory is laid out in detail, including the specific assumptions upon which it is based, and then those assumptions are examined in terms of how well they have held up under empirical scrutiny. The purpose of this analysis is to determine how well deterrence and incapacitation serve as foundational rationales justifying crime and criminal-justice policy.

ASSUMPTIONS AND EMPIRICAL TESTS OF DETERRENCE THEORY

Deterrence is the oldest theory of crime and punishment. It formed the basis for the Classical school of criminology, which dominated European thought about crime and justice in the eighteenth century (see Pratt, Gau, & Franklin, 2010). Deterrence conceptualizes individuals as rational actors capable of calculating the rewards and costs associated with a particular action, weighing those rewards and costs against each other, and engaging in only those actions yielding net benefits. Deterrence-based policies aim to prevent crime by attaching costs (criminal punishments) to illegal acts, thereby convincing would-be offenders that the drawbacks of the contemplated criminal act outweigh the expected benefits (Beccaria, 1764/1986).

There are two types of deterrence: general and specific (also called special). General deterrence occurs when the threat of detection is high enough and the punishment is sufficiently unpleasant to convince people that crime is not worth the negative consequences;. In other words, general deterrence is a form of crime prevention. When general deterrence fails, specific deterrence is intended as a fail-safe. This theory holds that people who have committed crimes and been subjected to penalty will seek to avoid being punished again in the future and, therefore, will refrain from further illegal behavior. According to this logic, punishment sensitizes one-time offenders to the pain of criminal sanctions and causes them to stay out of trouble for fear of experiencing sanctions again.

The three elements of effective deterrence are certainty, severity, and swiftness (Beccaria, 1764). Certainty is critical because, according to deterrence theory, would-be offenders will only be dissuaded from crime when they believe they will be apprehended and punished. Severity is important because the punishment must be unpleasant enough to tip the cost–benefit analysis in favor of costs. In the case of special deterrence, penalties must be severe enough to convince the one-time offender that punishment is something to avoid in the future. Swiftness operates to minimize the amount of time between offense and punishment. People are more cognizant of short-term consequences than of ramifications they might face in the long term.

Deterrence theory is intuitive on its face, but a parsimonious examination reveals additional layers that add substantial complexity to this seemingly straightforward punishment rationale. These layers revolve around three assumptions built into deterrence theory that turn out to be problematic in practice. Each assumption has flaws that undermine policies resting on deterrence rationales.

First, deterrence theory assumes offenders always premeditate their crimes and carefully map out anticipated risks and rewards. In reality, many crimes result from impulse, emotion, or intoxication (Loeber et al., 2012; Zimring, 1968). When offenders do plan in advance, they often display cognitive distortions leading them to downplay potential costs and focus exclusively on expected benefits (Copes & Vieraitis, 2009 see also Decker, Wright, & Logie, 1993). An increase in anticipated rewards can offset an increase in certainty or severity, motivating people to commit crimes they view as particularly lucrative even when they think there is a realistic chance they will be caught and punished (Decker et al., 1993).

Second, deterrence theory presupposes that would-be offenders are aware of arrest probability and sanction severity. If deterrence is to work, people must believe they stand a high chance of apprehension and punishment (Walker, 2001). Research has shown, however, that people do not correctly estimate sanction risk or severity (Kleck & Gertz, 2013; Kleck, Sever, Li, & Gertz, 2005), which undercuts the effectiveness of general deterrence. Specific deterrence does not seem to fare any better, as those who have been arrested in the past are no better (Kleck et al., 2005) and possibly even worse (see Pogarsky & Piquero, 2003 for a review) than persons with no previous criminal-justice contact at judging the probability of being arrested for a future crime.

Third, deterrence theory seems to suggest that incremental rises in certainty and severity (the two most examined elements of deterrence) will produce corresponding linear reductions in crime. In other words, every increase in the probability of arrest or the length of a prison sentence should consistently yield crime declines proportionate to the increase in the system variables. This assumption also fails when examined closely. There is some evidence to support absolute deterrence, which is the deterrent value achieved through the process of criminalizing a particular act (e.g., burglary) and attaching a penalty to it (Walker, 2001). All else being equal, people do tend to avoid behaviors that are criminal, serious, and carry weighty penalties. However, increases in severity from previous levels (called marginal deterrence) do not offer greater crime-suppressive effects. Research has not supported the prediction that crime rates drop when sentences become harsher, which calls marginal deterrence into question (Tonry, 2008).

Given the three problems in fundamental deterrence assumptions outlined above, it is unsurprising that empirical tests of deterrence yield weak support for the theory. A large portion of these studies have been macrolevel in nature, meaning they sought to determine whether there was a relationship between aggregate (e.g., city or state) levels of arrest probability or sanction severity and subsequent crime rates. Problems trying to test for such an association hit immediate roadblocks. Scholars in the 1970s complained that police records are unreliable data sources, that plea bargaining creates a disjuncture between arrest rates and incarceration rates, and that the macrolevel impacts of deterrence and incapacitation cannot be disentangled in analyses of incarceration rates (Nagin, 1975). Two decades later, the situation had not improved; in fact, scholars had identified even more impediments to methodologically rigorous empirical evaluation (Nagin, 1998).

Evidence favoring deterrence is not absent (e.g., Levitt, 1996), but studies have produced mixed results and critics have identified severe methodological flaws. The results are highly sensitive to model specification (Chamlin, Grasmick, Bursik, & Cochran, 1992), meaning that the findings are unstable across studies (Pratt & Cullen, 2005). In addition, the average magnitude of the effect for certainty of punishment is low. There seems to be some possible impact of prison-sentence lengths on aggregate crime rates, but it is impossible to determine whether this is due to deterrence, incapacitation, or some other factor (Pratt & Cullen, 2005; see also Nagin, 1975). Even those firmly convinced of the crime-control capacity of deterrence are quick to point out that the pertinent question is not whether deterrence works as a general premise but, rather, how effective specific policies and programs are at producing deterrent effects (Nagin, 1998).

Absent the ability to reach trustworthy conclusions on the basis of macrolevel research, many scholars turned to perceptual research. At its heart, deterrence is about perception—would-be offenders will be deterred only if they perceive there is a high likelihood of being caught and feel that the penalty is too harsh to make them want to risk being subjected to it. As noted previously, this research has shown that people are not good at judging apprehension risks or punishment levels (Kleck & Gertz, 2013; Kleck et al., 2005). Much of the research on perceptions also suffers methodological weaknesses. Researchers sometimes survey people about their perceptions of certainty and severity, and then they ask those individuals whether they have ever engaged in criminal acts or how likely they would be to do so in the future. Many of these studies reveal negative relationships between certainty and past crime commission or the likelihood of future offending. This method fails to disentangle temporal ordering. It is not necessarily true that people who think they have a high chance of being caught commit less crime; rather, people who have committed crime, and not been arrested, may now see their apprehension probability as being quite low (Paternoster, 1987). In panel designs, where people are tested over two or more points in time, perceived certainty is a weak or nonexistent predictor of crime commission (Paternoster, 1987, 1989).

Tests of perceived severity and crime commission or likelihood also fall short because they—like most of the certainty research—fail to account for variables beyond those pertaining to the criminal-justice system (Hochstetler & Bouffard, 2010). Many acts classified as crimes (robbery, sexual assault, burglary, and so on) are morally reprehensible. Most people would not fathom attacking another person or breaking into homes, not because such an act is illegal but because it is wrong. They would feel guilt and their family and friends might express disappointment in them. Perhaps they would lose their jobs. Studies have found that moral attitudes significantly predict people's offending probability (Mocan & Rees, 2005). In many cases, the effect of perceived severity of punishment on crime commission or likelihood of offending disappears once moral-attitude variables are included in the model (Patenoster, 1987). Overall, then, compared to macrolevel deterrence research (Pratt & Cullen, 2005; Tonry, 2008), perceptual-deterrence studies similarly suffer widespread model misspecification and support for deterrence tends to emerge only in weak, flawed models (Paternoster, 1987). The inclusion of variables tapping into informal social control (e.g., religious beliefs) and economic conditions or opportunities suppresses the impact of system variables on offending likelihood (Mocan & Rees, 2005).

In sum, the classical formulation of deterrence receives a low grade in terms of empirical support. It rests on several untenable assumptions about the nature of criminal behavior and offenders' response to the criminal-justice system. Tests have produced mixed findings that, overall, are weak and inconsistent. Policies grounded in this theory of punishment, then, suffer serious flaws in their guiding principles.

This is not to say that deterrence will never work; to the contrary, some crimes (and some people) may be more "deterrable" than others (Mocan & Rees, 2005; Nagin, 1998; Tonry, 2008). Classical deterrence has given rise to a modern conceptualization of rational-choice theory that could be a ticket to crime prevention. The new rational-choice model focuses on the criminal situation. According to this view, an offender (as a rational actor) attracted to a certain criminal opportunity evaluates the immediate social and physical environment to gauge how feasible the crime will be, the chances of being interrupted, and the chances of being caught or thwarted in the act (Cornish & Clarke, 2008). Structural or situational approaches to crime prevention could increase the difficulty of committing crime and thus prompt offenders to reconsider their plans (Clarke & Cornish, 1985). The overriding lesson is that deterrence is more complex than it seems on the surface, and deterrence-grounded policies are doomed from the start if they fail to account for relevant nuances.

ASSUMPTIONS AND EMPIRICAL TESTS OF INCAPACITATION THEORY

Incapacitation as a theory of punishment posits that society can prevent crime by physically restraining offenders. This might be accomplished through incarceration or other means, such as house arrest, that creates a barrier between an offender and the opportunity or ability to engage in crime. Incapacitation, then, is a future-oriented approach, though the duration of the effect is limited to the length of the sentence.

Incapacitation is commonly invoked to justify the widespread use of incarceration and increased sentence length for certain crimes. The premise behind incapacitation as a theory of crime control is straightforward: Prevent crime by physically restraining offenders and making it impossible for them to engage in illegal acts. Incarceration is advanced as a means of ensuring that offenders do not continue to pose a threat to society.

Incapacitation can be broken down into two types: collective and selective. *Collective incapacitation* happens when broad categories of offenders are subject to prison, without consideration of their level of risk. Collective incapacitation entails the use of prison sentences for multiple types of offenses and offenders. There is no effort to determine risk level or to tailor sentence length to the offender's probability of future offending. Collective incapacitation produces higher prison populations and, in the United States, has led to the current state of mass incarceration in which numerous offenders of varying degrees of potential danger are sentenced to terms of confinement (Pratt, 2009).

Selective incapacitation occurs when high-rate offenders are targeted for long prison sentences. Selective incapacitation has been touted as a promising approach to crime control because, so the argument goes, prison space can be reserved for the "worst of the worst" and lower-risk offenders can be sentenced to much shorter prison terms or channeled into lesser penalties, such as community supervision. This balance would seem to appeal broadly to people of various political orientations and social attitudes (see Wilson, 1985; see also Pratt et al., 2010).

Incapacitation theory rests on several assumptions about offenders' behavior, and all must hold true for incapacitation to be an effective, efficient method of crime control. Empirical tests of these assumptions, however, have revealed serious weaknesses that undermine the incapacitation argument. It has been demonstrated that both collective and selective incapacitation suffer important gaps in their underlying logic.

Collective incapacitation is premised on the notion that all offenders who are incarcerated would be committing new crimes if they were free in society rather than confined in prison. The technical term for offending rates in research on incapacitation theory is *lambda*, which is measured as the number of crimes each imprisoned person is projected to have committed per year if that person were not in prison. For instance, if a prisoner has a lambda of 5, then incarcerating that person for 5 years prevents $5 \times 5 = 25$ crimes (see Blumstein & Nagin, 1978). The problem is that this hypothesis is impossible to test, because there is no way to know with certainty what any given prisoner would be doing if he or she were not incarcerated. In other words, there is no way to discover the true value of lambda. If lambda equals 10 for a certain prisoner, then incarcerating that person might be a good idea; however, if that prisoner's lambda is actually 0, then incarcerating him or her is useless because no crimes are being prevented. Because it sweeps so wide, collective incapacitation scoops up low-rate offenders along with high-rate ones.

This leads to the second, related, problem with collective incapacitation: *diminishing returns*. In addition to assuming a high value of lambda, collective incapacitation presumes that this value is constant across offenders; that is, it presumes all prisoners would be committing the same number of crimes each year were they not incarcerated. This assumption has been proven wrong by the large body of research showing that some offenders commit crimes at high rates, while others commit a moderate number of crimes, and still others engage in just a few illegal acts and then never reoffend again (Laub & Sampson, 2003; Moffitt, 1993). Because lambda is much smaller for some offenders than for others, the addition of lower-risk offenders to the higher-risk pool causes a deterioration in the overall effectiveness of the incapacitation strategy.

An example helps illustrate diminishing returns. Suppose a warden is operating a prison with ten beds. Because the available space is so restricted, the warden reserves the beds for offenders who have committed several serious crimes and, thus, can reasonably be seen as requiring imprisonment for the good of society. For sake of argument, let us say that each offender's lambda is 10; thus, $10 \times 10 = 100$ crimes are prevented each year (10 per prisoner). Now suppose that the warden's prison capacity doubled to twenty beds, so ten additional offenders can be brought in. Given the increased space, the warden can relax the criteria and admit prisoners who are less serious in nature, so a group with lambdas of 5 is brought in. Now, the total number of crimes prevented is $(10 \times 10) + (10 \times 5) = 150$, or 7.5 crimes per prisoner. The per-prisoner prevention impact declined with the addition of the new prisoners. This example can be carried further if we assume the bed space increased to thirty and so ten new prisoners with lambdas of 2 were admitted, for a total of $(10 \times 10) + (10 \times 5) + (10 \times 2) = 170$ prevented crimes and a per-prisoner prevention rate of 5.7. Diminishing returns occur when less-serious offenders are scooped up into the widened incapacitation net and reduce the overall impact of incarceration. This represents a severe flaw in collective incapacitation theory. Not only will high rates of imprisonment not be very effective, but incarceration will be a very inefficient method of crime control, requiring massive infusions of resources for relatively small crime-reduction benefits. Indeed, incarceration does appear to reduce crime (Pratt & Cullen, 2005), but the effect is small (Spelman, 2000) and the impact of diminishing returns significantly dampens crime-control benefits when incarceration is used on a large scale rather than being limited to demonstrably serious offenders (Liedka, Piehl, & Useem, 2006).

Selective incapacitation has also fallen short in empirical tests. The primary flaw in selective incapacitation is its central assumption that it is possible to reliably predict which people will become high-rate offenders and which ones will dabble in crime briefly before moving on to law-abiding lives. Prediction is the crux of selective incapacitation, since the theory only holds up if the high-rate offenders can be accurately distinguished from the low-rate ones. In the 1970s and 1980s, substantial effort went into the search for valid, reliable predictors; however, these efforts proved fruitless and the pursuit has been abandoned (Pratt et al., 2010).

To be sure, there are correlates of high-rate offending. People who were arrested as juveniles, have drug-abuse histories, and have problems maintaining employment are more likely to persist in a criminal career (Auerhahn, 1999). Gender, race, and age also predict involvement in certain types of crime (Mocan & Rees, 2005). These factors, however, only correlate with high-rate offending; they do not *cause* it. Even if someone possesses a set of risk factors known to enhance the probability that the person will reoffend, there is no guarantee that the person actually will engage in future crime. Risk-prediction instruments designed to categorize offenders as high, medium, or low risk are notoriously inaccurate. They produce both false positives (low-risk offenders mistakenly labeled as being high-risk) and false negatives (high-risk offenders erroneously classified as low-risk). Selective incapacitation, then, has intuitive appeal but is not viable in practice.

Incapacitation theory also presumes that the removal of offenders via incapacitation produces a net reduction in the total number of crimes committed. In other words, taking an offender out of circulation is predicted to stop a certain number (lambda) of crimes from being committed. This assumption proves problematic in practice, primarily because of the phenomena of co-offending and replacement. Co-offending undermines incapacitation because the removal of one or even a few members of gangs and other criminal groups will not hamper the antisocial activities of those groups. A substantial portion of offenders commit their offenses in concert with criminal peers (McGloin & Piquero, 2009; Stolzenberg & D'Alessio, 2008; van Mastrigt & Farrington, 2009), meaning co-offending reduces the impact of incapacitation on total crime rates. Replacement effects occur when an incarcerated offender's vacant position in a criminal enterprise is filled by a new recruit (Spelman, 2000). When criminal networks—drug traffickers, for instance—lose a member, they replace that person with someone new and continue business as usual, producing no net reduction in total crimes committed. Moreover, when the incarcerated individual returns to society, he or she may return to the criminal trade, thus producing an overall net *gain* in offenders and crimes (Spelman, 2000).

Overall, the evidence clearly shows that incapacitation theory is not as straightforward as it seems on the surface. There are good reasons to question its effectiveness at reducing crime.

The theory rests on several assumptions about offenders and offending networks, all of which must be true in order for incapacitation to exert beneficial impacts on crime rates. Unfortunately, research shows that these presumptions are either incorrect or of questionable validity due to the infeasibility of subjecting them to empirical tests. Incapacitation, like deterrence, may have some potential merit, but more and better information is needed about the circumstances under which incapacitation might (and might not) be a viable policy solution.

POLICY IMPLICATIONS

The problems with deterrence and incapacitation that have been discussed in this chapter are not merely the armchair musings of detached academics caught up in fancy statistics and abstract theories; quite the contrary, the identified empirical failings have direct, serious implications for crime and criminal-justice policy. Deterrence and incapacitation are the underpinning logic for many policies intended to reduce crime. For instance, police use random motorized patrol and certain hot-spot techniques with the belief that such tactics deter crime. Widespread use of incarceration for multiple types of offenders and offenses is carried out under the auspices of crime prevention through incapacitation. If the theories are flawed, so too are the policies premised upon them.

Few would disagree that criminal law or punishment is necessary in any ordered society. People may disagree on the precise rationale justifying the existence of this system (retribution, prevention, and so on), but nobody would seriously argue that the solution is to do away with the system entirely. Rather, the policy question turns on the *what* and *how much* of criminal punishment. *What* penalties should be used? *What* should society do to prevent people from offending? *How much* punishment should be applied to someone who has committed an offense? These and similar questions form the heart of the policy debate (von Hirsch, 1998).

Empirical evidence can be used to craft policies capitalizing on various aspects of deterrence or incapacitation that might hold promise. For instance, the deterrence research showing that people are generally unaware of the severity of a sentence they would face if they committed a crime (Kleck et al., 2005) could be translated into public-information campaigns designed to disseminate information about prison-sentence lengths for certain types of crime. Research suggests, too, that certain types of offenders may need deterrence messages tailored to them. Some identity thieves, for example, know that banks reimburse credit-card theft victims so these victims do not ultimately lose any money, which from the offenders' point of view means these victims suffer no harm (Copes & Veiraitis, 2006). Deterrence in this context, then, might involve better public information about the long-term consequences for victims (such as damaged credit scores) to sensitize would-be offenders to the harm their actions would inflict upon others. This strategy could play upon would-be offenders' moral sensibilities (see Nagin, 1998) and turn them away from crime.

CONCLUSION

This chapter noted the widespread dependence of crime and criminal-justice policy on the theories of deterrence and incapacitation. Most policies rely (either wholly or in part) upon some element of one of these theories. When assessing the overall effectiveness of a policy, it is important to evaluate the strength of the logic guiding it. If that logic is weak, then the policy itself is threatened. In this chapter, a review of the rationales underlying deterrence and incapacitation, and of the results of empirical tests of these theories and policies grounded upon them, revealed several weaknesses on both theoretical and practical levels. Neither theory is utterly hopeless to the point of being irredeemable, however. For instance, deterrence may have merit as applied to rational calculations offenders make based upon the immediate physical surroundings of a contemplated crime. Where possible, making crimes harder to commit could be a way to put deterrence to good use. Incapacitation, likewise, may offer some crime-control benefits if used sparingly and only for serious, repeat offenders. Mass incarceration creates diminishing returns and dramatically undercuts the impact of incapacitation on crime.

In analyzing policies throughout the following chapters, we will examine both empirical outcomes and the soundness of the underpinning theory or logic to determine how well a particular policy is working and, moreover, whether there is any reason to believe that it could work. By thinking critically about crime and policies, we can begin to develop a rational sanctioning system grounded in evidence, theory, and logic. This chapter might be a helpful reference point for later chapters that deal with deterrence and incapacitation.

DISCUSSION QUESTIONS

1. Researchers have pointed out that one of the problems in trying to empirically assess the impact of incapacitation on crime is that incarceration rates and crime rates are reciprocally related; that is, each one affects the other. Identify and describe at least two reasons for this relationship.
2. Within deterrence theory, severity and certainty tend to operate inversely of one another. In particular, when punishments become harsher, the certainty of them actually being applied to people who commit crimes diminishes. Identify and describe at least two ways in which this inverse relationship might operate. Think about arrest, prosecution, and sentencing decisions.
3. Starting in the 1980s, incarceration rates rose dramatically and reached record levels. Starting in the 1990s, violent crime nationwide fell dramatically. Many politicians and commentators claimed that the increased use of prison caused the violent-crime drop. Examine this claim using what you learned in this chapter. Point out specific reasons to question it and specific reasons to believe it might have merit.
4. Using the concepts covered in this chapter, construct an ideal policy scenario. Identify the strengths in deterrence, incapacitation, or both that policymakers should incorporate into crime and criminal-justice policies. Think about ways in which different elements can be combined and balanced with one another.

CHAPTER 3

DRUG POLICY

INTRODUCTION

The United States population has a voracious appetite for psychoactive substances, both legal and illegal; 86 percent of adults report having tried alcohol (National Institute on Alcohol Abuse and Alcoholism, n.d.[a]) and 6 percent receive treatment for a diagnosed alcohol-use disorder each year (National Institute on Alcohol Abuse and Alcoholism, n.d.[b]). More than 9 percent of Americans age 12 and older use illegal drugs annually (National Institute on Drug Abuse [NIDA], 2015). Two-thirds of people booked into jail report regular alcohol use and 69 percent use illicit drugs. Approximately 33 percent were drinking at the time of the offense, and 29 percent were under the influence of drugs (James, 2004). Legal and illicit drugs are used in all manner of socially acceptable and socially harmful ways.

The efforts to control drug use through criminalization and strict regulation have been bumpy and erratic. At times, the legislative response is so slow that people's use of the drug is already in decline by the time laws are enacted (see Musto, 1989). States, municipalities, and the federal government are often out of sync with one another. In the United States today, marijuana remains illegal at the federal level, yet twenty-eight states and the District of Columbia have enacted laws decriminalizing or legalizing marijuana either for medicinal or recreational use (Rubin, 2016). Because federal drug laws supersede those enacted by states, each U.S. president—and the attorney general serving under him—has discretion over whether or not to pursue federal cases against people growing or using marijuana within the bounds of applicable state law. Drug law and policy continue to be subject to the shifting winds of public sentiment and political decisions.

This chapter discusses the major historical and contemporary trends in drug use and policy. We will see that the most popular (and infamous) approach—the war on drugs—has been declared a failure. Drug courts may have a bright future as an alternative to harshly punitive approaches, but typically produce only modest reductions in drug use.

The prescription-pill problem has been largely overlooked and recent efforts at control have produced mixed results. Overall, this chapter will demonstrate that the best methods for curbing illegal drug use and addiction have yet to be discovered. Before diving into drug laws and policies, we will first review the history of drugs in the United States in order to lend context to the government's antidrug actions.

A BRIEF HISTORY OF DRUG TRENDS

Most of today's most-vilified drugs used to be legal, popular, and a staple of medicinal remedies. In the 1800s, before the advent of modern medicine, physicians had rudimentary knowledge about diseases and injuries, and knew of few or no remedies for most types of physical ailments. Drugs, in particular opium and cocaine, which possess remarkable anesthetic properties—played an outsized role in treatment regimens because physicians often could do little more for patients than alleviate their symptoms (Hodgson, 2001).

Opium is found in the sap of the poppy plant and, in its natural state, has been used for at least 2,500 years to quell pain, coughing, and diarrhea. In the early 1800s, scientists developed a method to extract morphine (the active ingredient in opium) to create a powerful analgesic. Morphine and other opium products produce a pleasant sensation of relaxation; opium syrups were even marketed to parents seeking ways to soothe their fussy infants (Hodgson, 2001). These drugs, however, quickly sparked a rash of abuse and addiction. The invention of the hypodermic syringe in the late 1800s further facilitated addiction (Musto, 1991), because injection is the most effective route of administration (compared to smoking or oral ingestion).

Coca leaves contain a mild stimulant and have been popular for thousands of years. In 1860, scientists learned how to isolate the active ingredient from coca leaves to make a concentrated stimulant. Physicians raved about cocaine's healing properties—it could act as a local anesthetic for small surgeries, alleviate asthma, and serve as a nonaddictive substitute for opiates to allow addicts to recover. Only at the turn of the century did the medical community and general public become starkly aware that cocaine was, in fact, highly addictive and that its medical advantages had been exaggerated. Cocaine's public image flipped from "wonder drug" to social malignancy. So many states and cities banned cocaine in the late 1800s and early 1900s that by the time Congress enacted legislation in 1914 to restrict it, the federal legislation was mostly redundant (Musto, 1989).

Marijuana, amphetamines, LSD/acid, and MDMA/ecstasy have similar historical trends. There is the initial introduction—often accompanied by enthusiasm about the drug's medicinal properties—followed by a surge in use, which in turn is followed by a public outcry about the damage the drug is causing. The next step is usually some form of regulation or criminalization (or both) enacted to curtail the problem (see generally, Lassiter, 2015; Musto, 1989, 1999; Rosenbaum, 2002).

LEGAL AND POLITICAL ORIGINS OF FEDERAL
DRUG LAWS AND POLICIES

Although Americans' affinity for psychoactive substances dates back centuries, federal laws are relatively recent. Most came about in the 1900s, particularly in the latter decades of the century. The reasons for the delay and the timing of criminalization and regulation, as well as the drugs that ultimately were (or were not) selected for criminalization, are matters of controversy. The debate is particularly heated because of the massive impact of the war on drugs (described in the next section). The drug war is not the United States' only policy approach to reducing drug sales and use, but it is by far the most impactful and controversial. It is also a notable example of the federal government imposing its political will upon the states (Gest, 2001), a controversial action in a federal system of government. The federal government's intense involvement in antidrug efforts requires explanation.

The cause for the delay in enacting federal laws and policies can be found in early constitutional politics. Until the mid-1900s, the federal government had very little constitutional authority to impose legislative remedies upon the states. This powerlessness was due to the U.S. Supreme Court's narrow view of Congress' authority under the Commerce Clause to enact legislation affecting the states. Under the auspices of preventing the federal government from infringing upon states' rights or private companies' business interests, the Court struck down every congressional act that affected states' economic enterprises (even laws prohibiting child labor). President Franklin D. Roosevelt's efforts to protect the states from the Great Depression fell victim to the Court's hands-off doctrine until Roosevelt launched his now-infamous campaign to increase the size of the Court so he could stack it with justices who would support him (National Archives, n.d.). In a series of cases (*West Coast Hotel Co. v. Parrish*, 1937; *National Labor Relations Board v. Jones & Laughlin Steel Corp.*, 1937; *Wickard v. Filburn*, 1942), the Court gave in and widened its interpretation of Congress' authority to regulate interstate economic transactions. Congress was finally positioned to criminalize and regulate mind-altering substances. The legal precedent these cases set is far reaching; in fact, it is the basis for the constitutionality of federal laws maintaining marijuana's illegal status even as numerous states legalize this substance within their own borders (*Gonzales v. Raich*, 2005).

Another source of antidrug momentum is the way crime and drugs were portrayed in the American political arena in the 1960s. As a maneuver to garner votes and ensure their election (or reelection), presidential and congressional candidates harnessed the power of fear and convinced the public that a scourge of crime and drugs was tearing apart America's cities and neighborhoods (Gest, 2001). Facts about the prevalence and origins of crime, and the danger of drugs, were distorted or ignored as these social problems were stripped of substantive meaning and transformed into political footballs (see Currie, 1998; Pratt, 2009. "Getting tough" became a requirement for getting elected.

Some historians allege that the war on drugs was a veneer for military action against communist groups attempting to take control of governments in Central and South America. The McCarthy era's abusive persecutions of suspected communists in the 1950s soured the public on governmental efforts to suppress communism. By the 1980s, however, U.S.

government officials perceived the spread of communism throughout Latin America as a significant threat to U.S. interests, but it needed an excuse to intervene (Morales, 1989). Thanks to decades of antidrug propaganda (Lassiter, 2015), the public was primed to throw its weight behind a war on drugs. Because Central and South America were significant sources of illegal drugs, it was easy for the U.S. government to disguise its true intentions and fight the war on communism behind a façade of a war on drugs (Morales, 1989).

Critical explanations for the way the war has played out domestically revolve around race and social class (Peterson, 1985). The modern war on drugs, a war targeting impoverished inner-city neighborhoods (Elwood, 1995), rests upon a long history of the demonization of marginalized segments of the population. In the 1850s, a Protestant-led temperance movement was fueled by the widespread belief that Irish immigrants (most of whom were Catholic) were incorrigible drunkards and led to the criminalization of alcohol in more than a dozen states (McPherson, 1988). Anti-Chinese sentiments were tied to the public's condemnation of opium in the early 1900s (Morgan, Wallack, & Buchanan, 1989; Musto, 1989, 1991); the federal government's actions against cocaine in the first years of the 1900s painted this substance as black Americans' drug of choice (Musto, 1989); and the federal ban on marijuana was related to concerns about immigration from Mexico in the early decades of the 1900s (Musto, 1999). Drug policy is frequently packaged along with inflammatory rhetoric fanning fears of some "alien minority" (Musto, 1999, p. 229). We will see later in this chapter that drug policy in the United States remains closely tied to race. While some federal drug laws spring from good-faith efforts to regulate dangerous substances, many are corrupted by legislative recklessness and failure to correct problems that take serious tolls on individuals, families, and communities (Peterson, 1985).

DRUG LAWS AND POLICIES

BEFORE THE WAR ON DRUGS: EARLY LAWS

The Pure Food and Drug Act of 1906 was the federal government's first effort to address cocaine and heroin use and addiction. This act did not prohibit or regulate these drugs' use, but instead simply required all medicinal remedies containing them to be labeled accurately (Musto, 1991). As described previously, during this time period the federal government had little ability to regulate state matters and so its 1906 law was largely insubstantial. However, domestic and international forces underway in the late 1800s and early 1900s would ultimately coalesce to create conditions favorable to the next significant piece of federal drug legislation.

On the domestic front, the early years of the 1900s were characterized by a darkening of the national mood toward opium and cocaine. Misuse, abuse, and addiction were spreading, while at the same time medical advancements and the advent of painkillers such as aspirin meant opium and cocaine were causing more problems than they were curing (Musto, 1991). On the international scene, changes began in 1898 when the United States acquired the Philippines from Spain, which had held the island nation for more than 300 years. This move touched off combat between U.S. troops and Filipino activists who opposed another colonial regime. As part of its efforts to establish control, the United States forbade Filipinos from nonmedical opium use. At the same time, the U.S. started collaborating with China to support that country's antiopium efforts. An international co-alition produced a treaty under which each participating nation agreed to enact domestic laws regulating opium within its borders. The resulting legislation in the United States was the Harrison Act of 1914 (Musto, 1991; see also Musto, 1989).

The Harrison Act taxed the importation and sale of all coca and opium derivatives and prohibited physicians from prescribing cocaine and opium to patients for the sole purpose of managing their addictions (Musto, 1989). Congress argued that the Harrison Act would aid the states in addressing problems of drug abuse (King, 1952) by making cocaine and heroin prohibitively expensive. To drum up public support, the Harrison Act's backers shamelessly exploited stereotypes linking various minority groups to different drug types (Brown, 1981). After the act's passage, cocaine and heroin became far less available than they had been (Ball, 1965), and the use and abuse of these drugs declined significantly (Musto, 1991), but this achievement came at a price. The Harrison Act was enforced with a zeal that critics contend terrorized doctors and addicts alike and singlehandedly trans-formed a medical problem into a criminal one (Brown, 1981; King, 1952). The Harrison Act drove drug addiction underground and a black market rose to meet the demand of a still-strong customer base (Ball, 1965).

Congress next turned its sights to alcohol. The Temperance Movement originated in the 1800s and had been gaining momentum. Temperance was bound up in Progressive ideol-ogy, which took a paternalistic (one could say pejorative) view of urban immigrants con-gregating in neighborhood saloons that served as centers for gambling and prostitution, both of which contributed to and benefitted from police corruption (Burnham, 1968). Progressives triumphed in 1917 when Congress passed the Eighteenth Amendment to the U.S. Constitution (ratified by the requisite number of states in 1919 and implemented in 1920) establishing Prohibition (Burnham, 1968). The Volstead Act, which provided for Prohibition's enforcement, took effect in 1920.

Prohibition criminalized the manufacture and sale of alcohol but not the consump-tion of it. Progressives' expressed intention was to "kill off the liquor business in general and the saloon in particular" while still permitting those who enjoyed libations within the comfort of their homes (the mode employed by middle- and upper-class drinkers) to continue their tradition (Burnham, 1968, p. 55). Thousands of arrests were made in the first few years, leading many observers to defend the law as a success (Hobart, 1923). En-forcement was highly localized, however, since the federal government had not adequately funded the Volstead Act (Burnham, 1968) and states did not appreciate being stuck with the bill. Because of state-by-state variation in enforcement, it is nearly impossible to evalu-ate Prohibition's effectiveness on a national scale (Burnham, 1968). Since alcohol was still lawful to purchase and consume, there was substantial incentive for black-market trade (Kleiman, Caulkins, & Hawken, 2011). Several cities experienced massive problems with bootlegging, backdoor liquor establishments, and violence between rival organized-crime syndicates (Cressey, 1969). Americans' liquor consumption declined substantially during the Prohibition period, but it is unclear what contribution Prohibition itself made to this reduction (Burnham, 1968). Flagging popular and political support for Prohibition, frustration with enforcement's high price tag, and widespread violations of the law eventually led Congress to repeal the Eighteenth Amendment in 1933 by passing the Twenty-first Amendment.

The next federal move in the area of drugs was passage of the Marihuana Tax Act of 1937, which placed prohibitively high taxes on the import and sale of the substance. It is not clear why this act ever came into existence, since marijuana was already illegal in all U.S. states (Galliher & Walker, 1977) or taxed so highly it was virtually unaffordable. Some claim that this act had racial origins. During the Great Depression, jobs were scarce and blue-collar workers in the United States saw Mexican immigrants as a threat to their livelihoods, so they attempted to deter Mexican immigrants from coming to the U.S. by outlawing their drug of choice (Musto, 1973). Others dispute this conclusion and assert that the tax act was merely a symbolic gesture Congress used to bring federal law into congruence with state laws (Galliher & Walker, 1977).

The federal Drug Abuse Control Amendments of 1965 targeted LSD and other hallucinogens that had become popular among middle-class youth and college students. These laws were not intended to put privileged youth behind bars, a move policymakers considered unconscionable (Lassiter, 2015); rather, they were designed to tamp down on the countercultural attitudes popular among many young people in the 1960s (see Peterson, 1985 for a review). Another Drug Abuse Control Amendment in 1968 combined the Federal Drug Administration's Bureau of Drug Abuse Control and the Treasury Department's Bureau of Narcotics, transferred them to the Department of Justice, and subsumed them under a new Bureau of Narcotics and Dangerous Drugs. This bureau would eventually become the Drug Enforcement Administration (DEA).

In 1970, Congress passed the Comprehensive Drug Abuse Prevention and Control Act (CDAPCA). The previous year, the U.S. Supreme Court had held the Marihuana Tax Act unconstitutional (*Leary v. United States*, 1969), providing the impetus for Congress to revisit federal drug law. The CDAPCA largely replaced earlier laws and became the single, reigning legislative framework. Part of this act was Title II, the Controlled Substances Act, which established a scheduling system. The schedules range from I to V, in decreasing levels of restriction (Rasmussen, 2008). The determination of where to place a drug in the tiers rests on a comparison of its level of danger (potential for abuse and dependence) and the extent to which it is accepted as having a legitimate medical use. Congress set down an initial categorization of certain drugs into particular schedules, but since then the DEA and the Food and Drug Administration (FDA) have had primary control over classifications.

Schedule I drugs are those deemed harmful and as having no accepted medical uses. Marijuana, heroin, MDMA (ecstasy), and LSD (acid) are among the Schedule I drugs. Schedule II contains those substances that are recognized as carrying high potential for danger but that possess limited medicinal properties. Cocaine, opioids (e.g., hydrocodone, hydromorphone), methamphetamine, and amphetamines are Schedule II substances. Schedule III includes drugs considered to have moderate or low potential for abuse or dangerous use, but that the government feels still require regulation. Examples of Schedule III drugs include anabolic steroids, ketamine, medications containing small amounts of codeine, and testosterone. Schedule IV drugs have low potential for misuse or addiction and include anxiolytics (e.g., Xanax) and sleep aids (e.g., Ambien). Finally, Schedule V contains a mixture of prescription-only and over-the-counter drugs, including cough syrups with small amounts of codeine and some analgesic medications (Drug Enforcement Administration, n.d.).

THE WAR ON DRUGS

The enactment of the CDAPCA came at a turning point in U.S. history. Antidrug efforts took on a decidedly punitive spin, and events unfolded at the national level that would send out ripple effects still felt today. President Richard Nixon launched the war on drugs in 1971 (Lassiter, 2015), a trend followed with enhanced vigor by Presidents Ronald Reagan in 1986 and George H. W. Bush in 1989 (Elwood, 1995). President Bill Clinton doubled down on the war in the 1994 Violent Crime Control and Law Enforcement Act. Presidents George W. Bush and Barack Obama largely maintained their predecessors' policies, although Obama voiced criticism of mass incarceration and pushed for legislative changes that would reduce prison sentences for low-level drug offenders. The war corresponded to the penalty structure laid out in the CDAPCA and was later supplemented with additional congressional sentencing legislation. The war on drugs and related policy shifts were enshrouded in a distinctly conservative political ideology (Elwood, 1995) that conflicted with traditional leftist ideals about government's role in assisting disadvantaged people and communities (Humphreys & Rappaport, 1993). Nevertheless, the war enjoyed substantial bipartisan enthusiasm. Democrats joined their Republican colleagues in crafting new "get-tough" legislation, such as mandatory minimum sentencing schemes (Lassiter, 2015).

The rhetoric surrounding the war divided the drug market into sellers and users. There was widespread recognition that users were demographically diverse, as well as a common stereotype of sellers as minorities either from other countries or from inner-city America. Lawmakers waged a bifurcated war in which harsh penalties would be visited upon traffickers and dealers, while users would face milder penalties (Lassiter, 2015; Peterson, 1985) and be offered treatment. Federal funding was redirected from community-based mental health programs to in-patient drug-treatment facilities (Humphreys & Rappaport, 1993) via the Office of Substance Abuse Prevention, which was created by the Omnibus Anti-Drug Abuse Act of 1986 (Johnson et al., 1990).

This 1986 act was passed by Congress with bipartisan support and became the basis for harsh sentencing policies for drug offenders. This law instituted the so-called 100:1 rule, which treated 500 grams of cocaine as the equivalent of 5 grams of crack (Lassiter, 2015), with 5-year minimum prison sentences to both. Likewise, fifty grams of crack or five kilograms of powder carried a 10-year minimum prison sentence (Beaver, 2010). The origins of this arbitrary 100-to-1 ratio trace back to the congressional hearings in the months leading up to the passage of the act, during which legislators heard testimony from a so-called expert, Johnny St. Valentine Brown. Brown claimed to have proven through independent research that 20 grams of crack was as dangerous as 1,000 grams of powder cocaine. Brown was later discredited when it was discovered that he lied about possessing a doctorate and board certification in pharmacology and had perjured himself numerous times during his appearances as an expert witness in criminal trials. He was later sent to prison (Beaver, 2010). Congress, however, did not immediately revisit the debunked ratio, so the damage Brown inflicted was left to reverberate throughout the ensuing decades. It was not until 2010 that Congress finally took corrective action. The Fair Sentencing Act left the disparity in place but reduced it from a ratio of 100:1 down to 18:1 (American Civil Liberties Union, n.d.).

The war on drugs fundamentally altered the nature of urban policing. The Comprehensive Crime Act of 1984 allowed local police agencies to keep proceeds generated from assets confiscated during drug investigations. This incentivizes police administrators to redirect their operational priorities toward drug enforcement (Benson, Rasmussen, & Sollars, 1995). Since dealers were the intended targets of the war, and the domestic drug trade was assumed to be an exclusively urban phenomenon, police resources were allocated toward street-level enforcement in inner-city neighborhoods. Inner-city drug markets have traditionally been open-air (Beckett, Nyrop, & Pfingst, 2006), in contrast to the better-concealed drug transactions in suburban communities (Lassiter, 2015). Therefore, intensive suppression efforts in inner cities generated enormous quantities of arrests, numbers that drug-war advocates interpreted as proof that their efforts were paying off.

As the war on drugs progressed, the prison population ballooned. Due to legislative changes to federal and state criminal codes, more people were sent to prison, and prison sentences were longer (Cahalan & Parsons, 1986). Prison construction could not keep pace, and state prison systems descended into disorder and violence. Prisoner litigation alleging that conditions of confinement had become so decrepit that they violated the Eighth Amendment's prohibition on cruel and unusual punishment (e.g., *Ruiz v. Estelle*, 1979) led to court orders requiring prisons to ameliorate the problems. While a portion of the increase in prison populations was attributable to the get-tough movement on crime overall, the bulk of it was the consequence of soaring rates of incarceration for drug offenses (Currie, 1993).

DRUG COURTS

Against the backdrop of the war on drugs and bloated prison populations, drug courts emerged. The first one started in Miami, Florida, in 1989, and the model quickly spread. There are currently more than 3,000 drug courts operating nationwide (National Institute of Justice, n.d.). Drug courts emphasize the role of rehabilitation and problem solving in combating drug addiction (Goldkamp, White, & Robinson, 2001). The expansion of drug courts occurred in spite of an absence of evidence about their effectiveness (Mitchell, Wilson, Eggers, & MacKenzie, 2012), suggesting that the ideology behind them enjoyed popular appeal.

The central feature of drug courts that separates them from traditional courts is the prominent role judges play in actively monitoring defendants (Wilson, Mitchell, & MacKenzie, 2006). The prosecutor and defense attorney occupy supporting roles in nonadversarial proceedings. Drug courts typically accept only lower-level drug offenders whose charges involve personal use. Defendants appear in open court at scheduled intervals to have their progress evaluated. Judges review reports from the treatment staff to determine if defendants have been meeting the requirements of their terms of supervision (such as mandatory drug counseling and testing). Judges praise defendants for good work, and penalize them if they slip. Punishment for violations (e.g., failing urine tests, not meeting with treatment providers) may result in short stays in jail or ejection from the program and transfer to traditional court. There are three general types of drug courts (e.g., Wilson et al., 2006). In one, the treatment program takes place preadjudication and defendants who complete the program successfully have the charges against them dropped. Another type is postadjudication, where defendants plead guilty to the charges, but can have the conviction expunged if they graduate from the program. Finally, some courts let judges decide on a case-by-case basis what the best outcome for each defendant should be.

DECRIMINALIZATION AND LEGALIZATION

Some opponents of the drug war criticize criminalization itself and advocate decriminalization and legalization of certain substances. Decriminalization can entail legalizing the possession of small amounts of a certain drug, or turning possession into a civil offense rather than a criminal one. Manufacturing, selling, and possessing large quantities would remain unlawful. On the surface, decriminalization seems like an attractive way to purge the system of low-level users while still fighting to disrupt drug markets, but in truth, decriminalizing a drug can increase the demand for it and incentivize trafficking (Kleiman et al., 2011).

Legalization represents a return to the days before drug regulation began. Critics of legalization allege that its advocates forget the serious, widespread problems with drug addiction that plagued society when drugs were unregulated (Musto, 1999). Alcohol also offers an instructive illustration. Approximately 6.2 percent of adults have an alcohol-use disorder characterized by heavy drinking and associated problems (National Institute on Alcohol Abuse and Alcoholism, n.d.[b]). This exacts enormous social and financial tolls (Kleiman et al., 2011). If cocaine and heroin were legal, abuse and its consequences for individuals, families, and communities would probably rise, though by how much and whether the increase would be offset by the harm reduction gained through ending the drug war are legitimate questions.

Marijuana presents a potentially different set of circumstances compared to other illegal street drugs, since marijuana's psychotropic effects are milder and it does not have the same physically addictive qualities as heroin and cocaine (though dependence is still possible). A full 58 percent of the U.S. public supports legalization (Jones, 2015). Marijuana is currently legal in some form (medicinally, recreationally, or both) in twenty-eight states (Rubin, 2016). Rates of use have risen (NIDA, 2015), a predictable result of legalization. As yet, it is not clear whether this rise is harmless or consequential. Pediatric research has found that infants and toddlers exposed to second-hand marijuana smoke at home test positive for THC metabolites, which has unknown implications for their brain development. Marijuana legalization might be increasing the number of young children with detectable THC metabolite levels (Wilson et al., 2016).

PRESCRIPTION DRUGS

The bulk of antidrug policy in the United States is targeted toward traditional street drugs (cocaine, heroin, and marijuana) and various fad, club, and designer drugs. Prescription drugs, especially opioids and benzodiazepines, have remained under the radar until recently. Even today, they have not garnered the notoriety of street drugs, even though they kill tens of thousands of people annually. Policy efforts have not kept pace with the wave of prescription-drug abuse and addiction.

Opioids surged in popularity throughout the 1990s and early 2000s as companies invented and produced increasingly large selections and quantities of these Schedule II substances. The medical profession embraced opioids for the treatment of pain (Mularski et al., 2006) arising from everything from terminal cancer to routine dental surgery. OxyContin (the proprietary name for oxycodone) dominated the scene (Cicero, Inciardi, & Muñoz, 2005), followed closely by competing drugs such as Vicodin, Percocet, and Lorcet (hydrocodone and acetaminophen combinations), fentanyl (found under multiple proprietary labels), and several other molecular and compositional variants. The increasing medical use of opioids corresponded to an alarming rise in the prevalence of abuse and dependence (Van Zee, 2009). Benzodiazepines are Schedule IV drugs commonly prescribed for anxiety. They go under proprietary names such as Xanax and Valium. Benzodiazepine prescriptions are increasing in both quantity and potency (Bachhuber, Hennessy, Cunningham, & Starrels, 2016; Kaufmann, Spira, Depp, & Mojabai, 2016). While their potential for abuse and dependence is lower than that for opioids, they remain perilous, especially when combined with alcohol or opioids.

The rates of abuse, dependence, and overdoses involving opioids and benzodiazepines has been rising steadily since at least the late 1990s. Approximately 2 million people nationwide have abused or are dependent upon opioids, and nearly 25 percent of people prescribed opioids for noncancerous pain become addicted. Prescription drugs cause more deaths each year than street drugs do. In 2014, there were 49,714 deaths attributable to all drug types (Kochanek, Murphy, Xu, & Tejada-Vera, 2016). Nearly two-thirds were caused by opioids (including heroin), and most of those were prescription drugs. Heroin abuse appears to be on the rise as a consequence of the prescription opioid problem (Rudd, Aleshire, Zibbell, & Gladden, 2016). In 2013, approximately 11,000 people died as a result of benzodiazepine overdoses (Bachhuber et al., 2016). Benzodiazepines and opioids are frequently abused concurrently; in 2011, approximately 34 people per 100,000 population were treated in emergency departments for overdoses involving both drugs, and benzodiazepines are present in 31 percent of opioid-caused deaths (Jones & McAninch, 2015).

Policies to curb prescription-drug abuse are in their infancy. Several states have enacted prescription drug monitoring programs (PDMPs), which are databases operated by state regulatory agencies. Physicians can check their state's PDMP to determine whether patients have received controlled substances from other providers. Pharmacists can use the PDMP to find out if a patient has been filling an unusual quantity of prescriptions or to flag certain physicians as producing a large number of suspicious prescriptions. Law-enforcement personnel authorized to access the database can see links between physicians, patients, and pharmacists (Gau & Brooke, 2017). Other state-level efforts to reduce prescription-drug misuse are difficult to summarize since they vary depending on the severity of a state's problem and the strength of its commitment to reducing that problem. Federally, the DEA operates several programs within its Diversion Control Division. The DEA can tighten control of certain drugs by moving them upward in the scheduling classification, monitoring physicians' prescribing of controlled substances, and taking administrative or criminal action against prescribers deemed to be acting outside of their authority. The Obama administration was active in attempting to raise awareness about the dangers of prescription drugs (particularly opioids). In general, the tone of the national discourse on prescription-drug misuse and addiction has been rehabilitative and emphasizes improving public awareness about these substances' dangerousness.

EXAMINING THE RATIONALES

For present purposes, drug policies are divided into those targeting traffickers and street-level dealers and those aimed at users. The rationales underlying policy efforts against narcotrafficking and street dealing are deterrence and incapacitation. The intended deterrent purpose of the war on drugs is evident in the rhetoric surrounding the war. Presidential speeches repeatedly refer to notions such as "sending a message" to those contemplating bringing drugs into communities (Elwood, 1995). The incapacitation intent is apparent in the long prison sentences, such as those mandated by the Anti-Drug Abuse Act of 1986. Criminal-justice policy approaches to reducing and preventing the use of drugs are grounded in deterrence and treatment. We will discuss each of these rationales in turn.

DETERRENCE

The greatest deterrence effect of antidrug laws likely lies in the very fact of criminalization itself. Criminalization stigmatizes a particular behavior (Room, 2005), which can repel people away from that behavior. It is unknown how many people today would use cocaine, heroin, and other potentially dangerous substances were these drugs legal; however, we have seen how prevalent the use of cocaine and opium was prior to their being banned (Musto, 1989, 1999), and marijuana legalization and decriminalization appear to be associated with a rise in use (NIDA, 2015). Criminalization has a role in reducing usage.

How far the positive impacts of deterrence might span remains a question. In this answer, less confidence can be placed. On its face, involvement in the drug trade does seem to bear the hallmarks of choice: A person opts to make or sell drugs rather than participate in the legitimate labor market. A deeper examination, however, reveals the socioeconomic backdrop at play. For instance, nearly all heroin sold on the street in the United States contains opium grown in Afghanistan. The U.S. has been unable to put a dent in opium farming there despite pouring billions of dollars into the attempt. The intractability of the problem owes to this crop being impoverished Afghan farmers' only means of survival. Because opium is a low-maintenance plant that is inexpensive to grow and that sells for more per unit than most other crops, farmers have an economic incentive to devote their land to it rather than to other, less-profitable crops. Additionally, the Taliban tightly controls much of the country and extorts high taxes from farmers no matter what they grow (or even if they grow nothing at all), so farmers are forced into opium cultivation even against their will (Chuck, 2015).

In the United States, urban street-level drug sales operate within a milieu of intergenerational poverty and lack of employment opportunities. In the decades following World War II, manufacturing jobs vanished as companies moved factories overseas and mechanized their assembly lines. Deindustrialization has been accompanied by a steady decline in other entry-level jobs that have been outsourced or eliminated, as well as a downsizing of the public-sector workforce. This devastation to the blue-collar sector of the economy was especially harmful to black Americans, who by the 1950s had achieved a fragile upward mobility. The cuts sent many black workers and their families spiraling downward (Wilson, 1987). As this was occurring, black Americans were still suffering the effects of racist housing policies that deliberately concentrated blacks in certain neighborhoods in order to keep them away from white areas (Massey & Denton, 1993). They were also disadvantaged by public-housing policies that were race neutral on their face but, in practice, trapped poor blacks in low-income housing and created a perverse incentive structure that encouraged people to *not* obtain formal employment for fear of losing what precious little housing assistance they receive (Schill & Wachter, 1995). Many inner-city neighborhoods are physically and socially isolated and have been taken over by entrenched poverty.

In these areas, the incentive to sell drugs is strong and the opportunities are abundant (Anderson, 1999). The drug economy is firmly embedded. There is a steady supply of customers because drug use offers a psychological respite from the daily struggles of being extremely poor or homeless (Humphreys & Rappaport, 1993). Suburbanites travel into the inner city to purchase drugs for personal use or to sell in their middle-class neighborhoods (Lassiter, 2015). Many black youth grow up believing that this is their only realistic employment opportunity (Anderson, 1999). This perception largely accords with reality, given the educational disadvantages hampering children and adolescents in impoverished neighborhoods (Shedd, 2015) as well as systemic racial discrimination in hiring practices (Pager, 2008).

Even apart from the socioeconomic backdrops that push many people into the drug trade, there is a general tendency for offenders of all types to be less deterred by formal penalties (even stiff ones) when a crime proves lucrative (Decker, Wright, & Logie, 1993). Selling drugs is a way to earn quick money that can buy status symbols like expensive clothing and jewelry (Anderson, 1999. Although many drug dealers do end up serving jail or prison time at some point, most of the transactions they engage in are covert and carry minimal risk of arrest. Many see an occasional arrest or stint behind bars as a hazard of the business.

Another problem with deterrence-based approaches to reducing drug use is that this orientation overlooks the physiological component of drug dependence. Slogans like "Just say no" portray substance use as a simple choice. While this may be a reasonable depiction of some people's use, it is wildly inaccurate for those who have become physically dependent. Experimenters and casual users constitute the greatest portion of the total group of substance consumers (Inciardi, 2002), but the majority of illegal drugs purchased nationally is consumed by the relatively small group of heavy users and addicts (Kleiman et al., 2011). Between 5 and 6 percent of people who try cocaine become addicted within the first year, and approximately 15 or 16 percent of those who have been using cocaine for 10 years or more meet the diagnostic criteria for dependence (Wagner & Anthony, 2002).

The addictiveness of street drugs and some prescription medications arises from their chemical composition. Opiates (e.g., heroin) and opioids (e.g., oxycodone) are synthetic versions of endogenous morphine (commonly called endorphins) that the human body produces naturally to suppress pain. The introduction of external sources of these chemicals causes some people's bodies to develop a physical dependence, which makes quitting extremely painful (Volkow, 2014). Cocaine and amphetamines trigger releases of neurotransmitters (most importantly, dopamine) in the limbic system (Grilly, 2002), producing a burst of positive emotion. Chronic use over time suppresses the brain's natural release mechanisms and leads to dopamine depletion (Martinez et al., 2009). Dopamine is vital to mood; low levels cause severe depression (Diehl & Gershon, 1992). The dopamine depletion cocaine addicts experience when they are not consuming this substance is likely the main reason they relapse (Martinez et al., 2007). The possible legal consequences for buying and using these drugs is secondary to the intense physical need that addicts develop.

Overall, then, deterrence has some ability to curb the use of dangerous and addictive substances, but we should be wary of antidrug efforts so heavily reliant upon this one philosophy of punishment. The criminal law and criminal-justice system are blunt instruments too clunky to effectively eliminate a significant social ill with complex, multifaceted origins (see Morris & Tonry, 1991). For additional consideration of policy approaches that might fill some gaps left by deterrence, we turn to incapacitation.

INCAPACITATION

One goal of the drug war is to shrink the supply side of the drug trade by removing traffickers and dealers from the streets and imprisoning them for long periods of time. Theoretically, this will reduce drug supplies and drive up prices. There are several assumptions built into this line of reasoning. First is the presumption that removing a few links in the supply chain will significantly disrupt the market. This is wrong. Replacement is a well-recognized phenomenon for crimes committed by groups (see generally McGloin & Piquero, 2009). If a street-level dealer is incarcerated, someone else might be recruited to fill the void. Other dealers might also increase the quantity they sell to compensate for the reduction. Even locking up an entire network probably would not noticeably impact supplies. Drug organizations have overlapping territory, so if one group is disbanded, others can shoulder the increased demand put on them (Poret, 2003).

A second assumption behind incapacitation is that it can wreck cartels by capturing the people at the top. This belief is based on an inaccurate vision of the drug trade as being controlled by tightly organized, hierarchical cartels. In reality, many drug operations are loose groups with no clear organizational structure (Poret, 2003). Within the cartels that do exist, even high-level traffickers can be replaced. Recently, Mexican authorities captured Sinaloa cartel boss Joaquin "El Chapo" Guzmán. Unfortunately, as El Chapo himself correctly pointed out, his arrest means little to the organization's future. The Sinaloa cartel, like other narcotrafficking organizations, contains elements of both horizontal and vertical organization. El Chapo relied upon numerous other people, and those individuals will continue their work in his absence (Alfred, 2016). Capturing and imprisoning cartel bosses is not useless—it would be difficult to argue they should be left to their own devices—but its effectiveness is inherently limited because of the focus on individuals embedded within large, complex networks that are not dependent upon any single person within them (Kleiman et al., 2011).

Even if incapacitation were effective at disrupting markets, the current approach to drug enforcement would undermine this effort. Most enforcement activities against sellers take place on the streets. Street-level dealers are the low-hanging fruit of the drug trade; they are relatively easy for police to identify and capture (see also Beckett et al., 2006). The majority of so-called "traffickers" sent to prison are actually minor dealers (Kleiman et al., 2011). Twelve percent of jail inmates are serving time for trafficking (James, 2004). Jail sentences are typically shorter than one year, which belies the seeming gravity of these inmates' offenses and suggests that "trafficking" has taken on an expansive definition that includes low-level dealers who are even less important to the supply network than genuine traffickers are.

In sum, incapacitation fares poorly as an antidrug strategy. The primary reason for this is that drug trafficking and sales are conducted by networks and groups. Once a network or group is in place, removal of one or even several members matters little to its operation. Incapacitation cannot be expected to noticeably impact the total supply of drugs on the streets.

PREVENTION AND TREATMENT

Drug-prevention programs abound. The most well-known is Drug Abuse Resistance Education (D.A.R.E.), a school-based program in which police officers deliver packaged content to grade-school classrooms. The D.A.R.E. curriculum has been expanded beyond drug use to include messages against violence, bullying, and other antisocial behaviors (D.A.R.E., n.d.). The rationale behind prevention is to keep children away from addictive or destructive substances so that they never become at risk for arrest or incarceration and never develop a need for treatment. At face value, prevention seems to contain obvious social utility: Reduce drug use by stopping people from ever consuming them to begin with. The problem is that, for many people, this commonsense approach is not merely simple but, rather, simplistic. As described previously, drug use (and dealing) has complex, multifaceted origins. For some people, it may begin as purely a recreational experiment; many drug users, however, are socialized into environments wherein drug abuse is prevalent and serves as a common form of self-medication (see Anderson, 1999). Drug-prevention programs may have limited power to influence youth raised in such environments, but remain on the table as potentially viable for lower-risk children and adolescents.

Treatment has been a guiding rationale of the drug war since the war's inception. While demanding harsh penalties for sellers, policymakers have simultaneously advocated treatment for people suffering substance dependence (Humphreys & Rappaport, 1993; Lassiter, 2015). This accords with public opinion. Two-thirds of Americans think cocaine and heroin addicts should be sent to treatment programs rather than to jail or prison (Pew

Research Center, 2014), with a mere 7 percent believing the government is winning the drug war (Rasmussen Reports, 2012). As noted previously, drug courts have been popular since they began in the late 1980s; there has always been a sentiment that antidrug efforts should contain room for more than mere punishment.

Treatment holds promise for many drug users, but its utility is circumscribed because the majority of people who use drugs do not meet diagnostic criteria for substance dependence (Wagner & Anthony, 2002). Certainly, many of those who fall short of a formal diagnosis may use drugs in a problematic way, such as causing disruption to their families or their ability to function at work or school. Treatment in some form might benefit this group. Many people's drug use, though, is occasional and recreational (Inciardi, 2002). For them, treatment is nonsensical. Inappropriate application to people who are at low risk for future misbehavior can cause new problems (e.g., Lowenkamp, Latessa, & Holsinger, 2006). The validity of the logic behind using treatment as an alternative to (or in conjunction with) traditional punishment rests on whether court personnel assess defendants accurately. Treatment should be reserved for those with demonstrated need, and nondependent users should be handled some other way.

THE EMPIRICAL STATUS OF DRUG POLICY

THE WAR ON DRUGS

The assessment of the "effectiveness" of the war on drugs is complicated by the search for an operational definition of "success." One intended outcome was the incarceration of more drug offenders than were imprisoned prior to the war's launch. Measured as such, the war on drugs has been a smashing success. As described earlier, the war massively increased the prison population. More than 2.2 million people are in jail or prison any given year (Carson, 2015). Approximately 18 percent of state prisoners and 51 percent of federal inmates are serving time for a drug offense (Guerino, Harrison, & Sabol, 2011), as are roughly 25 percent of jail inmates (James, 2004). In 2009, the median state-prison sentence for possession of illegal drugs was 36 months and that for trafficking was 48 months (Bonczar, Hughes, Wilson, & Ditton, 2011). Between 1998 and 2012, the number of drug offenders in federal prisons increased by 63 percent (Taxy, Samuels, & Adams, 2015). Half of male federal-prison inmates and 59 percent of female inmates are serving time for drug offenses (Carson, 2015), primarily trafficking; these inmates carry an average sentence of 11 years (Taxy et al., 2015). "Trafficking," as discussed earlier, has a broad interpretation and encompasses both serious drug dealers and lower-level street dealers (Kleiman et al., 2011). The war on drugs has been the primary force behind a sweeping, unprecedented expansion of jail and prison populations.

The war on drugs was also intended to reduce drug use, but data on drug availability and use has led to a general consensus that the war has not led to significant improvements and may have even backfired. The cost of street drugs has declined rather than increased (Boyum & Reuter, 2005) and drug supplies have increased rather than declined (Poret, 2003). Adolescents' drug-use trends vary across time with no apparent connection to rates of incarceration for drug crimes. According to youth surveys, adolescent drug use was at

55 percent in the 1970s and increased until 1981 (66 percent), then began a long decline through the next decade until it hit a low point in 1992 (41 percent) before reaching another peak (55 percent) in 1999. Rates fell during the first years of the 2000s (to 47 percent) and have generally stabilized at that level, displaying only mild year-to-year fluctuations (Johnston, O'Malley, Bachman, & Schulenberg, 2009). College students' and young adults' drug use fell during the 1980s and then varied little from 1991 to 2010; roughly half of college students have tried an illegal substance, and slightly less than two-thirds of young adults have done so (Johnston, O'Malley, Bachman, & Schulenberg, 2011). Prison admissions and populations rose steadily from the 1970s through the early 2000s (Carson & Golinelli, 2013). A look at the data shows there is no correspondence between changes in incarceration rates and dips or rises in drug use.

Drug-related violence was another problem the war was intended to fix. The impact, however, seems to have been a net *increase* in violence. A systematic review of multiple longitudinal studies of drug-market conflict in the United States and other nations revealed higher levels of violence accompanying enhancements in antidrug campaigns by law enforcement (Werb, Rowell, Guyatt, Kerr, Montaner, & Wood, 2011). Intensifying law enforcement may be beneficial up to a certain level of investment, at which point the impact levels off and additional increases suffer from diminishing marginal returns (Kleiman et al., 2011). Ironically, the war gave rise to a large number of the very same international and street-level trafficking networks it was designed to crush. Suppression efforts led by law enforcement drive up drug profitability and lucratively reward those willing to tolerate the risk of apprehension, thereby luring in more traffickers, which in turn engenders fiercer competition and violence. The Mexican government's primary strategy to destroy narcotrafficking in that country has been to capture or kill identified kingpins. The end result, however, has been a proliferation of smaller drug rings. These smaller operations lack the comfort their more seasoned predecessors enjoyed as the result of their established claims over particular territories. Because of their inexperience and sizable number, these newer drug rings battle viciously to carve out turf (Finnegan, 2012). The war on drugs has heightened competition and ramped up the violence in the international drug trade.

The collateral damage has been domestic as well as international. The use of incarceration for drug possession and low-level dealing has taken a toll on black and Latino Americans, their families, and many inner-city communities. Blacks are incarcerated at a rate of 2,724 per 100,000 and Latinos at 1,091, with whites trailing at 465 (Carson, 2015). The bulk of these disparities is attributable to the war on drugs. In federal prisons, blacks constitute 39 percent of those serving time for drug offenses (Taxy et al., 2015), even though they make up only 13 percent of the general population in the United States. Latinos are 37 percent of federal drug offenders (Taxy et al., 2015) and 18 percent of the population. Blacks make up 88 percent of inmates imprisoned for crack cocaine (Taxy et al., 2015), a predictable outcome of the 100:1 (or, more recently, 18:1) rule that levies harsh penalties for small amounts of crack, which is the most prevalent drug in inner-city, black neighborhoods (Bourgois, 2003). The situation is similarly bleak in jails: 31 percent of black jail inmates, 28 percent of Latino inmates, and 19 percent of white inmates are in for drug offenses (James, 2004). State prisons show the least amount of racial disparity: 16 percent of blacks, 15 percent of Latinos, and 15 percent of whites serving time in these facilities are there for drug crimes (Carson, 2015).

Racial disparities in imprisonment rates are exacerbated by the fact that black and Latino Americans display concentrated residential patterns. The concentration is particularly pronounced among urban-residing blacks, a large portion of whom live in mostly or entirely black neighborhoods that are socially and economically isolated (Wood & Brunson, 2011). Many Latinos, likewise, reside in majority-Latino neighborhoods and experience hostility from surrounding white neighborhoods (Vera Sanchez & Gau, 2015). These neighborhoods experience high incarceration rates; prison is a source of constant population turnover, with large chunks of the community cycling in and out of prison regularly. This tumult disrupts families and severs the ties between neighbors that make up the fabric of a community, thereby worsening crime rates (Clear, Rose, Waring, & Scully, 2003). Constant police scrutiny and high rates of arrest and incarceration generate an atmosphere of ever-present government surveillance and control that damages the psyches of those residing in these areas (Rios, 2011). The drug war has had dramatic, devastating impacts on many black and Latino communities.

DRUG COURTS

The question of whether drug courts "work" is complicated. First, drug courts vary across jurisdictions (e.g., Mitchell et al., 2012). Some are dedicated to adults, and some to juveniles. Some focus solely on certain offense types (e.g., driving under the influence) while others accept a wide array of offenders. This variation makes sense, given drug courts' goal of dispensing justice that accords with community values (Goldkamp et al., 2001), but makes it difficult to assess this heterogeneous conglomeration as a single category. Second, the matter of drug-court effectiveness inevitably leads to another question, "Compared to *what*?" It is not clear if participants' outcomes should be evaluated against those of people who went to jail, prison, or probation. It is similarly difficult to select an appropriate recidivism threshold. It is unrealistic to expect no future drug use at all among drug-court graduates; relapse is a strong possibility even for the most motivated recovering addicts. There is no standard regarding what rates of recidivism are considered acceptable or unacceptable (Goldkamp et al., 2001). It is also not true that a single relapse is indicative of failure—a drug-treatment participant can pull through and continue on the road toward recovery.

Third, and most importantly from an empirical standpoint, most of the research on drug courts suffers from varying gradations of methodological weakness. Experimental designs employing random assignment to treatment (drug court) and control (processed through regular court) groups are rare (Gottfredson & Exum, 2002; Gottfredson, Najaka, & Kearley, 2003). The absence of random assignment means that there is no valid comparison group, because drug-court participation is voluntary and requires defendants to commit to an extended regimen of treatment and regular court appearances. Drug-court participants may do better than those who went through regular channels simply because the former were more motivated to succeed, a phenomenon called selection bias. To correct for this as best as possible, researchers employ quasiexperimental research designs whereby drug-court graduates are matched on key characteristics (gender, drug-use history, and so on) to controls who did not go through the program (or who started but dropped out). Matching is not a perfect solution to the absence of random assignment, but it is superior to using control groups composed of convenience samples, results of any such comparisons being wholly untrustworthy. Drug-court evaluations vary markedly in quality, with rigorous studies being far outnumbered by medium and weak ones (e.g., Mitchell et al., 2012). Unfortunately, weaker ones tend to produce larger apparent positive results for drug-court participants, while stronger ones yield smaller or null results (Lowenkamp, Holsinger, & Latessa, 2005).

With the above caveats in mind, there are some general conclusions that can be drawn about drug courts' effectiveness. There are a small handful of studies using experimental designs. Two of these studies focused on a drug court in Baltimore and found that at a 12-month follow-up 64 percent of controls but only 48 percent of drug-court participants had been arrested for a new drug offense (Gottfredson & Exum, 2002), a difference that remained substantively significant at 24 months (Gottfredson et al., 2003). It is also clear that program quality matters for outcomes; programs must be evidence-based and closely adhere to treatment protocol or they will not work (Goldkamp et al., 2001; Gottfredson et al., 2003).

Evaluations of individual drug courts have yielded inconsistent results, so meta-analyses are instructive. Meta-analyses are "studies of studies" that compile published and unpublished evaluations to quantitatively synthesize the sum total of the evidence. A meta-analysis can reveal whether the bulk of the evidence leans toward effectiveness or ineffectiveness. (Chapter 14 contains a detailed description of meta-analytic techniques.) Mitchell et al. (2012) found that participants in adult and juvenile drug courts had lower general and drug-specific recidivism rates than comparison groups did, but that these summary findings were attributable primarily to methodologically weak studies that produced misleading results due to selection bias and other flaws (see also Lowenkamp et al., 2005). Juvenile courts' effects were small even among weak studies. Lowenkamp et al. (2005) found that the most effective programs were those that targeted high-risk drug users, a result that calls into question the standard practice of reserving drug courts for minor, first-time offenders. Wilson et al. (2006) discovered that the drug courts employing standardized preadjudication or postadjudication policies appear to be more effective than those allowing judges to decide the terms of supervision on a case-by-case basis, likely because predictability and consistency offer an advantage over the unknowns of an idiosyncratic system. Overall, the evidence leans in favor of drug courts' ability to reduce drug use and rates of re-arrest for all crime types, but the effects are modest in size and contingent upon program quality.

PREVENTION PROGRAMS

Prevention programs are so diverse that it is not possible to say whether, as a group, they "work" or not. Most are not effective (White & Pitts, 1998), but there are program characteristics that appear to reliably differentiate successful from unsuccessful programs (Tobler, Roona, Ochshorn, Marshall, Streke, & Stackpole, 2000), and thus offer helpful policy guides. Using a packaged curriculum that has been shown to work in the past is a smart move for school administrators (see Cuijpers, 2002 for a review). Interaction seems to be a key ingredient to a successful program. Children absorb information better when they engage in dialogue and receive constructive feedback than when they are merely lectured at about the dangers of drug use (Cuijpers, 2002; Tobler et al., 2000). Social-influence approaches also appear to be superior. This perspective recognizes that children's attitudes toward drugs are formed from a combination of exposure to media, peers, parents, siblings, and other sources. Program tactics revolve around guiding children into developing negative attitudes toward drugs. It is thought that if they adopt normative beliefs that illegal substances are detrimental for multiple reasons, they will stay away from them. There seems to be merit in this (Botvin, 2000; Tobler et al., 2000). Even effective programs, however, do not produce stunning reductions in the rates at which adolescents try drugs for the first time or in the quantities of drugs consumed among those who use them. Effects tend to be very small (Tobler et al., 2000; White & Pitts, 1998). They are usually also short lived and wear off unless students are periodically exposed to booster sessions (Botvin, 2000).

EFFORTS TO REDUCE PRESCRIPTION-PILL ABUSE

This area of policy is new and represents a multitude of local, state, and federal efforts, so the discussion of effectiveness is tentative and preliminary. The state of Florida stands out as a recent example of how a state wracked by an opioid problem initiated new policies and made significant improvements. This state once contained some of the nation's highest per capita rates of opioid prescriptions and deaths. From 2009 to 2011, the state legislature created a PDMP and tightened regulations on physicians prescribing opioids. There was also a statewide, ground-level campaign by law enforcement to arrest and prosecute physicians who were prescribing pills for profit. These combined efforts appear to have dramatically reduced the total number of pain clinics in the state (Gau & Brooke, 2016) and opioid-caused deaths (Delcher, Wagenaar, Goldberger, Cook, & Maldonado-Molina, 2015; Johnson et al., 2014).

Unfortunately, this decline may have exerted its own set of collateral consequences. Corrupt physicians looking for easy pill profits can easily set up shop in other states with fewer regulations; the state of West Virginia, for instance, has seen a rise in opioid prescriptions and overdose deaths and is now experiencing a veritable crisis (Eyre, 2016). Prescription opioids' decline in availability and spike in price also seems to have stimulated the heroin market and, in particular, a strand of heroin containing fentanyl, a powerful and often lethal opioid. Deaths from fentanyl have surged (Leger, 2015). The United States has yet to devise an effective method of reducing prescription pill misuse, addiction, and overdose.

CONCLUSION

The approach to drug policy in the U.S. has been a twisting road that has forked off in many directions. Historically, Congress invoked its powers of taxation to stem the flow of drugs into and throughout the nation. Then in the 1970s, it rolled out a stringent regulatory framework, followed closely by the launch of the original punitive antidrug measures.

By the 1980s, the war on drugs was in full swing. The only measurable output of the war on drugs has been an enormous increase in the prison population, chiefly among black and Latino Americans, which has visited extreme consequences upon the relatively small number of neighborhoods from which the bulk of the prison population is pulled. The prison boom has not suppressed drug markets to a prohibitive extent. Drugs are available and affordable, street-level dealing is common in many urban and suburban neighborhoods, and the violence associated with international narcotrafficking is staggering. Drug use and street-level dealing are inextricably bound up in poverty, victimization, and systemic racial and economic discrimination.

Drug courts and school-based prevention programs appear to have benefits, as long as they adhere to evidence-based practices. Currently, many programs do not. Even those effects that do emerge tend to be modest in magnitude and to decay over time.

Perhaps the most significant flaw in the reasoning atop which the war on drugs, and even treatment and prevention, stands is that the criminal-justice system cannot be expected to solve problems caused by larger social, economic, and political forces, yet a solution from the criminal-justice system is precisely what the backers of antidrug programs and policies claim they will accomplish. Ameliorating the drug problem requires better social and economic policies that, among other things, make employment a realistic possibility for all and that eliminate racial bias in hiring and housing. Until the federal and state governments adopt more creative, nuanced, evidence-based approaches, there will likely be no noteworthy reduction in drug use, trafficking, or violence in the foreseeable future.

DISCUSSION QUESTIONS

1. Former President Barack Obama made several moves to scale back drug enforcement and reduce the use of prison for nonviolent drug offenders. He also instructed federal prosecutors to turn their attention away from marijuana in states that had legalized the drug. President Donald Trump's administration, by contrast, announced plans to ramp up the enforcement of drug laws and enforce federal marijuana laws in all states, irrespective of state law. Do you think this will significantly reduce drug use, availability, or the illegal drug market? What impact could it have on prison populations? Explain your answers.

2. Critics of modern drug policies claim that there is inherent racial bias built into the differences in governmental approaches to the misuse of prescription pills (opioids and benzodiazepines, in particular) as compared to the use of street drugs (powder cocaine, crack, heroin, and marijuana). Prescription-pill misuse and addiction is primarily concentrated among whites, while street drugs have historically been associated with minorities. The primary approach to street drugs has been strict enforcement and suppression, while conversations about pill misuse revolve around finding ways to cure the disease, not about implementing harsher penalties for misusing these drugs. Critics see this as a direct result of the racial patterns of drug use. Do you see merit in this argument, or do you think there is a good reason for the two different approaches? Defend your position.

3. The proper role of the federal government in directing and controlling state activities has been debated since the founding of the country. Federalists contend that federal mandates ensure consistency across states and prevent arbitrariness and confusion. States-rights advocates, on the other hand, think states should be free to decide what happens within their own borders

and should be largely free of federal control and regulation. Analyze this debate within the context of drug policy. What are the merits of each side of the argument? What are the drawbacks or weaknesses of each side? Ultimately, what do you think the best approach would be, and why?

4. Marijuana has been a Schedule I drug for decades, which means it is officially declared as having no medical utility, yet more than half the states and the District of Columbia have legalized medical marijuana. There has been significant public and political support for reclassifying marijuana and placing it in a lower tier, which would lift restrictions on use and on laboratory research, but federal lawmakers and policymakers have thus far refused to do so. Congress only just introduced a bill in 2017 proposing to move it to Schedule III. Why do you think the federal government has kept marijuana a Schedule I drug for so long despite substantial public support for moving it to a lower tier?

CASES CITED

Gonzales v. Raich, 545 U.S. 1 (2005).
Leary v. United States, 395 U.S. 6 (1969).
National Labor Relations Board v. Jones & Laughlin Steel Corp., 301 U.S. 1 (1937).
West Coast Hotel Co. v. Parrish, 300 U.S. 379 (1937).
Wickard v. Filburn, 317 U.S. 111 (1942).

CHAPTER 4

SEX-OFFENDER POLICY

INTRODUCTION

On September 3, 2016, authorities in Minnesota announced they had located and positively identified the remains of Jacob Wetterling. Jacob had not been seen since he was abducted at gunpoint by a masked assailant in 1989. He was 11 years old. In the course of the investigation, police attention focused on Danny James Heinrich, a local man who matched the description provided by victims of similar kidnappings that had taken place around the time of Jacob's disappearance. Lacking sufficient evidence to formally arrest and charge Heinrich, police released him. In July 2015, authorities analyzed a DNA sample found on a sweater belonging to one of the other victims—it was a match to Heinrich. The execution of a search warrant on Heinrich's home revealed a cache of child pornography. Heinrich later confessed to sexually assaulting and murdering Jacob, and he led authorities to the remains.

The appalling crime perpetrated against Jacob Wetterling was a turning point in the nation's approach to sex-offender legislation. While it could not be proven in the wake of the kidnapping that Jacob had fallen victim to a sex crime, his abduction occurred in the midst of a spate of other crimes in which young boys were grabbed from public locations, sexually assaulted, and released. The natural inference was that Jacob had been similarly abused. The public's fury soon translated into sweeping national legislation requiring all persons convicted of sex offenses to register with local authorities upon their release from prison. Between 1994 and 2006, the federal government continuously ramped up the severity of sex-offender registration and community notification laws. During this same period and since, states and many cities and counties also enacted residency restrictions prohibiting convicted sex offenders from living within a certain distance (anywhere from 500 to 2,500 feet, depending on the jurisdiction) from schools, daycare centers, and other locations where children congregate. The overriding purpose of these sex-offender registration and notification (SORN) laws and residency restrictions (RRs) is to crack down on sex offenders in the name of community protection.

Empirical evaluations of SORN and RRs have yielded dismal results. These laws do not appear to impact on sex-offender (SO) recidivism. Furthermore, there is some evidence that the laws can increase the chances of reoffending by disrupting offenders' reentry processes and preventing them from accessing the social stability and services necessary for successful rehabilitation. It is tremendously difficult to publicly denounce SO laws, as there are few criminal offenders the public considers more revolting than those who sexually prey on others, particularly upon children. Contemporary SO laws are the product of this scorn, which is understandable on an emotional level. Sex-offender policy is a uniquely problematic sphere because emotions are so strong, and yet the stakes are too high to allow ineffective, counterproductive laws to persist merely because they make the public feel better. This chapter will critically examine SORN and RR laws. We will trace the history of sex-offender laws and policies, examine the rationales underlying them, review empirical tests of their effectiveness, and discuss promising avenues for future policy approaches. While most of the policies covered here affect people convicted of all kinds of sex crimes perpetrated against both adults and children, offenses against children occupy a central role in public dialogue and policymaking activity. This chapter reflects that focus.

HISTORY OF SEX-OFFENDER LAWS AND POLICIES

Criminal laws and policies have traditionally been localized; that is, they have been treated as matters for states and cities to control within their own borders. The federal government dictates policy for federal crimes, but typically does not meddle with state criminal codes. In accord with this tradition, SO laws originated with the states and initially existed solely at this level. Washington State pioneered the use of SORN in 1990. Several states soon followed with their own versions of the Washington approach (Jerusalem, 1995). During this decade, many states also passed civil-commitment laws (Jerusalem, 1995; Levenson, 2004) allowing SOs clinically assessed as being extraordinarily dangerous to be confined in mental hospitals indefinitely upon the expiration of their prison sentences.

In the 1990s, the nation saw a dramatic surge in the federal government's involvement in criminal laws that impacted state and local operations (Logan, 2008). Federal mandates for the ways states handle sex offenders were a part of this surge (A. J. Harris & Labanov-Rostovsky, 2010; Jerusalem, 1995). The goal was to impose harsh, standardized penalties on SOs no matter where in the United States they resided. Nevertheless, states continue to evince variation in the ways in which they implement and carry out federal mandates (A. J. Harris & Labanov-Rostovsky, 2010). SO policies are a mix of national standards and state-by-state (even city-by-city) diversity.

The push at the federal level began with Jacob Wetterling. Jacob's abduction and presumptive (now confirmed) sexual assault prompted Congress to pass the Jacob Wetterling Crimes against Children and Sexually Violent Offender Registration Act (also known as the Wetterling Act) in 1994. This law required states to maintain registries that track people convicted of sex offenses after their release from prison or probation. That same year, 7-year-old Megan Kanka of New Jersey fell victim to a horrific rape and murder, which further fueled the nation's outrage. Her killer, who had previous convictions for sexual assaults on children, lived next door to the Kankas, but they were unaware of his past. The ensuing 1996 federal legislation, known as Megan's Law, amended the Wetterling

Act by adding community notification to the registration requirement, thus allowing local residents access to the names and addresses of known sex offenders.

In 2006, the Adam Walsh Child Protection and Safety Act (also known as the Walsh Act, and as the Sex Offender Registration and Notification Act [SORNA]) replaced the Wetterling Act and Megan's Law with an even stricter set of requirements. Adam Walsh had been abducted and murdered in Florida in 1981, and this new legislation was named in his honor 25 years after his tragic death. (Adam was not sexually assaulted and his killer had no known sex-offense history. The naming of the act in his memory was supported by several parents whose children had fallen victim to repeat sex offenders.) The Walsh Act established tiers that states must follow for assessing sex offenders' risk levels (Harris, Lobanov-Rostovsky, & Levenson, 2010) and requires states to publicly release information about offenders who meet certain criteria. This law also allows federal courts to civilly commit offenders deemed sexually dangerous. The U. S. Supreme Court confirmed the constitutionality of civil commitment in *Kansas v. Hendricks* (1997). Since civil commitment is for treatment, not punishment, it does not violate the prohibition on double jeopardy.

The Walsh Act is a sweeping set of highly specific criteria that the federal government imposes upon the states (Harris & Lobanov-Rastofsky, 2010). Some of its provisions have been argued to be unconstitutional (Fetzer, 2010) and some have been challenged in court. In *United States v. Comstock* (2010), the U.S. Supreme Court affirmed Congress' authority to enact federal civil-commitment laws. There have been an array of federal-court decisions pertaining to the registration provision, particularly the requirement that offenders registered in one state subsequently register within any other state to which they travel. Several lower courts have struck down this provision as an unconstitutional overreach by Congress' (see Fetzer, 2010 for a review). Recently, the U.S. Supreme Court ruled in favor of a registered SO who moved and failed to notify his old jurisdiction of his new address (*Nichols v. United States*, 2016). It seems likely that the Walsh Act will continue facing legal challenges, and some of its provisions could be struck down.

Residency restrictions are a relatively new addition to the set of approaches taken against sex offenders. These laws are an outgrowth of SORN laws–once people realized they could identify who the sex offenders were, they began wanting to keep SOs away from schools and other places where children congregate. The federal government does not require RRs; these laws exist at the state and local levels only. Nearly half of states restrict where people with sex-offense histories can reside (Nieto & Jung, 2006). These laws vary substantially in severity and scope. Illinois, for example, prohibits those who have committed offenses against children from residing within 500 feet of schools, while Alabama prohibits all sex offenders from residing or working within 2,000 feet of schools or daycares. Some states allow parole officials to decide on a case-by-case basis which offenders should be subject to RRs and which should not, while others outline classification schemes for determining which offenders are high risk and should be restricted (National Conference of State Legislatures, 2006). Where state laws are absent, many cities and counties have passed ordinances specifying their own local RRs. There are hundreds of such ordinances nationwide (Nieto & Jung, 2006).

These restrictions, like some of the SORN requirements, have encountered resistance in the courts. Most legal challenges arise out of studies showing that RRs dramatically reduce (in some states and cities, nearly eliminate) available housing for sex offenders, forcing them into homelessness (California Sex Offender Management Board, 2008) and creating severe social instability in their lives (Edwards & Hensley, 2001). The California Supreme Court declared a local ordinance prohibiting all sex offenders from living within 2,000 feet of schools and parks unconstitutional because of the enormous toll it took on offenders as they attempted to reenter society. The justices cited studies showing how the draconian RR created a barrier between parolees and necessary services, such as drug and mental-health counseling centers. By contrast, the court found the provision of the law allowing parole officials to initiate residency restrictions on a case-by-case basis depending on parolees' risk levels to be acceptable (*In re Taylor,* 2015). Despite ongoing debates about RRs' possible negative impacts on public safety and emerging legal challenges to these laws' constitutionality, many cities continue to implement new ordinances restricting SOs' living arrangements. Some jurisdictions allow restrictions only for repeat and violent SOs, while others cast wide nets that capture lower-level offenders (e.g., those convicted of indecent exposure) as well (Fifield, 2016). As with the Walsh Act, cases involving RRs may keep cropping up in the courts.

Critics have contended that sex-offender laws are purely symbolic, intended only to pacify the public and deceive people into believing that the government is "doing something" about the sex-offender problem (Sample, Evans, & Anderson, 2011). This deceit is likely intentional in some cases, while in others it may be an outgrowth of politicians' own lack of knowledge about the realities of sex offending. Research suggests that politicians, like most of the public, rely on the media for information about sex offenders and their crimes; they get swept up in an emotional response and fall into the belief that registration and notification are effective, necessary policy responses (Sample & Kadleck, 2008). Rather than being entirely symbolic, SO laws might be better characterized as expressive. Expressive laws are the public's effort to send a message. By criminalizing and harshly penalizing certain actions, the citizenry can collectively display its condemnation of those behaviors. Instrumental laws, by contrast, are designed to achieve an identified set of objectives and goals. Expressive laws can bring people together and reaffirm the social morals of a culture. This has some benefits in terms of fostering solidarity and a shared sense of normative beliefs; however, laws designed to merely soothe the public's anger and fear do not improve public safety in the long run, and can even reduce it by taking up legislative space that could be occupied instead by laws with true substance that intelligently connect strategies with identified target outcomes.

EXAMINING THE RATIONALES

The rationales invoked to justify sex-offender policy center more on the offenders themselves than on traditional philosophies about the purposes of punishment. This is not to say that deterrence, retribution, incapacitation, and rehabilitation do not have their place in policy discussions; they most certainly do. But digging deeper into the issue reveals that at its core, SO policy rests on the assumptions that sex offenders are mentally disordered and uniformly pose high risks of recidivism (e.g., Petrunik, 2003). Somewhat contradicting the "sex offenders are sick" hypothesis, however, is the assertion that tough penalties for sex offenses will have both general and specific deterrent effects. Because deterrence theory presumes offenders are rational, the presumption of pervasive, severe mental illness is incompatible with the notion that harsh penalties will effect deterrence. There are also several assumptions built into the "sex offender" label, including assumptions about the homogeneity of this class of offenders and the accuracy of criminal convictions as indicative of actual crimes committed, as opposed to approximations settled upon during the charging and plea bargaining process. The public expresses widespread endorsement of assumptions about sickness, deterrence, and accuracy (Levenson, Brannon, Fortney, & Baker, 2007). We will examine each in turn.

THE ASSUMPTION THAT SEX OFFENDERS ARE "SICK"

The answer to the question of whether SOs are "sick" is that some are and some are not. There is a prevalent presumption among policymakers that sex offenders commit these acts because they have genetic or psychological abnormalities that cause dysfunctional sexual urges (Jerusalem, 1995; Sample & Bray, 2003; Simon, 2000; Zgoba, 2011). Embedded within the very existence of the label "sex offender" is an assumption that people who commit sex offenses are specialists; that is, it is commonly believed that sex crimes are the only offenses these people commit. This is not true. People who commit sex offenses are often generalists, meaning they commit multiple types of crimes (Harris, Smallbone, Dennison, & Knight, 2009; Simon, 2000). Their sex crimes might be evidence more of a pattern of antisocial behavior than of a mental pathology specifically relating to deviant sexual desires.

Nevertheless, there could be something unique about some sex offenders' cognitive processes; indeed, many display cognitive distortions such as a belief that the victim wanted the contact (Jerusalem, 1995). The psychological treatment delivered to sex offenders mandated to therapy as part of a court order is fundamentally different from that provided to other categories of offenders (English, Jones, & Patrick, 2003). Sex offenders display a variety of mental illnesses, and a sizable portion of them abuse drugs and alcohol (Simon, 2000). However, aside from pedophilia's obvious relevance to sexually deviant behavior, it is not clear whether or how psychological disorders or substance abuse are linked to sexual offending. More research is needed to uncover the prevalence of mental illness among SOs, the types of disturbances they have, and the nature of the connection (if any) between their psychological troubles and their negative behaviors.

THE ASSUMPTION THAT SEX OFFENDERS WILL REOFFEND

Sex-offender recidivism rates are a matter of considerable debate. Different studies have painted disparate pictures of reoffending among SOs (Vásquez, Maddan, & Walker, 2008). The criteria the Walsh Act requires states to use when placing SOs into tiers have been criticized for failing to include several relevant pieces of information and, consequently, overestimating offenders' risk levels (Harris, Lobanov-Rostovsky, & Levenson, 2010). There is also ambiguity about what, exactly, constitutes recidivism.

Recidivism must be broken down into general and offense-specific categories. General recidivism is the commission of any new crime, while offense-specific recidivism is the perpetration of additional offenses that are the same as the original one. Official statistics (that is, arrest and conviction data) show that sex offenders' general recidivism rates are high (Caldwell, 2010; Maddan, Miller, Walker, & Marshall, 2011), but are no different from the rates found among other types of offenders (Sample & Bray, 2003). The rate at which SOs sexually reoffend, however, is low. Some studies have uncovered sexual-recidivism rates of 8 percent for new charges and 5 percent for new convictions (Letourneau, Levenson, Bandyopadhyay, Sinha, & Armstrong, 2010a). Others have found 10 percent or less for rearrests for any sex offense and below 6 percent for a new sex offense matching the original one (Sample & Bray, 2006). Still others have documented rates of 9.5 percent and 8.2 percent for new sex-offense arrest and conviction, respectively (Maddan et al., 2011). Approximately 7 percent of juveniles convicted of sex offenses reoffend. Importantly, their highest-risk period is during the years immediately following the original conviction; as time progresses, the risk diminishes (Caldwell, 2010). The official statistics suggest that people convicted of sex offenses are at relatively low risk of repeating this behavior.

Official numbers are somewhat unreliable, however, because many of the people sex offenders are guilty of more crimes than those for which they are arrested and convicted, so the statistics may underestimate recidivism rates. Under polygraph examination, SOs frequently admit to a greater number of offenses and victims than that reflected in their formal criminal records (Cooley-Towell, Pasini-Hill, & Patrick, 2000). Sexual assault and abuse are typically low-visibility crimes that are difficult to detect, especially because most victims do not go to the police (English et al., 2003; Tabachnick & Klein, 2011). Many SOs get away with their crimes or are able to offend several times before getting caught.

Finally, sex offending itself is poorly understood and there is no solid evidence about which types of offenders may be at higher risk for recidivism than others. Crime type, victim characteristics, and situational factors seem to play a role in offenders' recidivism likelihood (Nieto & Jung, 2006; Sample & Bray, 2006). There are important questions lingering about whether a sex-offender typology exists whereby offenders could be classified according to their behavioral patterns and risk for future offending. Overall, then, we are left with a hazy picture regarding how often sex offenders repeat their crimes and which offenders (or categories thereof) pose the greatest threat to the public.

THE ASSUMPTION THAT THE SEX-OFFENDER LABEL IS ACCURATE

Sex-offender policy also rests upon the additional assumption that sex offenders are properly labeled and that the label accurately reflects each person's past. This assumption is problematic for several reasons. First, high rates of nonreporting introduce unreliability into the label. The majority of sex-crime victims do not report the incident. For instance, only about 35 percent of rape victims go to the police (Truman & Langton, 2014). Estimates of the reporting of child sexual abuse are as low as 12 percent. Many victims are ashamed, and some perpetrators physically threaten their victims to deter them from reporting the crime (see Tabachnick & Klein, 2011 for a review). Victims often feel embarrassed and fear that they will be blamed for what happened. Most victims are acquainted with their assailants—even related to them—and a large portion of sex offenses represent not isolated incidents but, rather, extended patterns of repeated abuse. Victims' complex relationships with their abusers make it difficult for them to disclose their victimization (English et al., 2003). Ironically, the severity of the criminal-justice response to sex offending can itself discourage victims and their families from reporting, because the abuser may be a loved one (such as an older sibling of the victim) and the family wants to see him or her receive treatment, not prison time followed by registration requirements (Tabachnick & Klein, 2011). This undermines the major SO policies, because a substantial segment of people who have committed sex crimes and might be dangerous do not have criminal records and therefore do not appear in SORN databases and are not subject to RRs. The vast majority of people arrested for sex crimes are first-time offenders, meaning much sexual victimization is perpetrated by people who are not on community-notification websites (Sandler, Freeman, & Socia, 2008). Someone who is not a registered sex offender is not necessarily innocent—he or she simply may not have (yet) been caught.

Second, the crime for which someone is convicted is an unreliable indicator of the offense they actually committed. Police, prosecutors, and defense attorneys make several discretionary judgments that can alter (sometimes drastically) the nature and number of criminal charges against a defendant. For instance, a police officer may arrest a suspect for sexual assault, but a prosecutor might decline to file charges out of concern that a jury would not find the victim credible (see Frohman, 1997). The prosecutor could also proceed with a different charge, such as an assault or abuse charge that does not contain a sexual element. If sex-crime charges are filed, they might be dropped during the plea-bargaining process. Rape charges, for instance, are frequently pled down to kidnapping (Simon, 2000). The very harshness of SO penalties heightens the probability that plea bargaining will result in offenders pleading down to nonsexual offenses in order to avoid SORN requirements and RRs (Cohen & Jeglic, 2007). Evidentiary problems play a role in this process. A prosecutor might agree to drop or reduce sex-crime charges exchange for a defendant's guilty plea if the evidence is weak and conviction at trial is doubtful, or if testifying at trial would traumatize the victim. For many reasons, then, people guilty of sex offenses can be convicted of non sexual types of crimes.

Finally, SO policy has faced widespread criticism for relying on mischaracterizations about the nature of most sex offenses. Media and politicians frame the violent horrors inflicted upon murdered children featured in news broadcasts as typical of sex offenses. However, these terrible acts are outliers unrepresentative of the majority of sexual predation. Sex crimes range widely in severity and circumstances, but this variation is largely omitted from public discourse. Media-generated moral panics vilify people convicted of sex offenses and fire up the public (Fox, 2013), whose main source of information about sex offending is television (Sample & Kadleck, 2008; Schiavone & Jeglic, 2009). The public, in general, holds inaccurate beliefs about sex offenders' behaviors and risk levels

(Levenson et al., 2007). People are particularly vulnerable to the emotional manipulation in sensationalized sex crimes (Malinen, Willis, & Johnston, 2014).

Most SO policy is driven by a desire to express society's moral outrage against those who commit sex crimes, not by a carefully reasoned analysis of the evidence (see Leon, 2011 for a review). Myths and misunderstandings about sex offenders fuel punitive attitudes (Quinn, Forsyth, & Mullen-Quinn, 2004), and fear of these offenders—especially those who have victimized children—significantly increases people's support for registration and notification laws (Kernsmith, Craun, & Foster, 2009). In an unfortunate circularity, media coverage of serious, atypical sex offenses sometimes spikes after new laws are enacted (Ducat, Thomas, & Blood, 2009). Thus, distortions and misinformation give rise to off-the-mark policies, which in turn reify the underlying misconceptions. Crafting policy based on outliers and then uncritically applying it to thousands of people whose crimes look nothing like those upon which the policy was built is counterproductive.

Another downside of overgeneralizing is that laws based on sensationalized cases fail to adequately account for the diversity in offending. Self-reports from convicted SOs reveal substantial heterogeneity. An offender convicted of sexual abuse of a female child may also have abused a male child; some people caught for assaulting strangers have histories of sex crimes against family members (Cooley-Towell et al., 2000). Arrest data likewise show that people convicted of different charges (e.g., child pornography, rape) are rearrested for new sex offenses at sharply different rates (Sample & Bray, 2006). The sex-offender stereotype obscures this variety and frustrates efforts to learn more about what causes sex offending and how to tailor punishment and treatment to accurately match each offense. Indiscriminate application of the SO label also reduces the public's ability to figure out which offenders pose a credible threat and which ones do not (Levenson, 2011).

SHAMING AND DETERRENCE (SORN)

Registration, notification, and residency restrictions do not spring from any single or widely agreed upon rationale. As described previously, they reflect several popular beliefs about sex offenders themselves. Many proponents also point to the supposed deterrent effects of these laws (see Letourneau et al., 2010b). Indeed, SORN laws are modern versions of the historical practice of public shaming. In the 1600s, most nations and communities penalized behavior considered deviant (sexually and otherwise) by humiliating and degrading the offender. Sometimes the punishment was temporary (e.g., spending time in the pillory) and sometimes it was permanent (e.g., having one's face branded). It was popularly presumed that public embarrassment was an effective deterrent. After the Revolutionary War, the United States rejected public shaming as an outdated, inhumane ritual. The rise of SORN beginning in the 1990s represents a return to this long-ago abandoned practice (Jerusalem, 1995).

The deterrence justification for current SO laws clashes with the hypothesis that SOs' crimes spring from psychological sickness. There is an inherent contradiction in the claim that SOs are intractably mentally ill and behaviorally disordered, but that they can nevertheless be deterred by harsh sanctions. Given the flaws in the "sick hypothesis" described earlier, however, it is reasonable to believe that some SOs may indeed be rational offenders, so it is worth considering whether, in theory at least, they may be deterrable.

Deterrence, as a general crime-prevention strategy, has well-known limitations. Offenders often commit crimes on impulse with little or no planning, and many are under the influence of drugs or alcohol and thus operating with impaired judgment (Loeber et al., 2012; Zimring, 1968). Many offenders will carry out a crime even if they think they might be arrested, as long as they perceive the payoff to be worth the risk (Decker, Wright, & Logie, 1993). Offenders of all types respond more to the certainty of punishment than to the severity of it, which is particularly problematic for this class of crimes. Sex offenses usually take place in private; most sex abuse occurs within the home and is perpetrated by people known to the victim (Tabachnick & Klein, 2011). The secrecy undermines certainty of arrest. State and federal governments' emphasis on the severity of punishment diverts attention away from laws and policies that could enhance the probability of detection, such as programs encouraging victims to report abuse or educating childcare providers on recognizing the signs of abuse. Since only a small percentage of offenders are subject to SORN and RRs, these laws' deterrent values are likely modest at best.

GEOGRAPHIC PROXIMITY (RESIDENCY RESTRICTIONS)

Residency restrictions, like SORN, represent a return of an age-old practice. These restrictions are a modern version of banishment (Nieto & Jung, 2006; Zgoba, 2011). Centuries ago, nations commonly exiled individuals who engaged in disruptive or deviant behavior. Convicts were sent to designated islands to live together in isolated colonies, or were ferried to other continents as indentured servants. The goal was not to reform offenders but, rather, to simply get rid of them.

The rationale for residency restrictions is sometimes articulated in terms of the routine activities model of crime commission (Cohen & Felson, 1979). This model posits that SOs' residential proximity to schools, daycare centers, and other places that host daily flows of children allow these offenders to develop familiarity with the circumstances and timing of activities within that area. Another, related, criminological model is that of distance decay, which suggests that, all else being equal, offenders will commit crimes closer to home and will not travel great distances to offend (Berenson & Appelbaum, 2011). An SO who resides next to a school might learn that at 1 PM every weekday, children are released for recess and there are not enough adults to furnish adequate supervision. A predator living near a park might likewise figure out what time parents arrive for playgroups and be able to discern the level of supervision parents exercise over their children.

These are valid concerns that should be addressed through law and policy; however, RRs are not a logical solution. These laws contain gaping loopholes and have no ability to prevent SOs from living near children or being in places where children congregate. For instance, an offender can live in an apartment building full of children, so long as it is not near a school or other prohibited location. There is also nothing stopping SOs from spending time in parks, even if they have to travel to get there. In fact, contrary to the distance decay principle, offenders benefit from leaving their neighborhoods when scouting for opportunities to offend, because they have a lower chance of being recognized when they are in unfamiliar territory. Sex offenders themselves tend to agree that residency restrictions would not stop them from reoffending if they were motivated to do so (Mercado, Alvarez, & Levenson, 2008). Residency restrictions are a crude policy approach that may have a trace amount of validity in terms of creating access barriers between offenders and victims, but they have been applied so uncritically and indiscriminately that they have come uncoupled from any core logic that might support a more tailored, thoughtful application of them. In addition to their aforementioned deficits, RRs are problematic in their focus on controlling offenders rather than protecting potential victims. We will return to this point later in the chapter.

TREATMENT AND INCAPACITATION (CIVIL COMMITMENT)

Civil commitment is grounded in the rationale that some sex offenders are so severely psychologically disturbed that they cannot be safely released back into society. The ostensible goal of civil commitment is treatment, but since there are no proven therapies for sexual pathologies, the true goal may simply be incapacitation (see Levenson, 2004). Critics of civil commitment generally approach the topic from a legal or civil-rights perspective, arguing that these laws represent an unjust expansion of the criminal law and are nothing more than the government's effort to circumvent due process by confining people under the façade of treatment (Wright, 2008). These skeptics also question the rationale and ethics of targeting sex offenders alone for this unique form of post-incarceration confinement (Jackson & Covell, 2013; Wright, 2008). Since most sex offenders are generalists who commit a variety of offenses (sexual and nonsexual alike), it seems odd to focus exclusively on one of the crimes they have committed and ignore the rest (Harris et al., 2009).

The logic underpinning civil commitment is subject to some of the same doubts as that for SORN and RRs. In particular, the utility of civil commitment hinges upon psychiatric authorities' ability to accurately diagnose offenders and predict each person's probability of recidivism, as well as on the validity of the presumption that severely mentally disturbed offenders are likely to commit new sex offenses. There is evidence pointing to the general accuracy of diagnoses (Jackson & Hess, 2007; Levenson, 2004), which supports a portion of the argument. On the other hand, much is still unknown about the dimensions of risk, the proper ways to clinically assess offenders along these dimensions, and the extent to which actuarial risk-assessment instruments correctly predict recidivism (Roberts, Doren, & Thornton, 2002). As such, the rationale underlying civil commitment (whether that rationale be treatment or incapacitation) is not conclusively refuted, but cannot be said to rest on firm ground.

THE EMPIRICAL STATUS OF SEX-OFFENDER POLICIES

REGISTRATION AND NOTIFICATION

Registration and notification laws, as described earlier, rest on the twin (and seemingly incompatible) assumptions that sex offenders are psychologically disturbed recidivists and that their behavior can be quelled through the use of harsh penalties. Of course, the contradiction may be reconciled by conceding that deterrence is probably not useful due to SOs' compromised mental status and, as a result, that the burden must be shifted onto communities if they are to protect themselves from known offenders. Under this scenario, SORN is not intended as a deterrent; in fact, it is an admission that deterrence is not a viable approach. The logic underpinning SORN is slippery.

One study uncovered apparent support for general deterrence. Letourneau et al. (2010b) found a significant decline in first-time sex crime arrests in one state after that state passed SORN laws. People at risk of committing sex offenses may be influenced by the existence of registration and community notification. However, critics have alleged that harsh SORN (and RR) laws increase victims' reluctance to report sexual assaults and abuse. Abuse of one family member by another, for instance, may be dealt with informally (or not dealt with at all), because the abuser is integral to the family unit and the tolls that are exacted financially (e.g., fathers removed from the home) or emotionally (e.g., adolescents removed for abusing their younger siblings) are too great to bear (Tabachnick & Klein, 2011). It is not clear, then, whether a reduction in sex-crime arrests after the enactment of SORN is indicative of a true decline in offending or whether it suggests a spike in victim nonreporting (or a combination of both). A similar study of aggregate trends in sex-crime arrests in a different state showed no change after the state's passage of its SORN law (Sandler et al., 2008). An assessment of the impacts of federal registration requirements under Megan's Law found inconsistent changes in reported rapes across states; three showed significant reductions, while in several rape reporting increased, albeit not enough to find the effect statistically significant (Vásquez, Maddan, & Walker, 2008).

Specific recidivism does not appear to be impacted by SORN. Many studies have analyzed the impacts of registration and notification on SOs' recidivism likelihood. This research spans multiple states, time periods, and offender groups and uses different measures of recidivism (e.g., a new arrest, a new conviction). Maddan, Miller, Walker, and Marshall (2011), studying a single state's passage of SORN laws, assembled a pre-SORN group of sex offenders and a post-SORN group. They found that SOs convicted in the SORN era did not sexually reoffend less than those who were not subject to these laws; however, the post-SORN group did show a reduction in arrests and convictions for nonsex crimes. Zevitz (2006) matched a sample of sex offenders convicted after Megan's Law to one processed prior to its enactment and found no differences in general recidivism (returns to prison) between the groups. The group subject to the more extensive notification requirement actually had a slightly higher rate of sex-specific reimprisonments, but the difference was not statistically significant and so it is not clear whether this finding indicated a true effect or was attributable purely to chance. Tewksbury and Jennings (2010) likewise uncovered no differences in recidivism patterns among pre-SORN and post-SORN sex offenders.

Another area of evaluation focuses on the impact of SORN on community members' self-protective behaviors. One of the goals of SORN is to equip members of the public with the ability to protect themselves and their loved ones from known offenders. A handful of studies have assessed the public's use of sex-offender registries and the steps they take to manage their personal risks. It seems that the public is knowledgeable about the existence of such registries; however, only about one-third actually check the database (Anderson & Sample, 2008; Kernsmith, Comartin, Craun, & Kernsmith, 2009), and those who have accessed it have done so only once or a few times (Anderson & Sample, 2008). Being notified that a sex offender has moved into the neighborhood appears to significantly heighten people's fear of sexual victimization (Beck & Travis, 2004), but does not increase their adoption of self-protective behaviors (Anderson & Sample, 2008; Bandy 2011). Most of the measures that are taken are minimal, such as sharing the information with neighbors (Anderson & Sample, 2008). On the other hand, parents who are notified by law enforcement that a sex offender has moved into their neighborhood may ramp up the steps they take to protect their children (Bandy, 2011). Overall, despite strong support for SORN, the public does not seem to actually use the information made available by this law.

RESIDENCY RESTRICTIONS

As explained earlier, residency restrictions are found sporadically across the United States. Some are state laws and others are local ordinances. Most studies evaluating RRs employ geocoding and spatial analysis. A body of evidence has emerged showing that residency restrictions have dramatic impacts on SOs' housing availability. Zandbergen and Hart (2006) found that RRs eliminated 95 percent of housing for SOs within a particular county, and Zgoba, Levenson, and McKee (2009) demonstrated that the implementation of RRs in one large county would displace 88 percent of registered sex offenders. Berenson and Appelbaum (2011) discovered that between 80 and 90 percent of residences within two urban areas were within restricted zones; perhaps not surprisingly, compliance with RRs was extremely low and the majority of registered SOs in each city resided inside restricted zones. Hughes and Burchfield (2008) also found evidence of widespread noncompliance with RRs.

Noncompliance might not be as problematic as it sounds, though. Huebner, Kras, Rydberg, Bynum, Grommon, and Pleggenkuhle (2014) compared sex-offender residential patterns and recidivism trends in two states before and after the passage of RRs. They found that many SOs lived within restricted zones, but that offense-specific recidivism was not impacted by the passage of RRs. Zandbergen, Levenson, and Hart (2010) matched a sample of sexual recidivists to one-time sex offenders to compare the two groups' residential proximity to schools or daycares. No differences emerged. The distance between SOs' homes and places where children congregate does not, by itself, appear to be a risk factor for sexual recidivism. Nobles, Levenson, and Youstin (2012) evaluated one city's expansion of its RRs to include larger buffer zones around a greater number of locations. Their analyses revealed an increase in the total number of sex-crime arrests (both first-time and recidivistic) after the new RRs went into effect. This seemingly counterintuitive finding could be explained by the heightened risk of detection in the postpolicy period.

An additional consideration pertains not only to the availability of housing but also to the types of areas that are more or less available to SOs subject to residency restrictions. Densely populated urban areas are most heavily affected by these housing limitations (Hughes & Burchfield, 2008). Areas on the outskirts of cities, such as counties (Berenson & Appelbaum, 2011) and rural and suburban enclaves (Socia, 2011), also experience an impact, but the magnitude is smaller. Heavily restricted areas tend to have higher concentrations of economic disadvantage and social disorganization (Hughes & Burchfield, 2008; Socia, 2011). There are a few implications of these findings. It could be good that potentially dangerous SOs are largely kept out of socially disorganized areas, as these are the locations most conducive to crime. Guardianship of children is low, and informal social controls are weak (Zgoba, 2011). On the other hand, treatment services, jobs, and public transit are located in urban centers, so forcing SOs to live outside these areas may significantly disrupt their reentry process and increase the likelihood of recidivism (Socia, 2011).

CIVIL COMMITMENT

Evaluations to date offer little in the way of either supporting or refuting the efficacy of civil commitment. Outcome evaluations (such as comparing recidivism rates across matched samples of treated and untreated SOs) have yet to appear in the scientific literature. As described previously, the overall level of accuracy of diagnoses, predictions, and the presumed connection between diagnosis and future behavior is not known with certainty. It does seem that forensic psychiatrists evaluating SOs for possible civil commitment properly utilize validated risk-assessment tools and diagnostic criteria, and that the procedures used for these evaluations are reasonably consistent across the experts using them (Jackson & Hess, 2007), as are experts' diagnostic decisions (Packard & Levenson, 2006). One study found evidence that civilly committed offenders scored significantly higher than noncommitted ones on risk assessments and measures of psychopathy, and had more victims, younger victims, and longer histories of arrests for sex and nonsex crimes (Levenson, 2004).

On the other hand, because having multiple victims and ongoing deviant sexual thoughts increases the chances that a civilly committed sex offender will be continually confined, SOs have strong incentives to lie during treatment sessions and not fully disclose thoughts and behaviors that could be used against them in recommitment hearings. Because it is impossible for therapists to effectively treat patients who withhold important information, the treatment delivered to civilly committed sex offenders may be misconceived or misdirected (Miller, 2010). Indeed, some empirical evidence suggests that therapy delivered in institutional environments is less effective than that provided in outpatient settings (Grossman, Martis, & Fichtner, 1999). This evidence is all indirect, though, and the absence of well-designed, scientific evaluations looms large in the discussion of the forcible confinement of SOs for treatment purposes.

COLLATERAL CONSEQUENCES

Registration, notification, and residency restrictions laws have produced several unintended consequences. The damage is largely done in the very areas most closely linked with recidivism likelihood. One impact is that RRs force many SOs into untenable and destructive living arrangements. Onerous RRs may either leave SOs with virtually nowhere to live (e.g., Zandbergen & Hart, 2006), or push them to the outer rings of urban areas and impede their access to treatment services, employment opportunities, and affordable housing (e.g., Socia, 2011). They are often barred from residing with family members who could offer a stable, socially supportive environment (Levenson & Hern, 2007). Instead, they experience significant economic and housing instability, as well as painful social isolation (Levenson & Cotter, 2005). Cities that have enacted strict RRs have seen sharp increases in homelessness among SOs (California Sex Offender Management Board, 2008). Sex offenders subject to SORN and RRs report that these laws create residential, employment, and social instability for them (Levenson & Hern, 2007; Mercado, Alvarez, & Levenson, 2008). Transience and an inability to stay connected with supportive family are risk factors for recidivism. Residency restrictions can backfire by sending SOs who are motivated to reoffend away from the neighborhood in search of new victims in areas where they are not known. This makes the new crimes harder to solve because victims and witnesses may not recognize the offender (Edwards & Hensley, 2001).

Registration and notification inspire significant feelings of shame and embarrassment. Registered sex offenders feel stigmatized, isolated, and vulnerable (Tewksbury, 2005; Tewksbury & Lees, 2006). Strong negative emotions can hamper offenders' recovery processes by making them feel hopeless. People in the process of self-reformation need to be optimistic about their recovery if they are to stay motivated. Making SOs feel that they will never live normal lives or be allowed back into mainstream society is discouraging and can dampen their intrinsic drive for self-improvement (Tabachnick & Klein, 2011). The instability and isolation SORN and RRs create in people's lives likewise may trigger relapse (Levenson & Cotter, 2005). Harsh penalties could also deter victims and offenders alike from seeking help. Victims may be reluctant to report incidents, and families that become aware of abuse may cover it up or try to handle it informally without police involvement. An entire family can feel shamed when one member is revealed to be sexually abusive; all other members of the family experience stigmatization and, sometimes, blame (Edwards & Hensley, 2001). The family might also believe that the offender is not dangerous and needs treatment rather than a punitive criminal-justice response that will haunt him or her for life (Tabachnick & Klein, 2011). Victims, offenders, and families have trouble accessing treatment services, however, because of mandatory-reporting laws requiring therapists to disclose to police any incident of sexual abuse of a minor that they learn of (Edwards & Hensley, 2001). An adult who previously abused a minor and wants psychiatric help to avoid repeating the behavior cannot comfortably discuss the problem with a therapist out of fear that the therapist will alert the authorities. This creates a catch-22. Full disclosure is crucial to effective treatment, but patients cannot be honest with therapists because candor may land them in jail.

Finally, SORN and RRs divert the public's attention away from real threats toward highly unlikely ones. The narrow focus on high-profile tragedies like those that befell Jacob Wetterling and Megan Kanka fosters widespread adherence to the "stranger danger" narrative (Edwards & Hensley, 2001; Tabachnick & Klein, 2011). Certainly, parents and teachers should educate children to use due caution around strangers; however, this is only a small portion of the total effort needed to keep children safe. A parent steeped in the "stranger danger" message may overlook blatant signs that his or her child is being victimized by the babysitter because this type of abuse does not meld with the "stranger danger" scenario. As such, SORN and RRs offer little more than a false sense of security (Leon, 2011), and they help perpetuate myths that are detrimental to people's ability to protect their own safety and that of their children.

ALTERNATIVE SO POLICIES

Sex-offender policy is not all doom and gloom. We have seen that SORN and RRs do not achieve their stated goals and, worse, may be making the public less safe by increasing recidivism risk and promoting inaccurate beliefs about sex offenders' predatory habits. The search for effective policy is not futile, however. Alternative policies are in use and additional ones could be constructed on the basis of scholarly knowledge about sex offending.

An alternative approach currently in use in many states is the containment method. Containment is a community-based strategy to simultaneously supervise and treat SOs. Sometimes it is used as an alternative to incarceration for those convicted of lower-level sex offenses, and other times it is part of a postincarceration reentry plan. An offender undergoing the containment method receives a case-management team consisting of a probation or parole officer, a polygraph examiner, and a treatment provider. The polygraph examiner attempts to uncover comprehensive information about SOs' past misdeeds in order to facilitate effective therapy and to help ensure that SOs refrain from new crimes (English, Jones, & Patrick, 2003; English, Jones, Patrick, & Pasini-Hill, 2003). The case-management team pushes offenders to accept responsibility for their crimes and meaningfully participate in treatment, while using the threat (and, when necessary, swift application) of punishment for transgressions (Cooley-Towell et al., 2000; English, 1998; English, Jones, & Patrick, 2003). There is also an effort to gain a clear grasp on SOs' offending patterns so as to monitor them vigilantly for any sign that they are reverting to old habits (English, 1998). Outcome evaluations of the containment method have yet to be conducted, so its effectiveness is unknown. It remains an unproven but potentially worthwhile policy approach.

The containment method, although potentially valuable as an alternative to SORN and RRs, suffers from one critical weakness just as the other policies do: It is reactive. Something bad has to happen before these laws can be applied (Jerusalem, 1995). The situational crime prevention model (Clarke, 1995), bounded rationality perspective (Clarke, 2014), and crime-commission script model (see Leclerc, Wortley, & Smallbone, 2011) offer a vision for making children safer proactively. Bounded rationality holds that offenders engage in a risk–benefit calculus as deterrence theory suggests, but that their information is frequently imperfect and their judgment prone to error (Cornish & Clarke, 2017).

The implication of this for policy is that safety can be improved by arranging social and physical environments in manners that are visibly inhospitable to crime. Situational models emphasize the characteristics of places and interpersonal interactions that can increase or reduce the opportunities for sex crimes to occur (Wortley & Smallbone, 2006). Crime scripts could be used to understand typical offender behavior within certain settings (Leclerc et al., 2011) in order to build empirically validated physical, social, and situational barriers that reduce sex-offending opportunities. Educating parents and teachers about the typical scripts followed by different types of offenders (e.g., strangers, family members) would help them prevent the coalescing of opportunities that combine to create the crime event (Leclerc et al., 2011). To prevent attacks by strangers, parks and playgrounds can be constructed in such a way that access points are controlled and parents and guardians have full view of their children at all times. Bus stops located in places where parents cannot wait with their children can be moved, or designated school officials could be assigned to monitor each stop when children are present. These examples represent a shift away from reactive, offender-centered approaches that focus on recidivism reduction toward proactive strategies to prevent victimization from occurring in the first place.

The federal government may need to loosen its grip on states in order to promote innovative, evidence-based practices. States have trouble finding the money and personnel to implement and enforce SORN laws (Harris & Lobanov-Rostovsky, 2010); with such a large portion of total resources dedicated to SORN, there is little left for experimentation with alternative approaches. The federal SORN classification scheme tends to place offenders in higher tiers compared to where they would be under state-issued tier systems (Harris et al., 2010), so states are pressed to incarcerate offenders who might, in fact, be good candidates for community-based punishments such as the containment method. Federal laws mandating notification for all SOs in certain groups neglect the devastating impact that notification may have on victims; a localized approach could allow authorities with knowledge about the offender and victim to decide when notification is and is not warranted (see English, 1998). The federalized system also offers no incentive for states and cities to innovate by trying new methods. With respect to other types of crimes (e.g., youth gang involvement, gun violence) the federal government has developed sets of best practices and identified specific programs that have fared well in empirical evaluations, and it offers grants to cities and community workgroups wishing to implement a proven or promising program. Rather than forcing states to adhere to the Walsh Act, the federal government could provide funding for states and cities seeking to test new sex-offender policies or adopt programs that worked well in other jurisdictions. This, of course, would require policymakers to admit the faults in existing SO policies and publicly support trying new strategies.

CONCLUSION

Sex offenses garner significant and warranted public concern. Even the lower-level forms of these crimes are upsetting, particularly when the victim is a child. Many of the laws enacted to prevent sex offending are products of widespread outrage over highly publicized incidents in which children were brutally assaulted and killed. These laws have been primarily symbolic and expressive, intended to let policymakers openly demonstrate their concern and to allow the public to feel that it has effectively voiced its condemnation of sexual assault and abuse. There may be social benefit in employing the criminal law to reinforce widespread intolerance of any sexual transgression against children or unwilling adults. These policies, though, need to go beyond being merely symbolic or expressive—they need to be instrumental and effective. Sex-offender laws and policies should rest upon scientific research about the targeted problem, comprehensive analyses of victimization patterns and trends, and proven or promising solutions derived from theory and empirical evidence.

Sex-offender registration and notification, residency restrictions, and civil commitment are the primary policies currently used in the United States to prevent SO recidivism. Registration and notification have produced null results in evaluations, and residency restrictions also seem ineffective. Civil commitment has not been thoroughly evaluated. SORN and RRs might impede convicted sex offenders' rehabilitation and reintegration process by disrupting their social networks and making it difficult for them to access treatment and other services. Promising alternatives include the containment method for convicted SOs, and situational approaches aimed at preventing victimization from ever occurring. The federal government would be wise to relax its control over states' handling of sex offenders. The better approach is one encouraging and incentivizing innovation. The federal government should partner with states to develop, implement, and evaluate new strategies with the goal of ultimately producing a set of evidence-based best practices that will truly offer community protection.

DISCUSSION QUESTIONS

1. One impediment to a community-based approach to the punishment and rehabilitation of sex offenders is public fear. The public expresses much concern about people convicted of sex crimes remaining in the community, even if they are on probation and subject to periodic polygraph testing. Suppose you work for a local law-enforcement or corrections agency and have been tasked with raising public support for a community-based treatment program for convicted sex offenders. Your agency knows the program will generate controversy, so your job is to explain to the public the reasons why they should be receptive to the program and not be afraid that it will endanger local residents. What will you say to them? How will you calm their fears and convince them to give the program a chance?

2. The media are significant sources of public misperceptions that paint the "typical" sex offender as a severely violent predator and serial recidivist. Media organizations' coverage practices are driven by ratings and readership; the phrase "if it bleeds, it leads" directs reporters to focus on the most sensationalistic stories and to ignore the ones that would not produce eye-grabbing headlines. This practice distorts the public image of sex offending and leads to widespread support of punitive, ineffective policies. Do you think the media have an ethical obligation to change their coverage of sex offenders? That is, do they have a social responsibility to generate more accurate information, given that the stories they produce end up impacting public policy?

3. Civil commitment of sex offenders has been legally and ethically controversial. Proponents claim civil commitment protects the public from dangerous sexual predators who have serious

psychological disturbances. Opponents contend that there are no reliable diagnostic tools to predict which people convicted of sex offenses will reoffend and which will not; they argue that no other types of offenders are subject to postincarceration civil confinement so it is unfair to single out sex offenders. Does it seem justifiable to treat sex offenders as fundamentally different from other types of offenders? Why or why not? If diagnostic instruments existed and recidivism could be predicted accurately, would civil commitment be ethically permissible?

4. The public is largely unaware of the ineffectiveness and collateral consequences of SORN and RRs. Why do you think this is? Do you think that the public would stop supporting these policies if people knew that they not only are ineffective, but also have negative impacts on people, including offenders' families? Or do you believe that the public would continue supporting existing policies even if this information was disseminated? Explain your answer.

CASES CITED

In re Taylor 60 Cal. 4th 1019 (2015).
Kansas v. Hendricks 521 U.S. 346 (1997)
United States v. Comstock 560 U.S. 126 (2010)

CHAPTER 5

GANG POLICY

INTRODUCTION

Street gangs occupy a unique place in American fear. Residents of communities gripped by gangs live the fear daily; those not directly exposed to the threat experience it vicariously through movies, music, news media, and urban legend. Movies and rap songs glorify gangster life, although sometimes the nostalgia is tinged with bittersweet emotions. Gang life is dangerous, both for gang members and those living in places where gangs are prevalent. Gangs have proliferated in the past few decades and have spread from their traditional urban territories into suburban and rural areas. Gangs inspire so much fear because of their heavy involvement with violence. Gangs use violence internally as a tool of social control to ensure conformity among their own members, and externally to prevent community members from taking actions against them.

Most of what is "known" about gangs, however, is only partially factual, and some of it is entirely incorrect. The dialogues taking place in the news media, among legislators and local politicians, and in police briefing rooms are generally grounded in anecdotes, assumptions, and selective observations. Some of this information is accurate, but some is off point or incomplete. Genuine scientific theory and evidence about the realities of gangs is usually either missing or present only in snippets or side notes.

Policy suffers as a result of the widespread failure to fully consider the scholarly research on gangs and gang members. As this chapter will show, there are a multitude of antigang initiatives in existence, yet only a small handful have shown promising capacities to reduce gang membership or gang activity. This can be traced to divisions between scholars, practitioners, and policymakers. We will see that research has uncovered important knowledge that lends itself helpfully to policy efforts, although researchers must continue evaluating programs to achieve a greater understanding of what works and what does not. Policy approaches that capitalize on scientific research can suppress violence by tapping into gangs' and gang members' vulnerabilities, while simultaneously offering troubled youths alternatives to gang life.

This chapter describes some of the most widely used antigang policies and programs, but the focus is on the logic and evidence underlying those initiatives more than the

initiatives themselves. For instance, rather than attempting to exhaustively list all intervention or suppression strategies that that have been utilized, we will critically examine
the feasibility of intervention and suppression and the conditions that must be present
for any policy or program grounded in these principles to hold promise. As will be seen
throughout the chapter, policymakers and criminal-justice officials often rush to propose
solutions without first analyzing the problem and acquiring a solid understanding of it.
Therefore, this chapter takes a step back and seeks a detailed understanding of gangs' organization, behavior, and social processes. From there, we will examine the ways in which
tactics grounded in prevention, intervention, and suppression strategies can be tailored
to achieve certain goals that are realistic within their contexts. The analytical framework
employed here can be applied to the evaluation of any antigang policy or program.

THEORETICAL EXPLANATIONS FOR GANG MEMBERSHIP AND ACTIVITY

The theories advanced to explain youths' involvement in gangs and the behavior of the
groups themselves are divided into three units of analysis: individual level; macrolevel
(i.e., community); and microlevel (i.e., group). We will discuss each in turn. After doing so,
we will consider the perennial question of whether gangs cause elevated levels of violence
among their members or, conversely, whether gang violence occurs because these groups
attract people already prone to violence.

INDIVIDUAL-LEVEL PREDICTORS OF GANG INVOLVEMENT AND DESISTANCE

The individual level of explanation speaks to the question of why certain youths join gangs,
what sets gang-involved youths apart from those not in gangs, and why some gang members desist. Contrary to much popular belief, gang membership is generally a transient
state rather than a lifelong one. Most youths who join gangs drift back out within one year
(Melde & Esbensen, 2011, 2013; Peterson, Taylor, & Esbensen, 2004; Thornberry, 1998).

   Individual-level theories of gang membership have not received the scholarly attention they deserve (McGloin & Decker, 2010). Most research focuses on the period during
which youths are part of gangs and neglects the pregang and postgang phases of their
lives, which stymies theoretical inquiry (Thornberry, 1998). There is a small bit to go on,
though. Early work suggested that troubled youths joined gangs in a search for pseudofam-
ily networks and a sense of belonging (Thrasher, 1927). Dominant contemporary theories
in this area are life course and self-control. Both of these theories have garnered strong
empirical support in regard to general criminal offending (Moffitt, 1993, 2003; Pratt &
Cullen, 2000). People with low self-control are more likely to become victims, which is
largely due to their engagement in risky activities (Pratt, Turanovic, Fox, & Wright, 2014).
Gang membership certainly constitutes a risky activity, so if youths with low self-control
join gangs, their victimization rates elevate. Some empirical evidence seems to support
the applicability of life-course (Melde & Esbensen; 2011; Pyrooz, Decker, & Webb, 2010)
and self-control theories (Kissner & Pyrooz, 2009), at least partially. The individual-level

factors predicting gang membership and desistance are sorely in need of theoretical and empirical development. Researchers are still grappling with unknowns such as the factors that differentiate youths who join gangs from similarly situated ones who do not, the predictors of whether a gang member will remain involved long-term or will separate from the group after a short period, and the consequences for youthful gang involvement on a person's life trajectory even after leaving the gang.

MACROLEVEL AND MICROLEVEL EXPLANATIONS FOR GANG BEHAVIOR

Macrolevel theories offer explanations for the existence of gangs in certain communities. Research on gangs is nearly as old as American criminology itself. Sociologists took up the study of street-level criminal groups in the early 1900s. The field was originally dominated by the Chicago school (McGloin, 2007a; McGloin & Decker, 2010), which invoked social disorganization theory to explain gangs. According to this line of thought, concentrated socioeconomic disadvantage (low education, poverty, single-parent households, residential instability, and the like) eroded social cohesion. Breakdowns in social cohesion undermined a community's capacity to exert both informal and formal social control. Adults could not or would not supervise neighborhood youths or call the police to report problems. A community incapable of self-regulation is fertile ground for deviance and crime.

Social disorganization theory offers some insight, but leaves gaps. For one thing, research in the early- and mid-1900s revealed that gang-heavy communities are not disorganized so much as *differentially* organized (Suttles, 1968; see McGloin & Decker, 2010 for a review). Residents of socioeconomically troubled communities adapted to their circumstances and developed patterns, habits, and moral values that helped them navigate these environments. In some areas where gangs were prominent, local ties were a mesh of legal and illegal alliances The heart of the problem was the community's inability to productively interact with larger society (Whyte, 1943), a problem exacerbated by the community's internal fragmentation and cultural clashes (Suttles, 1968). Decades later, researchers pointed out that the study of macrolevel conditions omitted the role of situational factors (McGloin & Decker, 2010) as well as the group processes and collective behavior that are central to gangs' activities and violence (Decker, 1996). Macrolevel factors may help predict the existence of gangs in certain areas, but they are unhelpful in revealing the reasons why gangs function the way they do.

There are unique cultural dynamics of disadvantaged inner-city neighborhoods (most of them predominantly black or Latino) where crime flourishes. Concentrated disadvantage and pervasive, systemic racism produce pockets of severe deprivation. Residents of these isolated neighborhoods have few opportunities to participate in mainstream society or in the legitimate labor market (Massey, 1995; Wilson, 1987). In some neighborhoods, these conditions provide the groundwork for a culture of opposition (called the code of the street), which rejects the values and mores of wider society and embraces a code of conduct that prizes respect and legitimizes the use of violence to maintain one's status and stave off challenges to one's authority (Anderson, 1999). Those residents who do not endorse the code are nonetheless trapped by it because they feel alienated from the police (Kirk

& Matsuda, 2011; Sampson & Bartusch, 1998) and fear violent reprisal should they attempt to take formal or informal action to stop violence or other criminal activities (Anderson, 1999; see also Kubrin & Weitzer, 2003). The oppositional culture takes social disorganization a step further in explaining the conditions that give rise to the formation of gangs and in helping to understand gangs' violent propensities.

For a deeper understanding of gang behavior, we turn to microlevel processes (McGloin & Decker, 2010). Microlevel processes are group-level dynamics. Studies of these processes uncover the mechanisms driving behavior and the reasons why certain activities are so central to gang identities (McGloin, 2007a). Gangs are groups; therefore, their behavior can be understood within a broader framework of collective action.

Gangs' social identities revolve around carving out and defending turf, and establishing a reputation for violence (Decker, 1996). Turf serves practical purposes (such as being territory for drug transactions) and is symbolically important as well, because it represents a sense of home and identity. Gangs' status and reputations generally center on their capacity for violence. Similar to the street code in general (Anderson, 1999), gang members earn prestige for themselves and their gangs by issuing verbal threats and periodically following through on them (Decker, 1996; see also Kubrin, 2005). Collective behavior escalates violence through rivalries. Slights from enemy gangs inspire fury. The collective-behavior model explains that most gang homicides occur when personal rivalries, competition for turf, and struggles for corners of the drug market lead to deadly altercations (Pizarro & McGloin, 2006; see also Decker, 1996). The passion for vengeance helps reinforce gang members' cohesion and loyalty (Decker, 1996). Violence is normative within gangs (Decker, 1996; Kubrin, 2005), meaning it is embedded in their cultural scripts and is a preferred and often mandatory means of dispute resolution.

ENHANCEMENT: THE CRIMINOGENIC PROPERTIES OF GANGS

Gangs commit more crime and violence than lone individuals or other types of groups. Gang members, while a minority of all youths in any given city, account for the majority of delinquent offenses (Thornberry, Huizinga, & Loeber, 2004). Many scholars and commentators have pondered whether this is the result of something unique about the gang that causes its members to do things they would not otherwise do, or whether gang members already possess a proclivity for crime and violence and are merely "birds of a feather flocking together." Research reveals truth in both of these perspectives.

Gang members self-select into gangs, meaning there are qualitative differences between gang members and people who are not in gangs. This is called the "selection model" (see Melde & Esbensen, 2011 for a review). Those who join gangs display higher pregang delinquent involvement (DeLisi, Barnes, Beaver, & Gibson, 2009; Melde & Esbensen, 2013). Gangs do seem to attract people with a penchant for antisocial behavior.

Gangs also exacerbate crime and violence among their members. This is called "enhancement" (see Melde & Esbensen, 2011 for a review). Enhancement has received substantial empirical support. Although most gang members are far from model citizens prior to joining a gang (but see Thornberry, Krohn, Lizotte, & Chard-Wierschem, 1993), their participation in crime and violence spikes during the period of their gang affiliation (DeLisi et al., 2009; Gordon, Lahey, Kawai, Loeber, Stouthamer-Loeber, & Farrington, 2004; Melde & Esbensen, 2013; Thornberry et al., 1993). Those who leave the gang likewise display a reduction in illegal activities (Gordon et al., 2004; Melde & Esbensen, 2013; Thornberry et al., 1993). The enhancement model squares with the research on co-offending, which finds that group-based offending carries a higher likelihood of violence when compared to lone offending, even when the individual actors do not have histories of violence (McGloin & Piquero, 2009a).

The enhancement model has implications for policy, as it shows that effective antigang programs could reduce overall rates of crime and violence. This result would not be possible if the selection thesis were true and individual gang members would be wreaking havoc even if they did not band together to co-offend. Similarly, interventions that pull youths and young adults out of gangs (or prevent them from joining in the first place) could yield better outlooks for youths' futures. We will revisit this point later in the chapter when we discuss antigang policies.

THE ROLES OF VIOLENCE AND DRUGS IN GANG OPERATIONS

While gangs commit all manner of crime and delinquency, and generally do not specialize in any one type of offending (Klein, 1993, 1995), they do construct their identities around violence. Violence attains a mythical status in gangs' ceremonies and discourse (Decker, 1996). Gang members use hard, brash language to foster their reputations as loose cannons, and they must periodically engage in violence to prove they are capable of more than mere talk and bravado (Decker, 1996; Kubrin, 2005). The street code requires a gang member to cultivate a reputation as someone who easily comes unhinged—even outright crazy (Kubrin, 2005)—and unleashes mortal violence against enemies and anyone who has shown disrespect (see also Kubrin & Weitzer, 2003). Failing to retaliate against insults or attacks reveals weakness and increases the risk of future victimization (Anderson, 1999). In this way, the street code holds that the use of violence is self-protective (Kubrin, 2005), although research reveals that youths who adhere to the code have higher rates of victimization than those who do not (Stewart, Schreck, & Simons, 2006). Similarly, gang involvement, which gang members often believe buffers them from attack, heightens their risk for violent victimization (Peterson, Taylor, & Esbensen, 2004; Taylor, Peterson, Esbensen, & Freng, 2007).

Guns play a central role in gangs. Gang members are more likely than nongang members to own guns for protection (Bjerregaard & Lizotte, 1995) and gang involvement is a significant correlate of illegal gun ownership and carrying (Lizotte, Howard, Krohn, & Thornberry, 1997; Lizotte et al., 2000). Guns also serve a symbolic function in the myths built up around the gangster lifestyle. Gang members tote guns as symbols of their masculinity and toughness (Fagan & Wilkinson, 1998). Gangsta-rap music glorifies guns as sources of power and dominance (Kubrin, 2005). Consistent with the enhancement model, individuals who join gangs are more likely to already own guns for self-protection, but upon joining the gang, their rates of gun ownership and carrying sharply increase (Bjerregaard & Lizotte, 1995). Most gang homicides (Decker & Curry, 2002; Fagan & Wilkinson, 1998) and violence in general (Klein, 1995) are perpetrated with guns.

Drugs are also a reality in the life of the urban poor, especially in predominantly black neighborhoods. The drug economy is strong in urban areas characterized by extreme sociostructural disadvantage (Anderson, 1999), brought about by decades of entrenched, systemic racism and residential segregation (Massey, 1995; Massey & Denton, 1993; Wilson, 1987). Drugs are a source of revenue for many who lack legitimate means of earning income (Anderson, 1999).

There is variation in—and some debate about—the importance of drugs to gangs (see Decker & Curry, 2002 for a review). Street gangs typically do not specialize in drug dealing (Klein, 1993, 1995). On the other hand, several studies have documented gang involvement in the drug trade (Decker & Curry, 2002). One source of confusion could be that in gang-heavy communities, buying, selling, and using illegal drugs is common among both gang members and those who are not gang affiliated (Anderson, 1999). In these areas, gang members' involvement with drugs may be coincidental. In some cities, though, gangs are reliant upon drug markets for revenues (Kennedy, 1997).

GANG STRUCTURE, ORGANIZATION, AND RIVALRIES

It is commonly presumed that gangs are hierarchically structured and tightly organized. Members of the public and even law-enforcement officers frequently cast gangs as possessing high levels of cohesion (McGloin, 2007b). This assumption, however, is faulty in many cases. Gangs are arranged horizontally more often than vertically (McGloin & Decker, 2010; see also Howell, 2010). Gang networks tend to be loose associations. Within a larger gang (such as Bloods or Crips), there are usually smaller sets or cliques. Sets exhibit internal cohesion and close ties among their members, but they generally function independently of one another. Large gangs look like constellations—small clusters linked together in a larger network, with set members loyal more to their subgroups than to the gang as a whole (Decker, 1996; McGloin, 2005, 2007b). Many gangs and sets evince internal variation in structure and cohesion, often being constructed of a few core members orbited by several less-involved affiliates (see Thrasher, 1927).

Gang violence is widely misunderstood. Lore abounds about the bloodthirsty rivalries between gangs like the Crips and Bloods; however, a slain gang member's killer is often a fellow Blood or Crip (Decker & Curry, 2002). This may be related to the decentralized, constellation-type nature of gangs—individual sets fracture off from the larger whole, claim turf, and promote their own agendas. Rivalries between sets are often more salient than those between gangs themselves (Shakur, 2007). In some cities, however, it does seem that most gang violence is attributable to intergang (rather than intragang) rivalries (Kennedy, 1997). The relationship between organization and violence is, as yet, not fully understood. Some researchers find that members of tightly organized gangs commit more violence (Decker, Katz, & Webb, 2008), while others document that neighborhoods with more loosely organized gangs experience more conflict (Howell, 2010; Hughes, 2013).

This may reflect the variation in gang organization and violence from city to city, and among the gangs in a single city (Weisel, Painter, & Kusler, 1997).

GANG POLICIES

Gang policies in the United States have generally not been driven by theory or empirical evidence and so have not capitalized upon—or benefitted from—scientific knowledge about the structure and cohesiveness of gangs (McGloin & Decker, 2010). Cities seeking to implement new antigang initiatives usually do not start with a comprehensive analysis of the nature of gang behavior in their jurisdiction (McGloin, 2005). This presents problems for these policies and programs. Gangs' characteristics and behaviors differ from city to city (Curry & Thomas, 1992; Weisel et al., 1997), so an initiative that seemed effective in one jurisdiction cannot be automatically transplanted to another area and expected to be equally successful. Poorly planned programs can backfire (Klein, 1995).

The various strategies employed in antigang efforts fall into three general categories: prevention, intervention, and suppression. Prevention is intended to stop youths from joining gangs, intervention is an effort to extract gang-involved youths from their deviant peers, and suppression is an attempt to forcibly stop gang activity through enhanced law enforcement or use of criminal penalties. With a few notable exceptions, antigang programs contain only one element and do not incorporate multiple approaches (Klein & Maxson, 2010).

There are more gang policies and programs than can be brought together in a single summary, so this chapter includes the most prominent ones. Schools, in particular, host a multitude of antigang programs (Esbensen, Peterson, Taylor, & Osgood, 2012). Schools are important staging grounds for social conflicts. Interpersonal and intergroup rivalries established at school may boil over into violence either on or off school grounds (Brunson & Miller, 2009).

One of the most popular school-based initiative is the Gang Resistance Education and Training (G.R.E.A.T.) program. The program began in 1991 and originally borrowed heavily from the national Drug Abuse Resistance Education (D.A.R.E.) program. Roughly 10 years after its inception, G.R.E.A.T. was significantly revised and now operates in an updated format. Students undergo G.R.E.A.T. as a group (Esbensen, Osgood, Taylor, Peterson, & Freng, 2001). Curriculum content is delivered by uniformed police officers, sometimes with assistance from prosecutors and federal law-enforcement agents. The goal is to convince youths of the dangers of gang membership and to keep them out of delinquency, generally by helping them learn techniques to resist peer pressure (Esbensen, Peterson, Taylor, & Osgood, 2012). The G.R.E.A.T. program is funded by the Office of Juvenile Justice Delinquency Prevention (OJJDP), the agency within the U.S. Department of Justice that funds and oversees juvenile-delinquency prevention initiatives.

The OJJDP also promotes the Comprehensive Gang Model, which was developed by a research team at the University of Chicago and originally dubbed the Spergel Model. The Comprehensive Gang Model is a set of directions offering guidance to communities wishing to implement antigang programs. The best practices listed in the model include steps such as mobilizing the community and all potential partners, obtaining a broad base of support from diverse agencies, and promoting formal and informal social control (Office of Juvenile Justice Delinquency Prevention, 2010). The Comprehensive Gang Model offers a recipe for communities to follow, but local officials must also tailor the core components to meet their jurisdictions' unique needs.

In the early 2000s, OJJDP launched a spinoff of the Comprehensive Gang Model called the Gang Reduction Program. The Gang Reduction Program started as a pilot project to test its predecessor in four demonstration sites around the country. Research arising out of the pilot program formed a new set of best practices, which detail the elements communities should include and how to best set up and run those elements. The OJJDP recommends, among other things, that communities form steering committees and task lead agencies with overseeing program development and implementation (OJJDP, 2010).

Another one of the best-known strategies is the pulling-levers approach, which was made famous by Boston's Operation Ceasefire (Kennedy, 1997) and is an element of various other suppression programs (Braga, 2008; McGarrell, Chermak, Wilson, & Corsaro, 2006). Pulling levers has its roots in problem-oriented policing (Braga, 2008; Braga & Weisburd, 2012) and revolves around turning gangs' strengths into vulnerabilities. Gang members participate in various types of criminal activity. This is a strength insofar as they enjoy substantial "criminal capital" (Decker, 2007, p. 730), meaning they have wide networks of criminal associates. However, their chronic offending also means that most serious gang members have outstanding warrants, are on probation or parole, or are known to police. Gang members' offending is a weakness that police, prosecutors, and community agencies, working together, can exploit (Kennedy, 1997). This is the core of pulling levers.

Pulling levers is focused deterrence (Braga & Weisburd, 2012), whereby police and prosecutors bring their resources to bear against specific offenses and offenders. In Ceasefire, violence (specifically homicide) is the crime selected for suppression, and the message is delivered directly to the individuals known to be involved in violence. Pulling levers begins with the convening of an interagency working group consisting of police, prosecutors, probation and parole personnel, and community social-service agencies. Next is an information-gathering and analysis phase whereby the level of gang involvement in local homicide is assessed, as is the specific nature of gang violence (whether it generally arises from rivalries or drugs, whether it is mostly intragang or intergang, and so on). The working group constructs a logical set of responses to violence based on the results of the analysis. Finally, the message is communicated to the gang(s) that violence will not be tolerated and will bring a swift, powerful response. At the same time, community-service agencies offer counseling, job training, and education services to gang members. The idea is to simultaneously scare them out of gang violence and entice them into turning their lives around (Braga, 2008; Braga & Weisburd, 2012; Kennedy, 1997).

The deterrence element of pulling levers is predicated upon using gang members against one another by creatively levying sanctions when the prohibition on violence is violated. In Boston, Operation Ceasefire's city of origin, police (with the help of probation, parole, and prosecution personnel) responded to incidents of gang violence by descending upon drug markets. Boston gangs depended heavily on drug sales for revenues, so shutdowns hurt (Kennedy, 1997). Police also launched order-maintenance crackdowns aimed at known gang members, flanked out to enforce outstanding warrants, and used civil laws to seize assets and properties suspected of being involved in illegal operations. Federal prosecutors charged the offenders in federal courts, where prison sentences tend to be longer compared to state courts (Braga, Kennedy, Waring, & Piehl, 2001). This menu of penalties far exceeded the punishments for gang violence meted out in the past, and penalized the entire gang for the actions of individuals. Pulling levers has been implemented in cities across the nation.

Civil abatement is another popular strategy. Civil gang injunctions (CGIs) are the legal tool of abatement. Southern California cities pioneered CGIs and remain a leader in their use (Maxson, Hennigan, & Sloane, 2005). Police and prosecutors collect evidence that a gang is presenting a public nuisance and petition a judge for an order enjoining members of that gang from engaging in certain activities, such as wearing gang colors or flashing gang signs, or even just being together in public (Maxson et al., 2005). Violation can result in fines, incarceration, or both. The goal is to make gang membership effectively illegal. This is murky territory, as it is unconstitutional to criminalize a status (*Robinson v. California*, 1962). Some cities have experimented with antiloitering ordinances designed to give police legal grounds for arresting gang members seen together in public. Many ordinances were struck down as unconstitutionally vague because they gave police too much discretion in determining whom to arrest (*City of Chicago v. Morales*, 1999). To sidestep these legal hurdles, CGIs must be highly detailed in the gang, people, and area they cover. They can include large numbers of gang members and significant land areas (Maxson et al., 2005) so long as the evidence supports it. Civil gang injunctions vary substantially in scope. One of their attractive features is that they are flexible and can be adapted to suit each city's unique gang problem (Maxson, Hennigan, & Sloane, 2003).

EXAMINING THE RATIONALES

Each of the three rationales—prevention, intervention, and suppression—proceeds from its own set of premises and assumptions. In this section, we examine these premises for strengths and weaknesses in light of the available theory and evidence about gang membership and behavior. The goal is to determine the extent to which each one would be expected to provide fruitful avenues for policy.

PREVENTION

Prevention, as one would expect, is an approach designed to keep youths away from gangs. The G.R.E.A.T. program is an example of a prevention-based initiative (Esbensen et al., 2012), although intervention is also possible, since some of the adolescents in the program are already in gangs or join during the course of the program (see Melde & Esbensen, 2013). Several scholars agree that prevention is the most effective method of keeping youths away from gang activity and that the best approach is to aim antigang programming at children younger than 14 years of age (see Esbensen et al., 2012 for a review).

Prevention seems to meet a few important criteria supporting the internal logic of this goal. Research documents how difficult it is for those already embroiled in gang life to extract themselves, particularly if they are heavily involved (Pyrooz et al., 2010; 2013). Leaving a gang may be harder than never joining in the first place. Additionally, since gang-involved youth typically display higher rates of delinquency prior to joining the gang (DeLisi et al., 2009; Gordon et al., 2004; Melde & Esbensen, 2013), at-risk youths are identifiable and thus feasible to target for prevention programming (Thornberry, 1998). Most youths who join gangs do so voluntarily, and do so because the gang appears to offer attractive benefits such as opportunities to earn money and have fun (Howell, 2010). These adolescents could be receptive to prevention programs if those programs offered accurate information about the perils of gang membership sufficiently compelling to counteract youths' fantasies about the lifestyle. At-risk youths might also benefit from diversion programs that funnel them into prosocial activities and groups.

At the same time, there are some features of gangs and gang members that may undermine prevention policies. First, gangs are prevalent in distressed, urban neighborhoods (Thornberry, 1998). Youths with familial ties to gangs are more likely to themselves become gang members (Thornberry, 1998), probably due to the social learning that occurs when one is raised in an environment where attitudes favorable toward gangs are prevalent (Kissner & Pyrooz, 2009). It may be unrealistic to expect a prevention program to counterbalance family and neighborhood influences. Second, prevention efforts generally target youths at the individual level, whereas the risk factors for gang membership are diverse and come from the community and family levels (Howell, 2010; Thornberry, 1998). For example, suffering abuse as a child is a risk factor for later gang involvement (see Howell, 2010 for a review), so a prevention program teaching the adolescent about the negative aspects of gangs might not be effective unless it was coupled with a method of addressing the youth's underlying psychological needs. Gang involvement cannot be treated as occurring in a vacuum independent of other processes in youths' lives.

Prevention programs like G.R.E.A.T. may be adequate for youths at low risk for gang involvement (or at least for serious, long-term involvement). More targeted prevention may be necessary for adolescents who have multiple risk factors (such as familial gang ties and low attachment to school). Targeted prevention may also require wrap-around services that include the child's parents and siblings, as well, to ensure all risk factors are being addressed.

INTERVENTION

Intervention-oriented programs seek to extract youths from gangs and steer them in a better direction. The OJJDP's Gang Reduction Program (OJJDP, 2010; see also McGloin & Decker, 2010) is a popular intervention strategy. Operation Ceasefire, an approach to gang-violence reduction that focuses on chronic offenders (Kennedy, 1997), is a suppression strategy but contains some tactics consistent with an intervention goal (namely, offering social services to gang members). Intervention generally consists of mechanisms to try to push gang-involved youths out of the gang, such as by helping them recognize the risks they incur for themselves and the harm they pose to others by being in the gang. Coupled with the push is a pull, or an effort to draw them into prosocial activities like employment, school, and drug counseling.

One drawback to intervention is that it is possible for the cure to be worse than the disease. Most youths who join gangs leave within a fairly short time (Melde & Esbensen, 2011, 2013; Peterson et al., 2004; Thornberry, 1998). Gang membership is not a dichotomous state whereby a youth is either in a gang or not. Gang involvement is a continuum of embeddedness ranging (at the low end) from simple contact with a gang or its members to (at the high end) active participation in gang violence. Less-immersed gang members are more likely to leave the gang than are those who are deeply embedded, and they take shorter amounts of time to extract themselves (Pyrooz, Sweeten, & Piquero, 2013). Irrespective of a youth's level of involvement, the desistance process occurs gradually and involves a severing of ties over time.

Intervention programs that do not properly account for the complex nature of gang affiliations and ties may fail or even exacerbate the problem. Casting a wide intervention net that scoops up lesser-involved youths and labels them gang members could increase, rather than reduce, their attachment to the gang (see Klein, 1995). Similarly, people and groups implementing prevention programs must not expect youths to abruptly declare themselves gang free. They will need time to undergo this change, and they may have setbacks along the way.

Intervention programs also must confront gangs' group-level dynamics. As Klein (1993, p. 312) states, "The gang world is not a rational choice model, but a social psychological one." Intervention programs do not adequately account for group processes, which has hampered these efforts (McGloin & Decker, 2010). Each gang member is enmeshed in a complex, multilayered web of peer networks buoyed by history, lore, turf, colors, and signs that are symbols of unity. Gangs frequently frame their violence as self-protective (Decker, 1996). The self-defense narrative makes it hard for individual members to see that what they are doing is destructive, not noble. Many gang members reject mainstream society as unfair, racist, and classist. These attitudes may have originated prior to their involvement with the gang (see Anderson, 1999) and they are reinforced by the gang's celebration of its outsider status (Klein, 1993; Matsuda, Melde, Taylor, Freng, & Esbensen, 2013). These social-psychological phenomena undermine intervention and nullify the impact of an intervention program that fails to address the group aspect of gangs (see also Klein & Maxson, 2010).

A final reason to question the rationale of intervention is that while gang membership tends to be transient for individual youths (Thornberry, 1998), gangs themselves show stability over time (Decker, 2007; Klein & Maxson, 2010). Co-offending undermines the intervention logic because the removal of one or even a few members of gangs will not dampen the antisocial activities of those groups (see generally McGloin & Piquero, 2009b; Stolzenberg & D'Alessio, 2008; van Mastrigt & Farrington, 2009). Gang members who quit may be replaced by new recruits (see Spelman, 2000). Even if interventions pull an occasional youth out of a gang, then, the gang itself will continue unabated.

SUPPRESSION

Suppression involves cracking down on gangs and forcing them to cease their activities or to disband entirely. Suppression-based strategies are generally led by police (Kennedy, 1997). Suppression is one of the most widely employed antigang approaches, and deterrence is the most commonly cited rationale for it (Klein, 1993). Police use tactics such as street sweeps, drug buy-busts, covert surveillance, confidential informants, and overt surveillance of gang members who are on probation or parole (Klein, 1993). Most commonly, these activities are conducted by specialized police gang units (Katz & Webb, 2006).

Policymakers and police leaders talk the language of sending messages and increasing the certainty and severity of punishment, but their version of deterrence is out of sync with the scholarly research (Klein, 1993). This is a problem, as the limits of deterrence are well known (Zimring & Hawkins, 1973). Many crimes are the product of impulse, not drawn-out planning, and most people—including those who have had previous run-ins with the law—are uninformed about the probability of being caught and punished (Kleck, Sever, Li, & Gertz, 2005). Additionally, police crackdowns can backfire by increasing gang cohesion and solidarity (Klein, 1995). Sweeps of gang neighborhoods wherein police use traffic, code, and other laws against low-level offenses as pretexts for arresting gang members may promote the view that police are too powerless or inept to tackle gangs directly and so must resort to indirect measures (Klein, 1993). Police are not painted in a favorable light if all they can do to punish chronic gang offenders is jail them briefly for reckless driving or possession of open containers of alcohol in public.

Certain types of deterrence have shown promise, though, and suppression's viability as a rationale supporting antigang efforts may turn on the type of deterrence being utilized (Klein, 1993). Unfocused police patrol has no deterrent value against crime in general (Kelling, Pate, Dieckman, & Brown, 1974) or against gang crime in particular (Fritsch, Caeti, & Taylor, 1999). Similarly, gangs can subvert crackdowns and surveillance. Gangs cleverly "convert stigmata into status symbols" (Zimring & Hawkins, 1973, p. 317). Arrest, conviction, and even prison become badges of honor. Officers in police gang units use harsh language invoking images of war (KIein, 1993) and employ military-style tactics (see Decker, 2007). Their stated missions are often to stomp out or eradicate gangs, a scorched-earth depiction of antigang efforts that encourages gang members to visualize themselves as fighting for their lives, not merely against rivals but against the police. Gangs' internal cohesion benefits from the existence of a common enemy (Klein, 1995).

Focused deterrence contains a stronger logic than general deterrence does. Focused deterrence is behind the pulling-levers approach (Braga, 2008; Braga & Weisburd, 2012). Focused deterrence directs resources at gang violence and the individuals known to be most active in it. There is logic in honing in on specific actions and people (Kennedy, 1997). Police cannot be everywhere at once, and prosecutors and judges cannot send every gang member to prison, so broad-based threats are not credible. Zeroing in on a small handful of identified gang members generates a realistic threat of detection and punishment. Pulling levers also transfers some of the enforcement burden from police to gangs themselves—when anybody errs, everybody suffers. Police might punish entire gangs by raiding drug markets, ramping up patrol in gang territories, or any number of other tactics police can bring to bear upon gangs. This motivates gangs to regulate their own members' behavior.

Civil gang injunctions, in theory, suppress gangs at the individual, group, and community levels (Maxson et al., 2005). Injunctions may improve individual-level deterrence because being identified by name theoretically makes gang members believe they are under surveillance and run a high risk of detection. Violations usually carry fairly small penalties, which may undermine perceived sanction severity (Grogger, 2005). At the group level, CGIs can help negate the protective psychological buffer that allows gang members to feel that they are not doing anything wrong or bear no personal responsibility for the actions of the group. Finally, communities may benefit from CGIs. The process of obtaining a CGI often requires police to enlist community assistance, which may foster partnerships. If a CGI does quell gang activity, community members may feel less fearful and start spending more time outside, which promotes informal social control.

The viability of focused deterrence and CGIs rests upon an additional requirement, however: Proper analysis must be conducted, and the local gang structure, organization, cohesiveness, and criminal activities must be vulnerable to these types of suppression strategies (McGloin, 2005). Collective-accountability approaches, such as Ceasefire, have an impact because they use individual gangs and gang members as leverage against other ones. This will not work where gangs are too loosely structured for police and other authorities to exert meaningful leverage and pressure. Communication is also integral to CGIs, focused deterrence, and collective accountability. Police and others who are part of the initiative must get their message out (Kennedy, 1997).

Similarly, CGIs require that gangs be sufficiently cohesive and active to allow for identification of the specific gangs and members to be named in the injunction (see Maxson et al., 2005). A gang might be so loosely organized that a CGI would exert little impact. Even worse, CGIs may inadvertently increase cohesion among loose gangs (Klein, 1995; see also Swan & Bates, 2017). In a city where gangs are horizontal and constellation-like, suppression might not be feasible.

Another pitfall for CGIs is the potential for police and courts to mislabel a loosely affiliated group of friends as a gang, or to incorrectly assume that a gang member's close friends or family members are criminal associates. In these instances, prohibitions on public congregation, wearing common colors, and otherwise communicating with each other are pointless. They may also be racially discriminatory and reflect assumptions made by police officers, prosecutors, and judges that minority youth living in neighborhoods with a visible gang presence are themselves gang involved (Stewart, 1998). In Southern California, the first CGI to ever be used was in a black neighborhood and had overt racial components. While modern CGIs appear race neutral on their face, many of the profiles and behaviors used as criteria for labeling someone a gang member are vestiges from this racialized past (Muniz, 2014). For CGIs to have a rational basis, the lists of people named in them must be constructed on the basis of clear evidence of demonstrable gang-related behavior and not on assumptions, profiles, or preconceived notions.

THE EMPIRICAL STATUS OF MODERN GANG POLICY

A caveat about definitions is in order before we dive into the evaluations of antigang policies and strategies. There is no universally accepted conceptualization of what constitutes gang crime or even what a gang is (Klein & Maxson, 2010; Sullivan, 2006). Gang members themselves often do not use the word "gang" and opt instead for alternatives like "crew" (Papachristos, 2005). Some practitioners and researchers use more inclusive definitions of gangs and gang crimes, while others employ more narrow criteria (Decker & Curry, 2002). The definition selected can materially alter a study's results and conclusions about program effectiveness. Thus, the empirical literature should be approached with a measure of caution.

The majority of school-based prevention programs have not been evaluated. School officials are prey for pseudoexperts peddling nonsense wrapped in pretty packages (see Esbensen et al., 2013). Scholars have produced research to guide school administrators' decisions about which programs to trust and which to avoid (Esbensen et al., 2012). Many evaluations, though, are methodologically weak, and only a few meet criteria for scientific rigor (Esbensen et al., 2013). Most that have been evaluated produce no discernable positive outcomes (Esbensen et al., 2013).

One of the most extensively evaluated programs is G.R.E.A.T. As described earlier, the program began in the early 1990s. Initial evaluations of G.R.E.A.T. suggested the program was modestly effective, but effect sizes were small in magnitude (Esbensen & Osgood, 1999) and follow-up studies utilizing more sophisticated methodology found no difference between the treatment and control groups on gang membership or delinquency (Esbensen et al., 2001).

In response, the curriculum underwent revisions, including the addition of evidence-based strategies (Esbensen, Osgood, et al., 2013; Esbensen, Peterson et al., 2012). An evaluation of the implementation of the revised curriculum showed police officers and others involved in content delivery adhered well to the curriculum (Esbensen, Matsuda, Taylor, & Peterson, 2011). Outcome evaluations found that the revised program produced a statistically significant and substantively meaningful reduction in gang membership among G.R.E.A.T. participants one year after they graduated from the program (Esbensen et al., 2012). A four-year follow-up revealed that the lowered likelihood of joining a gang persisted, albeit somewhat attenuated from the one-year period (Esbensen et al., 2013). G.R.E.A.T. appears to have positive impacts on several behavioral and attitudinal measures, including favorable attitudes toward police, fewer associations with delinquent peers, less anger, and less use of neutralization techniques, among others (Esbensen, Osgood, et al., 2013; Esbensen, Peterson, et al., 2012). The fact that G.R.E.A.T. has fared well in evaluations despite the diversity of methods and outcome measures used has led to widespread agreement that schools looking for an antigang program should turn to G.R.E.A.T. (Howell, 2013).

G.R.E.A.T., however, is not without limitations. It appears to work in some cities better than in others, and it puzzlingly reduces gang participation without concomitantly suppressing delinquency (Maxson, 2013; Papachristos, 2013; Pyrooz, 2013). Those it deters may be the students who would have been weakly tied to gangs and not active in criminal behavior. In other words, G.R.E.A.T. might only work for the "low-hanging fruit" (Pyrooz, 2013, p. 431; but see Maxson, 2013 for a competing argument and see also Klein & Maxson, 2010). More importantly, G.R.E.A.T. assumes that gang membership is a binary status—either a youth is a gang member or not. This conceptualization of gang membership is flawed; gang involvement exists on a continuum (Pyrooz et al., 2010), which has implications for the desistance process (Pyrooz et al., 2013; see also Decker, Pyrooz, & Moule, 2014). Gang members do not simply decide one day that they are no longer in a gang. It can take time for them to remove themselves.

Accordingly, G.R.E.A.T. might miss the mark in two ways. First, it may speak more to lower-risk youths than to higher-risk ones, thus targeting those who might never have joined a gang or if they did, would have been only peripheral members. Second, the program could—by fostering more negative attitudes toward gang membership—convince less-embedded members to stop calling themselves gang members without meaningfully altering their behavior (Pyrooz, 2013). More research is needed to assess how well G.R.E.A.T. translates into genuine behavioral differences, particularly among those who are, or who are at risk of becoming, deeply embedded in gang lifestyles.

Interventions, such as OJJDP's Gang Reduction Program, have received mixed reviews. The evidence-based nature, specificity, and detail of OJJDP's best-practices model has proven helpful to communities. This model is both structured and flexible, allowing communities to adapt the key elements to meet local needs (Cahill & Hayeslip, 2010; Howell, 2010). Intervention in general, however, has proven problematic in practice. Two factors contribute to this. First, as Maxson et al. (2005, p. 578) epxlain, "Gang members are notoriously resistant to intervention." The collective processes of the gang (Decker, 1996) and the social-psychological forces that pull gang members together (Klein, 1993) make it hard for youth to leave gangs, particularly if they are deeply immersed (Pyrooz et al., 2013). Interventions such as the Gang Reduction Model and its variants (the Spergel Model and the Comprehensive Gang Model) operate primarily at the individual level and do not adequately account for group-level processes (Klein & Maxson, 2010). Joining a gang is indeed generally a voluntary choice (Howell, 2010); however, it requires a misreading of the gang literature to arrive at the conclusion that a program need only highlight the costs of gang membership and the rewards of a gang-free life in order to make youths desist.

Second, scholars have had a notoriously hard time evaluating intervention programs (Klein & Maxson, 2010; Maxson et al., 2005). Interventions are often nebulous, making it impossible for researchers to define and operationalize key concepts. Program goals may be ambiguous or too broad to be useful for research. Data limitations may make it difficult to differentiate between total crime in a city and those incidents related to gangs. Evaluation deficiencies hinder effective programming because researchers cannot discern what works and what does not (or, in the case of ineffective programs, what went wrong and how it could be fixed). Overall, intervention-based antigang programs lack sufficient empirical evidence to support their effectiveness. They cannot be categorically ruled out as having no impact, but there are good reasons, grounded in the scholarly research on gangs and gang membership, for being skeptical that formal intervention is a viable approach.

Gang-suppression programs and policies can be grouped into two general categories for evaluation purposes. The first is traditional police-led antigang efforts, which are typically spearheaded by specialized gang units (Decker, 2007). Since gang units are not programs or policies with a definitive beginning and end, their effectiveness cannot be tested. There is, though, indirect evidence suggesting that gang units fall short of ideal. They tend to rely on intelligence and surveillance, which are tactics devoid of long-term strategic planning. Units are often isolated from the community and even from other divisions within their own department, narrowing their options for creative problem solving. Their isolation, independence, and image of themselves as soldiers in a war against gangs sometimes leads to misconduct and even high-profile scandals (Decker, 2007). Additionally, police crackdowns that lack sufficient focus (Fitsch et al., 1999) or are grounded in misunderstandings of the group dynamics of local gangs (Klein, 1995) have no effect and can even make the situation worse. Many gang units could be operating smarter and more effectively than they presently are.

The second category of suppression encompasses strategies that are often led by police but that are more strategic and evidence based. These include pulling levers and civil gang injunctions. Pulling levers has received mixed but generally positive empirical support. All evaluations suffer from two methodological weaknesses attributable to the nature of this type of program: lack of random assignment and control groups. Pulling-levers operations target all gangs in a city, not a random selection of them, and there is no predetermined set of treatment and control neighborhoods. Most evaluators examine gang crime data before and after the intervention to discern whether the implementation corresponded to a reduction in crime, and compare crime trends in the treatment city to those in comparable cities that did not experience any gang-policy change during the study period. Researchers employing these methods uncovered evidence that Boston Ceasefire significantly reduced youth homicide (Braga et al., 2001), an impact that also surfaced in evaluations of Ceasefire and other pulling-levers based approaches in cities nationwide (Braga, 2008; McGarrell et al., 2006; Papachristos, Meares, & Fagan, 2007). Some scholars have questioned the magnitude of the contribution Ceasefire made to the reduction in youth homicides, noting that violence of all types was on a downward trend throughout the 1990s and that the influence of police-led initiatives was probably overstated (Fagan, 2002; see generally Levitt, 2004). There are also doubts about the sustainability of the reductions that accompany the initial drop in violence after program implementation; some evidence suggests that the benefits decay over time (Braga, 2008). A recent systematic review of the entire body of literature built around pulling levers concluded that the strategy appears effective, but that caution is warranted due to the absence of randomized controlled trials (Braga & Weisburd, 2012).

Civil gang injunctions rest on shaky empirical grounds. Relatively few evaluations exist, and many of the pertinent questions about effectiveness remain unanswered (Grogger, 2005). The evaluations that have been conducted have yielded mixed, inconsistent results (Esbensen, 2013). Studies attempting to assess CGIs' impact on violent crime have alternately revealed modest reductions (Grogger, 2002), null effects (Maxson & Allen, 1997), and increases (American Civil Liberties Union, 1997). One found decreases in certain types or measures of crime (that is, calls for services as compared to crimes uncovered by police) and increases in others, for an overall uninterpretable picture of the CGI's impact (Goulka, Heaton, Tita, Matthies, Whitby, & Cooper, 2009). A longitudinal analysis of violent-crime trends in two areas of a city that were both put under CGIs in the same year revealed a significant drop in violence in one of the areas followed by a rebound to near pre-intervention levels. Violence in the other area spiked after the CGI took effect and then slid downward. The authors interpreted these discrepancies to mean that police and courts need to do a better job assessing the social and organizational aspects of gangs before issuing CGIs (Hennigan & Sloane, 2013). An evaluation of community members' quality of life and fear of crime showed small but consistent improvements after the implementation of a CGI, suggesting some support for the positive outcomes of CGIs under a social-disorganization framework (Maxson et al., 2005).

By contrast, there is evidence that CGIs have deleterious consequences for the people listed on them, as well as for the friends and family of those individuals. As noted previously, CGIs have been criticized for sweeping too wide and scooping up people merely presumed—commonly because of their race and residence in certain neighborhoods—to be gang members (Muniz, 2014; Stewart, 1998). The stigma of being named in a CGI, and the fear that a listed person is being watched by police, can damage relationships between friends and family members. Many listed gang members are teenagers, and being monitored by police interferes with their schooling (Swan & Bates, 2017). Echoing Klein (1993), one study found that many people angered by the perceived injustice of being put on a CGI rebelled by becoming even more involved in their gangs (Swan & Bates, 2017). In Southern California, injunctions have become entrenched in the local law-enforcement culture. Prosecutors and police can pull up boilerplate injunctions and implement them with minimal tailoring to the specifics of the gang at hand (Muniz, 2014), which enhances the probability of collateral consequences, including increased gang solidarity.

CONCLUSION

This chapter discussed and evaluated gang policy within the context of contemporary scholarly findings about the organization and behavior of gangs. Gangs are perennially difficult to define, and often look more like loosely associated constellations of groups rather than the hierarchical, tightly organized criminal enterprises they are frequently portrayed as being. Gangs' origins and behavior can be traced to macrolevel (community), microlevel (group), and individual-level factors. Microlevel or group processes are powerful forces shaping gangs' and gang members' behavior, yet they are overlooked in many antigang programs. Many antigang initiatives, moreover, do not begin with comprehensive analyses of the nature of local gangs and are therefore in danger of failing. Many also target only one level of risk factor (e.g., individual) and neglect the others.

Effective antigang policy may be achieved with realistic, accurate, timely knowledge about local gangs. Policymakers, practitioners, school officials, and community advocates seeking to implement a program or policy must start with a thorough analysis of the local gang problem. This would include, but not be limited to, the number and size of gangs; how hierarchical versus horizontal or constellation-like their organization tends to be;

whether rivalries exist more between different gangs or between different sets of the same gang; the level of involvement each gang has in the drug market; and the average depth of embeddedness among the majority of gang-affiliated youth. Local initiatives also must be grounded in evidence-based practices. Some gang approaches (such as pulling levers) rest on reasonably sound scientific support, while others (such as most intervention strategies targeting individual gang members) fall short in both theory and empirical evidence. Researchers should increase their attention to gang programs and produce more and higher-quality evaluations. Local politicians, police, school officials, and community leaders who pay attention to the research and appreciate the importance of evidence-based practices could help reduce gang activities and violence and improve the quality of life for residents of troubled neighborhoods.

DISCUSSION QUESTIONS

1. Some police officers working in cities with gang problems have a colloquial saying that "Gang members don't retire; they expire." This expression is used to describe gang members' (supposed) lifetime involvement in their gangs and represents the assumption that once a person joins a gang, he or she is in it for life. Analyze the correctness of this claim. Does it apply to all gang members in all types of gangs? Are there certain types of gang members it might accurately describe?

2. Suppose you live in an urban area with a gang problem. After a recent increase in gang-related homicides and assaults, the local police chief and mayor declared their intentions to implement Operation Ceasefire as a means of reducing the violence. The chief and mayor have asked you to coordinate the implementation. What information do you need in order to do this? Identify all the things you would need to know about local gangs and their activities in order to first determine whether Ceasefire is appropriate for this city and then, assuming you found it to be appropriate, what additional information you would need to implement this program.

3. This chapter made clear that research is sparse with respect to many aspects of gangs, the people who join and leave them, gang organizations and activities, and the effectiveness of gang interventions. Identify three gaps in the research as described in the chapter, and propose research methods which could be used to collect data that could shed light on these important voids in our understandings of gangs.

4. Drawing from what you have learned about policies grounded in prevention, intervention, and suppression, propose an antigang program that incorporates at least two of these policy approaches. Describe the elements of your program, the evidence- or theory-based reasons why you selected those elements, and the reasons why you believe this program would work.

CASES CITED

City of Chicago v. Morales. 527 U.S. 41 (1999)
Robinson v. California. 370 U.S. 660 (1962)

CHAPTER 6

JUVENILE JUSTICE

INTRODUCTION

Criminal justice in the United States is split into one system for adults and one for youths. The adult system is bound by formal procedural rules, most of which derive from the U.S. Constitution's Bill of Rights and the various U.S. Supreme Court cases laying out what states must do to ensure compliance with those amendments. The juvenile system, by contrast, is relatively informal and displays a great degree of localization. The result is an uneven administrative and operational landscape, which is further compounded by the substantial discretion vested in police, caseworkers, judges, and other criminal-justice and social-service officials who decide how to handle youth who come into conflict with the law.

Informality and decentralization originate from the underlying rationale of the statutory distinction between adults and juveniles. The adult system is intended to deter, incapacitate, punish, control, and (at times) rehabilitate. By contrast, rehabilitation is the primary guiding philosophy of the juvenile system. This ideological underpinning does not always translate into practice; indeed, punishment and control have assumed central roles in the system's handling of juveniles (Bonnie, Johnson, Chemers, & Schuck, 2013). Nonetheless, rehabilitation remains central to the stated mission of the juvenile-justice system.

Juvenile courts have jurisdiction over most youths (typically defined as up to age 18, but sometimes 17 or 16, depending on state statutes) who break the law. It is estimated that juvenile courts handled 1,058,500 delinquency cases in 2013, or about 2,900 every day. A steady decline has taken place over recent years and the number of cases is at its lowest since 1997 (Hockenberry & Puzzanchera, 2015). Approximately 383,000 juveniles are placed on probation and another 78,700 held in custody annually (Sickmund, Sladky, & Kang, 2015). In 2010, juvenile courts handled 137,000 status-offense cases, 36 percent of which were for truancy and 22 percent for underage drinking (Salsich & Trone, 2013). The juvenile-justice system impacts the lives of millions of young people and their families.

This chapter reviews the history and ideological origins of the juvenile-justice system. The juvenile court, in particular, is a central locus of decision making and played an outsized role in the initial response to wayward and miscreant youth in the United States. A summary of some modern critiques of the system will be presented, and we will critically parse the underlying rationales of the system to arrive at a conclusion about whether those guiding philosophies seem sound. Finally, the empirical evidence is examined to determine whether the programs and policies in place to prevent juvenile offending and recidivism are working as planned.

HISTORY AND ORIGINS OF THE JUVENILE SYSTEM

The juvenile court has its roots in the Progressive movement that guided the development of a treatment-centered approach to adult criminal justice at the turn of the twentieth century. The end of the 1800s and first decades of the 1900s saw the United States transform from an agrarian society into an industry-dominated economy. Urban centers rose up around factories and plants. Rural migrants and European immigrants searching for jobs flooded these new cities. The Progressives were middle- and upper-class reformers concerned about urban children's wellbeing. Progressive observers perceived an increase in unsupervised youngsters in urban areas, and feared these children were not receiving proper education and family support. This concern was not free from classist and ethnocentric sentiments that poor immigrants were not instilling in their children the "proper" moral and religious beliefs. Childhood took on a status as a vital period of formative development, and the Progressives devoted themselves to "saving" urban children (Feld, 1983; Platt, 1977).

The social and legal concept of a "juvenile" arose as Progressives assembled a system to handle wayward youth who disobeyed their parents and teachers, were truant from school, and made public nuisances of themselves. Various efforts to curtail juvenile misbehavior had been explored before, but the Progressives were the first to consolidate these interventions into a single system (Platt, 1977). Criminal courts handled youths who broke criminal laws, but there was no formalized mechanism for exerting state control over youths whose parents would not or could not control them. The civil courts cobbled together an imperfect solution grounded in the doctrine of *parens patriae* that allows the state to assume custody of wayward children. *Parens patriae* vests the state with legal authority to assume custody of orphaned children and to take children away from their parents when the state deems such action necessary for the children's wellbeing. Civil-court control over needy youth constituted the original approach to juvenile status offending (Ferdinand, 1991). Status offenses are activities that are illegal for youths to engage in because of their young age, but are lawful for adults (such as drinking alcohol). Progressives saw the civil court as the optimal mechanism because it allowed for flexibility, informality, and the tailoring of state responses to meet each juvenile's unique needs (Feld, 1983).

Throughout the 1800s, civil and criminal courts were overwhelmed with status offenders and delinquents. Calls went out for the creation of a new court system devoted entirely to juveniles. In addition to relieving civil and criminal-court caseloads, the juvenile court was thought to be an ideal way to ensure that troubled children's needs were met. Progressive ideals held that the standardization seen in adult courts was improper for the administration of the juvenile court (Feld, 1983). Procedures in the juvenile court would be informal and tailored to the individual needs of each adolescent. Judges and caseworkers would be educated about the familial and psychological origins of juvenile misbehavior, and would determine the most appropriate outcome that would help set juveniles on a path for a more promising future (Feld, 1983; Ferdinand, 1991). In 1899, Illinois became the first state to establish a juvenile court (which was located in Cook County) and adopt a legal code devoted entirely to juveniles. Other states followed, and by 1945 all had juvenile courts (Ferdinand, 1991).

Enthusiastic reformers did not adequately consider the social or legal ramifications of pooling low-level status offenders and serious juvenile delinquents together in a legal system that existed outside the criminal law, and this critical error embedded a serious flaw in the juvenile-justice system (Ferdinand, 1991). From the start, rehabilitation and punishment have been strange companions in the juvenile system. Likewise, the Progressives' faith in the benevolence of the state and its ability to rehabilitate troubled youth gave rise to a system rife with uncertainty, inequity, and undue control over (immigrant and minority) children and adolescents (Feld, 1983). The juvenile-court system of the Progressive era was headed for an overhaul.

The juvenile system soon came under fire for stripping juveniles of their freedom without affording them legal rights (Ferdinand, 1991). Because *parens patriae* holds that the purpose of confining young law-breakers is for treatment and care, not criminal punishment, states denied youths the procedural protections that the U.S. Constitution and Bill of Rights extend to adults accused of crimes. In contrast to the public nature of adult courts, juvenile-court proceedings were conducted in private (Feld, 1983). Juveniles, including status offenders, might be held in custody for years. Delinquents could be incarcerated for longer terms than adults would be for the same offenses, yet the juvenile courts did not afford accused youths full opportunities to defend themselves against the charges (Feld, 1999). The absence of standardized constitutional rights also exacerbated the lack of uniformity in juvenile-court proceedings and outcomes. Juvenile courts operate locally, generally at the county level, and this decentralization resulted in the development of substantial idiosyncrasy as each court established its own customs. Fragmentation and unpredictability followed (Ferdinand, 1991).

In the 1960s and 1970s, the adult correctional system (also operating under Progressive ideology) disintegrated in the wake of the "nothing works" movement that left academics and policymakers alike convinced that it was impossible to rehabilitate offenders. The now-infamous Martinson (1974) report purporting to prove the hopelessness of correctional intervention coincided with a series of discouraging evaluations of community-based early-intervention and treatment programs for juveniles (Ferdinand, 1991). Even though the claim that "nothing works" was incorrect and supportable only through a highly selective reading of the empirical evidence, it permeated public opinion because of a generalized failure to understand the characteristics that separated effective programs from ineffective ones (Fagan, 1990). The "nothing works" mantra was also a convenient vehicle for get-tough proponents to justify reorienting correctional budgets (Levesque, 1996). The increasingly right-leaning electorate and their conservative politicians—led by Presidents Richard Nixon and Ronald Reagan—replaced rehabilitation with an expanded system of punishment and control.

The U.S. Supreme Court's *In re Gault* (1967) decision proved to be a turning point in the history of juvenile courts. Fifteen-year-old Gerald Gault, who was on probation after a previous run-in with the law, made an obscene telephone call and for this offense was remanded to an institution for juvenile delinquents until he turned 21. An adult convicted of the same offense would have been fined between $5 and $50, or jailed no longer than 2 months. During the adjudication process, Gault was denied formal hearings or the ability to confront the complainant who accused him of making the call. The Court reaffirmed the rehabilitative mission of the juvenile system, but rejected the claim that *parens patriae* justifies secrecy and a complete absence of procedural standards. The justices declared that juveniles called into court have the right to due process, to be represented by legal counsel (including court-appointed attorneys if their families are indigent), to be free from compelled self-incrimination, and to cross-examine witnesses. A few years later, in *In re Winship* (1970), the Court raised the legal standard necessary to formally adjudicate a juvenile as a delinquent from the very low "preponderance of the evidence" up to "beyond a reasonable doubt," the standard of proof required to convict an adult of a crime. In *McKeiver v. Pennsylvania* (1971), though, the justices refused to give juveniles the right to trial by jury under the rationale that doing so would turn juvenile courts into adversarial forums and ruin the "intimate, informal protective proceeding" (*McKeiver*, p. 545). The Court expanded juveniles' rights in *Breed v. Jones* (1975), where it found functional equivalence between delinquency proceedings and criminal trials and extended the right to be free of double jeopardy. In spite of these rulings, juvenile offenders remain in legal limbo: They can be punished severely, but they cannot avail themselves of the panoply of constitutional rights available to adults (Feld, 1999). Some critics have called the juvenile court a "scaled-down, second-class criminal court" (Feld, 1993, p. 403; see also Feld, 1999) because it has shifted toward a more punitive ideology than originally intended, without concomitantly securing solid procedural protections for juveniles charged with breaking the law.

The absence of full procedural protections for juvenile delinquents is particularly troubling given that the juvenile system has become expressly punitive toward young offenders. In the 1980s and 1990s, juvenile arrests for violent crime spiked (Baer & Chambliss, 1997). In response, the public demanded the system "get tough" on youthful offenders (Ferdinand, 1991). Criminal-justice practitioners and researchers who claimed subject-matter expertise issued inflammatory rhetoric and dire predictions of a coming apocalypse of rampant youth violence. The label "superpredator" circulated widely, and pundits warned the nation to brace itself for disaster (see Baer & Chambliss, 1997; Jordan & Myers, 2011 for reviews). All states enacted new laws and policies directing prosecutors and judges to send juveniles accused of violent acts to adult court, where they would face the same prison terms as adults (Bernard & Kurlycheck, 2010; Levesque, 1996). Prevention and rehabilitation programs also received an infusion of resources (Butts & Mears, 2001), but the dominant tone was one of getting tough (Merlo, Benekos, & Cook, 1997a, 1997b) by finding ways to put juveniles behind bars for longer periods of time (Torbet, Gable, Montgomery, & Hurst, 1996), either by sending them to adult courts or making juvenile-court penalties harsher.

Doomsday never came, though. Juvenile violence did not rise; in fact, it did the opposite: it plummeted (Blumstein, 2000). Get-tough proponents created a punishment-oriented system designed to handle a generation of superpredators that never materialized. Rather than admit error, however, policymakers and practitioners put this new system to use in spite of the fact that the apparent need for it (i.e., high rates of juvenile-perpetrated violence) was gone. Many youths are now transferred to adult court and treated severely. Those remaining in juvenile courts are subject to largely informal proceedings that are now infused with a punitive orientation not seen prior to the juvenile get-tough movement. This contrasts sharply with youths' diminished constitutional rights and inability to adequately defend themselves (Feld, 1999). Youths taken into custody remain largely helpless to challenge court officials' decisions to prosecute them, to detain them while they await their day in court, or to find them guilty of a crime without the benefit of a jury trial.

Some scholars argue that the juvenile court should be abolished and that juveniles should be tried in adult court (Ainsworth, 1991; Feld, 1993, 1999). Criticism has also been aimed at what the juvenile system represents. Symbolically, watered-down rights convey a message to youth of being devalued by society (Ainsworth, 1994). If processed through the adult system, youths would enjoy full procedural protections. To account for their young age and underdeveloped decision-making capacity, their youth could be considered a mitigating factor justifying lighter sentences than what adults would receive for the same offenses (Feld, 1993, 1999). Unification of adult and juvenile courts is unlikely to occur, however, because the public opposes it, partly out of a lingering faith in juvenile courts' rehabilitative capacity (Mears, Hay, Gertz, & Mancini, 2007). Unification would also eliminate individualized treatment and probably pull the policy approach to juvenile offenders even further off its rehabilitation moorings.

DEFINITIONS AND OVERVIEW OF JUVENILE-COURT PROCEDURES

The juvenile-justice system possesses a unique vocabulary and set of practices. The two types of misbehavior that can land an adolescent in the system are status offending and delinquency. Status offenses are misbehaviors committed by youth that would not be crimes if engaged in by adults. Drinking alcohol, being out in public past curfew, and being truant from school are examples. State laws and local ordinances determine the types of conduct juveniles are prohibited from engaging in. Juvenile delinquency occurs when a person under the age of majority breaks the criminal law. The same action by an adult would be called a crime.

The localized nature of the juvenile system precludes a detailed description of the process by which juveniles are handled, but there are enough common elements to construct a model of typical case flow. Youths come into contact with the system through arrest or referral. Referrals are written complaints made by third parties (e.g., school officials) who allege that the juvenile has broken the criminal law or demonstrated a pattern of status offending.

When a youth is arrested or referred, the intake process begins. The case is reviewed by an intake officer, who is usually a probation officer. The intake officer examines the alleged offense and might administer a risk-assessment instrument. The intake officer writes a report containing a recommendation for the prosecutor about how to proceed with the case. The prosecutor is not bound to this recommendation, but will take it seriously.

The juvenile-court analog to the prosecutorial charging decision in adult court is called a petition. If the intake officer decides the case requires formal processing, the officer advises petitioning the case; otherwise, the officer suggests the juvenile be diverted for informal handling or that the case be dropped entirely. A juvenile against whom a petition has been filed moves to the adjudication portion of the process, which is the functional equivalent of pretrial proceedings.

During adjudication, a juvenile may be detained in a secure facility or allowed to return home. This decision may be informed by the risk assessment performed during intake. A judge holds a detention hearing, typically between 24 and 72 hours from arrest or referral, to determine whether the juvenile seems dangerous to self or others or is a flight risk. In many states, judges can dismiss petitions or divert juveniles during the adjudication process if formal processing seems inappropriate. Sometimes judges can arrange for informal dispositions involving some type of requirement (e.g., victim restitution) and dismiss the charges once the terms have been met.

If a plea bargain is not struck, the case proceeds to an adjudicatory hearing (trial). Since juveniles do not have a constitutional right to a trial by jury, the adjudicatory hearing happens before a judge unless a state statutorily grants juveniles jury trials. If the judge (or jury) believes the juvenile is guilty, or if the juvenile pleads guilty as the result of a plea arrangement, the juvenile is adjudicated delinquent (convicted).

A juvenile who has been adjudicated delinquent moves forward to a disposition (sentencing) hearing. In the time leading up to the hearing, a probation officer reviews the case, evaluates the youth, and prepares a sentencing recommendation (called a disposition plan) for the predisposition report. At the disposition hearing, the prosecutor, judge, probation officer, and juvenile can put options forward. These may include probation, drug treatment, mental-health counseling, victim restitution, community service, confinement in a residential facility or detention center, and so on. Youths given community sanctions must return to court periodically for review hearings until they have successfully completed the terms of the arrangement, at which point their cases are closed. Those placed in residential or detention facilities serve their sentences and then should be released into aftercare (the juvenile version of parole), during which they receive services and are supervised during their transition back into the community. In many communities, resources are insufficient and aftercare is less structured in practice than on paper.

DISPROPORTIONATE MINORITY CONTACT

There are racial disparities in juvenile-justice system contact and in punishment severity. Concerns about racial disparities (technically termed disproportionate minority contact) are as old as the juvenile system itself. As previously described, clashes between well-to-do U.S. citizens and poor immigrants fueled the rise of the child-saving movement that formed the juvenile court. Today, racial disparities and the overrepresentation of minority youth in the juvenile system are readily apparent. In 2014, the arrest rate among white juveniles was 2,538 per 100,000 youths aged 10–17, while that for black juveniles was 6,444 per 100,000 (Office of Juvenile Justice and Delinquency Prevention, 2015). Descriptive statistics indicate that minority youths are more likely to be arrested, petitioned, held in secure detention, and placed in residential facilities when compared to similarly situated white youths. Congress formally recognized disproportionate minority contact and confinement in 1989 when it attached a national mandate to its reauthorization of the 1974 Juvenile Justice and Delinquency Prevention Act (JJDPA). The mandate made receipt of federal grants contingent upon states' demonstrated efforts to identify the extent of the problem in their jurisdictions and to adopt best practices to curb it (Leiber & Rodriguez, 2011). The mandate has been amended in subsequent reauthorizations, but remains a core requirement for states seeking federal money (Peck, 2016).

Racial disparities are partially driven by real differences in offending rates. Differential offending accounts for a certain proportion of disproportionate minority contact (Leiber & Peck, 2015). The juvenile system exacerbates racial disproportionality, however, because police officers, judges, probation officers, caseworkers, and other officials possess a great deal of discretion in how they decide to deal with juvenile offenders. Mixed results emerge as to whether black and Latino youth are more likely than similarly situated white youth to be petitioned at intake, detained during adjudication proceedings, adjudicated delinquent, or given placement, even controlling for legal (e.g., prior record) and extralegal (e.g., school status, family situations) characteristics (Leiber & Peck, 2013a Leiber, Peck, & Rodriguez, 2016; Peck, Leiber, & Brubaker, 2014). Offense type affects the magnitude of racial disparities (Fix, Fix, Totura, & Burkhart, 2017) and impacts which groups are treated harsher than other ones (Leiber, Peck, & Baudry-Cyr, 2016) of racial disparities. Gender also factors in; harsher outcomes for black youths may be driven by punitive treatment directed at black males in particular (Cochran & Mears, 2015; Leiber et al., 2016).

There are multiple decision points at which white youths might be treated more leniently than their black or Latino peers, so it is wiser to consider the entirety of the process rather than limit the inquiry to any single decision point. Disproportionate minority contact is best explained by the cumulative-disadvantage perspective. (Leiber & Peck, 2013b). Disadvantageous decisions occurring earlier in the process can have consequences for later outcomes. For instance, youths detained during the adjudication process are more likely to later be adjudicated delinquent. Cumulative disadvantage for blacks and Latinos has been uncovered in the adult justice system as well (Kutateladze, Andilororo, Johnson, & Spohn, 2014). Youths of color, then, experience a similar set of disadvantages in the juvenile-court system as their adult counterparts encounter when they traverse the criminal courts.

JUVENILE-JUSTICE POLICIES

This section summarizes the primary approaches to juvenile justice in the United States. There are innumerable state and local efforts to prevent juvenile delinquency and deal with troublesome or criminal youth, so the following overview discusses policies and programs in broad terms and avoids delving into the details of any specific ones. Furthermore, we confine the discussion to policies and programs directly involving police, courts, or corrections. There are several proven and promising school and community programs (Blueprints for Healthy Youth Development, 2017; CrimeSolutions.gov, n.d.), but purely community- or school-based initiatives are outside the scope of the current discussion because they are not coordinated by criminal-justice officials. For present purposes, juvenile-justice policies are grouped into curfews, diversion, teen courts and status-offender programs, out-of-home placement, and waiver. Many of these categories overlap—and specific programs can fall into multiple categories—so this typology is intended solely to enhance the clarity of the description of juvenile policies and does not reflect an established or formalized differentiation.

CURFEWS

States and municipalities have attempted to prevent juvenile offending by enacting curfews. Curfew laws or ordinances require youths younger than a specified age (frequently 17, sometimes 16, and infrequently 15 or 14; Ruefle & Reynolds, 1996) to be indoors after a certain time at night unless accompanied by a parent or guardian. Exceptions are often made for travel to work, religious services, or other legitimate destinations (Kline, 2012). Curfews have been used since the 1800s (Scherr, 1992), but their popularity blossomed in the 1990s (Ruefle & Reynolds, 1996). Curfews enjoy broad public appeal and have been endorsed by both Democratic and Republican political candidates. Curfews are theorized to be effective because they eliminate criminal opportunities (McDowall, Loftin, & Wiersema, 2000), prevent the convergence of offenders and victims (Sherman, Gottfredson, MacKenzie, Eck, Reuter, & Bushway, 1998), and strengthen parental control over juveniles (Ruefle & Reynolds, 1996).

Critics argue—and some courts have held—that curfews violate juveniles' constitutional right to freedom of movement, due process, and equal protection (Horowitz, 1991; Stoddard, Steiner, Rohrbach, Hemmens, & Bennett, 2014). Additionally, police officers have wide discretionary latitude when they encounter a juvenile out past curfew. They can bring the youth into custody or transport him or her home (Ruefle & Reynolds, 1996). The low-visibility nature of these decisions (and the fact that they are rarely subject to review by supervisors or judges) raises concerns about biased enforcement. Additionally, if a juvenile is not carrying identification, police cannot discriminate between those just under and just over the minimum age, raising the possibility of wrongful arrests (Kline, 2012). Critics have also alleged that curfews will merely temporally displace juvenile misbehavior from nighttime to daytime, but this fear seems to be largely unfounded (Reynolds, Sydlitz, & Jenkins, 2000).

DIVERSION

Diversion was a major component of post-*Gault* reform. The federal government and individual states sought ways to keep delinquent youth out of secure confinement and to keep status offenders out of the system entirely or, at least, strictly limit the amount of state control to which they are subjected (Klein, 1979). The JJDPA of 1974, and its periodic reauthorizations, pushes states to divert status offenders from juvenile courts and find other ways to provide services to them (Feld, 1983).

Diverted juveniles are referred to organizations or agencies outside of the justice system. Diversion programs vary widely (Ray & Childs, 2015). Youths can be diverted either pre-charge or postcharge. Precharge diversion is the more common of the two (Hoge, 2016). Both entail sets of conditions involving mandatory programming, surveillance, or both. In precharge diversion, completion of the required programming or term of surveillance is rewarded with no charges being filed. In postcharge programs, charges are filed initially but lifted upon completion (Wilson & Hoge, 2013). Diversion used as an alternative to prosecution can help troubled juveniles avoid the stigma of a criminal history (Ray & Childs, 2015; Seroczynski, Evans, Jobst, Horvath, & Carozza, 2016) and saves money because diversion is less expensive than custodial confinement (Hoge, 2016). The severity of youths' offenses and their assessed recidivism risk levels are used to determine the length and intensity of treatment services and control (Wilson & Hoge, 2013). Most diversion programs require youths to voluntarily agree to the terms of diversion and admit guilt (Hoge, 2016), which has been criticized for coercing false confessions (Mears et al., 2016).

Skeptics of diversion argue that the existence of lower-control options generates a net-widening impact. Net widening occurs when youths who previously would have been released from state control entirely are now sentenced to various forms of programming (Klein, 1979; Mears et al., 2016; Ray & Childs, 2015). Whenever possible, police should simply warn low-risk youths and release them without further action (Mears et al., 2016).

WAIVERS

Juvenile waivers (also called transfers) arose in the post-*Gault* era and became widespread during the juvenile get-tough movement of the 1990s, as described earlier. Waivers move youth from juvenile courts to adult courts. Supporters contend that waivers help juvenile courts filter out serious, violent, and incorrigible juveniles who possess little potential for rehabilitation and thereby reserve juvenile-court resources for adolescents who have greater promise for desistance. Waivers also fit well with the rhetoric of the get-tough movement, as they provide for harsher penalties than what the juvenile courts can impose, including long terms of incarceration in adult prisons (Levesque, 1996).

There are three types of transfers: judicial waiver, legislative (or statutory) exclusion, and direct file (also called prosecutorial certification or waiver; Kupchik, 2004). Juveniles are constitutionally entitled to procedural fairness to guard against arbitrary or biased waiver decisions (*Kent v. United States*, 1966), but skeptics claim that judges and prosecutors retain undue amounts of discretion. The absence of strict guidelines to regulate waiver decisions has been alleged to cause racial disparities and cross-jurisdictional inconsistencies (Feld, 1987).

Waivers originally permitted the death penalty to be imposed upon juveniles convicted of murder (*Stanford v. Kentucky*, 1989), but the U.S. Supreme Court later outlawed this practice (*Roper v. Simmons*, 2005). The Court also prohibited sentences of life in prison without parole for juvenile offenders convicted of crimes other than homicide (*Graham v.*

Florida, 2010) and mandatory life-without-parole for youthful homicide offenders (*Miller v. Alabama*, 2012). States can incarcerate juveniles convicted in adult courts inside adult correctional facilities, but must house them separately from adult prisoners.

Waivers are controversial. Advocates employ catchphrases like "adult crime, adult time" to capture the sentiment that the juvenile system inadequately punishes juveniles who commit serious crimes. Opponents argue that it is dangerous to incarcerate juveniles with adult criminals even if efforts are made to keep them separate. Youths in adult jails and prisons suffer higher rates of violent and sexual victimization (Forst, Fagan, & Vivona, 1989) and suicide (Flaherty, 1983) than those committed to juvenile facilities. Some critics contend that waivers are symbolic policies that have no capacity to improve public safety (Kupchik, 2004; Titus, 2005). "Adult time" may also be fundamentally unjust, since juveniles' brains are not fully formed. Throughout childhood and adolescence, the brain's emotional centers and sensitivity to rewards develop quickly, while the areas responsible for impulse control and rational decision making lag behind. Juveniles are biologically less capable of controlling their behavior than adults are (e.g., Leshem, 2016).

TEEN COURTS AND STATUS-OFFENDER PROGRAMS

Teen courts are sometimes considered diversion programs and are other times seen as being under the auspices of status-offender programs. Status-offender programs, likewise, vary tremendously in content and operation. Because of these ambiguities, teen courts and status-offender programs are given their own section here, with the acknowledgement that other writings on juvenile programs might classify them differently.

Teen courts (sometimes called youth courts) are a type of problem-solving court. They emerged in the 1980s and met with instant popularity. Most of them target low-level, first-time offenders. They employ a peer-court model (Forgays & DeMilio, 2005) wherein many of the "officials" are teenagers, including former defendants (Butts, Buck, & Coggeshall, 2002), who volunteer to serve as clerks, attorneys, and jurors. They might also participate in sentencing recommendations (Hissong, 1991). Some teen courts require juveniles to plead guilty to the charges against them and a parent or guardian to agree to help the defendant complete the sentence (Forgays & DeMilio, 2005).

Teen courts operate under the ideological and theoretical frameworks of therapeutic jurisprudence, social control and social learning, and restorative justice. The therapeutic-jurisprudence perspective views the law and legal system as agents for positive change (Shift & Wexler, 1996). Social-control and social-learning theories posit that replacing adult officials with teenage ones will foster a greater sense of connection between the adolescent defendant and the people running the court, provide prosocial peer role models for defendants, and internalize within them a desire to comply with the terms of their sentences and refrain from further lawbreaking. Under a restorative-justice approach, an offender is held accountable for his or her deviance and then is welcomed back into the community and treated as an equal after the terms of the sanction have been met (Forgays & DeMilio, 2005). Victims, as applicable, play a central role in teen court as a way to help the victim recover and the juvenile understand the negative consequences his or her actions had for the victim (Shift & Wexler, 1996). The ultimate goal—aside from healing victims—is to keep teens out of future trouble by making them feel more strongly connected to their community.

Status-offender programs are a type of early intervention designed to keep youths whose violations were relatively minor out of custody, while providing services to help them avoid further trouble with the law. The juvenile system has been sharply criticized for holding status offenders in secure confinement, sometimes for longer periods than youths charged with delinquency (Matthews, 2000). The most common status offenses are truancy, curfew violations, underage drinking, running away, and incorrigibility. In spite of efforts to divert status offenders out of custody, nearly 10,000 youths experience confinement for status offenses annually. Ideally, these youths would be immediately referred to social-service agencies without any period of custody. If confinement cannot be avoided, custody should last no more than a day or two (Levin & Cohen, 2014) and should occur in a facility or unit separate from juveniles who have been alleged or adjudicated delinquent. Status-offender programs are operationally diverse. They can involve a short stay at a residential facility, where staff provide treatment and education courses, followed by family therapy (Druckman, 1979). State statutes alternately refer to status offenders and their families as PINS (persons in need of supervision), CHINS (children in need of services), or FINS (families in need of services; Chiu & Mogulescu, 2004).

Many states are turning away from status-offender programs toward community-based solutions that circumvent the courts (Chiu & Mogulescu, 2004; Salsich & Trone, 2013). In its 2002 JJDPA reauthorization, Congress admonished states to stop holding status offenders in detention. Some state legislatures outlawed confinement for status offenders and others greatly restricted its use. There was a broad-scale shift toward diversion to community-based services where youths' risk levels and needs would be evaluated and treatment plans developed accordingly (Salsich & Trone, 2013). Community agencies work with children and their families. Referral to the juvenile court is resorted to only after several layers of increasingly intense interventions have proven futile (Chiu & Mogulescu, 2004).

OUT-OF-HOME PLACEMENT

After a juvenile has been adjudicated delinquent, courts impose dispositions. Some adolescents can return home and perform community-based sentences (e.g., probation, counseling), but some require commitment to out-of-home placement. These youths may be too severely troubled for their families to realistically care for them, or the family environments are too toxic for the juveniles to live in anymore. Juveniles can also be detained pending adjudication if the court deems them to be at risk of hurting someone or being harmed. Youths can be placed in juvenile-corrections facilities, residential treatment facilities, foster homes, or group homes.

Approximately 26 percent of juveniles adjudicated delinquent are committed to some form of residential placement (Puzzanchera, 2002). Among juveniles in placement, 86 percent are delinquents and 3 percent are status offenders. (The remaining 11 percent are wards of the state because of abuse, neglect, or other reasons precluding them from living at home.) Of those held for delinquency, 37 percent are there for crimes against people, 24 percent for property offenses, and the remainder are held for drug and public order crimes, including technical violations of community sanctions. Committed youth are primarily in group homes (42 percent) and long-term secure facilities (37 percent). The placement rate for black youths is 4.5 times greater than that for white youths, and Hispanic youths' rate is 1.8 times larger than for white youths (Hockenberry, 2014). Committed youths of color are more likely to be sent to facilities emphasizing physical regimens (e.g., boot camps), while white youths have higher probabilities of being committed to therapeutic facilities (Cochran & Mears, 2015; Fader, Kurlychek, & Morgan, 2014).

EXAMINING THE RATIONALES

Prevention and rehabilitation are the primary principles guiding the operations of the juvenile system. Punishment became ingrained during the get-tough movement, but prevention and rehabilitation remain the stated justifications for having a separate juvenile system rather than folding juveniles into the regular criminal-justice apparatus. We will analyze each one's potential to keep youths out of trouble or help prevent reoffending. Additionally, we will consider the underlying logic used to justify the existence of laws that create status offenses. This inclusion furthers the chapter's goal of critically analyzing the rationale for treating youths differently than adults. Here, status offenses are subsumed under the rationale of child saving.

CURFEWS: PREVENTION

Curfews are debatable as a prevention method. Skeptics claim that curfews do not incentivize greater parental control because juveniles—not their parents—are the ones who are punished when they violate curfew. Nighttime streets devoid of juveniles should not be automatically interpreted to mean adolescents are home being parentally supervised (Scherr, 1992). There are many ways youths can get into trouble indoors. Additionally, if there is abuse occurring at home, barring adolescents from seeking refuge in public spaces could expose them to physical, emotional, or sexual harm (see generally Humphrey, 2004). Finally, curfews are difficult to enforce, since police officers cannot readily identify teens' ages merely by looking at them. Especially if they are driving or in a crowded public area, older curfew violators enjoy a low risk of detection unless police are engaged in a curfew-enforcement crackdown (see generally Fritsch, Caeti, & Taylor, 1999).

On the other hand, given that crime is opportunistic, keeping youth out of public spaces at night (to the extent curfews accomplish this goal) rests on reasonable assumptions about crime prevention through physical separation of victims (or targets) and offenders (e.g., see Felson, 1998). Even if adolescents are engaging in minor offending indoors (e.g., underage drinking), it is not impossible that the existence of a curfew would prevent more serious trouble (e.g., drunken vandalism) by keeping them inside. Opportunity theories are more about places than people, though (see Felson & Clarke, 1998; Lum,

Koper, & Telep, 2011), so their applicability to curfews might not be as straightforward as it seems at first glance. As a means to prevent delinquency and victimization, then, curfews have logical flaws but could make sense from the viewpoint of opportunity theories. The validity of the rationale behind curfews is murky.

TREATMENT AND REHABILITATION

The efficacy of evidence-based correctional intervention is one of the few truisms in recidivism prevention. Researchers have identified risk, need, and responsivity as the critical components of effective therapeutic intervention (Andrews, Zinger, Hoge, Bonta, Gendreau, & Cullen, 1990). The so-called RNR (*r*isk, *n*eed, *r*esponsivity) model holds that offenders' risk levels should be assessed upon entering the program so that the proper treatment "dosage" can be gauged. Intensive treatment should be reserved for medium- and high-risk offenders, while low-risk ones should receive the smallest amount of intervention possible (or none at all; see Cullen, Jonson, & Mears, 2017). Offenders' criminogenic needs should be addressed using cognitive-behavioral therapy, which seeks to help people improve their behavior by correcting negative thought patterns. Finally, treatment must be delivered in a manner that is responsive to offenders' learning styles, levels of education and literacy, and applicable learning or developmental disabilities. While the RNR model was developed primarily in adult correctional settings, the causes of adults' and juveniles' law-breaking behavior are substantially similar, so the model translates well into the juvenile context (see Gendreau, 1996 for a review). Rehabilitation only works when the RNR model is faithfully adhered to; deviation eliminates the positive outcomes of correctional treatment (Lipsey, 2009; Lowenkamp, Makarios, Latessa, Lemke, & Smith, 2010).

While the empirical support for rehabilitation makes this a sensible approach to use in juvenile justice, juvenile agencies and centers frequently do not employ the RNR model or, sometimes, any genuine effort at treatment. This parallels the trend in adult courts of making defendants' offenses a master status, part of a new penological paradigm that Feeley and Simon (1994) dubbed "actuarial justice" (see also Feeley & Simon, 1992). In the actuarial juvenile-justice system, administrative efficiency takes precedence over individualized treatment and the delivery of programs and services. Courts prioritize speed in the processing of cases, and confinement facilities seek to house as many juveniles as possible at as low a cost as possible. Treatment (and even punishment) is eliminated as a guiding philosophy and supplanted by the goal of saving money (Kempf-Leonard & Peterson, 2000).

Diversion may have collateral consequences for rehabilitation. When diversion successfully keeps lower-risk youth out of the court system (either by sending them to programming or doing nothing to them at all), the juvenile-court population becomes higher risk, since only the most serious offenders are processed and confined. This can fuel declines in rehabilitative services as institutions prioritize control and security over treatment and programming, and negatively impacts public opinion by lending the (false) impression that the "typical" juvenile offender is a serious threat to public safety (Ferdinand, 1991).

This effect, however, is actually good for the RNR model because rehabilitation works best with high-risk youth (Lipsey, 2009). If policymakers and juvenile-justice personnel break away from the erroneous belief that high-risk adolescents are lost causes (see Levesque, 1996), rehabilitation and waivers can work in tandem to reserve treatment resources for the neediest youth.

STATUS OFFENSES: CHILD SAVING

While the state's need to assume custody over children victimized by abuse and neglect is obvious, the legitimacy of state control over presumed "wayward" youth is more controversial. Status offenses expand the government's opportunities for restricting youths' freedoms, formally intervening in the family, and potentially impacting the trajectory of a juvenile's life. The rationale for this is child welfare, but dissecting this rationale uncovers significant errors in the assumption that status-offense laws and policies benefit youth.

Skeptics of status offenses argue that these laws do more to punish troubled adolescents than to protect them. Laws against running away, for instance, may be harmful to youths experiencing physical or sexual abuse in the home (Humphrey, 2004). Many status offenses are vague, such as disobedience or immorality, vesting significant (unwarranted, according to many) discretionary authority in officials when they encounter youths who fail to strictly conform to societal expectations. Historically, status-offender laws have been used more often against girls, particularly for sexual behavior and actions that violate the female gender role (Chesney-Lind & Shelden, 2013; Humphrey, 2004). Fears that status offenders escalate to become delinquents are unfounded. Nearly two-thirds of youths referred for status offenses have no subsequent court contact, and of those who do, only a minority graduate to more serious offenses (Shelden, Horvath, & Tracy, 1989).

Schools contribute to status offending and court contact by enacting zero-tolerance policies (Bonnie et al., 2013). These policies increase juvenile referrals to the court system directly (when school police officers file petitions to the court instead of handling disciplinary matters internally) and indirectly (through suspensions and expulsions that put youth at risk for dropping out of school). Youths of color are overrepresented among school referrals for violations of zero-tolerance policies, and are more likely to receive diagnoses for serious mental disorders, which makes then ineligible for many treatment programs (Bonnie et al., 2013). Schools are a significant source of the total number of status offenders referred to the juvenile courts (Childs, Frick, & Krupa, 2013).

The juvenile court has become a catch-all repository of last resort. Exasperated parents and frustrated school officials refer a persistently misbehaving youth to the juvenile court, only to find that the child is removed from the home, parents are denied access to the child, the judge lacks good options, and the child is held in a detention facility crammed full of other status offenders (Chiu & Mogulescu, 2004; Salsich & Trone, 2013). It strains rational judgment to advocate in favor of status offenses on grounds of child welfare. The argument that these laws promote youths' safety, improve parental control, and that the juvenile court is the proper vehicle for handling troubled adolescents is specious.

THE EMPIRICAL STATUS OF JUVENILE-JUSTICE POLICIES

CURFEWS

Juvenile curfews have met with generally disappointing empirical outcomes. McDowall et al. (2000) found that new curfew ordinances in a sample of cities and counties had no impact on any crime type. Revisions to existing ordinances were associated with statistically significant reductions in larcenies, but the effect on other crime types was mostly null. There was no decline in juvenile homicide victimization. Reynolds et al. (2000) evaluated one city's curfew enactment and did not find reductions in juvenile victimizations or arrests during the hours in which the curfew was in effect. There was an increase in some victimization types during noncurfew hours. In a city-level analysis carefully separating arrests of youths under and over each city's curfew age, Kline (2012) uncovered a spike in juveniles' curfew and loitering arrests following enactment, and a concomitant 10 percent reduction in juvenile arrests for violent and property crimes. Conversely, Wallace (2016) found an increase, rather than a decline, in nighttime juvenile arrests. Grossman, Jernigan, and Miller (2016) did not find a relationship between curfews and juvenile alcohol consumption.

A comprehensive review of existing studies evaluating curfews arrived at the conclusion that they are ineffective at reducing juvenile offending or victimization. There seemed to be slight crime increases during curfew hours (Wilson, Gill, Olaghere, & McClure, 2016; Wilson, Olaghere, & Gill, 2016). Carr and Doleac's (2014) creative comparison revealed that rainstorms were more effective than curfews at reducing juvenile gun violence during curfew hours. A review of studies assessing curfews' effects on traffic crashes and traffic fatalities—total and among youth in particular—revealed reductions during curfew hours. The authors cautioned, however, that only six studies had examined traffic-crash outcomes and all were of modest methodological quality, so these findings are tentative (Grossman & Miller, 2015).

DIVERSION

The empirical evidence is mixed with respect to the success of diversion programs at preventing future misbehavior. On average, diversion does not perform better than non-intervention or traditional punishments (e.g., probation) at reducing youths' reoffending (Lipsy, 2009; Schwalbe, Gearing, MacKenzie, Brewer, & Ibrahim, 2012; Wilson & Hoge, 2013). These aggregate findings mask diversity in program structure and content, so the correct question is not "Does diversion work?" but rather, "What types of diversion programs work?" Done correctly, diversion programs can yield beneficial outcomes (Petrosino, Turpin-Petrosino, & Guckenburg, 2010); done incorrectly, they are no better than traditional methods.

Diversion programs emphasizing personality development, relationship skills, and emotional insight outperform those trying to prevent recidivism through deterrence- and control-oriented measures (Landenberger & Lipsey, 2005). As with adult correctional-intervention programs (e.g., Andrews et al., 1990), cognitive-behavioral therapy works particularly well (Landenberger & Lipsey, 2005; Lowenkamp et al., 2010; Wilson, Bouffard, & MacKenzie, 2005). Therapies focusing on moral reasoning also produce positive outcomes (Wilson et al., 2005; see also Seroczynski et al., 2016) and there is some support for restorative justice (Bergseth & Bouffard, 20007; Schwalbe et al., 2012) and family-based therapies (Schwalbe et al., 2012). Emphasizing goal commitments and problem-solving skills may enhance program-completion rates (Belciug, Franklin, Bolton, Jordan, & Lehmann, 2016).

Diversion type appears to relate to adolescents' recidivism likelihood. A meta-analysis of a heterogeneous sample of diversion programs revealed less reoffending among youth in precharge, as opposed to postcharge, diversion. Low-risk youths, in particular, fared better in precharge programs and in diversion involving only formal warnings and no further government control, while medium- and high-risk youths responded well to more intensive intervention (Wilson & Hoge, 2013; see also Mears et al., 2016). This accords with the correctional-treatment literature highlighting the importance of putting as little formal burden on low-risk offenders as possible (Andrews et al., 1990; Lowenkamp, Latessa, & Holsinger, 2006). Fortunately, experts have developed risk-assessment instruments. These instruments have been validated across different groups of juveniles (Childs, Frick, & Gottlieb, 2016) and, as part of comprehensive assessments of propensity toward risky behavior (Sullivan, Childs, & O'Connell, 2010), help predict future offending (Wareham, Dembo, Poythress, Childs, & Schmeidler, 2009) and successful completion of probation (Childs Ryals, Frick, Lawing, Phillippi, & Deprato, 2013).

After a systematic, critical review of the evidence, Mears et al. (2016; see also Ray & Childs, 2015) concluded that diversion is causing net-widening. The researchers framed diversion as a modern form of child saving that continues the problematic tradition of low-visibility, high-discretion decision making that can produce unfair and incorrect outcomes (see Klein, 1979; Ray & Childs, 2015). Diversion programs, too, display wide variation in forms and functions. Some employ evidence-based practices and some do not (Mears et al., 2016; Ray & Childs, 2015). This unevenness is currently a serious problem hindering the juvenile-justice system and preventing diversion from reaching its potential.

WAIVERS

Since waivers are intended to serve two distinct but related functions—increased severity of penalties for transferred youth and reduced recidivism—we will consider both of these outcome measures here. Of course, a finding that waived juveniles are punished more severely would not necessarily be an indicator of "success," given the violence and harsh conditions to which they are subjected when housed in adult correctional facilities (Flaherty, 1983; Forst et al., 1989). This inquiry pertains solely to whether juvenile waivers are accomplishing the goals policymakers set out for them, which is to make punishment more severe for juveniles.

The picture is inconclusive as to whether juveniles eligible for transfer are, in fact, consistently sent to adult court. One study revealed that prosecutors direct filed only 23 percent of eligible cases (Sridharan, Greenfield, & Blakley, 2004). In a sample of automatically waived juveniles, judges decertified 42 percent and sent them to juvenile court (Jordan & Myers, 2007). Even in states with strict waiver policies, then, adult-level punishment is uncertain (see also Jordan & Myers, 2011).

There is also inconsistent evidence regarding whether transferred juveniles are treated more harshly in adult courts. Jordan and Myers (2011) compared decertified youths to those who stayed in the adult system. There were no group differences in the probability of conviction or incarceration; however, among youths sentenced to prison, youths processed by adult courts received significantly longer terms than those who were decertified. Fagan (1996) arrived at the opposite conclusion: His analyses showed adult-processed youths were more likely to be sentenced to prison, but that term lengths among imprisoned youths were similar across both contexts. In a state in which judges have the option to sentence waived youths as either adults or juveniles, Burrow (2008) found that judges opted to sentence them as juveniles 71 percent of the time. Kurlycheck and Johnson (2004) compared waived juveniles to young adults with similar charges and criminal histories, finding that juveniles were sentenced more severely than their similarly situated but slightly older counterparts. This suggests that transferred juveniles pay an unfair penalty in that judges and prosecutors interpret the very fact of waiver as evidence of increased culpability and dangerousness. Much of the muddled nature of the waiver research is likely due to between-state variation in laws and policies. Johnson and Kurlycheck (2012) found noteworthy differences between two states in whether waived juveniles were treated more or less harshly. This variability makes it hard to form solid conclusions about the effect waivers have on juvenile sanction severity.

Research tapping into waivers' impacts on recidivism is likewise inconclusive (Kurlycheck, 2016). Transfers do not have a clear specific-deterrent effect, overall (Zane, Welsh, & Drakulich, 2016). Some studies have found that youths sentenced as adults are less likely to be rearrested (Jordan, 2012); others have uncovered no difference (Johnson, Lanza-Kaduce, & Woolard, 2011; Loughran et al., 2010); and still others have discovered significantly lower recidivism rates among youths processed in juvenile courts (Fagan, 1996; Redding, 2008), and even increases in rates of violence among transferred youth (McGowan et al., 2007). Steiner and Wright (2006) tested for general deterrence and likewise were unable to detect an impact: States' enactment of juvenile-waiver policies did not reduce violent crime among youth (see also Redding, 2008). There is, however, variation in recidivism rates potentially caused by state-level differences in waiver policies (Redding, 2016), the impacts of graduated sanctions (Johnson et al., 2011), and whether transferred juveniles were convicted of crimes against persons versus property offenses (Loughran et al., 2010). Future research might produce evidence of deterrence for specific waiver policies or for certain types of juveniles.

TEEN COURTS AND STATUS-OFFENDER PROGRAMS

Teen courts appear to reduce recidivism (Bright, Morris-Compton, Walter, Falls, & Young, 2013; Bright, Young, Bessaha, & Falls, 2015; Butts et al., 2002; Evans, Smokowski, Barbee, Bower, & Barefoot, 2016; Shift & Wexler, 1996). Teen-court defendants report high levels of satisfaction with their experiences (Bright et al., 2015) and improved psychosocial functioning and social relationships, such as a reduction in delinquent friends, aggression, and depression (Evans et al., 2016). Teen courts are also associated with enhanced functioning and coping among youths and their families (Bright et al., 2013; see also Laundra, Rodgers, & Zapp, 2013).

There is, nonetheless, room for improvement. Although most of these courts only take first-time offenders, second-time offenders with somewhat serious charges are more likely to complete their sentences and less likely to reoffend if they are sent to teen court rather than through regular court proceedings (Forgays & DeMilio, 2005). Teen-court officials should consider accepting medium-risk youth. White teens (Hissong, 1991; Rasmussen, 2004), particularly males (Hissong, 1991), seem to be reaping the most benefits from teen court, raising questions about how well these courts are serving females and youths of color. Some courts lack a guiding theoretical focus, which risks compromising their missions and goals (DeFosset, Schooley, Abrams, Kuo, & Gase, 2017). Additionally, Rasmussen (2004) uncovered evidence of net widening—officials referred cases to teen court which, prior to the establishment of this court, they would have dismissed. Referral agents should send to teen courts only youths who would have been diverted or petitioned, and not those who otherwise would have been released without further action.

Status-offender programs vary so widely that they defy evaluation as a single group of interventions. One element common across most of them is family therapy, which has become especially common in states that have switched from court-based to community-based methods for handling status offenders. Addressing the root causes of status offenses, especially serious ones like running away from home, may avoid criminalizing youths whose misbehavior is a symptom of abuse and other problems occurring in the home (see Chesney-Lind & Shelden, 2013; Humphrey, 2004).

Not all family therapies are created equal or implemented properly. Early research was mixed. Some studies affirmed the importance of a family-based approach (Beal & Duckro, 1977), but others uncovered no support for this treatment modality (Gruher, 1979) or found high rates of recidivism even when family environments improved (Druckman, 1979). A systematic review of prevention and early-intervention programs identified community-based programs emphasizing positive family interactions as successful. They outperformed punishment-oriented approaches. The reason for their effectiveness likely lies in equipping parents with techniques for emotionally connecting with, and providing helpful structure to, their at-risk children (Greenwood, 2008). The positive impacts of family therapy may be short-term (Pommier & Witt, 1995). Permanent improvements in family functioning could require "booster" sessions to prevent family members from reverting back to dysfunctional habits.

The conversion from a court-centered approach to a community-based one has significantly reduced the number of status offenders under jurisdiction of the juvenile system (see Salsich & Trone, 2013 for a review). For instance, the MacArthur Foundation's Models for Change Initiative funded projects in Pennsylvania, Illinois, Louisiana, and Washington State to help states and counties adopt best practices for handling status offenders (Models for Change, n.d.). In Louisiana, several parishes reformed their FINS systems in 2007

(Hallstrom, Jenkins, Levison-Johnson, Ganey-Nola, Simpson, & Stubbs, 2012) and the ensuing years saw a reduction in the number of FINS handled formally and informally in the juvenile courts (Childs et al., 2013). The other states observed similar successes (Hurst, 2012). How well the community alternatives solved juveniles' and families' problems remains an open question, but keeping them out of the system is a success in its own right.

OUT-OF-HOME PLACEMENT

Placement situations vary substantially, so the answer to the question of whether placement "works" is nuanced. Being placed outside the home for child-welfare reasons (abuse, neglect, and so forth) is a risk factor for later justice-system involvement (see Kolivoski, Shook, Goodkind, & Kim, 2014 for a review), but foster-care placement is less harmful than confinement in secure facilities (Kolivoski et al., 2014). Foster care seems to be the best option for youths with significant mental-health needs (Barth, 2005). Juveniles' trauma histories impact their recidivism likelihoods, and severely traumatized adolescents who receive treatment in foster care fare better than those treated in residential facilities or hospitals (Robst, Armstrong, & Dollard, 2017).

Placement, in general, is associated with worse outcomes relative to leaving youths in their homes while they serve community sentences (Ryan, Abrams, & Huang, 2014). Many secure facilities, even those claiming to provide rehabilitative services, do little more than warehouse juveniles. Facilities expose youths to abuse by staff and other adolescents, and use isolation and restraints as punishment for disciplinary infractions (Mendel, 2011). This is not to say residential placement is inevitably hopeless; to the contrary, well-designed, therapeutic facilities that conform to the RNR model reduce recidivism (Lowenkamp & Latessa, 2004). Nonetheless, there is general consensus that out-of-home placement should be used sparingly and as a last resort, and that all efforts should be made to keep youths at home (e.g., Lee et al., 2014) while providing them care and service levels commensurate with the severity of their needs (see generally Stein et al., 2014).

CONCLUSION

Since its inception in the 1800s, the juvenile system has been fraught with controversies and dilemmas. It displays a schizophrenic inconsistency in whether the intention is to treat, punish, or merely control juveniles; rehabilitation is the overarching goal, but punishment and control frequently take precedence over treatment. Proponents argue that informality and localization are vital to the mission of protecting troubled children from the stigma of being labeled criminals. Critics, however, call the juvenile court second-class because it denies juveniles the full spectrum of constitutional rights, even though youths adjudicated delinquent can lose their freedom for the same or even longer periods of time than adults.

In terms of "what works" to prevent juvenile delinquency or recidivism, curfews fall short. Teen courts have generated positive results. Waivers produce mixed findings, with no specific or general deterrent effects apparent in the research that has been conducted. Evidence-based individual and family therapies produce beneficial outcomes. The recent movement to keep status offenders out of court and to handle them in community-based settings has markedly reduced the number of youths experiencing formal processing and sanctions. Disproportionate minority contact remains a troubling aspect of the juvenile system. Initiatives are under way in many states to ensure youths of color are not treated more harshly than their white counterparts. The modern juvenile-justice system has come a long way and continues to evolve in its efforts to achieve its goal of protecting and helping vulnerable youth, but there is still a pressing need for reforms to ensure fair processes and outcomes for juveniles.

DISCUSSION QUESTIONS

1. Critics of juvenile courts have called for their abolition. They claim that juveniles are treated harshly and not offered full constitutional protections, which in their view is a violation of youths' rights. Opponents of abolition counter that although the juvenile-court system needs some reforms, fixing it is better than dispensing with it entirely. Opponents argue that abolishing these courts would do away with the important rehabilitative, service-based approach and lead to a system in which juveniles are simply punished with no additional efforts to help address their needs and problems. What do you think? Analyze the benefits and drawbacks to abolishing the juvenile courts and, conversely, to continuing to handle juvenile lawbreakers in a separate court system dedicated to them. Which side of this debate do you think makes more sense? Why?

2. Schools' zero-tolerance stance toward student misbehavior has caused the phenomenon dubbed the "school-to-prison pipeline." Children are often suspended, expelled, arrested, or referred to court for minor offenses or for patterns of misbehavior that reflect undiagnosed learning disabilities or trouble at home. Being suspended, expelled, or put under juvenile-court control significantly increases the likelihood that youths will never finish high school; will become involved in status offending, delinquency, and eventually adult crime; and ultimately end up under some form of criminal-justice supervision. School officials and police argue these policies are critical to maintaining order and safety within schools, while opponents contend that schools' punishment-based approach sends many children down a bad path in life. Examine this dilemma. Based on what you know about punitive responses to misbehavior, do you think schools' zero-tolerance policies are effectively promoting safety? What role do police officers and the juvenile court play in schools, if any? Do you see room for collaboration to address student misconduct without imposing harsh penalties that can have lifelong negative consequences for youth?

3. Disproportionate minority contact has emerged as a serious issue being addressed around the country. There are many decision points within the juvenile-court system (and even prior to it, taking into account arrest and referral decisions) at which officials can treat minority youths harsher than white youths. Schools' zero-tolerance disciplinary practices also fall predominantly upon students of color; black and Latino students are overrepresented among those suspended, expelled, or arrested for misbehavior in school. Propose a solution to disproportionate minority contact. Identify two or three decision points that you think are particularly important and which could be targeted for reform. Explain the reasons for your proposed reforms and why you think they hold promise.

4. Waivers and harsher sentences for youth who remain in the juvenile system were implemented during a time when youth-perpetrated violence was extraordinarily high. Rates of violent

crime have since dropped among this group. Does it make sense to continue these punitive policies? What are the possible merits and drawbacks of doing away with get-tough approaches to serious offending among juveniles?

CASES CITED

Breed v. Jones, 421 U.S. 519 (1975)
Graham v. Florida, 560 U.S. 48 (2010)
In re Gault, 387 U.S. 1 (1967)
In re Winship, 397 U.S. 358 (1970)
Kent v. United States, 383 U.S. 541 (1966)
McKeiver v. Pennsylvania, 403 U.S. 528 (1971)
Miller v. Alabama, 567 U.S. 460 (2012)
Roper v. Simmons, 543 U.S. 551 (2005)
Stanford v. Kentucky, 492 U.S. 361 (1989)

CHAPTER 7

GUN POLICY

INTRODUCTION

Few topics evoke such controversy and furious public debate in the United States as guns. The use of guns in crime—and the extent to which violence might be reduced by restricting the availability of guns—is a point of continuing contention. The discussion is usually a political one, with conservatives lining up to defend easy access to guns and liberals advocating greater restrictions. Public discourse becomes especially heated in the wake of mass killings such as those at Sandy Hook Elementary School in Connecticut; the Aurora, Colorado, movie theater; state offices in San Bernardino, California; the Pulse nightclub in Orlando, Florida; and the music festival in Las Vegas, Nevada. Each shooting raises a different set of questions about killers' motives or states of mind—mental illness featured prominently in analyses of the Sandy Hook murderer, and the San Bernardino and Orlando massacres were determined to be inspired by terrorism. Inevitably, the debate turns to guns and gun policy and what, if anything, could have been done to prevent these tragedies.

The focus on high-profile incidents, however, obscures the reality of gun violence in the United States. As devastating as they are, mass shootings account for a miniscule fraction of all murders and assaults with firearms. In 2011, there were 11,101 homicides and 467,300 nonfatal violent victimizations perpetrated with firearms (Planty & Truman, 2013), though there is some uncertainty surrounding estimates of the number of nonfatal crimes committed with firearms (Kleck, 1997). Firearms account for 70 percent of homicides and 10 percent of nonfatal violence. Some 70 to 80 percent of homicides and 90 percent of nonfatal violence are carried out with handguns (Planty & Truman, 2013). Gun violence is geographically concentrated. In urban areas, which experience higher rates of firearm violence overall, certain microplaces (small geographic zones) are hot spots (Braga, Papachristos, & Hureau, 2010).

As we shall see in this chapter, there is a mismatch between the reality of gun violence in the United States and the policies that have been proposed or enacted to combat this type of crime (Piquero, 2005). Much gun legislation looks more symbolic than substantive (see also Kleck, 1997). *Symbolic laws* are crafted in such a manner so as to appear to address a particular issue while, in actuality, they lack internal logic or enforceability and therefore have no true impact on the problem at hand. Symbolic laws and policies are form without content. Gun policy's deep entrenchment in politics makes this area of crime policy particularly vulnerable to symbolic legislation and, as such, to policies that do little to reduce crime or make communities safer.

GUN POLICY AND THE CONSTITUTION

Gun policy is unique from other crime and criminal-justice policies in that it directly implicates a constitutional right. The Second Amendment to the U.S. Constitution was ratified in 1791, along with the other nine amendments in the Bill of Rights. The Second Amendment states in full:

> A well regulated Militia, being necessary to the security of a free State, the right of the people to keep and bear Arms, shall not be infringed.

Perhaps owing to its defiance of modern grammar rules and generally accepted proper comma usage, the Second Amendment has been the subject of extensive legal wrangling about its precise meaning. The challenge is in deciphering the meaning of the so-called "right to bear arms" within the parameters of constitutional doctrine.

Two U.S. Supreme Court cases stand out as having the greatest impact on this question and the most potential to impact laws and policies pertaining to gun regulation. In *District of Columbia v. Heller* (2008), the Court separated the right to bear arms from any matter pertaining to a militia or other group purpose; that is, the Court held that the Second Amendment grants individuals the right to own firearms for private purposes, such as hunting, sport, and self-defense. The *Heller* decision represented a large, significant step toward declaring that the Second Amendment guarantees all persons in the United States the right to own firearms and, concomitantly, that states cannot interfere or impinge upon individuals' gun acquisition or ownership. *Heller* stopped short of declaring a national right to ownership, however, because the plaintiffs resided in Washington, DC, which is federal territory. Thus, *Heller* did not create a rule binding on state governments.

This latter step was taken two years later in *McDonald v. Chicago* (2010). Here, the Court incorporated the Second Amendment, which means the Court made the Second Amendment binding upon the states. As such, gun ownership formally became an individual right upon which states cannot unreasonably infringe or impede.

It might be tempting to conclude that *Heller* and *McDonald* foreclose any chance at gun regulation. If the Second Amendment grants everyone in the United States the right to own guns free of state interference, then is it possible to have *any* gun policy that would pass constitutional muster? The answer is yes. No constitutional right is absolute. Even those rights most central to the nation's history and traditions have their limits. Your right to free speech, for instance, does not allow you to yell "Fire!" in a crowded theater or phone in bomb threats to an airport. Those actions are speech, but they are illegal. They are prohibited because they are harmful, and the state has a legitimate interest in protecting its citizens. The right to a free press, too, can sometimes be circumscribed, such as when media presence in a criminal courtroom is so disruptive that the defendant's right to a fair trial is imperiled. As such, there is no reason to stop the conversation about gun policy. Undoubtedly, some of the laws and policies states might attempt to use would be challenged in court and possibly struck down; however, there are many ideas worthy of consideration, and a healthy public discourse is both constitutionally permissible and socially beneficial.

PRIMARY AND SECONDARY GUN MARKETS

An important distinction needs to be made between the *primary gun market* and the *secondary gun market* (see Cook, Molliconi, & Cole, 1995). The primary market consists of licensed dealers, manufacturers, and importers. These sellers are immersed in the business of gun retail for profit. The secondary market consists of the myriad other gun sales and transfers that take place. These consist of occasional sales (such as when someone decides to downsize his or her private collection by selling some guns off) and gifts. Persons selling or gifting guns on the secondary market are not subject to regulation, other than being barred from transferring firearms to people they know to have criminal records, malicious intentions for the guns once acquired, or are otherwise prohibited from owning firearms (such as minors). We shall see in this chapter that most of the laws endeavoring to prevent guns from falling into the hands of high-risk persons are aimed at the primary market; the secondary market remains a black box wherein guns change hands in an off-the-radar fashion and generally leave no paper trail (see Cook et al., 1995). This point will resurface later when we evaluate the logic of existing gun policy.

GUN POLICIES

There is no single gun policy throughout the United States; instead, there are many approaches that have been tried in efforts to quell gun violence and reduce the use of guns in other illegal activities (such as drug sales). The variety in these efforts stems in part from the strong political currents swirling around the policy arena. Because lawmakers face competing demands from constituents, lobbyists, and other legislators, they must find creative methods of compromise if they are to have any hope of passing gun legislation. On the other hand, the diversity of viewpoints could be viewed in a positive light as being one area of crime policy where multiple ideas have been laid out for consideration. If the gun market is viewed as a leaky boat with multiple holes through which guns trickle from the legal market into, ultimately, unlawful usages, then each patched hole represents progress toward a solution.

This chapter will focus on the most common types of gun policies. This is not an exhaustive review of every policy that has ever been tried; instead, policies will be grouped according to their general approaches and overarching goals. This will permit an overview of the different options, and allow for a critical examination of the logic and evidence underlying each one.

EFFORTS TO MAKE GUNS UNAVAILABLE TO HIGH-RISK INDIVIDUALS

In the dizzying flurry of statistics lobbed by all sides of the gun debate, two facts emerge: First, the vast majority of gun owners never commit crimes (and certainly not violent crimes) with their weapons; and second, the vast majority of guns are not used in crime. The precise estimates of how many guns and owners end up involved in violence vary. Cook (1981a) estimated that 0.5 percent of handguns sold in any given year will end up being used in homicides. Kleck (1986) put the figure for handgun involvement in any crime type at between 2 and 6.7 percent of those sold annually. Whatever the exact numbers may be, the conclusion is clear that most guns and most gun owners are not involved in antisocial activity.

From this fact, many policymakers have drawn the conclusion that the key to reducing gun violence is keeping guns away from the minority of high-risk users. This notion has led to a category of gun policies focused on ways whereby high-risk individuals are targeted for restrictions, while law-abiding citizens' rights to gun ownership are not abridged. Efforts to identify a class of individuals for whom gun ownership is forbidden represent compromises between the rights of the general citizenry, and the rights of a relatively small group meeting certain criteria.

Federal efforts to ban sales of guns to people with certain background characteristics date back to the Federal Firearms Act (FFA) of 1938 and the Gun Control Act (GCA) of 1968 (see Jacobs, 2002). The FFA banned the sale of guns to persons with felony convictions, and the GCA added minors, drug abusers, and those with histories of commitment for mental illnesses to the list of prohibited persons. The GCA made it illegal for felons to possess guns, a provision that went hand-in-hand with the FFA's prohibition on selling guns to people with felony records. The GCA also created the Bureau of Alcohol, Tobacco, and Firearms (ATF; now known as the Bureau of Alcohol, Tobacco, Firearms, and Explosives) to enforce federal gun laws, and established licensing requirements for anyone involved in the business of selling guns for profit.

Under the GCA, anyone engaged in gun commerce was mandated to acquire a federal firearms license (FFL). While the intention of lawmakers who crafted the GCA was to maintain standards with respect to who was (and was not) permitted to participate in the gun market, FFL criteria were so lax that pretty much anybody who applied for a license would get one. Moreover, the ATF was severely underfunded from the start, so it has had virtually no ability to enforce FFL licensing requirements, such as through periodic inspections of business premises (Jacobs, 2002). The result was a largely hollow system of quality control.

The Firearm Owners' Protection Act (FOPA) of 1986 loosened FFL regulations by exempting from registration requirements anyone who occasionally sold guns or who sold or gifted guns from their private collections (Vizzard, 2015). This modification paved the way for gun shows and other secondary-market transactions to take place without ATF or other federal oversight. This made it easier for both law abiders and law breakers to acquire firearms on the secondary market.

The GCA made it the responsibility of FFL-holding dealers to ensure they did not sell guns to prohibited individuals. This was accomplished through the use of sworn statements whereby the purchaser signed a document promising that he or she did not meet any of the ineligibility criteria. Lying to a dealer was a crime; however, dealers were under no obligation to verify the truth of sworn statements, so there was little credible threat of detection or punishment. Any prohibited person willing to lie under oath could purchase a firearm through a federally licensed dealer, resulting in an "honor system" (Jacobs, 2002, p. 25) where the permitted and prohibited alike signed their names and received their guns.

The Anti-Drug Abuse Amendment Act of 1988 expanded limits on firearm sales by making it a federal crime for any individual—not just dealers—to knowingly transfer firearms to persons intending to use those weapons in crimes of violence or relating to drug trafficking (Kleck, 1997). Those convicted under this statute faced up to 10 years in prison, a fine, or both. The statute does not require individuals conducting such transfers to definitively determine the ends to which recipients plan to put their newly acquired firearms, so it seems plausible that gun sellers need only refrain from asking questions about buyers' intentions in order to comply with the letter of the law, even if violating it in spirit.

Probably the most talked-about piece of modern gun legislation is the Brady Act of 1993 (formally titled the Brady Handgun Violence Prevention Act). This law's origin lies in the 1981 assassination attempt on then-President Ronald Reagan. The president and his press secretary, James Brady, were both severely wounded. Reagan recovered fully, but Brady suffered permanent paralysis. Subsequently, Democratic members of Congress proposed the first versions of the Brady Bill, but the bill repeatedly fell flat either because it was voted down or never made it to the floor for a vote at all. In 1993, the bill finally passed and was signed into law by then-President Bill Clinton.

The Brady Act's largest and most enduring contribution has been the establishment of mandatory background checks for all persons purchasing firearms from FFLs, gun manufacturers, or gun importers. This closed the gaping loophole left by the GCA, where ineligible persons could buy guns merely by swearing (falsely) that they did not possess disqualifying characteristics. Under the Brady Act, licensed sellers could require would-be purchasers to wait up to 5 days while local law enforcement verified applicants' eligibility. In 1998, the FBI's National Instant Check System (NICS) went live, relieving the burden from local law enforcement and speeding up the background-check process. Shortly after the Brady Act went into effect, at the behest of lobbyists for women's-rights groups, Congress expanded the list of prohibited persons to include those convicted of misdemeanor domestic violence or subject to a current restraining order for domestic violence or stalking (Jacobs, 2002). The expanded ineligibility criteria and background-check requirement remain in full force today, although some other provisions of the Brady Act have since expired.

During this same time period, it became more difficult to acquire and maintain FFLs. The Brady Act raised the price of acquiring a license, with the intention of cracking down on persons who were abusing their authority as legally authorized retailers. The Clinton Administration also beefed up ATF enforcement activities to ensure FFL compliance and shut down rogue operators. By 1999, the number of FFLs had dropped by two-thirds (Jacobs, 2002).

ASSAULT WEAPONS BANS

Lawmakers and members of the public have long been concerned about the availability and use of certain classes of souped-up firearms that are—or at least appear—more deadly than standard handguns, rifles, and shotguns. The federal government's first attempt to outlaw certain types of guns was the National Firearms Act (NFA) of 1934. The NFA arose out of widespread worry about public shootouts between groups of gangsters from rival syndicates. The exchange of fire was often accomplished through the use of "tommy guns" (Jacobs, 2002), the street name for Thompson submachine guns. These fully automatic weapons fired large-caliber ammunition at a high rate of speed.

Congress determined that tommy guns—as well other submachine guns, all machine guns, and sawed-off shotguns—had no legitimate civilian use. Federal legislators sought to outlaw these weapons; however, they doubted their constitutional ability to ban them outright and so instead resorted to their taxation authority. Congress levied heavy taxes against the import, manufacture, sale, and transfer of these weapons, and required that all current and future owners of these guns register their weapons in a national database. Law-enforcement officials could not arrest and prosecute people for owning these weapons, but they could if owners had not registered their guns and paid the tax (Jacobs, 2002). Decades later, the Firearm Owners Protection Act (FOPA) of 1986 criminalized the manufacture and transfer of new weapons covered by the FFA (Jacobs, 2002).

In the 1980s and 1990s, various types of firearms were singled out in the media and public debates. These guns bear the label *assault weapon* (AW). (For present purposes, so-called "assault rifles" will be subsumed under the AW heading.) Some groups argue that assault weapons are particularly deadly and have no legitimate civilian usage in hunting, recreation, or self-defense. States have enacted bans on a variety of AWs and AW-type features (Kleck, 1997). In 1989, then-President George H.W. Bush outlawed the importation of certain models of semiautomatic rifles.

The Violent Crime Control and Law Enforcement Act of 1994 was the most significant federal legislation impacting AWs since the FFA. A provision of the 1994 act banned importation, manufacture, sale, and possession of certain firearms bearing a set of characteristics deemed to enhance their lethality. Congress singled out certain manufacturers (such as Uzi, Beretta, and Colt) known for their heavy involvement in the production and sale of enhanced armaments (Koper & Roth, 2002). The law also identified and prohibited specific features (such as flash suppressors, threaded barrels, and folding stocks) and authorized the ATF to employ a "features test" to examine and outlaw additional models on a case-by-case basis (Koper, Woods, & Roth, 2004). A grandfather clause in the 1994 legislation exempted AWs already in circulation and permitted existing owners to continue to possess these weapons and to transfer them on the secondary market. The AW ban contained a sunset clause setting the ban to expire in 2004 if not renewed. Congress declined to renew it, so the federal ban evaporated, though assorted bans still exist at the state level.

FIREARM SENTENCE ENHANCEMENTS

The federal government and nearly all states provide sentence enhancements for the use of deadly weapons in the commission of crimes. These laws vary widely from state to state (see Marvell & Moody, 1995). Some states impose enhancements only for firearms, while other states use broader definition of deadly weapons to include knives or other dangerous instruments. Additionally, the word "use" is sometimes interpreted expansively to include carrying a weapon during the commission of a crime, even if the offender does not actually employ it in any way; conversely, the federal government's (Jacobs, 2002) and some states' sentence enhancements are triggered only when an offender actively utilizes the weapon, such as by brandishing it or harming the victim with it.

Most states' firearm sentence enhancements (FSEs) appeared on the law books in the 1970s and 1980s (see Marvell & Moody, 1995). The idea behind FSEs is to discourage the use of guns in the commission of crimes, and to visit harsh penalties upon those who do use them. Generally, FSEs add on two or more years in prison on top of the sentence for the primary offense. For instance, an offender convicted of robbery with a firearm in a state with a two-year FSE add-on would receive the prison sentence allotted for robbery, plus two years.

Firearm sentence enhancements are one of the most prevalent forms of gun policy because they have broad political appeal since they affect only the unlawful use of firearms and in no way impact lawful gun acquisition or use. As such, they receive enthusiastic backing from political conservatives and progun organizations, although they are less well-received by left-leaning and libertarian groups skeptical of further enhancements to an already prison-heavy sentencing system.

The federal government has also supplied a variant on traditional FSEs by providing pathways by which people who use guns in crimes can be prosecuted in federal courts. Traditionally, offenders committing crimes involving guns in a single jurisdiction (that is, not spanning multiple cities, counties, or states) would be prosecuted in the court with authority over that area; only those whose crimes cross state boundaries would be eligible for transfer to federal court. Federally funded efforts such as Project Safe Neighborhoods (see Ludwig, 2005) established federal–local partnerships to encourage county and state courts to forward gun cases to federal courts so that offenders convicted of serious, gun-involved crimes will face federal penalties, which tend to be stiffer than those provided for by states.

CONCEALED CARRY AND GUN BUYBACKS

Popular and political antipathy toward gun laws that affect the manufacture, sale, or possession of firearms (such as restrictions on handguns or assault weapons), combined with the U.S. Supreme Court's decisions in *Heller* and *McDonald*, have had two major impacts on gun policy. First, they greatly reduce the probability—to basically zero—that there will be significant bans or major restrictions on firearms in the foreseeable future. Second, and because of the first, they have sparked a search for other, more politically palatable (and constitutionally permissible) means of suppressing firearm violence.

One of the alternatives that has proved enormously popular is the expansion of concealed carry laws (CCLs). States began toying with various forms of CCLs in the early 1900s. Initially, most states' laws were restrictive and limited lawful concealed carry to persons demonstrating need (such as those working in law-enforcement capacities). Starting in the 1980s, however, as the nation and its elected leaders shifted hard to the political right, states rapidly adopted so-called "shall-issue" policies, which require permits to be issued to any person meeting certain requirements (for instance, a person who is 21 years of age or older and has no history of felony convictions). Today, all states allow concealed carry, though they vary in legal requirements. Some states do not issue permits and instead allow all residents meeting minimum criteria to carry concealed weapons. Shall-issue states require permits and grant them to all eligible applicants. The rest (called may-issue states) have more restrictive license standards that require applicants to articulate a reasonable need to carry a concealed firearm. In these states, local or state authorities retain discretion to accept or reject applicants' requests.

Concealed carry owes its popularity to gun-policy skeptics who have successfully advanced the opinion that the best way to thwart violent attacks is to arm law-abiding citizens. Widespread concealed carry is intended to deter would-be offenders from crimes such as robbery out of the fear that the victim might be armed, and to stop in-progress attacks by allowing victims or bystanders to successfully defend themselves or others with deadly force. In the wake of mass shootings, it is common to hear progun groups advocate for greater use of concealed carry as a means of either deterring such attacks or reducing the carnage.

Gun buybacks (sometimes called gun exchanges) are another politically and ideologically "safe" option. They are touted as a way to reduce the overall supply of potential crime guns, while posing no threat to any constitutional rights. Buybacks are frequently operated by local police departments. Departments typically advertise the buyback in advance as a day of amnesty for people in illegal possession of firearms to relinquish them with no questions asked. Sometimes gift cards are offered as incentives. Submitted guns are destroyed, sometimes after being traced for determination of past involvement in crime. Supporters claim that buybacks reduce the total quantity of guns in circulation, thereby making it harder for those who with nefarious motives to acquire them. Buybacks provide a means by which a community can feel empowered in helping to remove unwanted guns and protecting public safety (Braga & Wintemute, 2013). Buybacks, as a gun-violence reduction strategy, garner significant public support even among gun owners (Callahan, Rivara, & Koepsell, 1994).

EXAMINING THE RATIONALES

EFFORTS TO MAKE GUNS UNAVAILABLE TO HIGH-RISK INDIVIDUALS

There are several assumptions built into the notion that gun violence can be curbed by screening out persons with certain types of histories or records. First, the classes of people identified as prohibited have to be correctly, reliably identified so that FFL dealers will not sell to them. Second, the classification schemes outlining who is allowed to purchase a firearm and who is not must bear an empirical association with dangerousness. In other words, felons, persons with domestic-violence histories, drug abusers, and those with severe mental illness have to be demonstrably more dangerous than those without such markers, or the prohibitions do not make sense. Third, persons denied purchase by primary-market sellers must not have a readily available alternative means of acquiring firearms. We will analyze each of these assumptions in turn.

First, there is the assumption that criminal records are accessible to FFL gun dealers and are complete and accurate. This assumption is reasonable with respect to felony convictions because of the FBI's automated NICS. This database is considered accurate. On the other hand, it is not clear that persons with domestic-violence misdemeanors or restraining orders will be reliably flagged in background checks. Many states do not separately classify assaults against intimate partners—these crimes merely go onto offenders' records as assaults, with no victim characteristic specified. Those with misdemeanor assault convictions can still purchase firearms from FFL dealers, meaning many people with histories of domestic violence might slip through the cracks (Jacobs, 2002). Problems also arise with the prohibition on FFLs selling guns to persons with histories of drug abuse or severe mental illness. There are no national or state databases containing the names of persons who have been treated for drug abuse or involuntarily committed to mental institutions. As such, many people who are technically barred from purchasing firearms can likely still do so simply by lying on the forms they fill out for FFL dealers.

The second assumption—that of a clear connection between the prohibited characteristics and elevated dangerousness—also proves shaky. There is no reliable connection between mental illness and violent crime—persons with mental illnesses are no more dangerous, on average, than persons who have never been diagnosed with or treated for a mental-health problem, and there is no empirically sound rationale for targeting the mentally ill for specific prevention efforts (Wolf & Rosen, 2015).

Similarly, it is erroneous to assume that all persons with felony convictions are equally dangerous (and are, as a group, more dangerous than persons without criminal records). It may serve the public interest to deny firearms to a person convicted of robbery last month, but it is harder to see the logic in prohibiting a sale to a middle-aged individual who stole a car for a joyride when he was a teenager (see Jacobs, 2002). The felony-conviction exclusion is a blunt instrument that likely excludes many nondangerous people (false positives) while giving FFL dealers the green light to sell to persons who are, in fact, untrustworthy (false negatives).

The third assumption likewise fails the logic test, because it is easy for a person denied a gun on the primary market to find one the secondary market instead (Cook et al., 1995). The single greatest weakness with the background-check approach is the fact that secondary-market sellers are not required to perform these checks. Gun owners can sell used firearms at gun shows, via newspaper ads, online ads, or by word of mouth. No paperwork accompanies these sales, and although sellers are prohibited from transferring guns to persons they know have criminal, drug, or mental-health histories, sellers can easily claim ignorance (whether that claim is true or not) if they do make a sale to a prohibited person. The "black box" of the secondary market means guns change hands constantly and there is no telling where a gun purchased on the primary market today will end up one month, one year, or five years from now.

ASSAULT WEAPONS BANS

There are a few assumptions built into the frame of logic that produces the conclusion that banning certain types of weapons will reduce firearm violence. First, other types of guns cannot be substituted for the banned weapons; in other words, those wishing to use banned AWs to commit violence must be effectively barred from accomplishing their gun-crime goals. Second, AWs need to constitute a sufficiently large proportion of crime guns to make their elimination have meaningful impact on total rates of gun violence. We will examine each assumption in turn.

The assumption regarding absence of substitution is not tenable. The problem boils down to the fact there is no such thing as an "assault weapon." The term defies definition (Jacobs, 2002). It was forged in the media and is not a technical category within the firearm-manufacturing industry (Kleck, 1997). This slippery label is used to describe semiautomatic long guns (generally rifles) with so-called "military style" characteristics. Most of these flourishes are cosmetic and do not affect the lethality of these weapons (see Jacobs, 2002). These include features such as plastic stocks and matte barrels (Kleck, 1997), folding stocks, flash suppressors, threaded muzzles, and bayonet mounts (Jacobs, 2002). Advocates of AW bans also cite these guns' ability to accept high-capacity magazines as greatly enhancing their lethal potential; however, most types of rifles and handguns can also utilize large magazines, so this criticism of AWs is dubious.

The end result is that assault-weapon bans prohibit certain types of guns while leaving substantially similar (even identical for all intents and purposes) guns untouched. The Assault Weapons Ban of 1994, the most expansive federal legislation outlawing these firearms, identified 18 models of assault weapons, and the ATF later criminalized 118 models that failed the features test (Koper, Woods, & Roth, 2004); however, at the time the ban went into effect, there were at least 387 models being manufactured (Kleck, 1997). Thus, assault-weapons bans violate the first element of the logic test because they only ban certain AWs and leave plenty of alternative options open for those wishing to obtain high-powered firearms.

The second assumption is that assault weapons account for a sizeable chunk of the total amount of gun violence such that banning them will effectively tug down the gun homicide and assault rates. This is not true. The vast majority of guns involved in violent crime are handguns (Planty & Truman, 2013). It is possible that assault weapons increase the lethality of mass shootings, but mass shootings account for a very small portion of gun homicides. Even if AWs were eliminated, aggregate rates of gun violence would likely be unaffected. Perpetrators of mass killings would also still have access to traditional firearms, so although there might be fewer victims, nothing would prevent the attack from occurring.

FIREARM SENTENCE ENHANCEMENTS

The rationale behind FSEs is twofold. First, these laws are meant to deter would-be offenders from using guns in the commission of crimes by increasing the severity of punishment and thus tipping the cost-benefit calculus in favor of leaving one's gun at home. Second, FSE proponents hope to heighten the incapacitation of serious offenders and thereby prevent them from committing any further acts endangering public safety. Because FSEs rest on deterrence and incapacitation rationales, they must be assessed according to the strengths and weaknesses within each of these punishment philosophies.

First, with respect to deterrence, one must analyze the assumptions built into the notion that would-be offenders will decide against using guns in crimes out of fear of extended prison terms. It seems unlikely that FSEs would deter the use of guns in homicide. Homicide is penalized with life (sometimes death) sentences, so it strains the imagination that anyone willing to risk life in prison—or execution—would find the additional 2 or 3 years so onerous that he or she would seek an alternative weapon. This same logic applies, with perhaps slightly diminished force, to other types of serious violence that also carry long prison sentences. There is no good reason to believe that an offender undeterred by an already lengthy term of incarceration would respond to the threat posed by a FSE.

A second problem with deterrence pertains to the unanswered question of whether increasing severity genuinely produces more effective deterrence. This is a matter of absolute versus marginal deterrence—a large-scale deterrent effect is likely achieved when a particular act is made illegal and subject to criminal punishment, but it does not follow that incrementally upping the severity of punishment will produce a concurrent reduction in that crime (see Marvell & Moody, 1995 for a review). There is no reason to believe that FSEs would deter the use of guns in crime beyond whatever deterrence impacts are already achieved through the prison sentences for the underlying crimes (robbery, assault, and so on).

Furthermore, for FSEs to be effective, violent offenders must be aware of their existence. Deterrence research shows that the general population—including those with previous arrests—possesses inaccurate perceptions of the severity of sentencing laws (Kleck, Sever, Li, & Gertz, 2005). This raises doubts as to the accuracy of active offenders' information about criminal sanctions of any sort, including FSEs; if offenders are unaware of the existence of FSEs, it is impossible for these sentence enhancements to have any deterrent value.

Finally, deterrence theory assumes all offenders' actions are premeditated. The notion of a rational, calculating offender presupposes that all acts of violence are thought out and planned in advance. This assumption is dubious, particularly with regard to homicide, since most killings occur during the course of heated disputes between friends, acquaintances, and spouses. Alcohol is involved in over half of these incidents (Zimring, 1968), further illustrating the clouded judgment and impulsivity entailed in these crimes. The angry, intoxicated, or impulsive offender is unlikely to stop to ponder how long his prison term might be if he uses a gun or whether he would benefit from switching to a different weapon to avoid a sentence enhancement. This, combined with the aforementioned general lack of awareness of criminal-sentence lengths, undercuts the perceptual side of FSEs.

The second argument, pertaining to incapacitation, rests on its own set of related assumptions. First, offenders eligible for FSEs must be receiving them. In other words, prosecutors and judges cannot adjust their charging and sentencing practices so as to mitigate the impact of FSEs on total sentence lengths. Second, offenders subject to extended prison terms under FSEs would need to be those who would otherwise be doing harm in society but for this sentence extension.

Research on the behavior of prosecutors and judges shows strong tendencies for new policies to be subverted in favor of business-as-usual methods of resolving cases and sentencing offenders. These court actors are aware of the impact their activities have on jail and prison populations, and they generally avoid changes to sentencing practices that would substantially increase confined populations in already-bulging correctional institutions (see Loftin, Heumann, & McDowall, 1983; Marvell & Moody, 1995). It is probable that FSEs would meet the same fate as other efforts to make prison sentences longer.

The second assumption of the incapacitation impact of FSEs is that the offenders who receive FSE add-ons would otherwise be out on the streets committing serious crimes during the FSE period. For instance, if someone received a prison sentence of five years for the primary offense and an additional two years for the use of a firearm in that crime, incapacitation due to the FSE is effective only if the offender would have engaged in violence during the final two years of the seven-year sentence. It is impossible to assess the accuracy of incapacitation claims of this sort, or to predict in advance which offenders will repeat their crimes if they are not behind bars (Auherhan, 1999). Thus, the incapacitation argument rests on shaky ground because core components of this rationale cannot be empirically tested.

CONCEALED CARRY AND GUN BUYBACKS

The logic behind CCLs can be boiled down to deterrence and enhanced ability to stop attacks once they start. The effectiveness of CCLs on deterring violent attacks rests upon offenders' perceptions of the likelihood that potential victims or bystanders are armed; if offenders are unaware of the status of CCL laws, or if they believe it is unlikely that any given victim is actually carrying a firearm, no change in their behavior would be expected. Deterrence would also require offenders to decide not to attack anybody at all, rather than merely substituting an unarmed victim for an armed one. Moreover, concealed carrying by law-abiding citizens must not encourage more widespread gun carrying by offenders who anticipate the possibility of encountering armed victims, thus creating an "arms race" of sorts between victim and offender populations. At this point, there is no evidence available to evaluate the credibility of these assumptions.

An additional element of deterrence requires that whatever crime-reduction impact CCLs may exert is not offset or outweighed by an increase in violence spurred by the easy availability of firearms. Interpersonal disputes may turn deadly when a gun is present (Zimring, 1968). An overall elevation in homicides and serious assaults due to increased presence of firearms in the general population could negate or even reverse any beneficial effect of CCLs. This assumption also remains an open question, as researchers have been unable to establish a link of any sort between concealed carrying and rates of firearm violence (Cramer & Kopel, 1995).

Gun buybacks lack logical basis. They are unfocused, whereas the evidence clearly shows that antiviolence strategies of all kinds require targeting the places and people at highest risk. Buybacks are operated under the assumption that the relinquished guns would have otherwise ended up being used in crime (or suicides or accidents), but the truth is that certain guns have much higher likelihood than others to end up being used illegally or otherwise harmfully (Sherman, 2001). Even if buybacks reduce gun ownership, as some scholars have suggested (Romero, Wintemute, & Vernick, 1998), it does not necessarily follow that this reduction translates into lower gun-lethality rates. The people who turn in guns are probably at very low risk of employing those guns in violent acts. Buybacks fall short on the rationality test.

THE EMPIRICAL STATUS OF MODERN GUN POLICY

In the previous section, we saw through a dissection of the underpinning logic of the major gun policies that they suffer weaknesses ranging from mild to severe. It is possible, however, that these policies succeede in spite of these seeming limitations. To explore this potential outcome, we now turn to an examination of the empirical evidence surrounding each policy to determine if the policy has produced meaningful reductions in the unlawful acquisition or use of guns.

EFFORTS TO MAKE GUNS UNAVAILABLE TO HIGH-RISK INDIVIDUALS

The background-check requirement established by the GCA, FOPA, and Brady Act (including Brady's follow-up amendments and subsequent launch of the NICS) represents the federal government's most widespread and lasting impact on gun markets. This tightening of controls on sales funneled through federally licensed dealers was intended to deny firearm access to persons deemed risky and untrustworthy. Many scholars have studied whether background checks accomplish the goal of reduced firearm violence. Most of these studies have focused on the Brady Act and related legislation.

Brady Act proponents tout the number of firearm-purchase denials attributable to the background-check system. The NICS has resulted in 100 million background checks in the past decade, and 700,000 denials (Federal Bureau of Investigation, n.d.). The problem, of course, is that there are no data proving that those persons denied purchase on the primary market did not merely shift to the secondary market—or to the black market or theft—to acquire a weapon. Moreover, it is not true that those denied a firearm would have, if granted firearm access, inevitably used the weapon in a criminal manner.

One method of analyzing Brady's impact is through a longitudinal or time-series design, in which researchers collect gun-crime data for a period before and a period after Brady's implementation to find out if gun violence fell during this period. A downward trend would suggest a beneficial impact. A problem has arisen in tests of the Brady Act, though, because violent crime nationwide began declining in the early 1990s and continued a steady descent throughout that decade. It would be easy to mistakenly attribute to Brady a violence-reduction trend that began *before* the law took effect.

Researchers have devised various means to get around this problem. One set of researchers compared homicide trends in states affected by Brady to those not impacted. Prior to Brady, 18 states and the District of Columbia already required background checks and waiting periods for handgun purchases, so the remaining 32 states saw a change in firearm-sales policy. The researchers found that total homicide and gun-homicide rates declined equally across all states (Ludwig & Cook, 2000). This suggests that Brady did not impact aggregate rates of total homicides or homicides with guns. Another study analyzed homicide data from Florida before and after that state adopted waiting periods and background checks in 1991. The researchers discovered a reduction in gun homicides after the law took effect; however, nongun homicides also declined somewhat, too, leaving the authors unable to conclude with certainty that the background-check law was the driving force behind the decline (McDowall, Loftin, & Wiersema, 1995).

Another technique to evaluate Brady is to analyze impacts at the micro (that is, individual) level. In one study, researchers compared a group of people who had been convicted of felonies and were denied handgun purchases to a group that had been arrested for (but not convicted of) felonies who were permitted to buy handguns. The group allowed to purchase handguns was more likely than the denial group to have new arrests for violence in general, and gun crimes specifically. This effect was limited to felons whose previous crimes involved weapons or violence. The authors concluded that background checks produce a moderate reduction in gun violence, though there is negligible benefit in denying handguns to felons with no histories of violence or weapons-related crimes (Wright, Wintemute, & Rivara, 1999).

Another study comparing handgun purchasers with misdemeanor convictions to purchasers with no criminal histories found elevated risk of new violent convictions among the misdemeanor group. The effect was strongest for misdemeanants with histories of violence, but was also present for nonviolent offenders (Wintemute, Drake, Beaumont, Wright, & Parham, 1998). These findings suggest potential positive impacts of background checks, though it is unclear to what extent offenders' new acts of violence may have been facilitated by their newly acquired guns or, instead, were merely a continuation of ongoing behavior patterns.

Overall, the preponderance of the evidence indicates mandatory background checks for all new handgun purchasers may reduce gun violence, but the reduction is modest at best. Reasons for the absence of strong effects are that persons blocked from purchasing firearms on the primary market may turn to the secondary market instead (Cook et al., 1995) or may steal guns or acquire them on the black market (Kleck, 1997). Additionally, evidence indicates that firearm availability may have little impact on nonlethal violence like assault and robbery, with homicide being the only crime likely to be noticeably affected by a constricted supply of guns (Cook, 1981b; Kleck, 1997). Background checks, therefore, get a cautious thumbs-up as a promising method of gun-violence suppression, but they clearly leave much to be desired.

ASSAULT WEAPONS BANS

Unlike background checks, where evidence is mixed but tips slightly in favor of the policy, the outlook on AW bans' effectiveness is dismal. The main reason for this was elucidated earlier in the analysis of the logic underpinning these bans—AWs play a miniscule role in gun violence. Even if AWs were eliminated entirely and offenders did not substitute other types of firearms (an unrealistic assumption), little social benefit would follow. Bans cover only certain features and manufacturers of AWs (Jacobs, 2002; Koper & Roth, 2002), so it is easy for someone to purchase a nearly identical legal version of a banned weapon, or to slightly modify the cosmetic appearance of a banned weapon to transform it into a legal firearm without altering its functionality in any way (Koper, 2004). Handguns are also readily available substitutes for anyone unable to acquire AWs.

Another method to evaluate AW bans is to determine whether bans impact the overall quantity and price (measures of accessibility) of these weapons. In theory, bans reduce the supplies and increase prices of affected weapons, since they are no longer legal to manu- facture and sell on the primary market. This should squeeze the secondary market via constriction of the flow of AWs from the primary market. However, bans fail this test, too. In the months leading up to the 1994 federal AW ban, production of soon-to-be-outlawed AW models soared. Prices rose, too, but soon fell again. In the end, the federal ban may have resulted in an *increase*, rather than a reduction, in the number of assault weapons circulating on the secondary market (Koper & Roth, 2002).

An expansion of the federal ban to include a wider array of AW models and features may have yielded positive impacts, as may have renewing the ban or codifying it into per- manent federal law. A broader ban would have been more meaningful and likely would have put greater pressure on the primary and secondary markets in terms of supply reduc- tion and price increase. Additionally, since there were so many grandfathered preban AWs in circulation, the supply drop and price rise would be gradual and it might have taken several years to see a slump in the criminal use of AWs (Koper, 2004). As it stands, though, the federal AW ban expired in 2004 after Congress declined to renew it. Current political sentiment in the United States is decidedly against new bans (Vizzard, 2015), so whatever value broad, permanent bans may have will likely remain an open question for the foresee- able future.

FIREARM SENTENCE ENHANCEMENTS

Firearm sentence enhancements are intended to reduce gun violence through a combi- nation of deterrence and incapacitation. Evaluations of FSEs have yielded disappointing results. One study found no impact of one state's FSE on rates of gun robberies or assaults, and unclear effects for firearm homicides (Loftin et al., 1983). A meta-analysis of FSE evaluations of varying methodology and quality uncovered a negative but extremely weak effect size (Makarios & Pratt, 2012), meaning that across the board, FSEs do not appear to reduce gun violence.

Firearm sentence enhancements also appear to suffer implementation problems. Studies show that FSEs do not produce consistent increases in the number or lengths of prison sentences handed out for convictions related to firearm violence (Loftin et al., 1983; Marvell & Moody, 1995). Various organizational pressures (Loftin et al., 1983), as well as fear of further overcrowding already bulging prison populations (see D'Alessio & Stolzenberg, 1995), lead prosecutors and judges to subvert sentence enhancements. Although the incapacitation rationale is potentially flawed, as discussed earlier, whatever incapacitation effects FSEs might potentially achieve in practice are blocked by these laws' failure to translate into increased time served for violent gun offenders.

CONCEALED CARRY AND GUN BUYBACKS

The empirical evaluations of what impact, if any, CCLs have on violent crime are discrepant and contradictory. On one side are those claiming to have proven that CCLs substantially reduce violent crime (Lott & Mustard, 1997) and on the other are those who sharply rebuke this assertion and demonstrate that CCLs have no overall impact on violent crime (Cramer & Kopel, 1995) or that they are associated with *increases* in homicide (Ludwig, 1998; McDowall et al., 1995). Concealed carry does not appear to reduce mass shootings (Duwe, Kovandzic, & Moody, 2002). Only between 1 and 4 percent of right-to-carry states' eligible populations actually do obtain permits (Cramer & Kopel, 1995), so the laws' ambiguous and seemingly weak impacts on violence might not be surprising given this low level of participation. In the end, concealed carry does not consistently contribute to either increases or reductions in violence.

There is no empirical evidence supporting the effectiveness of citywide gun buybacks either at removing crime guns from the street or reducing firearm violence. Romero et al. (1998) found that 23 percent of people who turned in guns reported that the firearms did not work. Older people and women—the groups least likely to commit violent crime—were overrepresented among those submitting firearms (see also Callahan et al., 1994). A substantial proportion of people who participate in buybacks continue to own guns and store loaded guns unlocked in the home (Green et al., 2017; Romero et al., 1998). Most buybacks attract fairly small numbers of guns, but even the confiscation of large quantities of guns appears to have no impact on subsequent rates of gun violence (see generally Plotkin, 1996). The null results are likely driven in large part by the fact that the guns given over during buybacks differ significantly from guns used in crime. Relinquished guns are more likely to be older, small-caliber long guns, as opposed to the relatively new, large-caliber handguns used in most firearm violence (Kuhn, Nie, O'Brien, Withers, Wintemute, & Hargarten, 2002; see Braga & Wintemute, 2013 for a review). Buybacks are extraordinarily expensive (Sherman, 2001). Given the absence of evidence suggesting effectiveness, this money would be better spent elsewhere.

There are very preliminary indications that gun buybacks targeted at specific people and neighborhoods could generate larger numbers of high-risk weapons (Sherman, 2001). In Boston, police specifically reached out to youth in advertisements about the upcoming buyback. They placed drop-off locations in churches and local community organizations so that people could hand over their weapons without entering the police station. This buyback produced a significantly greater number of high-caliber, relatively new handguns compared to a previous buyback in which the Boston police used the traditional citywide approach and did not gear their efforts specifically toward crime-involved populations. Many of the guns bore signs of having been trafficked across state lines, and police held them as potential evidence in subsequent cases against the traffickers. It was not possible to determine whether the buyback led to a reduction in gun violence (Braga & Wintemute, 2013), but this case study provides tentative support for targeted buybacks that are organized based on a well-researched understanding of local gun crime.

CONCLUSION

Gun policy is a dicey area to critically evaluate on the evidence, because so little empirical data and good theory are utilized in these policies' creation. Public debates are dominated by those on the extreme sides of the gun-control continuum: some declare that guns should be banned outright, while others push strongly for total deregulation. The result is widespread confusion of rhetoric with reality, and the concomitantly empty political debates wherein each side dedicates itself to "setting up and knocking down their respective straw men" (Kleck, 1997, p. xv). It is perhaps no surprise, then, that most of the laws passed in the wake of legislative battles are symbolic.

This chapter took a logic- and evidence-based approach to the evaluation of gun policy. Under this guiding framework, the chapter laid out the main categories of gun policy, the logic underlying each one, and the empirical evidence lending support (or lack thereof) to the approach. The conclusions were fairly dismal, and a key takeaway point is that current gun policy falls short. This fact alone, however, is insufficient for an indictment against modern gun policies; as Kleck (1997) put it, "[N]o one concludes that the thousands of homicides committed each year mean that laws prohibiting murder are ineffective and should be repealed" (p. 10). While we have seen that existing policies are flawed, it is not correct to leap to the conclusion that nothing works, or will ever work, and that the whole effort ought to be scrapped. The proper analytic strategy is to weighs costs and benefits of each law and use sound rationales and empirical facts about gun markets and gun-crime offenders to figure out how existing policies might be made better and what new policies might be put to the test.

DISCUSSION QUESTIONS

1. In the aftermath of mass shootings carried out with so-called assault weapons, victims and their families sometimes call for a ban on these military-style firearms. Suppose you are an elected official and have to make a public statement in response to a local advocacy group's push for an assault-weapon ban after a mass shooting. How will you advocate for evidence-based gun policies that make sense in light of the information about gun violence, while respecting the trauma and serious emotional toll these attacks take on people? Write a speech or series of points you would make.

2. Take the previous scenario and now imagine that the advocacy group is pushing for policies that would make guns more prevalent, such as arming teachers and relaxing regulations on concealed carry. Craft a rational, evidence-based response to this proposal.

3. Gun regulation is an area of law and policy in which the federal government must be involved, because individual states' actions either loosening or tightening restrictions on gun purchasing and ownership can have significant spillover effects on other states. Explain why this is; that is, why do one state's laws and policies have implications for gun availability and prices in other states? How might the federal government help mitigate these impacts?

4. Political and emotional arguments have been the primary forces behind the approach to gun policy in the United States. Science and reliable information typically get shut out of the debate. The deeply entrenched ideology behind both sides of the gun debate has produced laws and policies that do not have much or any promise of reducing gun violence. Propose a strategy for convincing the public (and, by extension, policymakers) that gun policy should be grounded in evidence, even if the evidence conflicts with what either side (or both sides) believe or feel about guns and their regulation. Take two of the policies covered in this chapter, or that you have heard about from other sources, and package them in a politically engaging manner. Explain why the policies make sense in light of the evidence and why they work (or hold promise), and explain why they either do not conflict with political or social ideologies or, if there is a conflict, why people should drop their preconceived notions and give these policies serious consideration.

CASES CITED

District of Columbia v. Heller, 554 U.S. 570 (2008)
McDonald v. Chicago, 561 U.S. 742 (2010)

CHAPTER 8

MASS INCARCERATION

INTRODUCTION

The United States has garnered notoriety for having the highest rates of incarceration among Western, industrialized democracies (Lynch & Pridemore, 2011; Tonry, 1999). In fact, the U.S. incarceration rate exceeds even those of undeveloped nations condemned throughout the world for promoting rampant human-rights abuses (see Hartney, 2006). The United States constitutes 5 percent of the world's population, yet accounts for 25 percent of the prisoners (Travis, Western, & Redburn, 2014). While there is debate about the specific reasons for the uniquely widespread use of imprisonment in the United States (Lynch & Pridemore, 2011), there is no question that this penalty is at the forefront of this country's so-called "war on crime."

Incarceration is the act of imprisoning a single individual; the term "mass incarceration" refers to the national practice of heavy reliance on prison as a key tool in the crime-control effort. Mass incarceration proponents generally cite deterrence or incapacitation (or both) as the rationale for prison. These commentators and policymakers contend that the harshness of imprisonment deters would-be offenders from crime. Where deterrence fails, incapacitation takes over; confinement physically prevents prisoners from committing new crimes and posing a threat to society. Some also tout prison as a means of rehabilitating offenders. While full-scale commitment to rehabilitation is a relic of the past, there remain significant segments of the public that support its use and believe the government should offer counseling, drug treatment, and educational and vocational programs to prisoners, particularly young ones (Moon, Sundt, Cullen, & Wright, 2000; Nagin, Piquero, Scott, & Steinberg, 2002).

In this chapter, mass incarceration is examined first historically and then in its modern morphology. The theoretical rationales underlying mass incarceration are then parsed to determine the strength of their premises and seeming promise to produce meaningful crime control in the United States. Importantly, we will critically analyze mass incarceration in terms of both *effectiveness* (how well or poorly it performs as a crime-control mechanism) and *efficiency* (the amount of monetary and human cost it takes to achieve crime reduction). This balance—effectiveness versus efficiency—is vital, because crime reduction that comes with an enormous social, economic, and human price tag might not be worth the cost in the end. Finally, the empirical status of mass incarceration will be discussed along with the question of whether this policy has had unintended negative consequences that may undermine it in the long run.

HISTORICAL TRENDS IN INCARCERATION

Mass incarceration is a relatively new phenomenon. Prior to the Age of Enlightenment in the 1700s, criminal penalties throughout Europe and the American colonies were a brutal, bloody affair. Corporal punishment dominated the scene. Whipping, branding, mutilation, and torture were common, as was execution. Judges handing down death sentences devised all manner of sadistic methods to effect the demise of the condemned. This state of affairs was so bad that the guillotine—the French method of dropping a heavy blade to decapitate the victim—was advanced as a method of *improving* the humaneness of capital punishment by ensuring death was swift and painless (Smith, 2003).

The Enlightenment and, particularly, persuasive writings by important thinkers like Voltaire brought about a newfound concern with the manner in which criminal trials were conducted and punishments dispensed (see Smith, 2003). Cesare Beccaria and Jeremy Bentham took up the reform mantle and made compelling cases for greater humanity in criminal justice and more judicious use of punishment. Beccaria, in particular, stressed the philosophical view that all humans possess free will and have the capacity to make calculated, informed, rational decisions. Criminal penalties, he urged, are justifiable only as a form of deterrence (Beccaria, 1764). His argument was timely and filled a growing need for a modernized approach to crime control and criminal justice. Industrialization and urbanization were expanding during this time period Urbanization's attendant crowding, crime, and disarray put pressure on governments around the world to find effective methods of crime control (Hirsch, 1992). The search was on for new methods of punishment.

One of the most important outcomes of this radical shift was the prison. Previously, prisons were used only to house offenders on trial or awaiting execution, as well as debtors unable to pay what they owed. When Western society shifted away from corporal punishment, prison arose as a seemingly civilized, enlightened alternative. It spared offenders from the bloody rituals of physical penalties society now viewed with distaste and simultaneously opened the possibility for offenders to be reformed. The word "penitentiary" has its roots in "penitence." Prisons, often run by religious sects, were domiciles of strict silence, obedience, isolation, and labor (Greene, 1977). This was intended to force the prisoner to admit his guilt, atone with God, and ultimately unlock his inner goodness. Female offenders (many of whom were caught up in the criminal-justice system for offenses like prostitution) were originally held inside men's prisons, where they were subject to constant sexual attack and other abuses. Later, women's institutions evolved into reformatories wherein "wayward females" were taught domestic skills like cooking and sewing. The theory was that immersing women in the rituals common to their gender role would eventually cause them to accept and internalize their "proper" place in society (Rafter, 1985).

At the turn of the nineteenth century, the tide of public opinion changed course yet again. The source was twofold. First was growing recognition of the horrors happening inside these so-called houses of correction. Some of them were haphazard warehouses that mashed together men, women, and children in squalid living conditions with no security and rampant physical and sexual violence perpetrated by both inmates and guards. Others (the more religious, penitence-oriented ones) enforced torturous solitary confinement that drove many inmates insane after years of isolation and silence. Many of those who entered prison—even for small offenses like petty theft or trivial debts—died there, and many of those who survived emerged worse off than they had been before.

The second reason for shifting public opinion was the rise of scientific positivism. Positivism had existed in certain forms for centuries, but gained a foothold in Western thought during the mid- and late-1800s. Positivism is a view of social reality dedicated to the conviction that there is objective truth. Even the most seemingly intangible aspects of the human psyche and the workings of social groups can be identified, quantified, and measured. (And, conversely for positivists, anything that cannot be studied scientifically is not "real" and is properly relegated to the realm of religion or philosophy.) The scientific method became the accepted modality of knowledge creation. The deterrence-based concept of free will was rejected as an outmoded, fuzzy idea that defied definition or measurement and therefore lacked scientific credence and had no place in criminal-punishment policy. Positivists pointed with approval to Sigmund Freud's popular theories holding that the etiology of deviant behavior being rooted in pathology of the mind and, therefore, treatable through intensive psychoanalytic therapy. Other reformers and early sociologists, too, saw people's social environments (in particular, the disorder and squalor of inner cities) as important creators of mental disease and criminal behavior.

These reformers, who prized science and believed psychopathology was the true cause of deviant and aberrant behavior, rejected the notion that intensive religious immersion for men and domestic-skills training for women could improve offenders' behavior. They instead embraced scientific approaches to the design of the content of in-prison programming. Progressive reformers believed prison should be a place for offenders to receive psychotherapy with the ultimate goal of rehabilitating them so that they would emerge from prison ready to participate in mainstream society in a positive way.

Rehabilitation thus became the dominant punishment philosophy. Judges possessed wide latitude in handing down sentences. Since the goal was to rehabilitate, judges were tasked with estimating how much time it would take for each individual offender to achieve significant mental-health gains. Judges frequently left this determination to parole boards. Parole boards were vested with enormous discretion to decide when a prisoner showed adequate signs of reform and readiness to reenter society. This system existed under the label "indeterminate sentencing," a moniker capturing the policy of tailoring sentences according to individual offenders' assessed level of need; they were released only after parole boards felt that they had been reformed. For the first two-thirds of the century, incarceration rates hovered at a rate of approximately 100 prisoners per 100,000 people in the general population (Wagner, 2014).

Then came the 1960s and 1970s. The Civil Rights Movement, the Vietnam War and associated protests, and clashes between the police and university students sent the nation into social turmoil. The protests and violent confrontations both spurred and reflected a widespread dissatisfaction with the existing social and political order. The public's confidence in government plummeted. In corrections, liberal academics and reformers took issue with the government's claim that it was rehabilitating prisoners. Discontented citizens raised fundamental questions about what right (if any) the government had to capture people and forcibly alter their minds. Adding insult to injury, the psychotherapies employed by prisons were seemingly discredited by empirical studies showing no overall improvement in offenders' thinking or behavior after treatment (Martinson, 1974). (The notion that "nothing works" in prisoner rehabilitation would later itself be disproven, but at the time, the public accepted the existing evidence. Chapter 14 contains a detailed description of the flaws in the "nothing works" doctrine.)

At the same time that liberal groups were decrying rehabilitation, indeterminate sentencing, and prisons, conservatives became vocal about the rising levels of crime and disorder in urban areas. They pointed to what they saw as lax criminal laws that provided minimal or no punishment for many offenders (particularly perpetrators of low-level offenses like aggressive panhandling and other forms of social disorder; see Kelling & Coles, 1996). While leftist reformers originally had more momentum in effectively dismantling the rehabilitation scheme, they faltered when it came time to propose a new system. In this vacuum, conservatives took action (see Pratt, Gau, & Franklin, 2011).

Spurred by conservative academics, commentators, and policymakers, prison reformers on the political right swiftly replaced rehabilitation policies with new laws touted as returns to deterrence, which they touted as having been unwisely rejected in favor of the rehabilitation philosophy. Incapacitation also gained popularity. An influential book by respected political scientist James Q. Wilson called *Thinking about Crime* (1983) eloquently advocated for a system of selective incapacitation whereby the "worst of the worst" would be issued severe prison sentences so as to remove them from society for a very long time. Those who posed minimal public-safety risks could be given short sentences sufficient to punish them for past deeds and then released so they did not take up unwarranted prison space that could be more productively used to house demonstrably dangerous people. A flurry of excitement over selective incapacitation ensued (Pratt et al., 2011), but never came to fruition. Its downfall was the discovery—following substantial academic inquiry and empirical analysis—that it is impossible to predict accuracy which offenders pose ongoing public-safety threats and which ones do not (e.g., Auherhan, 1999). Absent high-quality assessment instruments to reliably distinguish high-risk offenders from low-risk ones, selective incapacitation breaks down as a useful crime-control tool.

What the deterrence and incapacitation movement yielded, then, was a system of collective incapacitation. By the 1970s and 1980s, crime had become a core element of both major parties' platforms (Gest, 2001). Republican and Democratic lawmakers alike threw their weight behind a "war on crime" and a "war on drugs," policies promoting aggressive action to ferret out crime and visit severe punishment upon offenders. Under the banner of mantras like "a thug in prison can't shoot your sister," prison advocates rallied for the use of incarceration for a wide variety of crimes (Clear, 2016). The war on drugs, too, created a new class of crimes and criminal offenders eligible for prison sentences. The relentless pursuit of drug traffickers, dealers, and users became the single largest contributor to the prison-population explosion that began in the 1970s and continues nearly unabated today. The crime and violence beget by illegal drug markets likewise drove incarceration rates up.

CONTEMPORARY INCARCERATION TRENDS

In 2015, approximately 1,526,800 adults in the United States were confined in state and federal prisons. Rate calculations vary depending on the denominator used in the equation, but the 2015 rate was roughly 593 per 100,000 adults in the general population. This rate is the lowest in a decade and a decline from the year 2007, when it hit 670 per 100,000, the highest imprisonment rate in the 2000s (Carson & Anderson, 2016). Fifty-three percent of prisoners under state jurisdiction are serving time for violent offenses, 19 percent for property offenses, 16 percent for drug crimes, and 12 percent for various other criminal acts (such as weapons offenses). In federal prisons, 7 percent of inmates were convicted for violent crimes, 6 percent for property crimes, 50 percent for drug crimes, and 36 percent for other offenses (Carson, 2015).

Incarceration rates are distributed unevenly across race, age, and sex. By all accounts, black and Hispanic/Latino men (of all ages, though the rate spikes especially markedly in the 20–49 age group) are incarcerated at rates far exceeding that for white men. Hispanic/Latina women's incarceration rate is commensurate with white women's, while black women's rate is roughly double that of white women. The overall decline in incarceration rates, noted previously, is driven entirely by a drop in men's imprisonment rate; women's rate, by contrast, is on a steady rise (Carson, 2015).

The war on drugs has been the single most powerful force behind mass incarceration (Currie, 1998; Travis et al., 2014) and the racial divides in incarceration rates (Tonry, 1995). Drug policy in the United States combines aggressive enforcement by police with stiff and often mandatory prison sentences. This dual-pronged approach (an increase in the number of people sentenced to prison along with longer sentences) led to significant jumps in incarceration among all demographic groups, but hit minorities and women particularly hard. Twenty-four percent of women in state prisons are there for drug offenses (compared to 15 percent of men) as are 59 percent of female federal prisoners (and 50 percent of men). Across race, the percentage incarcerated for drug crimes is fairly consistent in state prisons (15 percent of whites, 16 percent of blacks, and 15 percent of Hispanics/Latinos), but diverges sharply at the federal level (40 percent of whites, 53 percent of blacks, and 57 percent of Hispanics/Latinos; Carson, 2015).

The racial differences in incarceration are partially attributable to variations in offending patterns, but differential offending alone does not explain the disparities in imprisonment patterns. Breaking the comparison of arrest and incarceration down by offense type, unexplained disproportionality (that is, the percentage of racial differences in incarceration rates *not* explainable by differential arrest rates) is highest among less-serious crimes. This makes sense because police, prosecutors, and judges have more discretion in property, drug, and public-order cases than they do in crimes of violence (Austin & Allen, 2000; Blumstein, 1982, 1993; Tonry, 1995). Every incremental increase in the amount of discretion present in a case concomitantly raises the risk of the abuse of that discretion. Importantly, however, unexplained disproportionality is present even among serious crimes (Austin & Allen, 2000). Official estimates of unexplained disproportionality are somewhat tentative, though. They do not account for the possibility that blacks, on average, have lengthier criminal histories, which would reduce the size of the gap. They also omit the fact that police tend to be more active in black neighborhoods, which would distort the data by creating artificially high estimates of blacks' offending rates (Sorensen, Hope, & Stemen, 2003). With these limitations in mind, however, the research paints a reasonably clear picture in which blacks' extraordinary rate of incarceration is caused by a combination of drug-crime sentencing practices, a higher average crime-commission rate, and racial discrimination. Less is known about the causes of Latinos' disproportionate imprisonment rates, but these same processes can probably be applied to explain this group's higher involvement as well.

Mental illness and drug addiction also factor into people's likelihood of incarceration. People with mental illnesses, as a group, have an elevated arrest rate (Wallace, Mullen, & Burgess, 2004). Mental-health problems are more common among prisoners than among the nonincarcerated population (Diamond, Wang, Holzer, & Thomas, 2001). Approximately 20 percent of state and federal prisoners suffer from a cognitive disability, compared to 5 percent of the general population (Bronson, Maruschak, & Berzofsky, 2015).

Low educational attainment is also a risk factor for incarceration. The most severe impacts are seen among people who do not finish high school, although rates of incarceration are also higher among those who graduate but do not go on for additional college-level schooling. The negative consequences of low education operate differentially across race. Blacks are hit particularly hard; their chances of incarceration spike sharply if they do not graduate high school or do not go on to earn a college degree (Lochner & Moretti, 2004; Petit & Western, 2004). The significant increase in black males' incarceration rates during the 1980s and 1990s fell primarily on the shoulders of those who had either dropped out of high school or had completed high school but never attended college (Petit & Western, 2004).

Incarceration has become a fact of life among the economically disadvantaged and within communities of color in urban areas. In 2014, 6 percent of all black males between the ages of 30 and 39 were in prison, as were 2 percent of Hispanic/Latino men and 1 percent of white men in this age group (Carson, 2015). Prison experience is so common in socioeconomically distressed minority communities that among some groups it is considered a rite of passage or a badge of honor—it is some young men's way of proving they can withstand the deprivation and violence of the institutional environment (Shakur, 2007). Many others bear intense and long-lasting shame, stigma, and financial crisis (Clear, Rose, & Ryder, 2001; Western, 2002). Most prison inmates have young children. These children may experience hardship and trauma when they first lose a parent and then that parent returns home, as most do. Former inmates frequently have trouble readjusting to regular life, and this rocky period can take a toll on children (Foster & Hagan, 2009).

Mass incarceration of minorities (especially black men imprisoned for drug crimes) has contributed to high rates of out-of-wedlock births and single-female households. Men who serve prison time are at a severe disadvantage in the labor market (Clear et al., 2001; Western, 2002). Given that men's earning potential plays a prominent role in young women's decisions about whether to marry (Edin, 2000; Wilson, 1987), male imprisonment severely hurts family units. Incarceration policies that cast a wide net and scoop up large numbers of people from certain neighborhoods may destabilize the social fabric of these communities (Clear, Rose, Waring, & Scully, 2003; Rose & Clear, 1998). Incarceration can plunge already vulnerable families and neighborhoods into even deeper crisis (Arditti, Lambert-Shute, & Joest, 2003). Mass imprisonment exacerbates racial and economic inequality because minorities and the poor are more likely to serve prison terms at some point in their lives; in turn, having a history of incarceration suppresses income earning over the life course (Western, 2002).

Recently, mass incarceration and its chief cause (the war on drugs) have come under fire on the political stage. Former President Barack Obama issued many high-profile statements and speeches criticizing mass incarceration and the race and wealth gaps in incarceration rates. He participated in or spearheaded new laws and Justice Department policies designed to draw attention away from lower-level offenders and refocus anticrime efforts at more serious lawbreakers (e.g., Hudson, 2015). During her 2016 bid for the presidency, Democratic nominee Hillary Clinton distanced herself from statements she made in 1994 when, as First Lady to President Bill Clinton, she lobbied on behalf of the Violent Crime Control and Law Enforcement Act. That 1994 act added fuel to the war on drugs and other get-tough measures, thereby perpetuating racially disproportionate mass incarceration. Democratic candidate Bernie Sanders, who was a U.S. senator in 1994, was likewise haunted by having voted for the bill (e.g., Williams, 2016). Some congressional lawmakers have likewise spoken out against the widespread deleterious impact of mass incarceration, particularly on men of color and their families (e.g., Geier, 2016).

To date, however, most of the talk has not translated into meaningful legislative or policy action. Most reforms that have occurred have been symbolic or are only partial fixes that barely scratch the surface of the real problem. Lawmakers of both parties have been loath to strongly criticize mass incarceration or the war on drugs, as the political debate has long been poisoned by an atmosphere of divisive, illogical rhetoric of the "If you disagree with this policy, you are soft on crime" variety. Those who dare to suggest that incarceration does not work risk being branded foolish and naïve about offenders' dangerousness and callous toward victims' suffering (see Pratt, 2009). This inflammatory rhetoric whips up vacuous political frenzy that benefits political campaigns, but it regretfully stalls progress and prevents productive conversation about promising improvements to correctional policy. It is certainly possible that some day, there will be an overhaul to the system; until then, mass incarceration appears here to stay.

EXAMINING THE RATIONALES

As noted previously, mass incarceration rests upon premises of deterrence and incapacitation. In the 1960s and 1970s, the rehabilitation philosophy fell out of favor. While liberals and conservatives agreed on the central premise—that rehabilitation was no longer an acceptable justification for imprisonment—they diverged sharply on proposed policy solutions. Conservatives, having recently won key positions in all three branches of government at the federal and many state levels, ultimately prevailed. Theirs was a "get-tough" approach that dictated longer prison sentences and prison as a possible or mandatory sentence for a larger number of offense types. Deterrence was resurrected after decades of dormancy and framed by the reigning political establishment as a wrongfully cast-aside goal of punishment that, unlike rehabilitation, held true potential to reduce crime. Simultaneously, proponents of the tough-on-crime initiative pointed to incapacitation as an equally important benefit of prison. In this section, we will take a close look at the logic underlying deterrence and incapacitation as they pertain to mass incarceration. (For a full treatment of deterrence and incapacitation theories, see Chapter 2.) We will also examine the soundness of rehabilitation as a correctional goal. This discussion will not touch upon matters of the effectiveness of correctional rehabilitation (that topic is the subject of Chapter 14). Rather, we will ask whether rehabilitation could ever be used as a principle to justify sending someone to prison.

DETERRENCE

On its face, deterrence theory seems like a simple proposition. The core premise of deterrence is that humans are rational actors who take time to consider whether or not to engage in a particular course of action and to weigh the costs and benefits to determine if, on balance, the if the rewards outweigh possible costs. The idea behind mass incarceration is that, in theory, facing a potential prison sentence will tip the calculus toward costs and convince a would-be offender that crime simply is not worth the risk.

This framing of deterrence (that crime is a choice and anyone who decides to offend is implicitly volunteering to be subjected to the consequences) fit conveniently into the larger social and economic changes taking place in the United States in the 1970s and 1980s. This era saw the rise of laissez faire capitalism (aka, Reaganomics) and the concomitant demise of a "society-centric" political framework to one more aptly described as "individual-centric." Personal accountability was the slogan of the day, not only in relation to crime but in all aspects of one's life. Poverty and joblessness had previously been cast as social ills requiring government programs such as those offering food stamps and housing assistance to low-income people and families. Now, what were once seen as social problems were framed as signals of personal failings resulting in pathological dependence on the government that drained taxpayer money and enabled laziness. In particular, unemployment and financial troubles among the lower classes came to be accepted as evidence of a poor work ethic and widespread desire among poor people to live off welfare checks rather than get jobs. Deterrence's rational-choice assumption was logically consistent with this line of economic argument; conservative lawmakers folded mass incarceration into their broader political agenda under the common theme of personal responsibility and individual choice (Garland, 2001; Pratt, 2009; see also Currie, 1998).

Deterrence, however, is more finely grained than policymakers and the general public tend to realize or acknowledge. Choice does play a critical role in crime. Many criminal-justice researchers concur that aside from cases of duress or other exigencies, people who break the law do so because they decide to (Cornish & Clarke, 2014). A compelling body of research has amassed around the concept of choice in crime (Clarke & Felson, 1993; for a review, see Hechter & Kanazawa, 1997). The pertinent question is not whether choice matters—it does—but, rather, whether the existence of harsh prison sentences truly does alter individual offenders' cost-benefit calculus. Evidence suggests that it does not. Impacts of deterrence should be analyzed in terms of both *absolute* and *marginal* effects. We will discuss each in turn.

Absolute deterrence pertains to the deterrent value of the mere fact that a particular act is illegal and carries a penalty. Evidence suggests that illegality deters, although part of this benefit derives not merely from the threat of punishment but, in addition, from the fact that illegal acts and punishments carry social stigma (Grasmick & Appleton, 1977). Most people shy away from criminal offenses to avoid both formal penalty and personal shame.

Marginal deterrence, as it relates to mass incarceration, exists in the *additional* deterrent value achieved beyond the marginal benefits when a penalty is increased. Absolute deterrence can be thought of as the floor (the basic level of deterrence resulting from the fact of illegality) and marginal deterrence can be thought of as an adjustable ceiling. The question is whether raising the ceiling (i.e., enhancing the severity of punishment) increases the deterrent power of the criminal law. This is where the logic of deterrence and, by extension, mass incarceration weakens significantly (see Pratt et al., 2011). There is no good way to empirically demonstrate that marginal deterrence works; it is impossible to set up a real-world experiment that would allow a causal analysis of the relative impacts of harsher penalties as compared to lighter ones. Efforts to identify potential marginal impacts take the form of esoteric theorizing about what *might* or *could* happen under different sets of hypothetical circumstances (e.g., Kramer, 1990; Wilde, 1992).

Lacking the ability to test marginal deterrence directly, some scholars have attempted to assess it indirectly to provide at least suggestive evidence about its potential utility as a crime-control mechanism. The question at hand is whether, all else being equal, people are more deterred by stiffer penalties than by lighter ones. Researchers have sought to answer this question using various methodologies. One method consists of vignettes that manipulate sentence severity to determine if people respond more aversely to longer terms of incarceration. Decker, Wright, and Logie (1993) found that people who self-reported participation in burglary were less likely to say that they would commit the crime described in the vignette when the punishment was more severe (e.g., five years in prison) compared to when it was less harsh (e.g., two years of probation). Nonetheless, even with the harshest sanction available, 60 percent of burglars still said they would do it if the gains were high. Even if the gains were low, 44 percent reported they would probably commit the crime. This suggests that at the level of individual offenders' perceptions, marginal deterrence has some merit, but clearly, increasing punishment severity, alone, will not markedly impact crime rates.

INCAPACITATION

Incapacitation is a punishment philosophy that justifies the use of prison as a means to physically prevent offenders from delivering future harm to society. Prison proponents hail incapacitation as critical to the war on crime (Clear, 2016). Incapacitation is of two types: selective and collective. Proponents of selective incapacitation urge that high-risk offenders be sentenced to long prison terms. In theory, the crime-prevention effects of incarceration are maximized when prisons are reserved for the offenders who will go on to have lengthy criminal careers. Locking up low-risk offenders, by contrast, does not produce significant incapacitation benefits, because they would not reoffend. Selective incapacitation rests on the assumption that there is a reliable sorting mechanism that can correctly and consistently categorize offenders into high-risk and low-risk categories. Such a mechanism has never been discovered; the best available evidence shows that even the most reliable covariates of offending (such as age of onset) are poor predictors of an individual's lifetime criminal trajectory (Auerhahn, 1999).

Some studies initially hinted at the promising potential to develop valid actuarial instruments. This area of research showed that chronic offenders tended to have prior convictions and incarcerations, spotty employment histories, criminal convictions prior to age 16, and a history of drug abuse (Greenwood & Abramse, 1982). The implication was that the background characteristics possessed by many high-rate offenders could be flipped to become predictors of future offending. However, it quickly became apparent that correlates are lousy predictors (Cohen, 1983; Greenwood & Abrahamse, 1982; Visher, 1986). It is a logical error to presume that because high-rate offenders bear certain characteristics, anyone with this profile is a high-rate offender. For example, many repeat offenders got in trouble as juveniles and experienced their first arrest when they were teenagers. Juvenile troublemaking is therefore a correlate of offending. It is not at all true, however, that youthful lawbreakers will inevitably have lengthy criminal careers; in fact, the majority do not. Thus, it is correct to note that adult offenders frequently have histories of juvenile delinquency, but it is incorrect to presume that someone who engaged in delinquency as a youth will become a recidivistic adult.

Even if valid and reliable actuarial instruments could be developed, there would be serious ethical dilemmas inherent in a policy of selective incapacitation (von Hirsch, 1984). First, the United States prides itself as a constitutional democracy governed by the rule of law. The rule of law holds that no punishment shall be imposed unless a crime has been committed. Putting someone in prison for a lengthy period of time on the premise that they are probably going to commit a crime in the future contrasts sharply with the principle of the rule of law that allows people to be punished only after being duly convicted of a crime. Second, selective incapacitation—instead of being a solution to the problem of sentencing disparities among similarly situated offenders—replicates and even may exacerbate such disparities. Two offenders with similar criminal histories and both recently convicted of similar crimes could face two quite different sentences if one of those offenders is deemed to be high risk and the other low. Such an outcome would violate many people's sense of fairness.

In contrast to selective incapacitation, collective incapacitation is the process of using long prison sentences as a punishment for a wide variety of crimes. The proprison policies of the 1970s and 1980s (many of which originally rested on the rationale of selective incapacitation) ultimately transitioned into its collective form. This set mass incarceration in motion as more people were sentenced to prison for longer periods of time. The increase in the number of people going to prison likely played a larger role in creating bulging prison populations than the expansion of sentences lengths did (Gordon, 1990). Compared to other Western democracies, the U.S. hands out more prison sentences that are, on average, longer. The most striking point of divergence is that the U.S. authorizes prison for a number of nonviolent offenses, such as property and drug crimes (Clear, 1998; Tonry, 1999), and tends to issue longer sentences to lesser and moderately serious offenders (Lynch & Pridemore, 2011). Other Western nations, by contrast, lean toward penalties involving shorter terms of incarceration or community-based alternatives that keep low- and mid-level offenders out of prison entirely.

Collective incapacitation skirts the thorny troubles plaguing selective incapacitation because no prediction of dangerousness is required. Additionally, it focuses entirely on the severity of an offense and the offender's criminal history, thereby sidestepping the dilemmas of prediction attached to its selective counterpart. Some may also view collective incapacitation as the safer bet in a reality where it is impossible to know who will reoffend and who will not; if a person's objective risk level cannot be determined, then putting that person in prison might appear to be better than gambling with the public's future safety.

Mass incarceration (aka, collective incapacitation) contains inherent logical flaws, chief of which is the phenomenon of diminishing returns. Diminishing returns in prison policy occurs when many people of widely varying risk levels are all treated equally. This causes the incarcerated group's average annual rate of offending (that is, the number of crimes they would be committing, on balance, if they were not in prison) to drop. When everyone convicted of a particular offense type is imprisoned, then people who would have committed fifty new crimes are mixed in with people who would have committed nine, two, or zero new offenses. Mass incarceration thus dilutes the crime-reduction benefit of incapacitation, because it is not clear that, for any given individual, any new crimes are in fact being prevented.

Another fallacy innate to the rationale of incapacitation is the age–crime curve (Pratt, 2009). Offenders' most crime-prone years are in their youth; after that, their involvement in crime tapers off to zero or close to it (Lilly, Cullen, & Ball, 2014). An offender captured in his early- or mid-20s may well be at the peak of his "career." Under a policy emphasizing long prison sentences, he will sit behind bars long past the point at which he would have ceased criminal involvement. On average, prisoners who are middle-aged and older are at low risk for future offending.

Finally, incapacitation is an extremely difficult theoretical proposition to test empirically. Doing so would necessitate objectively assessing the validity of its central notion: that each person currently in prison would present an ongoing public-safety threat were he or she not incarcerated. This would require the construction of a counterfactual or, in other words, an alternate version of reality in which an offender serves a shorter (or no) prison sentence and is free in society rather than locked in a prison cell. No such counterfactual is possible. It is pure speculation and guesswork as to what current prisoners would be doing if they were free in society. Because of this, the effectiveness of incapacitation can be neither proven nor disproven directly. As will be discussed shortly, some indirect methods have been devised; however, the absence of a counterfactual is a persistent problem that undermines efforts to figure out if incapacitation truly works.

REHABILITATION

Rehabilitation, while no longer the dominant punishment rationale advanced to justify incarceration, deserves mention. In spite of rehabilitation's fall from prominence in the 1970s and 1980s, the public continues to support this philosophy and programs that operate under it (Moon et al., 2000; Nagin et al., 2002). However, support for rehabilitation is not as prevalent as the desire to feel satisfied that these offenders have suffered for their crimes (Clear, 1998).

Above and beyond the fact that the public still prioritizes punishment over rehabilitation as the main justification for criminal sanctions, there are additional reasons why rehabilitation might not ever be considered acceptable as a sole basis for incarceration. There are some reasons to question the logic of rehabilitation as a goal of incarceration. First, rehabilitation rests on the premise that all offenders are "sick" and in need of this sort of intervention. This is not a tenable assumption; in fact, research into correctional rehabilitation shows that many offenders are not good candidates for this type of intervention. Imposing rehabilitation on people for whom it is inappropriate can actually make them worse off (see Lowenkamp & Latessa, 2004). Mass incarceration will inevitably sweep up numerous people who have no need for, and will not benefit from, in-prison programming. Second, and related to the first, rehabilitation assumes the existence of effective programs that will exert measurable improvements in offenders' future behavior. This assumption is partially met. There are high-quality programs and researchers have identified key principles of effective correctional treatment (e.g., Andrews, Zinger, Hoge, Bonta, Gendreau, Cullen, 1990), but even the best programs only reduce recidivism—none of them eliminate it.

These two logical weaknesses undermine the use of rehabilitation as a punishment philosophy adequate to independently justify mass incarceration. It would be hard to defend imprisoning millions of people as a means of subjecting them to treatments they might not need or benefit from. Rehabilitation programs help many people, but this philosophy is not enough, by itself, to rationalize mass incarceration.

THE EMPIRICAL STATUS OF MASS INCARCERATION

As noted in the chapter introduction, the discussion of whether mass incarceration "works" will be broken down into two considerations: *effectiveness* and *efficiency*. Effectiveness concerns mass incarceration's apparent ability to reduce crime, and efficiency refers to the quantity of resources that must be invested to reap beneficial crime-control outcomes. A policy that is effective would still fail the efficiency test if the investment outweighs the positive results.

First is the matter of effectiveness. Mass incarceration has inspired countless academic studies attempting to discern what (if any) impact widespread prison usage has on crime. These researchers often have difficultly disentangling the seeming effect incarceration exerts on crime from the impacts of deterrence. As a result, the exact relationship between prison and crime remains muddled. Older research pointed, on balance, to the conclusion that mass incarceration does exert some crime-reduction benefit (Pratt & Cullen, 2005). Spelman (2000), analyzing whether prison expansion could be credited for the major crime drop of the 1990s, concluded that the crime drop would have been approximately 27 percent smaller if incarceration had not increased as it did.

One hurdle researchers face is that crime rates and incarceration rates are mutually dependent—a statistical dilemma called "simultaneity." In other words, crime rates may drive incarceration rates, but incarceration rates might also affect crime rates. Marvell and Moody (1994) and Levitt (1996) produced two of the few studies widely considered to have successfully overcome this problem. Marvell and Moody used longitudinal data across forty-nine states and arrived at the conclusion that the prison increase of the 1980s prevented 680,000 crimes over the decade, although they based their analyses on the dubious assumption that all incarcerated offenders would be committing seventeen crimes each year for the duration of their confinement. For reasons already discussed, this assumption warrants skepticism.

Through a very complicated set of statistical analyses, Levitt (1996) found that each additional prisoner added to the incarcerated population prevented 5.54 crimes (although only 1.13 of them were violent offenses) and produced a resultant social benefit of $53,900. While many prison proponents tout Levitt's study as proof of the benefits of prison expansion, Levitt himself cautioned that, "An important caveat concerning the application of these results to public policy is that the social benefit of radically expanding the prison population through the incarceration of increasingly minor criminals is likely to be well below the estimates presented here" (p. 347). This admonition demonstrates the ever-present problem of diminishing returns.

Overall, older studies seemed to indicate that mass incarceration was effective, albeit modestly so. Newer research, however, does not support the findings of these earlier studies. Contemporary researchers have the advantage of better data and more sophisticated statistical capability, allowing them to delve deeper into the nuances of the crime–incarceration link than their predecessors could. Kovandzic and Vieraitis (2006) narrowed their analysis to a single state (unlike most previous research, which used crime and imprisonment data across multiple states) and found no relationship between prison rates and crime rates over time. Liedka, Piehl, and Useem (2006) uncovered evidence that diminishing returns may be worse than originally thought, for two reasons. First, they calculated that the magnitude of the impact was greater than those found in previous research. Second, the effect may kick in at a lower threshold—their analyses suggested that more than three-quarters of states' prison populations exceed the point at which further increases have virtually no impact on crime rates. Sundt, Salisbury, and Harmon (2016) found no significant or long-term crime increases after one state downsized its prison population through the selective release of thousands of nonviolent, nonserious, nonsex offender inmates. Incarcerating these lower-level offenders may merely increase costs without improving public safety. On balance, the most reasonable conclusion in light of the evidence seems to be that mass incarceration does not reduce crime. Lower prison rates and an exclusive focus on demonstrably dangerous offenders might be effective (Liedka et al., 2006), but elevated rates and a policy of indiscriminately imprisoning offenders of all levels of (non)dangerousness does not improve public safety.

Second is the analysis of efficiency. Here, too, mass incarceration seems to fail the test. The federal government and states invest enormous sums on prisons and other correctional institutions on an annual basis. In 2010, states spent $48.4 billion, roughly three-quarters of which went to prisons and jails (Kyckelhahn, 2014). Evidence suggests that this price tag, large as it is, is an underestimate because it conceals some of the money spent. The true cost to taxpayers might be 14 percent higher than what states claim (Henrichson & Delaney, 2012). The federal Bureau of Prisons' annual operating budget is $8.5 billion (U.S. Department of Justice, n.d.). Yet, recidivism rates are high and more than three-quarters of people released from prison in any given year are rearrested within 5 years. Similarly, 55 percent of released prisoners return to prison within 5 years for either a new offense or a parole violation (Durose, Cooper, & Snyder, 2014). These numbers paint a grim picture of prison effectiveness when compared to its cost.

Researchers have also analyzed efficiency from the perspective of the relationship between prison populations and crime rates. Early econometric analyses suggest that a 1 percent increase in the number of people imprisoned would achieve a 0.16 percent reduction in crime (Marvell & Moody, 1994). This itself is hardly cause for optimism, but the scene becomes even bleaker. More recent studies reveal flaws in this older research that may have overestimated the impact of prison increases on crime by ignoring diminishing returns. The true numbers may be that when incarceration rates are low, a 10 percent increase in the incarcerated population lowers crime by 1.01 percent. When rates are moderate, a 10 percent increase translates to a 1.35 percent reduction. Finally, when rates are high, a 10 percent rise corresponds to a trivial 0.36 percent drop (Liedka et al., 2006). While, again, this does not rule out the possibility that there is a "floor" effect (i.e., that prisons have some kind of absolute deterrence or selective incapacitation impact when reserved for serious offenders), the evidence is clear that expanding prison populations drains public coffers without offering a tangible benefit to balance out taxpayers' investment. Mass incarceration's meagre crime-control outputs are dwarfed by the massive expenditures required to achieve even the humblest of results.

There are also human costs to mass incarceration, and reasons to suspect that this policy may actually *contribute* to crime. This argument lies in the phenomenon of concentration effects. Incarceration is not evenly distributed across social groups and residential geographies; to the contrary, it heavily impacts poor, inner-city, minority communities. Blacks are especially affected, as are Hispanics/Latinos, albeit not as dramatically relative to whites (Carson, 2015). High rates of imprisonment concentrated in disadvantaged communities further destabilizes the already threadbare social and economic fabric in these areas. Inner-city minority neighborhoods suffer from the high rates of joblessness and poverty left by the decline in the U.S. industrial economy (Wilson, 1987). Social disorganization (Rose & Clear, 1998) and cultural turmoil that often pits neighbors against one another (Anderson, 1999) flourish under these conditions of isolation and intense economic strain. Violence, drug trafficking, and other crimes skyrocket (Massey, 1995).

High rates of incarceration mean constant population turnover, which further weakens neighborhood ties and family units and prevents the community from establishing a common set of core moral and social values (Rose & Clear, 1998). Ex-prisoners also have a hard time finding employment (Clear et al., 2001), and many turn to the drug economy as a means of providing for themselves and their families (Anderson, 1999). Because these effects are so geographically concentrated, they morph from problems faced by individuals and families into broader troubles experienced by entire communities. Mass incarceration therefore is a destabilizing, disrupting force that may push severely distressed communities even further down into social despair and help crime retain its grip. This speaks against both effectiveness and efficiency.

In sum, mass incarceration seems to exert some crime-control benefits. These impacts, however, are weak in magnitude and must be considered in light of the substantial fiscal costs (in terms of dollars expended) and human costs (in terms of people locked up) required to effect even modest reductions in crime. Mass incarceration is inefficient. Furthermore, there is indication that mass incarceration can have criminogenic impacts on the communities it affects most strongly. In the long run, incarceration may have become a generative source of the very ill it was designed to cure.

CONCLUSION

This chapter examined mass incarceration as a crime-control policy. Mass incarceration has caused unprecedented rates of imprisonment and moved the United States to the top of the global list in terms of its incarceration rate. Prison rates soared in the late 1970s through the early 2000s and remain high today, although they have declined somewhat in recent years. Sharp racial and income disparities emerged during the spike, largely due to the disproportionate impact the war on drugs exerted on low-income, minority communities. Proponents of using prison as a penalty for a wide variety of crimes, and of making sentences long, typically justify their position on grounds of deterrence or incapacitation. In this chapter, both of these punishment philosophies were parsed to evaluate their logical veracity, and although there may be some merit to them, each came up short of ideal. Rehabilitation, likewise, cannot be used to defend this policy. When evaluated on principles of effectiveness and efficiency, mass incarceration was found to be marginally effective but highly inefficient. Sound evidence supports the existence of diminishing returns, meaning that once a state's incarceration rate has reached a certain level, further increases have no meaningful impact on crime. Furthermore, there is cause to believe the substantial collateral consequences of mass incarceration for distressed urban neighborhoods increase crime and counteract some of the crime-reduction benefits prisons may have. Mass incarceration, it must be concluded, leaves much wanting in terms of a crime-control policy grounded in sound logic and demonstrably effective and efficient. Combined with its ineffectiveness and tremendous cost, significant collateral consequences should be the basis for state and federal policymakers to undertake serious revisions of existing sentencing laws.

DISCUSSION QUESTIONS

1. Most states restrict the voting rights of people convicted of felonies. Some states impose lifetime bans, while others allow voting rights to be restored after a period of disenfranchisement. The racial and geographic concentration of incarceration means that disenfranchisement is likewise most prevalent among racial minorities and disadvantaged communities, making disenfranchisement a collateral consequence of mass incarceration. Proponents of disenfranchisement claim that it is a reasonable penalty, because people who have demonstrated that they disrespect society's laws should not be allowed to participate in the political process (at least for a time). Critically examine felony disenfranchisement within the context of the evidence presented in this chapter. Does this seem like good policy? Should states continue to revoke or restrict the voting rights of people who have been convicted of felonies? Explain your answer.

2. The majority of criminal convictions are products of plea bargains, where prosecutors offer to reduce the number or severity of charges against defendants or let them take the lightest sentence possible for their current offense. In exchange for some level of leniency, defendants plead guilty instead of taking their case to trial. This can distort the apparent composition of the prison population, because many prisoners' crimes were more serious than the offenses for which they were ultimately convicted and imprisoned. How do you think plea bargaining might impact efforts to reduce prison populations through less punitive sentencing schemes? Given that plea bargaining is the dominant mode of case disposition, what laws or policies pertaining to plea bargaining do you think are necessary to ensure that the effort to reduce mass incarceration still results in tough penalties for people who commit serious crimes?

3. Even as more and more people recognize the flaws in mass incarceration as a crime-control policy and some states make efforts to reduce their prison populations, many policymakers and members of the public continue to support this policy and believe that it works. Craft a compelling, evidence-based argument that neatly encapsulates the critical information about mass incarceration's impact on crime and its collateral consequences for individuals, families, and communities. Be creative and persuasive.

4. A person's likelihood of engaging in crime and ultimately ending up in prison is significantly increased by factors such as poverty, low education, and suffering from a mental illness or substance-abuse disorder. Prison often reduces people's employment prospects even further, can worsen their mental state, and reduces their prospects for experiencing beneficial life events like marriage. What are some things that policymakers or members of the public could do to reduce prison's negative impact on the lives of many of the people who experience this punishment? What laws or policies might help improve the situation? What can communities, business owners, or other individuals or groups do?

CHAPTER 9

THE DEATH PENALTY

INTRODUCTION

Of all the ways in which the United States stands apart from other Western democracies, one of the starkest is its continued use of the death penalty. Cesare Beccaria—the father of deterrence theory whose thoughtful eruditions on the acceptable amount of control governments may exert over their citizens guided the crafting of the US Constitution—denounced the death penalty. On moral grounds, Beccaria (1764) pondered, "By what alleged right can men slaughter their fellows?" (p. 48). For practical purposes, Beccaria argued that the death penalty is an inferior deterrent compared to life in prison, because death is a penalty of the body lasting only until the offender's demise; prison, by contrast, is a punishment of the mind that can extend for several years.

Despite opposition from the very person who breathed intellectual life into a primary theory upon which the United States continues to justify this penalty, and amidst wavering public support and swirling controversy, capital punishment lingers. For how long is unclear. Nineteen states and the District of Columbia have abolished the death penalty, and executions have been declining steadily for several years. In the year 2000, 85 people were executed (Snell, 2013), but by 2016 that number was down to 20, with a mere 30 new admissions to death row (Death Penalty Information Center, 2016). The federal government rarely conducts executions, and has not put anyone to death since 2003. Only a handful of the states that authorize capital punishment carry out executions. Southern states (namely Texas, Oklahoma, Virginia, and Florida) have been the primary sources of executions over the years, followed by Midwestern states (in particular, Missouri and Ohio). Arizona stands out among Western states in its use of capital punishment. Virtually no executions have occurred in the Northeast in recent decades (Snell, 2013). Public support for capital punishment is at an all-time low (Oliphant, 2016).

Death-penalty proponents generally invoke retribution and deterrence to justify their position. Retribution (or just deserts) is a moral argument that someone who willfully takes a life automatically forfeits his or her own. Deterrence is founded on utilitarian principles whereby executing convicted murderers is justified because it averts future murders. These two opinions can exist in tandem as both support for capital punishment or as opposition to it (Hood, 1998). Someone who strongly believes in the morality of "a life for a life," for instance, would not be swayed by the utilitarian argument that punishment is not justified unless it serves a greater social good. Morality remains a key element of the death-penalty debate, which complicates the policy discussion because morals are not subject to empirical analysis and therefore cannot be proven or falsified.

This chapter situates the death penalty within an era of increased opposition and controversy. The public's awareness about racial disparities, wrongful convictions, and botched executions is fueling a tide of antideath penalty sentiment. States are experiencing trouble obtaining lethal-injection drugs because the pharmaceutical companies that make them refuse to sell their products for this purpose. States' existing supplies of drugs critical to the lethal-injection cocktail are expiring, and it is not clear where or when they will be able to buy more (e.g., Andone, 2017). With this background in mind, we examine the legal and social history of the death penalty, and whether this punishment functions as an effective deterrent. It should be noted that the application of the death penalty is a highly localized phenomenon shaped by state-level and even community-level factors. Because these factors vary widely and differ from state to state (and community to community), it is not possible to comprehensively examine them here. Thus, we discuss national trends and aggregate information while bearing in mind that these broader processes are, fundamentally, reflective of activity at the local level.

HISTORY AND ORIGINS OF THE DEATH PENALTY

HISTORICAL TRENDS IN CAPITAL PUNISHMENT IN THE WEST

The Western world's capital-punishment history is tied closely to the development of society at large. Governments began emerging in the 1400s and amassed political power and structure in the ensuing three centuries. They gradually expanded their authority to include a monopoly on criminal punishment. They used the death penalty as a symbolic reinforcement of their power, which meant executions were public and ceremonially grotesque (Garland, McGowan, & Meranze, 2011).

During the Age of Enlightenment, which began in the late 1700s, barbarous criminal penalties faded from Western cultures as Enlightenment ideals heightened people's sense of humanity. Expanding trade and industry simultaneously ushered in an era of urbanization, wealth accumulation, and governmental modernization (Pratt, Gau, & Franklin, 2011). The death penalty remained in place in many nations, but officials were pressured to restrict its use and find execution methods considered fast and humane (e.g., the guillotine). Beccaria's vocal opposition to the death penalty inspired temporary abolition in some European states, and Enlightenment ideals led many states in the fledgling United States to limit capital punishment solely to the crime of murder or to outlaw it entirely (Hood, 1998). Several states banned public executions and added life in prison as an alternative to death (Poveda, 2000). Prison expanded in popularity across the Western world as a favored penalty for many crimes (Garland et al., 2011). In the 1860s, a handful of European nations abolished capital punishment (Zimring, 2003).

World War II was a defining moment in Western democracies' views on the death penalty. The horrors of the Holocaust dramatically turned public sentiment against state-sanctioned killing (Garland et al., 2011) and the dictatorships in Germany and Italy soured Europeans' attitudes toward government force and coercion (Zimring, 2003). Many countries had been gradually phasing out executions for years, but the end of World War II brought about a wave of abolition. There were few executions in the ensuing years, and the final European one took place in France in 1977 (Poveda, 2000; Zimring, 2003).

THE DEATH PENALTY IN THE UNITED STATES

The U.S. bucked the international trend by not only retaining the death penalty but doubling down on it. Since the 1970s, lawmakers who support capital punishment have tried to make it easier for death sentences to be imposed and carried out. One aspect of the administration of capital punishment these lawmakers have targeted is the tendency for multiple appeals to draw out the time a condemned prisoner sits on death row. In this effort, habeas corpus has come under fire. Habeas corpus is a constitutional right granted to all prisoners. Sometimes called indirect appeals, habeas corpus suits are prisoners' pleas to the courts alleging that the government has inadequate legal basis for holding them in confinement. Prisoners must exhaust all other postconviction avenues of appeal before they are allowed to file petitions for writs of habeas corpus, and appellate courts have discretion when deciding whether to review petitioners' cases or not. To be successful in a habeas suit, a prisoner must convince the appellate court that serious errors were made during the trial or during sentencing.

Conservative lawmakers launched efforts to restrict habeas corpus during the Richard Nixon presidential administration and persisted through the Ronald Reagan years. Congressional Republicans originally did not have the numbers to pass legislation, but Nixon's appointees to the U.S. Supreme Court helped achieve judicially what conservatives were unable to do legislatively. In the 1990s, Republicans gained enough seats in Congress to pass legislation (Tushnet & Yackle, 1997) and received a political boost when the Oklahoma City bombings prompted President Clinton and several congressional Democrats to take public stances favoring punitive federal legislation (Beall, 1998). The result was the 1996 Antiterrorism and Effective Death Penalty Act (AEDPA).

The AEDPA cracked down on existing habeas restrictions that were unevenly enforced and enacted new prohibitions and time limits, including placing a one-year statute of limitations on filing, restricting the circumstances under which federal courts can review petitions from state prisoners, and laying out a general prohibition on successive filings that allege the same underlying issues (Beall, 1998; Tushnet & Yackle, 1997). The AEDPA gives appellate judges several options and requirements for rejecting petitions for writs of habeas corpus, such as refusing to review the merits of any suit filed after an expired time limit or raising an issue that an appeals court had already reviewed and rejected. In theory, this streamlines the death process, reduces the financial burden on prisons and the courts, and enhances the death penalty's deterrent value (Blume, 2006).

Critics allege that the AEDPA amounts to mere empty symbolism (Tushnet & Yackle, 1997) and was a knee-jerk reaction by the government to hastily constrict constitutional rights in the wake of a major disaster (Beall, 1998). The act has also reinforced a critical problem in prisoner litigation—it is exceedingly difficult to assert one's factual innocence in an appellate system designed to consider appeals based only on procedural errors. Prisoners who come into possession of DNA results that could exonerate them, but who have already filed unsuccessful habeas petitions, encounter trouble convincing courts to consider their cases again, as this falls within the prohibition on successive filing (Williams, 2000). The AEDPA did not cause this problem, but may have worsened it. In the years after the AEDPA's passage, observers noted that it did not have the dramatic impact its champions had hoped for or that its detractors had feared. One possible reason for this is that the U.S. Supreme Court and other federal courts had been limiting habeas corpus rights since the 1970s, and the AEDPA was redundant with many of these judicially imposed restrictions (Blume, 2006; see also Tushnet & Yackle, 1997).

THE LEGAL DEVELOPMENT OF CAPITAL PUNISHMENT IN THE UNITED STATES

The death penalty is atypical among other U.S. crime policies in that the federal courts—most notably the U.S. Supreme Court—have heavily shaped its form, scope, and implementation. While state and federal legislatures write the laws authorizing the death penalty and guiding its use (e.g., the specific circumstances under which a murder defendant is eligible for capital prosecution), many laws and rules governing death-penalty policy have been issued by the courts. The history of capital punishment, then, must be considered within the context of important court rulings.

The United States briefly outlawed the death penalty during the large-scale abolition in the Western world, but for quite different reasons. In *Furman v. Georgia* (1972), the U.S. Supreme Court declared capital punishment unconstitutional. After an analysis of the manner in which states were imposing death sentences, the Court decided that such procedures rendered the death penalty arbitrary and capricious and thus afoul of the Eighth Amendment's prohibition on cruel and unusual punishment. Importantly, *Furman* was not a declaration that capital punishment itself violates the Eighth Amendment; rather, it was a finding that state laws at the time did not adequately guide juries' decision making and thereby made it possible for juries to hand out sentences of death based on whim and bias.

After *Furman*, state legislatures set about rewriting their capital codes to bring them into compliance with the Court's decision. The first test of the new statutes came in a series of three companion cases in 1976 (*Gregg v. Georgia*, *Jurek v. Texas*, and *Proffitt v. Florida*). The Court upheld these states' new guided-discretion statutes, thus putting an end to the moratorium that had been in place since *Furman*. Pursuant to *Gregg* and its companions, states can administer the death penalty in compliance with the Eighth Amendment by giving juries clear guidelines to use when weighing whether to sentence an offender to death or to life in prison.

In subsequent years, the U.S. Supreme Court shaped the legal landscape of death-penalty policy. In *Coker v. Georgia* (1977), the Court announced that any capital sentence imposed for a crime other than murder is excessive and violates the Eighth Amendment. The Court also heard cases pertaining to felony murder, which is murder committed in the course of a different crime (such as robbery or rape). Several states authorize the death penalty for all persons engaged in the original crime, even if they had no direct involvement in the killing. The Court affirmed the constitutionality of death sentences for persons convicted of felony murder (*Tison v. Arizona*, 1987), but made it clear that this penalty may only be imposed upon co-conspirators whose involvement was sufficiently proximate to the killing so as to make plain they acted with a knowing and reckless disregard for the victim's life (*Enmund v. Florida*, 1982). More recently, the Court decided that states cannot execute murderers who were juveniles at the time of their crime (*Roper v. Simmons*, 2005) or who have mental retardation (*Atkins v. Virginia*, 2002). The debate about intellectual and developmental disability (the term that has supplanted the phrase "mental retardation" in the years since *Atkins*) persists today as lower courts wrestle with identifying a diagnostic boundary separating offenders who are mildly impaired but still capable of self-control and moral reasoning from those whose disabilities are severe enough to render them protected by *Atkins*. In *Hall v. Florida* (2014), the Court found Florida's classification system unconstitutional because it employed a rigid adherence to a rule holding that only those defendants with IQ scores 70 and below are intellectually disabled enough to avoid death. The Court required states to consider the margin of error in IQ tests and allow anyone whose IQ falls between 70 and 75 to present evidence of intellectual disability and adaptive deficits to make a case for the applicability of *Atkins*.

Courts and states continue wrangling over the legal aspects of capital punishment. For instance, the state of Florida has been in the news lately. The U.S. Supreme Court struck its capital-sentencing law down in 2016 because it allowed judges to override juries' decisions (*Hurst v. Florida*, 2016). Lawmakers revised the statute, only for the state supreme court to declare the new law unconstitutional because it allowed death to be imposed as long as ten of twelve jurors voted in its favor. The state court held that to be constitutional, the law must require unanimity (*Perry v. Florida*, 2016).

Legal battles are likely to be ongoing in upcoming years. The issues will vary, but one that is on the horizon is whether lethal injection, as currently practiced, violates the Eighth Amendment. There is conflicting evidence pertaining to whether the sedative commonly used to render offenders unconscious at the start of the execution procedure actually does put them into a deep sleep and prevent them from feeling pain while they die. News accounts and videos of botched executions reveal instances in which prisoners took several minutes to die and thrashed around in agony (e.g., Hanna, 2016; Willingham & Ellis, 2016). The U.S. Supreme Court has not yet been sympathetic to the claim that questionable lethal-injection drugs constitute cruel and unusual punishment (e.g., *Glossip v. Gross*, 2015), but as the traditional drugs become scarcer and states experiment with alternatives that might perform badly, prisoners and advocacy groups will likely put increasing pressure on the judiciary to take action.

CONTROVERSIES IN DEATH-PENALTY POLICY

The death penalty has always commanded intense disagreement over the morality of state-sanctioned killing. Debates have become more heated in recent years. One of the reasons for this is the aforementioned problem states are having obtaining the drug cocktails needed to kill prisoners quickly and painlessly, as well as doubts about the effectiveness of the sedatives being used. Four other points of controversy are racial disparities, wrongful convictions, judicial elections, and the brutalization hypothesis. We discuss each in turn.

RACIAL AND GENDER DISPARITIES

Racial disparities in capital sentencing have been empirically documented across many studies, times, and contexts. In an early study, Baldus, Pulaski, and Woodworth (1983) analyzed capital-sentencing data from Georgia and found that, controlling for relevant legal factors, people convicted of killing whites were significantly more likely to receive the death penalty than those whose victims were black. The so-called "Baldus study" was made famous in the U.S. Supreme Court case *McCleskey v. Kemp* (1987), wherein the petitioner was a black man accused of killing a white man in Georgia and was sentenced to die. McCleskey attempted to use Baldus et al.'s findings to demonstrate that Georgia's death penalty was implemented in a racially discriminatory way and was therefore unconstitutional.

The justices rejected the argument. They accepted the validity of the data, but concluded that aggregate trends were insufficient to demonstrate racial bias in Georgia's capital-sentencing procedures. Juries are allowed a measure of discretionary latitude when making their decisions, and the justices believed the Baldus study's findings were within acceptable parameters. Moreover, the Court pointed out that the study failed to prove racially discriminatory intent on the part of the jury that sentenced McCleskey to death. The discriminatory-intent requirement means that defendants of color bear the burden of proving that a particular person or group (prosecutor, jury, and so forth) deliberately treated them harshly because of their race. This is a virtually impossible legal hurdle for a defendant to clear.

There is an important distinction between warranted and unwarranted disparity. Warranted disparities are differences that have rational bases. For instance, if black murderers tended to be proximate killers while white murderers were more likely to be accomplices, then a racial difference in sentencing would arise because accomplices are treated more leniently than those directly responsible for victims' deaths (Sorensen & Wallace, 1999). This disparity would be warranted. An unwarranted disparity would exist if black defendants were more likely to be sentenced to die than white ones irrespective of the aggravating (and mitigating) factors that may be present. Unwarranted disparity is a sign of potential racial discrimination. Fortunately, researchers have statistical methods to control for legal factors (such as whether the killer caused the victim to suffer) so that the impacts of legitimate considerations can be removed from the statistical model. Controlling for relevant case characteristics in statistical analyses means that any racial differences left over indicate unwarranted disparities.

The Baldus study and the *McCleskey* decision touched off an avalanche of research into racial disparities in capital sentencing. The General Accounting Office (GAO; 1990) commissioned a study to present to the congress' judiciary committees. The GAO synthesized twenty-eight studies on the effects of race in capital cases and executions, and concluded that there was "a pattern of evidence indicating racial disparities in the charging, sentencing, and imposition of the death penalty" (p. 5). Consistent with Baldus et al. (1983), the

GAO's study revealed that victim race was a singularly powerful predictor of death-eligible charging decisions and imposition of death penalties; in particular, killers of whites were more likely to face capital punishment than killers of blacks, even controlling for legally relevant case variables. The GAO's results were less conclusive with respect to defendant race, a finding that would be confirmed by later research also concluding that victim race and the victim–offender racial dyad are the strongest race-based predictors of death sentences (e.g., Baldus & Woodworth, 2003; Paternoster, 1984).

Studies have uncovered unwarranted racial disparities starting at the beginning of the charging process. An analysis of case records from a single prosecutor's office revealed that the probability of a prosecutor filing first-degree murder charges, notice of aggravating circumstances, and notice of intent to seek the death penalty were highest when victims were white and defendants were black. By comparison, blacks who killed blacks were the least likely racial combination to receive these three outcomes (Sorensen & Wallace, 1999). Paternoster (1984) found that prosecutors were substantially less likely to seek the death penalty in black-victim cases than in white-victim ones. With respect to the dyad, blacks were substantially more likely to face death-eligible charges when they killed whites than when they killed blacks; black killers of black victims were the least likely of all racial combinations to be sentenced to die. White killers' probability was similar irrespective of whether their victims were black or white. Other studies of black–white comparisons have yielded similar results with respect to the probability of a prosecutor seeking death (Keil & Vito, 1989, 1990; Paternoster, 1983; Unah, 2009), as has research expanding minority status beyond blacks to consider other defendants and victims of color (Donahue, 2014; Petersen, 2016). The pattern persists at the sentencing stage when the jury, rather than the prosecutor, becomes the decision maker (Baldus, Woodworth, Zuckerman, & Weiner, 1997; Beckett & Evans, 2016; Donahue, 2014; Keil & Vito, 1989, 1990).

While not attracting as much attention as race, gender influences the probability that people convicted of murder are sentenced to die. Cases involving female victims are more likely to result in death sentences than those in which the victims were male (Stauffer, Smith, Cochran, Fogel, & Bjerregaard, 2006), especially when female victims are white (Holcomb, Williams, & Demuth, 2004; Williams & Holcomb, 2004). It is possible that the gender effect is intertwined with a rape effect, as juries are particularly harsh toward murders accompanied by sexual violence (Richards, Jennings, Smith, Sellers, Fogel, & Bjerregaard, 2016; Williams, Demuth, & Holcomb, 2007). The tendency for men's killers to be treated less punitively than those who kill women is even greater when the victim is both male and black—killers of black males appear to be the least likely to receive death (Williams et al., 2007).

WRONGFUL CONVICTIONS

Wrongful convictions have been at the forefront of public and academic conversations about the administration of justice in the United States. Erroneous convictions have been found in both life and death sentences, but understandably raise more alarm in the latter, since it is impossible to rectify a wrongful execution. The prevalence of wrongful convictions is not known with certainty. To date, 349 exonerations have taken place with the help of DNA evidence (Innocence Project, n.d.[a]). Exonerations occur by other means, as well, including pardons by governors, new evidence unrelated to DNA (e.g., witnesses recanting), and retrials in which previously convicted defendants are acquitted the second time around (Gross, Jacoby, Matheson, Montgomery, & Patil, 2005). Researchers estimate that between 1.5 percent and 2 percent of all felony convictions are incorrect (Zalman, 2012).

Since 1973, 159 people on death row have been exonerated and released (Death Penalty Information Center, 2017a). The rate of erroneous convictions in murder cases of all types has been suggested to be between 1 percent and 1.4 percent (Poveda, 2001), and a recent study placed the estimate of wrongful death sentences at 4.1 percent, a rate the researchers believed likely underestimated the true prevalence (Gross, O'Brien, Hu, & Kennedy, 2014). There have even been a small handful of death-penalty convictions overturned because the "victims" turned up alive (Radelet & Bedau, 1987). The pace of exonerations is far slower than the estimated rate at which wrongful convictions occur. Gross et al. (2014) found that between 1973 and 2004, 1.6 percent of people sentenced to die were later found innocent. This rate stands in sharp contrast to the 4.1 percent rate of erroneous capital sentence occurrences. Capital sentences are also overturned more often than noncapital ones. People sentenced to death are exonerated at 9 times the rate for other homicide offenders. Approximately 25 percent of overturned murder convictions had death sentences attached (Gross & Shaffer, 2012).

While difficult to prove conclusively, there is evidence that wrongful executions have taken place. The Death Penalty Information Center (2017b) places the number at 13. The first was Carlos DeLuna, put to death by the state of Texas in 1989. The murder scene had blood, yet there was no physical evidence of DeLuna's presence nor DNA or blood evidence on DeLuna's clothing or other personal effects. Police and prosecutors were sloppy, the court-appointed defense attorney was inexperienced and performed incompetently during trial, and several critical pieces of evidence were destroyed or withheld from the defense (Cohen, 2012). Recent potential erroneous executions include Cameron Willington (Texas; 2004), Troy Davis (Georgia; 2011), Lester Bower (Texas; 2015), Brian Terrell (Georgia; 2015), and Richard Masterson (Texas; 2016).

The reasons for wrongful convictions are varied and complex. Inaccurate eyewitness identification is a leading culprit (Innocence Project, n.d.[b]; Wells, Small, Penrod, Malpass, Fulero, & Brimacombe, 1998) and is particularly likely to occur in cases with white witnesses and black assailants (Gross & Shaffer, 2012). Faulty police procedures such as the use of unreliable informants (Natapoff, 2006) and coercive interrogation techniques that yield false confessions (Cassell, 1998; Drizin & Leo, 2003) contribute, as well. Low-quality laboratory analysis and incorrect expert testimony about lab results (Garrett & Neufeld, 2009; Giannelli, 2006) and police or prosecutorial misconduct (Huff, Rattner, Sagarin, & MacNamara, 1986; Joy, 2006; Perlin, 2016) factor in. Ineffective assistance of counsel bears some blame (West, 2010; see also Gould & Leo, 2010; Radelet, Bedau, & Putnam, 1992 for reviews). Most defendants facing capital sentences are too poor to retain private attorneys and must take whatever court-appointed attorneys they receive. These attorneys are frequently inexperienced with the criminal law and incapable of mounting compelling legal defenses even when prosecutors' evidence is weak (Bright, 1994; see also Bright, 1992, 2014).

Typically, wrongful convictions result from of a series of mistakes that accumulate to produce the erroneous outcome (Huff, 2002). Not everyone is convinced the death penalty should be abolished on the basis of being imperfectly administered, but the mounting evidence of wrongful convictions, death sentences, and potential executions of innocent people has left many people with reservations about capital punishment. Illinois lawmakers, for instance, abolished the state's death penalty after 13 exonerations of wrongly convicted death-row inmates (National Public Radio, 2011).

JUDICIAL ELECTIONS

Judicial elections have sparked a flurry of criticism of the impact that this selection method may have on judges' decisions in death-penalty trials and, especially, appeals. There are three methods used to select judges: appointment, election, and merit retention. The federal government uses only appointment. States use a combination of all three, and some states use multiple methods (e.g., elections for trial judges and merit retention for appellate judges). Appointment is touted as the best method for securing judicial independence, since judges can, in theory, make decisions based solely on facts and law without regard for what the public might think. Proponents of elections argue that this is a vital mechanism of holding judges accountable to the public. Merit-retention advocates see this method as balancing independence and accountability.

The concern with judicial elections (either poplar or in a merit system) is that judges who entertain appeals filed by people who have been sentenced to death may come under fire in the next election. Critics argue that this undermines judicial independence because judges who see merit in these appeals must choose between the law and their own continued service on the bench (Bright & Keenan, 1995). There have been instances in which appellate judges who overturned capital convictions on the basis of errors they believed were committed at trial were ousted in the next election after public outcry by death-penalty advocacy groups (Blume & Eisenberg, 1998). Critics have also accused elected trial judges in conservative states of appointing incompetent counsel for defendants facing the death penalty (Bright, 2000) and of failing to hold prosecutors accountable for misconduct committed in the course of capital trials (Perlin, 2016).

Some empirical support has been uncovered for the claim that elected judges are more responsive to public sentiment favoring the death penalty than appointed judges are (Brace & Boyea, 2008), but the evidence is mixed (Blume & Eisenberg, 1999). Since judges elected in conservative states where capital punishment enjoys popular appeal are probably personally aligned with that ideology, it is unclear to what extent they may rule against death-penalty appeals out of a genuine sense of public pressure or because they are themselves disinclined to find these claims meritorious. Indeed, studies have found that gubernatorial and prosecutorial election cycles are associated with sudden spikes in executions and death-penalty trials (see Brooks & Raphael, 2002 for a review), demonstrating the broadly political nature of capital punishment (see also Jacobs & Carmichael, 2002). Interest groups play an important role in mobilizing opposition to judges whose death-penalty rulings they oppose (Canes-Wrone, Clark, & Kelly, 2014), which may account for the inconsistent relationship between selection method and voting behavior. Voters will likely remain unaware of judges' decisions in capital appeals absent an interest group bringing this information to light.

THE BRUTALIZATION HYPOTHESIS

Some death-penalty opponents argue that, contrary to its intent, capital punishment might actually increase murder. This is called the brutalization hypothesis. Adherents to this hypothesis contend that states set a bad example when they execute their citizens because state-sanctioned killing devalues human life and sends the message that government officials approve of the use of lethal violence against one's enemies. According to this argument, states' use of violence disinhibits people who believe they have been the victims of wrongdoing and encourages them to seek vengeance (see Cochran, Chamlin, & Seth, 1994). Brutalization could offset any deterrent value of capital punishment, rendering executions meaningless in terms of improving public safety (Land, Teske, & Zheng, 2012). If brutalization outweighed deterrence, the death penalty would be a dangerous public policy.

EXAMINING THE RATIONALES

As noted previously, the primary penal justifications offered in support of capital punishment are retribution and deterrence. Since retribution is a moral argument revolving around whether someone who kills willfully thereby sacrifices his or her own right to live, we will not attempt to bring a logical analysis to bear upon it. Deterrence, by contrast, can be parsed for its soundness in providing a rational basis for the use of capital punishment. We will also consider public opinion as a rationale, since politicians and U.S. Supreme Court justices have referenced public support as part of their pro-death penalty laws and policy decisions. A critical examination of public-opinion research will determine whether this argument holds up.

DETERRENCE

An oft-quoted defense of the death penalty is that people will refrain from murder if they know they could lose their lives for it (i.e., general deterrence). Underlying this is the assumption of rational choice, which maintains that harsh penalties deter crime by increasing people's fear of harsh consequences. The empirical evidence as to whether the death penalty deters murder is presented in the next section; here, we consider the logic behind the claim that would-be killers are rational actors who are aware of and give substantial thought to the potential costs of their crimes.

Perception is key to deterrence theory (Apel, 2013). In order to be deterred, a would-be offender must first be aware of the penalty for a particular crime and believe he or she stands a high probability of incurring it. To this end, capital punishment seems, on the surface at least, to fare better than other types of severe penalties (e.g., long prison terms) because executions are more visible (but see Katz, Levitt, & Shustrovich 2003). Not all executions garner media coverage, however; media tend to focus on cases that are particularly sensational (Vining, Wilhelm, & Collens, 2015) and that conform to stereotypes about minority offenders brutally attacking innocent victims (Lin & Phillips, 2014). Media also prominently feature conviction reversals (Vining et al., 2015). Executions are infrequent, so if the media are only covering a portion of them, and are simultaneously informing the public about convictions that are overturned, would-be murderers might estimate their chances of receiving the death penalty as extremely low.

People arriving at this conclusion would be correct. The probability of any given murderer being sentenced to death—and then having that sentence carried out—is miniscule. For example, since 1978, California has condemned 900 people to die but executed only 13. The system is sluggish and prisoners languish on death row for years. These conditions led a federal judge to sarcastically describe California's death-penalty system as "life in prison, with the remote possibility of death" (*Jones v. Chappell*, 2014, p. 2). The backlog and uncertainty exist nationwide. In 2013, states executed 39 of the 2,979 people under sentence of death. Of all the people given capital sentences since the resumption of the death penalty after *Gregg* in 1976, only 17 percent ultimately received this fate, and did so after spending an average of 137 months on death row (Snell, 2014). One study found that death rates among state prisoners were more closely associated with crime reductions than were executions (Katz et al., 2003), potentially because prison (and death within it) is a more probable consequence for crimes of serious violence.

In addition to the low chance that someone who kills will receive the death penalty (and be executed), there is no predictable relationship between offense characteristics and the probability that a homicide defendant will be charged with first-degree murder as opposed to a lesser offense not eligible for death (e.g., Hans et al., 2015; see also the previously reviewed studies pertaining to unwarranted racial disparities). Likewise, there is no clarity as to which condemned prisoners will ultimately be executed and which will not be (*Jones v. Chappell*, 2014). Since the probability that a person who commits murder will die for the crime is remote and not reliably raised or lowered based on the characteristics of the offense, the certainty element of deterrence theory is undermined. This is a serious blow to the deterrent logic behind capital punishment, since certainty of punishment is the most important part of the rational-choice calculus (Apel & Nagin, 2011; Beccaria, 1764; Decker, Wright, & Logie, 1993; Durlauf & Nagin, 2011; Pratt et al., 2011).

In some states, many people on death row were convicted of felony murder (Bailey, 1998; Peterson & Bailey, 1991), meaning homicides committed (deliberately or accidentally) in the course of a different felony. Only a minority of states allow people who were not direct killers to be sentenced to death, and there are constitutional restrictions on the conditions under which those sentences may be imposed (*Enmund v. Florida*, 1982), but death sentences do arise from these situations. Three people who rob a store together, for instance, may all face capital charges if one of them kills the clerk. Felony-murder statutes are a point of controversy both in terms of justice—since people who do not take part in a killing can conceivably be sentenced to die for it nonetheless—and in the magnitude of their deterrent function (if any exists at all). The question of justice is outside the scope of the present discussion; we will confine our analysis to the deterrence question.

There are conflicting arguments as to whether felony-murder laws deter murder. Those who believe they do argue that this strict-liability approach to holding an entire group of criminals equally accountable for the potential violent actions of any individual person within the group deters people from engaging in felonies that could conceivably result in a death, whether accidental or deliberate. Proponents also think felony-murder laws encourage co-offenders within a group to pressure one another to avoid undue violence against the victim (Sidak, 2015). Critics, on the other hand, contend that felony-murder convictions are tantamount to holding people criminally liable for homicides they did not commit, could not have foreseen or were powerless to stop, and are only remotely related to the underlying felony (Robinson & Williams, 2017). This seems to run counter to the U.S. tradition of tying criminal punishment closely to offenders' *mens rea* (guilty mind), the doctrine holding that criminal defendants' penalties should be proportionate to their level of culpability (Robinson & Williams, 2017; see generally Packer, 1968).

The principle of proportionality, likewise, holds that maximum deterrence potential is achieved when punishment severity is matched to the seriousness of the crime (Beccaria, 1764). In a felony-murder, someone who did not pull the trigger (literally or metaphorically) might receive a harsher penalty than a different offender who was the direct perpetrator of violence—even deadly violence—upon the victim (if, for instance, the distal offender had a criminal record and the killer did not). This violates the proportionality principle. The uncertainty inherent in felony-murder situations also contradicts the underpinnings of deterrence theory. The certainty principle requires that offenders perceive themselves as facing a high risk for the death penalty. If certainty is low, deterrence is undermined. Offenders who commit crimes in groups might not anticipate the use of lethal violence or, possibly, any violence at all. Uncertainty, arbitrariness, or sheer bad luck ruin the consistency and predictability required for deterrence to operate as planned.

Finally, the death penalty's deterrence rationale bumps up against a large body of empirical research showing that harsh penalties do not reduce crime (Pratt & Cullen, 2005). Many crimes are the products of impulse, not careful premeditation (Loeber et al., 2012; Zimring, 1968), and offenders often display cognitive distortions whereby they downplay potential costs and focus exclusively on expected benefits (Apel, 2013; Copes & Vieraitis, 2009; see also Decker et al., 1993). Choice matters in the commission of crime, and offenders make several decisions in the actions leading up to an offense, but the bulk of these calculations pertain to proximal situational factors (Clarke & Felson, 1993; Cornish & Clarke, 2014; see Apel, 2013 for a review), leaving relatively little room for the consideration of remote punishments that might or might not occur several years in the future.

Thus, the death penalty's deterrence justification cannot be said to rest on sound logic. This punishment's implementation is rare and unpredictable, which undermines certainty. Criminal penalties in general possess modest deterrent properties, so although death is clearly the most severe punishment available (but see Beccaria, 1764), there is no apparent reason to think it has unique power to shape offender decision making.

PUBLIC OPINION

Policymakers and judges—including U.S. Supreme Court justices—frequently cite public support as a guiding rationale for the use of capital punishment in the United States, even as the abolition by other Western nations has left this country's continued employment of it anomalous. The death penalty, so goes this argument, is a legitimate expression of moral outrage. Executing murderers is said to be the public's way of symbolically reaffirming the value of human life. Research, however, reveals that there is more complexity in people's death-penalty attitudes than most policy and legal debates admit.

The public leans in a punitive direction, but that preference has been exaggerated and recent trends suggest that death-penalty supporters have become the minority. The public's favorable disposition toward capital punishment diminished throughout the 1990s and 2000s, and appears to have taken a sharp downward turn in the past decade. In 2005, 67 percent of the public supported capital punishment (Shirley & Gelman, 2015), but data from a 2016 survey show only 49 percent in favor and 42 percent opposed and the remainder undecided (Oliphant, 2016). The majority of the public opposes executing people with intellectual and developmental disabilities (Ellsworth & Gross, 1994). One study of people living in Michigan, which abolished the death penalty in 1846, found a near-even split in opinions about whether or not the state should reinstate capital punishment (Adinkrah & Clemens, 2016). Death-penalty attitudes vary across regions, states, and demographic characteristics (age, race, gender, and educational attainment). Support is low among blacks, women (particularly black women), young people, those holding graduate degrees, and those residing in the Northeast and West (Cochran & Chamlin, 2006; Shirley & Gelman, 2015; Soss, Langbein, & Metelko, 2003; Stack, 2000).

Selective media coverage of executions manipulates public opinion by distorting the public's view of the "typical" killer on death row. Defendant, victim, and case characteristics dramatically affect the probability of high-profile coverage. For instance, the media are nearly certain to give front-page coverage to a case in which a black man sexually assaulted and murdered a white, college-educated woman, but the probability of front-page coverage is virtually zero if the killer was a white man and the victim was a black woman without a college degree, even if sexual assault occurred. The media's selection of the most sensationalistic, racially charged cases biases public opinion by lending the impression that the death penalty is used only in cases where sympathetic victims (frequently white women) were cut down by cold-blooded murderers (often black males), typically involving a sexual or monetary motive (Lin & Phillips, 2014). The racial tilt of media coverage plays into larger-scale relationships between racial bias and support for the death penalty. Whites who feel animosity toward blacks are more likely to support the death penalty compared to those who do not harbor racial bias (Barkan & Cohn, 1994; Soss et al., 2003). Racially biased media coverage may fan the flames of the race–death penalty attitudinal link.

Public-opinion researchers have criticized the wording of survey items commonly used to measure death-penalty support. Most questions use wording such as "Do you favor or oppose the death penalty for people convicted of murder?" This wording forces respondents into a "favor/oppose" dichotomy and artificially polarizes a complex set of opinions (Cullen, Fisher, & Applegate, 2000). When survey respondents are offered execution as the only punishment option, they often endorse it simply because the absence of alternatives misleads them into thinking that the alternative to capital punishment is to do nothing at all (Radelet & Akers, 1996; see generally Cullen et al., 2017). This forced-choice scheme makes people appear more punitive than they actually are (Cullen et al., 2000). When offered the option of putting people convicted of murder into prison for life without the possibility of parole, even most death-penalty supporters choose prison; the effect is even more pronounced when respondents are told that murderers will have to perform prison labor and the money they earn will go to their victims' families (McGarrell & Sandys, 1996).

Many who support the death penalty on moral grounds oppose it for practical purposes because they see severe flaws in laws and policies (Zimring, 2003). Support for the death penalty also differs according to crime severity, and even those who support capital punishment express a desire to see it imposed on a case-by-case basis, not uniformly on everyone convicted of murder (Ellsworth & Ross, 1983). Attitudes appear to tick closer toward "oppose" when respondents are presented with evidence that the death penalty does not deter murder (Sarat & Vidmar, 1976; see Radelet & Akers, 1996 for a review).

Overall, research reveals that public opinion is not squarely in favor of the death penalty. A large portion of the public opposes or is ambivalent toward it, and even many who support its use have misgivings, want to see it applied carefully, and generally prefer life in prison as a punishment for most murderers. Public support is not strong enough to suffice, on its own, as a rationale for continued use of capital punishment.

THE EMPIRICAL STATUS OF THE DEATH PENALTY

Empirical assessments of capital punishment's potential crime-reduction benefits have focused on the question of deterrence, since the question of retribution or just deserts is an ideological debate that does not lend itself to empirical test (Radelet & Akers, 1996). Studies in this body of work have used diverse data, time periods, and statistical methods to determine whether murders appear to decline in the wake of high-profile executions or significant policy changes that materially affect the administration of the death penalty at the state or federal level. Researchers have also tested for evidence of brutalization effects. Despite a large body of research stretching back to the 1950s, the empirical status of the death penalty is murky. Researchers have questioned whether it is even worthwhile to attempt to analyze the impact of capital punishment on murder, given seemingly intractable conceptual and statistical problems (Chalfin, Haviland, & Raphael, 2013).

Most death-penalty evaluations employ aggregate data from one or multiple states over time to test for differences in murder rates across states that do and do not authorize capital punishment, or for correspondence between executions and murder rates in death-penalty states. A few of these early panel studies generated what appeared to be remarkable deterrent effects (e.g., Ehrlich, 1975), but sophisticated re-analyses revealed that their results were the product of methodological weaknesses. Once these errors were corrected, the apparent deterrence impact vanished (Donahue & Wolfers, 2006).

Studies using time-series and panel data are plagued by problems that seriously limit their utility. It is impossible to figure out what any given state's murder rate would be if its death-penalty status were reversed (Manski & Pepper, 2013). The impact of one state's use of capital punishment may spill over into other states, particularly if there is media coverage (Bailey, 1998). There is no way to disentangle whatever impacts executions may have on murder from the multitude of other factors that drive murder rates up and down over time (Passell, 1975; Donahue & Wolfers, 2006). The conditions that give rise to higher or lower murder rates (for instance, a state's level of poverty and racial segregation) are stable over time, and the absence of meaningful variation in these predictor variables can lead to inaccurate statistical results (Chalfin et al., 2013; Donahue & Wolfers, 2006). There is no consensus regarding the proper way to set up statistical models in death-penalty research (Manski & Pepper, 2013) and no theory guiding model specification (Cohen-Cole, Durlauf, Fagan, & Nagin, 2009). Different statistical specifications, restrictions, and assumptions materially impact the results of these tests, leading some studies to show a deterrent impact, some to show brutalization, and some to produce null results (Durlauf, Fu, & Navarro, 2013; Manski & Pepper, 2013). As it stands, both death-penalty supporters and opponents can point to panel and time-series studies seeming to prove their point of view as correct (Charles & Durlauf, 2013).

An alternative option to panel studies is to compare murder rates before and after highly publicized executions. In theory, these executions would have a strong deterrent impact, since the media attention they garner should make the possibility of death as a penalty for murder salient in the public imagination (though as discussed previously, this logic is not as structurally sound as it may seem on the surface). Cochran et al. (1994) evaluated the impacts of the execution of Troy Coleman in Oklahoma, who was put to death in 1990 and was the first person executed by that state since *Gregg* ended the moratorium in 1976. The event was highly publicized. The researchers tested for both a deterrence and a brutalization effect on incidents of murder among several different categories of killings. The results showed no reduction in any murder type in the years following the execution, and, in fact, uncovered an increase in murders wherein the victim and offender were strangers to one another. These findings were consistent with the brutalization hypothesis.

Bailey (1998) revisited the Coleman execution, but differentiated his study from Cochran et al.'s (1994) research by using the number of murder victims, rather than the number of murder events, as the outcome variable. Bailey also incorporated a measure of Oklahoma newspaper coverage of any executions in other states occurring near the time of Coleman's death. Bailey's analysis revealed that neither the Oklahoma execution nor any others occurring around that same time deterred future murders, and that certain types of murders increased as a result of both executions and media coverage. Like Cochran et al., then, Bailey's study suggested no deterrence and modest brutalization.

Some researchers have asked whether capital punishment's apparent lack of deterrent capacity is attributable to the small number of executions that occur and the significant delay between an offender receiving a death sentence and ultimately being executed (Shepherd, 2004). One study indicated that commutations and other removals of prisoners from death row increased homicide rates (Mocan & Gittings, 2003), but another found that neither the certainty of death nor the swiftness of its imposition exerted any deterrence effect (Bailey, 1980). Most of these studies use panel designs and thus suffer from the aforementioned methodological problems that preclude firm conclusions. There is general consensus among scholarly experts that the death penalty's deterrent value would not be improved if executions were to become faster and more numerous (Radelet & Akers, 1996). Research on offender decision-making processes consistently shows that penalties statutorily attached to crimes take a back seat to more immediate concerns such as the feasibility of committing the crime and the likelihood of being caught in the act (see Apel, 2013 for a review). Given that aggregate police and prison levels in general exert minimal impacts on crime (Pratt & Cullen, 2005), it seems unwise from a policy standpoint to invest resources into expanding and expediting executions.

CONCLUSION

The continued use of the death penalty in the United States sets this nation apart from its counterparts in the Western world. In the wake of World War II, while other developed democracies abandoned the death penalty as an overreach of governmental power, the U.S. heralded it as a critical element of crime-control policy. The federal courts—in particular the U.S. Supreme Court—have played a critical role in shaping the legal and practical contours of capital punishment. Modern death-penalty policy reflects the contributions of both legislatures and courts.

Policymakers point to retribution, deterrence, and public support as rationales for employing capital punishment in response to murder. Retribution is a moral claim that the public has the right to express its outrage when an innocent life is taken by putting the killer to death. This ideological position cannot be logically or empirically parsed to determine if it is "right" or "wrong." Deterrence and public support, on the other hand, can be evaluated in light of the evidence. Neither one holds as a strong justification for capital punishment. The empirical evidence for deterrence is equivocal; severe methodological shortcomings prevent a clear picture from emerging as to whether the death penalty reduces murder or, conversely, increases it through a brutalizing impact. Given the weak support research has found for the proposition that harsh penalties deter crime, it seems likely that the death penalty has little, if any, impact on murder rates. Public opinion also proves to be a shaky foundation for death-penalty policy. Contrary to claims frequently advanced by policymakers and judges, the public does not fully support capital punishment; to the contrary, there is substantial disagreement about whether capital punishment should ever be used an, if so, under what circumstances it may be appropriate. Even those who support it in theory frequently prefer to see murderers put in prison for life rather than executed.

Controversies swirl around this most final of penalties. Pervasive racial disparities have been uncovered. There is a tendency for prosecutors and juries to pursue the death penalty more often when victims are white than when they are black, which many feel sends the message that the criminal-justice system devalues black people's lives. Wrongful convictions are a topic of fierce debate; the possibility of executing innocent people looms large in the public conscience. The practice in many states of electing (by popular vote or merit retention) judges is alarming to scholars and commentators who contend that elections compromise judicial independence and make it likely judges will deny justice to capital defendants and death-row prisoners in capitulation to electoral pressure. Finally, the practical and legal status of lethal injections seems on the verge of encountering serious trouble. Several pharmaceutical companies refuse to allow states to use their products to conduct executions, and the alternative drugs to which states have turned may be responsible for gruesome botched executions. The number of prisoners executed annually is on a decline, suggesting the U.S. death penalty may have entered its twilight years.

DISCUSSION QUESTIONS

1. Many death-penalty opponents believe that the U.S. Supreme Court should declare capital punishment unconstitutional by labeling it cruel and unusual punishment. Others contend that if the death penalty is headed for abolition, this is a decision rightfully belonging to the states. Conversely, if states want to continue using this penalty, advocates feel that they should have the right to do so even if the rest of the country opposes its use. Critically evaluate the claim that the use of the death penalty is best left to the states and that the U.S. Supreme Court should not intervene to stop it. Identify strengths and weaknesses in this argument. What is your conclusion? Should the U.S. Supreme Court consider abolishing capital punishment, or should it continue to be left up to each state to decide?

2. Postconviction exonerations have highlighted a critical weakness in the appellate system. Appeals and habeas corpus claims are supposed to be premised upon procedural errors that allegedly violated defendants' constitutional rights. Postconviction exoneration on the basis of new evidence, such as DNA, is a substantive matter, and appellate courts are not well equipped to handle it. Making it easier for death-row inmates to raise substantive questions on appeal would probably cause a significant increase in appeals, and the appellate courts are already struggling to handle their enormous caseloads. What is a possible solution to this dilemma? How can postconviction appeals premised upon the discovery of new evidence be given the attention they deserve without completely overwhelming appellate courts?

3. Despite known racial disparities in the application of the death penalty that disproportionately impact offenders of color (particularly black offenders), it remains very difficult for minority defendants to successfully argue that prosecutors have discriminated against them by using their race (and that of their victims) in making the decision to pursue a capital sentence rather than life in prison. Defendants of color have to prove to the court that prosecutors deliberately acted in a prejudiced manner and intentionally discriminated against them, which is nearly impossible to do. On the other hand, absent proof that a prosecutor acted with deliberate prejudice, it is not clear how defendants could demonstrate a racial-discrimination claim to be true. What do you think? How can courts balance consideration of legitimate claims of discrimination with the requirement that defendants furnish conclusive proof to back their claims up, proof that is hard or impossible for most defendants to access?

4. In Florida in 2017, State Attorney Amaris Ayala announced that she would not bring death-eligible charges against Markeith Loyd, who murdered his pregnant girlfriend and gunned down a police officer to evade capture. Ayala stated that her office policy is to never seek capital punishment. The governor of this deeply conservative state removed Ayala from all the first-degree murder cases in her office, and Ayala responded with a lawsuit alleging that the governor overstepped his authority. The choice between seeking death or instead opting for life in prison belongs to the prosecutor, but Ayala's critics claim she abused her power when she declared that she would never seek death irrespective of individual cases' circumstances.

Examine the different sides of this controversy. If a prosecutor has the authority to choose death (or life) in individual cases, does she or he also have the authority to establish an office policy of never seeking death? Should the governor have the right to intervene and try to force the prosecutor to abandon the policy or face consequences? The state attorney (sometimes called a district attorney) is an elected position in Florida and most other states. Does the fact that state attorneys are typically elected influence your reasoning?

CASES CITED

Atkins v. Virginia, 536 U.S. 304 (2002)

Coker v. Georgia, 433 U.S. 584 (1977)

Enmund v. Florida, 458 U.S. 782 (1982)

Furman v. Georgia, 408 U.S. 238 (1972)

Glossip v. Gross, 576 U.S. ____ (2015)

Gregg v. Georgia, 428 U.S. 153 (1976)

Hall v. Florida, 572 U.S. ____ (2014)

Hurst v. Florida, 577 U.S. ____ (2016)

Jones v. Chappell, 31 F.Supp.3d 1050 (2014)

Jurk v. Texas, 428 U.S. 262 (1976)

McCleskey v. Kemp, 481 U.S. 279 (1987)

Perry v. Florida, 192 So.3d 70 (2016)

Proffitt v. Florida, 428 U.S. 242 (1976)

Roper v. Simmons, 543 U.S. 551 (2005)

Tison v. Arizona, 481 U.S. 137 (1987)

CHAPTER 10

INTERMEDIATE SANCTIONS

INTRODUCTION

As the U.S. criminal-justice system evolved over the decades after the country's founding, prison and probation developed into the two default punishment methods. Prison has been used for those offenders society deems dangerous or entrenched in a criminal lifestyle, and probation is for those whose conduct is seen as requiring punishment less onerous than incarceration. Today, there are approximately 6,741,400 adults under correctional control (1 out of every 37 adults), and 7 out of 10 are on probation or parole (Kaeble & Glaze, 2016). Even with this massive community-corrections apparatus, however, states still sink nearly 90 percent of their correctional resources into prisons (Petersilia, 2011).

Prisons continue to dominate policy debates. Scholars have decried mass incarceration, pointing to its ineffectiveness at preventing recidivism (Cullen, Jonson, & Mears, 2017; Mitchell, Cochran, Mears, & Bales, 2017) and its capacity as an engine of inequity that deepens employment and racial stratification (Wakefield & Uggen, 2010), worsening the social and economic morasses already plaguing the communities from which offenders are disproportionately drawn (Rose & Clear, 1998). Politicians from both the left and the right have recently advocated reducing prison populations. Whether out of concern for social justice, government spending, or beliefs about the permissible scope of government control over individual liberty, prisons are falling out of favor.

The decline in support for prisons, however, will not translate into noteworthy reductions in prison populations until reasonable alternatives are in place. Prison is overly harsh for many of the people sent there, yet probation is often too lenient (Morris & Tonry, 1990) and frequently fails to deliver meaningful punishment (Cullen et al., 2017). This is where intermediate sanctions come in. The U.S. criminal-justice system needs to evolve from a prison-or-probation dichotomy into a diverse array of punishment options that can be calibrated to construct nonincarceration penalties proportionate to the severity of offenders' crimes and, where appropriate, provide services offenders need in order to become productive members of society. If retooled, intermediate sanctions could reduce the prison population, appropriately penalize offenders for their misdeeds, and bring recidivism rates down, all at a cost savings compared to the current system.

This chapter discusses intermediate sanctions. Consistent with Morris and Tonry (1990) and other scholars who have written on the topic, intermediate sanctions are framed as alternatives to both prison and probation. In this chapter, intermediate sanctions are differentiated from community corrections. Intermediate sanctions as we will frame them include terms of supervision in the community, but also fines, restitution, sentencing combinations, and other new or currently underutilized penalty options. Creativity and innovation are the hallmarks of intermediate sanctions. We will discuss intermediate sanctions in terms of their effectiveness at reducing recidivism and their ability to save money relative to custodial sentences. Since intermediate sanctions are underdeveloped, this chapter is framed as a consideration of the organizational changes and programmatic requirements that would be necessary for such a system to achieve prominence in U.S. sentencing and correctional policy. We will see that these penalty options hold promise to fundamentally reorient the criminal-justice system toward evidence-based practices that reduce costs and improve public safety by holding both offenders and correctional officials accountable.

ORIGINS AND TYPES OF INTERMEDIATE SANCTIONS

The two-tiered, prison-or-probation system came under fire in the 1980s. Violent crime rates rose, the United States launched the war on drugs, and the prison population exploded. State budgets buckled under the weight, and states began funneling offenders into probation and parole programs to alleviate the pressure (Gordon, 1990). The annual per-person cost of community corrections is far lower than that for jails and prisons (Petersilia, 2011), yet probation is widely considered inadequate. It is overly lenient (Morris & Tonry, 1990) and offenders report finding the various conditions and requirements more of a nuisance than a punishment. The constant threat of being incarcerated for a minor infraction also leads many to prefer short stints of incarceration to more protracted terms of community control that might end in prison anyway (Cullen et al., 2017).

Intermediate sanctions are typically characterized as being between prison and probation in terms of severity (Caputo, 2004), although we will see evidence in this chapter that probation itself needs an overhaul. Under an intermediate-sanctions sentencing system, prison remains an option but is used sparingly and reserved only for serious crimes and dangerous offenders (Morris & Tonry, 1990). Likewise, probation may be employed—alone or in combination with other sanctions—for moderately serious crimes. Petty offenses (such as disorderly conduct) would be punished with nonsupervisory sentences like fines (see Cullen et al., 2017).

There are many types of punishments that can fit under the intermediate-sanctions umbrella. Caputo (2004) lists intensive-supervision probation, boot camps, day-reporting centers, house arrest, electronic monitoring, fines, restitution, community service, and halfway houses. Others have considered specialized courts, mandatory education, and technologies such as interlock devices for people convicted of driving under the influence (Miller, Curtis, Sønderlund, Day, & Droste, 2015). As the public discourse about intermediate sanctions advances, it will become necessary to devise definitions and boundaries governing the types of penalties subsumed under the intermediate-sanctions heading.

For now, we will take an expansive approach and consider various sanctions that do not entail prison or standard probation. We will start with Caputo's (2004) list and then consider other forms of intermediate sanctions. This coverage is not exhaustive, but offers a reasonably comprehensive summary of the most popular types of intermediate sanctions.

Intensive-supervision probation (ISP) is a popular method of adding bite to probation and diverting people from prison. (Intensive supervision can be applied to parole, too, so although the term probation is used here, the discussion is applicable to parole programs as well.) Many ISP programs take on more serious offenders than traditional probation can safely accommodate. There is wide variation in the specifics of ISP, but its essence is that probation officers have lower caseloads and monitor probationers more closely than what is typical under regular probation. It is presumed that this control-based approach will deter probationers from reoffending and violating the terms of their supervision (Hyatt & Barnes, 2017). Intensive-supervision probation has been critiqued on its emphasis on control to the exclusion of rehabilitation (Lurigio & Petersilia, 1992). Recidivism and violation rates tend to increase among probationers in these programs. This is likely because enhanced scrutiny affords ISP officers more opportunities to detect their clients' wrongdoing (see Bouchard & Wong, 2017 for a review), not because these individuals misbehave at higher rates than traditional probationers do. Intensive-supervision probation is still used, but it has fallen short of expectations and probation agencies continue searching for better options (Weinrath, Donatelli, & Murchison, 2016).

Boot camps (also called shock-incarceration programs) started in Georgia in 1983 (Gowdy, 1996) and spread rapidly throughout the nation (Travis, 1996). Boot camps are military-like programs that typically last between 3 and 6 months. They mirror the basic training that new military recruits go through, with demanding physical exercise, strict adherence to authority figures (Gowdy, 1996), and even enforced silence (MacKenzie & Parent, 2004). Boot camps are intended to save money through reduced prison usage and to prevent recidivism by altering offenders' attitudes (Parent, 2003). These programs are controversial, particularly for juveniles, because of the physical and mental toll they exact upon people. Some critics have alleged that boot camps' rigor crosses over into abuse and violates the Eighth Amendment's prohibition on cruel and unusual punishment (Lutze & Brody, 1999). Boot camps still exist, but their popularity has diminished dramatically (Cullen, Blevins, Trager, & Gendreau, 2005).

Day-reporting centers (DRCs) began in the United Kingdom in the 1960s (Boyle, Ragusa-Salerno, Lanterman, & Marcus, 2013) and gained popularity in the United States during the 1980s (Carr, Baker, & Cassidy, 2016). They subject offenders to high levels of control and requirements that they report to the center each day for counseling, vocational training, and other mandated activities (Caputo, 2004). Participants may be probationers or parolees (McGregor et al., 2016), though day reporting can be used as a form of pretrial diversion (Boyle et al., 2013). Day-reporting centers are generally treatment oriented and cater to offenders with substance-abuse disorders and mental illnesses (Carr et al., 2016; McGregor et al., 2016). Programmatic and administrative characteristics vary across states (Boyle et al., 2013), but the commonality is that programming is highly structured and offenders are monitored closely. In Georgia, for instance, DRCs are run by the state's Department of Corrections in collaboration with local law-enforcement agencies, nonprofits, and the faith community. Offenders start under the most intensive programming and supervision level, then graduate to a more flexible schedule, and finally transition to aftercare (McGregor et al., 2016).

House arrest confines offenders inside their homes. They might be permitted to leave at preapproved times, such as for work (Caputo, 2004). House arrest is frequently enforced with electronic monitoring (Nellis, Beyens, & Kaminski, 2013; Petersilia, 1986). One benefit of house arrest is its flexibility—it can be used in conjunction with community service, mandatory counseling, and so on. House arrest is seen as more punitive than probation alone, since it restricts arrestees' freedom of movement (Petersilia, 1986). In the 1980s, when house arrest was new to the United States, some judges resisted it because it historically had been used by repressive governments to silence political dissidents (Petersilia, 1986). Indeed, it remains a favored method by which tyrannical regimes and corrupt politicians oppress their opponents (see generally Osnos, 2012; Roth, 2014). Critics allege that it transforms the home into a prison and raises important questions about the permissible scope of government control over individuals' private lives (Ball, Huff, & Lilly, 1988). Advocates champion house arrest as superior to incarceration since it does not subject low- and mid-level offenders to the toxicity of the prison environment and also saves money (Ball et al., 1988; Petersilia, 1986).

Electronic monitoring was pioneered in the United States. Prototypes emerged in the 1960s and 1970s, then the technology developed rapidly in the 1980s (Feeley, 2014) and quickly spread throughout the world (Nellis et al., 2013). Electronic monitoring is not a punishment in and of itself but, rather, is used to enforce other types of restrictions (e.g., house arrest). Electronic monitoring met with limited success at first because the technology was underdeveloped, but as soon as it was paired with GPS technology, its popularity soared. Today, community-corrections agencies use electronic monitoring prevalently among convicted sex offenders who are required to stay away from locations where children congregate (Gies, 2016). Probation and parole officers can monitor the whereabouts of their clients in real time and receive alerts when those individuals enter prohibited territory. Highly sophisticated units can even detect blood-alcohol levels (Feeley, 2014).

Fines are monetary penalties imposed upon offenders. The amount of a fine depends upon the severity of the offense and can be tailored to an offender's financial means (Caputo, 2004). Proponents of fines argue that in a country like the United States, where money plays a prominent role in everyday life, fines make sense and should be a staple of sentencing policy (Morris & Tonry, 1990). The use of fines and fees has increased since the 1980s, and today approximately two-thirds of prison inmates owe fines or fees and forty-four states make probationers and parolees pay for a portion of their supervision costs (Furman & Black, 2015). Fines are problematic as used in the United States because they are not reasonably proportionate to offenders' economic means. The majority of criminal defendants are moderately or extremely poor. Moreover, having a criminal conviction (particularly a felony) and serving time in jail or prison dramatically increases the difficulty in obtaining employment, since many businesses categorically refuse to hire people with criminal histories (Pager, 2007). Some people end up owing tens of thousands of dollars as courts impose more fines for failing to pay previous fines, and possibly even add interest (Harris, 2016). Judges may simultaneously fine offenders and revoke their drivers' licenses (Markowitz, 2016), and people often lose their jobs once they acquire criminal records (Harris, 2016). This generates an impossible dilemma and downward spiral of financial desperation. Court and correctional personnel collect only a small fraction of the total debt they are owed (Furman & Black, 2015), meaning fines and fees are a no-win penalty as currently practiced in this country.

Restitution is a method by which an offender makes monetary payments to his or her victim through the court (Caputo, 2004). Restitution is an outgrowth of the victims' rights movement, which advocated placing more emphasis on helping victims rather than merely punishing offenders (Lollar, 2014). The Violence against Women Act passed by Congress in 1994 mandates restitution for victims of domestic violence and sex crimes. The Mandatory Victims Restitution Act of 1996 requires courts to consider affidavits submitted by victims (or on their behalf, if they are deceased) attesting to the losses they suffered as a result of the violent or property crime and requesting restitution. Restitution has become a standard feature of criminal convictions for a variety of property and violent offenses, and critics charge that its use has exceeded the original intentions of trying to mitigate financial and emotional harm to victims to the point where it is now merely another criminal punishment judges may elect to impose upon offenders (Lollar, 2014). There is also legal ambiguity as to the types of expenses for which defendants may be required to reimburse victims (DeLong, 2015). Restitution can generate the same problems arising from fines and fees with respect to poor defendants' inability to pay and the chain reaction of negative consequences this can spark (Piquero & Jennings, 2016).

Community-service orders require offenders to complete a certain number of hours of free labor in the community, typically in the service of governmental offices and nonprofits (Caputo, 2004). Tasks may include cleaning, maintenance work, and construction (Young, 1979). People given community-service orders typically serve a concomitant term of probation (Bazemore & Maloney, 1994) and possibly additional forms of punishment as well. Some states have adopted community service for certain types of offenders (e.g., juveniles) as a form of restorative justice. Advocates maintain that community service has rehabilitative potential if the type of work an offender performed and the link between that work and a larger treatment agenda were tailored to the unique needs of each person (Bazemore & Maloney, 1994).

Halfway houses are minimum-security facilities located in communities. Offenders reside in halfway houses either as an alternative to incarceration or after serving an incarceration sentence. They receive treatment services and assistance with employment and housing (Caputo, 2004). Halfway houses appeared in the 1960s and expanded dramatically in the 1970s. They became popular, in part, as a method of diverting low-risk offenders out of prison and jail and making parole supervision more effective (see generally Bonta & Motiuk, 1987; Latessa & Allen, 1982). They also garner support because many people note that since offenders clearly had difficulty adjusting to social life prior to incarceration, it is unrealistic to expect them to successfully transition from prison back into the community without assistance (Keller & Alper, 1970).

There are a variety of other penalties that can go under the heading of intermediate sanctions. Specialized courts, for instance, deliver targeted care to particular populations (drug addicts, military veterans, intimate-partner abusers) who may benefit more from tailored, treatment-oriented services than from traditional punishments affording minimal opportunity for rehabilitation. Specialized courts, such as drug courts, have gained widespread popularity in recent decades, demonstrating the public's appetite for criminal-justice outcomes that do more than merely punish (Mitchell, Wilson, Eggers, & MacKenzie, 2012). People convicted of driving under the influence of alcohol might avoid incarceration by agreeing to have an interlock device installed in their vehicles, which prevents the engine from starting until the driver has successfully demonstrated a zero or very low blood-alcohol content. Victim–offender mediation is a type of program intended to deliver restorative justice. The goal is to facilitate victim healing and participation in the court process, while also giving offenders greater voice in negotiating sentences. Satisfaction with outcomes—gained by feeling one had a say in the process—theoretically makes offenders more likely to comply with the terms of their sentences, and evidence indicates some support for this proposition (Mullane, Burrell, Allen, & Timmerman, 2014).

As noted previously, were intermediate sanctions to gain a foothold in U.S. sentencing and correctional policy, boundaries would be needed to create a clearly defined category. A rational sentencing system would require specification of what is and is not an intermediate sanction. For now, we recognize that there are many types of penalties that may fall into this classification.

POLITICS AND PUBLIC OPINION

The intermediate-sanctions surge in the 1980s was largely fueled by the aforementioned prison-overcrowding crisis, but the tough-on-crime politicians who dominated the scene during this and subsequent decades needed to sell community-based sanctions to a fearful public accustomed to viewing anything short of prison as "soft" on crime and a bleeding-heart effort to coddle unworthy, often dangerous, offenders. To accomplish this, they coopted the concept of community corrections in order to fit it into the get-tough political agenda (Cullen et al., 2017). Policymakers pushed a control-oriented approach that rejected rehabilitation in favor of deterrence, control, and surveillance. Even the terminology shifted: Probation is referred to as part of the "corrections" system, so politicians subtly dispensed with the idea that punishment should have rehabilitative components by strategically replacing the word "corrections" with "sanctions" in discussions about community-based alternatives (Cullen et al., 2005). They argued that intermediate sanctions were apolitical and purely regulatory, pragmatic, and administrative (Nellis et al., 2013). Traditional probation and the types of intermediate sanctions that entail supervision of offenders (ISP, for instance) can justly be viewed with skepticism as surveillance mechanisms that do not merely punish people for past misdeeds but seek to monitor and control their future conduct (see Gordon, 1990). Critics have long maintained that the extended reach of the U.S. criminal-justice system is part of a larger governmental tendency to overcontrol citizens (Garland, 2000). The future of corrections—institutional, community, and intermediate sanctions alike—may lie in a scaling back of punishments of all types, particularly those involving surveillance and control.

Skeptics of intermediate sanctions might argue that the public will not support a wholescale implementation and will particularly resist giving community-based sentences to offenders who otherwise would be incarcerated. However, there are good reasons to believe that public opinion is not a barrier to the institutionalization of intermediate sanctions within the criminal-justice system. For one thing, the public is not as favorably disposed toward prison as many politicians claim. People in the United States do express punitive attitudes, but their harshness has been falsely exaggerated by poorly worded survey questions. Most surveys ask respondents dichotomous "yes or no" questions such as, "Do you think serious offenders should be sent to prison?" Worded as such, a question like this will nearly always receive an affirmative answer. When survey items instead offer multiple sentencing options for respondents to choose from, strong support for alternatives to incarceration emerges (see Cullen et al., 2017 for a review). People in the United States display a pragmatism about the criminal-justice system needing to do more than merely punish. Even a recent survey conducted in Texas—a deeply conservative, crime-control oriented state—found that rehabilitation emerged as respondents' top-ranked priority for dealing with nonviolent offenders. More than 77 percent thought first-time, nonviolent offenders should be given treatment; only 17 percent thought they should be sent to prison. Even for repeat offenders, 62 percent of respondents chose treatment and 27 percent chose prison (Thielo, Cullen, Cohen, & Chouhy, 2015). The preference for rehabilitative policies over punitive ones remains evident even across changes in the ways survey questions are worded or scored (Pickett & Baker, 2014).

Another study using a national sample found that although 63 percent of the sample supported prevention and rehabilitation over punishment, people who reported feeling fearful or at high risk of victimization were significantly more punitive than those who perceived themselves as safer (Baker, Falco Metcalfe, Berenblum, Aviv, & Gertz, 2015; see also Baker, Cleary, Pickett, & Gertz, 2016). This finding accords with other work arguing that advocates of community-based sanctions bear the burden of proving to the public that these programs keep people safe. The rollout of new sentencing schemes should be accompanied by community outreach to inform the public of the new policy and explain the benefits of the transition away from the traditional prison-or-probation approach to a more innovative approach. Where practicable, too, communities should be given the opportunity to be involved, such as being allowed to volunteer for community-service work crews (Wood, 2015). Evidence-based practices and agency accountability will be key in convincing the public that intermediate sanctions are good policy (Cullen et al., 2017).

EXAMINING THE RATIONALES

Intermediate sanctions rest largely upon the logic of cost savings and of providing a greater array of midrange sentencing options that will spare less-serious offenders from prison, while simultaneously giving greater bite to community-based sentences. This second rationale requires some guiding principles to apply diverse penalties in a fair and impartial manner. Each rationale is examined separately here, but in practice they are closely intertwined.

COST-EFFECTIVENESS

Intermediate sanctions have the potential to significantly reduce correctional budgets by shrinking the prison population. There are a few nuances and qualifications to this claim, however. First, cost savings for diversion from prison into intermediate sanctions are a downward step function, not a linear slope. Second, keeping offenders in the local area rather than sending them to state prisons necessitates alteration to states' budget structures to ensure counties have enough money to handle these caseloads. Third, efficiency will not be achieved if the underlying logic of intermediate sanctions (particularly that with respect to interchangeability) is twisted and intermediate sanctions devolve into a mere net-widening mechanism. We will discuss each caveat in turn.

The cost efficiency of alternatives to incarceration is frequently "demonstrated" through a comparison of the per-person cost of prison as compared to the per-person cost of non-prison options. Prison costs vary by state and are difficult to estimate. The Vera Institute of Justice (Henrichson & Delaney, 2012) calculates the per-inmate annual cost to range from $14,603 to $60,076, with an average of $31,286. The Pew Center on the States (2009), likewise, puts the daily average per-inmate cost of prison at $78.95 (which works out to $28,816.75 annually). By contrast, probation costs an average of $3.42 per probationer, per day (approximately $1,240.30 per year). The difference between the per-offender cost of prison compared to probation is startling.

It is not the case, however, that prison expenditures will decline on a per-inmate basis as intermediate sanctions divert people into community-based punishments. While the per-inmate cost of prison offers a convenient way of understanding correctional budgets, they are technically inaccurate. The majority of prison budgets are allotted for staffing—employees' wages, healthcare benefits, and pensions account for the largest chunk of total correctional spending (Henrichson & Delaney, 2012). Prison expenditures would experience noticeable declines only if inmate populations were reduced so significantly that a substantial portions of staff could be laid off and wings of prisons (or entire facilities) were closed. This is why cost reductions are not linear. Although the average daily or annual cost per inmate can be computed, this number is something of a fiction because it is not true that removing an individual inmate from custody would pull the total operating budget down by that daily or annual dollar amount. As such, it is more realistic to view prison expenditure reductions as a step function—declines in incarceration will produce no cost savings until the prison population drops to a number low enough to justify staffing reductions and partial or complete closures of some facilities.

The second requirement for intermediate sanctions to be more cost-effective than prisons is that states find a way to reallocate correctional monies. A system that kept more offenders in the community would save *state* money on prisons, but would dramatically increase the amount of *local* money needed to supervise those people, provide treatment, collect fines, and so on. Currently, local governments have incentives to send offenders to prison whenever possible because this relieves them of the fiscal responsibility of caring for those individuals. It is not realistic to expect counties or other units of local government to embrace intermediate sanctions if they also have to foot the bill and all the cost savings go to states (Cullen et al., 2017).

New budget models would be necessary to institutionalize a system grounded in intermediate sanctions. There would need to be both carrots (incentives for keeping offenders local instead of sending them to prison) and sticks (penalties for overuse of prison space). A few options are available to accomplish this. States could limit the number of offenders each county is allowed to send to prison annually and charge counties money for each additional inmate beyond that cap. Counties could be allowed to sell their unused beds to other counties in a sort of cap-and-trade system. It may be more cost-effective for counties exceeding their limits to purchase unused beds from other counties than to pay the state a flat overuse fee. Finally, instead of allotting each county a certain number of beds each year, states could give them lump sums and let them figure out how to spend it. If counties exceed their allocations, they must pay the difference from local revenue. All of these budget models reduce correctional spending by forcing local governments to make incarceration decisions carefully and reserve prison space for the most serious offenders, while ensuring that the cost burden of community sanctions does not crush local governments' budgets (Cullen et al., 2017).

The third element underpinning the cost-efficiency rationale is that intermediate sanctions are not overused in a net-widening fashion. Net widening occurs when punishments or programs are used simply because they are available. Sending someone to a halfway house who would have received probation under the traditional sentencing system, for instance, would be net widening unless that person (and the community at-large) genuinely stands to benefit. Similarly, intermediate sanctions could ultimately be more expensive than a prison-based system if people are given community-based sentences with terms that they cannot realistically meet. If offenders are not matched appropriately with specific punishments and services that make sense for them, they will fail their conditions and be sent to jail or prison, which will cost taxpayers even more money than if these offenders had simply been sentenced to jail or prison in the first place (Gordon, 1990). Saving money will require reasoned decisions about how community-based sanctions are used. Judges (advised by appropriate parties such as social workers) need to assess offenders' risk and need levels and make accurate decisions about which of the interchangeable sanctions they will employ. In addition to the principle of rough equivalence, judicial decision making under an interchangeability system should be informed by risk and needs assessments to ensure money is not wasted and offenders do not experience more control than absolutely necessary (see generally Bonta & Motiuk, 1987). Budget-model reorientations that make counties more accountable for their correctional choices (Cullen et al., 2017) would help prevent net widening by forcing them to select the lowest amount of supervision and control possible within the bounds of the principle of rough equivalence and the results of risk-and-needs assessments. Local governments have finite amounts of money, so if states refuse to pick up the tab for correctional expenses, counties will have strong incentive to use their finite resources wisely and judiciously (see Feeley, 2014).

INTERCHANGEABILITY AND THE PRINCIPLE OF ROUGH EQUIVALENCE

We have seen some of the forms intermediate sanctions may take, but there is still the question of how a sentencing system shifting away from prison and probation and toward intermediate sanctions would operate (i.e., the legal mechanism guiding judicial discretion in sentencing decisions). Judicial decision making needs to be governed by policy and principle. Intermediate sanctions represent both a practical change to sentencing (that is, changes to penalty options) and an ideological one. With respect to the latter, offenders play a larger role in judges' sentencing decisions under an intermediate-sanctioning system than under a traditional one. In the 1970s and 1980s, courts employed indeterminate-sentencing policies, wherein judges had substantial discretion about who to send to prison and how long their sentences should be. Often, prison sentences were left wide open, and the release decision was left to parole boards. Parole boards periodically reviewed prisoners' progress and made discretionary decisions about whether they had demonstratedsufficient improvement to merit release (Tonry, 2000). In the get-tough movement of the 1970s and 1980s, emphasis turned to standardizing sentences by basing them on the severity of offenders' crimes and their record of previous convictions. Offenders' personal circumstances were largely rejected as legitimate influences on sentencing decisions. Mitigating factors like youth, parental status, mental illness, and so on can be considered at times, and judges in most states retain some level of discretion over the sentences they impose, but for the most part offense severity and criminal history are the guideposts.

Intermediate sanctions require reintroducing flexibility. Judges need room to tailor penalties to offenders' personal, social, and economic characteristics. This tailoring must be approached with caution, however, because discretion can easily give way to arbitrariness and bias. Research indicates that white defendants are more likely than black or Latino ones to receive intermediate sanctions (Franklin, Dittmann, & Henry, 2015; Johnson & DiPietro, 2012) and that the use of intermediate sanctions varies significantly across judges and courts (Johnson & DiPietro, 2012). Consistency, transparency, and fairness must guide the application of intermediate sanctions. The legitimacy of intermediate sanctions (indeed, of community-based sanctions in general) also hinges upon demonstrating to the public that these are credible punishments and not mere slaps on the wrist (Cullen et al., 2017). An organizing principle is necessary to guard against haphazardly throwing sentences at people with no clear rationale or overarching purpose.

To accomplish this, Morris and Tonry (1990) propose interchangeability and the principle of rough equivalence. Interchangeability means that judges should be given creative license to draw from multiple types of intermediate sanctions when crafting appropriate sentences. Rough equivalence refers to the ultimate goal of sentencing, which is to ensure the severity of offenders' punishments (that is, the amount of harm done to them) is approximately the same across all people convicted of like offenses. Rough equivalence is the philosophical principle that guides judges' selection from the array of available penalties. It shapes discretionary decision making and guards against arbitrariness.

In addition to being a necessity for the existence of a sentencing system based on intermediate sanctions, the principle of rough equivalence has the potential to increase justice.

Sentencing people on the basis of offense severity and criminal history seems fair at first glance because people's actions form the basis for their sentences. That is, sentences are based on what they did, not on who they are. In theory, this removes bias and ensures that all people are equal under the law. In practice, however, cracks open up and reveal this apparent fairness as a façade. Noted novelist Anatole France's (1894, n.p.) famous quotation about "the majestic quality of the law which prohibits the wealthy as well as the poor from sleeping under the bridges, from begging in the streets, and from stealing bread" eloquently encapsulates this dilemma. (Although France was referring to criminal laws, not sentences, the underlying logic extends to the latter.) Punishing with the intention of impacting everyone equally while failing to acknowledge the marked *inequalities* among people's social and economic stations in life inevitably delivers unjust outcomes (Sepielli, 2013). We will swiftly be disabused of the delusion that it is morally righteous to punish the theft of bread by rich and poor alike when we confront the reality that there are no rich people in jail for this crime—only poor ones. Morris and Tonry (1990) characterize this as the tension between fairness and justice. Meting out punishments on the basis of offense severity may be fair insofar as all people who commit this crime receive the same penalty, but it is not just, because the impacts on offenders and their families and futures are decidedly unequal.

Intermediate sanctions distributed according to the principle of rough equivalence would, theoretically, enhance justice by ensuring similar harm inflicted upon offenders convicted of like crimes even if the penalties themselves vary. For instance, a middle-class drunk driver might receive a fine of $1,000 because, based on her income and job type, the judge estimates that she can afford the fine and that the financial pain will be serious but not crippling. A lower-class drunk driver, on the other hand, might be sentenced to community service with no corresponding fine because he has no realistic ability to pay. The number of hours of community service might be determined according to a preset market rate, such as $10 per hour. To achieve rough equivalence between these two sentences, the second offender would be required to perform 100 hours of community service. State legislatures would provide a set of general guidelines and expectations about how much harm should be inflicted for set categories of crimes, and then judges would work within those guidelines to tailor sentences to meet the criterion of rough equivalence. Done carefully, this system could significantly improve the justice of criminal penalties, and would also be fair because offenders convicted of similar crimes experience similar amounts of pain even though, on paper, their sentences appear quite different.

THE EMPIRICAL STATUS OF INTERMEDIATE SANCTIONS

Since the United States currently does not employ intermediate sanctions on a broad scale, we cannot empirically evaluate them as a unified system. Instead, the examination of their effectiveness is confined to assessments of certain types of programs. As with any program, implementation is key. We will discuss the outcomes of studies that have analyzed impacts of IS on recidivism, and the empirical support for the risk, need, responsivity (RNR) model showing that this formula is critical to the creation of effective programs and proper deployment of interchangeability and the principle of rough equivalence.

Proper implementation (including adherence to RNR in sentencing) is also necessary for intermediate sanctions to be cost effective and to avoid the pitfalls of net widening. The review of the empirical evidence for each type of intermediate sanction conforms to Caputo's (2004) list (with the exception of house arrest, which has not been evaluated as a stand-alone penalty), followed by additional penalties that may form the basis for intermediate sanctions. First, though, we will cover the basics of the RNR model, since it has implications for the (in)effectiveness of certain types of intermediate sanctions.

In the 1970s, social scientists began publishing evidence that "nothing works" to rehabilitate offenders (e.g., Martinson, 1974). More methodologically sound research conducted in subsequent decades, however, disproved the original dismal findings (see Pratt, Gau, & Franklin, 2011 for a review). These studies found that rehabilitation can work *if* certain rules are followed (e.g., Andrews et al., 1990). In particular, the intensity of the treatment and control to which an offender is subjected should be tailored to his or her risk level (this is called the risk principle). The most intensive programs should be reserved for the highest-risk offenders, while low-risk offenders should receive minimal intervention or even none at all (Cullen et al., 2017). Risk-principle violations have seriousconsequences. Several studies document higher rates of recidivism among low-risk offenders erroneously placed in high-supervision programs (Cohen, Cook, & Lowenkamp, 2016). The second element of the RNR model is the matter of dynamic risk factors, or what are called criminogenic needs. Needs are ongoing problems in offenders' lives that increase the chances they will engage in deviant behavior (Andrews et al., 1990). Dynamic risk factors are changeable, unlike static risk factors (e.g., having started one's criminal involvement as a juvenile). Criminogenic needs include antisocial thinking, a propensity to view oneself as a perpetual victim of circumstance, and an inclination to interpret other people's actions as intentionally insulting or hurtful (Lipsey, Landenberger, & S. J. Wilson, 2007). Criminogenic needs are best addressed using cognitive-behavioral therapy (CBT), which revolves around changing behavior by altering thought processes. Offenders are taught to shed their maladaptive thought patterns and adopt more open-minded, prosocial approaches. They are taught that they have the power to make their own choices and to influence how well (or poorly) interpersonal interactions play out. Cognitive-behavioral therapy is the gold standard of correctional treatment (Landenberger & Lipsey, 2005; Lipsey, Chapman, & Landenberger, 2001; Lipsey & Landenberger, 2006; Lipsey et al., 2007).

The third element of RNR is responsivity, which means utilizing interventions that make sense in light of offenders' unique needs and are grounded in evidence. Programs that properly assess offenders' risk levels and employ CBT to target criminogenic needs help satisfy the responsivity principle. There may be further need to adapt services, such as for offenders with mental illnesses or below-average reading ability. Program administrators must ensure they are packaging programs in a manner that makes them accessible to offenders of all types (Andrews et al., 1990).

Scholars have added a fourth, implied, element to the RNR model, which is program fidelity or integrity. This means that programs must not only be correctly designed but, in addition, properly implemented so they adhere to the RNR principles. Staff must hold relevant educational credentials and be adequately trained, physical facilities need to be supportive of a therapeutic ambiance, and so on. A perfectly designed, RNR-based program will fall apart if it is administered poorly (Lowenkamp et al., 2010).

The RNR model should be integrated into intermediate sanctions of all types. The risk principle should be incorporated into sentencing so judges can determine the level of services different offenders require. Risk, along with the principle of rough equivalence, should guide judges' choices between more-intensive sentences (e.g., day-reporting centers), less-intensive ones (e.g., community service), and penalties that do not involve terms of supervision (e.g., fines). Care and mindfulness are needed when assessing risk, as some scholars have claimed that people raised on the margins of society may be incorrectly classified as high-risk merely because of their disadvantaged backgrounds (Hannah-Moffat, 2016; van Eijk, 2016). Risk assessments should be thorough and comprehensive, and officials performing them need to be on guard against stereotyping people or otherwise making assumptions about them based on their income, race, and so on.

Intensive-supervision probation and parole were intended as a method of keeping felons out of prison. These individuals are thought to be too high risk for traditional probation or parole, so ISP functions as a way to divert them from prison (or shorten their prison terms) while maintaining control over them. For those not sentenced to a prison term, ISP is more uncomfortable than traditional probation (Petersilia & Turner, 1993). In theory, ISP correctly targets high-risk offenders just as the RNR model directs. Intensive-supervision probation and parole programs, however, have fallen short of expectations. Early evaluations yielded disappointing results (e.g., Nath, Clement, & Sistrunk, 1976; Petersilia & Turner, 1993). Studies consistently find that ISP is implemented according to plan, meaning probationers and parolees experience significantly more control measures (contacts with their supervising officers, drug tests, and so on) than offenders on traditional community supervision do (Nath et al., 1976; Petersilia & Turner, 1993; Hyatt & Barnes, 2017). There is, however, no relationship between indicators of control and ISP clients' probability of recidivism (Petersilia & Turner, 1993). Studies, even when using random assignment, typically find no differences between ISP groups and traditional probationers/parolees (Bouchard & Wong, 2017; Miller et al., 2015; Nath et al., 1976; Petersilia & Turner, 1993; Hyatt & Barnes, 2017). Null results hold for special populations, too, such as sex offenders (Buttars, Huss, & Brack, 2016).

There may even be unintended consequences of ISP in the form of higher incarceration rates, since increased supervision brings a greater chance that probation/parole officers will detect their clients' misbehavior. For instance, Hyatt and Barnes (2017) found no group differences in the probability of being sent to prison for a new crime, but that ISP participants were accused of violating the terms of supervision more often, were more likely to be jailed, and had their probation revoked at significantly higher rates. If ISP results in a higher probability that a person will be jailed or imprisoned for technical violations, it is questionable how much money would be saved over the long run. Lattimore, MacKenzie, Zajac, Dawes, Arsenault, and Tueller (2016) likewise expressed skepticism about the monetary savings realized by enhanced-control probation, noting that these programs do not produce better recidivism outcomes compared to traditional probation, but cost more to administer.

On the other hand, Pearson, McDougall, Kanaan, Torgerson, and Bowles (2016) evaluated an ISP program grounded in the RNR model. Offenders' risks levels were assessed upon entry and the services had a cognitive-behavioral foundation. The researchers found that the ISP group recidivated less. Importantly, the high-risk offenders showed the greatest drop in the probability of reoffending. Buttars et al. (2016) and O'Connell, Brent, and Visher (2016) also uncovered evidence pointing toward the utility of incorporating the RNR model into ISP. These empirical findings confirm that control alone is not adequate. Policymakers should expand the goals of ISP to include evidence-based treatment and social services (see also MacKenzie & Farrington, 2015).

Empirical evidence unequivocally rejects boot camps as an effective method of preventing recidivism. Policymakers, too, have gradually rescinded their support for these military-style shock incarceration programs (Bergin, 2016; Cullen et al., 2005), though many jurisdictions retain them (Gascón & Rousell, 2016). MacKenzie, Wilson, and Kider (2001) conducted a meta-analysis of several boot-camp evaluation studies and found that, overall, boot-camp graduates recidivated at roughly the same rate as similar offenders who received different penalties. A systematic review of the evidence yielded the same outcome (Wilson, MacKenzie, & Mitchell, 2005). Some studies have even found that boot-camp graduates are more likely to reoffend than those who experience traditional prison or probation (Wright & Mays, 1998). The regimented, militaristic environment fails to reduce recidivism irrespective of whether additional components are included in the program or the methodological quality of the evaluation (Wilson et al., 2005; see also MacKenzie et al., 2001). There is some indication that people may benefit from boot camps when they are permitted to choose it over regular prison terms (MacKenzie & Shaw, 1990), as opposed to being forced into it. This finding is preliminary and its validity on a large scale is not known. Boot camps' ability to save costs depends on how well they reduce recidivism and the extent to which they pull offenders who would have served long sentences out of prison (Parent, 2003). The available evidence shows that recidivism reductions are not happening. No evidence exists pertaining to whether boot camps are being used as a substitute for long prison terms or are, instead, facilitating net widening.

Day-reporting centers may hold promise. McBride and VanderWaal (1997) found that drug-addicted offenders with disadvantaged educational and vocational backgrounds displayed reduced drug use, improved appearance at court dates, and were unlikely to be arrested for new offenses during their DRC stay. There was significant variation in length of stay. Most had moderate or lengthy criminal records, indicative of their being higher risk and therefore more appropriately targeted by the relative intensity of DRCs. Craddock (2004) estimated that DRCs save substantial correctional costs by diverting high-risk, high-needs offenders out of prison and by reducing their recidivism.

Not all DRCs are effective, however. Boyle et al. (2013) found that medium- and high-riskparolees assigned to DRCs were rearrested and reconvicted at significantly higher rates than those on traditional parole. The authors concluded that DRCs are financially unsound if they cost more than traditional parole and produce worse outcomes. Duwe (2013) and Ostermann (2013) argued that Boyle et al.'s (2013) findings are indicative of programmatic breakdown in the RNR model; the DRC which Boyle et al. evaluated may not have been targeting criminogenic needs or may have been going about it in the wrong way. Steiner and Butler (2013), likewise, pointed out that this DRC was probably engaged in net widening because it was taking in parolees who would have been assigned to regular parole, rather than those who would have otherwise been prison bound. Much remains to be understood about what types of programming and services are taking place inside DRCs and the extent to which DRCs adhere to RNR, are effective, and save money.

Evaluations of electronic monitoring have yielded mixed results (DeMichele, 2014). Gainey, Payne, and O'Toole (2000) found lower recidivism rates among offenders sentenced to EM compared to those punished with jail time. Bales et al. (2010) reported that one state's use of EM was associated with significantly less recidivism among offenders receiving this sentence, particularly when linked to GPS, although the benefit was not as noteworthy for violent offenders as it was for those convicted of other types of crime. The researchers found that only one in three offenders on EM received it as an alternative to incarceration and that signal failures caused frequent false alarms, suggesting that EM is not as cost-effective as it could be. In another state, Gies, Gainey, Cohen, Healy, Yeide, & Bekelman (2013) discovered that high-risk gang offenders on parole who were required to wear GPS devices were less likely to be arrested for a violent offense, but were more likely to be returned to prison for parole violations. The per-day, per-parolee cost of GPS was $21.20, compared to $7.20 per day for traditional parolees. If GPS reduces violent recidivism but increases the likelihood offenders will be reincarcerated for parole violations, it is not clear whether, on balance, this technology is cost-effective.

In a creative method of assessing EM's cost-effectiveness, Andersen and Andersen (2014) compared rates of welfare dependency among offenders sentenced to EM compared to those sentenced to prison. They found that EM reduced welfare dependency among young offenders, but not among older offenders. Although welfare and corrections are two separate budget lines on government ledgers, promoting financial independence among those with criminal histories has substantial merit and can lead to an overall dip in public spending. Smart policy at the state level and careful decision making at the judicial level is needed to ensure EM is used on the right offenders so that cost savings can be achieved (Padgett, Bales, & Blomberg, 2006).

In terms of effectiveness, it may be misleading to ask whether EM works or not. Some scholars argue that this is the wrong question because EM was never intended as a stand-alone penalty; its purpose is to enhance the effectiveness of other types of community-based sanctions. Monitoring also has the insidious potential to encourage probation and parole officers to merely rely on offenders' locations and not regularly check in with them to be sure they are not engaged in crimes inside their homes (DeMichele, 2014). Scholars urge policymakers and corrections officials to view EM as a tool that helps keep tabs on offenders, not as a punishment in and of itself (DeMichele, 2014; Payne, 2014) and not as a substitute for face-to-face interactions with probation and parole officers.

Fines, although a critical element of Morris and Tonry's (1990) proposal, have proven dismal in practice. Most existing evaluations of the effectiveness of fines have been conducted in the context of driving offenses, since these offenses are commonly punished with monetary penalties. Moffatt and Poynton (2007) uncovered no evidence that fines for driving offenses reduced offenders' tendency to commit future offenses. Weatherburn and

Moffatt (2011) found similar results for driving under the influence. Bouffard and Muftić (2007) discovered that drunk-driving offenders sentenced to community service recidivated less than those punished with fines. Taxman and Piquero (1998) argued that treatment-oriented sanctions are more effective than punishment-only approaches in preventing drunk-driving recidivism, so fines may not be the best approach to solving this problem.

It is customary for courts to levy fines and fees (which may include restitution) against people who are sentenced to incarceration or probation, even though most people convicted of crimes are moderately or severely impoverished. A person who cannot pay a fine may be sent (back) to jail, a penalty scholars have likened to debtor's prison (Feierman, Goldstein, Haney-Caron, & Columbo, 2016). Offenders have reported selling drugs and committing other crimes in order to pay their fines so they are not sent to jail (Markowitz, 2016; see also Furman & Black, 2015), and research appears to confirm that fines increase recidivism, at least among juveniles (Piquero & Jennings, 2016). The U.S. system of fines and fees is convoluted and traps poor people in downward spirals.

Fines could play a useful role in an intermediate-sentencing system if done smartly. Day fines, for instance, are a popular European sentencing scheme whereby the amount of the fine is set based on an offender's ability to pay. This ensures the harm is equally severe across offenders of different economic means (Cullen et al., 2017; Morris & Tonry, 1990). Day fines are calculated on the basis of offense severity and an offender's average daily income (Zedlewski, 2010) and can take into account the number of dependents an offender supports (Greene, 1988). That being said, day fines should be approached with caution, because research suggests that the financial impact of a criminal conviction is greater among people making more money prior to receiving a conviction (Lott, 1990). A person's income at the time of conviction may be an inaccurate estimate of what he or she will make in the future. A person who is, or will become, so poor that a fine is unrealistic should receive a different penalty (Morris & Tonry, 1990).

The success of fines in the United States may hinge on their being imposed in lieu of jail or prison rather than in addition to such penalties. In some European countries, day fines are the sole penalty in upwards of 80 percent of criminal convictions (Greene, 1988). Fines can be used as original penalties in order to keep people out of jail and off probation (Greene, 1988; Zedlewski, 2010), and as punishments for probation/parole violations in situations where the offender would ordinarily be sent to jail or prison for the violation (Zedlewski, 2010).

Community service has received little empirical attention in the United States (Bouffard & Muftić, 2007). Internationally, research suggests that stakeholders and offenders themselves view community service positively (Chui, 2017) or at least view their penalty as more positive relative to those who end up in prison (Killias, Aebi, & Ribeaud, 2000). Community service compares favorably to incarceration with respect to recidivism (Killias et al., 2000), but it performs about as well as other noncustodial sentences on this outcome measure (Bouffard and Muftić, 2007; see McIvor, 2016 for a review) and might not be better than short jail terms of fourteen days or less (Killias, Gilliéron, Villard, & Poglia, 2010).

There is room for creativity in community service. Washington State, for instance, sentences some juveniles to work crews that contain volunteers from the community so that wayward youth can interact with adults who might become prosocial role models (Wood, 2015). Little is known about how the content of community service and offenders' subjective evaluations of their experiences may impact recidivism (McIvor, 2016). Community service is sometimes used purely as a retributive penalty and sometimes as a form of reintegration (McIvor, 2016). Punishments that serve no purpose beyond inflicting discomfort upon or exerting control over offenders do not work as well as those with restorative or rehabilitative goals (MacKenzie & Farrington, 2015), so community service that merely exacts free labor from offenders without simultaneously benefitting them would probably not reduce recidivism.

Halfway houses can be stand-alone sentences or can serve as a transition for people released from jail or prison with the goal of helping them integrate into the community. Historically, halfway houses have been underutilized due to a general tendency for corrections officials to overestimate the risks offenders pose to the community and rather to incarcerate many who would have been good candidates for halfway houses (Bonta & Motiuk, 1987, 1990). There is wide variation in the intensity of treatment and supervision within halfway houses and other forms of transitional housing, and not all types are equally effective (Clark, 2015). Proper adherence to the RNR model is critical, both in terms of offenders' program completion and post-program recidivism (Bonta & Motiuk, 1985; Motiuk, Bonta, & Andrews, 1986). Staff should use established instruments (e.g., the Level of Service Inventory—Revised) to assess risk and needs, and then structure services to be responsive to those needs (Bonta & Motiuk, 1985).

Housing is an immediate need for returning prisoners, and many have problems obtaining stable places to live (see Clark, 2015 for a review), so the mere fact that halfway houses provide this stability is a point in their favor. Research supports halfway houses as being effective at transitioning parolees into the community. Costanza, Cox, and Kilburn (2015) found that those who completed halfway-house programs were significantly more likely than traditional parolees to be successfully discharged from parole and less likely to be arrested within one year of discharge. Hamilton and Campbell (2014) did not find differences between halfway houses and traditional parole in terms of offenders' likelihood of rearrest or reconviction, but did find that halfway-house participants were less likely to have their parole revoked and to be returned to prison for either parole violations or new offenses. Halfway houses can be effective with both low-risk offenders who do not need the highly controlled environment of prison or jail (Bonta & Motiuk, 1987, 1990) and with high-risk offenders and special populations (e.g., sex offenders) who need more intensive treatment than prisons provide but also more supervision than what traditional probation allows for (Clark, 2015).

Specialized courts may have a part to play as intermediate sanctions become mainstream, but evidence is equivocal. Some researchers have found that drug-treatment courts reduce recidivism compared to traditional community-based treatment, suggesting that the combination of treatment and supervision is ideal (Gottfredson, Najaka, & Kearley, 2003). Others have uncovered no impacts of judicial monitoring on drug-court participants' recidivism, but that judges are more likely to detect wrongdoing in the drug-court context (Marlowe et al., 2003). Systematic reviews of available drug-court evaluations have produced tentatively positive conclusions, but the researchers have stressed that high-quality evaluations are rare and more studies are needed (Brown, 2010; Wilson, Mitchell, & MacKenzie, 2006). As currently administered, drug courts may be exerting a net-widening effect (Lynch, 2012). Evaluations of domestic-violence courts produce conflicting findings, with some showing no effect on recidivism (Labriola, Rempel, & Davis, 2008) and others finding that these courts do seem to reduce future domestic violence (Gover, MacDonald, & Alpert, 2003). Similar to ISP, specialized courts are more expensive to administer than some other community-based sanctions, so if they do not produce a clear advantage in terms of recidivism reduction, they might not be worth the cost (see Gottfredson et al., 2003).

CONCLUSION

Intermediate sanctions are an attractive alternative to the current "in/out" system wherein prison and probation are the default criminal punishments. Prison is inappropriate for offenders posing a low or mid-level risk to the community, while probation is not a satisfactory penalty because caseloads are high and supervision sporadic. This undoubtedly contributes to the tendency for judges to send low- and moderate-risk offenders to prison where it is guaranteed they will be monitored and controlled. Intermediate sanctions emerged in the 1980s and gained traction, but most of them never became a fixture of sentencing in the United States. To the extent that some are widely used (e.g., fines), their practical application falls well short of ideal and merits significant rethinking. Done correctly, intermediate sanctions could infuse sentencing and correctional policies with a far greater ability to appropriately punish and rehabilitate criminal offenders.

Intermediate sanctions also offer the opportunity to improve justice. Interchangeability and the principle of rough equivalence can achieve what a sentencing system based solely upon offense severity and criminal history cannot. Under an intermediate-sanctioning approach, judges would account for offenders' personal circumstances when issuing sentencing decisions. Fines, community service, day reporting, and so forth would be selected on the basis of offenders' social, financial, and mental-health circumstances to ensure appropriate levels of punishment, control, and rehabilitation. Such a system would also reject a purely control-based approach in favor of one that emphasizes the RNR model and evidence-based practices. The intensity of treatment and control need to be matched to an offenders' risk levels and criminogenic needs. Low-risk offenders should be sentenced to very little or no control, such as fines or short terms of community service. For intermediate sanctions to significantly shrink correctional budgets, judges must default toward the sentences that represent the minimum level of control and intensity of treatment necessary to protect the public and help the offender. Intermediate sanctions require a reorientation of thought in the sentencing and corrections systems, but the ultimate outcome would be more effective, efficient, and just criminal punishment.

DISCUSSION QUESTIONS

1. Fines are an integral part of many other Western nations' punishment systems, but thus far have been highly problematic in the United States. The reason for the difference lies partially

in the fact that U.S. courts do not adequately take offenders' ability to pay into consideration when setting fines. Most offenders are poor, many are extremely impoverished, so paying hefty fines is difficult or impossible. Do you think fines have any chance of succeeding as a viable intermediate sanction in the United States? If not, why? If so, what laws, policies, or practices would be necessary to make fines a useful, just intermediate sanction?

2. Many people are concerned that intermediate sanctions promote net widening because people who would have ordinarily been given a very minor penalty are now being sentenced to more intensive criminal-justice supervision. On the other hand, a key argument behind intermediate sanctions is that many offenders are being let off too lightly and should be punished more harshly, short of sending them to prison. If an intermediate-sanctioning scheme were implemented and many offenders received harsher penalties as a result, how would you respond to the claim that this is an instance of net widening? What would need to be done to make sure net widening did not occur?

3. A big concern driving the political reluctance to endorse intermediate sanctions is the potential that dangerous people would remain in the community rather than being sent to prison. Politicians and other policymakers are risk averse and fear being held responsible for tragedies, even if they bear no direct fault for these events. A politician or policymaker would be out of a job if she or he endorsed a community-based program and then an offender in that program subsequently committed a terrible act. The public, likewise, is risk averse and generally thinks prison is the safer bet. What arguments would you make to quell these concerns? An intermediate-sanctions system would result in offenders who previously would have been sent to prison now remaining in the community. How would you defend this? What evidence and rationales would you offer?

4. The tension between fairness and justice seen within the modern popularity of determinate, mandatory, and guided-discretion sentencing statutes stands in contrast to the indeterminate sentencing that dominated judicial practices until the 1980s. Under indeterminate sentencing, judges and parole boards tailored sentences to each offender. This caused widespread sentencing variation that seemed to have no rational basis and displayed signs of arbitrariness and bias. How would you make sure intermediate sanctions avoided the problems seen with indeterminate sentencing? That is, how would you translate the principle of rough equivalence into practice to ensure that justice is done even though offenders convicted of similar crimes might receive different penalties? Develop some guidelines that would help implement this principle.

CHAPTER 11

WHITE-COLLAR OFFENDING

INTRODUCTION

A long time ago, Charles Ponzi got an idea. He wanted to start an investment business. Traditionally, entrepreneurs pay investors with dividends earned through stocks, real estate development, and the like. But this means entrepreneurs actually have to possess something to sell (such as a piece of land or a new invention). What if you could skip the hassle of obtaining assets and simply pay one person with someone else's money? This cunning bit of financial deviltry quickly made Charles Ponzi a millionaire. He set up a company to manage his sham investment business and promote the fiction that he was cleverly (and legally) profiting off the foreign-exchange rate on postage stamps. By the time Ponzi was arrested in 1920, his con job (which would become known as the infamous "Ponzi scheme") had bilked investors out of millions. Many of these people were working class. Untold numbers were financially ruined. In 2009, nearly a century after Charles Ponzi's downfall, Bernard Madoff pleaded guilty in criminal court to operating a Ponzi scheme several times the magnitude of the original. He, too, used a company as a front for his fraud to make himself appear legitimate to investors.

In 1973, executives at Ford Motor Company ran a cost-benefit analysis and concluded that it would be more expensive to fix a critical flaw in the fuel tanks of the Pinto model than to settle lawsuits they anticipated would result from burn injuries and deaths. As a result, several hundred people died when their Pintos were rear-ended and exploded into flames. In 2001, General Motors executives noted a defect in the ignition switches being installed in some of their cars. They considered fixing the problem, but decided the price tag was too high. Four years later, people driving certain models of General Motors vehicles started getting injured and killed. Faulty ignition switches slipped out of the "on" position, instantly shutting off the engine, often while the cars were traveling at high speeds on busy roadways. Over the next several years, General Motors tinkered with the switches in their new cars after noting the wrecks and the problems uncovered during product testing. Despite being aware of the danger, the company did not initiate a recall until 2014. Additional recalls soon followed, totaling millions of cars.

There is an unsettling sense of history repeating itself in the study of what is popularly called "white-collar crime." Over time, while governmental response to white-collar (WC) crime has improved in some ways, the United States remains gridlocked in the effort to effectively curb harms committed in pursuit of company or personal profits. The damage to people, property, and finances caused by the offending behavior of corporations and individuals in high-level positions are massive and far outstrip those associated with "regular" crimes (robbery, burglary, and so on).

Yet criminal prosecutions for WC crime are infrequent, and serious penalties rarer still. For instance, the government has not pursued criminal cases against any high-level executives in the major firms at the heart of the 2008 financial crisis (Breslow, 2013; Isidore, 2016). These "too big to fail" companies were bailed out by the federal government to the tune of $400 billion (Isidore, 2016) after widespread predatory lending created a housing bubble that subsequently burst and caused a housing-market crash and massive economic recession. Nearly 9 million people lost their jobs (Breslow, 2013). Millions of homeowners defaulted on their mortgages and lost their homes because the true interest rates were far higher than what their banks had promised them when the mortgages were originated. A few bankers have been convicted in connection to fraudulent or predatory lending, but there is debate about how high up in the chain they are, and critics claim they are mostly minor players (Breslow, 2013; Holland, 2013). This stands in stark contrast to the savings-and-loan scandal in the 1980s, after which the federal government aggressively prosecuted and successfully imprisoned several top executives (Breslow, 2013; Holland, 2013; Rakoff, 2014). Most of the criminal laws applicable to such crimes have short statutes of limitations, so in all likelihood there will never be criminal cases brought to bear against anyone to blame for the housing bubble and devastating crash (Cohan, 2015; Rakoff, 2014). The delicate treatment of WC offenders is out of step with public opinion and constitutes a significant policy deficiency. The public wants to see WC offenders punished in the same manner as others who break laws and hurt people, and more consistent application and enforcement of the criminal law could reduce the occurrence of these crimes.

In this chapter, we will confront the problem of WC crime. Actually, we will not use the word "crime"; instead, we will call it *white-collar offending*. Although many of the actions committed in the course of business are harmful to people, property, and the environment, they are not all statutorily defined as criminal. As we will see, one of the primary causes of lackluster criminal prosecution of WC offenses is the absence of a common understanding of the exact types of acts that constitute this category of bad behavior. The cases described at the beginning of this chapter hint at the marked variation in WC offending—from using a company as a façade for a Ponzi scheme to declaring that a perilous automotive defect will not be fixed due to cost constraints.

Additional challenges arise from the complexity of the laws regulating corporate activity, the dense corporate ties that make up the U.S. and global economies, and the uncertainty surrounding how to penalize errant companies without inflicting collateral damage on innocent people. In defending themselves from criticism for not filing criminal charges against any top executives implicated in the 2008 crash, federal prosecutors claim that investigators were unable to determine the extent to which misdeeds were truly intentional and malicious actions instead of mere negligence or recklessness (Cohan, 2015; see also Rakoff, 2014). These and other matters pertaining to WC offending and its control will be discussed. This chapter will be slightly different from the other chapters in this book because the criminal-law enforcement against WC offenders (and research on such criminal-law approaches) has been too sporadic and scant to allow for an evaluation of the current empirical status of WC offending policy. Instead, the chapter will end with a review of the research pertaining to promising approaches that might work and ways the criminal law could be strengthened. We begin with a description of the quest to define white-collar offending and offenders. As this section will demonstrate, the impediments to criminal-law approaches begin with the foundational issue of how to define this problem in order to craft laws and policies to address it.

WHAT IS WHITE-COLLAR OFFENDING?

White-collar offending defies easy definition. Little consensus exists about what WC offenses are, as a group. Some of the actions popularly referred to as "white-collar crime" are unethical but legal. Others straddle the fence between civil and criminal, allowing the government to choose either prosecution strategy (Cullen, Cavander, Maakestad, & Benson, 2015). Scholars and policymakers have made progress but remain mired in a "definitional morass" (Ivancevich, Duening, Gilbert, & Konopaske, 2003, p. 115). What are the commonalities between actions such as knowingly shipping salmonella-tainted produce to market, selling company secrets to rival organizations, and stealing money from investors? Should we even attempt to lump these acts together under one heading? These questions have puzzled scholars and policymakers for decades. The debate is highly consequential, because we cannot create criminal laws proscribing certain behaviors until we know what those behaviors are.

While not the first to broach the subject, sociologist Edwin Sutherland put predatory white-collar misbehavior on the academic map and, indeed, onto the list of things the public cares about. Sutherland coined the term "white-collar crime" and defined it as "a violation of the criminal law by a person of the upper socioeconomic class in the course of his occupational activities" (Sutherland, 1941, p. 112). He originally focused on the actions that constituted WC crime. He stated that,

> White-collar criminality in business is expressed most frequently in the form of misrepresentation in financial statements of corporations, manipulation in the stock exchange, commercial bribery, bribery of public officials directly or indirectly in advertising and salesmanship, embezzlement and misapplication of funds, short weights and measures and misgrading of commodities, tax frauds, misapplication of funds in receiverships and bankruptcies (Sutherland, 1940, pp. 1–2).

Already, one can see the problem in this description—the diversity of actions covered seems to contradict the logic of placing them into a single category. Sutherland argued that the common thread linking these seemingly disparate acts together was the offender: The white-collar criminal occupies a status of economic, social, and political prestige. Sutherland also stated that, "The most general, although not universal, characteristic of white-collar crime is a violation of trust" (Sutherland, 1941, pp. 112). The WC offender, in Sutherland's view, was a high-powered business executive who exploited the trust he enjoyed as a function of his privileged position to benefit himself, his employer, or both. Thus, WC crime was defined through a combination of the characteristics of both the offender and his offense.

Many have questioned the wisdom of including the offender's social status in the definition of WC crime. All other crimes are defined by actions alone—a suspected offender's net worth is immaterial to the determination of whether he or she committed a crime. Several scholars advocated eliminating consideration of the perpetrator and including only the nature and severity of the offense. But this reverts the discussion back to the original dilemma: How can all the bad acts people commit in the course of business be linked together? Reiss and Biderman (1980, p. xxviii) declared that WC crimes are

> [T]hose violations of the law to which penalties are attached and that involve the use of a violator's position of significant power, influence, or trust in the legitimate economic or political institutional order for the purpose of illegal gain, or to commit an illegal act for personal or organizational gain.

Similarly, Shapiro (1990) advanced the argument that WC crimes are acts committed against principals (clients) by their agents (the people and companies principals hire to represent them). In this framework, the crux of the crime is a violation of a fiduciary duty. A fiduciary duty exists wherever a principal has hired an agent to act as that principal's representative in navigating the complicated waters of the system, be it the stock market, the tax code, medical procedures, or whatever else. In such a relationship, the power is held asymmetrically—the agent has an informational advantage over the principal, and the principal is vulnerable to being misinformed, misled, or lied to. When the agent lies or otherwise deliberately misleads, the fiduciary duty is violated and, according to Shapiro, a white-collar crime has occurred.

One theme that emerges in the various proposed definitions is a violation of trust (Shover, 1998), one of Sutherland's (1941) few propositions that has endured over time. White-collar offenders take unfair advantage of their unique access to information and power over others. These "others" may be clients, consumers, or the company itself. Violation of trust (or fiduciary duty) may be a useful focal point; indeed, the entire financial system is predicated upon trust and a breakdown would mean market collapse (Shapiro, 1984). We likewise trust farmers to not adulterate their products and automakers to not sell us cars that will kill us. The need to identify a common linkage (be it trust violation or something else) is paramount in the crafting of criminal codes prohibiting certain white-collar conduct.

HISTORY OF WHITE-COLLAR OFFENDING LAWS AND POLICIES

The relationship (and the discrepancy) between law and policy is perhaps nowhere more evident than in the realm of WC offenses. The reason for this is that WC laws are primarily regulatory in nature, and thus are enforced by administrative agencies, not by police and courts (Cullen et al., 2015; Newman, 1958; Shover & Scroggins, 2009). Regulatory agencies establish internal policies and practices that shape the way they enforce the law. In the area of WC offending, while the U.S. Department of Justice has a hand in directing inspectors and agencies, these regulatory bodies work largely independently of any criminal-justice actors. Their enforcement practices and priorities are based on general goals (namely, to ensure compliance with federal and state law while simultaneously facilitating smooth operations and not interfering with companies' productivity) and practical constraints like budget and staffing.

To understand current WC offending policy, we must trace the historical origins of the modern approach. Until the mid-eighteenth century, crimes were largely confined to the damage one person or group could inflict upon some person, property, or government. The industrial revolution, which began in the mid-1700s, opened an entirely new realm of opportunities for people to prey upon one another (Newman, 1958; Shover & Hochstetler, 1998). Moreover, the potential scale of damage increased exponentially, as now offenders could harm hundreds or thousands of people using methods never before possible.

From the very beginning, governments were slow to respond to corporate wrongdoing. One reason for this is that businesspeople seem respectable. They travel in the same social circles as lawmakers and judges, and they display all the trappings (families, houses, cars) of upstanding citizens according to mainstream definitions. It is difficult for lawmakers and judges to view them as criminals in the same way they would see the average lower-class thief or burglar (Sutherland, 1940, 1941, 1945). Government and business are also closely interconnected and mutually dependent upon each other (Simon, 2006), so the government is loath to interfere with, and risk angering, the business community. Additionally, industry technologies move at lightning speed, and there is no way for the government and the law to keep pace with these rapid developments (McCormick, 1977). Victims of corporate crime, furthermore, often do not know they have been taken advantage of or do not find out until after substantial harm has already been done (Reiss, 1983). Finally, business practices are enormously complicated. It is difficult for the government to discern the internal workings of companies, and even harder to determine the line between legitimate and illegitimate business endeavors (Shapiro, 1990).

Despite these impediments, the U.S. government has enacted several laws designed to set outer boundaries on what is considered acceptable business enterprise. One of the first concerns to be raised during the nineteenth century as corporations developed was monopolism (Geis & Meier, 1977). Monopolies strip consumers of the ability to make choices about price and quality and to select those goods and services that are the best for them. In so doing, they violate free-market principles. The initial major law aimed at business was the Sherman Antitrust Act of 1890 (amended several times in the years since its passage). The Sherman Act is an attempt to prevent corporations from merging with or acquiring one another to such an extent that competition is significantly diminished.

The Sherman Act criminalized violations of its antitrust provisions; however, it also offered federal prosecutors the option to suspend criminal charges in favor of civil remedies. In some scholars' view, the suspension option undercut the law and vitiated the criminal provisions (Sutherland, 1945), though others writing in the early decades of the act's enforcement pointed out that the Department of Justice favored treating suspected violators as criminal defendants (Berge, 1940). Whichever of these opinions is correct, the fact was that the Sherman Act was not enforced with genuine rigor. McCormick (1977, p. 32) provided a summary of the literature documenting the implementation (or lack thereof) of the Sherman Act:

> In order to establish the viability of recently enacted legislation (especially one initiating an entirely new field of criminal law) the Sherman law should have been widely and vigorously enforced from the outset... This, however, was not the case... [G]overnment administrators in the years immediately following the passage of the Sherman Act were reluctant to act. No extra funds for antitrust enforcement were voted by Congress, nor was a separate Anti-Trust Division created within the Department of Justice until 1903... In consequence, corporate combination, consolidation, and monopolization not only continued, but increased.

Another landmark piece of legislation came in 1906 with the passage of the Food and Drugs Act, later replaced by the broader U.S. Federal Food, Drug, and Cosmetic Act of 1938. The 1938 act was meant to increase consumer protection by requiring true, accurate labeling of all foods, drugs, devices, and cosmetics. Enforcement of this act has been hampered by the absence of an accepted definition of an "ordinary purchaser." The ordinary purchaser is a legal fiction created by the courts to decide cases in which consumers file lawsuits alleging misleading labeling or advertising. Courts and juries wrangle with the notion of just how clear and precise companies' labels must be, given the wide variety of educational, literacy, and sophistication levels present among American consumers (Forte, 1966).

The National Labor Relations Act of 1935 was the first piece of federal legislation designed to protect workers' right to collective bargaining. This act created the National Labor Relations Board to carry out enforcement. Relationships between corporations and unions have a dark history fraught with conflicts and, at times, violence. The 1935 act established workers' right to unionize and restricted business owners' ability to retaliate against employees for union-related activities. Businesses, however, retained the right to protect themselves from union activity posing a significant economic threat, and unions are limited in the types of goals they are allowed to pursue using economic leverage. The line between legitimate union activity for which employers must not penalize employees and activity that disrupts business practices and thus can be lawfully quashed is unclear. The National Labor Relations Board and the courts have been spotty in their application of the law due to confusion and ambiguity surrounding these core concepts (Getman, 1967).

Various laws were enacted throughout the 1900s to protect the public and investors from nefarious practices pertaining to the selling and trading of securities. Securities are financial assets such as stocks and bonds. The financial meltdowns and public outrage following major scandals such as Enron, Tyco International, and WorldCom inspired the Sarbanes-Oxley Act of 2002. These calamities cost investors (many of whom depended on their investments for retirement) billions of dollars and seriously undermined public trust in the securities industry. One way that large, publicly traded companies illicitly attract new investors is by inflating assessments of their net worth. This deceives investors into believing their money is safe and will yield good returns. When the fraud finally collapses, the company tanks and everyone loses their money. The Sarbanes-Oxley Act tightened regulations on publicly held companies to ensure greater transparency and accountability. One element of the act obligates top executives to regularly evaluate the effectiveness of internal controls over financial reporting, and to disclose any weaknesses they uncover to the Securities and Exchange Commission (Ge & McVay, 2005). Sarbanes-Oxley also mandated that companies' chief executive officers and chief financial officers personally certify the accuracy of their firms' financial statements, and it criminalized and harshly penalized the certification of statements known to be inaccurate. Evidence suggests that Sarbanes-Oxley increased public companies' conservatism (Lobo & Zhou, 2006), meaning a reduction in companies' exaggeration of their worth. However, company chief executive officers are permitted to select their own auditors, so conflicts of interest remain (Levi, 2009).

In the aftermath of the 2008 global financial crisis and economic recession, Congress passed the 2010 Dodd-Frank Wall Street Reform and Consumer Protection Act. This act tightened regulatory scrutiny of financial institutions by merging some administrative agencies and creating new ones, as well as overhauling the methods credit-rating agencies use to calculate firms' scores. The act's provisions were aimed at financial institutions in particular, but several were broad in scope and have implications for government oversight of all publicly traded companies. Dodd-Frank is the most comprehensive financial regulation reform passed in this country since the Great Depression (Tarbert, 2010; see also Fein, 2010). Nonetheless, the act has been criticized for being narrowly focused on U.S. markets and overlooking the global reality of the modern financial system wherein companies that dislike the rules and regulations of one country can simply relocate their operations to a more "friendly" nation (Chaffee, 2011).

One victim repeatedly overlooked in federal and state—and, indeed, global—laws and enforcement of acceptable corporate conduct is the environment. In the United Nations' 1972 World Congress on the Environment, the world's major countries unanimously agreed that ongoing environmental destruction poses a grave threat to humanity. And yet they balked at proposals for criminal laws to empower nations to impose and enforce limits on air and water pollution and other environmental harms. Congress responded by enacting new regulatory and criminal laws applying to pollution and air quality, and states soon followed (Mueller, 1996). One of the major actions was an update to the 1948 Federal Water Pollution Control Act. In 1972, Congress strengthened the law and renamed it the Clean Water Act (Environmental Protection Agency [EPA], n.d.[a]). The Clean Water Act and other federal and state laws contains both regulatory and criminal provisions. Enforcement, however, remains primarily a regulatory matter and criminal cases are infrequent. Part of this is because it is difficult to quantify the magnitude of the violation (such as the amount of toxic waste dumped into a river) and specific type and magnitude of harm the violation causes (the number of animals killed, people whose drinking water was poisoned, increased rates of cancer among the local population, and so on). It is also difficult to prove causal connections and criminal culpability (*mens rea*) by identifiable individuals in the corporation (Mueller, 1996).

When the government does take action against environmental destruction, the most common resolution is assessment of hefty fines and damages against the corporation.

For instance, in 2010 the Deepwater Horizon underwater oil drilling platform exploded, killing 11 workers and pouring nearly 5 million barrels (roughly 200 million gallons) of crude oil into the Gulf of Mexico. The three companies that jointly owned and operated the rig (BP, Transocean, and Halliburton) paid significant fines after pleading guilty to several crimes; BP pleaded guilty to manslaughter (EPA, n.d.[b]). The government also charged BP with violating the Clean Water Act, and the company agreed to pay a $5.5 billion penalty, the largest fine the federal government has ever levied against a company under this act. Additional monetary penalties were likewise unprecedented, and included an $18.7 billion settlement with the federal government and several coastal states and $7.1 billion to assess the full extent of the damage (Rushe, 2015). Considering all settlements and penalties, the deaths and spill cost BP approximately $53.8 billion (Heavey, Rucker, & Stephenson, 2015).

Only five people were criminally charged, however, and just three of them were convicted. Two were sentenced to probation after pleading guilty to destruction of evidence (Grimm, 2015; Pavlo, 2015). Manslaughter charges filed against two rig supervisors were dropped, although they still faced allegations of having violated the Clean Water Act. One of them pleaded guilty to the pollution charge and was ordered to probation, community service, and restitution (Stempel, 2016). The other was acquitted. A BP executive charged with knowingly underestimating (i.e., lying about) the number of gallons of oil gushing into the Gulf daily was acquitted (Associated Press, 2015).

In spite of the dizzying array of laws, policies, regulatory agencies, and law-enforcement personnel dedicated to preventing and remedying corporate wrongdoing, WC offending continues to plague the nation. Estimates vary, but it is clear that the costs of crimes by corporations and their employees dwarf those exacted by street crime (Cullen et al., 2015; Levi, 2009). By any measurement, annual losses are in the tens of billions of dollars; by some estimates, they are in the hundreds of billions (Helmkamp, Townsend, & Sundra, 1997). Companies themselves lose anywhere from 1 percent to 6 percent of their profits to crimes by employees (see Schnatterly, 2003). The regulation and enforcement of laws against WC offending obviously contain serious weaknesses and requires strengthening.

The government's response to WC offending can be grouped into two rationales: compliance and deterrence. In the following section, we critically examine each rationale. The benefits and drawbacks of each system are outlined.

EXAMINING THE RATIONALES

In this discussion, we borrow heavily from Reiss' work (Reiss, 1983, 1984; Reiss & Biderman, 1980). Reiss helpfully draws a distinction between compliance-based systems and penalty-based systems. A downside to classifying and pursuing WC offenses as crimes is that effectively protecting the public requires the government to be forward looking (proactive), but the criminal law is inherently backward looking (reactive). As we will see in this section, compliance is a necessary component to WC offending prevention. Of course, the extent to which the government relies too heavily on compliance strategies and insufficiently on criminal avenues of correcting WC wrongdoing is open for debate. We will consider the potential benefits to a stronger and more predictable application of the criminal law to WC offending.

COMPLIANCE

The United States embraces the ideology of laissez-faire capitalism, which has at its core the belief that the government's job is to facilitate the smooth functioning of private enterprise in order to maximize companies' profitability. In theory, this creates jobs, supplies investment opportunities, and ensures the health of the nation's economy. Regulation is seen as antithetical to the capitalist ideal. Administrative "red tape" allegedly places unnecessary obstacles between companies and their profits, increases costs, and imposes all manner of ills upon the public via employment reductions and hikes in the prices of goods and services. Of course, on the flipside of the business community's opposition to regulation is the obvious need for the government to demand protection of workers, consumers, and investors. It may indeed cost more to run a coal mine, for instance, that utilizes the best safety precautions available, but the tradeoff is fewer deaths of mine workers. It also runs afoul of most business executives' wishes for a hands-off policy for the government to insist on strict procedures regarding annual financial reporting, but the enormous losses to the public when companies scam investors and then collapse demonstrate the need for government involvement. The government is thus in a precarious position: It must not allow industry and business to run amok, yet it cannot regulate so strictly that it stifles innovation, jobs, and profits (Berge, 1940).

Governmental regulation of business is primarily administrative in nature (Cullen et al., 2015; Shover & Scroggins, 2009). Most occupation-related crimes are not listed in criminal codes and instead are embedded within the administrative codes and civil laws governing business conduct (Geis & Meier, 1977). Generally, the "police" who enforce the law are not police at all—they are regulatory agencies and inspectors who do things like visit factories' premises to evaluate the facilities' physical safety, audit financial records to ensure accuracy, and analyze firms' requests for mergers in terms of their projected impacts on consumers. Agencies include, but are not limited to, the Federal Trade Commission, the Securities and Exchange Commission, the National Labor Relations Board, the Public Company Accounting Oversight Board, and the National Highway Transportation Safety Administration. The inspectors and auditors employed by these agencies are decisively regulatory in both their stated mission and their role orientation; they see their purpose as one of catching problems in advance so that those matters can be quickly corrected. They do not view their job as one of punishing violations or violators (Carson, 1970).

Administrative efforts to leverage compliance often take the form of warnings in which the inspector or auditor documents a violation and offers a window of time in which the company must proffer a corrective solution. If the problem is satisfactorily addressed, the matter is closed. Penalties play no part in this scheme, nor is there generally cause for the inspector to initiate formal legal action against the company or any employee. In fact, inspectors see formal action as draconian and counterproductive because the system relies so heavily on the maintenance of a good working relationship between businesses and oversight agencies (Braithwaite, 1982). Formal actions are slow and costly; informal notifications can result in faster corrections. Administrative agencies' work is viewed as more effective and efficient when enforcement is congenial and promotes voluntary compliance (Carson, 1970).

Compliance systems are grounded in proactive oversight by regulatory bodies. In fact, proactive enforcement (random and scheduled inspections, audits, and the like) are key to effective administrative regulation and to preventing small violations from ballooning into significant messes (Braithwaite, 1985; Carson, 1970; Reiss, 1983). A compliance system, then, is only as good as its inspectors. Regulatory agencies must be adequately funded and empowered.

When a violation does end up in court, civil remedies (generally in the form of injunctions and consent decrees) are often preferred over criminal ones; in fact, only a small fraction of WC offenders are charged with criminal offenses (Carson, 1970; Cullen et al., 2015; Levi, 2009; McCormick, 1977) and sentences for those who are convicted tend to be fairly lenient (Levi, 2009). This speaks to the tension between the desire to punish blameworthy wrongs and the need for the government to force companies to cease dangerous practices. It may seem in line with notions of justice to impose a crippling fine on a car company convicted of knowingly prioritizing profits over human lives, but there is also a clear need to have this company immediately stop manufacturing defective products and to fix the products that have already entered the marketplace and pose an imminent threat of harm to consumers. Civil remedies accomplish the latter objective. Those who see merit in a compliance-based system do not necessarily reject criminal penalties, but they may see a criminal charge as more useful if it remains an unpulled lever. The compliance system is more about the threat of punishment than the actual imposition of it (Reiss, 1984). Once the punishment has been delivered, the government no longer has leverage to coerce compliance. Civil remedies allow the government to fashion intricate and wide-reaching plans for reform that will not only help mitigate harm done (e.g., monetary compensation for victims) but will, importantly, prevent future damage (Berge, 1940; Newman, 1958).

Despite its many benefits, compliance systems premised in regulatory regimes and civil remedies lack a critical feature: the stigma of a criminal conviction (Berge, 1940; Chambliss, 1967). Stigma is what separates civil and criminal penalties (Sutherland, 1945). The stigma of criminal conviction may even be more important than the pain of the punishment itself (Berge, 1940). It is one thing to settle a legal matter in court and have to pay a fine and agree to corrective action; it is quite a different matter to walk away branded a criminal. Stigma is an oft-cited rationale for strict application of the criminal law against street offenders, yet it has largely fallen by the wayside in discussions of methods for handling those who commit wrongdoing in the course of their occupation. The absence of stigma helps WC offenders either deny their guilt (Benson, 1985; Shover, 1998) or feel unfairly singled out in an "everybody does it" world of often-shady business transactions (Benson, 1985; Coleman, 1987). Shame is a powerful motivator, but its potential remains untapped in systems grounded in regulation and civil remedies.

DETERRENCE

In contrast to (but not completely at odds with) a compliance-based system is a penalty-based one. Possessing a compliance orientation may lead one to view penalties as signs of failure; after all, the best penalty is one that need not be imposed (Reiss, 1984). The absence of penalties may flow from widespread voluntary conformity with the law and the informal, administrative, or civil negotiations that successfully remedy detected wrong-doing. Viewed in this way, virtually nonexistent criminal sanctions against violators is a good sign. The United States maintains a compliance orientation, yet all available evidence points to the widespread, systemic failure of this approach. Thousands of people are wounded, sickened, killed, and conned each year in acts of corporate malfeasance (Cullen et al., 2015). Civil remedies may be expedient in individual cases, but they do a disservice to the overarching goal of preventing WC harms because they fail to create a meaningful general deterrent (Braithwaite, 1985).

Deterrence-based systems may be uniquely suited to be effective against WC offending because these crimes are instrumental in nature (Coleman, 1987; Shover & Hochstetler, 1998). Instrumental crimes are planned for a specific purpose, such as pecuniary gain. White-collar perpetrators lead what appear on the surface to be respectable, law-abiding lives and have much to lose if their criminality is detected. Those who commit crime in the course of their occupation are plausibly the most deterrable offenders of all (Chambliss, 1967) because of the planning that goes into these crimes and the substantial losses offenders face if detected. That being said, some evidence indicates that prison sentences do not impact offenders' likelihood of recidivism compared to offenders who are not imprisoned, suggesting that specific deterrence might not prevent reoffending among WC offenders who have misbehaved in the past (Weisburd, Waring, & Chayet, 1995). However, there is also reason to believe that repeat WC offenders differ from those who only dabble in these crimes (Weisburd, Waring, & Chayet, 2001), so it is plausible that general deterrence serves a valuable function among all but the most incorrigible business executives. Heterogeneity among perpetrators of all types of crimes means deterrence may be more effective for some groups than others (Apel & Nagin, 2011). High-profile criminal investigations, arrests, and prosecutions carry symbolic and instrumental value in communicating to would-be offenders that the government takes WC crimes seriously and will not hesitate to prosecute and punish (Ivancevich et al., 2003).

Penalty-based systems premised on criminal laws, prosecutions, and punishments face hurdles, however. Four hindrances stand out in particular. First, the criminal law is, by its very nature, reactive. No criminal case can be launched and no conviction obtained absent an identified harm. In WC offending, it can be hard to figure out when a crime has occurred. The detection of wrongdoing is stymied by several factors. The financial market and taxation system are byzantine mazes (Shapiro, 1990), offenders are usually remote from and only indirectly tied to their victims (Levi, 2009; Shover, 1998), and many victims do not learn that they have been defrauded until long after the crime has occurred, if they ever become aware of it (Reiss, 1983; Sutherland, 1945; see also Shover & Scroggins, 2009). Related to this is the fact that the harm must be sufficiently severe to trigger a criminal investigation. Administrative regulators can inspect a factory and order a blocked fire exit be cleared, but criminal investigators can step in only after the inoperable door has caused injury or death.

Second, in cases other than embezzlement and fraud, it can be difficult to prove criminal intent (Braithwaite, 1982; Newman, 1958; Shover, 1998). The technical term for intent is *mens rea* or, translated, a "guilty mind." Intent is the basis for the criminal law;

blameworthiness sits at the fulcrum of the punishment decision for all crimes, including white-collar ones (von Hirsch, 1982). Society punishes the driver who deliberately or recklessly runs over a pedestrian in a crosswalk, not the prudent driver who was legitimately unable to avoid hitting a jaywalker. The outcome is the same (a wounded pedestrian), but the difference in the drivers' levels of culpability transforms them into completely different cases under criminal law. In WC offending, it can be exceedingly difficult to separate *mens rea* from accident, or even to prove that a defendant's actions were anything more than a perceived rational response to market movements and general business practices (Braithwaite, 1982). A discrepancy in financial records could be fraud or merely a sign that the suspect is an inept accountant; a sudden sale of stock right before the price of that stock plunged might be insider trading or simply a lucky guess about the stock's future viability. The civil law offers ways around the vexing matter of intent. The legal doctrines of vicarious liability, affirmative duties, and strict liability all permit authorities to hold a principal actor accountable for negative outcomes even if he or she was not directly involved in the wrongdoing (Reiss, 1983). In criminal court, however, intent is vital and yet often plausibly denied, even to the point of WC offenders themselves being convinced they did nothing wrong (Benson, 1985).

Third, it can be dauntingly laborious to build a criminal case against suspected WC offenders. Little is known about WC offenders' law-breaking techniques, but what evidence is available suggests they generally work alone or in very small groups (Benson, 1985; Daly, 1989). Excepting those officers and agents who work in financial-crimes units and have developed expertise, police are not equipped with the technology and skills necessary to investigate suspected WC offenses (Levi, 2009; Shover & Scroggins, 2009). Because of this, enforcers of the criminal law lean heavily on the corporation itself to aid in the investigation. When the corporation is the victim (as in the case of crimes such as embezzlement), this cooperation may be forthcoming and the working relationship between police and the corporation smooth and productive. When the corporation itself, or its executives, is the target of the investigation, cooperation is harder to gain. This is a situation unique from street crimes. "Regular" street criminals (those who commit burglary, auto thefts, robberies, and the like) are indeed an important source of their own downfall; police and prosecutors depend heavily upon confessions from suspects to obtain convictions. But the average street offender need not provide extensive documentation of emails, financial transfers, and tax returns in order to be convicted of a crime. By contrast, WC investigations require the defendant corporation or executives to assist in their own prosecution (Shapiro, 1990), which, of course, they are not terribly enthusiastic about doing. They also have an informational advantage over police and prosecutors and may be able to conceal evidence and thus undercut the criminal case against them, making conviction difficult or impossible (Braithwaite, 1982, 1985; Shapiro, 1990).

Finally, criminal penalties can be hard to apply. It is difficult to penalize corporations without imposing collateral damage that ends up harming innocent people. Corporations cannot be put in prison, so the seemingly most rational punishment is a fine. But there is nothing stopping a corporation from raising its prices and passing the fine onto consumers and stockholders (Sutherland, 1945). A steep fine could send a company into bankruptcy, whereupon tens or hundreds of people will lose their jobs (Braithwaite, 1982; Shover, 1998). Imprisoning a mine operator or supervisor whose breach of safety standards caused workers' deaths may satisfy the public's sense of justice, but it does not protect the lives of other workers still vulnerable to the ongoing danger (Braithwaite, 1985). The extent to which the criminal law can be put to good use in a corporate or industry setting depends entirely on the government's ability to craft criminal codes and punishment schedules that are utilitarian, meaning they do not merely penalize past conduct but also prevent future harm (Braithwaite, 1982) and are not easily negated by transferring them to innocent parties.

Another reason criminal penalties can be difficult to levy against businesses, particularly large corporations, is that financial giants are integral to the nation's economy because of the way the marketplace is structured. The case of Lehman Brothers is instructive. Lehman was a too-big-to-fail financial-services firm heavily involved in the subprime-mortgage lending that caused the 2008 recession. Just as the housing bubble reached untenable heights, Lehman fell under suspicion of irregular financial practices and subsequently lost clients and stock. Although no criminal charges were brought, the losses Lehman sustained forced it into bankruptcy. The federal government considered bailing Lehman out, but decided against it. The massive bankruptcy triggered a rapid downward spiral into market chaos. Upon realizing the dangers of allowing enormous corporations to fail, the government bailed out other embattled ones or brokered deals for stronger companies to buy insolvent ones and avoid bankruptcy (Wessel, 2010). The U.S. economy (indeed, the global economy) consists of dense networks between companies, meaning the government cannot levy criminal penalties that would risk sending a corporation into a financial tailspin and shooting out potentially severe ripple effects.

These challenges to the use of the criminal law in the realm of WC offending are not necessarily defensible justifications for failing to create or enforce meaningful criminal penalties for WC actions that harm people, property, and the environment. The hurdles to criminal investigation, prosecution, and penalization of WC offenders are often cited as excuses for not engaging the criminal law more rigorously; however, the compliance system has been the default since the industrial revolution and a true penalty-oriented system has never been tried, so it is premature to say that there is no hope for such an approach. Law enforcement has historically been sporadic and inconsistent, and it is reasonable to believe that most of the individuals and businesses engaged in illegal behavior do so with impunity (Sutherland, 1945; see Cullen et al., 2015 for a review). In the following section, we will review the evidence suggesting promising methods of strengthening the criminal law and its enforcement to effect a deterrence-based system with the goal of reducing white-collar offending.

THEORIES OF WHITE-COLLAR OFFENDING: IMPLICATIONS FOR LAW AND POLICY

This section is structured differently than in other chapters in this book, the latter of which are titled "The Empirical Status" of the policy at hand. Here, however, we must change course for a simple reason: The research on WC-policy effectiveness is threadbare

(Shover & Scroggins, 2009) and conclusions are tentative and untrustworthy. The primary cause of this situation is an absence of sound data (Shover, 1998; Shover & Scroggins, 2009). There is no Uniform Crime Report for white-collar offending. Victim surveys are at times of some utility, but suffer serious weaknesses that undermine their usefulness (Shover & Scroggins, 2009), such as victims' sense of shame that they allowed themselves to be taken advantage of (Shover, 1998) or their lack of awareness of having been a victim at all (Reiss, 1983; Sutherland, 1945). Sometimes there is no identifiable victim, such as in the case of antitrust violations (Newman, 1958). Certainly, nobody would know if they have been the "victim" of an illegal corporate merger. The basic fact is that we are unable to estimate with much accuracy how much WC crime there is or how often the different WC crime types occur. It is clear that criminal cases against, and convictions of, WC offenders are rare (Levi, 2009). Official actions taken against corporations and their employees are more likely to be civil than criminal (Shover, 1998) even where the government could pursue criminal charges (Sutherland, 1945). The mere fact that a case winds up in civil court, however, is not proof that it could not have been sent to criminal court instead; the standard in defining crime is not whether someone *was* convicted but, rather, whether he or she *could have been* (Cullen et al., 2015; Newman, 1958; Sutherland, 1940, 1945). It would be unwise to form a data set of the offenders who have been handled in criminal court, because those who are treated as criminal violators are a small subset of the total population. There is no telling how these offenders might systematically differ from those who are dealt with in civil court instead of the criminal arena. The data simply do not exist to permit high-quality investigations into these matters. Compiling such data is possible, but would be an onerous undertaking requiring researchers to acquire, sift through, and catalogue copious quantities of records from multiple agencies (Geis & Meier, 1977; Sutherland, 1940.

Additionally, research about organizational and occupational offending is minimal, and evaluations of specific criminal laws are virtually nonexistent. In spite of the efforts of Sutherland and a few others, white-collar crime never made it onto the sociological or criminological main stage (Weisburd et al., 2001). Theories have been proposed as explanations for crimes by businesspeople and organizations, but empirical testing of these theories to determine their validity has not kept pace (Shover & Scroggins, 2009). The shaky understanding of the reasons for white-collar offending renders the quest for effective policy responses akin to shooting in the dark; the solution is hard to find when the reason for the problem is not fully understood. At this point, there is minimal available evidence suggesting the reasons why some white-collar workers abuse their authority and some do not, or the characteristics that differentiate low-level offenders from serious ones (Weisburd et al., 2001).

Fortunately, there is enough theory and empirical evidence to cobble together some proposals for what might work. First and foremost, we need a definition of white-collar offending (Braithwaite, 1985). While categories of certain offenses are helpful (fraud, embezzlement, and so on), the universe of possible harmful acts is too vast to realistically parse into specific, separate offenses. Criminalize one form of swindling, and white-collar offenders will simply switch to some other method that is not (yet) illegal. Probably the most fruitful approach is to weave criminal laws into the array of administrative and civil codes already in effect. The fiduciary duty that agents owe to their principals (Shapiro, 1990), for instance, can form the basis for a criminal law penalizing the violation of that duty. This duty should be interpreted broadly to encompass all forms of trust individuals and the public place in individuals who occupy positions of power. Under such a scheme, it would not matter the specific form the breach of duty took. The investor who misleads clients into buying worthless stocks and the executive who orders the dumping of dangerous chemicals near a town's water supply in order to cut company costs would both be guilty of white-collar offenses because both used their positions to hurt people for pecuniary gain Many WC offenders lurk in the gray area between legal and illegal activity (Passas, 2002). Their actions are questionable and brush up against the outer boundaries of licit business, but they do not cross into plainly illegal territory. A precise, inclusive definition revolving around selfish motives and breaches of trust would unify diverse activities, more clearly draw the line between lawful and unlawful behavior, and have deterrent value.

Second, popular and political will is needed to spell out meaningful penalties and then impose them on offenders. While Sutherland (1945) noted a general public apathy toward this type of offending and contended that this was a main reason why political action was so weak, major scandals in the late 1900s such as Watergate and the Ford Pinto disaster pushed white-collar wrongdoing into the public spotlight, where it has remained. Additionally, although Sutherland's urging of criminologists to envelop white-collar offenders into their study of crime were largely in vain, his writings did appear to help educate the public about white-collar crime and incite some anger toward it (Braithwaite, 1985). The public strongly disapproves of WC offenders whose actions take tolls similar to those of street criminals (Braithwaite, 1982; Cullen, Link, & Polanzi, 1982; Cullen Clark, Mathers, & Cullen, 1983; Holtfreter, van Slyke, Bratton, & Gertz, 2008) and sometimes views WC offenders even more harshly (Rebovich & Kane, 2002). Some public-opinion research shows that citizens think the government should expend as many resources enforcing laws against WC crimes as it spends on street crime (Holtfreter et al., 2008). To the extent that the public at times displays ambivalence about how harshly WC crime should be treated, this may be due to lack of knowledge about the extent and severity of WC offending, rather than to lenient attitudes (Cullen et al., 1983). There is a prevalent tendency, too, for the public to see significant damage inflicted upon people, the planet, and animals as simply the cost of doing business or the price society pays for progress (Frank & Lynch, 1992). Undoubtedly, information distortion (i.e., propaganda) and harm minimization is the doing of industry and business leaders (abetted by sympathetic lawmakers) who control the means of communication and can thereby shape or even dominate the narrative delivered to the public (see Sutherland, 1945). Likewise, the government's often-flimsy response to this type of crime may also mislead the public into thinking WC crime is uncommon or innocuous (Braithwaite, 1982; Sutherland, 1945). Based on the government's seemingly reluctant use of the criminal law to penalize WC offenders, the public can be forgiven for its hazy grasp of the scale of the damage this misbehavior inflicts on people and the planet. Lawmakers' failure to act decisively cannot be attributed to an absence of public desire for better laws and enforcement. Greater political will is needed and, contrary to much common belief, need not necessarily be political suicide. The current tide of populism washing over the United States, combined with the evidence that people do take WC offending seriously, suggests that politicians could gain an electoral advantage by adding WC crime to their platform agenda (Levi, 2009; see also Cullen et al., 2015).

Third, ramped-up criminal-law enforcement against WC offending and offenders may have a strong deterrence capacity. This type of offending is instrumental, not expressive (Chambliss, 1967), meaning it is carefully planned and committed in anticipation of certain identified rewards; it is not an impulsive act committed in the heat of emotional turmoil (Coleman, 1987). Common academic wisdom presumes these offenders to be rational actors who make offending decisions on the basis of anticipated costs and rewards (Shover & Scroggins, 2009). Because WC offenders map out their crimes, they are sensitive to government actions that increase the certainty and severity of penalties (Shover & Hochstetler, 1998). These offenders also have prized status. Fear of losing their reputations and families may be a powerful disincentive if they perceive a high likelihood of detection. Additionally, the stigma of criminal conviction and punishment could be a deterrent beyond the threat of punishment itself (Benson, 1985). The thought of being branded a criminal and suffering the shame and embarrassment of that label is a powerful deterrent to people who place personal pride in their reputations. The government misses an opportunity when it utilizes the criminal law relatively rarely among the group that is (arguably, at least) the most deterrable (Chambliss, 1967). Ratcheting up the chances of arrest, prosecution, and criminal penalties could reduce WC offending.

Another promising avenue is to make WC crime harder to commit. White-collar offending is borne out of opportunity. People who steal money from their employers or investors do so because they are motivated *and* because they have the access and ability necessary to carry out the scheme (Levi, 2009). WC crime, like street crime, has an opportunity structure (Benson, Madensen, & Eck, 2009). Criminal geographies and spaces are harder to pinpoint in WC offending than in street crimes where the offender and victim physically converge temporally and spatially (Benson et al., 2009; Shover & Hochstetler, 1998). In WC offending, criminal space may be the computer networks linking agents to their principals. A decision to reduce operating costs in a mine by skirting safety regulations might be made in one state, and the resulting injuries might occur in a different state. The physical distance between offenders and victims makes the WC space a harder for police to monitor or to alter in a fashion that makes crime more difficult. It is possible, however, for the government to structure the criminal law in a way that removes some opportunities and incentives for offending. One strategy ties back to the suggestion made earlier to devise useful definitions of white-collar misdeeds that constitute criminal-law violations. Cleaning up the definition would reduce offenders' ability to locate and exploit legal loopholes, while making ethically dubious behavior clearly unlawful rather than allowing it to continue floating in uncertainty. Other methods may involve the use of a combination of criminal and administrative law, such as creating greater distance (and prohibiting ties) between boards of directors and chief executive officers so that these boards can function as truly independent bodies that hold executives accountable (Ivancevich et al., 2003). Compensation for directors' and chief executive officers can also be tied to their performance to encourage everyone to work for the best interests of the company (Schnatterly, 2003). Conflicts of interest can be minimized through various channels, such as the government appointing financial auditors instead of permitting companies to select their own (Levi, 2009).

In some respects, WC crime may be easier to detect than many other types of offenses because potential offenders are identifiable and their crimes predictable (Reiss, 1983). If a company specializes in oil drilling, then chances are any crime it commits will pertain to that activity, such as by cutting corners in quality control and thereby increasing the risk of a spill or fire; likewise, a factory that produces large quantities of waste has an incentive to find ways to cheaply and illegally dispose of these chemicals. Criminal and regulatory enforcement agencies can monitor both potential offenders (the companies) and their potential "victims" (e.g., drilling sites or places where toxic waste could be hidden). Their visibility and predictability open WC offenders up to enhanced government surveillance in a way street crime does not.

Finally, better education of all business executives about the toll WC offenses take on victims could yield crime-prevention effects. Many of these offenders utilize techniques of neutralization to rationalize their crimes. They may paint themselves as the victims of overly demanding work or a cutthroat business culture where profits trump morals (Benson, 1985; Coleman, 1987; Weisburd et al., 2001). Some deny having harmed anyone; they may emphatically distinguish themselves from "regular" criminals by arguing that they never entered someone's home or threatened residents' personal safety. They feel their actions were more distant and thus less harmful (Benson, 1985; see also Copes & Vieraitis, 2009). The problem with this mentality is that WC offending does hurt people. Working- and middle-class citizens may lose their retirement funds. Even those not directly affected can experience the effects of vicarious victimization. White-collar scandals—particularly those in which the perpetrators escape with little or no punishment—demoralize the public and foster widespread distrust in companies, markets, and the economy itself (Braithwaite, 1982; Sutherland, 1940, 1941), lending credence to the cynical proposition that people with money and power can buy immunity from the law (Simon, 2006). The government and business leaders should cultivate a culture of ethics in which it is understood that WC crimes take an enormous toll on society. Additionally, consistent criminal prosecutions and punishments can poke a hole in WC offenders' mental bubble by showing them and the public alike that companies and executives are beholden to the law just like everyone else. A more dedicated effort to criminal-law enforcement may also eventually lead to WC offenders being seen as "real" criminals just like the people who assault and burglarize.

CONCLUSION

This chapter dealt with white-collar offending and discussed promising policy avenues for reducing this form of law violation. We saw that the most pressing matter is the definition of WC offending: Before it can be effectively addressed through policy, this category of offenses requires a clearer and more useful articulation. It might be the case that the term "white-collar crime" has no utility whatsoever and should be thrown out and replaced with a series of more descriptive categories tied directly to certain bad actions taken in the course of one's employment.

This chapter traced the outlines of the history of anti-WC offending legislation, and delved into the two major classes of approaches: compliance and deterrence. The United States currently employs a compliance-oriented approach. Compliance systems are attractive because they are proactive and allow regulatory agencies to force companies to fix smaller problems before they spiral into bigger ones, and to make widespread changes in cases where serious harms occurred. Deterrence-based systems rely on the imposition of penalties to coerce obedience to the law. Penalty systems are well suited for WC offending, because these offenders plan their crimes based on anticipated risks, rewards, and opportunities. Civil remedies allow problems to be fixed and, occasionally, penalties to be levied, but criminal conviction carries a stigma. This shame might be critical to deterring WC offenders.

Criminal law and enforcement is currently insufficient in WC offending. Failure to adequately criminalize certain violations of trust and to consistently punish people who harm society for their own gain generates cynicism and distrust among the citizenry. A legitimate government penalizes all people who threaten the public good, not just a select few. The consistent application of the criminal law in all cases of harms to the public is necessary for any government to prove itself fair, neutral, and just. On this count, the United States has a lot of room for improvement.

DISCUSSION QUESTIONS

1. Many people are dissatisfied with the government's explanations for the relatively infrequent criminal prosecutions of white-collar offenders. They believe that if the government invested more resources, law-enforcement personnel could effectively detect, investigate, and prosecute these crimes, even if the typical investigation was longer and more difficult than those required for street crimes. What do you think? Are white-collar offenses genuinely so clandestine that the government cannot reasonably be expected to prosecute them consistently, or is the rarity of prosecution evidence of policymakers' unwillingness to hold wealthy people accountable for their bad actions? Explain your answer.

2. A sad outcome of many large-scale investment frauds is that thousands of middle- and working-class people lose some or all of their retirement money when the fraud is exposed and the sham company collapses. Most people never recoup their losses because their money was absorbed into company operations and the company is now bankrupt. What should be done about this? Should the government reimburse victims? Should the government require investment companies to have savings accounts or insurance policies to protect investors? Offer some creative policy solutions that would protect small-scale investors whose personal finances depend heavily upon their invested money.

3. A benefit of the compliance-based approach to preventing and correcting white-collar offending is that civil remedies can entail extensive changes and compliance measures. Criminal punishments are more limited. Judges and the government cannot be as creative in crafting criminal penalties as they can be when drawing up civil ones. On the other hand, criminal convictions carry a stigma that can act as an important deterrent; executives do not want that kind of branding on themselves or their companies. Should the government stop relying so greatly on compliance and switch over to an approach that more heavily emphasizes criminal-law enforcement, convictions, and punishment? Or is compliance better because of its flexibility?

Weigh the strengths and weaknesses of each type of approach and decide which one you think has more merit and should be the one the government uses most often. Defend your position.

4. One of the obstacles to assessing the extent of white-collar offending and the effectiveness of the government's policies toward enforcing the law and punishing violators is the lack of reliable data. No governmental agency collects, compiles, and disseminates offending data the same way the FBI collects data on crimes like assaults and burglaries. Private citizens would likely face significant access barriers, so researchers and advocacy groups are limited in their ability to fill this gap in the data. What are the solutions to this? Should the government collect and release these data? Should it find ways to make it easier for private citizens to do so? Propose two or three creative options for resolving the data problem.

CHAPTER 12

HUMAN TRAFFICKING

INTRODUCTION

Humans have been enslaving one another for thousands of years. The emergence of city-states in approximately 7000 BCE introduced the world to the phenomenon of war. When wars were fought, the victors claimed the losers as their spoils. Competition for territory, colonialism, and trade expansion brought groups around the world into conflict with one another. The economies of ancient Greek and Roman societies depended upon slave labor. In the mid-1400s, slavery emerged as a global trade whereby (mostly) European countries sailed to Africa and the Americas to colonize tribal communities and enslave the natives into forced labor or to kidnap mass quantities of them for transport to Europe and its colonies. Christopher Columbus, the revered "discoverer" of the Americas, was the architect of the American slave trade (Loewen, 2007). Indentured servitude was also common in the American colonies and early years of the republic (see O'Connell Davidson, 2010 for a review).

The gradual global abolition of slavery took place over the course of several centuries and ultimately culminated in international criminalization of forced labor. The ban on using humans as chattel did not, however, eliminate the demand for cheap labor obtained through exploitation and coercion. Economic globalization and widening wealth gaps between the rich and the poor throughout the world generated incentives for poor migrants to seek new horizons, thus creating opportunities for predators and unscrupulous employers to take advantage of these vulnerable people. Human trafficking arose as an international black market.

This chapter discusses what human trafficking is (and is not) and the laws and policies used domestically and internationally to combat it. We will organize anti-trafficking efforts as being grounded in either criminal justice or in human rights. Effective anti-trafficking policies and enforcement require international cooperation and multilateral actions. We therefore situate the discussion as one in which we consider the role the United States currently plays on the global stage and the ways in which it should improve its approach both domestically and abroad.

DEFINING HUMAN TRAFFICKING AND THE ROLE OF CONSENT

Human trafficking is a direct outgrowth of globalization and migration, particularly labor migration (Chacón, 2006; Cho, 2012; Feingold, 2005). As one scholar put it, "More often than not, trafficking is labor migration gone horribly wrong" (Chuang, 2006a, p. 138). Wealth is increasingly concentrated among a small number of countries and individuals, creating sharp disparities between the rich and the poor both between nations and within them (Chuang, 2006a). The quest for jobs is a pervasive pull factor drawing hopeful aspirants to certain countries in search of greater economic opportunity.

There are also several push factors that drive many migrants away from their homes. Migrants exiting impoverished nations around the world are commonly fleeing starvation, desperate for survival (Chuang, 2006a; Ghosh, 1998). The governments of their native countries may be steeped in corruption and incompetent at providing even the most basic public services or protections (Agbu, 2003). Female migrants are frequently trying to escape gender-based oppression, employment discrimination, and violence (Chuang, 2006a). Climate change is wreaking havoc upon local ecosystems around the world. It is upending agriculture, drying up water supplies in some areas while flooding other communities, and making many populated lands uninhabitable. The consequences of environmental damage are hitting poor nations and communities hard because they lack the resources to absorb the shock. Experts believe the number of environmental refugees to be in the millions worldwide (Brown, 2008). Wars and ethnic or religious conflicts around the world generate untold numbers of displaced and persecuted people, including children (Rathgeber, 2002). Many of the people who get labeled "migrants" are actually refugees, even if they do not meet international definitions that would qualify them for formal refugee status.

Migrants and refugees are vulnerable to human traffickers. They might be kidnapped outright, lured to specific locations with false promises and then imprisoned, or fall into the hands of someone they mistakenly believed was a human smuggler. Most trafficking victims taken across national borders started off as voluntary migrants (Chacón, 2006; Gozdziak, 2012). Trafficking victims are subjected to conditions ranging from inhumane to unimaginable, with many of them experiencing deplorable working conditions, crippling on-the-job injuries, rape and other sex abuse, and torture (e.g., U.S. Department of State, 2016). Women are particularly imperiled because they have fewer options in more formalized segments of the economy (e.g., field labor) and so often end up in low-visibility jobs like domestic work and prostitution (Chuang, 2006a; Rathgeber, 2002).

Defining human trafficking is a persistent roadblock to domestic and international efforts to eliminate this problem and has stymied multilateral collaboration (Doezema, 2002; Raymond, 2002; Weitzer, 2015). One source of confusion is the qualifying labor conditions. Sweat shops, child labor, and other dangerous and exploitative practices may be illegal but do not necessarily constitute trafficking. The International Labour Organization (ILO) defines forced labor as "All work or service which is extracted from any person under the menace of any penalty and for which the said person has not offered himself voluntarily" (ILO, 2014, p. 3). The definition used by the United States and the United Nations (UN) do not require geographic movement; trafficking can occur even if offenders do not relocate their victims (Weitzer, 2015).

It is often difficult to separate trafficking from smuggling (Salt & Stein, 1997), voluntary prostitution (Capous Desyllas, 2007), and labor migration (Gozdziak, 2012). The fact that most trafficking victims originally started off voluntarily adds further confusion to the definition. Many countries maintain that victim consent is irrelevant to the definition of trafficking, while the U.S. insists that only those who were involuntary from the very beginning qualify for protection (Chacón, 2006). The distinction between trafficking victims and voluntary migrants—even those working in difficult or exploitative conditions—is of material importance. Governments that interfere with voluntary labor under the guise of trafficking enforcement face opposition from individuals and communities dependent upon local economic arrangements for their livelihoods (Gozdziak, 2012).

TRAFFICKING PREVALENCE AND VICTIMS

The true prevalence of trafficking is unknown because operations are shadowy, many victims are never found, and a large portion of those who escape or are released do not report their victimization to authorities. Definitional problems also preclude accurate counts. The ILO (2014) estimates that there are approximately 21 million people held in slave-like conditions. Most are in the private economy, with roughly 68 percent in labor roles (agriculture, construction, mining, and so on) and 22 percent being sexually exploited (such as forced prostitution). Women and girls constitute 55 percent of forced-labor victims, and 74 percent of victims are adults. The Asia-Pacific region contains the largest number, followed in descending order by Africa, Latin America and the Caribbean, developed Western countries, Central and Eastern Europe, and the Middle East. Within the U.S., metropolitan areas are hubs for commercial sex industries and are therefore attractive to sex traffickers (Newton, Mulcahy, & Martin, 2008; see also Cole & Sprang, 2015). Because of the flaws in the data, it is not possible to conduct a fully reliable state-by-state analysis; however, based on one database of reported incidents, California ranks highest, followed by Texas and Florida (Ali, 2017). New York City's large immigrant population is thought to contain a substantial number of trafficking victims as well (Pierce, 2014). Border states (California and Texas) and those with significant international activity (Florida and New York) are prime areas for transporting smuggled and trafficked people.

According to U.S. records of trafficking cases brought to the attention of law enforcement, 80 percent of known trafficking incidents involve sex trafficking and about 10 percent are labor trafficking (e.g., Feingold, 2005). Approximately two out of every five cases reported to federal task forces entail sex trafficking of minors. Victims of sex trafficking are most likely to be black or white, and victims of labor trafficking are more likely to be Hispanic or Asian. Sixty-two percent of known sex traffickers are male, and 48 percent of identified labor traffickers are Hispanic (Banks & Kyckelhahn, 2011). These numbers are based only on known offenses and likely over represent sex trafficking and underrepresent labor trafficking. Police and prosecutors are more likely to investigate sex trafficking than other forms of this crime (Farrell, Owens, & McDevitt, 2014; Farrell & Pfeffer, 2014) and frequently equate human trafficking with sex trafficking and prostitution

(Farrell, Pfeffer, & Bright, 2015; see also Capous Desyllas, 2007). The preoccupation with sex trafficking (and concomitant downplaying of labor trafficking) occurs in other countries, as well (Blanchette, Silva, & Bento, 2013).

IS HUMAN TRAFFICKING A FORM OF ORGANIZED CRIME?

It is frequently presumed that trafficking is conducted by tightly organized, international cartels (Feingold, 2005), but the reality is that "trafficking involves mostly 'disorganized crime': individuals or small groups linked on an ad hoc basis… Traffickers are as varied as the circumstances of their victims" (Feingold, 2005, p. 28; see also Zhang, 2016). These individuals and groups are globally connected, but only loosely associated, and often traffic in other illegal goods such as weapons and narcotics (Agbu, 2003; Salt & Stein, 1997). Complicity on the part of corrupt police officers and border-control agents is common (Agbu, 2003; Feingold, 2005; Rathgeber, 2002). Family members sometimes serve as facilitators (Gozdziak, 2012). The *modus operandi* most popular among traffickers varies by nation and region, and lawful business entities can become unwitting accomplices, such as airlines that unknowingly transport victims (Salt & Stein, 1997). Some domestic trafficking entails no international travel, such as when women are forced into prostitution by boyfriends and husbands (Raymond, 2002).

Assisted migration is a booming transnational business with both legal and illegal elements. Any given organization might simultaneously facilitate lawful migration, illegally smuggle people across borders, and traffic humans. Salt and Stein (1997) proposed a theoretical model dividing commercial migration (legal and illegal) into three stages: mobilization; en route activities; and insertion and integration. During mobilization, migrants are recruited and the logistical groundwork is laid for their transport. En route activities are the steps taken to move the migrants within countries and across borders. Some are planned in advance (e.g., the route to be traveled) and others are unanticipated (e.g., a newly fortified border crossing). Insertion and integration occur once migrants have arrived in destination countries. This requires the existence of local agents already embedded in the destination country. Trafficking may begin at any stage; frequently, facilitators hold migrants captive upon arriving in the destination country under the auspices of making them pay for their journey (Campana, 2016). Large international organizations might coordinate activities in all three stages, while smaller local or international groups might only perform a single designated task (Salt & Stein, 1997).

There is no agreed-upon definition of organized crime (Finckenauer, 2005), which undoubtedly accounts for part of the confusion about whether trafficking is a form of this type of enterprise. The Federal Bureau of Investigation (FBI) defines transnational organized crime as:

> Those self-perpetuating associations of individuals who operate transnationally for the purpose of obtaining power, influence, and monetary and/or commercial gains, wholly or in part by illegal means, while protecting their activities through a pattern of corruption and/or violence, or while protecting their illegal activities through a transnational organizational structure and the exploitation of transnational commerce or communication mechanisms (FBI, n.d.).

The FBI's description likely applies to some of the groups involved in trafficking, but trafficking operations span too broad an array of people and operations to be accurately encapsulated within this relatively narrow definitional framework. It is more appropriate to say that organized criminal groups sometimes participate in trafficking than that trafficking is itself a type of organized crime.

This is not to imply that human trafficking lacks organization; to the contrary, it appears patterned. Plans, affiliations, and prior experience are all required to carry out these operations. Trafficking seems to conform to the model of crime as scripted. Crime scripts are the "complete sequence[s] of instrumental actions preceding, including, and following the defining act" (Cornish & Clarke, 2012, p. 47). There are end goals and several subgoals along the way that must be met in order to reach the final objectives (Cornish & Clarke, 2012; see also Salt & Stein, 1997). There are also costs involved, which can fluctuate at each stage depending on circumstances (Campana, 2016), such as whether traffickers encounter border guards who must be bribed. The scripted, cost-laden nature of trafficking is a weakness that could be usefully leveraged by smart policy and law enforcement.

HUMAN-TRAFFICKING POLICIES AND THEIR ORIGINS

There are two general lenses through which human trafficking can be viewed: criminal justice and human rights. The criminal-justice response emphasizes the apprehension and punishment of traffickers, while the human-rights orientation focuses on protecting vulnerable populations by addressing the root causes of trafficking (namely, labor migration and conditions giving rise to mass numbers of refugees). The two approaches are not mutually exclusive and would ideally operate symbiotically (Agbu, 2003). In practice, however, the rights orientation has been superseded by the punitive one (Chacón, 2006; Chuang, 2006a, 2006b). Laws and policies worldwide rest more upon popular assumptions and myths about trafficking than on sound empirical evidence (Blanchette et al., 2013; Weitzer, 2015).

From its inception, the public discourse about human trafficking has been wrapped up with arguments over whether prostitution should or should not be legal. In the so-called "white slave trade," white women and girls were allegedly abducted and forced into commercial sex work. Debates in the late 1800s and early 1900s revolved around whether criminalizing prostitution would end this practice (Capous Desyllas, 2007), and from there the discussion evolved into a dispute over consent. Feminist activists argued that true consent to participate in sex work is impossible because the patriarchy oppresses women and is inherently coercive. These abolitionists wanted governments to outlaw prostitution (Doezema, 2002). The abolitionists ran up against those who believed it insulted women to flatly deny their ability to consent to sex work and reasoned that legalized prostitution allows governments to monitor the industry and protect women's safety (Capous Desyllas, 2007). France, for instance, maintained a regulationist position and helped push through agreements in 1904 and 1910 emphasizing that the distinction between prostitution and "white slavery" turns on the matter of consent.

Ultimately, the regulationists lost to the abolitionists. In the United States, Congress passed the Alien Prostitution Importation Act in 1895, outlawing the importation of women from other countries for purposes of engaging in sex work (Chacón, 2006), and the

White Slave Traffic Act in 1910, which prohibited unmarried women from interstate travel conducted for immoral purposes and banned interracial sexual relationships (Saunders & Soderlund, 2003). Both of these laws ostensibly protected women from slave-like exploitation in the sex industry, but in reality reflected an interweaving of moral panic about the perceived social evils of prostitution with racist and anti-immigrant sentiments (Capous Desyllas, 2007; Chacón, 2006; Saunders & Soderlund, 2003).

In 1933, the *International Convention for the Suppression of the Traffic in Women* criminalized the international recruitment and transport of female sex workers irrespective of their consent. European countries and the United States also passed their own legislation banning people from profiting off of prostitution. Contrary to their stated goal of protecting women from pimps and others who exploit them, the new laws merely drove prostitution underground and increased the perils to women in the sex trade (Doezema, 2002; Feingold, 2005). There is no solid evidence as to whether criminalizing prostitution reduces sex trafficking or whether legalizing it increases the demand for trafficked women (Cho, Dreher, & Neumayer, 2013; Feingold, 2005).

The 1949 UN *Convention on the Suppression of Trafficking in Persons and the Exploitation of the Prostitution of Others* doubled down on the 1933 Convention's abolitionist stance. Despite being couched in language touting prostitution as a violation of human dignity, the 1949 Convention further restricted prostitutes' ability to work together in groups for protection or seek legal redress for breaches of their legal rights. These standards were used as models for many nations' domestic prostitution laws (Doezema, 2002). Human trafficking then receded from the global agenda for nearly five decades (Chuang, 2006b).

Trafficking reemerged as an issue in the late 1990s, leading to two important actions in 2000. First was the UN's *Protocol to Prevent, Suppress and Punish Trafficking in Persons especially Women and Children* (also known as the Palermo Protocol; hereinafter referred to as the Protocol). This was the first major, international agreement since the 1949 Convention and reflected a new, fragile agreement among nations (Chuang, 2006b). The Protocol defines human trafficking (Article 3) as:

(a) "Trafficking in persons" shall mean the recruitment, transportation, transfer, harbouring or receipt of persons, by means of the threat or use of force or other forms of coercion, of abduction, of fraud, of deception, of the abuse of power or of a position of vulnerability or of the giving or receiving of payments or benefits to achieve the consent of a person having control over another person, for the purpose of exploitation. Exploitation shall include, at a minimum, the exploitation of the prostitution of others or other forms of sexual exploitation, forced labour or services, slavery or practices similar to slavery, servitude or the removal of organs;

(b) The consent of a victim of trafficking in persons to the intended exploitation set forth in subparagraph (a) of this article shall be irrelevant where any of the means set forth in subparagraph (a) have been used;

(c) The recruitment, transportation, transfer, harbouring or receipt of a child for the purpose of exploitation shall be considered "trafficking in persons" even if this does not involve any of the means set forth in subparagraph (a) of this article;

(d) "Child" shall mean any person under eighteen years of age.

The Protocol expressly rejects consent as a factor that could obviate someone's claim that she or he has been the victim of trafficking. This distinction between voluntary prostitution and coerced sex work was somewhat tepid (Doezema, 2002), but nonetheless enraged anti-prostitution groups worldwide (Raymond, 2002). There have been instances in which U.S. police failed to take action against traffickers running prostitution rings because the women originally consented to being smuggled into the country and only afterward realized they were prisoners. Watering down the consent–coercion distinction can help protect women in situations like this (Raymond, 2002). On the other hand, the Protocol's failure to assertively separate sex trafficking from prostitution paved the way for nations to enact laws curtailing women's freedom of movement and to deport female migrants found to be involved in sex work (voluntary or not) under the guise of anti-trafficking efforts (Doezema, 2002).

The Protocol is rooted in a criminal-justice orientation and stresses international information sharing, extradition agreements, and law-enforcement communication. Preventing trafficking by addressing social and economic inequities is framed as something that nations should "endeavor" to do (Chuang, 2006a, p. 148). The Protocol stresses the protection of victims (Raymond, 2002), but does not offer immunity from criminal prosecution to trafficking victims who may engage in prostitution, illegal migration, or other offenses they are forced to commit (Chuang, 2006a).

The second major action in 2000 was the U.S.' Victims of Trafficking and Violence Protection Act (also known as the Trafficking Victims Protection Act or TVPA; reauthorized in 2003). The TVPA, like the Protocol, adopts the view of trafficking as a crime problem, not a human-rights problem. The TVPA admonishes nations to tend to victims' needs and includes a comprehensive set of policies for giving foreign victims rescued in this country temporary or even permanent residency (Chuang, 2006b; Farrell & Cronin, 2015). Providing for victim services, however, is not the same as adopting a rights-centered orientation. The TVPA is silent as to the role of social, economic, gender, and environmental inequality in promoting both trafficking and the circumstances that furnish traffickers with a steady supply of victims (e.g., oppression, famine). The TVPA (Section 103) offers a definition of trafficking notably absent of reference to consent:

(8) SEVERE FORMS OF TRAFFICKING IN PERSONS.—The term "severe forms of trafficking in persons" means—

   (A) sex trafficking in which a commercial sex act is induced by force, fraud, or coercion, or in which the person induced to perform such act has not attained 18 years of age; or

   (B) the recruitment, harboring, transportation, provision, or obtaining of a person for labor or services, through the use of force, fraud, or coercion for the purpose of subjection to involuntary servitude, peonage, debt bondage, or slavery.

(9) SEX TRAFFICKING.—The term "sex trafficking" means the recruitment, harboring, transportation, provision, or obtaining of a person for the purpose of a commercial sex act.

Two elements of the TVPA stand out. First, it classifies voluntary prostitution as sex trafficking, something the Protocol explicitly did not do because there is not an international consensus that countries should outlaw prostitution (Chuang, 2006a). The TVPA's linkage of prostitution with sex trafficking and severe human trafficking also complicates prostitution and trafficking enforcement by local police agencies (Farrell & Cronin, 2015). Its focus on sex trafficking is problematic, moreover, because most trafficking victims are in other labor arrangements such as domestic work and agriculture (Feingold, 2005; ILO, 2014; see also Chacón, 2006). Although the U.S. Department of State recently declared that it no longer considers voluntary prostitution to be a form of trafficking irrespective of a country's prostitution laws (U.S. Department of State, 2010), the TVPA's affirmation of the abolitionist position sets a detrimental example for other countries crafting their own trafficking legislation (Blanchette et al., 2013).

Second, the TVPA's enforcement mechanism is the use of unilateral sanctions against countries it declares violate its minimum standards for addressing trafficking (according to the U.S. definition). The United States can withdraw its nonhumanitarian, nontrade related aid from noncompliant countries. The United States is an enormous source of aid to many poor nations, so this threat is significant. The TVPA's sanctioning regime amounted to the United States proclaiming itself the "global sheriff on trafficking," forcing nations around the world to conform to its definition of trafficking and standards for eliminating it (Chuang, 2006b, p. 439).

Pursuant to the TVPA, the State Department publishes annual Trafficking in Persons (TIP) reports in which it describes the current status of trafficking globally and classifies countries into three tiers. Tier 1 contains those countries fully in compliance with the TVPA, Tier 2 includes those that deviate somewhat but are demonstrably addressing the problem, and Tier 3 is reserved for those that are out of compliance and doing nothing about it. Countries in Tier 3 are considered for cuts to their nonhumanitarian, nontrade related aid (U.S. Department of State, 2016).

At the same time it was pursuing international anti-trafficking strategies, the federal government tasked local law-enforcement agencies with being the front line of domestic efforts and poured $80 million into training officers and supporting multiagency task forces. In 2004, the U.S. Department of Justice promulgated a "Model State Anti-Trafficking Criminal Statute," suggesting language for states to use when crafting their own legislation. All fifty states subsequently passed laws criminalizing trafficking and establishing enforcement mechanisms (Farrell, 2014), although these laws vary widely (Farrell et al., 2014) and do not contain well-specified enforcement provisions to guide police and prosecutors in investigating and bringing charges against suspected traffickers (Farrell, 2014; Farrell et al., 2014).

EXAMINING THE RATIONALES

This section characterizes anti-trafficking policies as being either criminal-justice oriented or human-rights oriented and examines them within a framework casting trafficking as a direct result of migration done either in search of better economic opportunities or to escape governmental, social, or environmental crises. Then we turn to a critical analysis of Western nations being at the forefront of defining trafficking (and deciding whether or not the definition includes voluntary prostitution) and concluding what to do about the problem with little or no input from developing and impoverished nations. While the leadership is certainly laudable, an unfortunate outcome has been the disenfranchisement of undeveloped nations, and a perceived "Western bias" that can undermine global collaboration in anti-trafficking policies.

THE CRIMINAL-JUSTICE RESPONSE: PUNISHING THE TRAFFICKERS

Worldwide, the primary response to trafficking has been to treat it as a crime-control problem and intensify law enforcement and border security. Countries have placed far less priority on helping and protecting victims and still less on preventing trafficking by addressing migration motivations and laws (Chacón, 2006). To be sure, a victim-rights angle exists; the State Department's 2016 TIP report heavily emphasizes protecting vulnerable groups, avoiding misguided prosecution of trafficking victims, and helping victims deal with the trauma of their experiences (U.S. Department of State, 2016). Even efforts to assist and protect victims, though, are reactive and require that trafficking occur before the government takes action.

Punishment advocates argue that governments should fight trafficking through a massive law-enforcement campaign involving strict scrutiny of international travelers and their vehicles, undercover stings, and the like. This wide sweep, however, does not deter migrants and instead only makes the journey more perilous. To avoid border crossings, migrants and refugees take to tumultuous seas in makeshift rafts and overcrowded vessels (O'Connell Davidson, 2010). In the Mediterranean alone, 3,800 lost their lives in 2016 and 3,771 the year before that (Smith-Spark, 2016). Migrants crossing the Mexican border into the United States avoid security checkpoints and physical barriers by altering their routes and attempting to pass through terrain that is more dangerous (Chacón, 2006). Because of the increased risk, border-enforcement measures make migrants more dependent upon smugglers, many of whom are traffickers in disguise (Chacón, 2006; Chuang, 2006a; Feingold, 2005).

The criminal-justice response relies heavily on victims in prosecutions because there is generally little or no physical evidence. Without victims explaining the situation, law enforcement cannot do much (Chuang, 2006a; Farrell et al., 2016). Victims might be expected to testify during trials, too, if defendants refuse to plead guilty. Victims, though, are often uncooperative. One reason for this arises from the complicated relationships they can have with their abusers (Farrell, DeLateur, Owens, & Fahy, 2016). There is a counterintuitive connection (called Stockholm Syndrome) that can form over the course of an extended period of physical or psychological bondage, such as in cases of domestic violence (Graham, Rawlings, & Rimini, 1988) or child sexual abuse (Jülich, 2005). Trafficking victims describe incidents that may seem bizarre to outsiders. One victim of sex trafficking reported that after she was arrested for prostitution, her pimp bailed her out (Alvarez, 2016). Victims suffering from psychological distortions or manipulations may be unwilling to help authorities compile cases against their former captors. Another cause of victims' reluctance is that many are undocumented immigrants. They might have voluntarily and knowingly entered the country illegally or overstayed temporary visas. Some are legal residents, but have no way of proving it because their captors stole their documents. Their actual or apparent illegal status dissuades them from coming forward (Chuang, 2006a).

Lacking voluntary cooperation from victims, law-enforcement officials often turn to coercion. Police frequently arrest victims to prevent them from fleeing and to leverage them into testifying (Farrell et al., 2016). The TVPA provides for T visas, which allow victims meeting the TVPA's definition of severe trafficking to obtain temporary or permanent residency if they help law enforcement build a case against their captors. Victims' family members may also be eligible for T visas (U.S. Department of State, 2016). Other countries offer similar deals. Victims applying for T visas have several administrative and security hurdles, including the burden of proving that they would be in serious danger if they returned to their country of origin. Congress allows up to 5,000 T visas to be issued annually (U.S. Citizenship and Immigration Services, n.d.). The vast majority of the yearly allotment goes unused (Chacón, 2006). In 2015, for instance, the Department of Homeland Security issued T visas to 610 victims and 694 family members; in 2014, those numbers were 613 and 788, respectively (U.S. Department of State, 2016). Residency options like the T visa are commonly used to coerce victims into cooperating with law enforcement (Chuang, 2006a). Victim-advocacy groups attribute the paltry issuance of T visas to law-enforcement personnel's failure to submit applications on victims' behalf (U.S. Department of State, 2016).

For perpetrators, human trafficking is a low-risk, high-reward crime (Agbu, 2003; Feingold, 2005). Labor laws in the United States enable trafficking by stripping undocumented migrants of rights and allowing executives—largely through the widespread practice of subcontracting—to deny knowledge of their companies' use of undocumented workers (Chacón, 2006). There is minimal risk for companies to force labor from illegal or undocumented immigrants, since the government's only response is to deport the workers back to their countries of origin. Facilitators who move migrants and victims across borders likewise earn enormous sums (Salt & Stein, 1997), as do the captors who hire victims out for labor and prostitution. The global profits from forced labor are roughly $32 billion annually (ILO, 2014). Deterrence research shows that the promise of a lucrative payoff looms large in offenders' decision-making calculus (Decker, Wright, & Logie, 1993), so profits from trafficking are attractive to the criminal element and unethical company owners.

Traffickers also enjoy relative impunity. Out of the estimated 21 million trafficking victims worldwide (ILO, 2014), there were only 77,823 victims identified and a mere 18,930 prosecutions (resulting in 6,609 convictions) of suspected traffickers in 2015. These numbers do represent marked increases over previous years (U.S. Department of State, 2016), but remain well below what would be needed to create a credible threat of punishment. Criminal sanctions and victim protection are vital elements of an effective policy response, but they cannot stand alone. We turn now to examine the potential utility of a rights-based approach.

THE HUMAN-RIGHTS RESPONSE: PREVENTING TRAFFICKING

As noted previously, human trafficking is entwined with migration. There is both a "push" side to migration (the harsh conditions that give rise to migrants' wish to leave their countries of origin) and a "pull" side (the features of destination countries that make them attractive to migrants). The strongest push and pull factors pertain to the economies and political stability of origin and destination countries. The flow of migrants begins in undeveloped and underdeveloped countries with flagging economies, systemic governmental corruption, and, often, endemic oppression of women, and it ends in developed nations with strong demand for manual labor in industries such as agriculture, mining, and manufacturing (Agbu, 2003; Cho, 2012). Many poor countries encourage emigration because workers send money home to their families and these remittances subsidize these nations' economies (Chuang, 2006a).

The human-rights approach involves addressing the needs of origin countries. This reflects a macrolevel view of governments and institutions that can affect migrant flow, rather than a microlevel emphasis on the migrants themselves (see Salt & Stein, 1997). Instead of eliminating aid to troubled nations, the United States and other strong nations could invest in struggling countries' economies, help them broker peace and trade deals, and assist them in eliminating sectarian violence and religious, gender, or racial persecution. For instance, the West African nation of Mauritania—notorious for its flagrant use of slavery—finally held free elections in 2007 and saw slavery abolished, only to suffer a military coup the following year and see the practice reinstated. The U.S. and France both heavily subsidize this small, poor country, yet neither have forced change (Bales, 2012). Under a human-rights approach, aid and other assistance would be strategically offered (or withheld) pursuant to a nation adhering to international laws against slavery. A human-rights approach would shift resources from border security and strict immigration policies toward alleviating the push factors (Chuang, 2006b). This reorientation could dramatically reduce the number of at-risk people and traffickers' ability to exploit them.

UNILATERAL SANCTIONS VERSUS INTERNATIONAL COLLABORATION

Globalization means nations need ways of holding one another accountable. In all but the most extreme circumstances, military aggression is not considered an acceptable means of conflict resolution. Economic sanctions are now the globally endorsed method for settling disputes (Miyagawa, 2016). Sanctions, however, are complicated by the power imbalance that exists on the world stage. Wealthier (mostly Western) nations routinely set the global economic, political, and human-rights agendas. When economic sanctions are applied by the West, developing countries regularly reject them as imperialistic and illegitimate (Cleveland, 2001). Treating developing nations more like chastised children than equal partners chills international relations and discourages cooperation. Economic sanctions, moreover, have no effect on humanitarian crises like genocide and politicide (Krain, 2017). The privileged classes in sanctioned countries suffer minimally, if at all. Sanctions strain the meager resources of those already eking out an existence, and are particularly dangerous for women because they increase poverty and political instability (Drury & Peksen, 2016). Even well-intentioned sanctions intended to protect human rights can instead worsen the living conditions of vulnerable people (Parker, Foltz, & Elsea, 2016).

For these reasons, the Protocol and TVPA face pushback. Many poor and non-Western nations see the TVPA and the Protocol as wealthy Western countries' attempts to impose their "domineering policies and imperialistic frameworks and ideologies... upon the rest of the world" (Capous Desyllas, 2007, p. 58). The TVPA's unilateral sanctioning regime reinforces the U.S.' appearance as the global punisher (Chuang, 2006b). Many countries subject to trafficking sanctions are already sanctioned for other reasons, and stacking on new ones further strains these tumultuous relationships (Feingold, 2005). It also negatively impacts public-awareness campaigns alerting migrants to the risk they face from traffickers, as these migrants often see such campaigns as nothing more than wealthy countries' efforts to keep poor immigrants out (see Chuang, 2006a; see also Capous Desyllas, 2007). It is not rational to continue trying to punish underperforming countries into compliance.

What holds greater promise is an egalitarian dialogue that gives voice to disadvantaged countries and places weight on understanding the political, social, and economic barriers preventing them from reducing emigration and preventing trafficking. Incentives work better than penalties, and many countries are eager for an alliance with the United States (Feingold, 2005). The country would have a better chance at securing cooperation if it actively helped distressed nations improve their anti-trafficking measures rather than merely punishing them for not doing so.

Of course, there must be an internationally understood set of expectations and ability to hold countries accountable for failing to protect their citizens. Sanctions can help promote compliance when they are imposed carefully and fairly (Cleveland, 2001). Through a global agreement on how to define and prevent trafficking—including adoption of universal human-rights standards—and collaboration in apprehending and punishing those who engage in it, nations committed to eliminating trafficking would have the means to do so and could leverage recalcitrant countries without resorting to overly punitive or unilateral actions.

THE EMPIRICAL STATUS OF HUMAN-TRAFFICKING POLICIES

Human-trafficking research is relatively new and evaluations of anti-trafficking policies are all but nonexistent (Laczko, 2005; see also Chuang, 2006b). A lot has been written on the topic, but most research is based on convenience samples, and methodologically rigorous research articles and reports are outnumbered by sensationalistic publications intended to draw attention and evoke outrage (Gozdziak & Bump, 2008; Weitzer, 2011). Policymakers (Chuang, 2006b) and researchers (Gozdziak & Bump, 2008; Laczko, 2005) tend to emphasize sex trafficking to the neglect of labor trafficking, which distorts the public's understanding of the problem. Many claims made by policymakers, nongovernmental organizations (NGOs), and others are questionable or false (Snajdr, 2013; Weitzer, 2013, 2014) and most policies are not evidence based (Weitzer, 2015). Data limitations are severe because of selective law enforcement and because most of the data that do exist are from the small portion of victims who ultimately come to the attention of authorities (Laczko, 2005). Most studies are conducted at the national or international level, and this large scope leads researchers to confine their analyses to aggregate trends that do not speak to the characteristics of victims, offenders, or situations (Weitzer, 2014, 2015).

This section will summarize the (scant) empirical evidence about the effectiveness of anti-trafficking efforts. The discussion is organized along two dimensions: international and domestic; and criminal-justice versus human-rights orientations. International policies will revolve around the role the United States plays in global anti-trafficking efforts. There are many international coalitions and policies that do not involve the U.S., but our focus here is on those in which this country is directly involved.

THE TVPA AND THE U.S. ROLE IN INTERNATIONAL POLICIES

The TVPA is useful, and has more bite than the Protocol does, but falls short as a method of promulgating and enforcing standards. The United States routinely fails to condemn any nation, even those it determines have violated anti-trafficking standards (Chuang, 2006b). For instance, the 2016 TIP report, which concerns itself primarily with the human-rights side of trafficking, states, "While Tier 1 is the highest ranking, it does not mean that a country has no human trafficking problem or that it is doing enough to address the problem" (U.S. Department of State, 2016, p. 36). It seems to belie the stated hardline stance against trafficking when the criteria themselves allow countries with known problems to be in the top tier.

Similarly, the Tier 2 criteria are very broad. Human-rights organizations blasted the State Department for its seemingly lenient treatment of countries that languished in this category, taking no steps toward improvement and yet enjoying immunity from sanctions (Chuang, 2006b). In 2008, Congress mandated that any country classified as Tier 2 for two consecutive years and failing to improve in the third year be demoted to Tier 3. This change took effect in 2013 (U.S. Department of State, 2016).

Still, however, there are concerns that classification is politicized and that the U.S. routinely extends high rankings to its allies and punishes governments with which it has political disagreements by issuing low grades (Chuang, 2006b). Differential treatment undermines the credibility of the sanctioning regime (Cleveland, 2001). Credibility requires consistent, rational application of clear principles; arbitrariness and apparent political motivation erode the TIP rankings' legitimacy (Chuang, 2006b). Additionally, nations in Tier 3 are not automatically sanctioned; rather, the President decides whether sanctions are warranted and, if so, which ones will be levied and how severe they will be (U.S. Department of State, 2016). Sanctioning decisions, like the classification process, have been criticized as politically motivated (Chuang, 2006b). The TVPA offers important protections to victims, but it should be viewed as a starting point rather than the final word on the U.S. role in promoting anti-trafficking efforts worldwide.

DOMESTIC POLICIES IN THE UNITED STATES

As is the case internationally, human-trafficking arrests and prosecutions are rare in the United States. Agency responses are hampered by a general lack of understanding about what human-trafficking is and what to do about it. One study found that 44 percent of police leaders and 50 percent of prosecutors in states with anti-trafficking statutes either did not know whether their state had such a law or incorrectly believed that it did not. There was also widespread confusion about the definition of trafficking and how trafficking differs from human smuggling (Newton et al., 2008). Another study found that

40 percent of police agencies had conducted human-trafficking trainings, 17 percent had adopted human-trafficking policies, and 13 percent had specialized units or personnel dedicated to the problem. Only 28 percent had investigated a trafficking case (Farrell, 2014).

In part, low investigation and prosecution rates are attributable to the time-consuming nature of these complex cases. In a sample of 150 suspects arrested on suspicion of trafficking and prosecuted in state courts, Farrell et al. (2016) found that only about one-fifth were charged with trafficking (all of them sex trafficking) and the rest were charged with various other offenses relating to prostitution, sexual assault, kidnapping, or drugs (see also Farrell et al., 2014). Interviews with prosecutors and police revealed that trafficking laws were complex and evidence was difficult to obtain. Judges and juries were unfamiliar with trafficking and had trouble determining when a defendant was guilty. Prosecutors felt their chances of obtaining convictions were better if they stuck to traditional charges than if they entered unchartered legal territory (see also Farrell et al., 2014; Farrell & McDevitt, 2014). The TVPA authorizes harsh penalties for convicted traffickers, but these penalties are useless if traffickers are not convicted of qualifying offenses.

Inadequate training and experience in fighting trafficking are a serious barrier. Police, lacking a clear understanding of what trafficking is, fail to recognize the signs of it in the traditional vice crimes they investigate (prostitution, drugs, money laundering, and so on) and incorrectly develop the impression that human trafficking is not a problem in their community (Farrell et al., 2015) or arrive at erroneous conclusions about the nature of local trafficking operations. Critics claim that many local law-enforcement agencies' anti-trafficking activities aggravate the criminalization of racial minorities and immigrants (Chacón, 2017). Without the ability to see trafficking for what it is, police may inaccurately interpret situations as involving only prostitution or illegal immigration.

Individual actors also face a variety of informal pressures (see Farrell et al., 2014 for a review). Prosecutors, for instance, are evaluated on their conviction rates. If they try a defendant on trafficking charges and lose, their professional reputation suffers. Police and prosecutors often blame victims and feel that there is no point investigating trafficking because the victim will probably refuse to testify (or will disappear), and so it would be pointless to devote resources to these cases (Farrell et al., 2014).

FUTURE DIRECTIONS FOR HUMAN-TRAFFICKING POLICIES

IMPROVING LABOR-MIGRATION AND HUMAN-RIGHTS LAWS

International policies must combine criminal-justice and human-rights perspectives and situate trafficking within the larger matter of global migration. One rights-based anti-trafficking policy option involves international reform to migration and immigration laws. Wealthy nations are heavily dependent upon immigrant labor and will become even more so in the upcoming decades as their populations age and their fertility rates decline (Chuang, 2006a). Migration policies that increase trafficking reduce demand for U.S. workers and drive down wages, since U.S. citizens compete with trafficking victims whose labor is cheap or free (Taran, 2000). Better immigration policies would be a win–win for migrants, the economies dependent upon them, and workers within both origin and destination countries.

The immigration laws and policies of both origin and destination countries are complex and require layers of screenings and documentation. Legal documents such as birth certificates are a universal requisite for travel and immigration, yet many developing countries' governments are highly disorganized (Agbu, 2003) and babies frequently do not receive birth certificates, making it impossible for them to prove their citizenship status and country of origin as adults (Feingold, 2005). Several developing nations limit the time their citizens are permitted to spend abroad and prohibit them from visiting certain countries (Ghosh, 1998). Smugglers and traffickers feed these migrants false promises of safe passage. Employers within destination countries can also keep immigrants enslaved by threatening to turn them over to authorities, since they might have an illegal status in their home countries even if they are legal residents of the country in which they currently reside (Ghosh, 1998).

A human-rights orientation could pivot the discussion toward trafficking prevention through broader enforcement of principles pertaining to international expectations for the protection of people's dignity and safety (Chuang, 2006b). The UN's *Convention on the Rights of the Child* (1989) is one starting point (Feingold, 2005; Sanghera, 2016). This Convention declares that, "[T]he child… should grow up in a family environment, in an atmosphere of happiness, love and understanding… The child shall be registered immediately after birth and shall have the right from birth to a name, the right to acquire a nationality and, as far as possible, the right to know and be cared for by his or her parents" (n.p.). Instead of being assessed on the rate at which children are trafficked out of or into a country—a nearly impossible number to obtain—nations can be evaluated on measures such as the percentage of children provided with official birth certificates and the percentage raised by their natural parents or other close relatives in family settings. These are more accurate benchmarks by which to gauge countries' protection of children and they sidestep the thorny problem of defining trafficking. Likewise, the UN's *Recommended Principles and Guidelines on Human Rights and Human Trafficking* (2002) is a detailed, rights-based model policy that countries and international coalitions could use to build a comprehensive framework that addresses the causes of migration and trafficking and ensures that anti-trafficking efforts do not infringe upon refugees, asylum seekers, or labor migrants.

The United Nations should also expand its criteria for conferring refugee status. Current international law does not adequately differentiate labor migrants seeking greater opportunity in another country from those whose very survival is at stake (see Chuang, 2006a for a review). According to the UN, "A refugee is someone who has been forced to flee his or her country because of persecution, war, or violence. A refugee has a well-founded fear of persecution for reasons of race, religion, nationality, political opinion or membership in a particular social group" (United Nations Refugee Agency, n.d.). This definition excludes people leaving because of starvation or serious discrimination (see Ghosh, 1998). Widening the criteria would help migrants achieve safe, lawful passage and resettlement (see also Taran, 2000).

SMART USE OF ECONOMIC SANCTIONS

While the imposition of unilateral sanctions in the form of the withdrawal of aid is generally considered ineffective and even counterproductive, targeted sanctions can effect change. International economic sanctions can be invoked to generate a normative endorsement of the need to protect people and their rights. The United States and other industrialized countries can help developing nations protect human rights by employing sanctions strategically (Hufbauer, Schott, & Elliott, 1990). Instrumental compliance (that is, compliance arising out of target nations' fear of incurring penalties) is insufficient. Targeted nations must internalize a normative sense of obligation to uphold human rights. Koh's (1997) transnational legal process theory offers a method for achieving this. The process begins with an ongoing interaction between the nations, which produces a common interpretation of the applicable global norm. This interpretation becomes a legal rule that then structures future transactions in an iterative process until the principle is internalized by all nations. Repetition of the principle during all transactions ensures its continued relevance.

The United States and other developed nations can apply transnational legal process theory to garner reluctant nations' compliance by embedding prorights and anti-trafficking language into global dialogue so that it becomes a standard feature of diplomats' and policymakers' parlance. Powerful nations further institutionalize these principles by weaving them into economic and political transactions, such as trade and aid negotiations. Sanctions should not be used unilaterally except as a last resort, and must be employed fairly and consistently. The U.S.' laws and policies on human rights must coincide with international views. Uneven, politicized, or arbitrary definitions and sanctions erode the legitimacy of the United States on a global scale (Cleveland, 2001). The United States also must engage a variety of NGOs, private parties, and others with vested interests in human rights and trafficking prevention, as these groups are important sources of information about nations' current human-rights and anti-trafficking activities. They can also help pressure reluctant governments to take action (Chuang, 2006b). Adhering to these transactional principles, the United States can help create genuine, lasting change on the world stage.

DOMESTIC LAW-ENFORCEMENT ACTIVITIES

There are ways to make investigating and prosecuting human trafficking more effective. One method is for police and prosecutors to make trafficking a higher priority so they are involved in more cases and develop expertise. Farrell et al. (2015) found that police officers working trafficking cases developed a clearer understanding of the problem and started recognizing the connections between trafficking and other crimes, such as prostitution and drug sales. They also became more adept at distinguishing between voluntary prostitution and sex trafficking. There is something to be said, then, for law enforcement diving into these cases even if they are difficult and messy at first.

Police also need to be more proactive and creative. Traditional vice strategies, such as undercover stings to arrest prostitutes and force them to give up their captors' names, are misguided approaches that retraumatize victims and reinforce their distrust of police (Farrell et al., 2015). Additionally, street-level prostitutes are less likely to be trafficking victims than are those working in clandestine environments (e.g., massage parlors) or who are available only through internet transactions. Smarter policing would direct resources toward the locations most likely to contain victims. Police should develop partnerships and task forces with regulatory, code-enforcement, and business-oversight agencies (Newton et al., 2008). Police can work with licensing agencies, for instance, to find out where the labor-trafficking "hot spots" are and then initiate proactive monitoring and investigations (Farrell et al., 2014).

Local and federal law enforcement could capitalize upon trafficking organizations' patterned behavior. As described earlier, trafficking is generally not a form of hierarchical, organized crime, but there is a routinization—or script—to the acquisition, transport, and exploitation of trafficked persons (Salt & Stein, 1997). Most individual offenders move in and out of the networks, and yet there are signs that the networks themselves remain stable over time. Each offender must coordinate with others in order to complete the process. Networks have nodes, which are small numbers of highly involved offenders who are particularly important to networks' functioning (Campana, 2016). This behavioral patterning and interdependence are weaknesses law enforcement could exploit to disable the network.

Personnel working in medicine, juvenile justice, corrections, social service, and other occupations wherein employees may come into contact with victims should be trained to recognize the signs of trafficking (Ahn et al., 2013). These frontline workers bring victims to the authorities' attention and help build cases against traffickers by creating documentation that will become critical pieces of evidence (e.g., photographs of physical injuries that may have healed by the time the jury sees the victim in court). The Department of Corrections in Florida trains correctional and probation staff about trafficking and educates jail inmates about the ways that they or others could be misled by predators posing as friends and offering them a place to stay when they are released from jail. The department recently reduced specificity of details about jail inmates that are available on the public online database as a means of protecting vulnerable individuals (Chavez, 2017).

The United States needs to adopt a strong emphasis on protecting victims. Victim services are lacking. It can take months to compile a trafficking case, and prosecutors generally have no way of housing victims. Even states with comprehensive anti-trafficking statutes fail to adequately provide for victims' needs (Farrell et al., 2014). In addition to being unjust to victims, this systemic weakness undermines attempts to punish traffickers because victims who cannot be housed securely for long periods of time are likely to flee, thus dismantling the prosecution's case (Farrell et al., 2014; Farrell et al., 2016). Rescued victims often return to trafficking situations (Farrell et al., 2015). Victims cannot be simply put back out onto the streets; they need follow-up services as they transition out of the victim mindset and work through their trauma. Better legal, social, and physical protection for victims is imperative if the United States is to become truly serious about fighting human trafficking within its borders.

CONCLUSION

Human trafficking is a persistent, global problem. The intricacy of the trafficking requires an equally complex, nuanced policy solution. Blunt instruments such as unilateral economic sanctions are not enough and can even backfire. No nation can fight trafficking alone; it will take global cooperation to design and implement genuine solutions.

The United States can be a leader in anti-trafficking efforts. First, there needs to be greater respect shown for the UN's definition of trafficking and the opinions of countries that do not believe prostitution should be criminalized. The TVPA's sanctioning regime will forever be limited in its capacity to promote the normative legitimacy of anti-trafficking sentiment if the United States looks more condescending than collabortive. Second, the United States needs to work with its allies to infuse the current criminal-justice orientation with an equally powerful human-rights framework. Requiring troubled nations to address the domestic crises that imperil their citizens and cause massive outmigration is tantamount to mandating them to crack down on trafficking, but from a different perspective that holds more promise. It is untenable to combat trafficking by trying to identify and capture the perpetrators; the real solution lies in depriving the perpetrators of victims. Finally, the United States needs smarter, more strategic domestic law enforcement. Training and education are lacking, as are the resources necessary to launch in-depth investigations and protect victims during lengthy trials. Revisions to the ways in which T visas are granted might be warranted. Human-trafficking networks, though not sufficiently tight and hierarchical to be considered organized crime, endure over time and display predictable behavior patterns, thus making them susceptible to infiltration by law enforcement. These three policy avenues are not the only means by which the United States can reduce human trafficking domestically and abroad, but they are good starting points.

DISCUSSION QUESTIONS

1. When police discover a human-trafficking ring, it is frequently by accident. They stumble upon it during the course of a different investigation, or when a victim escapes and seeks help. What are some ways police can be more proactive in preventing and detecting human trafficking? Propose creative solutions for police at local, state, and federal levels.

2. One of the reasons for the relatively lackluster impact the United States has had on human-rights laws in countries known to be engaged in widespread violation is that these nations strongly resist such criticism. Raising theissue can impede international conversations. Diplomats might avoid or downplay discussions about human rights in order to prompt leaders from these countries to negotiate on other matters of importance. Do you think the United States should take a stronger stance on human rights when negotiating with nations that have poor track records in this area? Should U.S. diplomats be ready to walk away from proposed deals that do not sufficiently emphasize improvements to these nations' treatment of their citizens? What are the possible downsides of such an approach? Identify the benefits and possible negative consequences that might occur if the United States were more demanding about human rights.

3. Labor trafficking in the United States is facilitated by employment laws containing loopholes company owners can exploit to avoid legal culpability for employing undocumented workers, including trafficking victims. Turning a blind eye toward immigrant employees' documentation status boosts profits because these employees make very little money; additionally, thoroughly reviewing all workers' immigration status is costly. Voluntary immigrants who do not have legal status also win because they can find jobs, even if the pay and conditions are poor. Many of these immigrants are not illegal by choice but, rather, because the process of obtaining documentation is difficult. Some accidentally allowed temporary visas to lapse and now fear deportation should they reapply. How might the United States be more effective at preventing companies from

hiring trafficked workers (which would reduce traffickers' incentive to commit this crime), while not unduly burdening employers with regulations or shutting down an important source of work for immigrants and their families? What efforts aimed at businesses might help? Are there laws and policies other than those relating to business regulations that might alleviate the problem?

4. International human trafficking requires coordination among several individuals and groups. There are also patterns, such as specific routes traffickers travel to transport their victims from an origin to a destination. Identify ways in which the coordinated, scripted nature of trafficking could be leveraged in order to disrupt networks and hamper trafficking. What would governments need to do to make it easier for police and border-control agents to uncover and investigate trafficking operations? Identify governmental laws, policies, and resources that would assist ground-level law enforcement.

STATUTE CITED

Victims of Trafficking and Violence Prevention Act of 2000, 22 USC 7101 (2000)

CHAPTER 13

POLICE POLICY

INTRODUCTION

Police policies in the United States have been diverse in type, target, scale, and scope. Some policies are local and derived from the unique challenges facing particular communities, while others have been adopted nationally. Some focus on specific offense types while others are intended to reduce crime more generally. Still others are aimed at improving police–community relations and reducing local residents' fear of crime. There is also variation in whether a given policy is a pre-packaged set of tactics that police apply according to preset instructions, or whether it is a general model or theory requiring each police agency to adapt and innovate to suit its own unique circumstances.

This chapter summarizes and critically examines some of the most popular and widely used contemporary police policies. Because of the immense number of policing approaches that have been tried and are currently in use (there are entire books devoted to the subject), this chapter is not exhaustive in either breadth or depth. This chapter also defines "police policy" as innovations in and models of policing; we will not discuss administrative policies such as the rules governing the use of force. Emphasis will be placed on the importance of evidence-based practices and the need to balance crime control with community relationships to find solutions to local problems that bring police and citizens together.

A BRIEF HISTORY OF POLICING IN THE UNITED STATES

To understand contemporary police policies, we first need to review major historical developments. Policing in the United States has been evolving since its inception in the mid-1800s. An important distinction between policing in the United States and other nations is that the U.S. adheres to a decentralized model; instead of a single, national police force, each individual jurisdiction (state, county, and municipality) establishes, operates, and funds its own police force. The federal government has police (the Federal Bureau of Investigation, the Drug Enforcement Administration, the Bureau of Alcohol, Tobacco, Firearms and Explosives, and so on), but federal agents' jurisdictions are limited by geography and subject matter. In other words, a crime must contain specific elements that make it eligible for federal intervention; otherwise, it is handled at the local level (i.e., the county or municipality in which it occurred).

Local control over police is a function of the doctrine of federalism, which holds that the federal government should largely leave the states to handle their own affairs. The Tenth Amendment to the Constitution states, "The powers not delegated to the United States by the Constitution, or prohibited by it to the States, are reserved to the States respectively, or to the people." In other words, whatever requirements or prohibitions binding on the states that are not contained in the Constitution are left to the states to deal with on their own. Since the Constitution did not establish a national police force with jurisdiction over state matters, the Tenth Amendment confers this right and obligation upon each state. As a result of decentralization, policing is highly localized. Although key characteristics appear nationally (e.g., the use of a paramilitary command structure, uniforms, marked cars), each police agency is organized and operated in its own way (Langworthy & Travis, 2003), based on community characteristics, local politics, and the needs most prevalent in the area (Wilson, 1968).

The history of U.S. policing is divided into eras (Kelling & Moore, 1988). The first was the political era (1800s to early 1900s). During this time, police were tools of local politicians and parties. Police jobs were handed out as rewards for loyalty, and officers in some cities were required to campaign on behalf of the incumbents to whom they owed their livelihood. Police officers were primarily engaged in order maintenance; they responded to a wide variety of problems and served many local functions (Kelling & Moore, 1988). There were essentially no legal restrictions on officers' actions. They routinely accepted bribes as payment for turning a blind eye toward certain forms of crime (e.g., gambling operations) and doled out "curbside justice" as they saw fit. Pay was low, training nonexistent, and corruption rampant (Wilson, 1968). Policing, in short, was altogether too localized.

Starting in the 1920s, police reformers advanced the professional (or legalistic) model, signaling the phasing out of the political era. In the professional era, officers were envisioned as detached from communities in order to prevent corruption. Administrative controls tightened to reduce officer discretion (Manning, 1988). The police mission was seen as limited to enforcement of the criminal law (Kelling & Moore, 1988; Wilson, 1968). Officers' job was to respond to calls for service and apprehend offenders. When not engaged in these activities, officers conducted randomized motor patrol, which was thought to help deter crime by establishing a sense of police omnipresence. Policing was thus reshaped into a detached, reactive, law-enforcement operation.

The cracks in the professional era became evident in the 1960s and 1970s. All governmental institutions were facing a legitimacy crisis. Police experienced community-relations problems as the Civil Rights Movement and opposition to the Vietnam War brought crowds pouring into streets and college campuses for mass protests, marches, and demonstrations. Newspapers regularly featured photographs of police turning dogs and firehoses on peaceful demonstrators, and police abuse of black citizens became a national topic of conversation and debate (Paoline, Gau, & Terrill, 2016). Crime was increasing, especially in urban areas, and the public put increasing pressure on the police to do something about it.

Police leaders were also coming to grips with the added problem that the professional model conflicted with the reality of policing. Police officers, in truth, never fully lost their order-maintenance function (Walker, 1984). The legalistic or professional model was a veneer that misrepresented the job to the public and to officers themselves. Most of the people who called the police for help had problems like lost children, car crashes, and disputes with neighbors. Additionally, a high-profile field experiment in which research-ers empirically tested the effectiveness of randomized vehicle patrol revealed that patrol had no impact on crime, fear of crime, response times, or any other metric (Kelling, Pate, Dieckman, & Brown, 1974). The mismatch between the professional model and the realities of police work, as well as the evidence that preventive patrol is not preventive at all, ushered in a new era.

In the 1970s and 1980s, police leaders returned to the idea that the officers are most effective when they have strong working relationships with communities. In this community problem-solving era, police administrators accepted that the job inevitably includes disorder and fear of crime (Kelling & Moore, 1988). Two highly influential publications helped popu-larize community and problem-solving policing. The first was Goldstein's (1979) persuasive argument that police should approach their work by first seeking to understand the origins of community problems and then fashioning and implementing creative solutions, and evalu-ating the success of their efforts. The second was Wilson and Kelling's (1982) broken windows model of crime causation, wherein they argued that police should occupy themselves with putting checks on neighborhood disorder (e.g., vandalism, graffiti, panhandling) in order to prevent crime. These compelling ideas—that police should prevent crime by focusing on dis-order and should seek to understand the causes of problems and develop tailored solutions—took U.S. policing into a radically new direction. We will see later that some of these reforms failed to alter police behavior in any fundamental or lasting way, and others spiraled out of control and ultimately widened the police–community gap instead of closing it.

Although not a policy per se, police militarization warrants discussion because it dra-matically reshaped the policing landscape. In the 1960s, the federal government declared a war on crime and set in motion a major conservative crime-control movement that accel-erated in the 1970s through the 1990s, eventually encompassing the war on drugs as well. The word "war" carries important symbolism. By defining a subset of the population as the enemy, the war metaphor encourages police to embrace the accoutrements of military con-flict and adopt the image of themselves as soldiers embroiled in urban combat. The 1980s and 1990s saw a blurring of the line between international military action and domestic law enforcement until the existence of militarization became normalized in police opera-tions (Kraska, 2007; Kraska & Kappeler, 1997). This trend intensified after the 9/11 terrorist attacks on the World Trade Center. Many police agencies today possess armored vehicles and military rifles that they swiftly bring out for raids and manhunts (Filkins, 2016). These militarized actions do not appear to have much value as crime-control measures (Kim, Phillips, & Wheeler, 2016), though of course certain deployments may improve officer safety when serving warrants or conducting raids in places known to be dangerous.

Militarization has made the war metaphor a self-fulfilling prophecy—the heavy-handed approach to urban policing legitimized by the war metaphor contributed to a reality in which police and low-income, urban minorities (particularly blacks) are in perpetual con-flict (Meeks, 2006). Controversial killings of black men who were unarmed or otherwise seemingly not posing a serious threat (e.g., Michael Brown in Ferguson, Missouri), some of whom were entirely innocent of wrongdoing (e.g., Donnell Thompson in Compton, California), have sparked mass protests and were the impetus behind the Black Lives Matter movement. Critics allege that militarization has corrupted urban policing, glorifies violence against vulnerable minorities, and leads police to devalue the lives and safety of those living in low-income, high-crime neighborhoods (Hill, 2016).

Post-9/11 militarization exacerbates longstanding tensions between police and communities of color. Within black neighborhoods and communities, police have historically been viewed as an occupying army. The problems trace to before the Civil War, when police actively participated in the enforcement of slavery laws and conducted slave patrols to round up and return slaves who had escaped. After the Civil War, the police vigorously enforced Southern Jim Crow laws and other racially biased laws and policies (Williams & Murphy, 1990). By the mid-1960s, things had not improved much. The situation finally boiled over and massive riots swept several major cities, including Detroit, Los Angeles, and Newark. In the aftermath, President Lyndon Johnson assembled a commission to study the deep-rooted problems between police and black communities. The Kerner Commission, as it was called, concluded that,

> The police are not merely a "spark" factor. To some Negroes police have come to symbolize white power, white racism, white repression. And the fact is that many police do reflect and express these white attitudes. The atmosphere of hostility and cynicism is reinforced by a widespread belief among Negroes in the existence of police brutality and in a "double standard" of justice and protection—one for Negroes and one for whites (Kerner Commission, 1967, p. 5).

The mutual hostility between police and black communities appears to have abated somewhat since the 1960s, but it still remains firmly entrenched. There is a widespread conviction among blacks in urban areas that police are racist (Brunson, 2007; Gau & Brunson, 2010). Militarization, along with some of the other strategies police have adopted for street-level law enforcement in troubled urban neighborhoods (which will be discussed shortly), are interpreted by many observers as tangible proof of police officers' lack of regard for people of color.

And yet, police enjoy a peaceful relationship with much of suburban and rural America. Whites express high levels of trust in and satisfaction with police (Skogan, 2005; Tyler, 2005). Neighborhood-level policing practices and people's individual experiences with officers are one of the main causes of attitudinal discrepancies (Weitzer & Tuch, 2002, 2005). Blacks and Latinos are stopped on foot and in vehicles at higher rates than are whites (e.g., Skogan, 2005). The level of respect—or disrespect—shown to citizens can vary widely between placid suburbs and distressed inner-city neighborhoods. Black and Latino Americans, however, do not hate police (Tyler, 2005; Weitzer & Tuch, 2005) and people of color living in troubled areas express a strong desire for an effective police presence in their communities (Carr, Napolitano, & Keating, 2007). Police need policies that are effective against crime, disorder, and fear but at the same time boost public confidence in police and avoid the pitfalls of the "war" model. It is against this backdrop that we turn to contemporary policing policies.

CONTEMPORARY POLICE POLICIES AND THEIR ORIGINS

As noted previously, this review will focus on the most popular and widely utilized policies. It should be kept in mind that many theories, tactics, and strategies overlap. Foot patrol and police–community partnerships, for instance, can be part of community policing, order maintenance, or hot spots. Police departments utilize multiple policies or mix and match tactics from different ones. The current review categorizes the different approaches for the sake of organization, but this separation is artificial in many ways.

ORDER-MAINTENANCE POLICING

Policing has historically been reactive—officers spend their shifts driving their patrol cars waiting to be dispatched to calls for service. Police agencies have devoted far more resources to crime investigation than prevention (Ratcliffe, 2016). As reviewed earlier, the 1970s and 1980s saw a loss of support for reactive policing. The time was right for a new model, and Wilson and Kelling (1982) proposed one. They argued that the police should act as the guardians of public civility by reining in disruptive individuals such as vandals, aggressive panhandlers, and prostitutes. By tamping down on low-level crimes and disorders, they maintained, police could prevent serious crime. Wilson and Kelling's so-called "broken windows" theory ultimately became one of the most influential policing theories of all time (Pratt, Gau, & Franklin, 2010).

Wilson and Kelling's policy recommendations lacked specificity, leaving individual departments to figure out how to implement these ideas. The policing strategies grounded in Wilson and Kelling's broken-windows principles vary widely and go by names such as order-maintenance, zero-tolerance, and broken-windows policing. Ultimately, the one tactic that united most of them was the street stop. Street stops are temporary detentions of pedestrians or motorists made when officers observe someone behaving strangely and have reasonable suspicion to believe that the individual is engaged in criminal activity. The legal justification for this practice is found in the landmark U.S. Supreme Court case *Terry v. Ohio* (1968). The *Terry* Court carved out an exception to the Fourth Amendment requirement that officers possess probable cause to seize and search someone suspected of criminal behavior. *Terry* permitted officers to conduct brief street stops on the basis of reasonable suspicion, a standard of proof that is lower than probable cause, and possibly frisk (i.e., quickly pat down) a suspect during a stop. A later expansion of *Terry* (*Illinois v. Wardlow*, 2000) allowed officers to use an individual's presence in a high-crime location as a factor in determining whether there is legal justification for a stop. *Terry* permits officers to frisk during a stop only if they have reasonable suspicion to believe the suspect is armed and dangerous; the stop itself does not automatically justify a frisk. The Court relaxed this standard in *Minnesota v. Dickerson* (1993). Today, frisks frequently accompany stops and are often illegal, but they escape judicial scrutiny because contraband is rarely uncovered during these searches and, therefore, arrests are infrequent (Gould & Mastrofski, 2004).

Order-maintenance policing (OMP) in general, and the street stop in particular, owe their fame to the New York City Police Department (NYPD), which in the early 1990s launched a massive order-maintenance campaign designed to reclaim the city's streets, parks, and subways. At first, NYPD officers used a number of different approaches. For instance, they ramped up enforcement in subways and arrested anyone attempting to jump the turnstile to avoid paying the fare, and they started handing out citations to curb the practice, popular among the city's homeless, of pouring dirty water on car windshields and then charging drivers a fee for them to clean up the mess (Kelling & Coles, 1997).

It is not clear at what point OMP devolved into a massive stop-and-frisk sweep of minority neighborhoods, but in 1999, the New York State Attorney General initiated an investigation and uncovered marked racial differences in stop rates that were not explainable by area crime rates, and found that the vast majority of stops led neither to arrest nor to the discovery of contraband (Office of the Attorney General of New York, 1999). The report's key findings were replicated in subsequent studies (Fagan & Davies, 2000; Gelman, Fagan, & Kiss, 2012). Stop and frisk hit its final crisis in 2013 when a federal court found that the NYPD's actions were so racially lopsided that they violated the equal-protection clause of the Fourteenth Amendment to the U.S. Constitution (*Floyd v. City of New York*, 2013). The court did not rule stop and frisk unconstitutional in a broad sense—only its current application by the NYPD—so police agencies are free to utilize this tactic so long as they are mindful to avoid racialization. Still, the *Floyd* decision tainted stop and frisk and turned much of the public against it.

The future of order-maintenance policing is difficult to predict. The troubles it has caused are not unique to New York City; police departments nationwide have alienated black and Latino residents under the guise of order maintenance (Gau & Brunson, 2010, 2015; Vera Sanchez & Gau, 2015). Commentators observe that, "The concept of broken windows long ago lost its moorings" (Hill, 2016, p. 54) and even Kelling eventually conceded that OMP got out of hand (Roberts, 2014; see also Thacher, 2014). Nonetheless, order maintenance has become ingrained in U.S. policing and will likely persist in some form, even if more subtly from here out. Nothing requires order maintenance to be carried out in an aggressive manner, and police agencies may still rely on the broken-windows concept using different tactics that do not erode their relationship with the community.

PROBLEM-ORIENTED POLICING

Problem-oriented policing (POP) also grew out of the belief that police could be more effective by being proactive, and that their powers of arrest represent a mere slice of their total competencies. Rather than simply enforce the criminal law, according to POP proponents, officers should employ a variety of creative approaches to community problems, and should seek to eliminate root causes. Recurring crimes are perceived to be indicative of underlying problems. The best solution is the one tailored to the unique features of a specific problem (Goldstein, 1979). Problem-oriented policing is distinguished from order-maintenance policing by its emphasis on identifying and gaining in-depth understanding of certain troublesome locations or behaviors, as opposed to a generalized plan to reduce crime and disorder more broadly (Goldstein, 1990). Advocates of POP also urge police to step outside the criminal law in deciding upon the problems to address. As noted earlier, police deal with myriad issues outside of the criminal law's realm (disputes, traffic and parking issues, and so on). This operational reality requires that the police not unduly restrict their activities by using the criminal law as a central organizing feature (Eck & Clarke,

2003; Goldstein, 1979). Instead, POP supporters urge police to redefine their role from law enforcers to problem solvers (Clarke & Eck, 2005; Goldstein, 1979, 1990).

One of the challenges the POP concept has faced in the process of becoming a reality of street-level policing is confusion over how to properly define "problems." The problems to which POP are best suited meet certain criteria. For one thing, the problem must be repetitive (Eck & Clarke, 2003). For instance, it has been noted that the majority of calls for service that a police department receives emanate from a relatively small percentage of the addresses within the municipality. Certain locations (e.g., taverns where patrons regularly become rowdy) or people (e.g., elderly individuals fearful of their young, boisterous neighbors in a demographically diverse apartment building) generate the bulk of all 911 calls and thus should be the focus of POP initiatives (Goldstein, 1990). Another criterion is that there must be an identifiable harm (Eck & Clarke, 2003). Harm identification is a requisite step in planning the intervention and is necessary so that police can assess their impact and determine whether their proposed solution was effective or whether they need to regroup and try again.

Scholars have proposed operational strategies and models of POP-based approaches to assist police in putting problem-based policing to work on the streets. Eck and Spelman (1987) created the SARA model (*s*canning, *a*nalysis, *r*esponse, *a*ssessment) to guide officers through the POP process. Scanning and analysis entail gaining a full understanding of the issue at hand. The response should be creative and tied closely to the results of the analysis. Assessment is crucial because police need to know if the response worked; if it did not, they need to start the SARA process again.

Eck and Clarke (2003) outlined a two-dimensional classification scheme intended to help police accurately describe problems. They classified problems according to behaviors and environments. Behaviorally, there must be some type of criminal, violent, or disorderly activities that threaten public peace and safety. Environmentally, police need to accurately describe the features of the place in which the problem is occurring (e.g., residential areas, businesses, parking structures). It is the intersection of a specific type of disruptive behavior and the characteristics of the location in which it takes place that defines a problem and forms the groundwork for its solution. Clarke and Eck (2005, 2014) wrote manuals to guide crime analysts in helping police officers analyze problems and evaluate the effectiveness of solutions. These practical guides were intended to ease the transition from traditional policing to POP.

COMMUNITY POLICING

It would be difficult to overstate the dramatic influence community policing (CP) has had on police agencies in the past few decades (Skogan, 2006). This was due in large part to former President Bill Clinton, who championed CP during his 1991 bid for the White House and, after being elected, allotted funds for hiring 100,000 new community-policing officers nationwide (Cordner, 2014). Initial implementations of CP spurred opposition from line-level officers, who were not on board with the reorientation of mission or mentality (Rosenbaum, Yeh, & Wilkinson, 1994), or remained unconvinced of the utility of CP (Wilson & Bennett, 1994). Nonetheless, early CP efforts seemed to have a small, positive effect on officers' attitudes that steadily increased the longer a department espoused a CP philosophy (Rosenbaum et al., 1994; Wilson & Bennett, 1994). Today, CP is widely endorsed.

Community policing emphasizes "consensus, community empowerment, and public safety" (Greene & Mastrofski, 1988, p. xi). Proponents of CP argue that police should view their role as promoting not merely public safety and order but public welfare; they should be intimately involved in helping improve and maintain quality of life (Goldstein, 1979). The ascendance of CP was spurred by research in the 1970s and 1980s showing that foot patrol and other tactics that increase the frequency of friendly contacts between officers and community members reduced citizens' fear of crime and enhanced their satisfaction with local police (see Kelling & Moore, 1988 for a review). Community policing entailed increasing patrol officers' use of discretion in handling day-to-day matters, thus reversing the reform-era's emphasis on reducing discretion.

Community policing is an organizational strategy. There is no predetermined goal or outcome; rather, the CP philosophy informs the process police agencies and officers should use when identifying problems and working toward solutions. The primary organizational elements of CP are decentralized command (e.g., neighborhood substations), participatory management wherein beat officers and midlevel managers are actively involved in gathering information and proposing solutions, and two-way communication with the local citizenry and business community (Kelling & Moore, 1988; Skogan, 2006; Skogan & Hartnett, 1997). Community policing, in theory, reduces crime indirectly by eliminating the problems that lead to it, such as citizens' distrust of police and their unwillingness to spend substantial time occupying public spaces. Problem solving is a critical element of CP; CP can be seen as organizational and operational changes that facilitate POP activities. Community policing advocates also subscribe to the broken-windows theory, believing that police must work with residents to keep disorder in check (Mastrofski, 1988).

Because CP is amorphous both conceptually and in practice, it is difficult to describe how prevalent it is (since there really is no "it" to speak of). Sixty-eight percent of police departments explicitly reference CP in their mission statements and 32 percent have a partnership or agreement with one or more local organizations (Reaves, 2015). The tactics a department uses, the number of such tactics employed, and the extent to which the department has genuinely embraced the philosophy of CP or merely pays it lip service vary widely. To some extent, this makes sense: CP is supposed to be flexible, so tactics should change over time both quantitatively and qualitatively (Skogan, 2006). On the other hand, this fuzziness makes it difficult to determine how effectively an agency has adopted CP. Many agencies form CP units, run foot-patrol programs, partner with neighborhood watches, and so forth, yet never fully commit to the organizational philosophy. From the very beginning, critics have alleged that community policing is largely a "façade" (Manning, 1988, p. 29).

DATA-DRIVEN POLICING

This section covers hot-spots policing, Compstat, and intelligence-led policing. These three strategies contain different tactics and operational angles, but they are all based on the analysis of data to identify likely troublemakers and determine the locations of high-crime areas. Data-driven strategies are designed to be proactive; although they rely upon information about crimes that have already occurred, data-driven policing methods are intended to facilitate the formation of new understandings about crime problems and of creative solutions to them (Ratcliffe, 2016).

Data-driven policing came about largely as a function of an increasing realization that police agencies collect large quantities of information (arrest reports, criminal investigations, calls for service, and so on) but have historically done little with it (Ericson & Haggerty, 1997). Computer hardware and software has gradually become cheaper, more sophisticated, and more user friendly, dramatically expanding police agencies' ability to not only collate data but also to analyze it in depth. Increasing public pressure has spurred police leaders to start putting data to work on the streets. Risk management, too, has fully infiltrated local policing and heavily shapes operational decisions. Police administrators and managers face intense pressure to avert disaster, and they are hit by the fallout when a seemingly preventable tragedy occurs (Ericson & Haggerty, 1997; Flood, 2004). In the wake of a string of unsolved burglaries that culminates in the assault of a homeowner or an abused wife murdered by her recently paroled husband, the community, media, and politicians point an accusing finger at local police. Police, moreover, face a demand gap created by ever increasing workloads (much of it paperwork) that outpace resource expansion, so police administrators must find ways to do more with less (Ratcliffe, 2016). Performance pressure, risk aversion, and strategic resource allocation now constitute major organizing principles for police operations.

Hot-spots policing arose from scholars' dissatisfaction with reform-era police tactics (e.g., randomized patrol; see Weisburd & Braga, 2006 for a review) and from criminological research showing that offender-based strategies were largely ineffective because much crime results from the characteristics of places, not of people. Crime rates vary across neighborhoods and, even more markedly, across smaller locations within neighborhoods (see Sherman, Gartin, & Buerger, 1989 for a review). So-called "microplaces" can be apartment complexes, abandoned buildings, convenience stores, or other small areas that attract crime because of their physical or social characteristics. In addition to place, time has been identified as contributing to crime; there are both "hot spots" and "hot times" (Sherman & Eck, 2002). For example, a local tavern might be calm from 5 PM to 9 PM each day, but the patrons exiting at 2 AM are a raucous bunch who get in fights and crash their cars.

Hot-spots policing is a data-driven resource-allocation strategy (Sherman & Weisburd, 1995). It is a method of figuring out where police should be (and when), but it does not tell them what to do once they arrive. Police administrators must decide this second part, and the decision matters greatly. Some place-based (and time-based) strategies are more effective than others (Groff, Ratcliffe, Haberman, Sorg, Joyce, & Taylor, 2015). Fortunately, an abundance of research has been conducted evaluating various police activities and while these efforts are ongoing and no unequivocal conclusions about whether "this works" or "that does not work" are possible yet, police administrators can gain a general sense of what types of activities seem more promising than others. Officers might simply try to take advantage of a deterrent impact by increasing their visibility in these areas (Sherman & Weisburd, 1995) or they might engage in problem solving, foot patrol, or focused deterrence aimed at known offenders (Groff et al., 2015; see also Sherman & Eck, 2002).

Compstat was pioneered in New York City in the early 1990s by William Bratton (police commissioner at the time) and Rudy Giuliani (then the mayor). Compstat took advantage of technology breakthroughs offering novel ways for police administrators to understand crime in their jurisdictions. Compstat is an administrative approach. It is a managerial mechanism for enhancing higher-ranking police officers' accountability for reducing crime (Magers, 2004). The basic idea is that the chief designates individuals of a certain rank within midlevel management (for instance, lieutenants) as responsible for their areas (precincts, districts, or beats). Crime mapping is used to determine the location of crime incidents and track their occurrence over time. At periodic (e.g., weekly) briefings, each manager makes a presentation to the chief and the rest of the group about recent crimes and what the manager did about them (Bratton, 1998). In theory, this open airing of problems puts pressure on each manager to seek creative ways to reduce crime in his or her assigned area. Critics of Compstat, however, contend that chiefs tightening control over their subordinates does nothing more than increase the rigidity of the hierarchy in police agencies' paramilitary bureaucracies (Weisburd, Mastrofski, McNally, Greenspan, & Willis, 2003).

Intelligence-led policing (ILP) originated in the United Kingdom. Originally designed as an operational tactic to help police objectively and effectively dedicate resources to the most active offenders, it gradually expanded to become a more comprehensive framework that can support other types of policing operations (Ratcliffe, 2016), although it continues to be used for offender identification (Groff et al., 2015). This approach is intended for utilization in everything from terrorism to international organized crime to local crime problems (Maguire, 2000). The types of information collected under ILP vary beyond traditional crime reports, informants, and so forth to include novel sources such as newspaper articles. Under an ILP approach, the systematic analysis of data is critical. A collection of information is meaningless unless a trained analyst rigorously organizes the data into actionable intelligence (Ratcliffe, 2016). Intelligence is then used to inform community and problem-based initiatives (Carter & Carter, 2009; McGarrell, Freilich, & Chermak, 2007).

Data-driven policing strategies have proliferated across the United States and many other countries. The advent of Compstat in the NYPD coincided with a remarkable drop in violent crime in New York City. Although, as we will see later in the chapter, there is little empirical evidence that Compstat contributed to the crime drop (e.g., Eck & Maguire, 2000), politicians and police leaders leapt to the conclusion that Compstat was the ticket to crime reduction, and they scrambled to implement it in their own jurisdictions (see Ratcliffe, 2016 for a review). Compstat's popularity was also fueled by the general trend, as noted previously, of increasing public expectations that the police take advantage of enhanced computing capabilities and start using data to inform their activities (Weisburd et al., 2003; Willis, Mastrofski, & Weisburd, 2007). Similarly, ILP's popularity skyrocketed after the 9/11 terrorist attacks and the ensuing national push for better information sharing between law-enforcement agencies (Carter & Carter, 2009; Ratcliffe, 2016). It became widely accepted that to effectively manage risks and demonstrate accountability to the public, police must collect, analyze, and share data. We will see later that most of the "changes" to police operations have been largely symbolic; nonetheless, the claim to be involved in data-driven policing and the utilization of at least lower-level forms of data collection and crime mapping have become commonplace among police agencies.

EXAMINING THE RATIONALES

We now turn to a discussion of the primary lines of logic driving the most popular policing approaches. There is overlap between these rationales (e.g., place-based strategies and order maintenance both have deterrent properties), so the following discussion creates an artificial categorization necessary to facilitate the presentation. The main rationales are deterrence; the logic underlying the broken-windows model (grounded in precepts of social psychology); place-based prevention; and the need for citizen involvement in the fight against crime and disorder.

OFFENDER-BASED DETERRENCE

In theory, police have the greatest ability of all criminal-justice agencies to prevent crime through deterrence. This is because certainty of apprehension is more powerful in turning would-be offenders away from crimes than the severity or swiftness of sanctions are. If police can create a credible threat of arrest, they will bring crime rates down (Durlauf & Nagin, 2011).

The question then becomes what police can do to generate a credible threat. Unfortunately, police nationwide rely primarily upon the reform-era techniques of random motorized patrol and rapid response to calls for service (Ratcliffe, 2016), which are designed to effect deterrence by convincing would-be offenders that they will be caught should they decide to follow through on their plans for criminal activity. These tactics were discredited long ago as having no impact on the probability that police will successfully identify and apprehend offenders (see Weisburd & Eck, 2004 for a review). Moreover, the public in general, including those who have been arrested in the past, are notoriously bad at assessing the likelihood that they would be caught if they committed a crime (Kleck, Sever, Li,, & Gertz, 2005).

The impact of arrest, too, is debatable. Some people who have been arrested in the past are likely to offend again in the future (Sherman, 1993; see Pogarsky & Piquero, 2003 for a review). There is no consensus among scholars as to whether, in general, arrest reduces, increases, or has no effect on the likelihood that a person will commit another criminal offense in the future (see Paternoster, Brame, Bachman, & Sherman, 1997 for a review). General, offender-based deterrence holds little promise for meaningful crime prevention or reduction. We will revisit the concept of creating a credible threat in the section on place-based policing.

THE BROKEN WINDOWS THESIS

Order-maintenance policing has, as previously described, come detached from its original theoretical basis. The discussion of OMP's rationale, then, is bifurcated into the conceptual notion behind this strategy, on the one hand, and the practical application of it (zero-tolerance policing grounded in deterrence; Greene, 2014) on the other. This policy is based on the broken-windows thesis, so we will focus on that here and preserve the matter of the effectiveness of order-maintenance policing for later in the chapter. In examining the broken-windows thesis, we endeavor to discern whether OMP would be a promising strategy even if it were implemented in a manner true to its theoretical origins.

The broken-windows thesis is grounded in social psychology. Wilson and Kelling (1982) contended that physical disorder (vandalism, graffiti, abandoned cars, and the like) and social disorder (prostitution, public drunkenness, aggressive panhandling, and so on) signal that nobody cares enough about the area to exert any control. A collective fear sets in among local residents who no longer feel safe in public spaces, and they retreat to their homes, ceding the streets to the criminal element.

The broken-windows thesis also reflects tenets from macrolevel criminology in which it is assumed that the social and economic characteristics of an environment shape the behavior of residents and those passing through it. While this theory of social disorganization has proven robust in predicting crime (Sampson & Groves, 1989), Wilson and Kelling's "mini" version oversimplifies critical concepts (Pratt & Gau, 2009). Social disorganization theory explains how socioeconomic disadvantage, such as poverty and broken families, significantly disrupts a neighborhood's social fabric. The broken-windows thesis, by contrast, suggests that lower-level crimes and disruptions can be divorced from their socioeconomic backdrop and suppressed without tending to the deeper conditions. This is probably not true. Aggressively enforcing the law prohibiting unwanted window washing, for instance, may lend the impression that police are improving quality of life (certainly to the relief of local motorists) when in fact they have not changed the fact that homeless people need money to survive (yesterday's window washer is today's purveyor of knock-off Prada purses). Single-minded applications of OMP may inadvertently increase violence, such as by driving open-air drug dealers into secluded locations and thereby raising the risk of violence during drug transactions (Mastrofski, 1988) and forcing homeless people to sleep in alleys and other hidden spots where they face high probabilities of victimization (Duneier, 1999).

The broken-windows thesis has met with poor empirical support. One famous study claiming to prove that disorder causes crime (Skogan, 1990) was later discredited (Harcourt, 2001) and research since then has uncovered significant flaws in the thesis (Gau, Corsaro, & Brunson, 2014; Gau & Pratt, 2008, 2010; Sampson & Raudenbush, 1999, 2004; Taylor, 2001). Given the problems with the logic of broken windows, it is doubtful that OMP would work even had it not gone astray.

PLACE-BASED AND PROBLEM-BASED PREVENTION

Some types of place-based policing may prevent crime (see Sherman & Eck, 2002 for a review). Place-based strategies rest upon multiple rationales. One is deterrence. Saturating a high-crime area with police officers creates a visible reminder to offenders that the police are nearby and closely attuned to possible criminal activity. This type of deterrence may solve some of the problems noted earlier with regard to general deterrence through techniques such as random patrol. Targeted, place-based strategies are more effective than diffuse, unfocused ones (Lum, Koper, & Telep, 2011). Officer presence makes the threat of arrest more credible compared to the remote possibility that perhaps a police car will happen to pass by.

Opportunity theories—the routine-activity approach, crime-pattern theory, and the rational-choice perspective—have also been advanced as a lens through which to view the merits of place-based approaches (Felson & Clarke, 1998). The routine-activity approach highlights the situational nature of crime in that offenders and targets (vulnerable people or objects) must converge in time and space absent a capable guardian (police officer, security guard, or witness; Felson, 1998). Crime-pattern theory adds to the routine-activity approach by noting that offenders' predatory behavior will be concentrated in, around, and between the places and pathways they frequent (home, work, school, and so on). Offenders' familiarity with these locations (and ease of access to them) allows them to locate attractive targets and assess the level of guardianship (Felson & Clarke, 1998).

The rational-choice perspective within the context of opportunity theory argues that offender decision making is far more complex than what is allowed for in deterrence theory's rather one-dimensional depiction of individuals weighing the benefits of the crime against the likelihood and severity of punishment and then choosing the course of action that wins out. In reality, decision making is bounded by the immediate situation and the choice-structuring properties of certain crimes (Clarke & Cornish, 1985; Cohen & Felson, 1979). The factors entering an offender's rational calculus vary depending on the reasons for the crime and whatever situational constraints may be present (Felson & Clarke, 1998). Offenders select targets on the basis of concrete, practical considerations, such as how easy or hard the crime will be to commit and how profitable it will be (Copes & Vieraitis, 2006). A car thief might choose one car over another merely because he does not know how to drive a standard transmission and so opts for an automatic instead. Place-based policing capitalizes upon opportunity theories by seeking to remove physical or social facilitators of crime and by instating barriers between offenders and potential targets (e.g., advising drivers of cars with automatic transmissions to take extra precautions).

Place-based prevention has distinct logical advantages over offender-based strategies like deterrence and order maintenance. Places are easier to control than people are, and more predictable. For instance, research shows that in the days following a residential burglary, the risk is high that the same house or one close to it will be targeted again (Moreto, Piza, & Caplan, 2014). Increasing police presence in the area during the risk window could prevent a second victimization or create an opportunity for police to catch the perpetrator.

Place-based prevention means that police do not chase amorphous, ambiguous goals like "preventing crime" and "maintaining order" (Goldstein, 1979). Place-based policing also sidesteps the ethical problems inherent in the requirement that officers decide who is "disorderly" and who is not (see Harcourt, 2001), as well as OMP's possible unintended consequences for police–community relations. In a problem-based approach to nonconsensual window washing, for instance, police might work with the city and advocacy organizations to increase the number of meals the homeless shelter offers each day and thereby cut down on the amount of money homeless individuals need to earn. A crackdown on window washing can certainly be a component of this initiative, but the problem-based solution is superior to the OMP one because it reflects an understanding of the reasons for the problem and creativity in the response. Problem-based strategies constructed around the characteristics of places and specific bad behaviors or conditions (Eck & Clarke, 2003) possess an internal logic for reducing crime, disorder, and fear.

CITIZEN AND COMMUNITY INVOLVEMENT

Police-community partnerships come in many forms. Some are voluntary, such as police having direct lines of communication with neighborhood-watch groups. Others contain an element of coercion, such as third-party policing whereby police bring threats of civil penalties to bear upon owners and managers of residential properties where drugs have become a serious problem (Green, 1996). Partnerships rely on the logic that because many local problems have multifaceted origins, police require community assistance (Goldstein, 1979; Green, 1996).

Community involvement makes sense in many respects. Police cannot be everywhere at all times (and society would devolve into a police state if they were), so self-policing mechanisms must be in place. Spheres of social control include private (e.g., the family), parochial (e.g., ties between neighbors), and public (e.g., the police). Each one operates independently of the other two and yet is dependent upon them in important ways (Bursik & Grasmick, 1993). Parochial social control increasingly relies upon assistance from the police to effectively maintain public order and address local problems (Carr, 2003). Police, likewise, rely upon citizens for information about crimes and offenders. When people do not trust the police, they stop reporting problems and offering information (Sampson & Bartusch, 1998). It is no coincidence that inner-city neighborhoods plagued by crime and disorder are also places where the relationship between the police and local residents is contentious or broken (Brunson & Gau, 2015; Gau & Brunson, 2010; Sampson & Bartusch, 1998). Police and communities possess a natural symbiosis requiring them to pull together for the preservation of public peace.

The downside of community involvement is that "community" is hard to define (Greene & Taylor, 1988). The CP and broken-windows frameworks admonish police to find out what "the community" wants, but in reality it is difficult to figure out who or what the community actually is. Clearly, the entire city cannot be considered "the community," so police need to parse out smaller geographic or social units. In many places, people living in close residential proximity to one another (meeting the geographic definition of a neighborhood) manifest heterogeneity in cultural values and have no social ties. Some neighborhoods have "communities," but many do not (Mastrofski, 1988). Absent a clear definition of community and a sense of shared responsibility among residents of the same neighborhood, it is hard for police to form partnerships or motivate collective action. This represents a potential barrier to community-based approaches.

THE EMPIRICAL STATUS OF POLICE POLICIES

Implementation failures have been pervasive among all the police innovations discussed in this chapter. Implementations contain some of the elements of the conceptual frameworks, but usually fall short of full utilization (e.g., the SARA model of POP is typically more "SAR") or have deviated in practice from their underlying theoretical origins (e.g., in many cities, OMP looks quite different from the vision of policing articulated in the broken-windows thesis). The quality of evaluation designs also varies. This section should be read with recognition of these limitations.

ORDER-MAINTENANCE POLICING

Support for OMP is equivocal (Greene, 2014). Most research designs are not very strong (Sherman & Eck, 2002) and weaker designs tend to produce stronger effect sizes (Braga, Welsh, & Schnell, 2015). Braga et al. (2015) grouped disorder-reduction approaches into aggressive order maintenance and community problem solving. Their meta-analysis of evaluations of both approaches found that only the community problem-solving initiatives reduced crime or disorder—aggressive order maintenance had no impact. Rosenfeld, Fornango, and Rengifo (2007) revisited New York City's marked violent-crime drop in the 1990s—a reduction OMP proponents attribute to NYPD's adoption of this strategy in the early 1990s—and found that OMP probably contributed to between 1 percent and 5 percent of the decline in robberies and between 6 percent and 12 percent of the homicide drop.

Some researchers have evaluated OMP-based stop, question, and frisk practices using microplaces (such as street segments and intersections) rather than entire cities. The logic of this methodology is that since crime is concentrated in small hot spots, policing activity is likely to be more prevalent in these same areas and, therefore, this unit of analysis is more precise than trying to examine the entire city or large segments of it. Weisburd, Telep, and Lawton (2014) confirmed that stops and frisks are concentrated in crime hot spots. Weisburd, Wooditch, Weisburd, and Yang (2016) found evidence that stops deter crime in microplaces, but this effect was very weak. The authors concluded that other policing strategies are more fruitful.

Order-maintenance policing has worsened relationships between police and minority communities. Stops (and frisks) of blacks and Latinos have soared under this policy (Fagan & Davies, 2000; Gelman et al., 2012). Blacks in urban areas express anger that they cannot walk down the street in their own neighborhoods without fearing potential confrontations with police (Gau & Brunson, 2010). As mentioned earlier, OMP may increase violence by driving public acts into secluded areas (Duneier, 1999; Mastrofski, 1988). It can be culturally insensitive, as well, by criminalizing longstanding pastimes like playing ball in the street, an activity that unites entire Latino neighborhoods (Vera Sanchez & Gau, 2015). Moreover, the strategy is not efficient; an analysis of New York City Police Department's OMP program found that approximately 6 or 7 percent of stops result in arrests (Weisburd et al., 2014). An entire year's worth of stops in this city (686,000) is associated with a 2 percent reduction in crime (Weisburd et al., 2016). This modest or weak crime-reduction impact of OMP might be outweighed by its criminogenic side effects (Howell, 2009) and the damage to police legitimacy and police–community relations it causes, in addition to being an inefficient use of police agencies' resources (Weisburd et al., 2016).

PROBLEM-ORIENTED POLICING

Goldstein (1979) proposed POP after observing that police departments were obsessed with administrative matters (how many officers were on the streets, average response times to 911 calls, and so on) and neglected the development of effective strategies for achieving public safety and order. After decades of POP efforts, Eck (2003) finally concluded that, "Problem-oriented policing has become the victim of the disease it was meant to cure, the 'means over ends syndrome'" (p. 79). Police departments typically fall short of the SARA idea. Problem identification and response creation are usually superficial and rely upon traditional strategies (such as arrest, programs for at-risk youth, and the like). For instance, San Diego Police Department officers were found to be selecting small-scale problems, conducting minimal analyses or investigations, and employing traditional rather than creative solutions (Cordner & Biebel, 2005). The "assessment" part of SARA is usually cursory or is missing entirely (Scott, 2003), so most agencies are actually employing SAR instead of SARA.

Where it has been properly implemented and evaluated, however, POP has produced promising results (Weisburd, Telep, Hinkle, & Eck, 2010). Problem-based approaches can reduce crime (Braga, Weisburd, Waring, Mazerolle, Spelman, & Gajewski, , 1999) as well as citizen complaints about police (Jesilow, Meyer, Parsons, & Tegeler, 1998), even within public-housing areas (Mazerolle, Ready, Terrill, & Waring,, 2000). Problem-oriented policing may be most effective when directed at specific problems pervasive in particular areas (Avdija, 2008). Boston's Operation Ceasefire, for instance, is a famous program that appears to have reduced homicides among the city's young people by targeting gang-involved youth (Braga, Kennedy, Waring, & Piehl, 2001). Open-air drug markets and accompanying disorder and property crimes can be ameliorated with POP (Corsaro, Brunson, & McGarrell, 2009).

COMMUNITY POLICING

As mentioned previously, community policing is an organizational strategy, not a specific program or policy. There is general consensus among police researchers that CP has not been implemented (Schaefer Morabito, 2010). With the notable exception of Chicago (Skogan, 2006), police agencies have not made the organizational alterations subsumed under the CP framework (Maguire, 1997). Many have undertaken a few measures that speak to this organizational model, but it is difficult to determine whether those changes are genuine or merely symbolic (Maguire & Mastrofski, 2000).

In spite of the general absence of significant organizational change, most police departments participate in some form of community engagement (Cordner, 2014) and the results are typically positive. In one city, the police department's program to reach out to disadvantaged youths significantly improved participating children's sense of responsibility for their community (Thurman, Giacomazzi, & Bogen, 1993). In two other cities, police–community collaboration significantly reduced citizens' perceptions of disorder in their neighborhoods and increased their sense of safety (Reisig & Parks, 2004). An evaluation of community policing in one suburban area showed declines in violent and property crime, but not in drug offenses (Connell, Miggans, & McGloin, 2008), a finding bolstered by other research demonstrating that CP has to be targeted to achieve reductions in specifically identified types of crime (Zhao, Scheider, & Thurman, 2002). Civilian patrols, wherein trained community members wear uniforms and patrol in official vehicles, may reduce crime in hot spots (Ariel, Weinborn, & Sherman, 2016). Neighborhood watches can also bring crime down, though the effect is inconsistent (Bennett, Holloway, & Farrington, 2006) and these organizations do not always successfully increase residents' commitment to their neighborhoods (Donnelly & Kimble, 2006).

Foot patrol has garnered positive reactions from citizens (Trojanowicz & Baldwin, 1982) and officers (Trojanowicz & Banas, 1985). Foot patrol may also reduce violence in violent-crime hot spots (Piza & O'Hara, 2014; but see Groff et al., 2015). This effect might be achieved through enhanced deterrence (Ratcliffe, Taniguchi, Groff, & Wood, 2011) or the fact that officers on foot have more contact with community members and obtain better information about crimes and offenders (Groff, Johnson, Ratcliffe, & Wood, 2012; Wood, Sorg, Groff, Ratcliffe, & Taylor, 2014). The initial benefits of foot patrol in violence hot spots, however, may wear off over time (Novak, Fox, Carr, & Spade, 2016; Sorg, Haberman, Ratcliffe, & Groff, 2013).

DATA-DRIVEN POLICING

Compstat has been widely implemented nationally (Weisburd et al., 2003) after it seemed to work in New York City; however, rigorous analysis of that city's crime drop in the 1990s found that Compstat, in fact, contributed very little to the decline (Eck & Maguire, 2000). Other analyses of Compstat's crime-reduction benefits have also arrived at null conclusions (Rosenfeld, Fornango, & Baumer, 2005). It is possible that Compstat helps facilitate the implementation of other approaches (e.g., POP). One study found that departments invested in Compstat had better-specified goals than those not using this model (Weisburd, Mastrofski, Greenspan, & Willis, 2012), suggesting that this managerial approach may be an important component of total organizational reorientation of street-level priorities and supervision strategies; however, other research indicates that most departments' Compstat models fall short of meaningful organizational change (Willis et al., 2007).

The research on place-based approaches is favorable (Lum et al., 2011). Importantly, crime displacement almost never occurs (e.g., Braga, 2005); in fact, place-based strategies commonly produce a diffusion of benefits such that surrounding areas also experience crime reductions (Weisburd & Green, 1993; Worrall, 2016). Hot-spots policing has met with general support, although positive results are not uniform across studies. Some research finds that ramping up police presence in hot spots reduces crime and disorder (Braga, 2005), presumably through the deterrent impact of increased police visibility (Sherman & Weisburd, 1995), while other studies uncover no effect (Taylor, Koper, & Woods, 2011). There are indications that hot-spots policing is most effective when officers focus on a specific type of crime (Avdija, 2008). Drug enforcement in hot spots has produced positive outcomes (Green, 1996; Weisburd & Green, 1993) as has gun-law enforcement (Sherman & Rogan, 1995), although this impact might not be consistent across all types of gun crimes (Rosenfeld, Deckard, & Blackburn, 2014).

It is also advisable for police to employ a specific plan that is tailored to the needs of the area. Problem-oriented policing seems to work better than saturated patrol (Braga & Bond, 2008; Braga, Papachristos, & Hureau, 2014), although saturated patrol is not necessarily entirely ineffective despite its smaller impact (Taylor, Koper, & Woods, 2011). The size of the targeted area matters, with microplaces (e.g., street segments) being superior to larger units such as patrol beats. Also, crime hot spots can move around, so police need constant, timely information to ensure they are targeting the right crime at the right place (Groff et al., 2015).

The few studies that have evaluated ILP are process evaluations, which makes sense because ILP is about the procedure used to allocate resources, not the outcome of that procedure. Most departments claiming to do ILP actually only utilize a diluted version (Carter, Phillips, & Gayadeen, 2014; Ratcliffe, 2016). Most of the research comes from countries outside the United States. One study identified impediments to ILP implementation within the Ugandan Wildlife Authority, the governmental organization responsible for the welfare of the country's protected species. Among these hindrances were line-level rangers' lack of access to the equipment (e.g., handheld GPS devices) they need to provide the information asked from them, and lack of understanding about the information-gathering process and precise definition of "intelligence" (Moreto, 2015). An examination of officers and analysts in the New Jersey State Police revealed slow and modest, yet noticeable, changes in officers' and analysts' attitudes after the agency radically reoriented its Investigations Branch to embrace ILP. Many officers and analysts welcomed the opportunity to share information and reported feeling more productive and effective, while several others resisted the changes or remained skeptical that ILP was anything more than the latest fad (Ratcliffe & Guidetti, 2008). A study of the UK Environment Agency's Securing Compliant Waste Exports Project found that this agency successfully launched an ILP initiative designed to reduce the illegal export of electronic waste, such as computers. Steps to information collection and analysis were mapped out, and information was collected from multiple sources. Importantly, in accordance with ILP precepts (Ratcliffe, 2016), the agency prioritized problems and devoted the bulk of its resources toward the most problematic offenders (Gibbs, McGarrell, & Sullivan, 2015). Finally, an examination of England and Wales' National Intelligence Model found that although this program embedded the concepts of ILP into British police agencies, police practice had not noticeably shifted in this direction and, in fact, seemed to be reverting back toward traditional tactics (Maguire & John, 2006).

CONCLUSION

This chapter critically examined the origins, implementation, and effectiveness of several of the most popular recent innovations in policing. One of the biggest challenges facing police today is how to be both effective and fair. Many historical and recent mistakes starkly reveal how misguided police are when they take a scorched-earth approach to crime control and lay waste to their relationships with communities. Some communities enjoy peaceful, mutually beneficial relationships with their local police forces, while in other cities, police and community members clash publicly and sometimes violently. Even within communities harboring substantial distrust of police, however, there is a strong desire for better police protection. Police agencies need ways to reduce local crime and disorder while also alleviating fear and promoting quality of life and positive police–citizen relations.

We saw in this chapter that the police role should be about much more than responding for calls to service, patrolling randomly, and making arrests; this is an overly narrow construction of the police role and seriously limits officers' ability to make a beneficial impact. The most promising approaches entail organizational changes that reorient police toward the identification of problems and constructive solutions grounded in an understanding of opportunity theories and well-researched, carefully analyzed intelligence. Citizen groups and private third parties should be leveraged when warranted. Goals need to be concrete and feasible, and evaluations must always follow interventions to determine if the problem has been alleviated or if a new approach needs to be devised. Multiple innovations should be combined to tailor responses based on particular problems. Officers on foot patrol, for instance, may obtain useful information that they convey to analysts, who combine the information with that from other sources to produce intelligence which is then used to construct a solution to a local problem. Creativity, proactivity, and relationship building are the tickets to a bright future for policing.

DISCUSSION QUESTIONS

1. A persistent obstacle to the implementation of innovative policing policies is time. Patrol officers spend their shifts answering calls for service, and most officers in urban areas do not have enough time to engage in high-quality problem solving, community engagement, and so on. If they do these things at all, it is cursory and not a genuine application of innovative practices. What can be done about this? Propose ways police organizations can address the fact that it is unrealistic to expect patrol officers to answer calls for service and simultaneously carry out innovations.
2. A dilemma in police innovations is that the neighborhoods most in need of police help in reducing crime and improving quality of life are the least able to support these changes in the police approach. They are socioeconomically distressed, often socially disorganized, and have high levels of mistrust toward the police. How might police in these areas combine different innovations as a means of effectively implementing promising police policies in distressed, high-crime neighborhoods? Combine the core elements of at least two policies, and explain how each one supports the other.
3. Although police feature prominently in the overarching efforts to suppress crime in the United States, harsh penalties (such as prison) typically predominate in policy debates. Discussions are more about the severity portion of deterrence, and less so about the certainty portion. States spend enormous sums on prisons. Police agencies face resource shortages and do not have the personnel or money to fully dedicate themselves to innovative practices. What should states do about this? In what ways might increased spending on police reduce correctional expenditures if police use the additional resources to implement innovations?
4. Recent protests and riots have starkly revealed the damage that police militarization and aggressive policies like stop-and-frisk have inflicted on police agencies' relationships with disadvantaged communities, particularly communities of color. A popular presumption that started in the 1990s and accelerated in the post-9/11 era is that police are most effective when they are tough, forceful, and intolerant. This attitude and approach, however, drives a wedge between police and the communities in which tough tactics are employed most frequently. How might police agencies turn toward innovative policies to simultaneously reduce crime and improve (or at least not worsen) their relationships with communities? Identify ways in which certain innovations offer improvements over the aggressive, crime-fighting model that has contributed to police–community tensions.

CASES CITED

Floyd v. City of New York, 959 F. Supp. 2d 540 (2013)
Illinois v. Wardlow, 528 U. S. 119 (2000)
Minnesota v. Dickerson, 508 U.S. 366 (1993)
Terry v. Ohio, 392 U.S. 1 (1968)

CHAPTER 14

CORRECTIONAL TREATMENT AND REHABILITATION

INTRODUCTION

Each week in the United States, more than 10,000 people exit state and federal prisons to restart their lives. This adds up to 650,000 returning prisoners every year (U.S. Department of Justice, n.d.). The vast majority of people sentenced to prison eventually reenter society. Dismally, the overwhelming majority of ex-prisoners reoffend, and more than half end up right back in prison within a few years and sometimes even within a few months of their release (Durose, Cooper, & Snyder, 2014). Neither deterrence nor incapacitation—the two reigning theories of punishment in the United States—offers a means of curbing recidivism or improving ex-offenders' prospects for succeeding in life after prison. Correctional treatment and rehabilitation holds promise to alleviate this situation.

Rehabilitation has a complicated and tumultuous relationship with correctional policy. Rehabilitation bears commonalities with other crime-related policies in that the public's opinion is contradicted by research studies and general academic understanding. At the same time, it stands apart from many other crime-related policies in that, thanks to the volume and meticulousness of the research it has inspired, rehabilitation boasts a clear set of "what works" principles. The process of implementing an evidence-based, effective treatment program is not quite as simple as applying a formula, but is akin to following a recipe. Using the correct ingredients and proper process will produce the desired outcome, and minor modifications are permitted so long as there is no substantial deviation from the directions. The programs that utilize the principles of correctional intervention show positive outcomes, and the ones that do not use them have poor outcomes. The world of empirical study of crime policy is often murky. Rehabilitation is a refreshingly clear policy prescription, though of course some areas of knowledge remain in need of further development.

Despite the existence of a roadmap to effective programming, many correctional-rehabilitation efforts fall short. Owing to multiple factors (inadequate budgets, insufficient training, misunderstandings by staff, and so on), rehabilitation programs nationwide suffer from a lack of the core components necessary to effect positive change. This situation can be remedied through education and training of policymakers and staff members who, collectively, design and implement treatment programs.

This chapter considers correctional rehabilitation as a criminal-justice policy. Rehabilitation can take place in correctional institutions (prisons and jails) and the community, so we will cover programs pertaining to each of these settings. Rehabilitation is delivered under diverse circumstances. Sometimes it is a program that prison or jail inmates can opt to participate in during their term of incarceration, sometimes it is a voluntary portion of probation or parole, and other times it is a mandatory element of a community-based sentence that functions as an alternative to incarceration for offenders offered the choice either to participate in programming or to serve a sentence of incarceration. As we will see, the key elements to effective rehabilitation require some adaptation to the context but, overall, span all treatment settings.

We will begin by examining the relationship between mental illness, substance abuse, and crime. An appreciation for the importance of this complicated set of factors will illuminate the importance of addressing the underlying factors that contribute to antisocial behavior. Not all offenders in need of correctional programming suffer from diagnosed mental illnesses; later in the chapter, we will see how maladaptive thought patterns contribute to antisocial behavior even absent a formal psychological disorder. Treatment is therefore beneficial to a broad spectrum of people. That being said, mental illness does play a role in crime, albeit one that is not fully understood as of yet. For this reason, we will start off with a discussion of the rates of mental illness and substance abuse among correctional populations.

MENTAL ILLNESS AND SUBSTANCE ABUSE AMONG CRIMINAL OFFENDERS

Most people with mental illness do not commit crime, but this group does have a higher arrest rate relative to people without such diagnoses (Wallace, Mullen, & Burgess, 2004). Mental-health problems are prevalent among known offenders (that is, jail, prison, and probation populations), and rates exceed those found in the general community (Diamond, Wang, Holzer, & Thomas, 2001). Estimates vary, but researchers believe that 20 percent of state and federal prisoners suffer from a cognitive disability, compared to 5 percent of the general population (Bronson, Maruschak, & Berzofsky, 2015). With respect to severe mental illness, the estimates are 6 to 15 percent of jail inmates and 10 to 15 percent of state prisoners (Lamb & Weinberger, 1998). Psychotic illnesses (which entail hallucinations, delusions, and other severe disruptions to one's functioning) are present among approximately 3.6 percent of male prisoners and 3.9 percent of female prisoners (Fazel & Seewald, 2012). A high proportion of those with mental-health problems are diagnosed as comorbid, meaning they have two or more psychiatric disorders (Diamond et al., 2001; Lovell, Gagliardi, & Peterson, 2002).

The arrest rate among people with mental illness rose sharply in the 1960s and 1970s, likely due to the deinstitutionalization movement (Steadman, Cocozza, & Melick, 1978). This movement involved a nationwide closing of state-run psychiatric hospitals. Deinsitutionalization was popularized by major stories revealing hidden horrors occurring within these hospitals. The documentary film *Titicut Follies*, in particular, captured national attention in its graphic depiction of patients tied to beds and locked in cells for indefinite periods, given careless and even reckless medication levels, and subject to emotional abuse by staff, even including social workers and psychiatrists. At the same time, major advances in psychiatric medication were suggesting unprecedented potential for individuals with serious mental illnesses (such as schizophrenia) to lead at least seminormal lives. Spurred by the widespread belief that institutionalized mental-health care was doing more harm than good and that drug therapies were the treatment modality of the future, states shuttered many of their psychiatric hospitals (Dear & Wolch, 1987).

The proposed alternative was a system of community-based mental-health care centers where former patients would receive the assistance they needed in an outpatient setting; however, these community clinics never appeared in the numbers needed to serve the scope of the need and those that did open failed to coordinate with hospitals to ensure continuity of care for recently released patients (Bassuk & Samuel, 1978). The practical effect was that thousands of mentally ill people, some of them plagued by crippling psychiatric disturbances, were dumped onto the streets (Dear & Wolch, 1987; Johnson, 1990). The scant number of agencies offering services bloomed into small ghettos as mentally ill, homeless individuals encamped around them (Dear & Wolch, 1987).

Mentally ill individuals face many obstacles in life that increase their chances of committing crime and becoming involved in the criminal justice system. Homelessness is associated with a risk of criminal-justice contact because, by definition, homeless people have to do things outside (use the restroom, drink alcohol, and so on) that people who have homes generally do indoors. Many of these activities are crimes when performed in public. Drug addiction is also common among mentally ill populations (Lovell et al., 2002), further enhancing their rate of arrest, conviction, and punishment. Mentally ill and drug-addicted offenders often receive a modicum of treatment in jail or prison and afterward, but the follow-up care for released offenders is substandard and unlikely to meaningfully assist these individuals (Lovell et al., 2002). Recidivism is common (Lovell et al., 2002) and parolees and probationers with mental-health problems are more likely than those without these issues to violate the terms of their community sentences and be committed or returned to prison (see Skeem, Manchak, & Peterson, 2011 for a review).

As the next section will show, the prevalence of mental illness among correctional populations is nothing new. Throughout history, jails and prisons have been the default repository for the people society does not know how to handle. While the underlying etiology of criminal justice contact among those with mental illness is complex and requires a broader-based effort than what the system alone can accommodate, jails, prisons, and community-based supervision agencies seem ideally situated to help those who come through their doors. The quest to transform a period of criminal-justice custody into a life-changing experience is an old and ongoing one.

HISTORY OF CORRECTIONAL TREATMENT AND REHABILITATION

Correctional rehabilitation experienced its zenith in the mid-1900s. From the early 1900s until the 1960s and 1970s, policymakers and the public embraced the notion that offenders' deviant behavior originated from mental defects instilled in them by deleterious life circumstances. This belief was grounded in psychological and criminological concepts and research. In the early 1900s, the field of psychiatry, led most notably by the famous Austrian neurologist Sigmund Freud, inspired the view that aberrant social behavior can be traced to illnesses of the mind; furthermore, those illnesses were treatable and, eventually, curable. Psychoanalysis (Freud's intensely popular psychiatric treatment method) was championed as a gold standard for uncovering the deep-seated etiology of pathological thinking and behavior and for either eliminating the problem or, at the least, improving the patient enough so that she or he could lead a reasonably normal life.

In the 1920s, researchers in the Chicago school of criminology began documenting the relationship between macrolevel socioeconomic disadvantage and rates of crime and delinquency. Sociologists Robert E. Park and Ernest Burgess were two of the pioneers of this school of thought, followed in ensuing decades by other famous criminologists such as Edwin Sutherland, Clifford Shaw, and Henry D. McKay. The theories and evidence linking offending to criminogenic ecological conditions bolstered the psychological viewpoint of crime as an outcome of mental disorders which, in turn, are produced by stress and trauma. In spite of this linkage to the macrolevel, however, rehabilitation proponents turned their attention entirely to the psychological side of the equation. Correctional rehabilitation targeted the offender and (to the detriment of these programs) paid relatively little attention to the social circumstances giving rise to pathological mental conditions.

During its heyday, rehabilitation was the dominant punishment rationale. People convicted of crimes were sent to prison so they could reap the (supposed) benefits of correctional programming. To help accomplish the goal of successfully rehabilitating offenders, judges, prison wardens, parole boards, and, at the community level, probation officers were granted wide latitude in making decisions pertaining to sentencing, release, and treatment protocol. The Model Penal Code, established in the 1950s, codified indeterminate sentencing as the fulcrum of rehabilitation. Indeterminate sentencing permitted authorities the discretion to tailor each sentence to the individual offender (Tonry, 2000). The assumption was that effective treatment required the state to respond to the individual needs of the offender.

In the 1960s, cracks started to open in the rehabilitation paradigm. The decay ran parallel with the deinstitutionalization movement described earlier. This decade was a time of social unrest and widespread public dissatisfaction with the government. The Civil Rights Movement highlighted the deep racial divisions still marring society and shaming governmental policies, and the U.S. involvement in the Vietnam War (and the associated draft that forced thousands of young men to fight against their will) dramatically damaged the government's legitimacy in the eyes of its citizenry. People also began questioning

what right the government had to capture people and alter their minds. This philosophical dilemma was captured poignantly in the popular films *A Clockwork Orange* and *One
Flew over the Cuckoo's Nest* as the tumult continued into the 1970s. Alongside these social
upheavals, urban crime rates were rising swiftly. Cities had become dangerous and—by
middle-class standards—places of disorder and decay. The government's crime-control
policies, it seemed, were not working.

In 1974, a report was published that posterity has labeled the death knell of the rehabilitation era. Robert Martinson, a criminologist skeptical of corrections officials' ability to
"fix" offenders, published a famous (in hindsight, infamous) treatise in which he delivered
a scathing critique of correctional rehabilitation. He reviewed 231 studies evaluating rehabilitation programs, and his pessimistic concluding remarks spawned the phrase "nothing
works." It would later be revealed that his study suffered serious methodological flaws
and his conclusions were premised upon faulty analyses. At the time, however, "nothing
works" quickly became the slogan of liberals and conservatives alike, all of whom (though
for differing reasons) wanted rehabilitation to meet its demise.

The end of the 1960s saw a national shift to the political right, and in subsequent years
the conservative drift turned into a veritable lurch. While liberal and conservative camps
agreed in wanting to dismantle rehabilitation and replace it with something else, they dif-
fered sharply on their reasons and proposed solutions. Conservatives saw the rising tide of
urban crime and disorder as proof that the government was "soft on crime" and needed to
get tough (e.g., Kelling & Coles, 1996); their policy proposal was to replace rehabilitation
with a punishment-oriented approach that would ride under the banners of deterrence
and incapacitation. They saw prison (without programming) as critical to accomplishing
these goals. (For a full treatment of deterrence, incapacitation, and mass incarceration, see
Chapter 8.) Liberals failed to articulate a competing set of proposals. There was no major
push from the left on a scale or with a forcefulness rivaling that which issued from the
conservative camp. As a result, crime policy veered away from rehabilitation and began its
journey into the "get-tough" era (Pratt, Gau, & Franklin, 2011).

CURRENT TRENDS IN CORRECTIONAL TREATMENT
AND REHABILITATION

The get-tough era championed deterrence and incapacitation as the sole acceptable rationales for punishment. Rehabilitation was considered discredited and debunked. And yet, it
was never *truly* disproven. In fact, the science behind correctional treatment was only just
beginning to gain ground in the 1960s and 1970s with the development of criminological
and psychological theories and research about the causes of criminal behavior (Gendreau,
1996). Rehabilitation was abandoned right at the moment when it was moving in a good
direction. Martinson's grim diagnosis of correctional therapy was but one of many empirical studies being published at the time, many of which cast rehabilitation in a positive light.
Yet these other sources of information, though no less (and quite possibly more) authorita-
tive than Martinson's report, were largely ignored. Martinson received widespread attention for two reasons. First, he was already something of a celebrity for his outspoken views
on rehabilitation and he accompanied the publication of his "nothing works" paper with a

talk show tour that distributed his message widely. Second, his argument fit well with the conservative movement's search for a way to knock the last, final leg out from under rehabilitation. What did not get glitzy media coverage were the studies immediately following Martinson's work that revealed the flaws in his methods and, by extension, his conclusions (e.g., Gendreau & Ross, 1979). Quite simply, Martinson was wrong.

While policymakers and the public gave up on rehabilitation and turned to ideologies grounded in deterrence and incapacitation, many academics continued the push for better understanding of what works. Some treatments were indeed ineffective; to that end, Martinson and other critics had a point. But some rehabilitation regimens *did* work. The goal became to figure out what elements, specifically, distinguished effective programs from ineffective ones. This is where Martinson had erred: He lumped all rehabilitation programs into a single group and tallied up the number of positive and negative outcome evaluations. He ignored (or, at least, failed to recognize the importance of) the fact that roughly half of the programs he reviewed did reduce recidivism, and he neglected to critically examine the literature for reasons why outcome evaluations were so split in their findings about program effectiveness (see Bonta, Wallace-Capretta, & Rooney, 2000). Researchers, largely consisting of a group of Canadian psychologists (Petersilia, 2004), took up the challenge and yielded some critical successes that put rehabilitation back on the radar of many researchers and some policymakers in the United States.

Rehabilitation today is experiencing something of a rejuvenation in public support. Part of this is due to a growing recognition of the high rates of mental illness, physical disability, educational disadvantage, and substance-abuse histories among jail and prison inmates. As described earlier, prisoners have higher rates of mental illness than that found in the general population. Estimates suggest that 40 percent of female prisoners and 31 percent of male prisoners have one or more mental or physical disabilities (these numbers are 49 percent and 30 percent, respectively, among jail inmates). The majority of these disabilities are cognitive (Bronson et al., 2015). Offenders have educational deficits, too. Roughly 41 percent of jail and prison inmates (and 31 percent of probationers) do not have a high-school or equivalency diploma. Among adults in the general population, 18 percent lack a diploma (Harlow, 2003). Both policymakers and the public at large have begun to realize that offenders, as a group, need help.

Substantial portions of the U.S. population feel rehabilitation should be a part of correctional intervention, particularly for younger offenders (Moon, Sundt, Cullen, & Wright, 2000; Nagin, Piquero, Scott, & Steinberg, 2006; Piquero et al., 2010). The federal government and many states have invested in various forms of in-prison programs and reentry services to increase the chances of successful transition from prison back into the community (Petersilia, 2004). Rehabilitation is in the midst of a reemergence (Pratt et al., 2011).

REHABILITATION TECHNIQUES AND PROGRAMS

A core set of techniques forms the basis for the various offender-therapy programs in existence. These modalities manifest in various forms, but share common underlying theoretical precepts. Cognitive-behavioral therapy (CBT) is the most popular. This treatment modality is grounded in a model that traces antisocial behavior back to errors of cognition.

All people develop cognitive shortcuts (called schemas) that organize the manner in which information is processed and stimuli are responded to. For some (often people with histories of being abused, neglected, or victimized) these schemas are maladaptive. People who fall into a trap of cognitive errors are prone to reacting strongly to unpleasant stimuli. Conflict or obstacles trigger automatic thoughts about being unlovable, being a failure in life, having no friends, and so on. Ambiguous events are interpreted in the most negative light possible. These cognitive errors, in turn, lead to internalizing (e.g., depression) and externalizing (e.g., aggression) emotions and subsequent behaviors (e.g., drug use, violence; see Dozois & Beck, 2011 for a review).

Cognitive therapy targets the automatic thoughts that are at the heart of the progression from unpleasant stimuli to antisocial behavior. The theory is that getting people to become aware of these automatic thoughts will help them control and, ultimately, change the way they process and react to incoming information. Programs grounded in CBT teach offenders how to analyze their thoughts for negative patterns, slow down and think carefully about their reactions to negative events, and start employing more prosocial cognitive, affective, and behavioral means of coping (Beck, Liese, & Najavits, 2016).

Dialectical-behavior therapy (DBT) is another popular method routinely applied in correctional settings. This therapy is specifically geared toward people with borderline personality disorder (BPD), a mental illness in which the individual persistently interprets others' words and actions as personal attacks and blames others for his or her problems. People with this disorder are at high risk for suicide, so DBT was developed to both improve functioning and reduce suicide rates among this population. The therapy has also successfully treated substance-abuse disorders and other problems, even including binge eating and purging (bulimia). There is a high rate of comorbidity between BPD and substance abuse, and a unique DBT model has been developed specifically for people who have both disorders (Hunter, Rosenthal, Lynch, & Linehan, 2016). The theory at the core of DBT is that emotional dysregulation is the central cause of negative thoughts and actions. When people with BPD or other forms of emotional distortions experience real or imagined conflicts with others, they quickly resort to aggressive or depressive emotions, which they then attempt to quell through destructive behavioral responses such as drug use, self-injury, or extreme overeating. Importantly, DBT is premised upon a biosocial theory of mental illness in which emotional dysregulation of the sort seen in BPD originates from malfunction in the region of the brain responsible for processing and regulating emotions. Thus, there is no cure for this illness and the goal is to help patients manage it (Robins & Rosenthal, 2011).

The DBT model focuses on acceptance and change (Hunter et al., 2016; Robins & Rosenthal, 2011). Therapists frequently draw from Zen Buddhist ideas about coming to terms with the negative aspects of life and being content with one's present circumstances instead of obsessing over things that were lost or never attained. Change involves therapists teaching patients how to solve problems. Therapists take patients step-by-step through recent events in their lives when emotional reactions were extreme or distorted and led to subsequent maladaptive behaviors. Through dialogue, therapists attempt to help patients see that their emotions were out of proportion and that their behaviors were destructive to themselves and their personal relationships with others (Robins & Rosenthal, 2011).

The "dialectic" is a philosophical mode of discourse intended to reconcile apparent contradictions by talking in a point–counterpoint fashion until a fundamental truth emerges. In DBT, the dialectic process is one in which the therapist guides the patient to the realization that every emotional and behavioral response has an opposite option and that no response is inevitable or uncontrollable (Hunter et al., 2016). Elements of CBT may be incorporated into the DBT regimen if it appears that negative schemas are also at play (Robins & Rosenthal, 2011).

Therapeutic-community (TC) treatment is popular with offenders who have serious substance-use disorders. Most TC programs are conducted in prison, although the effectiveness of institutional models spurred a gradual extension of TCs into community settings (Martin, Butzin, Saum, & Inciardi, 1999). The hallmark of TCs is that inmates are separated from the general prison population in a special area containing only other inmates also in the TC program and staff assigned solely to it. It is a "total treatment environment that can be isolated from the rest of the prison population—separated from the drugs, the violence, and the norms and values that rebuff attempts at rehabilitation" (Inciardi, Martin, & Surratt, 2000, p. 3).

The TC intervention is, ideally, a three-stage process that begins in prison, continues as the offender transitions into work release, and tapers off during parole (Inciardi et al., 2000; Martin et al., 1999). It is important to continue the therapy during work release, as this is the point at which the individual leaves the total institutional environment of the prison TC and is again exposed to potential triggers and criminogenic influences. The transitioning offender is highly vulnerable during this time. Once individuals have been paroled, out-patient therapy and group counseling should be used, and individuals should be encouraged to return to the work-release TC periodically for refresher courses (Inciardi et al., 2000). This three-stage continuum of care is optimal for preventing relapse and recidivism upon release from prison.

There is no single treatment modality used uniformly in all TCs. Behavioral, cognitive, and emotional therapies are the most appropriate approaches (Hooper, Lockwood, & Inciardi, 1993). The idea is to treat the whole person, not merely the substance-use disorder, and to see the abuse of substances as a symptom of deeper issues rather than the primary locus of the problem (Hooper et al., 1993; Inciardi et al., 2000). Self-help and personal accountability are emphasized. Inmates in TCs must earn privileges and rewards through prosocial behavior, and the inmates are responsible for the daily maintenance of the unit (Hooper et al., 1993).

Cognitive-behavioral therapy, dialectical-behavior therapy, and the TC model are not the only available approaches, but they are the most common in terms of forming the basis for the majority of treatment programs in use. In particular, CBT is a staple of correctional programming. Programs frequently draw from multiple modalities for approaches tailored to the needs of offenders and the institutional or community setting. Some programs used by prisons, jails, and community-corrections agencies are prepackaged, evidence-based curriculums, and others are local creations that might or might not be effective.

A multitude of prison, jail, and community-based treatment programs are in use around the nation. At the federal level, the Bureau of Prisons offers several options. The Challenge

Program is a CBT regimen for male prison inmates that targets mental illness, substance abuse, and criminal thinking errors that give rise to antisocial behaviors. It is limited to inmates with diagnosed substance-abuse or major mental-health disorders. The Mental Health Step Down Unit Program assists inmates with severe mental illness who cannot reasonably function in the general-population environment of the prison but are not so impaired as to require confinement in a psychiatric unit. This program utilizes CBT, skills training, and a form of TC to help inmates manage their mental-health issues and prevent the need for inpatient hospitalization. Several drug-treatment options are also available, ranging from basic educational classes to treatment in the form of the moderately intensive Nonresidential Drug Abuse Program and the intensive Residential Drug Abuse Program. Both treatment programs are CBT based. The Resolve Program uses a combination of CBT, cognitive processing therapy, and DBT to help offenders who are experiencing the effects of exposure to trauma. Finally, federal prisons provide both residential and non-residential, CBT-based sex-offender treatments. The residential program uses a TC design (Federal Bureau of Prisons, 2016).

Several high-quality, evidence-based programs have been developed that combine the elements of "what works" and lay out a clear set of instructions for corrections officials to implement in their institutions or agencies. These programs come prepackaged to guide corrections personnel in implementing them. This removes much of the burden and uncertainty (see D. B. Wilson, Bouffard, & MacKenzie, 2005), thus facilitating more widespread use of correctional programming. Most of these programs have a CBT core, and they differ from one another in the additional therapeutic elements added on and the specific types of thoughts, emotions, and behaviors they target for change.

One of the packaged treatment plans is Moral Reconation Therapy® (MRT). This program is grounded in the belief that healthy behavioral functioning requires a positive self-identity and strong moral values. It has been claimed to be especially useful for people who are resistant to psychotherapy (Little & Robinson, 1988). More than 1 million offenders have reportedly participated in MRT programs (Ferguson & Wormith, 2013).

Reasoning and Rehabilitation (R&R) is grounded in cognitive theories that cite maladaptive thought patterns as the primary cause of poor social functioning and low impulse control. It was developed using high-risk probationers and draws from a number of established therapeutic techniques designed to improve cognitive skills and functioning (Ross, Fabiano, & Ewles, 1988). The original R&R program has been updated over the years as new research emerges into the causes of and effective treatments for various disorders among different groups. The R&R2 uses fifteen sessions instead of the standard thirty-five. The short version was created on the logic that thirty-five sessions is an overkill for most offenders and that treatment that extends beyond what is absolutely necessary can be counterproductive (Ross, Hilborn, & Liddle, n.d.). The R&R2 Short Version for Youths is an adaptation for young people in criminal-justice settings (Ross & Hilborn, n.d.).

Thinking for a Change (T4C) combines cognitive restructuring with training to improve problem solving and social skills. This program was developed by the National Institute of Corrections (NIC). In addition to providing full kits for program implementation, the NIC offers training for corrections personnel to teach them about cognitive theories and techniques for effective delivery of the T4C curriculum (Bush, Glick, & Taymans, 2002).

This list of programs is not exhaustive, but highlights some of the most commonly used packaged programs. As will be seen later in the chapter, all have received empirical support. It is wise for administrators in prisons, jails, and probation and parole agencies to use evidence-based programs rather than attempting to develop new ones, unless they are partnered with experts in a formal effort to generate a novel program that serves a specific need or population that currently is not adequately provided for. New programs should always be rigorously evaluated to determine whether they are effective.

EXAMINING THE RATIONALE

The effectiveness of rehabilitation revolves around certain key principles. These principles are risk, need, and responsivity (Andrews, Zinger, Hoge, Bonta, Gendreau, & Cullen, 1990). Program integrity (including, but not limited to, staff quality) has also been shown to be crucial for success (Lowenkamp, Makarios, Latessa, Lemke, & Smith, 2010). We will discuss each of these in turn, after we first address a philosophical question pertaining to rehabilitation as a justification for the imposition of criminal punishment. The purpose of this brief detour is to clarify the boundaries of the discussion about the benefits of correctional rehabilitation..

REHABILITATION AND ETHICAL JUSTIFICATIONS FOR CRIMINAL PUNISHMENT

The debate about the legitimacy of correctional intervention begins with the premise that it is unethical for society to harm or severely impinge upon individuals and their freedom unless there is an objective, compelling reason to do so. The existence of criminal punishments, and the sentencing of individual offenders to receive particular penalties, must rest upon some logical rationale that legitimizes imposing a restriction of freedom or loss of liberty upon that person (Packer, 1968). Absent a legitimizing rationale, criminal penalties are unethical because the state has failed to offer a convincing reason for its actions. A rationale also provides an organizing principle that facilitates creation of policies ensuring fair and consistent treatment of similarly situated offenders.

Correctional rehabilitation programs that adhere to the three principles of risk, need, and responsivity and are administered with fidelity should (and do, as we will see) reduce recidivism among offenders in both institutional and community-based settings. However, the effectiveness of well-designed, well-implemented programs may not, in and of itself, constitute a rationale for correctional intervention. It is not clear that rehabilitation can or should serve as the primary justification for imposition of criminal penalties, particularly onerous ones like incarceration. Treatment was, indeed, the dominant rationale during the rehabilitation era; however, the thought of the government forcibly confining people and subjecting them to involuntary cognitive restructuring rightfully sits uneasily in the public's conscience. There is also a certain hypocrisy inherent in coercing or forcing people to do something that is against their own interest (serve jail time or be on probation, for instance) while claiming that "it's for their own good." History is rife with horrors inflicted with beneficent intentions.

It is not clear what the legitimizing principle of criminal sanctions is or should be (Packer, 1968). The United States has been disjointed and inconsistent in defining such principles, alternately pointing to different rationales, many of which are irreconcilable with the others. Despite its effectiveness, rehabilitation might not be an ethical justification for criminal punishment. In the present discussion, we confine the analysis to the narrower question of what types of services could be provided to offenders who have been sentenced to a term of state control (prison, jail, or probation). In other words, it will be assumed that these offenders are already under this control for other reasons (such as deterrence or incapacitation). Admittedly, this amounts to dodging the question, but wrangling with the philosophical dilemma would distract us from the central purpose of this chapter, which is to evaluate the empirical evidence pertaining to the capacity of rehabilitation to produce positive outcomes. The discussion thus proceeds with this caveat in mind.

THE PRINCIPLES OF EFFECTIVE CORRECTIONAL REHABILITATION

The first principle of correctional treatment is risk. The risk principle holds that treatment should be matched to offenders' criminal propensities. It might seem like common sense that low-level troublemakers are more "fixable" than serious, repeat criminals are; however, the reverse proves true empirically. Higher-risk individuals are the ones who should be targeted for intense treatment. Those at lower risk levels should receive very small doses of correctional rehabilitation, or none at all. Medical analogies are often invoked to illustrate this seemingly counterintuitive argument. For example, if you visit your physician complaining of a sinus infection and she blasts you with radiation intended to treat cancer, your physical condition as you exit the office will have deteriorated from what it was when you arrived. The basic idea in correctional rehabilitation is the same—people with minor conditions require minimal or no intervention; the intensive treatments must be reserved for the people clearly in need of them.

A large body of research confirms the centrality of the risk principle to effective rehabilitation. Andrews et al. (1990) provided the first methodologically rigorous evidence favoring the risk principle, and their research was followed by a flood of other studies that advanced the understanding of risk even further. The success of the approach of tailoring treatment intensity to match offenders' likelihood of reoffending has been affirmed multiple times (Landenberger & Lipsey, 2005; Lowenkamp, Latessa, & Holsinger, 2006) and is equally applicable to adults and juveniles (Landenberger & Lipsey, 2005; Lowenkamp et al., 2010) and to males and females (Lovins, Lowenkamp, Latessa, & Smith, 2007). Violating the risk principle either by putting low-risk offenders into an intensive program or simply failing to adequately assess risk at all and lumping all types of offenders into a single program group will not merely render treatment ineffective—it actually will make people *worse* (Bonta et al., , 2000; Lowenkamp & Latessa, 2004; J. A. Wilson & Davis, 2006).

The needs principle is the second pillar of effective correctional rehabilitation. Needs are a category of risk factor that are dynamic and changeable. Static, unchangeable risk factors are things like having been arrested as a juvenile, being male, and having a history of employment problems. Dynamic risk factors (i.e., needs) can be changed. Not all needs are created equal, though. Needs are of two types: criminogenic and noncriminogenic (e.g., Andrews et al., 1990; Bonta et al., 2000). Noncriminogenic needs are lousy targets for correctional intervention. They include issues such as offenders' self-esteem and anxiety levels, which bear little or no relationship to their criminality and, when changed, fail to exert any impact on recidivism (Bonta et al., 2000). Criminogenic needs, by contrast, are fruitful for intervention. These needs include problems such as antisocial thinking, a tendency to persistently misinterpret other people's actions as personal insults, and a worldview that casts one as a victim of circumstance (Lipsey, Landenberger, & S. J. Wilson, 2007). These cognitive distortions predispose people to lash out and to feel that their anti-social behavior is justified because they attribute fault to others and never to themselves. When these criminogenic thoughts are changed so that offenders begin to see themselves as in control of their own thoughts, responsible for their own lives, and aware of their errors in reasoning (a metacognition of sorts), their behavior improves.

The third principle of effective correctional rehabilitation is responsivity. Responsivity means correctly matching the treatment modality with offenders' needs. There are two interrelated requirements. First, the treatment must target criminogenic needs, as previously described. A program designed to improve noncriminogenic needs (such as a therapy focused on building self-esteem) violates the responsivity principle. Second, the treatment modality must be grounded in evidence-based practices using techniques shown to produce positive outcomes. A program grounded in psychoanalysis, for instance, would violate the risk principle because psychoanalysis has not been shown to effectively modify behavior. Related to responsivity is service type—services must be matched to offenders' learning styles (Andrews et al., 1990). As noted previously, many offenders have mental illnesses and low educational attainment. These disadvantaged individuals might not be able to immediately process detailed concepts that require abstract thinking; instead, complex ideas should be broken down and introduced gradually. Staff members need to deliver treatment content in a manner consistent with offenders' skill levels.

Finally, program integrity (also referred to as fidelity) matters. Program integrity refers to how well a program adheres to risk, need, and responsivity principles, as well as the quality of the staff. A rehabilitation program that looks excellent on paper can become an abject failure in practice if the people charged with implementing the protocol are poorly trained or inept. Programs must be both well designed and adeptly administered (Lowen-kamp et al., 2010) or they will not achieve their stated goals.

THE EMPIRICAL STATUS OF CORRECTIONAL TREATMENT AND REHABILITATION

The previous section laid out the principles of effective rehabilitation (risk, need, responsivity, and program integrity). In the current section, we will examine the empirical evidence pertaining to those principles and to programs that do (and do not) adhere to them. First, though, a brief deviation from substantive discussion to statistical methodology is needed. The advance of the scholarly research on correctional rehabilitation has depended heavily on a technique called meta-analysis, so a basic grasp of this statistical method is necessary in order to understand rehabilitation-program evaluations and the current status of the empirical literature.

A meta-analysis is, basically, a study of studies. A researcher conducting a meta-analysis searches for studies (both published and unpublished) evaluating correctional programs and records pertinent information about each of those studies. This information includes the outcome measure (criminal offending, drug relapse, and so on), characteristics of the program (namely, to what extent it adhered to all three principles), the research design (most are experiments or quasiexperiments) and methodological strength of that design, and the findings (recidivism among the treatment group as compared to control group). The researcher combines these pieces of information from each study into a single data file.

The subsequent statistical analysis allows for a detailed examination across multiple domains. Total treatment effects (that is, absolute differences between of the recidivism rates of treatment subjects and control subjects) can be calculated across the entire sample of studies. The researcher can also break the sample down to answer questions such as whether programs that adhered to the risk principle or that used a particular treatment modality appeared to produce better outcomes. Meta-analysis allows researchers to not only reveal *whether* programs worked but also *why* (or why not). This, as we saw earlier, is where Martinson went astray. He merely noted total effect sizes and did not take the analysis to the next level by uncovering specific attributes that determine whether or not a program reduces recidivism. Meta-analysis has helped contemporary researchers parsimoniously examine these details. Most, though not all, of the studies that will be reviewed here are meta-analyses. Evaluations of single programs are useful and relevant, but individual studies are like trees in a forest; meta-analysis examines the entire forest to discern patterns and commonalities.

Meta-analytic results are clear and consistent: Well-designed programs that adhere to the three principles and are implemented with fidelity work. On average, properly constructed and administered programs cut recidivism by 53 percent (Andrews et al., 1990). This result stands in marked contrast to criminal punishments that are purely intended to restrain people or inflict discomfort upon them. Studies comparing offenders who received treatment to those who were sentenced to jail, prison, or probation without treatment demonstrate that rehabilitation is not only effective in its own right but actually performs *better* than standard correctional supervision (Lipsey & Cullen, 2007). In fact, sanctions alone without a treatment component actually make people worse off (Andrews & Dowden, 2007).

The scholarly literature has yielded some main conclusions about "what works." First, the risk principle has been repeatedly demonstrated to be a critical element of an effective program. Risk must be measured through the use of standardized actuarial instruments rather than through clinical interviewing and judgments. One such instrument is the Level of Service Inventory–Revised (LSI–R), which is popularly used to classify offenders as low, medium, or high risk. Adherence (or lack thereof) to the risk principle can make or break a program. As noted previously, inclusion of low-risk offenders in intensive treatment programs (or failure to conduct any sort of risk assessment at all before assigning offenders to treatment) not only sabotages the program—it *increases* recidivism. Bonta et al. (2000) found that 32 percent of low-risk offenders placed in a community-based treatment program were convicted of a new offense within one year, compared to 15 percent of low-risk individuals who did not go through the program. By contrast, among high-risk offenders, 51 percent of those who did not receive treatment recidivated, compared to

32 percent of those who received treatment. Lowenkamp and Latessa (2004), in a meta-analysis of community-based residential programs, arrived at the same conclusion: On balance, interventions delivered to high-risk offenders produced positive results, those targeting moderate-risk individuals were sometimes effective and sometimes not, and those aimed at low-risk offenders generally produced increases in recidivism. J. A. Wilson and Davis (2006) evaluated a prison reentry program and found that treatment participants recidivated at higher rates than controls, a finding they attributed, in part, to the failure of program implementers to adequately assess offenders' risk levels. Similar findings have been reported in many other studies (e.g., Lovins et al., 2007; J. A. Wilson & Davis, 2006). Clearly, it is critical to accurately assess risk and correctly identify the type and intensity of treatment offenders will receive.

A second conclusion is the importance of treatment modality to correctly address criminogenic needs. A strong consensus has emerged holding up CBT as the gold standard of correctional treatment (Landenberger & Lipsey, 2005; Lipsey, Chapman, & Landenberger, 2001; Lipsey & Landenberger, 2006; Lipsey et al., 2007). CBT works because it targets the maladaptive thinking (criminogenic needs) that are the direct, immediate antecedents of antisocial behavior. This satisfies the need and responsivity criteria. There is some ambiguity about which CBT-based programs work best. Some evidence suggests no differences between brand-name and generic ones (Landenberger & Lipsey, 2005). Among the brand-name ones, one meta-analysis indicated that MRT and R&R both work but that MRT's effect sizes are consistently larger than R&R's, suggesting that MRT is slightly better. This finding is tentative because of potential variations in implementation quality (D. B. Wilson et al., 2005), but other R&R evaluations have uncovered fairly weak effects (Tong & Farrington, 2008). Effect sizes for MRT vary widely but are frequently small to moderate in magnitude. This program may work better for adults and in institutional settings rather than community settings. It is possible MRT works better with women than with men, but the data are preliminary (Ferguson & Wormith, 2013).

Rehabilitation programs can contain additional elements (such as education or vocational training) to complement core content grounded in CBT. Supplementation may enhance treatment's effectiveness (Landberger & Lipsey, 2005). Treatment modalities lacking a central cognitive and behavioral component, though, are generally ineffective (Andrews et al., 1990; Andrews & Dowden, 2007). Behavioral therapy alone, without a cognitive element, is also insufficient (Pearson, Lipton, Cleland, & Ye, 2002).

The third main conclusion is the importance of program integrity. Risk, need, and responsivity must all be present in proper form for a program to work. Additionally, staff must be educated and capable of translating the written protocol into a high-quality service. Importantly, it is not enough to have just one or two of the principles present. CBT programs fail when there is no (or only sporadic) use of a risk-assessment instrument (J. A. Wilson & Davis, 2006). Unfortunately, many (possibly most) programs violate the risk principle by substituting true assessment such as the LSI–R with alternative, less-useful criteria, like the checklists prisons use to make security classifications (Gendreau, 1996). The most widely used instrument to evaluate program integrity is the Correctional Program Assessment Inventory (CPAI). The CPAI evaluates programs according to six areas of service delivery (program implementation, preservice risk assessment, program characteristics, staff characteristics, existence of an outcome evaluation, and miscellaneous items; see Lowenkamp et al., 2010). Programs can score anywhere between 0 and 100 percent on the inventory.

Research confirms that program quality significantly predicts recidivism outcomes. Although some of the six domains seem to be stronger, more reliable predictors than others (Lowenkamp, Latessa, & Smith, 2006), programs with good-to-excellent CPAI scores consistently outperform those with moderate or low scores (Lowenkamp, Latessa, & Smith, 2006; Lowenkamp et al., 2010). The quality of staff also matters. Staff must be educated, trained, and capable of using discretion to adapt the treatment protocol where necessary to ensure appropriate service delivery (Andrews & Dowden, 2007). Unfortunately, most programs that have been evaluated score badly on the CPAI. Lowenkamp et al. (2006) found that the majority of residential programs in their meta-analysis fell into the "unsatisfactory" category on the scale, which means scores between 0 and 49 percent. This may foretell an even more disappointing result across the full landscape of programs, as the ones which have been evaluated constitute a nonrandom and probably nonrepresentative sample that likely overestimates the prevalence of high-quality programs currently in place (see Landenberger & Lipsey, 2005). While we know that fidelity is critical, then, the typical program may be one that scores poorly on this measure (Lipsey & Cullen, 2007).

Two other points deserve mention. First, the three principles appear to be equally effective for both juveniles and adults. The majority of the research reviewed in this section has been conducted on adult offenders, but the results are the same for juveniles. Programs that target high-risk youth, that are grounded in CBT, and that implement the protocol effectively reduce recidivism among these young offenders (Lowenkamp et al., 2010). There also seems to be promise for school-based prevention efforts. The objects of intended change for these programs are usually aggressive and disruptive behavior in the school setting, such as bullying and unruliness. Cognitive-behavioral techniques have been shown to reduce anger-related problems in children and adolescents (Sukhodolsky, Kassinove, & Gorman, 2004). Interestingly, CBT programs help reduce problem behavior irrespective of whether they are delivered to all students in a classroom irrespective of their individual behavioral histories (called universal programs) or, instead, target those children who have already begun acting out (S. J. Wilson & Lipsey, 2007). This curious finding could be explained by the fact that most universal programs are utilized in schools located in high-risk areas, such as those characterized by prevalent poverty and crime (Hahn et al., 2007). All children in these schools and classrooms might be at elevated risk based on their social circumstances, even if they have not yet started evincing problem behavior.

Second, programs in institutions and in community settings both seem to work equally well (Landenberger & Lipsey, 2005); however, the timing of treatment matters a great deal for incarcerated offenders (J. A. Wilson & Davis, 2006). There is a "treatment window" that spans each side of the release date. Treatment should begin a few weeks prior to release and should continue. This is referred to as a "continuum of treatment" (Butzin, Martin, & Inciardi, 2002, p. 63) that combines in-prison classes with transition or reentry services. The importance of reentry assistance cannot be overstated; it may mean the difference between successful reintegration and return to incarceration. Reentry programs vary widely in setting and duration, as well as in focus (job-skills training, substance-abuse counseling, and so on). There is evidence that vocational training, substance-abuse treatment, and halfway houses reduce recidivism. Educational assistance effectively increases ex-offenders' educational achievement, but does not seem to translate into lower recidivism rates (Seiter & Kadela, 2003). Like in-prison treatment, transitional and reentry services should contain a CBT component. One evaluation of a six-month boot camp found that offenders who went through a residential aftercare following boot-camp completion recidivated at a rate of 22 percent, compared to 33 percent among offenders who went through the boot camp only and did not receive aftercare (Kurlychek & Kempinen, 2006). It has also been found that in-prison treatment is more effective when combined with reentry assistance (Butzin et al., 2002). One evaluation of MRT in a reentry program found no significant differences between the treatment and control groups in recidivism rates, but did find that the MRT group committed fewer probation violations (H. V. Miller & J. M. Miller, 2015).

Another consideration that should be taken into account in discussing correctional treatment is the social, political, and legal setting ex-prisoners enter upon release. A long history of criminological research has demonstrated the criminogenic impacts of concentrated economic and social disadvantage (Anderson, 1999; Sampson & Groves, 1989) and systemic racial inequality (W. J. Wilson, 1987). Recent studies show that not only does concentrated disadvantage promote offending, it also elevates *re*offending among ex-prisoners (Kubrin & Stewart, 2006; Mears, Wang, Hay, & Bales, 2008; Reisig et al., 2007). Racial inequality also adds to the reintegration obstacles facing black ex-offenders (Reisig, Bales, Hay, & Wang, 2007). There is reason to believe that disadvantage also reduces the effectiveness of community residential programs; in particular, programs located in distressed areas appear to be of lower quality and, therefore, less effective at reducing recidivism (Wright, Pratt, Lowenkamp, & Latessa, 2012).

From a political and legal perspective, people who have been convicted of crimes (particularly felonies) face penalties and barriers beyond their formal criminal punishment (probation, prison, and so on). Many are forced to pay fines, fees, and restitution. Since most criminal offenders are impoverished, monetary penalties can be devastating to these individuals' lives (Harris, 2016). People leaving prison might not have drivers' licenses. Some states charge hundreds or even thousands of dollars for people who lose their licenses pursuant to criminal convictions to have their driving privileges reinstated (e.g., Adcock, 2015). Most states disenfranchise people convicted of felonies, so they cannot vote for a certain period of time or, possibly, ever again. Individuals with felonies have trouble getting jobs and finding stable housing, and many are disqualified for public housing or school loans. Commentators note that "having a criminal history continues to mark individuals for treatment as second-class social, political and economic citizens" (Geiger, 2006, p. 1194). States and the federal government need to revisit the economic, legal, and political tolls that are currently piled upon people in addition to formal criminal punishments. Even a high-quality rehabilitation program cannot combat the severe strain produced by the collateral consequences of criminal convictions and time spent in jail or prison.

A final barrier to full-scale implementation of rehabilitation is that the United States is currently divided about its desired approach to correctional intervention. There is no single, universally agreed upon paradigm justifying and guiding correctional policy (Garland, 2001; Packer, 1968). System goals are broken up into bits of deterrence, incapacitation, retribution, and rehabilitation. Criminal-justice actors (police, prosecutors, judges, probation officers, and the like) all possess substantial discretion in how they perform their jobs (Walker, 1993). Without a guiding paradigm, the treatment of suspects and offenders is doomed to be idiosyncratic and disorganized. Some actors will proceed from the notion that behaviorally troubled individuals are in need of a swift, severe response that will deter them from future crime and put them on the right path in life. Others will view crime as a type of erratic behavior characteristic of someone in need of treatment. There can be no systemwide consistency in policy and practice until there is broad agreement about what, exactly, the criminal justice system is supposed to be doing.

In sum, correctional rehabilitation enjoys a strong empirical foundation. While not a panacea to eliminating recidivism, rehabilitation produces better results than punishment alone does (Andrews et al., 1990). There are areas in need of further research (for instance, whether CBT should be tailored to meet the unique needs of certain groups, such as sex offenders; e.g., Seiter & Kadela, 2003). Program quality also remains a significant barrier to the aggregate success of in-prison, community-based, and transitional treatment services (see Gendreau, 1996). Policy efforts should concentrate on ensuring that all programs are designed according to risk, need, and responsivity and are properly implementing the protocol.

CONCLUSION

Merely punishing people is not enough. By itself, punishment has generally does not reduce recidivism and may even worsen criminal behavior. Hundreds of thousands of people exit prison and reenter society every year, most of whom will be reincarcerated within a few years (sometimes even within a few months) of release.

Fortunately, rehabilitation offers a promising alternative approach. Offenders sentenced to prison, jail, or community-based sanctions can reap meaningful benefits from correctional treatment. Programs must adhere to risk, need, and responsivity principles and be implemented by trained staff members who adhere to protocol and can appropriately adapt the treatment depending on offenders' learning styles and individual educational and cognitive deficits, where applicable. Much remains to be learned about effective interventions, and this area of research is in a state of perpetual development.

There are challenges to correctional rehabilitation that should become a focal point for policymakers. First, many or most rehabilitation programs in the United States are running at suboptimal levels. The next step forward in advancing rehabilitation policy is investing the resources necessary to bring these programs up to standard. Rehabilitation might not suffice as a philosophical grounding to justify the infliction of criminal penalties; however, in country heavily reliant upon incarceration and community supervision, we are remiss to not take advantage of the substantial promises rehabilitation holds for reducing recidivism, decreasing prison and jail populations, and improving public safety. Second, a microlevel view of individual treatment programs overlooks the broader social, legal, and economic barriers confronting people with criminal histories, especially those who have served time in jail or prison. The efficacy of correctional rehabilitation will be permanently stymied until policymakers remove the significant obstacles that prevent people with felonies from fully participating in economic and political enterprises. The search for ever-improved treatment programs should be coupled with a systematic trimming of the civil and collateral consequences that accompany criminal convictions.

DISCUSSION QUESTIONS

1. Correctional treatment is becoming increasingly common in prisons and jails, but transitional programs that continue to support released inmates during their reentry process are still relatively rare, despite important improvements in recent years. Parole or probation, by itself, does not provide the services ex-inmates need as they encounter barriers to starting life over again and avoiding the mistakes of the past. Among inmates who received high-quality treatment while incarcerated, what features of their return to society might threaten to undo the gains they made and set them back? What can corrections officials do to help people effectively ward off these negative influences?

2. Due to the mass-incarceration movement that began in the late 1970s, many prisons are overcrowded and understaffed. Administratively, maintaining order and control take precedence over providing services. Identify reasons why mass incarceration undermines the treatment approach, and why having more people in prison means that a smaller percentage of them will receive high-quality programming. What do you think should be done to fix this problem?

3. Suppose you and a friend are in a debate over correctional rehabilitation. He tells you that correctional treatment does not work and is a waste of time and money. He correctly points out that many inmates and probationers receive some type of programming while serving their sentences, but recidivism rates are high in spite of this. What is your response to your friend's statement that pervasive recidivism is proof that rehabilitation is useless? Identify specific, evidence-based counterpoints you would raise to refute this claim.

4. Some people raise the understandable concern that correctional treatment (and other services inmates and probationers receive, such as education and vocational training) is unfair because there are a lot of people who need this sort of help but do not commit crimes and so do not receive assistance. Placing so much emphasis on helping offenders can make it seem as if society has forgotten about the disadvantaged people who live law-abiding lives. What is your reaction to this dilemma? In what ways is correctional programming beneficial even for those who are not the direct recipients of it? Should governments invest more in community-based therapy programs for people who have never been involved in the criminal-justice system?

CHAPTER 15

NEW HORIZONS: THE PROMISE OF COMMUNITY-BASED CRIME CONTROL

INTRODUCTION

This final chapter wraps up the book with a discussion of contemporary policies that mobilize communities and neighborhoods for an approach to crime reduction that capitalizes upon the joint strength of formal and informal systems of control. One truism that should have emerged plainly in previous chapters is that purely punishment- and control-based approaches do not reduce recidivism, prevent crime, or enhance public peace. Even correctional rehabilitation (which can be efficacious) is an offender-based approach, and is thus limited because growing evidence shows that interventions targeting individual people are inferior to those grounded in the ecological aspects of places (e.g., Clarke, 1980; Lum, Koper, & Telep, 2011). There is also increasing recognition of the vital role citizens and communities play in promoting safety and quality of life. Some of these actions occur purely at the private level (e.g., installing residential burglar alarms) while others entail partnerships between citizens and public authorities (e.g., neighborhood watch).

Traditionally, informal and formal sources of control have been differentiated from one another as two separate vehicles through which people's public and private behavior is kept in check. In recent years, however, scholars have documented a confluence between the two (Carr, 2003). Some policing strategies, such as problem-oriented policing (Goldstein, 1990), explicitly call on officers to forge alliances with citizens, community groups, and business owners. Community policing, likewise, is valued for its ability to significantly improve quality of life (Reisig & Parks, 2004).

This chapter presents promising methods for community-based crime control premised upon partnerships between criminal-justice authorities and communities (including local agencies and nonprofit organizations). The term "community-based" is used broadly to include a variety of joint ventures. The theme linking them is a localized tailoring of justice-system activities to complement a community's unique strengths, deficits, tensions, and capacities for mobilization. Some communities may be well positioned to spearhead their own initiatives with minimal assistance, while others will require a substantial infusion of resources and support. The social, economic, and structural environment of a community or neighborhood should dictate the type and intensity of intervention. This chapter will demonstrate that crime control, public safety, and quality of life are responsibilities shared by the justice system and the public. Neither side can reach its full potential without help from the other one.

Before discussing developments in community-based crime prevention and control, we will review the weaknesses and collateral consequences of a purely punishment-oriented response to crime. The current system is rife with ideological and practical problems. This summary will serve as a launching point for a discussion of the promises of alternative policy approaches.

HARD LESSONS: HOW THE PUNISHMENT-ORIENTED SYSTEM IS BACKFIRING

The United States relies upon a dual-pronged approach to crime control. The first is the massive prison and jail infrastructure that is the state and federal governments' most visible manifestation of how it is keeping its promise to get tough on crime. Starting in the late 1970s and accelerating through the 1980s, a steady stream of new criminal statutes and sentencing schemes increased the number of offenders sent to prison and the amount of time most of them spent behind bars. It soon became apparent, however, that public funds could not keep pace with the rapid expansion of mass incarceration. This gave rise to the second prong: surveillance. Criminal-justice and other public authorities turned to technologies that allow them to subtly scrutinize citizens, frequently without their knowledge (Gordon, 1990). Closed-circuit television cameras are now a common fixture on street corners and in parking lots, stop lights in busy intersections sit next to license-plate readers that constantly scan the plates of passing cars, and police vehicles are equipped with mobile data terminals that make it easy for officers to run license plates. As these and other technologies have proliferated, law-breakers and law-abiders alike find themselves under constant surveillance.

The dual control-and-surveil approach has not markedly impacted the crime rate (Gordon, 1990). Violent crime fell steadily throughout the 1990s, but only a small fraction of the drop can be attributed to prison expansion (Spelman, 2000) or changes in policing (Eck & Maguire, 2000; Rosenfeld, Fornango, & Rengifo, 2007). The get-tough approach grounded in punishment, control, and surveillance has produced marginal benefits.

The system has also worsened circumstances for many individuals and families. Punishment, control, and surveillance reinforce social and racial inequalities (Gordon, 1991). People who are already marginalized run an elevated risk of entanglement in the criminal-justice system, and acquiring a criminal record—possibly including a stint in prison—subsequently reduces their chances for becoming gainfully employed (Pager, 2007) and experiencing the prosocial life activities that form protective barriers against criminal behavior, such as marriage and parenthood (Wilson, 1987).

Certain disadvantaged communities nationwide bear the brunt of justice-system policy gone awry. Communities already dogged by high rates of poverty, violence, and drug addiction are pushed even further down the social and economic ladder by aggressive policing strategies and mass incarceration. Aggressive policing tactics, such as pervasive pedestrian stops conducted under the banner of order maintenance, have fanned the flames of longstanding tensions between police and minority (particularly black) communities (Gau & Brunson, 2010). Observers of modern protests and riots like those seen in Ferguson in 2014 and in Baltimore in 2015 would be forgiven for thinking they had inadvertently traveled back in time and were witnessing the explosions occurring across the nation in the 1960s in places such as Watts, Newark, Chicago, and Detroit. Despite marked reductions in racism and improvements in police professionalism in recent decades, police continue to use higher levels of force against people in disadvantaged areas (Terrill & Reisig, 2003) and white officers employ more serious force against black suspects who resist officers' commands (Paoline, Gau, & Terrill, 2016) and are more cynical toward citizens than black and Latino officers are (Gau & Paoline, 2017).

Mass incarceration, likewise, perpetuates social, racial, and economic injustice by being a perpetual source of turmoil in distressed communities. These communities were weakened by devastating shifts in the labor market (Wilson, 1987), the rise of oppositional cultures that promote violence and impede prosocial forms of community control (Anderson, 2000; Stewart & Simons, 2010), and racism in official and unofficial housing-market policies that trap impoverished individuals and families of color in isolated pockets of severe deprivation (Schill & Watchter, 1995). High rates of incarceration are an additional source of social breakdown in these communities. Fathers are removed from families, marriages are prevented or ruined, and children grow up without strong male role models (Anderson, 2000; Wilson, 1987). Constant population turnover also destabilizes the social fabric of communities and prevents the fusion of social ties necessary for the development of healthy communities (Clear, Rose, Waring, & Scully, 2003; Rose & Clear, 1998).

Fortunately, none of the collateral consequences of punishment-based policies are inevitable. They can be avoided by transitioning away from using punishment as the primary method of protecting public safety. In high-crime areas, lawbreaking is a symptom with causes rooted in social, economic, and frequently race-based exclusion and isolation. The justice system is incapable of singlehandedly solving the full spectrum of ills that give rise to drug addiction and predatory behavior. Strengthening communities' capacities for self-regulation can form the basis for a comprehensive approach that prevents criminal activity, holds offenders accountable when they do break the law, and does not generate side effects. We now turn to a discussion of these alternative perspectives and policies. We focus on those entailing partnerships between criminal-justice officials and communities. There are many purely community-based approaches, but this chapter is concerned with policies and programs intended to foster collaboration between the justice system and the public.

THE THEORETICAL ORIGINS OF COMMUNITY-BASED CONTROL

The Chicago school kicked off the discipline of criminology in the United States in the 1930s. This school was grounded in observations that neighborhood-level socioeconomic disadvantage (poverty, residential instability, and ethnic or racial heterogeneity) consistently overlapped with area levels of delinquency and crime. It took some time to uncover the reasons for this relationship, but ultimately scholars tied it to community attachment (Kasarda & Janowitz, 1974; Sampson, 1988) and, relatedly, local social networks, unsupervised youth peer groups, and low neighborhood participation (Sampson & Groves, 1989;

Lowenkamp, Cullen, & Pratt, 2003). Neighborhood-level disadvantage disrupts neighborhood ties and thereby impedes social control. This process operates in a feedback loop: Disadvantage fuels fear, weakens social networks, and fosters crime, and those ills then reinforce socioeconomic distress (Bursik, 1986; Markowitz, Bellair, Liska, & Liu, 2001).

The two operative features of a neighborhood's social environment are cohesion and social control (Sampson, Raudenbush, & Earls, 1997; see also Gau, 2014a; Reisig & Cancino, 2004). Cohesion consists of the ties among neighbors that generate protective behaviors such as knowing who lives in the neighborhood and who is a stranger, keeping an eye on neighbors' houses while they are away, and collective supervision of youth. Informal social control refers to individuals' and neighborhoods' willingness to intervene, such as stepping in to break up a fight. Ultimately, the goal is social control. Social control is "the attempt to protect the area from threats that may undermine its regulatory ability" (Bursik & Grasmick, 1993, p. 15). Control operates at three levels (Hunter, 1985): private (family and close friends within the neighborhood), parochial (larger local networks, such as links between community groups, churches, and business owners), and public (services and resources provided by the government).

Social disorganization—while a reliable predictor of crime—does not operate uniformly across all types of troubled neighborhoods. Some socioeconomically distressed areas suffer high levels of disorganization, but others are better described as differentially organized. Digging under the surface of apparent disorganization often reveals a social order and culture linking residents together through common understandings of what constitutes "acceptable" public behavior. The crime and disorder in these neighborhoods may be a symptom of isolation from surrounding neighborhoods and city services (Whyte, 1943; see also Massey, 1995). Neighborhood problems may also spring from oppositional aspects of the local culture that reject mainstream social values and instead embrace defiance, self-help, and a willingness to use violence to defend one's honor (Anderson, 2000). It is not correct, then, to take a measurement of a neighborhood's socioeconomic status and presume that distress inevitably means an absence of organization. Neighborhoods should be evaluated internally and as a function of their relationship to the larger community or city (Bursik & Grasmick, 1993) and to public-sphere authorities like the police (Carr, 2003).

THE THEORETICAL ORIGINS OF PLACE-BASED CRIME PREVENTION

In the 1970s, several crime scholars voiced dissatisfaction with criminological theories' explanations for criminal behavior (Clarke, 1980) along with the apparent ineffectiveness of correctional rehabilitation at producing lasting improvement in offenders' behavior once they are released back into the community (Cornish & Clarke, 2008). Theses scholars embarked on a new path of inquiry. They argued that the crime event should play the most prominent role in understanding why crime occurs and how to stop it. A revised model of rational choice, adapted from traditional deterrence theory, was developed as a framework for understanding the factors people take into account when assessing a criminal opportunity for feasibility and anticipated reward.

Policing scholars added their voice to the burgeoning place-based movement. Problem-oriented policing (Goldstein, 1979, 1990) grew out of the empirical reality that police officers' time is disproportionately consumed by disturbances repeatedly occurring at a relatively small number of locations. Problem-oriented policing and place-based crime prevention dovetailed nicely: Identify locations with high incidences of disturbances, figure out what features of the social or physical environment are to blame, and fix those underlying causes to yield lasting solutions. Community-based crime strategies should capitalize upon the merits of situational prevention both because it is effective (Weisburd, Telep, Hinkle, & Eck, 2010) and because it avoids the conflicts and dilemmas posed by person-based strategies. One of the downsides of community approaches is that a neighborhood's grievances can quickly devolve into conflict, and proposed "solutions" are at times nothing more than demands for more arrests and harsher punishments (Goldstein, 1990; Rosenbaum, Lurigio, & Davis, 1998), which runs counter to the purpose and spirit of community-based initiatives.

Police, in particular, need to demonstrate leadership by directing the development of solutions revolving around places instead of people. For example, police in a disadvantaged Chicago neighborhood noticed consistently high rates of robberies outside the check-cashing facilities where residents cashed their paychecks and purchased money orders to pay bills, since most did not have bank accounts. Officers worked with a local bank to install an ATM inside the neighborhood police substation. Robberies declined, and residents gained access to a legitimate bank that did not charge them the exorbitant transaction fees imposed by check-cashing facilities (Skogan & Hartnett, 1997). A more traditional approach, such as undercover stings to catch robbers in the act, may have yielded several arrests but likely would have done little to affect the robbery rate because it would not have altered the true cause of the crimes: a constant supply of victims with cash. Police instead opted to give people a safe place to cash their checks and the ability to avoid carrying large amounts of money, which diminished opportunities for robbery.

TYING IT TOGETHER: COMMUNITIES AS PLACES

The justice system is generally conceptualized as an isolated entity that steps in after a crime has happened to penalize the person who violated the law. It then recedes and does not show up again until another illegal act occurs. The system is not frequently viewed as an extension of the community itself, and yet its most vital potential lies in this very capacity. Justice-system officials achieve their maximum effectiveness when they act as supporters of parochial forms of social control (Bursik & Grasmick, 1993; Carr, 2003). As a noted urban sociologist put it, "The first thing to understand is that the public peace—the sidewalk and street peace—of cities is not kept primarily by the police, necessary as police are. It is kept primarily by an intricate, almost unconscious, network of voluntary controls and standards among the people themselves, and enforced by the people themselves" (Jacobs, 1961, p. 32). The optimal scenario is one in which public-sphere resources operate in tandem with parochial-level neighborhood controls. Many people who want to help maintain order and security within their neighborhoods feel too fearful or uncomfortable to personally intervene, but they are willing to call the police for help (Carr, 2003). There may also be collaboration between community groups and other city departments (such as public works) to, for instance, fix sidewalks and clean up parks to encourage people to spend more time outside occupying public spaces. The ideal role justice-system officials and local leaders play in public safety is as facilitators of informal social control.

Informal control can be accomplished outside neighborhood networks, including within districts and the city at large, so long as public spaces are clean and orderly such that people feel safe using them. As Jacobs (1961) observed, "The bedrock attribute of a successful city district is that a person must feel personally safe and secure on the street among all these strangers" (p. 30). A sidewalk bustling with strangers contains ample "eyes upon the street" (Jacobs, 1961, p. 35), which deters many would-be offenders from preying upon any of those strangers. When an attempt is made, it may be quickly thwarted by locals, shop owners, or passersby. Widespread social control among strangers in city streets—like that within neighborhoods—requires smart public planning and resource allocation.

There is no single, proven method for accomplishing productive partnerships. Many fail because they lack theoretical basis, because their implementation is flawed, or both (Bursik & Grasmick, 1993). For example, with respect to problems caused by deficient theory, a program designed to create dense social ties among neighbors may seem like a logical extension of the centrality of cohesion in social-disorganization theory, but such a program would actually hold little promise. Research demonstrates that weak ties (Granovetter, 1973; Warner & Rountree, 1997) and infrequent interactions (Bellair, 1997) among larger networks are more productive than dense ties among smaller groups. The crime-repellant capacity of networks shrinks as those networks become tighter and denser (Browning, Feinberg, & Dietz, 2004). Additionally, social networks do not automatically translate into crime prevention; they first must lead to informal social control. Networks alone have marginal impacts on crime, but combined with informal control, they reach full potential (Bellair & Browning, 2010; see also Sampson et al., 1997).

An example of implementation failure can be seen in order-maintenance policing. Broken-windows theory posited that social and physical disorders (panhandling, graffiti, and so forth) generate fear among local residents, which causes residents to withdraw from public spaces, wrecks informal social controls, and opens up the neighborhood to predatory criminals. Police, in this framework, should fight crime by controlling disorder (Wilson & Kelling, 1982). The theory itself received inadequate testing and rests on some questionable assumptions (e.g., Gau & Pratt, 2008, 2010; Harcourt, 2001; Taylor, 2001), but it was put into practice nonetheless. Order-maintenance policing, as it is commonly called, quickly devolved into an aggressive street-stop campaign that disproportionately targeted minorities (Fagan & Davies, 2000; Gelman, Fagan, & Kiss, 2007) and damaged police relations with people and communities of color (Gau & Brunson, 2010; Vera Sanchez & Gau, 2015). These collateral consequences were insults added to injury, because aggressive order maintenance has minimal impact on serious crime (Rosenfeld et al., 2007).

As with any mistakes, past mistakes can be turned into learning opportunities to guide future actions. Continuing with the example of order-maintenance policing, research has shown that although disorder reduction accomplished through aggressive policing has negligible impacts on crime, community-based and problem-oriented initiatives work (Braga, Welsh, & Schnell, 2015). Collaborations between communities and the justice system can be effective and mutually beneficial. Furthermore, crime need not—indeed, *should* not—be the only intervention target; fear of crime, social cohesion and informal social control, quality of life, and positive police–community relations are worthy objects of repair and maintenance. Additionally, community courts have been established in many cities to prompt local participation in criminal justice. There are also restorative-justice efforts underway to afford victims a greater role in the court process and offer outcomes that benefit both victims and offenders rather than simply punishing the latter. Restorative justice may help forge stronger alliances between the justice system and the public it serves. Resources not currently being tapped to their fullest potential include local community leaders and nonprofit organizations. Finally, policymakers, local justice officials, and the public should consider the harm-reduction model as a guide to promoting the health of communities experiencing drug problems. We discuss each of these policy areas and conceptual guides in turn.

REDUCING FEAR OF CRIME

Fear diminishes people's quality of life and willingness to actively participate in neighborhood life (Skogan, 1986). Researchers in the 1970s and 1980s started recognizing fear as a tangible, independent threat to neighborhoods, separable from crime (e.g., Lewis & Salem, 1986). Fear is often disconnected from objective victimization risk (see Hale, 1996 for a review).

The first step in a fear-reduction program is to identify its source, since the initially apparent object of, or reason for, fear might not be the true cause. For instance, elderly people may become fearful when young adults move into the area, not because the newcomers are actually threatening, but because they are young and unfamiliar. Maybe they speak a foreign language (see Goldstein, 1990). Along the same lines, women's heightened fear stems from a sense of being vulnerable to sexual assault, either as a singular offense or in addition to a different type of victimization (e.g., robbery; Ferraro, 1996). Fear also frequently arises from social and physical disorder and signs of decay in the community, such as broken sidewalks and abandoned buildings (LaGrange, Ferraro, & Supancic, 1992; Lewis & Salem, 1986; Skogan, 1986).

Fear-reduction programs have taken numerous forms. One of the earliest initiatives was foot patrol. Noting that motorized patrol, rapid response to calls for service, and criminal investigations were all reactive and focused entirely on crime, reformers called for police to walk their beats, strike up conversations with locals, and become familiar with local norms, customs, and problems. Newark, New Jersey, and Flint, Michigan, served as the first testing grounds for foot-patrol experiments, and the magnitude of fear reduction was striking (Moore & Trojanowicz, 1988).

The impact of foot patrol may be even stronger when combined with other community-policing tactics like neighborhood cleanup programs and establishment of police substations. Increasing the quantity and quality of contacts between citizens and officers appears to be the key to fear reduction (Moore & Trojanowicz, 1988). To this end, community-policing strategies that make officers closer and more responsive to neighborhood residents consistently suppress fear (Weisburd & Eck, 2004). Problem-oriented policing has also been shown to reduce fear (Baker & Wolfer, 2003; Cordner, 1986), but this effect is not as reliable as that seen with community policing (see Stokes, Donahue, Caron, & Greene, 1996).

PROMOTING COHESION, INFORMAL CONTROL, AND QUALITY OF LIFE

Quality-of-life policing was one of the first strategies to emerge from broken-windows theory. This type of policing is intended to reduce the social and physical disorders that cause fear and a breakdown of social cohesion and control. As with fear-reduction initiatives like foot patrol, the goal of policing designed to promote cohesion and quality of life is not to have an immediate impact on crime. Instead, it is to reduce disorder, strengthen the social processes that protect communities from crime, enhance residents' long-term commitment to the area (see generally Kasarda & Janowitz, 1974), and encourage the use of public spaces (see Jacobs, 1961).

Early evaluations of quality-of-life policing produced mixed results, but this may have been because these programs were overly narrow in scope (Novak, Hartman, Holsinger, & Turner, 1999; Sherman, 1990). An assessment of a program that was comprehensive in targeting multiple types of disorders, employing officers dedicated to code enforcement, and enlisting trained citizens to assist in disorder reduction resulted in inconsistent changes in calls for service related to various forms of physical and social incivilities (e.g., vandalism, panhandling). Calls for some types of offenses went down, while complaints about other forms rose (Katz, Webb, & Schaefer, 2001). Increases are not necessarily signs of failure; in fact, they can be positive indicators of enhanced citizen involvement. The very point of many quality-of-life initiatives is to enhance neighborhood residents' protective behaviors, and one method of doing this is to call the police more often. Police departments launching quality-of-life initiatives should be prepared for an increase (at least a temporary one) in reports of disorder and lower-level crimes, and should not jump to the conclusion that this increase signals program failure.

Quality-of-life policing wherein officers pay close attention to incivilities and are willing to cite or arrest people who disrupt public life may exert a deterrent impact, at least as pertaining to the commission of disorderly offenses. As has been demonstrated throughout previous chapters, deterrence-based policies are largely ineffective. There is a difference, though, between abstract possibilities of arrest and punishment (which are weak deterrents) and tangible, credible threats created when police officers are deeply embedded in an initiative and have a visible presence on the street. Golub, Johnson, Taylor, and Eterno (2003) interviewed arrestees in a city undergoing a major quality-of-life policing program and found that nearly all of them were aware of the program and that half of those who previously engaged in disorderly behaviors had reduced or stopped these activities out of fear of arrest.

One persistent impediment to community-based efforts to promote cohesion, informal control, and quality of life is that most such programs exist in neighborhoods that are already relatively well off and safe. Many of them spring into life as the result of a tragedy or sudden appearance of crime (such as a string of burglaries) and then fade away when the shock has worn off or the perpetrator has been arrested (Gest, 2001). There is a common perception that distressed areas are poor candidates for community-based crime control, but this assumption is incorrect and hampers progress. There is nothing inevitable about neighborhood-level socioeconomic disadvantage destroying social organization; to the contrary, many poor and working-class areas boast thriving social atmospheres and low crime rates (see generally Jacobs, 1961). The majority of people living in high-crime areas disapprove of deviant and criminal behavior, but they feel powerless to stop it themselves and are cynical toward the justice system for its failure to take effective action (Anderson, 2000; Sampson & Bartusch, 1998). While trust in police and other officials in these neighborhoods is low, there is nonetheless a widespread desire for greater collaboration and effective working relationships (Carr, Napolitano, & Keating, 2007).

POLICE–COMMUNITY COLLABORATION

Social control may be fostered through formalized collaborative partnerships between police and local neighborhoods, business owners, or other important people or groups (such as the owners of large apartment complexes). A popular form of such partnerships is third-party policing, whereby a local police department transfers some of the burden of supervising public behavior onto private individuals and entities. The idea is to hold people such as landlords and bar owners accountable for problems occurring on their properties. This strategy entails leveraging civil and regulatory laws against the owners of locations where trouble recurs. Preferably, owners would willingly participate in ridding their properties of serial miscreants, but absent voluntary consent, police and the city council (possibly in conjunction with a citizen group, as well) can pursue noncriminal legal channels to force the owner into a choice between compliance and closure (Carr, 2003; Mazerolle & Ransley, 2006; Skogan & Hartnett, 1997). Because of this system of leverage, third-party policing is controversial and strikes critics as unduly coercive.

Third-party arrangements are typically ad hoc and spurred by pressure from citizen groups (Mazerolle & Ransely, 2006), which raises the specter of class, race, or cultural bias. There is also evidence that third-party policing pressure falls most heavily on landlords in black neighborhoods, and that domestic-violence calls for service are frequently an impetus for police to pressure landlords to evict certain tenants, a chillingly dangerous outcome for abused women (Desmond & Valdez, 2013). This is not to say third-party policing is a lost cause; the point is that it must be done with due caution, sound data, respect for civil liberties, and an awareness of the possibility for unintended harm to vulnerable people. Carried out in such a manner, third-party policing can be an important tool for quelling some types of neighborhood disturbances.

Positive police–community relations can reduce people's perceptions of incivilities and increase their feelings of safety, even in disadvantaged neighborhoods (Reisig & Parks, 2004). Neighborhoods suffering from serious or extreme socioeconomic distress benefit greatly from infusions of public resources and supports (Vélez, 2001). Undoubtedly, the challenges of partnerships are more daunting in distressed areas (Skogan, 1990), but the promise for gains in quality of life, social control, and crime reduction is significant. Modest improvements in control capacity and quality of life might not affect well-off areas much, but may be felt poignantly in troubled neighborhoods (Skogan & Hartnett, 1997).

Neighborhood watch is another form of police–community collaboration. Neighborhood watch garners enormous public support, even though there is insufficient empirical evidence to determine whether this strategy reduces crime, reduces fear, or fosters a sense of community. Neighborhood watch may increase fear by exposing residents to their neighbors' victimization experiences (Rosenbaum, 1987). A meta-analysis tentatively concluded that the evidence for crime reduction appears to tilt in favor of neighborhood watch, but that more research–especially of rigorous methodology—is needed before a firm statement can be made (Bennett, Holloway, & Farrington, 2006). Indirect evidence in favor of neighborhood watch may be derived from the fact that burglary follows a repeat and near-repeat pattern, meaning that in the days following a residential burglary, both the house that was originally targeted and the houses in proximity to it are at high risk for being broken into (Moreto, Piza, & Caplan, 2014). By informing residents about recent burglaries (and other property crimes), neighborhood watches could arm residents with the knowledge they need to take protective measures to prevent their property from becoming the next target.

The procedural-justice (or process-based) model of policing is an additional means by which police may establish community relationships that foster collaboration. A movement is underway in police agencies across the country to enhance their legitimacy by drawing from the principles of procedural justice. Legitimacy, broadly defined, is the public's respect for and willingness to comply with governmental institutions and agencies (Weber, 1978). Police need the public to see them as legitimate authority figures in order to promote citizen compliance during face-to-face interactions and to achieve cooperation on a larger scale, such as by residents' providing information about crimes and offenders and reporting suspicious behavior (Tyler, 2006; Tyler & Huo, 2002).

Principles of procedural justice guide the process and manner by which police engage with members of the public. Police anger the people they come into contact with when they engage in unjust treatment such as rudeness or undue physical coercion (Gau & Brunson, 2010), or when they stop motorists (Gau, 2013; Gau & Brunson, 2012) and pedestrians (Gau & Brunson, 2010) without sufficiently explaining the rationale for the stop. People are more likely to see the police as legitimate authority figures when they believe police treat members of the public fairly and respectfully, give them a voice in the decision-making process, and make neutral and transparent decisions (e.g., Gau, 2011, 2013, 2014b, 2015; Gau, Corsaro, Stewart, & Brunson, 2012; Hinds & Murphy, 2007; Mazerolle, Bennett, Davis, Sargeant, & Manning, 2013). Procedural justice helps people identify with police (Bradford, 2014) and feel a sense of shared moral purpose or alignment (Jackson, Bradford, Hough, Myhill, Quinton, & Tyler, 2012). The end result is a more positive attitude toward police and a greater desire to help and support them.

Police can improve relationships with offenders as a means of convincing them to refrain from crime. In Chicago, under the auspices of the federally funded Project Safe Neighborhoods program intended to reduce gun violence, local police and prosecutors met face-to-face with known troublemakers and threatened them with arrest and prosecution if they carried or used guns illegally. An evaluation revealed significant violent-crime declines largely attributable to these meetings (Papachristos, Meares, & Fagan, 2007). This illustrates the superiority of a personal approach over one in which police and prosecutors are passive, removed, and distant. In the meetings, law enforcement explicitly adopted the principles of procedural justice to convey an image of being tough but fair and to treat offenders respectfully. This may have improved offenders' perceptions of police and prosecutors' legitimacy and encouraged compliance with the law (Papachristos et al., 2007).

COMMUNITY COURTS

Community courts are an extension of the specialized courts (such as drug courts) that sprung up in the 1980s and remain popular today, but they differ from other specialized courts in important ways. Their overarching purpose is to provide localized justice sensitive to community wishes and problems, and to use arbitration, mediation, and restorative penalties like victim restitution in lieu of formal prosecution and punishment (Alper & Nichols, 1981). These courts are also intended to improve deterrence by ensuring prosecution and punishment of people who cause neighborhood disruption, including disorderly behavior and low-level crimes (Gest, 2001; Thompson, 2002). Offenses of this nature stand a low probability of prosecution in regular courts, so community courts are seen as a way for residents to take control and ensure punishment for people who violate the peace (Fagan & Malkin, 2002; Thompson, 2002). In theory, opening up the court to community involvement enhances the justice system's legitimacy, particularly in distressed neighborhoods where cynicism of police and courts is high (Fagan & Malkin, 2002).

Community courts have been criticized for taking on too broad a spectrum of case types. They do not limit their scope to certain crimes (such as drug use) or populations (such as people with mental illnesses). Additionally, they may foster net-widening because they ensure justice-system involvement for people whose crimes are minor and do not have direct victims, such as disorderly conduct (Thompson, 2002). As described earlier, there is no social utility—and a very real risk of harm—in prosecuting and punishing people who are not objectively threatening or dangerous. On the other hand, many community courts operate under a treatment model and are envisioned as places where individuals in need can be connected with appropriate services (Fagan & Malkin, 2002). A treatment approach does not eliminate the danger that net-widening will occur (it may in fact increase it), but judicious use of community-court resources and careful attention to bringing formal action against only those who are at risk for reoffending may be a productive approach.

RESTORATIVE JUSTICE AND VICTIM-CENTERED APPROACHES

Restorative justice and victim-centered approaches are numerous and diverse, but the basic idea is to use the legal process in a manner that does more than merely punish the offender. Punishment is an unreliable method of coercing behavioral change from people, and ignores the harm done to the victim. Restorative justice aims to aid victims in their path toward recovery. More than a change in mission, though, it represents a reorientation of court functioning. It dissolves the traditional adversarial courtroom atmosphere—a competition between the government and the accused—and reshapes it into something more resembling mediation (Van Ness & Strong, 2014).

Another way of thinking about this is to conceptualize court proceedings and sentencing decisions as quests for justice rather than for truth (Thibaut & Walker, 1978). The adversarial model pits each side against the other in a truth-seeking battle. This may be an accurate depiction of criminal cases in which facts are in dispute, such as homicide trials built upon forensic evidence. Most crimes, however, are interpersonal disputes or harms inflicted by a known offender. As such, court processes are more about the fair distribution of outcomes than a search for some singular "truth." Someone whose home has been vandalized, for instance, may benefit more if the perpetrator repairs the damage than if he or she is sent to jail. The vandal, likewise, may deserve leniency if he or she is young and was merely part of a group of troublemakers and did not personally engage in the destruction.

Related to the search for justice in place of truth is an emphasis on process in addition to outcome. A large body of research has shown that people's satisfaction with authority figures is driven primarily by how fair they feel the process was, not by the favorability of the outcome (see MacCoun, 2005 for a review). The amount of control people have over the court process weighs heavily upon their satisfaction with outcomes and their willingness to accept unfavorable decisions (Thibaut & Walker, 1978). Obviously, direct control is not feasible, since criminal proceedings are based on laws and not personal preferences; however, satisfaction can be enhanced by allowing both parties to express themselves and be heard. The concept of voice captures people's beliefs that they were given the chance to explain their side of the story. Voice promotes a sense of procedural justice (Baker, Pelfrey Bedard, Dhungana, Gertz, & Golden, 2014) and helps people feel satisfied with the process and outcome (Thibaut & Walker, 1978).

Many programs, case-by-case actions, and operational philosophies can be grouped beneath the "tent" of restorative justice (Bazemore & Schiff, 2001, p. 6; see also Daly, 2002). Many restorative-justice programs have no community component and instead employ a case-based approach to individualized justice and healing. Several advocates argue, however, that restorative justice promotes community justice by highlighting that a crime never has only one victim; rather, the victimization of a single person ripples outward and deleteriously impacts many people. Restorative justice may reinforce community bonds and promote cohesion and control, thereby bolstering an area's crime-prevention capacity (Crawford & Clear, 2001).

Additionally, advocates contend that the face-to-face interaction between offender, justice-system officials, and victims affords an opportunity for a teachable moment. That opportunity is lost when impersonal courtroom actors declare someone guilty of a crime and hand down a sentence accordingly. Restorative justice seizes these "opportunities for norm-clarification," whereby community norms can be reinforced through dialogue (Christie, 1977, p. 8). Similarly, the norm-reinforcement properties of restorative justice have been likened to regulatory forms of law enforcement such as those seen in the corporate world. In regulatory enforcement, officials typically work with owners, managers, and staff to gain an understanding of the problematic behavior and develop solutions. Drawing from regulatory theory, restorative justice may be seen as a mechanism to correct misbehavior by schooling and guiding offenders toward more acceptable behaviors (Braithwaite, 1999).

There are several ways justice officials may grant crime victims a more prominent place in the justice process and help them recover from their frightening or traumatic experiences, although this remains an area thin on empirical findings to guide evidence-based practices. Many of these methods are not policies or programs but, rather, case-by-case decisions and treatment. Research shows that victims respond to aspects of both procedure and outcome, but little is known about precisely what it is that victims need from officials in order to feel satisfied with the overall experience (Laxminarayan, Bosmans, Porter, & Sosa, 2013). Some recent research hints at future directions for policy development in this regard. For example, police, as the most frequent first responders to incidents of victimization, can mitigate victims' feelings of guilt, shame, and anger by being respectful, courteous, and polite. By dampening victims' negative emotions, police may help prevent them from becoming fearful of future victimization and experiencing social isolation (Barkworth & Murphy, 2016).

Restorative justice is not without its critics and implementation deficiencies. The entire concept of restorative justice has been criticized for being more myth than reality. It is couched in rhetoric that invokes nostalgia about ancient and indigenous tribal justice and tight-knit communities that enjoy collective identities. In truth, a substantial portion of victims come away from restorative-justice conferences feeling that the offender was treated too leniently. Few victims receive notification regarding whether or not offenders successfully completed their sentences (Daly, 2002). The evidence is mixed with respect to whether restorative justice reduces recidivism (see Wenzel, Okimoto, Feather, & Platow, 2008 for a review). Because restorative-justice programs and individual conferences are so varied, it is impossible to capture the full landscape of victims' satisfaction and offenders' future behavior. Probably the most accurate summary at this point is that restorative justice may be ideal for certain situations (for instance, youthful perpetrators of property crimes or minor assaults), but its appropriateness should be judged case by case.

ENLISTING LOCAL LEADERS, GROUPS, AND NONPROFITS

There is much the justice system could do to establish rapport and build partnerships with communities. This is particularly important in communities experiencing serious crime problems and historically rocky relationships with police and other governmental institutions. Local agencies, nonprofit organizations, and leaders can act as liaisons and contribute to the prevention or reduction of crime problems.

In Boston in the late 1990s, for example, police initiated a pulling-levers program to force gang-involved youth to refrain from using or carrying guns. Operation Ceasefire, as it was called, was multipronged and aimed to convince troubled youths to turn away from gangs and go back to school, obtain vocational training, and so on (Braga, Kennedy, Waring, & Piehl, 2001). Ultimately, though, police dominated the endeavor. As with order-maintenance and other forms of aggressive policing, tough crackdowns can outrage a community that feels besieged.

Boston police, therefore, enlisted local clergy to help obtain buy-in from the predominantly black neighborhoods in which gang violence was most prevalent and Ceasefire efforts were therefore most active. Churches are an important source of informal social control in many black neighborhoods. They serve as gathering places for religious worship and socializing, which strengthens bonds and networks. In Boston, black clergy assisted in the Ceasefire effort by acting as liaisons between police and the neighborhoods impacted by this program. Clergy funneled information in both directions and mediated disputes. The police–clergy relationship was not perfect, but serves as an example of an innovative method by which justice-system agencies can communicate and collaborate with distressed neighborhoods (Brunson, Braga, Hureau, & Pegram, 2015).

Project Safe Neighborhoods offers another example of an anticrime endeavor spearheaded by law enforcement and rounded out by community partnerships. Project Safe Neighborhoods was intended to reduce gun violence through innovative policing, harsh prosecution and sentencing, and community partnerships. Some of the cities that launched Project Safe Neighborhoods initiatives saw modest reductions in violent crime (McGarrell, Corsaro, Hipple, & Bynum, 2010; see also Papachristos et al., 2007). Cities that received money to implement this program all adapted it to meet unique local needs, so the partnerships varied and cannot be evaluated for their effectiveness independent of the policing and prosecution activities taking place at the same time. However, the fact that the federal government required local officials to reach out to social-service agencies, clergy, and community organizations as a condition for receiving funding (McGarrell et al., 2009) attests to policymakers' growing acknowledgement of partnerships' crucial role in crime reduction.

Nonprofit organizations have sprung up in numerous states and cities to assist with finding alternatives to incarceration. Their quantity and variation defy succinct summary; each one is organized and operated to serve a specific goal. Some receive government funding and others are sustained entirely through private donations. There is no scientific research on what, in general, nonprofits do and how efficacious they are, but anecdotal descriptions of certain agencies reveal a wide range of activities. A nonprofit in Florida, for instance, works with the juvenile courts to filter out youths who seem in danger of going astray and would benefit from prosocial opportunities and mentoring. Youths receive programming tailored to their needs and interests. They are paired with mentors and learn outdoor hobbies such as sailing (Gonzalez, 2016). New York State contains large nonprofits dedicated to keeping nondangerous offenders out of prison and ensuring their access to treatment and education (Berman, 2013). Absent rigorous evaluation, it is impossible to gauge the success of these efforts at reducing incarceration rates, promoting healthy family and community ties, and preventing recidivism; however, as creative, localized solutions, they hold promise to ameliorate the collateral consequences of imprisonment and help offenders reset their life trajectories.

ADJUSTING THE IDEOLOGY: APPLICATIONS FROM PUBLIC HEALTH

The shift toward community-based approaches would be assisted by expanding the ideological underpinnings of anticrime efforts. In the United States, crime-policy discussions are grounded in punishment, treatment, and prevention of criminal behavior, but these are not the only options. Public health is an area of theory and research with particular relevance to community-based policies. This discipline offers a harm-reduction model. Harm reduction "is a pragmatic approach that aims to reduce the adverse consequences of drug abuse and psychiatric symptoms . . . Consumers are allowed to make choices—to use alcohol or not, to take medications or not—and regardless of their choices, they are not treated adversely, their housing status is not threatened, and help continues to be available to them" (Tsemberis, Gulcur, & Nakae, 2004, p. 652). As this definition suggests, the greatest applicability of the harm-reduction model with respect to crimes is drug use. The central goal under such an approach would be to reduce the dangers associated with drug use, particularly HIV transmission and overdose.

As the war on drugs rages, people addicted to drugs continue to suffer serious health consequences. Even after substantial declines in the rate of HIV transmission among injection-drug users, one in twenty-three women who inject drugs will be infected at some point, as will one in thirty-six men (Centers for Disease Control and Prevention, 2016). Overdose deaths attributable to both illegal (namely, heroin and cocaine) and legal (mostly opioids and benzodiazepines) are on a steady upward climb nationwide (National Institute on Drug Abuse, 2017). Approximately 60,000 people died of overdoses in 2016 (Katz, 2017). Families and communities are rapidly losing loved ones to illness and death.

Harm reduction entails quelling these negative outcomes rather than trying to reduce drug use itself. People will still receive treatment if they want it, but the emphasis is on protecting them rather than trying to cure them. Needle-exchange programs are one option. These sites accept used needles and supply new ones, with no questions asked, so injection-drug users can access sanitary needles. Evaluations of needle exchanges reveal that they are associated with statistically significant reductions in new HIV diagnoses (Aspinall et al., 2014). Supervised injection facilities are locations wherein people can inject or otherwise consume the substances of their choice with medical staff on-site who can prevent overdoses and the reuse of old needles. There are currently ninety such facilities worldwide, most of them in Europe. They have been associated with significant reductions in several health problems (Shaw et al., 2015) and in public healthcare expenditures (Enns, Zaric, Strike, Jairam, Kolla, & Bayoumi, 2015).

Clearly, the harm-reduction model is at odds with traditional criminal-justice ideology. Adopting such an approach to drug use would require police and other justice-system officials to willfully ignore criminal behavior they know is taking place. This would require significant legislative and policy support, and support from local police and communities. The potential benefits, however, merit public discussion. Drug addiction and its associated consequences devastate communities with high rates of addiction. As uncomfortable as private citizens and public officials might feel when initially exposed to the harm-reduction model, it is a conversation communities with prevalent drug abuse should have with their local and state policymakers to determine if this model makes sense as one component of the larger effort against drug abuse and addiction.

CONCLUSION

The war on crime and drugs is currently being fought as a war on the people engaged in illegal behavior to the neglect of the social and economic conditions that give rise to it. Individuals, families, and communities have suffered the consequences, and the magnitude of the war's crime-reduction benefits are insufficient to justify the damages. The war metaphor itself is a rhetorical wedge representing an ideology in which criminal-justice officials and the nation's residents are pitted against one another as enemies on a battlefield.

In order to make genuine progress in the effort to improve public safety and quality of life, the language of war must be discarded and replaced with a spirit of cooperation, coproduction, and collaboration between criminal-justice authorities and communities.

Community-based policies and programs offer several promising options for reducing crime without incurring the costs of a system revolving around punishment and surveillance. These strategies operate upon crime through their influence on fear, social cohesion, and informal social control instead. Because they strengthen the forces of informal (private and parochial) control, community-based efforts are more sustainable. They equip neighborhoods with the ability to self-regulate.

The community-based approach emphasizes the use of public spaces. For this to occur, people must feel safe in public. Perceived safety is compromised by crime and disorder. Police and other local authorities can encourage the use of sidewalks, parks, and other open areas by using place-based tactics to remove criminal opportunities, keeping the physical environment clean and attractive, and employing methods such as foot patrol to foster casual, friendly encounters between police and citizens.

Community-based approaches may pose a challenge in severely distressed neighborhoods, but they should not be rejected out of preconceived assumptions that such neighborhoods are beyond reach. These neighborhoods, in fact, stand to profit enormously from even modest reductions in fear and improvements in cohesion and informal control. Empowering residents to take ownership over their areas and feel capable of mobilizing against unpleasant and threatening behaviors can set in motion the mechanisms of self-regulation that minimize crime over the long term.

Crime reduction and prevention is fundamentally a partnership-oriented venture where citizens and neighborhood groups contribute as much or more than public authorities to solidify, communicate, and reinforce community norms and values. Arrest and punishment will occur, but should be viewed as part of the overarching goal of community development rather than as end goals in and of themselves. Locally driven cohesion and control—coupled with infusions of outside assistance as needed—are where genuinely effective crime policy begins.

DISCUSSION QUESTIONS

1. Think about a disadvantaged neighborhood or community with which you are familiar. Identify features of the physical and social environment that diminish quality of life and make people feel afraid. Why do you think these problems exist, and why have they not been fixed? How might a partnership between the community and the justice system potentially help improve the area? Describe the type of partnership you think would be most effective in this particular neighborhood or community.

2. One method by which police can reach out to communities that need help to reduce disorder and crime and improve the quality of life is by connecting with locally based groups and individual community leaders to enlist them in the effort. These groups and individuals can act as liaisons between police and the community. Thinking about the neighborhoods and communities with which you have had experience, what are some groups and people police might contact to perform this function? Are there any differences across neighborhoods in the types

of groups and leaders that might be most relevant to such an effort? Explain how these liaisons might differ across neighborhoods, and why.

3. A frequent criticism of community-based approaches to crime control is that "community" is a poorly defined term and may vary across neighborhoods. Some neighborhoods are small and cohesive, while others are large and have fairly weak social networks (or networks are present only among small groups within the larger whole). Do you see this as an impediment to community-based crime control? Could police and city officials tailor policies and programs within each neighborhood to the unique characteristics of that area? Offer examples of a tailored approach.

4. Over the course of this book, evidence was presented showing that criminal punishments intended to do nothing more than inflict discomfort on offenders or control and monitor them do not work and often have collateral consequences that make things worse for individual offenders and, sometimes, entire communities. We have seen that policies such as correctional rehabilitation, intermediate sanctions, and place-based crime prevention are effective and do not have side effects. Why, then, do punishment and control continue to dominate crime and criminal-justice policy? In your view, what are the reasons for the ongoing focus by both the public at large and policymakers on policies that do not work? Why have better approaches not become the norm? Do you think they ever will? Why or why not?

REFERENCES

Adcock, C. (2015). Ex-offenders face steep price to reinstate drivers' licenses. *Oklahoma Watch* (23 February 2015). Available http://oklahomawatch.org/2015/02/23/for-released-offenders-a-steep-price-to-drive-again/ (accessed 12 May 2017).

Adinkrah, M., & Clemens, W. M. (2016). To reinstate or not reinstate? An exploratory study of student perspectives on the death penalty in Michigan. *International Journal of Offender Therapy and Comparative Criminology*. DOI: 10.1177/0306624X16643743.

Agbu, O. (2003). Corruption and human trafficking: The Nigerian case. *West Africa Review, 4*(1), 1–13.

Ahn, R., Alpert, E. J., Purcell, G., Konstantopoulos, W. M., McGahan, A., Cafferty, E., . . . & Burke, T. F. (2013). Human trafficking: Review of educational resources for health professionals. *American Journal of Preventive Medicine, 44*(3), 283–289.

Ainsworth, J. E. (1991). Re-imagining childhood and reconstructing the legal order: The case for abolishing the juvenile court. *North Carolina Law Review, 69*, 1083–1133.

Ainsworth, J. E. (1994). Youth justice in a unified court: Response to critics of juvenile court abolition. *Boston College Law Review, 36*, 927–951.

Alfred, C. (2016). Why the capture of "El Chapo" Guzman won't stop his cartel. *Huffington Post* (14 January 2016). Available at http://www.huffingtonpost.com/entry/el-chapo-mexico-steven-dudley_us_5697d867e4b0778f46f86d6b

Ali, S. S. (2017). Human trafficking increased in 2016, organization reports. NBC News (5 February 2017). Available at http://www.nbcnews.com/news/us-news/human-trafficking-increased-2016-organization-reports-n717026 (accessed 23 May 2017).

Alper, B. S., & Nichols, L. T. (1981). *Beyond the courtroom: Programs in community justice and conflict resolution.* Lexington, MA: Lexington Books.

Alvarez, P. (2016). When sex trafficking goes unnoticed in America. *The Atlantic* (February 23).

American Civil Liberties Union of Southern California (1997). False premises, false promises: The Blythe Street Gang injunction and its aftermath. Los Angeles, CA: ACLU of Southern California.

American Civil Liberties Union. (n.d.). Fair Sentencing Act. Available at https://www.aclu.org/feature/fair-sentencing-act?redirect=fair-sentencing-act (retrieved 27 December 2016).

Andersen, L. H., & Andersen, S. H. (2014). Effect of electronic monitoring on social welfare dependence. *Criminology & Public Policy, 13*(3), 349–379.

Anderson, A. L. & Sample, L. L. (2008). Public awareness and action resulting from sex offender community notification laws. *Criminal Justice Policy Review, 19*(4), 371–396.

Anderson, E. (1999). *Code of the street: Decency, violence, and the moral life of the inner city.* New York, NY: WW Norton & Company.

Anderson, E. (2000). *Code of the street: Decency, violence, and the moral life of the inner city.* New York, NY: W.W. Norton & Company.

Andone, D. (2017). *Arkansas plans to execute 8 men over 10 days* (3 March 2017). Available at http://www.cnn.com/2017/03/02/health/arkansas-eight-executions/index.html (accessed 10 March 2017).

Andrews, D. A., & Dowden, C. (2007). The risk-need-responsivity model of assessment and human service in prevention and corrections: Crime-prevention jurisprudence. *Canadian Journal of Criminology and Criminal Justice, 49*(4), 439–464.

Andrews, D. A., Zinger, I., Hoge, R. D., Bonta, J., Gendreau, P., & Cullen, F. T. (1990). Does correctional treatment work? A clinically relevant and psychologically informed meta-analysis. *Criminology, 28*(3), 369–404.

Apel, R. (2013). Sanctions, perceptions, and crime: Implications for criminal deterrence. *Journal of Quantitative Criminology, 29*(1), 67–101.

Apel, R., & Nagin, D. S. (2011). General deterrence: A review of recent evidence. In J. Q. Wilson & J. Petersilia (Eds.), *Crime and public policy* (pp. 411–436). Oxford, UK: Oxford University Press.

Arditti, J. A., Lambert-Shute, J., & Joest, K. (2003). Saturday morning at the jail: Implications of incarceration for families and children. *Family relations, 52*(3), 195-–204.

Ariel, B., Weinborn, C., & Sherman, L. W. (2016). "Soft" policing at hot spots—do police community support officers work? A randomized controlled trial. *Journal of Experimental Criminology, 12*, 277–317.

Aspinall, E. J., Nambiar, D., Goldberg, D. J., Hickman, M., Weir, A., Van Velzen, E., Palmateer, N., Doyle, J. S., Hellard, M. E., & Hutchinson, S. J. (2014). Are needle and syringe programmes associated with a reduction in HIV transmission among people who inject drugs: A systematic review and meta-analysis. *International Journal of Epidemiology, 43*(1), 235–248.

Associated Press. (2015). Ex-BP executive found not guilty of lying to investigators during 2010 gulf oil spill. *The New York Times.* Available at https://www.nytimes.com/2015/06/06/business/ex-bp-executive-found-not-guilty-of-lying-to-investigators-during-2010-gulf-oil-spill.html (accessed 6 May 2017).

Auerhahn, K. (1999). Selective incapacitation and the problem of prediction. *Criminology, 37*(4), 703–734.

Austin, R. L., & Allen, M. D. (2000). Racial disparity in arrest rates as an explanation of racial disparity in commitment to Pennsylvania's prisons. *Journal of Research in Crime and Delinquency, 37*(2), 200–220.

Avdija, A. S. (2008). Evidence-based policing: A comparative analysis of eight experimental studies focused in the area of targeted policing. *International Journal of Criminal Justice Sciences, 3*(2), 110–128.

Bachhuber, M. A., Hennessy, S., Cunningham, C. O., & Starrels, J. L. (2016). Increasing benzodiazepine prescriptions and overdose mortality in the United States, 1996–2013. *Journal Information, 106*(4), 686–688.

Baer, J., & Chambliss, W. J. (1997). Generating fear: The politics of crime reporting. *Crime, Law and Social Change, 27*(2), 87–107.

Bailey, W. C. (1980). Deterrence and the celerity of the death penalty: A neglected question in deterrence research. *Social Forces, 58*(4), 1308–1333.

Bailey, W. C. (1998). Deterrence, brutalization, and the death penalty: Another examination of Oklahoma's return to capital punishment. *Criminology, 36*(4), 711–734.

Baker, T. E., & Wolfer, L. (2003). The crime triangle: Alcohol, drug use, and vandalism. *Police Practice and Research, 4*(1), 47–61.

Baker, T., Cleary, H. M. D., Pickett, J. T., & Gertz, M. G. (2016). Crime salience and public willingness to pay for child saving and juvenile punishment. *Crime & Delinquency, 62*(5), 645–668.

Baker, T., Falco Metcalfe, C., Berenblum, T., Aviv, G., & Gertz, M. (2015). Examining public preferences for the allocation of resources to rehabilitative versus punitive crime policies. *Criminal Justice Policy Review, 26*(5), 448–462.

Baker, T., Pelfrey Jr, W. V., Bedard, L. E., Dhungana, K., Gertz, M., & Golden, K. (2014). Female inmates' procedural justice perceptions of the police and courts: Is there a spill-over of police effects? *Criminal Justice and Behavior, 41*(2), 144–162.

Baldus, D. C., & Woodworth, G. (2003). Race discrimination and the legitimacy of capital punishment: Reflections on the interaction of fact and perception. *DePaul Law Review, 53*, 1411–1496.

Baldus, D. C., Pulaski, C., & Woodworth, G. (1983). Comparative review of death sentences: An empirical study of the Georgia experience. *The Journal of Criminal Law and Criminology, 74*(3), 661–753.

Baldus, D. C., Woodworth, G., Zuckerman, D., & Weiner, N. A. (1997). Racial discrimination and the death penalty in the post-Furman era: An empirical and legal overview with recent findings from Philadelphia. *Cornell Law Review, 83*, 1638–1770.

Bales, K. (2012). *Disposable people: New slavery in the global economy* (rev. ed.). Berkeley, CA: University of California Press.

Bales, W., Mann, K., Blomberg, T., Gaes, G., Barrick, K., Dhungana, K., & McManus, B. (2010). *A quantitative and qualitative assessment of electronic monitoring*. Washington, DC: U.S. Department of Justice.

Ball, J. C. (1965). Two patterns of narcotic addiction in the United States. *The Journal of Criminal Law, Criminology, and Political Science, 56*(2), 203–211.

Ball, R. A., Huff, C. R., & Lilly, J. R. (1988). *House arrest and correctional policy: Doing time at home*. Newbury Park, CA: Sage Publications.

Bandy, R. (2011). Measuring the impact of sex offender notification on community adoption of protective behaviors. *Criminology & Public Policy, 10*(2), 237–263.

Banks, D., & Kyckehlhahn, T. (2011). *Characteristics of suspected human trafficking incidents, 2008–2010* (NCJ 233732). Washington, DC: Bureau of Justice Statistics.

Barkan, S. E., & Cohn, S. F. (1994). Racial prejudice and support for the death penalty by whites. *Journal of Research in Crime and Delinquency, 31*(2), 202–209.

Barkworth, J., & Murphy, K. (2016). System contact and procedural justice policing: Improving quality of life outcomes for victims of crime. *International Review of Victimology, 22*(2), 105–122.

Barth, R. P. (2005). Foster home care is more cost-effective than shelter care: Serious questions continue to be raised about the utility of group care in child welfare services. *Child Abuse & Neglect, 29*, 623–625.

Bassuk, E. L., & Samuel, G. (1978). Deinstitutionalization and mental health services. *Scientific American, 238*(2), 46–53.

Bazemore, G., & Maloney, D. (1994). Rehabilitating community service toward restorative service sanctions in a balanced justice system. *Federal Probation, 58*, 24–35.

Bazemore, G., & Schiff, M. (2001). Introduction. In G. Bazemore & M. Schiff (Eds.), *Restorative community justice: Repairing harm and transforming communities* (pp. 1–18). New York: Routledge.

Beal, D., & Duckro, P. (1977). Family counseling as an alternative to legal action for the juvenile status offender. *Journal of Marital and Family Therapy, 3*(1), 77–81.

Beall, J. A. (1998). Are we only burning witches? The Antiterrorism and Effective Death Penalty Act of 1996's answer to terrorism. *Indiana Law Journal, 73*(2), 693–710.

Beaver, A. L. (2009). Getting a fix on cocaine sentencing policy: Reforming the sentencing scheme of the Anti-Drug Abuse Act of 1986. *Fordham Law Review, 78*(5), 2531–2575.

Beccaria, C. (1764). *On crimes and punishments*. Indianapolis, IN: Hackett Publishing Company.

Beccaria, C. (1764/1986). *On crimes and punishments*. Indianapolis, IN: Hackett Publishing Company, Inc.

Beck, J. S., Liese, B. S., & Najavits, L. M. (2016). Cognitive therapy. In A. H. Mack, K. T. Brady, S. I. Miller, & R. J. Frances (Eds.), *Clinical textbook of addictive disorders* (4th ed.; pp. 563–587). New York: The Guilford Press.

Beck, V. S. & Travis, L. T., III. (2004). Sex offender notification and fear of victimization. *Journal of Criminal Justice, 32*, 455–463.

Beckett, K., & Evans, H. (2016). Race, death, and justice: Capital sentencing in Washington State, 1981–2014. *Columbia Journal of Race & Law, 6*, 77–114.

Beckett, K., Nyrop, K., & Pfingst, L. (2006). Race, drugs, and policing: Understanding disparities in drug delivery arrests. *Criminology, 44*(1), 105–137.

Belciug, C., Franklin, C., Bolton, K. W., Jordan, C., & Lehmann, P. (2016). Effects of goal commitment and solution building on the completion rates for a juvenile diversion program. *Criminal Justice and Behavior, 43*(7), 923–936.

Bellair, P. E. (1997). Social interaction and community crime: Examining the importance of neighbor networks. *Criminology, 35*(4), 677–704.

Bellair, P. E., & Browning, C. R. (2010). Contemporary disorganization research: An assessment and further test of the systemic model of neighborhood crime. *Journal of Research in Crime and Delinquency, 47*(4), 496–521.

Bennett, T., Holloway, K., & Farrington, D. P. (2006). Does neighborhood watch reduce crime? A systematic review and meta-analysis. *Journal of Experimental Criminology, 2*, 437–458.

Bennett, T., Holloway, K., & Farrington, D. P. (2006). Does neighborhood watch reduce crime? A systematic review and meta-analysis. *Journal of Experimental Criminology, 2*(4), 437–458.

Benson, B. L., Rasmussen, D. W., & Sollars, D. L. (1995). Police bureaucracies, their incentives, and the war on drugs. *Public Choice, 83*(1–2), 21–45.

Benson, M. L. (1985). Denying the guilty mind: Accounting for involvement in a white-collar crime. *Criminology, 23*(4), 583–607.

Benson, M. L., Madensen, T. D., & Eck, J. E. (2009). White-collar crime from an opportunity perspective. In *The Criminology of White-Collar Crime* (pp. 175–193). New York: Springer.

Berenson, J. A. & Appelbaum, P. S. (2011). A geospatial analysis of the impact of sex offender residency restrictions in two New York counties. *Law and Human Behavior, 35*(3), 235–246.

Berge, W. (1940). Remedies available to the government under the Sherman Act. *Law & Contemporary Problems, 7*, 104–111.

Bergin, T. (2016). *The evidence enigma: Correctional boot camps and other failures in evidence-based policymaking.* New York: Routledge.

Bergseth, K. J., & Bouffard, J. A. (2007). Examining the effectiveness of a restorative justice program for various types of juvenile offenders. *International Journal of Offender Therapy and Comparative Criminology, 57*(9), 1054–1075.

Berman, G. (2013). Alternatives to incarceration are cutting prison numbers, costs and crime. *The Guardian.* Available at https://www.theguardian.com/commentisfree/2013/jul/04/alternatives-incarceration-prison-numbers (accessed 8 June 2017).

Bernard, T. J., & Kurlychek, M. C. (2010). *The cycle of juvenile justice* (2nd ed.). New York: Oxford University Press.

Bjerregaard, B. & Lizotte, A. J. (1995). Gun ownership and gang membership. *The Journal of Criminal Law and Criminology, 86*(1), 37–58.

Blanchette, T. G., Silva, A. P., & Bento, A. R. (2013). The myth of Maria and the imagining of sexual trafficking in Brazil. *Dialectical Anthropology, 37*(2), 195–227.

Blueprints for Healthy Youth Development. (2017). Website. Available at http://www.blueprintsprograms.com (accessed 16 May 2017).

Blume, J. H. (2006). AEDPA: The "hype" and the "bite." *Cornell Law Review, 91*, 259–302.

Blume, J., & Eisenberg, T. (1998). Judicial politics, death penalty appeals, and case selection: An empirical study. *Southern California Law Review, 72*, 465–503.

Blumstein, A. (1982). On the racial disproportionality of United States prison populations. *Journal of Criminal Law and Criminology, 73*(3), 1259–1281.

Blumstein, A. (1993). Racial disproportionality of US prison populations revisited. *University of Colorado Law Review, 64*(3), 743–760.

Blumstein, A. (2000). Disaggregating the violence trends. In A. Blumstein & J. Wallman (Eds.), *The crime drop in America* (pp. 13–44). Cambridge, UK: Cambridge University Press.

Blumstein, A., & Nagin, D. (1978). On the optimum use of incarceration for crime control. *Operations Research, 26*(3), 381–405.

Bonczar, T. P., Hughes, T. A., Wilson, D. J., & Ditton, P. M. (2011). *National corrections reporting program: Sentence length of state prisoners, by offense, admission type, sex, and race.* Washington, DC: Bureau of Justice Statistics.

Bonnie, R. J., Johnson, R. L., Chemers, B. M., & Schuck, J. (2013). *Reforming juvenile justice: A developmental approach.* Washington, DC: The National Academies Press.

Bonta, J., & Motiuk, L. L. (1985). Utilization of an interview-based classification instrument: A study of correctional halfway houses. *Criminal Justice and Behavior, 12*(3), 333–352.

Bonta, J., & Motiuk, L. L. (1987). The diversion of incarcerated offenders to correctional halfway houses. *Journal of Research in Crime and Delinquency, 24*(4), 302–323.

Bonta, J., & Motiuk, L. L. (1990). Classification to halfway houses: A quasi-experimental evaluation. *Criminology, 28*(3), 497–506.

Bonta, J., Wallace-Capretta, S., & Rooney, J. (2000). A quasi-experimental evaluation of an intensive rehabilitation supervision program. *Criminal Justice and Behavior, 27*(3), 312–329.

Botvin, G. J. (2000). Preventing drug abuse in schools: Social and competence enhancement approaches targeting individual-level etiologic factors. *Addictive Behaviors, 25*(6), 887–897.

Bouchard, J., & Wong, J. S. (2017). Examining the effects of intensive supervision and aftercare programs for at-risk youth: A systematic review and meta-analysis. *International Journal of Offender Therapy and Comparative Criminology.* DOI: 0306624X17690449.

Bouffard, J. A., & Mufti , L. R. (2007). The effectiveness of community service sentences compared to traditional fines for low-level offenders. *The Prison Journal, 87*(2), 171–194.

Bourgois, P. (2003). Crack and the political economy of social suffering. *Addiction Research & Theory, 11*(1), 31–37.

Boyle, D. J., Ragusa-Salerno, L. M., Lanterman, J. L., & Marcus, A. F. (2013). An evaluation of day reporting centers for parolees. *Criminology & Public Policy, 12*(1), 119–143.

Boyum, D. & Reuter, P. (2005). *An analytic assessment of U.S. drug policy.* Washington, DC: AEI Press.

Brace, P., & Boyea, B. D. (2008). State public opinion, the death penalty, and the practice of electing judges. *American Journal of Political Science, 52*(2), 360–372.

Bradford, B. (2014). Policing and social identity: Procedural justice, inclusion and cooperation between police and public. *Policing and society, 24*(1), 22–43.

Braga, A. A. (2005). Hot spots policing and crime prevention: A systematic review of randomized controlled trials. *Journal of Experimental Criminology, 1,* 317–342.

Braga, A. A. (2008). Pulling levers focused deterrence strategies and the prevention of gun homicide. *Journal of Criminal Justice, 36,* 332–343.

Braga, A. A., & Bond, B. J. (2008). Policing crime and disorder hot spots: A randomized controlled trial. *Criminology, 46*(3), 577–607.

Braga, A. A., & Weisburd, D. L. (2012). The effects of "pulling levers" focused deterrence strategies on crime. *Campbell Systematic Reviews, 6,* 1–90.

Braga, A. A., & Wintemute, G. J. (2013). Improving the potential effectiveness of gun buyback programs. *American Journal of Preventive Medicine, 45*(5), 668–671.

Braga, A. A., Kennedy, D. M., Waring, E. J., & Piehl, A. M. (2001). Problem-oriented policing, deterrence, and youth violence: An evaluation of Boston's Operation Ceasefire.

Journal of Research in Crime and Delinquency, 38(3), 195–225.

Braga, A. A., Papachristos, A. V., & Hureau, D. M. (2010). The concentration and stability of gunviolence at micro places in Boston, 1980–2008. *Journal of Quantitative Criminology, 26*(1), 33–53.

Braga, A. A., Papachristos, A. V., & Hureau, D. M. (2014). The effects of hot spots policing on crime: An updated systematic review and meta-analysis. *Justice Quarterly, 31*(4), 633–663.

Braga, A. A., Weisburd, D. L., Waring, E. J., Mazerolle, L. G., Spelman, W., & Gajewski, F. (1999). Problem-oriented policing in violent crime places: A randomized controlled experiment. *Criminology, 37*(3), 541–580.

Braga, A. A., Welsh, B. C., and Schnell, C. (2015). Can policing disorder reduce crime? A systematic review and meta-analysis. *Journal of Research in Crime and Delinquency, 52*(4), 567–588.

Braithwaite, J. (1982). Challenging just deserts: Punishing white-collar criminals. *The Journal of Criminal Law and Criminology, 73*(2), 723–763.

Braithwaite, J. (1985). White collar crime. *Annual Review of Sociology, 11*, 1–25.

Braithwaite, J. (1999). Restorative justice: Assessing optimistic and pessimistic accounts. *Crime and Justice, 25*, 1–127.

Bratton, W. (1998). *Turnaround*. New York: Random House.

Breslow, J. M. (2013). Were bankers jailed in past financial crises? PBS Frontline. Available at http://www.pbs.org/wgbh/frontline/article/were-bankers-jailed-in-past-financial-crises/ (accessed 6 May 2017).

Bright, C. L., Young, D. W., Bessaha, M. L., & Falls, B. J. (2015). Perceptions and outcomes following teen court involvement. *Social Work Research, 39*(3), 135–146.

Bright, C., Morris-Compton, D., Walter, J., Falls, B., & Young, D. (2013). *Multijurisdictional teen court evaluation: A comparative evaluation of three teen court models*. Annapolis, MD: Administrative Office of the Courts.

Bright, S. B. (1992). In defense of life: Enforcing the Bill of Rights on behalf of poor, minority and disadvantaged persons facing the death penalty. *Missouri Law Review, 57*(3), 849–870.

Bright, S. B. (1994). Counsel for the poor: The death sentence not for the worst crime but for the worst lawyer. *The Yale Law Journal, 103*(7), 1835–1883.

Bright, S. B. (2000). Elected judges and the death penalty in Texas: Why full habeas corpus review by independent federal judges is indispensable to protecting constitutional rights. *Texas Law Review, 78*, 1805–1837.

Bright, S. B. (2014). The role of race, poverty, intellectual disability, and mental Illness in the decline of the death Penalty. *University of Richmond Law Review, 49*, 671–692.

Bright, S. B., & Keenan, P. J. (1995). Judges and the politics of death: Deciding between the Bill of Rights and the next election in capital cases. *Boston University Law Review, 75*, 759–835.

Bronson, J. & Maruschak, L. M. (2015). Disabilities among prison and jail inmates, 2011-12 (NCJ 249151). Washington, DC: US Department of Justice.

Bronson, J., Maruschak, L. M., & Berzofsky, M. (2015). Disabilities among prison and jail inmates, 2011–12 (NCJ 249151). Washington, DC: U.S. Department of Justice.

Brooks, R. R. W., & Raphael, S. (2002). Life terms or death sentences: The uneasy relationship between judicial elections and capital punishment. *The Journal of Criminal Law and Criminology, 92*(3/4), 609–640.

Brown, L. S. (1981). Substance abuse and America: Historical perspective on the federal response to a social phenomenon. *Journal of the National Medical Association, 73*(6), 497–506.

Brown, O. (2008). The numbers game. *Forced Migration Review, 31*(8), 8–9.

Brown, R. T. (2010). Systematic review of the impact of adult drug-treatment courts. *Translational Research, 155*(6), 263–274.

Browning, C. R., Feinberg, S. L., & Dietz, R. D. (2004). The paradox of social organization: Networks, collective efficacy, and violent crime in urban neighborhoods. *Social Forces, 83*(2), 503–534.

Brunson, R. K. (2007). "Police don't like black people": African-American young men's accumulated police experiences. *Criminology & Public Policy, 6*(1), 71–101.

Brunson, R. K., & Gau, J. M. (2015). Officer race versus macro-level context a test of competing hypotheses about black citizens' experiences with and perceptions of black police officers. *Crime & Delinquency, 61*(2), 213–242.

Brunson, R. K., & Miller, J. (2009). Schools, neighborhoods, and adolescent conflicts: A situational examination of reciprocal dynamics. *Justice Quarterly, 26*(2), 183–210.

Brunson, R. K., Braga, A. A., Hureau, D. M., & Pegram, K. (2015). We trust you, but not that much: Examining police–black clergy partnerships to reduce youth violence. *Justice Quarterly, 32*(6), 1006–1036.

Burnham, J. C. (1968). New Perspectives on the Prohibition" Experiment" of the 1920s. *Journal of Social History, 2*(1), 51–68.

Burrow, J. (2008). Reverse waiver and the effects of legal, statutory, and secondary legal factors on sentencing outcomes for juvenile offenders. *Crime & Delinquency, 54*(1), 34–64.

Bursik, R. J. (1986). Delinquency rates as sources of ecological change. In R. J. Sampson & J. M. Byrne (Eds.), *The social ecology of crime* (pp. 63–76). New York: Springer.

Bursik, R. J., & Grasmick, H. G. (1993). *Neighborhoods and crime: The dimensions of effective community control.* New York: Macmillan.

Bush, J., Glick, B., & Taymans, J. (2002). *Thinking for a Change: Integrated cognitive behavior change program.* Washington, DC: National Institute of Corrections.

Buttars, A., Huss, M. T., & Brack, C. (2016). An analysis of an intensive supervision program for sex offenders using propensity scores. *Journal of Offender Rehabilitation, 55*(1), 51–68.

Butts, J. A., & Mears, D. P. (2001). Reviving juvenile justice in a get-tough era. *Youth & Society, 33*(2), 169–198.

Butts, J. A., Buck, J., & Coggeshall, M. B. (2002). *The impact of teen court on young offenders.* Washington, DC: Urban Institute.

Butzin, C. A., Martin, S. S., & Inciardi, J. A. (2002). Evaluating component effects of a prison-based treatment continuum. *Journal of substance abuse treatment, 22*(2), 63–69.

Cahalan, M. W. & Parsons, L. A. (1986). *Historical corrections statistics in the United States, 1850–1984* (NCJ 102529). Washington, DC: U.S. Department of Justice.

Cahill, M., & Hayeslip, D. (2010). Juvenile Justice Bulletin: Findings from the evaluation of OJJDP's gang reduction program. Washington, DC: Office of Juvenile Justice and Delinquency Prevention.

Caldwell, M. F. (2010). Study characteristics and recidivism base rates in juvenile sex offender recidivism. *International Journal of Offender Therapy and Comparative Criminology, 54*(2), 197–212.

California Sex Offender Management Board. (2008). *Homelessness among registered sex offenders in California: The numbers, the risks and the response.* Sacramento, CA: California Sex Offender Management Board.

Callahan, C. M., Rivara, F. P., & Koepsell, T. D. (1994). Money for guns: Evaluation of the Seattle gun buy-back program. *Public Health Reports, 109*(4), 472.

Campana, P. (2016). The structure of human trafficking: Lifting the bonnet on a Nigerian transnational network. *British Journal of Criminology, 56*, 68–86.

Canes-Wrone, B., Clark, T. S., & Kelly, J. P. (2014). Judicial selection and death penalty decisions. *American Political Science Review, 108*(01), 23–39.

Capous Desyllas, M. (2007). A critique of the global trafficking discourse and US policy. *Journal of Sociology & Social Welfare, 34*(4), 57–79.

Caputo, G. A. (2004). *Intermediate sanctions in corrections.* Denton, TX: University of North Texas Press.

Carr, J. B., & Doleac, J. L. (2014). Keep the kids inside: Juvenile curfews, bad weather, and urban gun violence. *Batten Working Paper 2014-003.*

Carr, P. J. (2003). The new parochialism: The implications of the Beltway case for arguments concerning informal social control. *American Journal of Sociology, 108*(6), 1249–1291.

Carr, P. J. (2003). The new parochialism: The implications of the Beltway case for arguments concerning informal social control. *American Journal of Sociology, 108*(6), 1249–1291.

Carr, P. J., Napolitano, L., & Keating, J. (2007). "We never call the cops and here is why": A qualitative examination of legal cynicism in three Philadelphia neighborhoods. *Criminology, 45*(2), 445–480.

Carr, W. A., Baker, A. N., & Cassidy, J. J. (2016). Reducing criminal recidivism with an enhanced day reporting center for probationers with mental illness. *Journal of Offender Rehabilitation, 55*(2), 95–112.

Carson, E. A. (2015). *Prisoners in 2014* (NCJ 248955). Washington, DC: U.S. Department of Justice.

Carson, E. A., & Anderson, E. (2016). *Prisoners in 2015* (NCJ 250229). Washington, DC: U.S. Department of Justice.

Carson, E. A. & Golinelli, D. (2013). Prisoners in 2012: Trends in admissions and releases, 1991–2012 (NCJ 243920). Washington, DC: U.S. Department of Justice.

Carson, W. G. (1970). White-collar crime and the enforcement of factory legislation. *The British Journal of Criminology, 10*(4), 383–398.

Carter, D. L., & Carter, J. G. (2009). Intelligence-led policing conceptual and functional considerations for public policy. *Criminal Justice Policy Review, 20*(3), 310–325.

Carter, J. G., Phillips, S. W., & Gayadeen, S. M. (2014). Implementing intelligence-led policing: An application of loose-coupling theory. *Journal of Criminal Justice, 42*(6), 433–442.

Cassell, P. G. (1998). Protecting the innocent from false confessions and lost confessions: And from" Miranda." *The Journal of Criminal Law and Criminology, 88*(2), 497–556.

Centers for Disease Control and Prevention. (2016). *HIV and injection drug use*. Washington, DC: Centers for Disease Control and Prevention.

Chacón, J. M. (2006). Misery and myopia: Understanding the failures of U.S. efforts to stop human trafficking. *Fordham Law Review, 74*(6), 2977–3040.

Chacón, J. M. (2017). Human Trafficking, Immigration Regulation, and Subfederal Criminalization. *New Criminal Law Review: In International and Interdisciplinary Journal, 20*(1), 96–129.

Chaffee, E. C. (2011). The Dodd-Frank Wall Street Reform and Consumer Protection Act: A failed vision for increasing consumer protection and heightening corporate responsibility in international financial transactions. *American University Law Review, 60*, 1431–1457.

Chalfin, A., Haviland, A. M., & Raphael, S. (2013). What do panel studies tell us about a deterrent effect of capital punishment? A critique of the literature. *Journal of Quantitative Criminology, 29*(1), 5–43.

Chambliss, W. J. (1967). Types of deviance and the effectiveness of legal sanctions. *Wisconsin Law Review*, 703–719.

Chamlin, M. B., Grasmick, H. G., Bursik, R. J., & Cochran, J. K. (1992). Time aggregation and time lag in macro-level deterrence research. *Criminology, 30*(3), 377–396.

Charles, K. K., & Durlauf, S. N. (2013). Pitfalls in the use of time series methods to study deterrence and capital punishment. *Journal of Quantitative Criminology, 29*(1), 45–66.

Chavez, C. (2017). Probation officers get training to combat human trafficking. Available at http://www.wmfe.org/probation-officers-to-get-training-to-combat-human-trafficking/69450 (accessed 16 February 2017).

Chesney-Lind, M., & Shelden, R. G. (2013). Girls, delinquency, and juvenile justice (4th ed.). West Sussex, UK: John Wiley & Sons.

Childs, K. K., Frick, P. J., & Gottlieb, K. (2016). Sex differences in the measurement invariance and factors that influence structured judgments of risk using the structured assessment of violence risk in youth (SAVRY). *Youth Violence and Juvenile Justice, 14*(1), 76–92.

Childs, K. K., Ryals, J., Frick, P. J., Lawing, K., Phillippi, S. W., & Deprato, D. K. (2013). Examining the validity of the Structured Assessment of Violence Risk in Youth

(SAVRY) for predicting probation outcomes among adjudicated juvenile offenders. *Behavioral Sciences & the Law, 31*(2), 256–270.

Childs, K., Frick, P., & Krupa, J. (2013). *A summary of the Louisiana Models for Change (LaMfC) data deliverables (August 2013): 2006–2011.*

Chiu, T., & Mogulescu, S. (2004). *Changing the status quo for status offenders: New York State's effort to support troubled teens.* New York: Vera Institute of Justice.

Cho, S-Y. (2012). Modeling for determinants of human trafficking. *Economics of Security Working Paper, No. 70.* Berlin, Germany: German Institute for Economic Research.

Cho, S-Y, Dreher, A., & Neumayer, E. (2013). Does legalized prostitution increase human trafficking? *World Development, 41*, 67–82.

Christie, N. (1977). Conflicts as property. *British Journal of Criminology, 17*(1), 1–15.

Chuang, J. (2006b). The United States as global sheriff: Using unilateral sanctions to combat human trafficking. *Michigan Journal of International Law, 27*(2), 437–494.

Chuang, J. (2006a). Beyond a snapshot: Preventing human trafficking in the global economy. *Indiana Journal of Global Legal Studies, 13*(1), 137–163.

Chuck, E. (2015). As heroin use grows in U.S., poppy crops thrive in Afghanistan. *NBC News* (7 July 2015). Available at https://www.nbcnews.com/news/world/heroin-use-grows-u-s-poppy-crops-thrive-afghanistan-n388081 (accessed 25 December 2016).

Chui, W. H. (2017). Probation and community service orders. In W. H. Chui & T. W. Lo (Eds.), *Understanding criminal justice in Hong Kong* (2nd ed., n.p.). New York: Routledge.

Cicero, T. J., Inciardi, J. A., & Muñoz, A. (2005). Trends in abuse of OxyContin® and other opioid analgesics in the United States: 2002–2004. *The Journal of Pain, 6*, 662–672.

Clark, V. A. (2015). *The effect of community context and post-release housing placements on recidivism: Evidence from Minnesota.* St Paul: Minnesota Department of Corrections.

Clarke, R. V. (1995). Situational crime prevention. *Crime and Justice, 19*, 91–150.

Clarke, R. V. (2014). Introduction. In D. B. Cornish & R. V. Clarke (Eds.), *The reasoning criminal: Rational choice perspectives on offending* (pp. ix–xvi). New Brunswick, NJ: Transaction Publishers.

Clarke, R. V., & Cornish, D. B. (1985). Modeling offenders' decisions: A framework for research and policy. *Crime and justice: A review of the research*, vol. 6, 147–185.

Clarke, R. V., & Eck, J. E. (2005). *Crime analysis for problem solvers in 60 small steps.* Washington, DC: Center for Problem Oriented Policing.

Clarke, R. V., & Eck, J. E. (2014). *Become a problem-solving crime analyst.* New York: Routledge.

Clarke, R. V. & Felson, M. (1993). Introduction: Criminology, routine activity, and rational choice. In R. V. Clarke & M. Felson (Eds.), *Routine activity and rational choice.* New Brunswick, NJ: Transaction Publishers.

Clarke, R. V. G. (1980). "Situational" crime prevention: Theory and practice. *British Journal of Criminology, 20*(2), 136–147.

Clarke, R. V. G. & Felson, M. (Eds.). (1993). *Routine activity and rational choice* (Vol. 5). New York: Transaction Publishers.

Clear, T. R. (1998). *Harm in American penology: Offenders, victims, and their communities.* New York: State University of New York Press.

Clear, T. R. (2016). "A thug in prison can't shoot your sister." *Criminology & Public Policy, 15*(2), 343–347.

Clear, T. R., Rose, D. R., & Ryder, J. A. (2001). Incarceration and the community: The problem of removing and returning offenders. *Crime & Delinquency, 47*(3), 335–351.

Clear, T. R., Rose, D. R., Waring, E., & Scully, K. (2003). Coercive mobility and crime: A preliminary examination of concentrated incarceration and social disorganization. *Justice Quarterly, 20*(1), 33–64.

Cleveland, S. H. (2001). Norm internalization and U.S. economic sanctions. *Yale Journal of International Law, 26*(1), 3–102.

Cochran, J. C., & Mears, D. P. (2015). Race, ethnic, and gender divides in juvenile court sanctioning and rehabilitative intervention. *Journal of Research in Crime and Delinquency, 52,* 181–212.

Cochran, J. K., & Chamlin, M. B. (2006). The enduring racial divide in death penalty support. *Journal of Criminal Justice, 34*(1), 85–99.

Cochran, J. K., Chamlin, M. B., & Seth, M. (1994). Deterrence or brutalization? An impact assessment of Oklahoma's return to capital punishment. *Criminology, 32*(1), 107–134.

Cohan, W. D. (2015). How Wall Street's bankers stayed out of jail. *The Atlantic* (September). Available at https://www.theatlantic.com/magazine/archive/2015/09/how-wall-streets-bankers-stayed-out-of-jail/399368/ (accessed 6 May 2017).

Cohen, A. (2012). Yes, America, we have executed an innocent man. *The Atlantic* (14 May 2012). Available at https://www.theatlantic.com/national/archive/2012/05/yes-america-we-have-executed-an-innocent-man/257106/ (accessed 18 May 2017).

Cohen-Cole, E., Durlauf, S., Fagan, J., & Nagin, D. (2009). Model uncertainty and the deterrent effect of capital punishment. *American Law and Economics Review, 11*(2), 335–369.

Cohen, J. (1983). Incapacitation as a strategy for crime control: Possibilities and pitfalls. In M. Tonry & N. Morris (Eds.), *Crime and justice: A review of research* (vol. 2; pp. 1–84). Chicago: University of Chicago Press.

Cohen, L. E., & Felson, M. (1979). Social change and crime rate trends: A routine activity approach. *American Sociological Review, 44,* 588–608.

Cohen, L. E., & Felson, M. (1979). Social change and crime rate trends: A routine activity approach. *American Sociological Review, 44*(4), 588–608.

Cohen, M., & Jeglic, E. L. (2007). Sex offender legislation in the United States: What do we know? *International Journal of Offender Therapy and Comparative Criminology, 51*(4), 369–383.

Cohen, T. H., Cook, D., & Lowenkamp, C. T. (2016). The supervision of low-risk federal offenders: How the low-risk policy has changed federal supervision practices with compromising community safety. *Federal Probation, 80*(1), 3–11.

Cole, J., & Sprang, G. (2015). Sex trafficking of minors in metropolitan, micropolitan, and rural communities. *Child Abuse & Neglect, 40,* 113–123.

Coleman, J. W. (1987). Toward an integrated theory of white-collar crime. *American Journal of Sociology,* 406–439.

Collins, J. J.& Bowdoin, G. D. (1999). *Beyond unilateral economic sanctions: Better alternatives for US foreign policy.* Washington, DC: The CSIS Press.

Connell, N. M., Miggans, K., & McGloin, J. M. (2008). Can a community policing initiative reduce serious crime? A local evaluation. *Police Quarterly, 11*(2), 127–150.

Cook, P. J. (1981a). Guns and crime: The perils of long division. *Journal of Policy Analysis and Management, 1*(1), 120–125.

Cook, P. J. (1981b). The effect of firearm availability on violent crime patterns. *Annals of the American Academy of Political Science, 455,* 63–79.

Cook, P. J., Molliconi, S., & Cole, T. B. (1995). Regulating gun markets. *The Journal of Criminal Law and Criminology (1973-), 86*(1), 59–92.

Cooley-Towell, S., Pasini-Hill, D., & Patrick, D. (2000). The value of the post-conviction polygraph: The importance of sanctions. *Polygraph, 29*(1), 6–19.

Copes, H., & Vieraitis, L. M. (2009). Bounded rationality of identity thieves: Using offender-based research to inform policy. *Criminology & Public Policy, 8*(2), 237–262.

Cordner, G. (2014). Community policing. In M. Reisig & R. Kane (Eds.), *The Oxford handbook of police and policing* (pp. 148–171). Oxford, UK: Oxford University Press.

Cordner, G. W. (1986). Fear of crime and the police: An evaluation of a fear-reduction strategy. *Journal of Police Science and Administration, 14,* 223–233.

Cordner, G., & Biebel, E. P. (2005). Problem-oriented policing in practice. *Criminology & Public Policy, 4*(2), 155–180.

Cornish, D. & Clarke, R. (2014). Introduction. In D. Cornish & R. Clarke (Eds.), *The reasoning criminal: Rational choice perspectives on offending* (pp. 1–14). New Brunswick, NJ: Transaction Publishers.

Cornish, D. B., & Clarke, R. V. (2012). Analyzing organized crimes. In A. R. Piquero & S. G. Tibbetts, *Rational choice and criminal behavior: Recent research and future challenges* (pp. 41–64). New York: Routledge.

Cornish, D. B., & Clarke, R. V. (2017). The rational choice perspective. In R. Wortley & M. Townsley (Eds.), *Environmental criminology and crime analysis* (2nd ed.; pp. 29–61). New York, NY: Routledge.

Cornish, D. B., & Clarke, R. V. (Eds.). (2014). *The reasoning criminal: Rational choice perspectives on offending.* New York: Transaction Publishers.

Cornish, D. B., & Clarke, R. V. (2008). The rational choice perspective. In. R. Wortley & L. Mazerolle (Eds.), *Environmental criminology and crime analysis* (pp. 21–44). New York: Routledge.

Corsaro, N., Brunson, R. K., & McGarrell, E. F. (2009). Problem-oriented policing and open-air drug markets: Examining the Rockford pulling levers deterrence strategy. *Crime & Delinquency, 59*(7), 1085–1107.

Costanza, S. E., Cox, S. M., & Kilburn, J. C. (2015). The impact of halfway houses on parole success and recidivism. *Journal of Sociological Research, 6*(2), 39–55.

Craddock, A. (2004). Estimating criminal justice system costs and cost-savings benefits of day reporting centers. *Journal of Offender Rehabilitation, 39*(4), 69–98.

Cramer, C. E., & Kopel, D. B. (1995). "Shall issue": The new wave of concealed handgun permit laws. *Tennessee Law Review, 62,* 679–757.

Crawford, A., & Clear, T. (2001). Community justice: Transforming communities through restorative justice? In G. Bazemore & M. Schiff (Eds.), *Restorative community justice: Repairing harm and transforming communities* (pp. 127–150). New York: Routledge.

Cressey, D. R. (1969). *Theft of the nation: The structure and operations of organized crime in America.* New Brunswick, NJ: Transaction Publishers. *Crime & Delinquency, 25*(4), 463–489.

CrimeSolutions.gov. (n.d.). Website. Available at https://www.crimesolutions.gov (accessed 16 May 2017).

Cuijpers, P. (2002). Effective ingredients of school-based drug prevention programs: A systematic review. *Addictive Behaviors, 27*(6), 1009–1023.

Cullen, F. T., Blevins, K. R., Trager, J. S., & Gendreau, P. (2005). The rise and fall of boot camps: A case study in common-sense corrections. *Journal of Offender Rehabilitation, 40*(3-4), 53–70.

Cullen, F. T., Cavender, G., Maakestad, W. J., & Benson, M. L. (2015). *Corporate crime under attack: The fight to criminalize business violence* (2nd ed.). New York: Routledge.

Cullen, F. T., Clark, G. A., Mathers, R. A., & Cullen, J. B. (1983). Public support for punishing white-collar crime: Blaming the victim revisited? *Journal of Criminal Justice, 11*(6), 481–493.

Cullen, F. T., Fisher, B. S., & Applegate, B. K. (2000). Public opinion about punishment and corrections. *Crime and Justice, 27,* 1–79.

Cullen, F. T., Jonson, C. L., & Mears, D. P. (2017). Reinventing community corrections. *Crime and Justice, 46*(1), 27–93.

Cullen, F. T., Jonson, C. L., & Mears, D. P. (2017). Reinventing community corrections. *Crime and Justice, 46*(1), 1–67.

Cullen, F. T., Link, B. G., & Polanzi, C. W. (1982). The seriousness of crime revisited: Have attitudes toward white-collar crime changed? *Criminology, 20*(1), 83–102.

Currie, E. (1993). *Reckoning: Drugs, the cities, and the American future.* New York: Hill and Wang.

Currie, E. (1998). *Crime and punishment in America: Why the solutions to America's most stubborn social crisis have not worked—and what will.* New York: Owl Books.

Curry, G. D., & Thomas, R. W. (1992). Community organization and gang policy response. *Journal of Quantitative Criminology, 8*(4), 357–374.

D'Alessio, S. J., & Stolzenberg, L. (1995). The impact of sentencing guidelines on jail incarceration in Minnesota. *Criminology, 33*(2), 283–302.

D.A.R.E. (n.d.). Official organization website. Available at www.dare.com. Accessed (6 December 2016).

Daly, K. (1989). Gender and varieties of white-collar crime. *Criminology, 27*(4), 769–794.

Daly, K. (2002). Restorative justice: The real story. *Punishment & Society, 4*(1), 55–79.

Dear, M. J., & Wolch, J. R. (1987). *Landscapes of despair: From deinstitutionalization to homelessness.* Princeton, NJ: Princeton University Press.

Death Penalty Information Center (2017b). Executed but possibly innocent. Available at https://deathpenaltyinfo.org/executed-possibly-innocent REF>(accessed 18 May 2017).

Death Penalty Information Center. (2016). *The Death Penalty in 2016: Year End Report.* Washington, DC: Death Penalty Information Center.

Death Penalty Information Center. (2017a). Innocence and the death penalty. Available at https://deathpenaltyinfo.org/innocence-and-death-penalty (accessed 18 May 2017).

Decker, S. H. (1996). Collective and normative features of gang violence. *Justice Quarterly, 13*(2), 243–264.

Decker, S. H. (2007). Expand the use of police gang units. *Criminology & Public Policy, 6*(4), 729–734.

Decker, S. H., & Curry, G. D. (2002). Gangs, gang homicides, and gang loyalty: Organized crimes or disorganized criminals. *Journal of Criminal Justice, 30,* 343–352.

Decker, S. H., Katz, C. M., & Webb, V. J. (2008). Understanding the black box of gang organization: Implications for involvement in violent crime, drug sales, and violent victimization. *Crime & Delinquency, 54*(1), 153–172.

Decker, S. H., Pyrooz, D. C., & Moule, R. K. (2014). Disengagement from gangs as role

transitions. *Journal of Research on Adolescence, 24*(2), 268–283.

Decker, S., Wright, R., & Logie, R. (1993). Perceptual deterrence among active residential burglars: A research note. *Criminology, 31*(1), 135–147.

DeFosset, A. R., Schooley, T. S., Abrams, L. S., Kuo, T., & Gase, L. N. (2017). Describing theoretical underpinnings in juvenile justice diversion: A case study explicating Teen Court program theory to guide research and practice. *Children and Youth Services Review, 73,* 419–429.

Delcher, C., Wagenaar, A. C., Goldberger, B. A., Cook, R. L., & Maldonado-Molina, M. M. (2015). Abrupt decline in oxycodone-caused mortality after implementation of Florida's Prescription Drug Monitoring Program. *Drug and Alcohol Dependence, 150,* 63–68.

DeLisi, M., Barnes, J. C., Beaver, K. M., & Gibson, C. L. (2009). Delinquent gangs and adolescent victimization revisited a propensity score matching approach. *Criminal Justice and Behavior, 36*(8), 808–823.

DeLong, M. N. (2015). A closer look at the mandatory victims restitution act and whether the costs of a corporation's independent internal investigation should be included in a criminal defendant's mandatory restitution order. Available at http://www.turnpikelaw.com/assets/ABA_Contest_Article_MNDeLong.pdf (accessed 28 February 2017).

DeMchele, M. (2014). Electronic monitoring: It is a tool, not a silver bullet. *Criminology & Public Policy, 13*(3), 393–400.

Desmond, M., & Valdez, N. (2013). Unpolicing the urban poor: Consequences of third-party policing for inner-city women. *American Sociological Review, 78*(1), 117–141.

Diamond, P. M., Wang, E. W., Holzer III, C. E., & Thomas, C. (2001). The prevalence of mental illness in prison. *Administration and Policy in Mental Health and Mental Health Services Research, 29*(1), 21–40.

Diehl, D. J., & Gershon, S. (1992). The role of dopamine in mood disorders. *Comprehensive Psychiatry, 33*(2), 115–120.

Doezema, J. (2002). Who gets to choose? Coercion, consent, and the UN Trafficking Protocol. *Gender & Development, 10*(1), 20–27.

Donahue, J. J., & Wolfers, J. (2006). Uses and abuses of empirical evidence in the death penalty debate. *Stanford Law Review, 58,* 791–846.

Donnelly, P. G., & Kimble, C. E. (2006). An evaluation of the effects of neighborhood mobilization on community problems. *Journal of Prevention & Intervention in the Community, 32*(1–2), 61–80.

Donohue, J. J. (2014). An empirical evaluation of the Connecticut death penalty system since 1973: Are there unlawful racial, gender, and geographic disparities? *Journal of Empirical Legal Studies, 11*(4), 637–696.

Dozois, D. J. A., & Beck, A. T. (2011). Cognitive therapy. In J. D. Herbert & E. M. Forman (Eds.), *Acceptance and mindfulness in cognitive behavior therapy: Understanding and applying the new therapies* (pp. 26–56). Hoboken, NJ: John Wiley & Sons, Inc.

Drizin, S. A., & Leo, R. A. (2003). The problem of false confessions in the post-DNA world. *North Carolina Law Review, 82*(3), 891–1008.

Druckman, J. M. (1979). A family-oriented policy and treatment program for female juvenile status offenders. *Journal of Marriage and the Family, 41*(3), 627–636.

Drug Enforcement Administration. (n.d.). *Drug scheduling.* Available at https://www.dea.gov/druginfo/ds.shtml (accessed 5 December 2016).

Drury, A. C., & Peksen, D. (2016). Economic sanctions and women's status in target countries. In J. Steans & D. Tepe-Belfrage (Eds.), *Handbook on gender in world politics* (pp. 245–254). Cheltenham, UK: Edward Elgar Publishing.

Ducat, L., Thomas, S., & Blood, W. (2009). Sensationalising sex offenders and sexual recidivism: Impact of the Serious Sex Offender Monitoring Act 2005 on media reportage. *Australian Psychologist, 44*(3), 156–165.

Duneier, M. (1999). *Sidewalk.* New York: Macmillan.

Durlauf, S. N., & Nagin, D. S. (2011). Imprisonment and crime: Can both be reduced? *Criminology & Public Policy, 10*(1), 13–54.

Durlauf, S. N., Fu, C., & Navarro, S. (2013). Capital punishment and deterrence: Understanding disparate results. *Journal of Quantitative Criminology, 29*(1), 103–121.

Durose, M. R., Cooper, A. D., & Snyder, H. N. (2014). *Recidivism of prisoners released in 30 states in 2005: Patterns from 2005 to 2010* (NCJ 244205). Washington, DC: U.S. Department of Justice.

Duwe, G. (2013). What's inside the "black box"? The importance of "gray box" evaluations for the "what works" movement. *Criminology & Public Policy, 12*(1), 145–152.

Duwe, G., Kovandzic, T., & Moody, C. E. (2002). The impact of right-to-carry concealed firearm laws on mass public shootings. *Homicide Studies, 6,* 271–296.

Eck, J. (2003). Police problems: The complexity of problem theory, research and evaluation. *Crime Prevention Studies, 15,* 79–114.

Eck, J., & Clarke, R. V. (2003). Classifying common police problems: A routine activity approach. *Crime Prevention Studies, 16,* 7–39.

Eck, J., & Maguire, E. R. (2000). Have changes in policing reduced violent crime? An assessment of the evidence. In A. Blumstein and J. Wallman (Eds.), *The crime drop in America* (pp. 207–265). Cambridge, UK: Cambridge University Press.

Eck, J. E., & Spelman, W. (1987). *Problem-solving: Problem-oriented policing in Newport News.* Washington, DC: U.S. Department of Justice.

Edin, K. (2000). What do low-income single mothers say about marriage? *Social Problems, 47*(1), 112–133.

Edwards, W., & Hensley, C. (2001). Contextualizing sex offender management legislation and policy: Evaluating the problem of latent consequences in community notification laws. *International Journal of*

Offender Therapy and Comparative Criminology, 45(1), 83–101.

Ehrlich, I. (1975). The deterrent effect of capital punishment: A question of life or death. *The American Economic Review, 65*(3), 397–417.

Ellsworth, P. C., & Gross, S. R. (1994). Hardening of the attitudes: Americans' views on the death penalty. *Journal of Social Issues, 50*(2), 19–52.

Ellsworth, P. C., & Ross, L. (1983). Public opinion and capital punishment: A close examination of the views of abolitionists and retentionists. *Crime & Delinquency, 29*(1), 1–169.

Elwood, W. N. (1995). Declaring war on the home front: Metaphor, presidents, and the war on drugs. *Metaphor and Symbol, 10*(2), 93–114.

English, K. (1998). The containment approach: An aggressive strategy for the community management of adult sex offenders. *Psychology, Public Policy, and the Law, 4*(1/2), 218–235.

English, K., Jones, L., & Patrick, D. (2003). Community containment of sex offender risk: A promising approach. In B. J. Winick & J. Q. La Fond (Eds.), *Protecting society from sexually dangerous offenders: Law, justice, and therapy* (pp. 265–278). Washington, DC: American Psychological Association.

English, K., Jones, L., Patrick, D., & Pasini-Hill, D. (2003). Sexual offender containment: Use of the postconviction polygraph. *Annals of the New York Academy of Sciences, 989*, 411–427.

Enns, E. A., Zaric, G. S., Strike, C. J., Jairam, J. A., Kolla, G., & Bayoumi, A. M. (2015). Potential cost-effectiveness of supervised injection facilities in Toronto and Ottawa, Canada. *Addiction, 111*, 475–489.

Environmental Protection Agency [EPA]. (n.d.[a]). Summary of the Clean Water Act, 33 U.S.C. §1251 et seq. (1972). Available at https://www.epa.gov/laws-regulations/summary-clean-water-act (accessed 6 May 2017).

Environmental Protection Agency [EPA]. (n.d.[b]). Summary of criminal prosecutions. Available at https://cfpub.epa.gov/compliance/criminal_prosecution/index.cfm?action=3&prosecution_summary_id=2468 (accessed 6 May 2017).

Ericson, R. V., & Haggerty, K. D. (1997). *Policing the risk society.* Oxford, UK: Oxford University Press.

Esbensen, F. A. (2013). Civil gang injunctions. *Criminology & Public Policy, 12*(1), 1–4.

Esbensen, F. A., & Osgood, D. W. (1999). Gang Resistance Education and Training (GREAT): Results from the national evaluation. *Journal of Research in Crime and Delinquency, 36*(2), 194–225.

Esbensen, F. A., Matsuda, K. N., Taylor, T. J., & Peterson, D. (2011). Multimethod strategy for assessing program fidelity: The national evaluation of the revised GREAT program. *Evaluation Review, 35*(1), 14–39.

Esbensen, F. A., Osgood, D. W., Peterson, D., Taylor, T. J., & Carson, D. C. (2013). Short- and long-term outcome results from a multisite evaluation of the G.R.E.A.T. program. *Criminology & Public Policy, 12*(3), 375–411.

Esbensen, F. A., Osgood, D. W., Taylor, T. J., Peterson, D., & Freng, A. (2001). How great is G.R.E.A.T.? Results from a longitudinal quasi-experimental design. *Criminology & Public Policy, 1*(1), 87–118.

Esbensen, F. A., Peterson, D., Taylor, T. J., & Osgood, D. W. (2012). Results from a multi-site evaluation of the G.R.E.A.T. program. *Justice Quarterly, 29*(1), 125–151.

Evans, C. B., Smokowski, P. R., Barbee, J., Bower, M., & Barefoot, S. (2016). Restorative justice programming in teen court: A path to improved interpersonal relationships and psychological functioning for high-risk rural youth. *Journal of Rural Mental Health, 40*(1), 15.

Eyre, E. (2016). Drug firms poured 780M painkillers into WV amid rise of overdoses. *Charleston Gazette-Mail* (17 December 2016). Available at http://www.wvgazettemail.com/news-health/20161217/drug-firms-poured-780m-painkillers-into-wv-amid-rise-of-overdoses (accessed 27 December 2016).

Fader, J. J., Kurlychek, M. C., & Morgan, K. A. (2014). The color of juvenile justice: Racial disparities in dispositional decisions. *Social Science Research, 44,* 126–140.

Fagan, J. (1990). Social and legal policy dimensions of violent juvenile crime. *Criminal Justice & Behavior, 17*(1), 93–133.

Fagan, J. (1996). The comparative advantage of juvenile versus criminal court sanctions on recidivism among adolescent felony offenders. *Law & Policy, 18*(1–2), 77–114.

Fagan, J. (2002). Policing guns and youth violence. *The Future of Children, 12*(2), 133–151.

Fagan, J., & Davies, G. (2000). Street stops and broken windows: *Terry,* race and disorder in New York City. *Fordham Urban Law Journal, 28,* 457–504.

Fagan, J., & Malkin, V. (2002). Theorizing community justice through community courts. *Fordham Urban Law Journal, 30,* 897–953.

Fagan, J., & Wilkinson, D. L. (1998). Guns, youth violence, and social identity in inner cities. *Crime and Justice, 24,* 105–188.

Farrell, A. (2014). Environmental and institutional influences on police agency responses to human trafficking. *Police Quarterly, 17*(1), 3–29.

Farrell, A. & Cronin, S. (2015). Policing prostitution in an era of human trafficking enforcement. *Crime, Law, & Social Change, 64,* 211–228.

Farrell, A. & McDevitt, J. (2014). Hidden in plain sight: Challenges to identifying, investigating, and prosecuting human trafficking. *JRSA Forum, 32*(3), 1–6.

Farrell, A. & Pfeffer, R. (2014). Policing human trafficking: Cultural blinders and organizational barriers. *Annals of the American Academy of Political and Social Science, 653,* 46–64.

Farrell, A., DeLateur, M. J., Owens, C., & Fahy, S. (2016). The prosecution of state-level human trafficking cases in the United States. *Anti-Trafficking Review, 6,* 48–70.

Farrell, A., Owens, C., & McDevitt, J. (2014). New laws but few cases: Understanding the challenges to the investigation and prosecution of human trafficking cases. *Crime, Law, and Social Change, 61,* 139–168.

Farrell, A., Pfeffer, R., & Bright, K. (2015). Police perceptions of human trafficking. *Journal of Crime & Justice, 38*(3), 315–333.

Fazel, S., & Seewald, K. (2012). Severe mental illness in 33,588 prisoners worldwide: Systematic review and meta-regression analysis. *The British Journal of Psychiatry, 200*(5), 364–373.

Federal Bureau of Investigation [FBI]. (n.d.). Transnational organized crime. Available at https://www.fbi.gov/investigate/organized-crime (accessed 23 May 2017).

Federal Bureau of Investigation. (n.d.). National Instant Criminal Background Check System. Available at https://www.fbi.gov/about-us/cjis/nics

Federal Bureau of Prisons. (2016). *Directory of national programs.* Washington, DC: Federal Bureau of Prisons.

Feeley, M. M. (2014). Entrepreneurs of punishment: How private contractors made and are remaking the modern criminal justice system—An account of convict transportation and electronic monitoring. *Criminology, Criminal Justice, Law & Society, 17*(3), 1–30.

Feeley, M. M., & Simon, J. (1992). The new penology: Notes on the emerging strategy of corrections and its implications. *Criminology, 30*(4), 449–474.

Feeley, M. M., & Simon, J. (1994). Actuarial justice: The emerging new criminal law. In D. Nelkin (Ed.), *The future of criminology* (pp. 172–201). Thousand Oaks, CA: Sage.

Feierman, J., Goldstein, N., Haney-Caron, E., & Columbo, J. F. (2016). *Debtor's prison for kids? The high costs of fines and fees in the juvenile justice system.* Philadelphia, PA: Juvenile Law Center.

Fein, M.L. (2010) 'Dodd–Frank Wall Street Reform and Consumer Protection Act', mimeograph, available at http://ssrn.com/abstract=1357452 (accessed 16 January 2012).

Feingold, D. A. (2005). Human trafficking. *Foreign Policy, 150,* 26–30.

Feld, B. C. (1983). Criminalizing the American juvenile court. *Crime and Justice, 17,* 197–280.

Feld, B. C. (1987). Juvenile court meets the principle of offense: Legislative changes in juvenile waiver statutes. *Journal of Criminal Law and Criminology, 78,* 471–533.

Feld, B. C. (1993). Juvenile (in)justice and the criminal court alternative. *Crime & Delinquency, 39*(4), 403–424.

Feld, B. C. (1999). The honest politician's guide to juvenile justice in the twenty-first century. *Annals of the American Academy of Political and Social Science, 564,* 10–27.

Felson, M. (1998). *Crime in everyday life* (2nd ed.). Thousand Oaks, CA: Pine Forge Press.

Felson, M., & Clarke, R. V. (1998). *Opportunity makes the thief.* Police research series vol. 98. London: Home Office.

Ferdinand, T. N. (1991). History overtakes the juvenile justice system. *Crime & Delinquency, 37*(2), 204–224.

Ferguson, L. M., & Wormith, J. S. (2013). A meta-analysis of Moral Reconation Therapy. *International Journal of Offender Therapy and Comparative Criminology, 57*(9), 1076–1106.

Ferraro, K. F. (1996). Women's fear of victimization: Shadow of sexual assault? *Social Forces, 75*(2), 667–690.

Fetzer, L. B. (2010). The sexual offender registration and notification act: No more than "statutory 'lip service'" to interstate commerce." *Washington and Lee Journal of Civil Rights and Social Justice, 16,* 483–528.

Fifield, J. (2016). Despite concerns, sex offenders face new restrictions. Available at http://www.pewtrusts.org/en/research-and-analysis/blogs/stateline/2016/05/06/despite-concerns-sex-offenders-face-new-restrictions

Filkins, D. (2016). "Do not resist" and the crisis of police militarization. *The New Yorker* (13 May 2016).

Finckenauer, J. O. (2005). Problems of definition: What is organized crime? *Trends in Organized Crime, 8*(3), 63–83.

Finnegan, W. (2012). The kingpins. *The New Yorker* (2 July 2012).

Fix, R. L., Fix, S. T., Totura, C. M. W., & Burkhart, B. R. (2017). Disproportionate minority contact among juveniles adjudicated forsSexual, violent, and general offending: The importance of home, school, and community contexts. *Crime & Delinquency, 63*(2), 189–209.

Flaherty, M. G. (1983). The national incidence of juvenile suicide in adult jails and juvenile detention centers. *Suicide and Life-Threatening Behavior, 13*(2), 85–94.

Flood, B. (2004). Strategic aspects of the UK National Intelligence Model. In J. H. Ratcliffe (Ed.), *Strategic thinking in criminal intelligence* (pp. 37–52). Sydney: Federation Press.

Forgays, D. K., & DeMilio, L. (2005). Is teen court effective for repeat offenders? A test of the restorative justice approach. *International Journal of Offender Therapy and Comparative Criminology, 49*(1), 107–118.

Forst, M., Fagan, J., & Vivona, T. S. (1989). Youth in prisons and training schools: Perceptions and consequences of the treatment-custody dichotomy. *Juvenile and Family Court Journal, 40*(1), 1–14.

Forte, W. E. (1966). The ordinary purchaser and the federal Food, Drug and Cosmetic Act. *Virginia Law Review, 52*(8), 1467–1503.

Foster, H. & Hagan, J. (2009). The mass incarceration of parents in America: Issues of race/ethnicity, collateral damage to children, and prisoner reentry. *The ANNALS of the American Academy of Political and Social Science, 623*(1), 179–194.

Fox, K. J. (2013). Incurable sex offenders, lousy judges & the media: Moral panic sustenance in the age of new media. *American Journal of Criminal Justice, 38*(1), 160–181.

France, A. (1894). *The red lily.* South Australia: University of Adelaide.

Frank, N. K., & Lynch, M. J. (1992). *Corporate crime, corporate violence: A primer.* New York: Harrow and Heston.

Franklin, T. W., Dittmann, L., & Henry, T. K. S. (2015). Extralegal disparity in the application of intermediate sanctions: An analysis of U.S. district courts. *Crime & Delinquency.* DOI: 0011128715607533.

Fritsch, E. J., Caeti, T. J., & Taylor, R. W. (1999). Gang suppression through saturation patrol, aggressive curfew, and truancy enforcement: A quasi-experimental test of the Dallas anti-gang initiative. *Crime & Delinquency, 45*(1), 122–139.

Frohmann, L. (1997). Convictability and discordant locales: Reproducing race, class, and gender ideologies in prosecutorial decisionmaking. *Law and Society Review, 31*(3), 531–556.

Furman, J., & Black, S. (2015). *Fines, fees, and bail: An overlooked part of the criminal justice system that disproportionately impacts the poor.* Huffington Post Blog (03 December 2015). Available at http://www.huffingtonpost. com/jason-furman/fines-fees-and-bail-an-ov_b_8702912.html (accessed 25 February 2017).

Gainey, R. R., Payne, B. K., & O'Toole, M. (2000). The relationships between time in jail, time on electronic monitoring, and recidivism: An event history analysis of a jail-based program. *Justice Quarterly, 17*(4), 733–752.

Galliher, J. F., & Walker, A. (1977). The puzzle of the origins of the Marihuana Tax Act of 1937. *Social Problems, 24*(3), 367–376.

Garland, D. (2000). *The culture of control.* Oxford, UK: Oxford University Press.

Garland, D. (2001). *The culture of control: Crime and social order in contemporary society.* Chicago, IL: The University of Chicago Press.

Garland, D., McGowen, R., & Meranze, M. (Eds.). (2011). *America's death penalty: Between past and present.* New York, NY: New York University Press.

Garrett, B. L., & Neufeld, P. J. (2009). Invalid forensic science testimony and wrongful convictions. *Virginia Law Review, 95*(1), 1–97.

Gascón, L. D., & Roussell, A. (2016). An exercise in failure: Punishing "at-risk" youth and families in a South Los Angeles boot camp program. *Race and Justice.* DIO: 2153368716678289.

Gau, J. M. (2011). The convergent and discriminant validity of procedural justice and police legitimacy: An empirical test of core theoretical propositions. *Journal of Criminal Justice, 39*(6), 489–498.

Gau, J. M. (2013). Consent searches as a threat to procedural justice and police legitimacy: An analysis of consent requests during traffic stops. *Criminal justice policy review, 24*(6), 759–777.

Gau, J. M. (2014a). Unpacking collective efficacy: The relationship between social cohesion and informal social control. *Criminal Justice Studies, 27*(2), 210–225.

Gau, J. M. (2014b). Procedural justice and police legitimacy: A test of measurement and structure. *American Journal of Criminal Justice, 39*(2), 187–205.

Gau, J. M. (2015). Procedural justice, police legitimacy, and legal cynicism: A test for mediation effects. *Police Practice and Research, 16*(5), 402–415.

Gau, J. M., & Brooke, E. J. (2017). An assessment of the impact of a multipronged approach to reducing problematic pain clinics in Florida. *Journal of Drug Issues, 47*(2), 185–204.

Gau, J. M., & Brunson, R. K. (2010). Procedural justice and order maintenance policing: A study of inner-city young men's perceptions of police legitimacy. *Justice quarterly, 27*(2), 255–279.

Gau, J. M., & Brunson, R. K. (2012). "One question before you get gone . . . " Consent search requests as a threat to perceived stop legitimacy. *Race and Justice, 2*(4), 250–273.

Gau, J. M., & Brunson, R. K. (2015). Procedural injustice, lost legitimacy, and self-help: Young males' adaptations to perceived unfairness in urban policing tactics. *Journal of Contemporary Criminal Justice, 31*(2), 132–150.

Gau, J. M., & Pratt, T. C. (2008). Broken windows or window dressing? Citizens' (in)ability to tell the difference between disorder and crime. *Criminology & Public Policy, 7*(2), 163–194.

Gau, J. M., & Pratt, T. C. (2010). Revisiting broken windows theory: Examining the sources of the discriminant validity of perceived disorder and crime. *Journal of Criminal Justice, 38*(4), 758–766.

Gau, J. M., Corsaro, N., & Brunson, R. K. (2014). Revisiting broken windows theory: A test of the mediation impact of social mechanisms on the disorder–fear relationship. *Journal of Criminal Justice, 42*(6), 579–588.

Gau, J. M., Corsaro, N., Stewart, E. A., & Brunson, R. K. (2012). Examining macro-level impacts on procedural justice and police legitimacy. *Journal of Criminal Justice, 40*(4), 333–343.

Gau, J. M. & Paoline, E. A. III. (2017). Officer race, role orientation, and cynicism toward citizens. *Justice Quarterly, 34*(7), 1246 – 1271.

Ge, W., & McVay, S. (2005). The disclosure of material weaknesses in internal control after the Sarbanes-Oxley Act. *Accounting Horizons, 19*(3), 137–158.

Geier, B. (2016). *Why Rand Paul's debate comments on race, prisons make him a GOP outlier.* Available at http://fortune.com/2016/01/29/rand-paul-race-criminal-justice-republican-debate/.

Geiger, B. (2006). The case for treating ex-offenders as a suspect class. *California Law Review, 94*(4), 1191–1242.

Geis, G., & Meier, R. F. (1977). *White-collar crime: Offenses in business, politics and the professions* (rev. ed.). New York: The Free Press.

Gelman, A., Fagan, J., & Kiss, A. (2012). An analysis of the New York City police department's "stop-and-frisk" policy in the context of claims of racial bias. *Journal of the American Statistical Association, 102*(479), 813–823.

Gendreau, P. (1996). Offender rehabilitation: What we know and what needs to be done. *Criminal Justice and Behavior, 23*(1), 144–161.

Gendreau, P., & Ross, B. (1979). Effective correctional treatment: Bibliotherapy for cynics.

General Accounting Office. (1990). *Death penalty sentencing: Research indicates patterns of racial disparities.* Washington, DC: General Accounting Office.

Gest, T. (2001). *Crime & politics: Big government's erratic campaign for law and order.* Oxford, UK: Oxford University Press.

Gest, T. (2001). *Crime and politics: Big government's erratic campaign for law and order.* New York: Oxford University Press.

Getman, J. G. (1967). The protection of economic pressure by Section 7 of the National Labor Relations Act. *University of Pennsylvania Law Review, 115*(8), 1195–1250.

Ghosh, B. (1998). *Huddled masses and uncertain shores: Insights into irregular migration.* The Hague: Martinus Nijhoff Publishers.

Giannelli, P. C. (2006). Wrongful convictions and forensic science: The need to regulate crime labs. *Case Western Reserve University Faculty Publications, 149*, 163–235.

Gibbs, C., McGarrell, E. F., & Sullivan, B. (2015). Intelligence-led policing and transnational environmental crime: A process evaluation. *European Journal of Criminology, 12*(2), 242–259.

Gies, S. V. (2016). The use of electronic monitoring as a supervision tool. In E. L. Jeglic & C. Calkins (Eds.), *Sexual violence* (pp. 95–117). New York: Springer.

Gies, S. V., Gainey, R., Cohen, M. I., Healy, E., Yeide, M., & Bekelman, A. B. (2013). *Monitoring high-risk gang offenders with GPS technology: An evaluation of the California supervision program final report.* Washington, DC: U.S. Department of Justice.

Goldkamp, J. S., White, M. D., & Robinson, J. B. (2001). Do drug courts work? Getting inside the drug court black box. *Journal of Drug Issues, 31*(1), 27–72.

Goldstein, H. (1979). Improving policing: A problem-oriented approach. *Crime & Delinquency, 25*(2), 236–258.

Goldstein, H. (1990). *Problem-oriented policing.* New York: McGraw-Hill.

Golub, A., Johnson, B. D., Taylor, A., & Eterno, J. (2003). Quality-of-life policing: Do offenders get the message? *Policing: An International Journal of Police Strategies & Management, 26*(4), 690–707.

Gonzalez, F. (2016). Florida nonprofits offer alternatives to incarceration. *James Madison Journal, Winter*, 34–43.

Gordon, D. (1990). *The justice juggernaut.* New Brunswick, NJ: Rutgers University Press.

Gordon, D. R. (1990). *The justice juggernaut: Fighting street crime, controlling citizens.* New Brunswick, NJ: Rutgers University Press.

Gordon, R. A., Lahey, B. B., Kawai, E., Loeber, R., Stouthamer-Loeber, M., & Farrington, D. P. (2004). Antisocial behavior and youth gang membership: Selection and socialization. *Criminology, 42*(1), 55–88.

Gottfredson, D. C. & Exum, M. L. (2002). The Baltimore City drug treatment court: One-year results from a randomized study. *Journal of Research in Crime and Delinquency, 39*(3), 337–356.

Gottfredson, D. C., Najaka, S. S., & Kearley, B. (2003). Effectiveness of drug treatment courts: Evidence from a randomized trial. *Criminology & Public Policy, 2*(2), 171–196.

Gould, J. B., & Leo, R. A. (2010). One hundred years later: Wrongful convictions after a century of research. *The Journal of Criminal Law and Criminology, 100*(3), 825–868.

Gould, J. B., & Mastrofski, S. D. (2004). Suspect searches: Assessing police behavior under the U.S. Constitution. *Criminology & Public Policy, 3*(3), 315–362.

Goulka, J., Heaton, P., Tita, G., Matthies, C., Whitby, A., & Cooper, A. (2009). *Anti-gang initiative grants in the Central District of California*. Report to the U.S. Attorney, WR-660-DOJ, RAND Working Paper.

Gover, A. R., MacDonald, J. M., & Alpert, G. P. (2003). Combating domestic violence: Findings from an evaluation of a local domestic violence court. *Criminology & public policy, 3*(1), 109–132.

Gowdy, V. B. (1996). Historical perspective. In D. L. MacKenzie & E. E. Hebert (Eds.), *Correctional boot camps: A tough intermediate sanction* (pp. 1–16). Washington, DC: U.S. Department of Justice.

Gozdziak, E. (2012). Children trafficked to the United States: Myths and realities. *Global Dialogue, 14*(2), 1–12.

Gozdziak, E. M., & Bump, M. N. (2008). *Data and research on human trafficking: Bibliography of research-based literature: Final report to the U.S. Department of Justice*. Washington, DC: U.S. Department of Justice.

Graham, D. L., Rawlings, E., & Rimini, N. (1988). Survivors of terror: Battered women hostages and the Stockholm syndrome. In K. Yllo & M. Bograd (Eds.), *Feminist perspectives on wife abuse* (pp. 217–233). Thousand Oaks, CA: Sage Publications.

Granovetter, M. (1973). The strength of weak ties. *American Journal of Sociology, 78,* 1360–1380.

Grasmick, H. G. & Appleton, L. (1977). Legal punishment and social stigma: A comparison of two deterrence models. *Social Science Quarterly, 58*(1), 15–28.

Green, J., Damle, R. N., Kasper, R. E., Violano, P., Manno, M., Nazarey, P. P., . . . & Hirsh, M. P. (2017). Are "Goods for Guns" good for the community? An update of a community gun buyback program. *Journal of Trauma and Acute Care Surgery, 83(2),* 284–288.

Green, L. (1996). *Policing places with drug problems* (Vol. 2). Thousand Oaks, CA: Sage.

Greene, J. A. (1988). Structuring criminal fines: Making an "intermediate penalty" more useful and equitable. *Justice System Journal, 13*(1), 37–50.

Greene, J. R. (2014). Zero tolerance and policing. In M. Reisig & R. Kane (Eds.), *The Oxford handbook of police and policing* (pp. 172–196). Oxford, UK: Oxford University Press.

Greene, J. R., & Mastrofski, S. D. (1988). Preface. In J. R. Greene & S. D. Mastrofski (Eds.), *Community policing: Rhetoric or reality* (pp. xi–xiv). New York: Praeger.

Greene, J. R., & Taylor, R. B. (1988). Community-based policing and foot patrol: Issues of theory and evaluation. In J. R. Greene & S. D. Mastrofski (Eds.), *Community policing: Rhetoric or reality* (pp. 195–224). New York: Praeger.

Greene, W. R. (1977). Early development of the Illinois State Penitentiary System. *Journal of the Illinois State Historical Society, 70*(4), 185–195.

Greenwood, P. (2008). Prevention and intervention programs for juvenile offenders. *The Future of Children, 18*(2), 185–210.

Greenwood, P. W., & Abrahamse, A. (1982). *Selective incapacitation*. Santa Monica, CA: Rand.

Grilly, D. M. (2002). *Drugs and human behavior.* Boston, MA: Allyn & Bacon.

Grimm, A. (2015). BP oil spill: Criminal cases largely unresolved 5 years after Deepwater Horizon blowout. *The Times-Picayune*. Available at http://www.nola.com/environment/index.ssf/2015/04/bp_oil_spill_criminal_cases_la.html (accessed 6 May 2017).

Groff, E. R., Johnson, L., Ratcliffe, J. H., & Wood, J. (2012). Exploring the relationship between foot and car patrol in violent crime areas. *Policing: An International Journal of Police Strategies & Management, 36*(1), 119–139.

Groff, E. R., Ratcliffe, J. H., Haberman, C. P., Sorg, E. T., Joyce, N. M., & Taylor, R. B. (2015). Does what police do at hot spots matter? The Philadelphia policing tactics experiment. *Criminology, 53*(1), 23–53.

Grogger, J. (2002). The effects of civil gang injunctions on reported violent crime: Evidence from Los Angeles County. *Journal of Law and Economics, 45,* 69–90.

Grogger, J. (2005). What we know about gang injunctions. *Criminology & Public Policy, 4*(3), 637–642.

Gross, S. R., & Shaffer, M. (2012). *Exonerations in the United States, 1989–2012.* The National Registry of Exonerations.

Gross, S. R., Jacoby, K., Matheson, D. J., Montgomery, N., & Patil, S. (2005). Exonerations in the United States 1989 through 2003. *The Journal of Criminal Law and Criminology, 95*(2), 523–560.

Gross, S. R., O'Brien, B., Hu, C., & Kennedy, E. H. (2014). Rate of false conviction of criminal defendants who are sentenced to death. *Proceedings of the National Academy of Sciences, 111*(20), 7230–7235.

Grossman, E. R., & Miller, N. A. (2015). A systematic review of the impact of juvenile curfew laws on public health and justice outcomes. *American Journal of Preventive Medicine, 49*(6), 945–951.

Grossman, E. R., Jernigan, D. H., & Miller, N. A. (2016). Do juvenile curfew laws reduce underage drinking? *Journal of Studies on Alcohol and Drugs, 77*(4), 589–595.

Grossman, L. S., Martis, B., & Fichtner, C. G. (1999). Are sex offenders treatable? A research overview. *Psychiatric Services, 50*(3), 349–361.

group-oriented, cognitive-behavioral programs for offenders. *Criminal Justice and Behavior, 32*(2), 172–204.

Gruher, M. (1979). Family counseling and the status offender. *Juvenile & Family Court Journal, 30*(1), 23–27.

Guerino, P., Harrison, P. M., & Sabol, W. J. (2011). Prisoners in 2010 (NCJ 236096). Washington, DC: U.S. Department of Justice.

Hahn, R., Fuqua-Whitley, D., Wethington, H., Lowy, J., Crosby, A., Fullilove, . . . & Dahlberg, L. (2007). Effectiveness of universal school-based programs to prevent violent and aggressive behavior: A systematic review. *American Journal of Preventive Medicine, 33*(2S), S114–S129.

Hale, C. (1996). Fear of crime: A review of the literature. *International Review of Victimology, 4*(2), 79–150.

Hallstrom, K., Jenkins, E., Levison-Johnson, J., Ganey-Nola, D., Simpson, T., & Stubbs, K. (2012). *Families in need of services (FINS) commission report.* Baton Rouge, LA: Louisiana Legislature.

Hamilton, Z. K., & Campbell, C. M. (2014). Uncommonly observed: The impact of New Jersey's halfway house system. *Criminal Justice & Behavior, 41*(11), 1354–1375.

Hanna, J. (2016). Witness: *Condemned Alabama man coughed, heaved during execution.* CNN.com (9 December 2016). Available at http://www.cnn.com/2016/12/09/health/alabama-execution/(accessed 15 March 2017).

Hannah-Moffat, K. (2016). A conceptual kaleidoscope: Contemplating "dynamic structural risk" and an uncoupling of risk from need. *Psychology, Crime & Law, 22*(1-2), 33–46.

Hans, V. P., Blume, J. H., Eisenberg, T., Hritz, A. C., Johnson, S. L., Royer, C. E., & Wells, M. T. (2015). The death penalty: Should the judge or the jury decide who dies? *Journal of Empirical Legal Studies, 12*(1), 70–99.

Harcourt, B. E. (2001). *Illusion of order: The false promise of broken windows policing.* Cambridge, MA: Harvard University Press.

Harlow, C. W. (2003). *Educational and correctional populations* (NCJ 195670). Washington, DC: U.S. Department of Justice.

Harris, A. (2016). *A pound of flesh: Monetary sanctions as punishment for the poor.* New York: Russell Sage Foundation.

Harris, A. J. & Lobanov-Rostovsky, C. (2010). Implementing the Adam Walsh Act's sex offender registration and notification provisions: A survey of the states. *Criminal Justice Policy Review, 21*(2), 202–222.

Harris, A. J., Lobanov-Rostovsky, C., & Levenson, J. S. (2010). Widening the net: The effects of transitioning to the Adam Walsh Act's federally mandated sex offender classification system. *Criminal Justice and Behavior, 37*(5), 503–519.

Harris, D. A., Smallbone, S., Dennison, S., & Knight, R. A. (2009). Specialization and versatility in sexual offenders referred for civil commitment. *Journal of Criminal Justice, 37*(1), 37–44.

Hartney, C. (2006). *US rates of incarceration: A global perspective.* Report to the National Council on Crime and Delinquency.

Heavy, S., Rucker, P., & Stephenson, E. (2015). U.S. says BP to pay $20 billion in fines for 2010 oil spill. *Reuters.* Available at http://www.reuters.com/article/us-bp-usa-idUSKCN0RZ14A20151005 (accessed 6 May 2017).

Hechter, M. & Kanazawa, S. (1997). Sociological rational choice theory. *Annual Review of Sociology, 23,* 191–214.

Helmkamp, J. C., Townsend, K. J., & Sundra, J. A. (1997). *How much does white collar crime cost?* Morgantown, WV: National White Collar Crime Center.

Hennigan, K. M., & Sloane, D. (2013). Improving civil gang injunctions. *Criminology & Public Policy, 12*(1), 7–41.

Henrichson, C., & Delaney, R. (2012). *The price of prisons: What incarceration costs taxpayers.* Washington, DC: Vera Institute Center on Sentencing and Corrections.

Henrichson, C., & Delaney, R. (2012). *The price of prisons: What incarceration costs taxpayers.* New York: Vera Institute of Justice.

Hill, M. L. (2016). *Nobody: Casualties of America's war on the vulnerable, from Ferguson to Flint and beyond.* New York: Atria Books.

Hinds, L., & Murphy, K. (2007). Public satisfaction with police: Using procedural justice to improve police legitimacy. *Australian & New Zealand Journal of Criminology, 40*(1), 27–42.

Hirsch, A. J. (1992). *The rise of the penitentiary: Prisons and punishment in early America.* New Haven, CT: Yale University Press.

Hissong, R. (1991). Teen court: Is it an effective alternative to traditional sanctions. *Journal for Juvenile Justice and Detention Services, 6*(2), 14-23.

Hobart, G. S. (1923). The Volstead Act. *The Annals of the American Academy of Political and Social Science, 109,* 85–101.

Hochstetler, A., & Bouffard, J. A. (2010). Contemporary retrospective on rational choice theories: Classical and rational choice perspectives. In H. Copes and V. Topalli (Eds.), *Criminological theory: Readings and retrospectives* (pp. 19–35). New York: McGraw-Hill.

Hockenberry, S. (2014). *Juveniles in residential placement, 2011.* Washington, DC: U.S. Department of Justice.

Hockenberry, S., & Puzzanchera, C. (2015). *Juvenile court statistics, 2013.* Washington, DC: U.S. Department of Justice.

Hodgson, B. (2001). *In the arms of Morpheus: The tragic history of morphine, laudanum, and patent medicines.* Buffalo, NY: Firefly Books.

Hoge, R. D. (2016). Application of precharge diversion programs. *Criminology & Public Policy, 15*(3), 991-999.

Holcomb, J. E., Williams, M. R., & Demuth, S. (2004). White female victims and death penalty disparity research. *Justice Quarterly, 21*(4), 877–902.

Holland, J. (2013). Hundreds of Wall Street execs went to prison during the last bank-fueled crisis. Available at http://billmoyers.com/2013/09/17/hundreds-of-wall-street-execs-went-to-prison-during-the-last-fraud-fueled-bank-crisis/ (accessed 6 May 2017).

Holtfreter, K., van Slyke, S., Bratton, J., & Gertz, M. (2008). Public perceptions of white-collar crime and punishment. *Journal of Criminal Justice, 36,* 50–60.

Hood, R. (1998). Capital punishment. In M. Tonry (Ed.), *The handbook of crime and punishment* (pp. 739–776). New York, NY: Oxford University Press.

Hooper, R. M., Lockwood, D., & Inciardi, J. A. (1993). Treatment techniques in corrections-based therapeutic communities. *The Prison Journal, 73*(3), 290–306.

Horowitz, S. M. (1991). A search for constitutional standards: Judicial review of juvenile curfew ordinances. *Columbia Journal of Law & Social Problems, 24,* 381–417.

Howell, B. (2009). Broken lives from broken windows: The hidden costs of aggressive order-maintenance policing. *New York University Review of Law & Social Change, 33,* 271–329.

Howell, J. C. (2010). Juvenile Justice Bulletin: Gang prevention: An overview of research and programs. Washington, DC: Office of Juvenile Justice and Delinquency Prevention.

Howell, J. C. (2013). GREAT results: Implications for PBIS in schools. *Criminology & Public Policy, 12*(3), 413–420. http://www.businessinsider.com/where-is-marijuana-legal-2016–11

Hudson, D. (2015). *President Obama: "Our criminal justice system isn't as smart as it should be."* Available at https://www.whitehouse.gov/blog/2015/07/15/president-obama-our-criminal-justice-system-isnt-smart-it-should-be .

Huebner, B. M., Kras, K. R., Rydberg, J., Bynum, T. S., Grommon, E., & Pleggenkuhle, B. (2014). The effect and implications of sex offender residence restrictions. *Criminology & Public Policy, 13*(1), 139–168.

Hufbauer, G. C., Schott, J. J., & Elliott, K. A. (1990). *Economic sanctions reconsidered: History and current policy* (2nd ed.). Washington, DC: Institute for International Economics.

Huff, C. R. (2002). Wrongful conviction and public policy: The American society of criminology 2001 presidential address. *Criminology, 40*(1), 1–18.

Huff, C. R., Rattner, A., Sagarin, E., & MacNamara, D. E. (1986). Guilty until proved innocent: Wrongful conviction and public policy. *Crime & Delinquency, 32*(4), 518–544.

Hughes, L. A. (2013). Group cohesiveness, gang member prestige, and delinquency and violence in Chicago, 1959–1962. *Criminology, 51*(4), 795–832.

Hughes, L. A. & Burchfield, K. B. (2008). Sex offender residence restrictions in Chicago: An environmental injustice? *Justice Quarterly, 25*(4), 647–673.

Humphrey, A. (2004). The criminalization of survival attempts: Locking up female runaways and other status offenders. *Hastings Women's Law Journal, 15*, 165.

Humphreys, K. & Rappaport, J. (1993). From the community mental health movement to the war on drugs: A study in the definition of social problems. *American Psychologist, 48*(8), 892–901.

Hunter, A. (1985). Private, parochial and public social orders: The problem of crime and incivility in urban communities. In G. D. Suttles & M. Zald (Eds.), *The challenge of social control* (pp. 230–242). Norwood, NY: Ablex.

Hunter, D., Rosenthal, M. Z., Lynch, T. R., & Linehan, M. M. (2016). Dialectical behavior therapy for individuals with borderline personality disorder and substance use disorders. In A. H. Mack, K. T. Brady, S. I. Miller, & R. J. Frances (Eds.), *Clinical textbook of addictive disorders* (4th ed.; pp. 648–667). New York: The Guilford Press.

Hurst, H. (2012). *Models for Change update 2012: Headlines.* Pittsburgh, PA: National Center for Juvenile Justice.

Hyatt, J. M., & Barnes, G. C. (2017). An experimental evaluation of the impact of intensive supervision on the recidivism of high-risk probationers. *Crime & Delinquency, 63*(1), 3–38.

Inciardi, J. A., Martin, S. S., & Surratt, H. L. (2000). *Therapeutic communities in prisons and work release: Effective modalities for drug-involved offenders: Report to the U.S. Department of Justice.* Washington, DC: U.S. Department of Justice.

Innocence Project. (n.d.(a)). Webpage. Available at https://www.innocenceproject.org/#causes (accessed 11 March 2017).

Innocence Project. (n.d.(b)). Eyewitness identification reform. Available at https://www.innocenceproject.org/eyewitness-identification-reform/#resources (accessed 11 March 2017).

International Labour Organization [ILO]. (2014). *Profits and poverty: The economics of forced labour.* Geneva, Switzerland: International Labour Organization.

Isidore, C. (2016). 35 bankers were sent to prison for financial crisis crimes. CNN Money. Available at http://money.cnn.com/2016/04/28/news/companies/bankers-prison/ (accessed 6 May 2017).

Ivancevich, J. M., Duening, T. N., Gilbert, J. A., & Konopaske, R. (2003). Deterring white-collar crime. *The Academy of Management Executive, 17*(2), 114–127.

Jackson, J., Bradford, B., Hough, M., Myhill, A., Quinton, P., & Tyler, T. R. (2012). Why do people comply with the law? Legitimacy and the influence of legal institutions. *British Journal of Criminology, 52*(6), 1051–1071.

Jackson, R. L. & Covell, C. N. (2013). Sex offender civil commitment. In K. Harrison & B. Rainey (Eds.), *Handbook of legal and ethical aspects of sex offender treatment and management* (pp. 406–423). Chichester, UK: John Wiley & Sons.

Jackson, R. L. & Hess, D. T. (2007). Evaluation for civil commitment of sex offenders: A survey of experts. *Sex Abuse, 19*(4), 425–448.

Jacobs, D., & Carmichael, J. T. (2002). The political sociology of the death penalty: A pooled time-series analysis. *American Sociological Review, 67*(1), 109–131.

Jacobs, J. (1961). *The death and life of great American cities.* New York: Vintage Books.

Jacobs, J. B. (2002). *Can gun control work?* Oxford, UK: Oxford University Press.

James, D. J. (2004). *Profile of jail inmates, 2002.* NCJ 201932. Washington, DC: Bureau of Justice Statistics.

Jerusalem, M. P. (1995). A framework for post-sentence sex offender legislation: Perspectives on prevention, registration, and the public's "right" to know. *Vanderbilt Law Review, 48,* 219–248.

Jesilow, P., Meyer, J., Parsons, D., & Tegeler, W. (1998). Evaluating problem-oriented policing: A quasi-experiment. *Policing: An International Journal of Police Strategies & Management, 21*(3), 449–464.

Johnson, A. B. (1990). *Out of bedlam: The truth about deinstitutionalization.* New Y: Basic Books.

Johnson, B. D., & DiPietro, S. M. (2012). The power of diversion: Intermediate sanctions and sentencing disparity under presumptive guidelines. *Criminology, 50*(3), 811–850.

Johnson, B. D., & Kurlychek, M. C. (2012). Transferred juveniles in the era of sentencing guidelines: Examining judicial departures for juvenile offenders in adult criminal court. *Criminology, 50*(2), 525–564.

Johnson, C. A., Pentz, M. A., Weber, M. D., Dwyer, J. H., Baer, N., MacKinnon, D. P., Hansen, W. B., & Flay, B. R. (1990). Relative effectiveness of comprehensive community programming for drug abuse prevention with high-risk and low-risk adolescents. *Journal of Consulting and Clinical Psychology, 58*(4), 447–456.

Johnson, H., Paulozzi, L., Porucznik, C, Mack, K., Herter, B., (2014). Decline in drug overdose deaths after state policy changes—Florida, 2010–2012. *Morbidity and Mortality Weekly Report, 63*(26), 569–574.

Johnson, K., Lanza-Kaduce, L., & Woolard, J., (2011). Disregarding graduated treatment: Why transfer aggravates recidivism. *Crime & Delinquency, 57,* 756–777.

Johnston, L. D., O'Malley, P. M., Bachman, J. G., & Schulenberg, J. E. (2009). *Monitoring the Future: National results on adolescent drug use: Overview of key findings, 2008* (NIH Publication No. 09-7401). Bethesda, MD: National Institute on Drug Abuse.

Johnston, L. D., O'Malley, P. M., Bachman, J. G., & Schulenberg, J. E. (2011). *Monitoring the Future national survey results on drug use, 1975–2010: Volume II, College students and adults ages 19–50.* Ann Arbor: The University of Michigan.

Jones, C. M., & McAninch, J. K. (2015). Emergency department visits and overdose deaths from combined use of opioids and benzodiazepines. *American Journal of Preventive Medicine, 49*(4), 493–501.

Jones, J. M. (2015). *In U.S., 58% back legal marijuana use.* Gallup. Available at http://www.gallup.com/poll/186260/back-legal-marijuana.aspx (accessed 3 December 2016).

Jordan, K. L. (2012). Juvenile transfer and recidivism: A propensity score matching approach. *Journal of Crime and Justice, 35*(1), 53–67.

Jordan, K. L., & Myers, D. L. (2007). The decertification of transferred youth: Examining the determinants of reverse waiver. *Youth Violence and Juvenile Justice, 5*(2), 188–206.

Jordan, K. L., & Myers, D. L. (2011). Juvenile transfer and deterrence: Reexamining the effectiveness of a "get-tough" policy. *Crime & Delinquency, 57*(2), 247–270.

Joy, P. A. (2006). Relationship between prosecutorial misconduct and wrongful convictions: Shaping remedies for a broken system. *Wisconsin Law Review, 2006*, 399–427.

Jülich, S. (2005). Stockholm syndrome and child sexual abuse. *Journal of Child Sexual Abuse, 14*(3), 107–129.

Kaeble, D., & Glaze, L. (2016). *Correctional populations in the United States, 2015* (NCJ 250374). Washington, DC: U.S. Department of Justice.

Kasarda, J. D., & Janowitz, M. (1974). Community attachment in mass society. *American Sociological Review, 39*, 328–339.

Katz, C. M., & Webb, V. J. (2006). *Policing gangs in America*. New York: Cambridge.

Katz, C. M., Webb, V. J., & Schaefer, D. R. (2001). An assessment of the impact of quality-of-life policing on crime and disorder. *Justice Quarterly, 18*(4), 825–876.

Katz, J. (2017). Drug deaths are rising faster than ever. *New York Times*. Available at https://www.nytimes.com/interactive/2017/06/05/upshot/opioid-epidemic-drug-overdose-deaths-are-rising-faster-than-ever.html?_r=0 (accessed 8 June 2017).

Katz, L., Levitt, S. D., & Shustrovich, E. (2003). Prison conditions, capital punishment, and deterrence. *American Law & Economics Review, 5*(2), 318–343.

Kaufmann, C. N., Spira, A. P., Depp, C. A., & Mojtabai, R. (2016). Continuing versus new prescriptions for sedative-hypnotic medications: United States, 2005–2012. *American Journal of Public Health, 106*(11), 2019–2025.

Keil, T. J., & Vito, G. F. (1989). Race, homicide severity, and application of the death penalty: A consideration of the Barnett scale. *Criminology, 27*(3), 511–535.

Keil, T. J., & Vito, G. F. (1990). Race and the death penalty in Kentucky murder trials: An analysis of post-Gregg outcomes. *Justice Quarterly, 7*(1), 189–207.

Keller, O. J., & Alper, B. S. (1970). *Halfway houses: Community-centered correction and treatment*. Lexington, MA: Heath Lexington Books.

Kelling, G. L., & Coles, C. M. (1996). *Fixing broken windows: Restoring order and reducing crime in our communities*. New York: Simon and Schuster.

Kelling, G. L., & Moore, M. H. (1988). The evolving strategy of policing. In *Perspectives on Policing*. Washington, DC: National Institute of Justice.

Kelling, G. L., Pate, T., Dieckman, D., & Brown, C. E. (1974). *The Kansas City preventive patrol experiment*. Washington, DC: The Police Foundation.

Kempf-Leonard, K., & Peterson, E. S. L. (2000). Expanding the realms of the new penology: The advent of actuarial justice for juveniles. *Punishment & Society, 2*(1), 66–97.

Kennedy, D. M. (1997). Pulling levers: Chronic offenders, high-crime settings, and a theory of prevention. *Valparaiso University Law Review, 31*, 449–484.

Kerner Commission. (1967). *Report of the National Advisory Commission on Civil Disorders*.

Kernsmith, P. D., Comartin, E., Craun, S. W., & Kernsmith, R. M. (2009). The relationship between sex offender registry utilization and awareness. *Sexual Abuse: A Journal of Research and Treatment, 21*(2), 181–193.

Kernsmith, P. D., Craun, S. W., & Foster, J. (2009). Public attitudes toward sexual offenders and sex offender registration. *Journal of Child Sexual Abuse, 18*, 290–301.

Killias, M., Aebi, M., & Ribaud, D. (2000). Does community service rehabilitate better than short-term incarceration? Results of a controlled experiment. *The Howard Journal, 39*(1), 40–57.

Killias, M., Gilliéron, Villard, F., & Poglia, C. (2010). How damaging is imprisonment in the long-term? A controlled experiment comparing long-term effects of community service and short custodial sentences on re-offending and social integration. *Journal of Experimental Criminology, 6*, 115–130.

Kim, D., Phillips, S. W., & Wheeler, A. P. (2016). Using "symbolic" SWAT raids as a crime reduction strategy: Are their effects "instrumental" in nature?

Criminal Justice Policy Review. DOI: 10.1177/0887403416664567

King, R. G. (1952). Narcotics bureau and the Harrison Act: Jailing the healers and the sick. *The Yale Law Journal, 62,* 736.

Kirk, D. S., & Matsuda, M. (2011). Legal cynicism, collective efficacy, and the ecology of arrest. *Criminology, 49*(2), 443–472.

Kissner, J. & Pyrooz, D. C. (2009). Self-control, differential association, and gang membership: A theoretical and empirical extension of the literature. *Journal of Criminal Justice, 37,* 478–587.

Kleck, G. (1986). Evidence that "Saturday night specials" not very important for crime. *Sociology and Social Research, 70*(4), 303–307.

Kleck, G. (1997). *Targeting guns: Firearms and their control.* New York: Aldine de Gruyter.

Kleck, G., Sever, B., Li, S., & Gertz, M. (2005). The missing link in general deterrence research. *Criminology, 43*(3), 623–659.

Kleck, G., Sever, B., Li, S., & Gertz, M. (2005). The missing link in general deterrence research. *Criminology, 43*(3), 623–660.

Kleiman, M. A., Caulkins, J. P., & Hawken, A. (2011). *Drugs and drug policy: What everyone needs to know.* Oxford: Oxford University Press.

Klein, M. (1993). Attempting gang control by suppression: The misuse of deterrence principles. In M. W. Klein, C. L. Maxson, & J. Miller (Eds.), *The modern gang reader* (p. 304–313). Los AngelesA: Roxbury.

Klein, M. (1995). *The American street gang.* New York: Oxford.

Klein, M. W. (1979). Deinstitutionalization and diversion of juvenile offenders: A litany of impediments. *Crime and Justice, 1,* 145–201.

Klein, M. W., & Maxson, C. L. (2010). *Street gang patterns and policies.* New York: Oxford University Press.

Kline, P. (2012). The impact of juvenile curfew laws on arrests of youth and adults. *American Law and Economics Review, 14*(1), 44–67.

Kochanek, K. D., Murphy, S. L., Xu, J., & Tejada-Vera, T. (2016). Deaths: Final data for 2014. *National Vital Statistics Reports, vol. 65 no. 4.*

Washington, DC: U.S. Department of Health and Human Services.

Koh, H. H. (1997). Why do nations obey international law? *Yale Law Journal, 106*(8), 2599–2659.

Kolivoski, K. M., Shook, J. J., Goodkind, S., & Kim, K. H. (2014). Developmental trajectories and predictors of juvenile detention, placement, and jail among youth with out-of-home child welfare placement. *Journal of the Society for Social Work and Research, 5*(2), 137–160.

Koper, C. S. (2004). Updated assessment of the federal assault weapons ban: Impacts on gun markets and gun violence, 1994–2003. Washington, DC: National Institute of Justice.

Koper, C. S., & Roth, J. A. (2002). The impact of the 1994 federal assault weapons ban on gun markets: An assessment of short-term primary and secondary market effects. *Journal of Quantitative Criminology, 18*(3), 239–266.

Koper, C. S., Woods, D. J., & Roth, J. A. (2004). An updated assessment of the federal assault weapon ban: Impacts on gun markets and gun violence, 1994–2003: Report to the National Institute of Justice. Washington, DC: U.S. Department of Justice.

Kovandzic, T., & Vieraitis, L. M. (2006). The effect of county-level prison population growth on crime rates. *Criminology & Public Policy, 5*(2), 213–244.

Krain, M. (2017). The effect of economic sanctions on the severity of genocides or politicides. *Journal of Genocide Research, 19*(1), 888–111.

Kramer, S. (1990). An economic analysis of criminal attempt: Marginal deterrence and the optimal structure of sanctions. *The Journal of Criminal Law and Criminology, 81*(2), 398–417.

Kraska, P. B. (2007). Militarization and policing—its relevance to 21st century policing. *Policing, 1*(4), 501–513.

Kraska, P. B., & Kappeler, V. E. (1997). Militarizing American police: The rise and normalization of paramilitary units. *Social Problems, 44*(1), 1–18.

Kubrin, C. E. (2005). Gangstas, thugs, and hustlas: Identity and the code of the street in rap music. *Social Problems, 52*(3), 360–378.

Kubrin, C. E., & Stewart, E. (2006). Predicting who reoffends: The neglected role of neighborhood context in recidivism studies. *Criminology, 44*(1), 171–204.

Kubrin, C. E., & Weitzer, R. (2003). Retaliatory homicide: Concentrated disadvantage and neighborhood culture. *Social Problems, 50*(2), 157–180.

Kuhn, E. M., Nie, C. L., O'Brien, M. E., Withers, R. L., Wintemute, G. J., & Hargarten, S. W. (2002). Missing the target: a comparison of buyback and fatality related guns. *Injury Prevention, 8*(2), 143–146.

Kupchik, A. (2004). Direct file of youth to criminal court: Understanding the practical and theoretical implications. *Criminology & Public Policy, 3*(4), 645–650.

Kurlychek, M. C. (2016). Effectiveness of juvenile transfer to adult court. *Criminology & Public Policy, 15*(3), 897–900.

Kurlychek, M. C., & Johnson, B. D. (2004). The juvenile penalty: A comparison of juvenile and young adult sentencing outcomes in criminal court. *Criminology, 42*(2), 485–515.

Kurlychek, M., & Kempinen, C. (2006). Beyond boot camp: The impact of aftercare on offender reentry. *Criminology & Public Policy, 5*(2), 363–388.

Kutateladze, B. L., Andiloro, N. R., Johnson, B. D., & Spohn, C. C. (2014). Cumulative disadvantage: Examining racial and ethnic disparity in prosecution and sentencing. *Criminology, 52*(3), 514–551.

Kyckelhahn, T. (2014). *State corrections expenditures, FY 1982–2010* (NCJ 239672). Washington, DC: U.S. Department of Justice.

Labriola, M., Rempel, M., & Davis, R. C. (2008). Do batterer programs reduce recidivism? Results from a randomized trial in the Bronx. *Justice Quarterly, 25*(2), 252–282.

Laczko, F. (2005). Data and research on human trafficking. *International Migration, 43*(1/2), 5–16.

LaGrange, R. L., Ferraro, K. F., & Supancic, M. (1992). Perceived risk and fear of crime: Role of social and physical incivilities. *Journal of*

Research in Crime and Delinquency, 29(3), 311–334.

Lamb, H. R., & Weinberger, L. E. (1998). Persons with severe mental illness in jails and prisons: A review. *Psychiatric Services, 49*(4), 483–492..

Land, K. C., Teske, R. H., & Zheng, H. (2012). The differential short-term impacts of executions on felony and non-felony homicides. *Criminology & Public Policy, 11*(3), 541–563.

Landenberger, N. A., & Lipsey, M. W. (2005). The positive effects of cognitive–behavioral programs for offenders: A meta-analysis of factors associated with effective treatment. *Journal of Experimental Criminology, 1*(4), 451–476.

Langworthy, R. H., & Travis, L. F. III. (2008). *Policing in America: A balance of forces* (4th ed.). Upper Saddle River, NJ: Prentice Hall.

Lassiter, M. D. (2015). Impossible Criminals: The suburban imperatives of America's war on drugs. *Journal of American History, 102*(1), 126–140.

Latessa, E., & Allen, H. E. (1982). Halfway houses and parole: A national assessment. *Journal of Criminal Justice, 10*(2), 153–163.

Lattimore, P. K., MacKenzie, D. L., Zajac, G., Dawes, D., Arsenault, E., & Tueller, S. (2016). Outcome findings from the HOPE demonstration field experiment. *Criminology & Public Policy, 15*(4), 1103–1141.

Laub, J. H., & Sampson, R. J. (2003). *Shared beginnings, divergent lives: Delinquent boys to age 70.* Cambridge, MA: Harvard University Press.

Laundra, K., Rodgers, K., & Zapp, H. (2013). Transforming teens: Measuring the effects of restorative justice principles in a teen court setting. *Juvenile and Family Court Journal, 64*(4), 21–34.

Laxminarayan, M., Bosmans, M., Porter, R., & Sosa, L. (2013). Victim satisfaction with criminal justice: A systematic review. *Victims & Offenders, 8*(2), 119–147.

Leclerc, B., Wortley, R., & Smallbone, S. (2011). Getting into the script of adult child sex offenders and mapping out situational prevention measures. *Journal of Research in Crime and Delinquency, 48*(2), 209–237.

Lee, B. R., Ebesutani, C., Kolivoski, K. M., Becker, K. D., Lindsey, M. A., Brandt, N. E.,

Cammack, N., Strieder, F. H., Chorpita, B. F., & Barth, R. P. (2014). Program and practice elements for placement prevention: A review of interventions and their effectiveness in promoting home-based care. *American Journal of Orthopsychiatry, 84*(3), 244–256.

Leger, D. L. (2015). DEA: Deaths from fentanyl-laced heroin surging. *USA Today* (18 March 2015). Available at http://www.usatoday.com/story/news/2015/03/18/surge-in-overdose-deaths-from-fentanyl/24957967/ (accessed 27 December 2016).

Leiber, M. J., & Peck, J. H. (2013a). Probation violations and juvenile justice decision making: Implications for blacks and Hispanics. *Youth Violence and Juvenile Justice, 11*(1), 60–78.

Leiber, M. J., & Peck, J. H. (2015). Youth in the juvenile court and adult court. In M. D. Krohn & J. Lane (Eds.), *The handbook of juvenile delinquency and juvenile justice* (pp. 439–458). Malden, MA: John Wiley & Sons, Inc.

Leiber, M. J., & Rodriguez, N. (2011). The implementation of the disproportionate minority confinement/contact (DMC) mandate: A failure or a success? *Race and Justice, 1*(1), 103–124.

Leiber, M. J., Peck, J. H., & Beaudry-Cyr, M. (2016). When does race and gender matter? The interrelationships between the gender of probation officers and juvenile court detention and intake outcomes. *Justice Quarterly, 33*(4), 614–641.

Leiber, M. J., Peck, J. H., & Rodriguez, N. (2016). Minority threat and juvenile court outcomes. *Crime & Delinquency, 62*(1), 54–80.

Leon, C. (2011). The contexts and politics of evidence-based sex offender policy. *Criminology & Public Policy, 10*(2), 421–430.

Leshem, R. (2016). Brain development, impulsivity, risky decision making, and cognitive control: Integrating cognitive and socioemotional processes during adolescence. *Developmental Neuropsychology, 41*(1–2), 1–5.

Letourneau, E. J., Levenson, J. S., Bandyopadhyay, D., Armstrong, K., & Sinha, D. (2010 [Letourneau et al., 2010b]). Effects of South Carolina's sex offender registration and notification policy on deterrence of adult sex crimes. *Criminal Justice and Behavior, 37*(5), 537–552.

Letourneau, E. J., Levenson, J. S., Bandyopadhyay, D., Sinha, D., & Armstrong, K. (2010 [Letourneau et al., 2010a]). Effects of South Carolina's sex offender registration and notification policy on adult recidivism. *Criminal Justice Policy Review, 21*(4), 435–458.

Levenson, J. S (2004). Sexual predator civil commitment: A comparison of selected and released offenders. *International Journal of Offender Therapy and Comparative Criminology, 48*(6), 638–648.

Levenson, J. S. & Cotter, L. P. (2005). The effect of Megan's Law on sex offender reintegration. *Journal of Contemporary Criminal Justice, 21*(1), 49–66.

Levenson, J. S. & Hern, A. L. (2007). Sex offender residence restrictions: Unintended consequences and community reentry. *Justice Research and Policy, 9*(1), 59–73.

Levenson, J. S. (2011). Sex offender policies in an era of zero tolerance: What does effectiveness really mean? *Criminology & Public Policy, 10*(2), 229–233.

Levenson, J. S., Brannon, Y. N., Fortney, T., & Baker, J. (2007). Public perceptions about sex offenders and community protection policies. *Analyses of Social Issues and Public Policy, 7*(1), 1–25.

Levesque, R. J. (1996). Is there still a place for violent youth in juvenile justice? *Aggression and Violent Behavior, 1*(1), 69–79.

Levi, M. (2009). Financial crimes. In M. Tonry (Ed.), *The Oxford handbook of crime and public policy* (pp. 223–246). Oxford, UK: Oxford University Press.

Levin, M., & Cohen, D. (2014). Kids doing time for what's not a crime: The over-incarceration of status offenders. *Texas Public Policy Foundation, March*, 4–12.

Levitt, S. D. (1996). The effect of prison population size on crime rates: Evidence from prison overcrowding litigation. *The Quarterly Journal of Economics, 111*(2), 319–351.

Levitt, S. D. (2004). Understanding why crime fell in the 1990s: Four factors that explain the decline and six that do not. *The Journal of Economic Perspectives, 18*(1), 163–190.

Lewis, D. A., & Salem, G. (1986). *Fear of crime: Incivility and the production of a social problem.* New Brunswick, NJ: Transaction Books.

Lieber, M. J., & Peck, J. H. (2013b). Race in juvenile justice sentencing policy: An overview of research and policy recommendations. *Law & Inequality, 31,* 331–368.

Liedka, R. V., Piehl, A. M., & Useem, B. (2006). The crime-control effect of incarceration: Does scale matter? *Criminology & Public Policy, 5*(2), 245–276.

Lilly, J. R., Cullen, F. T., & Ball, R. A. (2014). *Criminological theory: Context and consequences* (6th ed.). Sage Publications.

Lin, J., & Phillips, S. (2014). Media coverage of capital murder: Exceptions sustain the rule. *Justice Quarterly, 31*(5), 934–959.

Lipsey, M. W. (2009). The primary factors that characterize effective interventions with juvenile offenders: A meta-analytic overview. *Victims and Offenders, 4*(2), 124–147.

Lipsey, M. W., & Cullen, F. T. (2007). The effectiveness of correctional rehabilitation: A review of systematic reviews. *Annual Review of Law and Social Science, 3,* 297–320.

Lipsey, M. W., & Landenberger, N. A. (2006). Cognitive-behavioral interventions. In B. C. Welsh & D. P. Farrington (Eds.), *Preventing crime: What works for children, offenders, victims, and places* (pp. 57–71). Dordrecht, Netherlands: Springer.

Lipsey, M. W., Chapman, G., & Landenberger, N. A. (2001). Cognitive-behavioral programs for offenders. *The Annals of the American Academy of Political and Social Science, 578,* 144–157.

Lipsey, M. W., Landenberger, N. A., & Wilson, S. J. (2007). Effects of cognitive-behavioral programs for criminal offenders. *Campbell Systematic Reviews.* The Campbell Collaboration.

Little, G. L., & Robinson, K. D. (1988). Moral Reconation Therapy: A systematic step-by-step treatment system for treatment resistant clients. *Psychological Reports, 62*(1), 135–151.

Lizotte, A. J., Howard, G. J., Krohn, M. D., & Thornberry, T. P. (1997). Patterns of illegal gun carrying among urban males. *Valparaiso University Law Review, 31*(2), 375–393.

Lizotte, A. J., Krohn, M. D., Howell, J. C., Tobin, K., & Howard, G. J. (2000). Factors influencing gun carrying among young urban males over the adolescent–young adult life course. *Criminology, 38*(3), 811–834.

Lobo, G. J., & Zhou, J. (2006). Did conservatism in financial reporting increase after the Sarbanes-Oxley Act? Initial evidence. *Accounting Horizons, 20*(1), 57–73.

Lochner, L., & Moretti, E. (2004). The effect of education on crime: Evidence from prison inmates, arrests, and self-reports. *The American Economic Review, 94*(1), 155–189.

Loeber, R., Menting, B., Lynam, D. R., Moffitt, T. E., Stouthamer-Loeber, M., Stallings, R., Farrington, D. P., & Pardini, D. (2012). Findings from the Pittsburgh Youth Study: Cognitive impulsivity and intelligence as predictors of the age-crime curve. *Journal of the American Academy of Child & Adolescent Psychiatry, 51*(11), 1136–1149.

Loewen, J. W. (2007). *Lies my teacher told me: Everything your American history textbook got wrong.* New York: The New Press.

Loftin, C., Heumann, M., & McDowall, D. (1983). Mandatory sentencing and firearms violence: Evaluating an alternative to gun control. *Law & Society Review, 17*(2), 287–318.

Logan, W. A. (2008). Criminal justice federalism and national sex offender policy. *Ohio State Journal of Criminal Law, 6,* 51–122.

Lollar, C. E. (2014). What is criminal restitution? *Iowa Law Review, 100,* 93–154.

Lott, J. R. (1990). The effect of conviction on the legitimate income of criminals. *Economics Letters, 34*(4), 381–385.

Lott, J. R., Jr., & Mustard, D. B. (1997). Crime, deterrence, and right-to-carry concealed handguns. *Journal of Legal Studies, 26,* 1–68.

Loughran, T. A., Mulvey, E. P., Schubert, C. A., Chassin, L. A., Steinberg, L., Piquero, A. R., Fagan, J., Cota-Robles, S., Cauffman, E., & Losoya, S. (2010). Differential effects of adult court transfer on juvenile offender recidivism. *Law and Human Behavior, 34*(6), 476–488.

Lovell, D., Gagliardi, G. J., & Peterson, P. D. (2002). Recidivism and use of services among persons with mental illness after release from prison. *Psychiatric services, 53*(10), 1290–1296.

Lovins, L. B., Lowenkamp, C. T., Latessa, E. J., & Smith, P. (2007). Application of the risk principle to female offenders. *Journal of Contemporary Criminal Justice, 23*(4), 383–398.

Lowenkamp, C. T., & Latessa, E. J. (2004). Increasing the effectiveness of correctional programming through the risk principle: Identifying offenders for residential placement. *Criminology & Public Policy, 4*(2), 263–290.

Lowenkamp, C. T., & Latessa, E. J. (2004). Increasing the effectiveness of correctional programming through the risk principle: Identifying offenders for residential placement. *Criminology & Public Policy, 4*(1), 501–528.

Lowenkamp, C. T., Cullen, F. T., & Pratt, T. C. (2003). Replicating Sampson and Groves's test of social disorganization theory: Revisiting a criminological classic. *Journal of Research in Crime and Delinquency, 40*(4), 351–373.

Lowenkamp, C. T., Holsinger, A. M., & Latessa, E. J. (2005). Are drug courts effective: A meta-analytic review. *Journal of Community Corrections, 15*(1), 5–28.

Lowenkamp, C. T., Latessa, E. J., & Holsinger, A. M. (2006). The risk principle in action: What have we learned from 13,676 offenders and 97 correctional programs? *Crime & Delinquency, 52*(1), 77–93.

Lowenkamp, C. T., Latessa, E. J., & Smith, P. (2006). Does correctional program quality really matter? The impact of adhering to the principles of effective intervention. *Criminology & Public Policy, 5*(3), 575–594.

Lowenkamp, C. T., Makarios, M. D., Latessa, E. J., Lemke, R., & Smith, P. (2010). Community corrections facilities for juvenile offenders in Ohio: An examination of treatment integrity and recidivism. *Criminal Justice and Behavior, 37*(6), 695–708.

Lowenkamp, C. T., Makarios, M. D., Latessa, E. J., Lemke, R., & Smith, P. (2010). Community corrections facilities for juvenile offenders in Ohio: An examination of treatment integrity and recidivism. *Criminal Justice and Behavior, 37*(6), 695–708.

Ludwig, J. (1998). Concealed-gun-carrying laws and violent crime: Evidence from state panel data. *International Review of Law and Economics, 18*, 239–254.

Ludwig, J. (2005). Better gun enforcement, less crime. *Criminology & Public Policy, 4*(4), 677–716.

Ludwig, J., & Cook, P. J. (2000). Homicide and suicide rates associated with implementation of the Brady handgun violence prevention act. *JAMA, 284*(5), 585–591.

Lum, C., Koper, C. S., & Telep, C. W. (2011). The evidence-based policing matrix. *Journal of Experimental Criminology, 7*(1), 3–26.

Lurigio, A. J., & Petersilia, J. (1992). The emergence of intensive supervision programs in the United States. In J. Byrne, A.J. Lurigio, & J. Petersilia (Eds.), *Smart sentencing: The emergence of intermediate sanctions* (pp. 3–17). Newbury Park, CA: Sage Publications.

Lutze, F. E., & Brody, D. C. (1999). Mental abuse as cruel and unusual punishment: Do boot camp prisons violate the Eighth Amendment? *Crime & Delinquency, 45*(2), 242–255.

Lynch, J. P., & Pridemore, W. A. (2011). Crime in international perspective. In J. Q. Wilson & J. Petersilia (Eds.), *Crime and public policy* (pp. 5–52). Oxford, UK: Oxford University Press.

Lynch, M. (2012). Theorizing the role of the "war on drugs" in U.S. punishment. *Theoretical Criminology, 16*(2), 175–199.

MacCoun, R. J. (2005). Voice, control, and belonging: The double-edged sword of procedural fairness. *Annual Review of Law and Social Science, 1*, 171–201.

MacKenzie, D. L., & Farrington, D. P. (2015). Preventing future offending of delinquents and offenders: What have we learned from experiments and meta-analyses? *Journal of Experimental Criminology, 11*(4), 565–595.

MacKenzie, D. L., & Parent, D. G. (2004). Boot camp prisons for young offenders. In D. L. MacKenzie & G. S. Armstrong (Eds.), *Correctional boot camps: Military basic training or a model for corrections?* (pp. 16–25). Thousand Oaks, CA: Sage Publications.

MacKenzie, D. L., & Shaw, J. W. (1990). Inmate adjustment and change during shock incarceration: The impact of correctional boot camp programs. *Justice Quarterly, 7*(1), 125–150.

MacKenzie, D. L., Wilson, D. B., & Kider, S. B. (2001). Effects of correctional boot camps on offending. *The ANNALS of the American Academy of Political and Social Science, 578*(1), 126–143.

Maddan, S., Miller, M., Walker, J. T., & Marshall, I. H. (2011). Utilizing criminal history information to explore the effect of community notification on sex offender recidivism. *Justice Quarterly, 28*(2), 303–324.

Magers, J. S. (2004). Compstat: a new paradigm for policing or a repudiation of community policing? *Journal of Contemporary Criminal Justice, 20*(1), 70–79.

Maguire, E. R. (1997). Structural change in large municipal police organizations during the community policing era. Justice Quarterly, 14(3), 547–576.

Maguire, E. R., & Mastrofski, S. D. (2000). Patterns of community policing in the United States. *Police Quarterly, 3*(1), 4–45.

Maguire, M. (2000). Policing by risks and targets: Some dimensions and implications of intelligence-led crime control. *Policing and Society: An International Journal, 9*(4), 315–336.

Maguire, M., & John, T. (2006). Intelligence led policing, managerialism and community engagement: Competing priorities and the role of the National Intelligence Model in the UK. *Policing & Society, 16*(1), 67–85.

Makarios, M. D., & Pratt, T. C. (2012). The effectiveness of policies and programs that attempt to reduce firearm violence: A meta-analysis. *Crime & Delinquency, 58*(2), 222–244.

Malinen, S., Willis, G. M., & Johnston, L. (2014). Might informative media reporting of sexual offending influence community members' attitudes towards sex offenders? *Psychology, Crime & Law, 20*(6), 535–552.

Manning, P. K. (1988). Community policing as a drama of control. In J. R. Greene & S. D. Mastrofski (Eds.), *Community policing: Rhetoric or reality* (pp. 27–46). New York: Praeger.

Manski, C. F., & Pepper, J. V. (2013). Deterrence and the death penalty: Partial identification using repeated cross sections. *Journal of Quantitative Criminology, 29*(1), 123–141.

Markowitz, E. (2016). The long-term costs of fining juvenile offenders. *The New Yorker* (24 December 2016). Available at http://www.newyorker.com/business/currency/the-long-term-costs-of-fining-juvenile-offenders (accessed 28 February 2017).

Markowitz, F. E., Bellair, P. E., Liska, A. E., & Liu, J. (2001). Extending social disorganization theory: Modeling the relationships between cohesion, disorder, and fear. *Criminology, 39*(2), 293–319.

Marlowe, D. B., Festinger, D. S., Lee, P. A., Schepise, M. M., Hazzard, J. E., Merrill, J. C., Mulvaney, F. D., & McLellan, A. T. (2003). Are judicial status hearings a key component of drug court? During-treatment data from a randomized trial. *Criminal Justice and Behavior, 30*(2), 141–162.

Martin, S. S., Butzin, C. A., Saum, C. A., & Inciardi, J. A. (1999). Three-year outcomes of therapeutic community treatment for drug-involved offenders in Delaware: From prison to work release to aftercare. *The Prison Journal, 79*(3), 294–320.

Martinez, D., Greene, K., Broft, A., Kumar, D., Liu, F., Narendran, R., Slifstein, M., van Heertum, R., & Kleber, H. D. (2009). Lower level of endogenous dopamine in patients with cocaine dependence: Findings from PET imaging of D 2/D 3 receptors following acute dopamine depletion. *American Journal of Psychiatry, 166*(10), 1170–1177.

Martinez, D., Narendran, R., Foltin, R. W., Slifstein, M., Hwang, D., Broft, A., Huang, Y., Cooper, T. B., Fischman, M. W., Kleber, H.D., & Laruelle, M. (2007). Amphetamine-induced dopamine release: Markedly blunted in cocaine dependence and predictive of the choice to self-administer cocaine. *American Journal of Psychiatry, 164*(4), 622 –629.

Martinson, R. (1974). What works? Questions and answers about prison reform. *The public Interest*, (35), 22–54.

Marvell, T. B., & Moody Jr, C. E. (1994). Prison population growth and crime reduction. *Journal of Quantitative Criminology, 10*(2), 109–140.

Marvell, T. B., & Moody, C. E. (1995). The impact of enhanced prison terms for felonies committed with guns. *Criminology, 33*(2), 247–281.

Massey, D. S. & Denton, N. A. (1993). *American apartheid: Segregation and the making of the underclass.* Cambridge, MA: Harvard University Press.

Massey, D. S. (1995). Getting away with murder: Segregation and violent crime in urban America. University of Pennsylvania Law Review, *143*(5), 1203–1232.

Mastrofski, S. D. (1988). Community policing as reform: A cautionary tale. In J. R. Greene & S. D. Mastrofski (Eds.), *Community policing: Rhetoric or reality* (pp. 47–68). New York: Praeger.

Matsuda, K. N., Melde, C., Taylor, T. J., Freng, A., & Esbensen, F. A. (2013). Gang membership and adherence to the "code of the street". *Justice Quarterly, 30*(3), 440–468.

Matthews Jr, H. T. (2000). Status offenders: Our children's constitutional rights versus what's right for them. *Seattle University Law Review, 27*, 201.

Maxson, C. L. (2013). Do not shoot the messenger: The utility of gang risk research in program targeting and content. *Criminology & Public Policy, 12*(3), 421–426.

Maxson, C. L., & Allen, T. L. (1997). An evaluation of the city of Inglewood's Youth Firearms Violence Initiative. Los Angeles: University of Southern California's Social Science Research Institute.

Maxson, C. L., Hennigan, K. M., & Sloane, D. C. (2005). "It's getting crazy out there": Can a civil gang injunction change a community? *Criminology & Public Policy, 4*(3), 577–605.

Maxson, C. L., Hennigan, K., & Sloane, D. C. (2003). *For the sake of the neighborhood?: Civil gang injunction as a gang intervention tool in Southern California.* Belmont, CA: Wadsworth Publishing.

Mazerolle, L. G., Ready, J., Terrill, W., & Waring, E. (2000). Problem-oriented policing in public housing: The Jersey City Evaluation. *Justice Quarterly, 17*(1), 129–158.

Mazerolle, L., & Ransley, J. (2006). *Third party policing.* Cambridge, UK: Cambridge University Press.

Mazerolle, L., Bennett, S., Davis, J., Sargeant, E., & Manning, M. (2013). Procedural justice and police legitimacy: A systematic review of the research evidence. *Journal of experimental Criminology, 9*(3), 245–274.

McBride, D., & VanderWaal, C. (1997). Day reporting centers as an alternative for drug using offenders. *Journal of Drug Issues, 27*(2), 379–397.

McCormick, A. E. (1977). Rule enforcement and moral indignation: Some observations on the effects of criminal antitrust convictions upon societal reaction processes. *Social Problems, 25*(1), 30–39.

McDowall, D., Loftin, C., & Wiersema, B. (1995). Easing concealed firearm laws: Effects on homicide in three states. *The Journal of Criminal Law and Criminology, 86*(1), 193–206.

McDowall, D., Loftin, C., & Wiersema, B. (2000). The impact of youth curfew laws on juvenile crime rates. *Crime & Delinquency, 46*(1), 76–91.

McGarrell, E. F., & Sandys, M. (1996). The misperception of public opinion toward capital punishment: Examining the spuriousness explanation of death penalty support. *American Behavioral Scientist, 39*(4), 500–513.

McGarrell, E. F., Chermak, S., Wilson, J. M., & Corsaro, N. (2006). Reducing homicide through a "lever-pulling" strategy. *Justice Quarterly, 23*(2), 214–231.

McGarrell, E. F., Corsaro, N., Hipple, N. K., & Bynum, T. S. (2010). Project safe neighborhoods and violent crime trends in U.S. cities: Assessing violent crime impact. *Journal of Quantitative Criminology, 26*(2), 165–190.

McGarrell, E. F., Freilich, J. D., & Chermak, S. (2007). Intelligence-led policing as a framework for responding to terrorism. *Journal of Contemporary Criminal Justice, 23*(2), 142–158.

McGarrell, E. F., Hipple, N. K., Corsaro, N., Bynum, T. S., Perez, H., Zimmermann, C. A., & Garmo, M. (2009). *Project safe neighborhoods: A national program to reduce gun crime: Final project report*. Washington, DC: U.S. Department of Justice.

McGloin, J. M. (2005). Policy and intervention considerations of a network analysis of street gangs. *Criminology & Public Policy, 4*(3), 607–636.

McGloin, J. M. (2007a). The continued relevance of gang membership. *Criminology & Public Policy, 6*(2), 231–240.

McGloin, J. M. (2007b). The organizational structure of street gangs in Newark, New Jersey: A network analysis methodology. *Journal of Gang Research, 15*(1), 1–34.

McGloin, J. M., & Decker, S. H. (2010). Theories of gang behavior and public policy. In H. D. Barlow & S. H. Decker (Eds.), *Criminology and public policy: putting theory to work* (pp. 150–165). Philadelphia, PA: Temple University Press.

McGloin, J. M., & Piquero, A. R. (2009). On the relationship between co-offending network redundancy and offending versatility. *Journal of Research in Crime and Delinquency, 47*(1), 63–90.

McGloin, J. M., & Piquero, A. R. (2009). On the relationship between co-offending network redundancy and offending versatility. *Journal of Research in Crime and Delinquency, 47*(1), 63–90.

McGloin, J. M., & Piquero, A. R. (2009a). "I wasn't alone": Collective behaviour and violent delinquency. *The Australian and New Zealand Journal of Criminology, 42*(3), 336–353.

McGloin, J. M., & Piquero, A. R. (2009b). On the relationship between co-offending network redundancy and offending versatility. *Journal of Research in Crime and Delinquency, 47*(1), 63–90.

McGowan, A., Hahn, R., Liberman, A., Crosby, A., Fullilove, M., Johnson, R., Moscicki, E., Price, L., Snyder, S., ... & Lowy, J. (2007). Effects on violence of laws and policies facilitating the transfer of juveniles from the juvenile justice system to the adult justice system: A systematic review. *American Journal of Preventive Medicine, 32*(4), 7–28.

McGregor, B., Brown, E., Yan, F., Mitchell, C., Robinson, C., DeGroot, J., & Braithwaite, R. (2016). Program success of mental health clients in day reporting centers. *Journal of health care for the poor and underserved, 27*(2), 194–213.

McIvor, G. (2016). What is the impact of community service? In F. McNeill, I. Durnescu, & R. Butter (Eds.), *Probation: 12 essential questions* (pp. 107–128). London: Macmillan Publishers Ltd.

McPherson, J. M. (1988). *Battle cry of freedom: The Civil War era*. New York: Oxford University Press.

Mears, D. P., Hay, C., Gertz, M., & Mancini, C. (2007). Public opinion and the foundation of the juvenile court. *Criminology, 45*(1), 223–257.

Mears, D. P., Kuch, J. J., Lindsey, A. M., Siennick, S. E., Pesta, G. B., Greenwald, M. A., & Blomberg, T. G. (2016). Juvenile court and contemporary diversion: Helpful, harmful, or both? *Criminology & Public Policy, 15*(3), 953–981.

Mears, D. P., Wang, X., Hay, C., & Bales, W. D. (2008). Social ecology and recidivism: Implications for prisoner reentry. *Criminology, 46*(2), 301–340.

Meeks, D. (2006). Police militarization in urban areas: The obscure war against the underclass. *The Black Scholar, 35*(4), 33–41.

Melde, C., & Esbensen, F. (2011). Gang membership as a turning point in the life course. *Criminology, 49*(2), 513–552.

Melde, C. & Esbensen, F. (2013). Gangs and violence: Disentangling the impact of gang membership on the level and nature of offending. *Journal of Quantitative Criminology, 29*(2), 143–166.

Mendel, R. A. (2011). *No place for kids: The case for reducing juvenile incarceration*. Baltimore, MD: The Annie E. Casey Foundation.

Mercado, C. C., Alvarez, S., & Levenson, J. (2008). The impact of specialized sex offender legislation on community reentry. *Sexual Abuse: A Journal of Research and Treatment, 20*(2), 188–205.

Merlo, A. V., Benekos, P. J., & Cook, W. J. (1997a). Waiver and juvenile justice reform: Widening the punitive net. *Criminal Justice Policy Review, 8*(2–3), 145–168.

Merlo, A. V., Benekos, P. J., & Cook, W. J. (1997b). 'Getting tough' with youth: Legislative waiver as crime control. *Juvenile and Family Court Journal, 48*(3), 1–15.

Miller, H. V., & Miller, J. M. (2015). A promising jail reentry program revisited: Results from a quasi-experimental design. *Criminal Justice Studies, 28*(2), 211–225.

Miller, J. A. (2010). Sex offender civil commitment: The treatment paradox. *California Law Review, 98*(6), 2093–2128.

Miller, P. G., Curtis, A., Sønderlund, A., Day, A., & Droste, N. (2015). Effectiveness of interventions for convicted DUI offenders in reducing recidivism: A systematic review of the peer-reviewed scientific literature. *The American journal of drug and alcohol abuse, 41*(1), 16–29.

Mitchell, O., Cochran, J. C., Mears, D. P., & Bales, W. D. (2017). The effectiveness of prison for reducing drug offender recidivism: A regression discontinuity analysis. *Journal of Experimental Criminology, 13*(1), 1–27.

Mitchell, O., Wilson, D. B., Eggers, A., & MacKenzie, D. L. (2012). Assessing the effectiveness of drug courts on recidivism: A meta-analytic review of traditional and non-traditional drug courts. *Journal of Criminal Justice, 40*, 60–71.

Miyagawa, M. (2016). *Do economic sanctions work?* New York: Springer.

Mocan, H. N., & Gittings, R. K. (2003). Getting off death row: Commuted sentences and the deterrent effect of capital punishment. *The Journal of Law and Economics, 46*(2), 453–478.

Mocan, H. N., & Rees, D. I. (2005). Economic conditions, deterrence and juvenile crime: Evidence from micro data. *American Law and Economics Review, 7*(2), 319–349.

Models for Change. (n.d.). Website. Available at www.modelsforchange.net (accessed 27 March 2017).

Moffatt, S., & Poynton, S. (2007). Deterrent effect of higher fines on recidivism: Driving offences. *The Crime and Justice Bulletin, 106*, 1–15.

Moffitt, T. E. (1993). Adolescence-limited and life-course-persistent antisocial behavior: A developmental taxonomy. *Psychological Review, 100*, 674–701.

Moffitt, T. E. (2003). Life-course-persistent and adolescence-limited antisocial behavior: A 10-year research review and a research agenda. In B.B. Lahey, T.E. Moffitt, & A. Caspi (Eds.), *Causes of conduct disorder and juvenile delinquency* (pp. 49–75). New York: Guilford Press.

Moon, M. M., Sundt, J. L., Cullen, F. T., & Wright, J. P. (2000). Is child saving dead? Public support for juvenile rehabilitation. *Crime & Delinquency, 46*(1), 38–60.

Moore, M. H., & Trojanowicz, R. C. (1988). *Policing and the fear of crime.* Washington, DC: U.S. Department of Justice.

Morales, W. Q. (1989). The war on drugs: a new US national security doctrine? *Third World Quarterly, 11*(3), 147–169.

Moreto, W. (2015). Introducing intelligence-led conservation: Bridging crime and conservation science. *Crime Science 4*(15). DOI 10.1186/s40163-015-0030-9

Moreto, W. D., Piza, E. L., & Caplan, J. M. (2014). "A Plague on both Your Houses?": Risks, Repeats and Reconsiderations of Urban Residential Burglary. *Justice quarterly, 31*(6), 1102–1126.

Morgan, P., Wallack, L., & Buchanan, D. (1989). Waging drug wars: Prevention strategy or politics as usual. Drugs & Society, 3(1–2), 99–124.

Morris, N., & Tonry, M. (1990). *Between prison and probation: Intermediate punishments in a rational sentencing system.* Oxford, UK: Oxford University Press.

Motiuk, L. L., Bonta, J., & Andrews, D. A. (1986). Classification in correctional halfway houses: The relative and incremental predictive criterion validities of the Megargee-MMPI and LSI systems. *Criminal Justice and Behavior, 13*(1), 33–46.

Mueller, G. O. W. (1996). An essay on environmental criminality. In S. M. Edwards, T. D. Edwards, & C. B. Fields (Eds.), *Environmental crime and criminality: Theoretical and practical issues* (pp. 3–34). New York, NY: Routledge.

Mularski, R. A., White-Chu, F., Overbay, D., Miller, L., Asch, S. M., & Ganzini, L. (2006). Measuring pain as the 5th vital sign does not improve quality of pain management. *Journal of General Internal Medicine, 21*, 607–612.

Mullane, R., Burrell, N. A., Allen, M., & Timmerman, L. (2014). Victim–offender mediation. In N. Burrell, M. Allen, B. M. Gayle, & R. W. Preiss (Eds.), *Managing interpersonal conflict: Advances through meta-analysis* (pp. 106–125). New York: Routledge.

Muniz, A. (2014). Maintaining racial boundaries: Criminalization, neighborhood context, and the origins of gang injunctions. *Social Problems, 61*(2), 216–236.

Musto, D. F. (1973). *The American disease: Origins of narcotic control.* New Haven: Yale University Press.

Musto, D. F. (1989). America's first cocaine epidemic. *The Wilson Quarterly, 13*(3), 59–64.

Musto, D. F. (1991). Opium, cocaine and marijuana in American history. Scientific American, 265(1), 40–47.

Musto, D. F. (1999). *The American disease: Origins of narcotic control* (3rd ed.). New York: Oxford University Press.

Nagin, D. S. (1975). *General deterrence—a review of the empirical evidence.* Washington, DC: U.S. Department of Justice.

Nagin, D. S. (1998). Deterrence and incapacitation. In M. Tonry (Ed.), *The handbook of crime and punishment* (pp. 345–368). Oxford: Oxford University Press.

Nagin, D. S., Piquero, A. R., Scott, E. S., & Steinberg, L. (2006). Public preferences for rehabilitation versus incarceration of juvenile offenders: Evidence from a contingent valuation survey. *Criminology & Public Policy, 5*(4), 627–651.

Natapoff, A. (2006). Beyond unreliable: How snitches contribute to wrongful convictions. *Golden Gate University Law Review, 37,* 107–129.

Nath, S. B., Clement, D. E., & Sistrunk, F. (1976). Parole and probation caseload size variation: The Florida Intensive Supervision Project. *Criminal Justice Review, 1*(2), 61–71.

National Archives. (n.d.[a]). *Constitutional issues—separation of powers.* Available at https://www.archives.gov/education/lessons/separation-powers (accessed 5 December 2016).

National Conference of State Legislatures. (2006). States with sex offender residency restriction laws. Available at https://www.google.com/url?sa=t&rct=j&q=&esrc=s&source=web&cd=5&ved=0ahUKEwj79_LMmoXPAhWELSYKHSYNC04QFgg7MAQ&url=http%3A%2F%2Fwww.npr.org%2Fprograms%2Fmorning%2Ffeatures%2F2006%2Foct%2Fprop83%2Fncsl_residency.pdf&usg=AFQjCNExMLIVJDYNt0Y1Iy-tnse7OqOGxg&sig2=-NGY-VTSXf2cDbVgdhaa-w&cad=rja

National Institute of Corrections (n.d.). Thinking for a Change. Available at http://nicic.gov/t4c

National Institute of Justice. (n.d.). *Drug courts.* Available at http://www.nij.gov/topics/courts/drug-courts/pages/welcome.aspx

National Institute on Alcohol Abuse and Alcoholism. (n.d.[a]). *Alcohol facts and statistics.* Available at https://www.niaaa.nih.gov/alcohol-health/overview-alcohol-consumption/alcohol-facts-and-statistics

National Institute on Alcohol Abuse and Alcoholism. (n.d.[b]). *Alcohol use disorder.* https://www.niaaa.nih.gov/alcohol-health/overview-alcohol-consumption/alcohol-use-disorders

National Institute on Drug Abuse [NIDA]. (2015). *Drug facts—nationwide trends.* Available at https://www.drugabuse.gov/publications/drugfacts/nationwide-trends

National Institute on Drug Abuse. (2017). Overdose death rates. Available at https://www.drugabuse.gov/related-topics/trends-statistics/overdose-death-rates (accessed 8 June 2017).

National Public Radio. (2011). *Illinois abolishes the death penalty* (9 March 2011). Available at http://www.npr.org/2011/03/09/134394946/illinois-abolishes-death-penalty (accessed 16 March 2017).

Nellis, M., Beyens, K., & Kaminski, D. (2013). Introduction: Making sense of electronic monitoring. In M. Nellis, K. Beyens, & D. Kaminski (Eds.), *Electronically monitored punishment: International and critical perspectives* (pp. 1–18). London: Routledge.

Newman, D. J. (1958). White-collar crime. *Law and Contemporary Problems, 23*(4), 735–753.

Newton, P. J., Mulcahy, T. M., & Martin, S. E. (2008). *Finding victims of human trafficking: Final report to the U.S. Department of Justice.* Washington, DC: U.S. Department of Justice.

Nieto, M. & Jung, D. (2006). *The impact of residency restrictions on sex offenders and correctional management practices: A literature review.* Sacramento, CA: California Research Bureau.

Nobles, M. R., Levenson, J. S., & Youstin, T. J. (2012). Effectiveness of residence restrictions in preventing sex offense recidivism. *Crime & Delinquency, 58*(4), 491–513.

Novak, K. J., Fox, A. M., Carr, C. M., & Spade, D. A. (2016). The efficacy of foot patrol in violent places. *Journal of Experimental Criminology, 12,* 465–475.

Novak, K. J., Hartman, J., Holsinger, A., & Turner, M. (1999). The effects of aggressive policing of disorder on serious crime. *Policing, 22,* 171–190.

O'Connell Davidson, J. (2010). New slavery, old binaries: Human trafficking and the borders of "freedom." *Global Networks, 10*(2), 244–261.

O'Connell, D. J., Brent, J. J., & Visher, C. A. (2016). Decide your time: A randomized trial of a drug testing and graduated sanctions program. *Criminology & Public Policy, 15*(4), 1073–1102.

Office of Juvenile Justice and Delinquency Prevention [OJJDP]. (2010). Best practices to address community gang problems:

OJJDP's Comprehensive Gang Model. Washington, DC: Office of Juvenile Justice and Delinquency Prevention.

Office of Juvenile Justice and Delinquency Prevention [OJJDP]. (2015). *Juvenile arrest rate trends [data file].* Available at https://www.ojjdp.gov/ojstatbb/crime/JAR_Display.asp?ID=qa05200 (accessed 24 March 2017).

Office of the Attorney General of New York. (1999). *New York City Police Department's "stop & frisk" practices: A report to the people of the State of New York from the Office of the Attorney General.* Albany, NY: New York State Office of the Attorney General.

Oliphant, B. (2016). *Support for death penalty lowest in more than four decades.* Pew Research Center (29 September 2016). Available at http://www.pewresearch.org/fact-tank/2016/09/29/support-for-death-penalty-lowest-in-more-than-four-decades/ (accessed 15 March 2017).

Osnos, E. (2012). The Burmese spring. *The New Yorker* (6 August 2012). Available at http://www.newyorker.com/magazine/2012/08/06/the-burmese-spring (accessed 24 February 2017).

Ostermann, M. (2013). Using day reporting centers to divert parolees from revocation. *Criminology & Public Policy, 12*(1), 163–171.

Packard, R. L. & Levenson, J. S. (2006). Revisiting the reliability of diagnostic decisions in sex offender civil commitment. *Sexual Offender Treatment, 1*(3), 1–15.

Packer, H. (1968). *The limits of the criminal sanction.* Stanford, CA: Stanford University Press.

Padgett, K. G., Bales, W. D., & Blomberg, T. G. (2006). Under surveillance: An empirical test of the effectiveness and consequences of electronic monitoring. *Criminology & Public Policy, 5*(1), 61–91.

Pager, D. (2007). *Marked: Race, crime, and finding work in an era of mass incarceration.* Chicago: University of Chicago Press.

Paoline, E. A. III, Gau, J. M., & Terrill, W. (2016). Race and the police use of force encounter in the United States. *British Journal of Criminology.* DOI 10.1093/bjc/azw089

Papachristos, A. V. (2005). Interpreting inkblots: Deciphering and doing something about modern street gangs. *Criminology & Public Policy, 4*(3), 643–652.

Papachristos, A. V. (2013). Two decades of GREAT. *Criminology & Public Policy, 12*(3), 367–371.

Papachristos, A. V., Meares, T. L., & Fagan, J. (2007). Attention felons: Evaluating Project Safe Neighborhoods in Chicago. *Journal of Empirical Legal Studies, 4*(2), 223–272.

Papachristos, A. V., Meares, T. L., & Fagan, J. (2007). Attention felons: evaluating project safe neighborhoods in Chicago. *Journal of Empirical Legal Studies, 4*(2), 223–272.

Parent, D. G. (2003). *Correctional boot camps: Lessons from a decade of research.* Washington, DC: U.S. Department of Justice.

Parker, D. P., Foltz, J. D., & Elsea, D. (2016). Unintended consequences of economic sanctions for human rights. *WIDER Working Paper 2016/124.* Helsinki, Finland: UNU-WIDER.

Passell, P. (1975). The deterrent effect of the death penalty: A statistical test. *Stanford Law Review, 28*(1), 61–80.

Paternoster, R. (1983). Race of victim and location of crime: The decision to seek the death penalty in South Carolina. *The Journal of Criminal Law and Criminology, 74*(3), 754–785.

Paternoster, R. (1984). Prosecutorial discretion in requesting the death penalty: A case of victim-based racial discrimination. *Law and Society Review, 19*(3), 437–478.

Paternoster, R. (1987). The deterrent effect of the perceived certainty and severity of punishment: A review of the evidence and issues. *Justice Quarterly, 4*(2), 173–217.

Paternoster, R. (1989). Decisions to participate in and desist from four types of common delinquency: Deterrence and the rational choice perspective. *Law & Society Review, 23*(1), 7–40.

Paternoster, R., Brame, R., Bachman, R., & Sherman, L. W. (1997). Do fair procedures matter? The effect of procedural justice on spouse assault. *Law and Society Review, 31*(1), 163–204.

Pavlo, W. (2015). Government drops obstruction charges against former BP engineer Kurt Mix. *Forbes.* Available at https://www.forbes.com/sites/walterpavlo/2015/11/06/government-drops-obstruction-charges-against-former-bp-engineer-kurt-mix/#6a37fbb20e94 (accessed 6 May 2017).

Payne, B. K. (2014). It's a small world, but I wouldn't want to paint it: Learning from Denmark's experience with electronic monitoring. *Criminology & Public Policy, 13*(3), 381–391.

Pearson, D. A., McDougall, C., Kanaan, M., Torgerson, D. J., & Bowles, R. A. (2016). Evaluation of the Citizenship evidence-based probation supervision program using a stepped wedge cluster randomized controlled trial. *Crime & Delinquency, 62*(7), 899–924.

Pearson, F. S., Lipton, D. S., Cleland, C. M., & Yee, D. S. (2002). The effects of behavioral/cognitive-behavioral programs on recidivism. *Crime and Delinquency, 48*(3), 476–496.

Peck, J. H. (2016). The importance of evaluation and monitoring with the disproportionate minority contact (DMC) mandate. *Race and Justice.* DOI: 10.1177/2153368716675923

Peck, J. H., Leiber, M. J., & Brubaker, S. J. (2014). Gender, race, and juvenile court outcomes: An examination of status offenders. *Youth Violence and Juvenile Justice, 12*(3), 250–267.

Perlin, M. L. (2016). "Merchants and thieves, hungry for power": Prosecutorial misconduct and passive judicial complicity in death penalty trials of defendants with mental disabilities. *Washington and Lee Law Review, 73*(3), 1501–1545.

Petersen, N. (2016). Examining the sources of racial bias in potentially capital cases: A case study of police and prosecutorial discretion. *Race and Justice, 7*(1), 7–34.

Petersilia, J. (1986). Exploring the option of house arrest. *Federal Probation, 50*(2), 50–55.

Petersilia, J. (2004). What works in prisoner reentry—Reviewing and questioning the evidence. *Federal Probation, 68*(2), 4–8.

Petersilia, J. (2011). Community corrections: Probation, parole, and prisoner reentry. In J. Q. Wilson & J. Petersilia (Eds.), *Crime and public policy* (pp. 499–531). Oxford, UK: Oxford University Press.

Petersilia, J., & Turner, S. (1993). *Evaluating intensive supervision probation/parole: Results of a nationwide experiment.* Washington, DC: National Institute of Justice.

Peterson, D., Taylor, T. J., & Esbensen, F. (2004). Gang membership and violent victimization. *Justice Quarterly, 21*(4), 793–815.

Peterson, R. D. (1985). Discriminatory decision making at the legislative level: An analysis of the Comprehensive Drug Abuse Prevention and Control Act of 1970. *Law and Human Behavior, 9*(3), 243.

Peterson, R., & Bailey, W. C. (1991). Felony murder and capital punishment: An examination of the deterrence question. *Criminology, 29*(3), 367–395.

Petrosino, A., Turpin-Petrosino, C. &, Guckenburg, S. (2010). *Formal system processing of juveniles: Effects on delinquency.* Oslo, Norway: The Campbell Collaboration Library of Systematic Reviews.

Petrunik, M. (2003). The hare and the tortoise: Dangerousness and sex offender policy in the United States and Canada. *Canadian Journal of Criminology and Criminal Justice, 45*(1), 43–72.

Pettit, B., & Western, B. (2004). Mass imprisonment and the life course: Race and class inequality in US incarceration. *American Sociological Review, 69*(2), 151–169.

Pew Center on the States. (2009). *One in 31: The long reach of American corrections.* Washington, DC: Pew Charitable Trusts.

Pew Research Center. (2014). *America's new drug policy landscape.* Washington, DC: Pew Research Center.

Pickett, J. T., & Baker, T. (2014). The pragmatic American: Empirical reality or methodological artifact? *Criminology, 52*(2), 195–222.

Pierce, S. (2014). Top 4 states for human trafficking. Human Trafficking Search (3 November 2014). Available at http://www.humantraffickingsearch.net/wp1/top-4-states-for-human-trafficking (accessed 23 May 2017).

Piquero, A. R. (2005). Reliable information and rational policy decisions: Does gun research fit the bill? *Criminology and Public Policy, 4*(4), 779–798.

Piquero, A. R., & Jennings, W. G. (2016). Research note: Justice system–imposed financial penalties increase the likelihood of recidivism in a sample of adolescent offenders. *Youth Violence and Juvenile Justice.* DOI: 10.1177/1541204016669213

Piquero, A. R., Cullen, F. T., Unnever, J. D., Piquero, N. L., & Gordon, J. A. (2010). Never too late: Public optimism about juvenile rehabilitation. *Punishment & Society, 12*(2), 187–207.

Piza, E. L., & O'Hara, B. A. (2014). Saturation foot-patrol in a high violence area: A quasi-experimental evaluation. *Justice Quarterly, 31*(4), 693–718.

Pizarro, J. M., & McGloin, J. M. (2006). Explaining gang homicides in Newark, New Jersey: Collective behavior or social disorganization? *Journal of Criminal Justice, 34*(2), 195–207.

Planty, M., & Truman, J. L. (2013). Firearm violence, 1993–2001 (NCJ 241730). Washington, DC: Bureau of Justice Statistics.

Platt, A. M. (1977). *The child savers: The invention of delinquency.* Chicago: University of Chicago Press.

Plotkin, M. R. (Ed.). (1996). *Under fire: Gun buy-backs, exchanges and amnesty programs.* Washington, DC: Police Executive Research Forum.

Pogarsky, G., & Piquero, A. R. (2003). Can punishment encourage offending? Investigating the "resetting" effect. *Journal of Research in Crime and Delinquency, 40*(1), 95–120.

Pommier, J. H., & Witt, P. A. (1995). Evaluation of an outward bound school plus family training program for juvenile status offender. *Therapeutic Recreation Journal, 29*(2), 86–103.

Poret, S. (2003). Paradoxical effects of law enforcement policies: The case of the illicit drug market. *International Review of Law and Economics, 22,* 465–493.

Poveda, T. G. (2000). American exceptionalism and the death penalty. *Social Justice, 27*(2), 252–267.

Poveda, T. G. (2001). Estimating wrongful convictions. *Justice Quarterly, 18*(3), 689–708.

Pratt, T. C. (2009). *Addicted to incarceration: Corrections policy and the politics of misinformation in the United States.* Thousand Oaks, CA: Sage.

Pratt, T. C. (2009). *Addicted to incarceration.* Thousand Oaks, CA: Sage.

Pratt, T. C., & Cullen, F. T. (2000). The empirical status of Gottfredson and Hirschi's general theory of crime. *Criminology, 38*(3), 931–964.

Pratt, T. C., & Cullen, F. T. (2005). Assessing macro-level predictors and theories of crime: A meta-analysis. *Crime and justice: A review of research, 32,* 373–450. Chicago: University of Chicago Press.

Pratt, T. C., & Gau, J. M. (2009). Social disorganization theory. In J. H. Copes & V. Topalli (Eds.), *Criminology theory: The reader* (pp. 104–112). New York: McGraw-Hill.

Pratt, T. C., Gau, J. M., & Franklin, T. W. (2011). *Key ideas in criminology and criminal justice.* Thousand Oaks, CA: Sage.

Pratt, T. C., Turanovic, J. J., Fox, K. A., & Wright, K. A. (2014). Self-control and victimization: A meta-analysis. *Criminology, 52*(1), 87–116.

Project Greenlight reentry program. *Criminology & Public Policy, 5*(2), 303–338.

Puzzanchera, C. M. (2002). *Juvenile court placement of adjudicated youth, 1989–1998.* Washington, DC: U.S. Department of Justice.

Pyrooz, D. C. (2013). Gangs, criminal offending, and an inconvenient truth: Considerations for gang prevention and intervention in the lives of youth. *Criminology & Public Policy, 12*(3), 427–436.

Pyrooz, D. C., Decker, S. H., & Webb, V. J. (2010). The ties that bind: Desistance from gangs. *Crime & Delinquency, 60*(4), 491–516.

Pyrooz, D. C., Sweeten, G., & Piquero, A. R. (2013). Continuity and change in gang membership and embeddedness. *Journal of Research in Crime and Delinquency, 50*(2), 239–271.

Quinn, J. F., Forsyth, C. J., & Mullen-Quinn, C. (2004). Societal reaction to sex offenders: A review of the origins and results of the myths surrounding their crimes and treatment amenability. *Deviant Behavior, 25*(3), 215–232.

Radalet, M. L., & Bedau, H. A. (1987). Miscarriages of justice in potentially capital cases. *Stanford Law Review, 40*(1), 21–179.

Radelet, M. L., & Akers, R. L. (1996). Deterrence and the death penalty: The views of the experts. *The Journal of Criminal Law and Criminology, 87*(1), 1–16.

Radelet, M. L., Bedau, H. A., & Putnam, C. E. (1992). *In spite of innocence.* Boston, MA: Northeastern University Press.

Rafter, N. H. (1985). *Partial justice: Women in state prisons, 1800–1935.* Boston: Northeastern University Press.

Rakoff, J. S. (2014). The financial crisis: Why have no high-level executives been prosecuted? *The New York Review of Books* (9 January 2014).

Rasmussen, A. (2004). Teen court referral, sentencing, and subsequent recidivism: Two proportional hazards models and a little speculation. *Crime & Delinquency, 50*(4), 615–635.

Rasmussen, N. (2008). America's first amphetamine epidemic 1929–1971. *American Journal of Public Health, 98*(6), 974–985.

Rasmussen Reports. (2012). *7% think U.S. is winning war on drugs.* Available at http://www.rasmussenreports.com/public_content/lifestyle/general_lifestyle/november_2012/7_think_u_s_is_winning_war_on_drugs

Ratcliffe, J. H. (2016). *Intelligence-led policing.* New York: Routledge.

Ratcliffe, J. H., & Guidetti, R. (2008). State police investigative structure and the adoption of intelligence-led policing. *Policing: An International Journal of Police Strategies & Management, 31*(1), 109–128.

Ratcliffe, J. H., Taniguchi, T., Groff, E. R., & Wood, J. D. (2011). The Philadelphia foot patrol experiment: A randomized controlled trial of police patrol effectiveness in violent crime hotspots. *Criminology, 49*(3), 795–831.

Rathgeber, C. (2002). The victimization of women through human trafficking—an aftermath of war? *European Journal of Crime Criminal Law and Criminal Justice, 10*(2–3), 152–163.

Ray, J. V., & Childs, K. (2015). Juvenile diversion. In M. Krohn & J. Lane (Eds.), *The handbook of juvenile delinquency and juvenile justice* (pp. 422–438). West Sussex, UK: John Wiley and Sons, Inc.

Raymond, J. G. (2002, October). The new UN trafficking protocol. *Women's Studies International Forum, 25*(5), 491–502.

Reaves, B. A. (2015). *Local police departments, 2013: Personnel, policies, and practices* (NCJ 248677). Washington, DC: Bureau of Justice Statistics.

Rebovich, D. J. & Kane, J. L. (2002). An eye for an eye in the electronic age: Gauging public attitude toward white collar crime and punishment. *Journal of Economic Crime Management, 1*(2), 1–19.

Redding, R. E. (2008). *Juvenile transfer laws: An effective deterrent to delinquency?* Washington, DC: U.S. Department of Justice.

Redding, R. E. (2016). One size does not fit all: The deterrent effect of transferring juveniles to criminal court. *Criminology & Public Policy, 15*(3), 939–948.

Reisig, M. D., & Parks, R. B. (2004). Can community policing help the truly disadvantaged? *Crime & Delinquency, 50*(2), 139–167.

Reisig, M. D., & Cancino, J. M. (2004). Incivilities in nonmetropolitan communities: The effects of structural constraints, social conditions, and crime. *Journal of Criminal Justice, 32*(1), 15–29.

Reiss, A. J., Jr., & Biderman, A. (1980) *Data sources on white collar law-breaking.* Washington DC: National Institute of Justice.

Reisig, M. D., Bales, W. D., Hay, C., & Wang, X. (2007). The effect of racial inequality on black male recidivism. *Justice Quarterly, 24*(3), 408–434.

Reiss, A. J., Jr., (1983). The policing of organizational life. In M. Punch (Ed.), *Control in the Police Organization* (pp. 78–97). Cambridge, MA: The MIT Press.

Reiss, A. J., Jr. (1984). Selecting strategies of social control over organizational life. In K. Hawkins & J. M. Thomas (Eds.), *Enforcing Regulation* (pp. 23–35). Boston: Kluwer-Nijhoff Publishing.

Reynolds, K. M., Seydlitz, R., & Jenkins, P. (2000). Do juvenile curfew laws work? A time-series analysis of the New Orleans law. *Justice Quarterly, 17*(1), 205–230.

Richards, T. N., Jennings, W. G., Smith, M. D., Sellers, C. S., Fogel, S. J., & Bjerregaard, B. (2016). Explaining the "female victim effect" in capital punishment: An examination of victim sex–specific models of juror sentence decision-making. *Crime & Delinquency, 62*(7), 875–898.

Rios, V. (2011). *Punished: Policing the lives of black and Latino boys.* New York: New York University Press.

Roberts, C. F., Doren, D. M., & Thornton, D. (2002). Dimensions associated with assessments of sex offender recidivism. *Criminal Justice and Behavior, 29*(5), 569–589.

Roberts, S. (2014). *Author of 'broken windows' policing defends his theory.* New York Times. Available at https://www.nytimes.com/2014/08/11/nyregion/author-of-broken-windows-policing-defends-his-theory.html?_r=0 (accessed 18 January 2017).

Robins, C. J., & Rosenthal, M. Z. (2011). Dialectical behavior therapy. In J. D. Herbert & E. M. Forman (Eds.), *Acceptance and mindfulness in cognitive behavior therapy: Understanding and applying the new therapies* (pp. 164–192). Hoboken, NJ: John Wiley & Sons, Inc.

Robinson, P. H., & Williams, T. S. (2017). Mapping American criminal law: An exploration of the diversity among the states: Ch. 5 felony-murder rule. *University of Pennsylvania Law School Faculty Scholarship, 1719*, 1–8.

Robst, J., Armstrong, M., & Dollard, N. (2017). The association between type of out-of-home mental health treatment and juvenile justice recidivism for youth with trauma exposure. *Criminal Behaviour and Mental Health*. DOI: 10.1002/cbm.2024

Romero, M. P., Wintemute, G. J., & Vernick, J. S. (1998). Characteristics of a gun exchange program, and an assessment of potential benefits. *Injury Prevention, 4*(3), 206–210.

Room, R. (2005). Stigma, social inequality and alcohol and drug use. *Drug and Alcohol Review, 24*(2), 143–155.

Rose, D. R., & Clear, T. R. (1998). Incarceration, social capital, and crime: Implications for social disorganization theory. *Criminology, 36*(3), 441–480.

Rosenbaum, D. P. (1987). The theory and research behind neighborhood watch: Is it a sound fear and crime reduction strategy? *Crime & Delinquency, 33*(1), 103–134.

Rosenbaum, D. P., Lurigio, A. J., & Davis, R. C. (1998). *The prevention of crime: Social and situational strategies*. Belmont, CA: Wadsworth.

Rosenbaum, D. P., Yeh, S., & Wilkinson, D. L. (1994). Impact of community policing on police personnel: A quasi-experimental test. *Crime & Delinquency, 40*(3), 331–353.

Rosenbaum, M. (2002). Ecstasy: America's new "reefer madness". *Journal of psychoactive drugs, 34*(2), 137–142.

Rosenfeld, R., Deckard, M. J., & Blackburn, E. (2014). The effects of directed patrol and self-initiated enforcement on firearm violence: A randomized controlled study of hot spot policing. *Criminology, 52*(3), 428–449.

Rosenfeld, R., Fornango, R., & Baumer, E. (2005). Did Ceasefire, Compstat, and Exile reduce homicide? *Criminology & Public Policy, 4*(3), 419–449.

Rosenfeld, R., Fornango, R., & Rengifo, A. F. (2007). The impact of order-maintenance policing on New York City homicide and robbery rates: 1988–2001. *Criminology, 45*(2), 355–384.

Ross, R. R., Fabiano, E. A., & Ewles, C. D. (1988). Reasoning and rehabilitation. *International Journal of Offender Therapy and Comparative Criminology, 32*(1), 29–35.

Ross, R. R., & Hilborn, J. (n.d.). *Reasoning & Rehabilitation 2 Short Version for Youths: Program overview*. Program manual [no publisher].

Ross, R. R., Hilborn, J., & Liddle, P. (n.d.). *Reasoning & Rehabilitation2 Short version for adults: Program overview* Program manual [no publisher].

Roth, A. (2014). Court orders house arrest, and no Internet, for fierce critic of Putin. *The New York Times* (28 February 2014). Available at https://www.nytimes.com/2014/03/01/world/europe/aleksei-navalny.html?_r=0 (accessed 24 February 2017).

Rubin, R. (2016). Many states have legalized medical marijuana, so why does DEA still say it has no therapeutic use? Retrieved from http://www.forbes.com/sites/ritarubin/2016/11/16/many-states-have-legalized-medical-marijuana-so-why-does-dea-still-say-it-has-no-therapeutic-use/#187ae09635a1 (accessed 6 December 2016).

Rudd, R. A., Aleshire, N., Zibbell, J. E., & Matthew Gladden, R. (2016). Increases in drug and opioid overdose deaths—United States, 2000–2014. *American Journal of Transplantation, 16*(4), 1323–1327.

Ruefle, W., & Reynolds, K. M. (1996). Keep them at home: Juvenile curfew ordinances in 200 American cities. *American Journal of Police, 15*, 63–84.

Rushe, D. (2015). BP set to pay largest environmental fine in US history for Gulf oil spill. *The Guardian*. Available at https://www.theguardian.com/environment/2015/jul/02/bp-will-pay-largest-environmental-fine-in-us-history-for-gulf-oil-spill (accessed 6 May 2017).

Ryan, J. P., Abrams, L. S., & Huang, H. (2014). First-time violent juvenile offenders: Probation, placement, and recidivism. *Social Work Research, 38*(1), 7–18.

Salsich, A., & Trone, J. (2013). *From courts to communities: The right response to truancy, running away, and other status offenses*. New York: Vera Institute of Justice.

Salt, J., & Stein, J. (1997). Migration as a business: The case of trafficking. *International Migration, 35*(4), 467–494.

Sample, L. L., & Bray, T. M. (2003). Are sex offenders dangerous? *Criminology & Public Policy, 3*(3), 59–82.

Sample, L. L., & Bray, T. M. (2006). Are sex offenders different? An examination of rearrest patterns. *Criminal Justice Policy Review, 17*(1), 83–102.

Sample, L. L., & Kadleck, C. (2008). Sex offender laws: Legislators' accounts of the need for policy. *Criminal Justice Policy Review, 19*(1), 40–62.

Sample, L. L., Evans, M. K., & Anderson, A. L. (2011). Sex offender community notification laws: Are their effects symbolic or instrumental in nature? *Criminal Justice Policy Review, 22*(1), 27–49.

Sampson, R. J. (1988). Local friendship ties and community attachment in mass society: A multilevel systemic model. *American Sociological Review, 53*(5), 766–779.

Sampson, R. J., & Bartusch, D. J. (1998). Legal cynicism and (subcultural?) tolerance of deviance: The neighborhood context of racial differences. *Law and Society Review, 32*(4), 777–804.

Sampson, R. J., & Groves, W. B. (1989). Community structure and crime: Testing social-disorganization theory. *American Journal of Sociology, 94*(4), 774–802.

Sampson, R. J., & Raudenbush, S. W. (1999). Systematic social observation of public spaces: A new look at disorder in urban neighborhoods. *American Journal of Sociology, 105*(3), 603–651.

Sampson, R. J., & Raudenbush, S. W. (2004). Seeing disorder: Neighborhood stigma and the social construction of "broken windows." *Social Psychology Quarterly, 67*(4), 319–342.

Sampson, R. J., Raudenbush, S. W., & Earls, F. (1997). Neighborhoods and violent crime: A multilevel study of collective efficacy. *Science, 277*(5328), 918–924.

Sandler, J. C., Freeman, N. J., & Socia, K. M. (2008). Does a watched pot boil? A time-series analysis of New York State's sex offender registration and notification law.

Psychology, Public Policy, and Law, 14(4), 284–302.

Sanghera, J. (2016). Unpacking the trafficking discourse. In K. Kempadoo, J. Sanghera, & B. Pattanaik (Eds.), *Trafficking and prostitution reconsidered: New perspectives on migration, sex work, and human rights* (2nd ed; pp. 3–24). Abingdon, Oxon, UK: Routledge.

Sarat, A., & Vidmar, N. (1976). Public opinion, the death penalty, and the Eighth Amendment: Testing the Marshall hypothesis. *Wisconsin Law Review, 1976*, 171–206.

Saunders, P., & Soderlund, G. (2003). Threat or opportunity? Sexuality, gender and the ebb and flow of trafficking as discourse. *Canadian Woman Studies, 22*(3/4), 16–24.

Schaefer Morabito, M. (2010). Understanding community policing as an innovation: Patterns of adoption. *Crime & Delinquency, 56*(4), 564–587.

Scherr, P. L. (1992). The juvenile curfew ordinance: In search of a new standard of review. *Washington University Journal of Urban & Contemporary Law, 41*, 163–192.

Schiavone, S. K. & Jeglic, E. L. (2009). Public perception of sex offender social policies and the impact on sex offenders. *International Journal of Offender Therapy and Comparative Criminology, 53*(6), 679–695.

Schill, M. H., & Wachter, S. M. (1995). The spatial bias of federal housing law and policy: Concentrated poverty in urban America. *University of Pennsylvania Law Review, 143*(5), 1285–1342.

Schnatterly, K. (2003). Increasing firm value through detection and prevention of white-collar crime. *Strategic Management Journal, 24*(7), 587–614.

Schwalbe, C. S., Gearing, R. E., MacKenzie, M. J., Brewer, K. B., & Ibrahim, R. (2012). A meta-analysis of experimental studies of diversion programs for juvenile offenders. *Clinical Psychology Review, 32*(1), 26–33.

Scott, M. S. (2003). Getting the police to take problem-oriented policing seriously. *Crime Prevention Studies, 15*, 49–78.

Seiter, R. P., & Kadela, K. R. (2003). Prisoner reentry: What works, what does not, and what is promising. *Crime & Delinquency, 49*(3), 360–388.

Sepielli, A. (2013). The law's "majestic equality." *Law and Philosophy, 32*(6), 673–700.

Seroczynski, A. D., Evans, W. N., Jobst, A. D., Horvath, L., & Carozza, G. (2016). Reading for Life and adolescent re-arrest: Evaluating a unique juvenile diversion program. *Journal of Policy Analysis and Management, 35*(3), 662–682.

Shakur, S. (2007). *Monster: The autobiography of an LA gang member.* Grove/Atlantic, Inc.

Shapiro, S. P. (1984). *Wayward capitalists: Target of the Securities and Exchange Commission.* New Haven: Yale University Press.

Shapiro, S. P. (1990). Collaring the crime, not the criminal: Reconsidering the concept of white-collar crime. *American Sociological Review, 55*(3), 346–365.

Shaw, A., Lazarus, L., Pantalone, T., LeBlanc, S., Lin, D., Stanley, D., Chepesiuk, C., Patel, S., & Tyndall, M. (2015). Risk environments facing potential users of a supervised injection site in Ottawa, Canada. *Harm Reduction Journal, 12*(1), 49–58.

Shelden, R. G., Horvath, J. A., & Tracy, S. (1989). Do status offenders get worse? Some clarifications on the question of escalation. *Crime & Delinquency, 35*(2), 202–216.

Shepherd, J. M. (2004). Murders of passion, execution delays, and the deterrence of capital punishment. *The Journal of Legal Studies, 33*(2), 283–321.

Sherman, L. (1990). Police crackdowns: Initial and residual deterrence. *Crime and Justice, 12*, 1–48.

Sherman, L. W. (1993). Defiance, deterrence, and irrelevance: A theory of the criminal sanction. *Journal of Research in Crime and Delinquency, 30*(4), 445–473.

Sherman, L. W. (2001). Reducing gun violence: What works, what doesn't, what's promising. *Criminology and Criminal Justice, 1*(1), 11–25.

Sherman, L. W., & Eck, J. E. (2002). Preventing crime at places. In L. W. Sherman, D. P. Farrington, B. C. Welsh, & D.L. MacKenzie (Eds.), *Evidence-based crime prevention* (pp. 295–329). New York: Routledge.

Sherman, L. W., & Rogan, D. P. (1995). Effects of gun seizures on gun violence: "Hot spots" patrol in Kansas City. *Justice Quarterly, 12*(4), 673–693.

Sherman, L. W., & Weisburd, D. (1995). General deterrent effects of police patrol in crime "hot spots": A randomized, controlled trial. *Justice Quarterly, 12*(4), 625–648.

Sherman, L. W., Gartin, P. R., & Buerger, M. E. (1989). Hot spots of predatory crime: Routine activities and the criminology of place. *Criminology, 27*(1), 27–56.

Sherman, L. W., Gottfredson, D. C., MacKenzie, D. L., Eck, J., Reuter, P., & Bushway, S. D. (1998). *Preventing crime: What works, what doesn't, what's promising.* Washington, DC: U.S. Department of Justice.

Shift, A. R., & Wexler, D. B. (1996). Teen court: A therapeutic jurisprudence perspective. *Criminal Law Bulletin, 32*, 342–357.

Shirley, K. E., & Gelman, A. (2015). Hierarchical models for estimating state and demographic trends in U.S. death penalty public opinion. *Journal of the Royal Statistical Society, 178*(1), 1–28.

Shover, N. (1998). White-collar crime. In M. Tonry (Ed.), *The handbook of crime and punishment* (pp. 133–158). Oxford, UK: Oxford University Press.

Shover, N., & Hochstetler, A. (2006). *Choosing white-collar crime.* New York: Cambridge University Press.

Shover, N., & Sroggins, J. (2009). Organizational crime. In M. Tonry (Ed.), *The Oxford handbook of crime and public policy* (pp. 273–303). Oxford, UK: Oxford University Press.

Sickmund, M., Sladky, A., & Kang, W. (2015). *Easy access to juvenile court statistics: 1985–2013.* Available at http://www.ojjdp.gov/ojstatbb/ezajcs/ (accessed 24 March 2017).

Sidak, J. G. (2015). Two economic rationales for felony murder. *Cornell Law Review Online, 101*, 51–63.

Simon, D. R. (2006). *Elite deviance* (8th ed.). Boston: Pearson.

Simon, L. M. J. (2000). An examination of the assumptions of specialization, mental disorder, and dangerousness in sex offenders. *Behavioral Sciences and the Law, 18*, 275–308.

Skeem, J. L., Manchak, S., & Peterson, J. K. (2011). Correctional policy for offenders with mental illness: Creating a new paradigm for recidivism reduction. *Law and Human Behavior, 35*(2), 110–126.

Skogan, W. (1986). Fear of crime and neighborhood change. *Crime and Justice, 8*, 203–229.

Skogan, W. G. (1990). *Disorder and decline: Crime and the spiral of decay in American neighborhoods.* Berkeley, CA: University of California Press.

Skogan, W. G. (1990). *Disorder and decline.* Berkeley, CA: University of California Press.

Skogan, W. G. (2005). Citizen satisfaction with police encounters. *Police Quarterly, 8*(3), 298–321.

Skogan, W. G. (2006). *Community policing in Chicago: A tale of three cities.* Oxford, UK: Oxford University Press.

Skogan, W. G., & Hartnett, S. M. (1997). *Community policing, Chicago style.* Oxford, UK: Oxford University Press.

Skogan, W. G., & Hartnett, S. M. (1997). *Community policing, Chicago style.* New York: Oxford University Press.

Smith, P. (2003). Narrating the guillotine: Punishment technology as myth and symbol. *Theory, Culture, & Society, 20*(5), 27–51.

Smith-Spark, L. (2016). Mediterranean migrant deaths reach record level in 2016 (26 October 2016). Available at http://www.cnn.com/2016/10/26/world/mediterranean-refugees-2016-record-migrant-deaths/ (accessed 27 January 2017).

Snajdr, E. (2013). Beneath the master narrative: Human trafficking, myths of sexual slavery and ethnographic realities. *Dialectical Anthropology, 37*(2), 229–256.

Snell, T. (2013). *Prisoners executed under civil authority in the United States, by year, region, and jurisdiction, 1977–2013* (data set). Washington, DC: U.S. Department of Justice.

Snell, T. (2014). *Capital punishment, 2013—Statistical tables.* Washington, DC: U.S. Department of Justice.

Socia, K. M. (2011). The policy implications of residence restrictions on sex offender housing in upstate NY. *Criminology & Public Policy, 10*(2), 351–389.

Sorensen, J., & Wallace, D. H. (1999). Prosecutorial discretion in seeking death: An analysis of racial disparity in the pretrial stages of case processing in a Midwestern county. *Justice Quarterly, 16*(3), 559–578.

Sorensen, J., Hope, R., & Stemen, D. (2003). Racial disproportionality in state prison admissions: Can regional variation be explained by differential arrest rates? *Journal of Criminal Justice, 31*(1), 73–84.

Sorg, E. T., Haberman, C. P., Ratcliffe, J. H., & Groff, E. R. (2013). Foot patrol in violent crime hot spots: The longitudinal impact of deterrence and posttreatment effects of displacement. *Criminology, 51*(1), 65–102.

Soss, J., Langbein, L., & Metelko, A. R. (2003). Why do white Americans support the death penalty? *Journal of Politics, 65*(2), 397–421.

Spelman, W. (2000). The limited importance of prison expansion. In A. Blumstein & J. Wallman (Eds.), *The crime drop in America* (pp. 123–125). Cambridge, UK: Cambridge University Press.

Sridharan, S., Greenfield, L., & Blakley, B. (2004). A study of prosecutorial certification practice in Virginia. *Criminology & Public Policy, 3*(4), 605–632.

Stack, S. (2000). Support for the death penalty: A gender-specific model. *Sex Roles, 43*(3–4), 163–179.

Stauffer, A. R., Smith, M. D., Cochran, J. K., Fogel, S. J., & Bjerregaard, B. (2006). The interaction between victim race and gender on sentencing outcomes in capital murder trials a further exploration. *Homicide Studies, 10*(2), 98–117.

Steadman, H. J., Cocozza, J. J., & Melick, M. E. (1978). Explaining the increased arrest rate among mental patients: The changing clientele of state hospitals. *American Journal of Psychiatry, 135*, 816–820.

Stein, R. E., Hurlburt, M. S., Heneghan, A. M., Zhang, J., Rolls-Reutz, J., Landsverk, J., & Horwitz, S. M. (2014). Health status and type of out-of-home placement: informal kinship care in an investigated sample. *Academic Pediatrics, 14*(6), 559–564.

Steiner, B., & Butler, H. D. (2013). Why didn't they work? Thoughts on the application of New Jersey day reporting centers. *Criminology & Public Policy, 12*(1), 153–162.

Steiner, B., & Wright, E. (2006). Assessing the relative effects of state direct file waiver laws on violent juvenile crime: Deterrence or irrelevance? *The Journal of Criminal Law and Criminology, 96*(4), 1451–1477.

Stempel, J. (2016). No prison terms for Gulf spill as final defendant gets probation. *Rueters.* Available at http://www.reuters.com/article/us-bp-spill-sentencing/no-prison-terms-for-gulf-spill-as-final-defendant-gets-probation-idUSKCN0X3241 (accessed 6 May 2017).

Stewart, G. (1998). Black codes and broken windows: The legacy of racial hegemony in anti-gang civil injunctions. *The Yale Law Journal, 107*(7), 2249–2279.

Stewart, E. A., Schreck, C. J., & Simons, R. L. (2006). "I ain't gonna let no one disrespect me": Does the code of the street reduce or increase violent victimization among African American adolescents? *Journal of Research in Crime and Delinquency, 43*(4), 427–458.

Stewart, E. A., & Simons, R. L. (2010). Race, code of the street, and violent delinquency: A multilevel investigation of neighborhood street culture and individual norms of violence. *Criminology, 48*(2), 569–605.

Stoddard, C., Steiner, B., Rohrbach, J., Hemmens, C., & Bennett, K. (2014). All the way home: Assessing the constitutionality of juvenile curfew laws. *American Journal of Criminal Law, 42*, 177–211.

Stokes, R., Donahue, N., Caron, D., & Greene, J. R. (1996). *Safe travel to and from school: A problem-oriented policing approach.* Philadelphia: Temple University Center for Public Policy.

Stolzenberg, L., & D'Alessio, S. J. (2008). Co-offending and the age-crime curve. *Journal of Research in Crime and Delinquency, 45*(1), 65–86.

Sukhodolsky, D. G., Kassinove, H., & Gorman, B. S. (2004). Cognitive-behavioral therapy for anger in children and adolescents: A meta-analysis. *Aggression and Violent Behavior, 9*(3), 247–269.

Sullivan, C. J., Childs, K. K., & O'Connell, D. (2010). Adolescent risk behavior subgroups: An empirical assessment. *Journal of Youth and Adolescence, 39*(5), 541–562.

Sullivan, M. L. (2006). Are "gang" studies dangerous? Youth violence, local context, and the problem of reification. In J. F. Short, Jr. & L. A. Hughes (Eds.), *Studying youth gangs* (pp. 15–35). Oxford, UK: AltaMira Press.

Sundt, J., Salisbury, E. J., & Harmon, M. G. (2016). Is downsizing prisons dangerous? The effect of California's Realignment Act on public safety. *Criminology & Public Policy, 15*(2), 315–341.

Sutherland, E. H. (1940). White-collar criminality. *American Sociological Review, 5*(1), 1–12.

Sutherland, E. H. (1941). Crime and business. *The Annals of the American Academy of Political and Social Science, 217*(1), 112–118.

Sutherland, E. H. (1945). Is "white collar crime" crime? *American Sociological Review, 10*(2), 132–139.

Suttles, G. D. (1968). *The social order of the slum: Ethnicity and territory in the inner city.* Chicago, IL: The University of Chicago Press.

Swan, R. S., & Bates, K. A. (2017). Loosening the ties that bind: The hidden harms of civil gang injunctions in San Diego County. *Contemporary Justice Review, 20*(1), 132–153.

Tabachnick, J., & Klein, A. (2011). *A reasoned approach: Reshaping sex offender policy to prevent child sexual abuse.* Beaverton, OR: Association for the Treatment of Sexual Abusers.

Taran, P. A. (2000). Human rights of migrants: Challenges of the new decade. *International Migration, 38*(6), 7–47.

Tarbert, H. (2010). Financial regulatory reform: An overview of the Dodd-Frank Wall Street Reform and Consumer Protection Act. Available at https://www.google.com/url?sa=t&rct=j&q=&esrc=s&source=web&cd=2&cad=rja&uact=8&ved=0ahUKEwj3pM2vsJbOAh

VCQCYKHc3-CdEQFgglMAE&url=http%3A%2F%2Ffinancial-reform.weil.com%2Fwp-content%2Fuploads%2F2011%2F05%2F9357-FRROverview_v1.pdf&usg=AFQjCNEIcYMG67vtRP4qV1cEqsTOm2BVIA&sig2=hvh2BYq4qvzouvcWSK4fAg (accessed 8 May 2017).

Taxman, F. S., & Piquero, A. (1998). On preventing drunk driving recidivism: An examination of rehabilitation and punishment approaches. *Journal of Criminal Justice, 26*(2), 129–143.

Taxy, S., Samuels, J., & Adams, W. (2015). Drug offenders in federal prison: Estimates of characteristics based on linked data (NCJ 248648). Washington, DC: U.S. Department of Justice.

Taylor, B., Koper, C. S., & Woods, D. J. (2011). A randomized controlled trial of different policing strategies at hot spots of violent crime. *Journal of Experimental Criminology, 7*(2), 149–181.

Taylor, R. B. (2001). *Breaking away from broken windows: Baltimore neighborhoods and the nationwide fight against crime, grime, fear, and decline.* Boulder, CO: Westview Press.

Taylor, T. J., Peterson, D., Esbensen, F., & Freng, A. (2007). Gang membership as a risk factor for adolescent violent victimization. *Journal of Research in Crime and Delinquency, 44*(4), 351–380.

Terrill, W., & Reisig, M. D. (2003). Neighborhood context and police use of force. *Journal of Research in Crime and Delinquency, 40*(3), 291–321.

Tewksbury, R. (2005). Collateral consequences of sex offender registration. *Journal of Contemporary Criminal Justice, 21*(1), 67–81.

Tewksbury, R., & Lees, M. (2006). Perceptions of sex offender registration: Collateral consequences and community experiences. *Sociological Spectrum, 26*, 309–334.

Tewksbury, R., & Jennings, W. G. (2010). Assessing the impact of sex offender registration and community notification on sex-offending trajectories. *Criminal Justice and Behavior, 37*(5), 570–582.

Thacher, D. (2014). Order maintenance policing. In M. Reisig & R. Kane (Eds.), *The Oxford handbook of police and policing* (pp. 122–124). Oxford, UK: Oxford University Press.

Thibaut, J., & Walker, L. (1978). A theory of procedure. *California Law Review, 66*(3), 541–566.

Thielo, A. J., Cullen, F. T., Cohen, D. M., & Chouhy, C. (2015). Rehabilitation in a red state. *Criminology & Public Policy, 15*(1), 1–34.

Thompson, A. C. (2002). Courting disorder: Some thoughts on community courts. *Washington University Journal of Law & Policy, 10*, 63–103.

Thornberry, T. P. (1998). Membership in youth gangs and involvement in serious and violent offending. In R. Loeber & D. P. Farrington (Eds.), *Serious & violent juvenile offenders: Risk factors and successful interventions* (pp. 147–166). Thousand Oaks, CA: Sage Publications.

Thornberry, T. P., Huizinga, D., & Loeber, R. (2004). The causes and correlates studies: Findings and policy implications. *Juvenile Justice, 9*(1), 3–19.

Thornberry, T. P., Krohn, M. D., Lizotte, A. J., & Chard-Wierschem, D. (1993). The role of juvenile gangs in facilitating delinquent behavior. *Journal of Research in Crime and Delinquency, 30*(1), 55–87.

Thrasher, F. M. (1927). *The gang: A study of 1313 gangs in Chicago.* Chicago, IL: Chicago University Press.

Thurman, Q. C., Giacomazzi, A., & Bogen, P. (1993). Research note: Cops, kids, and community policing—An assessment of a community policing demonstration project. *Crime & Delinquency, 39*(4), 554–564.

Titus, J. J. (2005). Juvenile transfers as ritual sacrifice: Legally constructing the child scapegoat. *Youth Violence and Juvenile Justice, 3*(2), 116–132.

Tobler, N. S., Roona, M. R., Ochshorn, P., Marshall, D. G., Streke, A. V., & Stackpole, K. M. (2000). School-based adolescent drug prevention programs: 1998 meta-analysis. *Journal of Primary Prevention, 20*(4), 275–336.

Tong, L. S. J., & Farrington, D. P. (2008). Effectiveness of "Reasoning and Rehabilitation" in reducing offending. *Psicothema, 20*, 20–28.

Tonry, M. (1995). *Malign neglect: Race, crime, and punishment in America*. New York: Oxford University Press.

Tonry, M. (1999). Why are U.S. incarceration rates so high? *Crime & Delinquency, 45*(4), 419–437.

Tonry, M. (2000). Reconsidering indeterminate and structured sentencing. *Alternatives to Incarceration, 6*(3), 17–21.

Tonry, M. (2008). Learning from the limitations of deterrence research. *Crime and justice: A review of research, 37*, 279-311. Chicago: University of Chicago Press.

Torbet, P., Gable, R., Montgomery, I., & Hurst, H. (1996). *State responses to serious & violent juvenile crime*. Washington, DC: Office of Juvenile Justice and Delinquency Prevention.

Travis, J. (1996). Forward. In D. L. MacKenzie & E. E. Hebert (Eds.), *Correctional boot camps: A tough intermediate sanction* (pp. v–vi). Washington, DC: U.S. Department of Justice.

Travis, J., Western, B., & Redburn, F. S. (2014). *The growth of incarceration in the United States: Exploring causes and consequences*. Washington, DC: The National Academies Press.

Trojanowicz, R. C., & Baldwin, R. (1982). *An evaluation of the neighborhood foot patrol program in Flint, Michigan*. East Lansing, MI: Michigan State University.

Trojanowicz, R. C., & Banas, D. W. (1985). *Job satisfaction: A comparison of foot patrol versus motor patrol officers*. East Lansing, MI: Michigan State University.

Truman, J. T., & Langton, L., (2014). *Criminal victimization, 2013* (NCJ 247648). Washington, DC: Bureau of Justice Statistics.

Tsemberis, S., Gulcur, L., & Nakae, M. (2004). Housing first, consumer choice, and harm reduction for homeless individuals with a dual diagnosis. *American Journal of Public Health, 94*(4), 651–656.

Tushnet, M., & Yackle, L. (1997). Symbolic statutes and real laws: The pathologies of the Antiterrorism and Effective Death Penalty Act and the Prison Litigation Reform Act. *Duke Law Journal, 47*(1), 1–86.

Tyler, T. R. (2005). Policing in black and white: Ethnic group differences in trust and confidence in the police. *Police Quarterly, 8*(3), 322–342.

Tyler, T. R. (2006). *Why people obey the law.* Princeton, NJ: Princeton University Press.

Tyler, T. R., & Huo, Y. (2002). *Trust in the law: Encouraging public cooperation with the police and courts*. New York, NY: Russell Sage Foundation.

U.S. Citizenship and Immigration Services (n.d.). Questions and answers: Victims of human trafficking, T nonimmigrant status. Available at https://www.uscis.gov/humanitarian/ victims-human-trafficking-other-crimes/ victims-human-trafficking-t-nonimmigrant-status/questions-and-answers-victims-human-trafficking-t-nonimmigrant-status-0 (accessed 11 February 2017).

U.S. Department of Justice (n.d.). *FY 2015 budget request*. Washington, DC: U.S. Department of Justice.

U.S. Department of Justice (n.d.). Prisoners and prisoner reentry. Available at https://www.justice.gov/archive/fbci/progmenu_reentry.html

U.S. Department of State. (2010). *Trafficking in Persons Report, 2010*. Washington, DC: Department of State.

U.S. Department of State. (2016). *Trafficking in Persons Report—June 2016*. Washington, DC: U.S. Department of State.

Unah, I. (2009). Choosing those who will die: The effect of race, gender, and law in prosecutorial decision to seek the death penalty in Durham County, North Carolina. *Michigan Journal of Race & Law, 15*(1), 135–179.

United Nations Refugee Agency. (n.d.). Definitions. Available at http://www.unrefugees.org/what-is-a-refugee/ (accessed 11 February 2017).

United Nations. (1949). *Convention for the suppression of the traffic in persons and of the exploitation of the prostitution of others*. New York: UN Office of the High Commissioner for Human Rights.

United Nations. (1989). *Convention on the rights of the child*. New York: UN Office of the High Commissioner for Human Rights.

United Nations. (2000). *Protocol to prevent, suppress and punish trafficking in persons, especially women and children, supplementing the United Nations Convention against Transnational Organized Crime.* New York: UN Office of the High Commissioner for Human Rights.

United Nations. (2002). *Recommended principles and guidelines on human rights and human trafficking.* New York: UN Office of the High Commissioner for Human Rights.

van Eijk, G. (2016). Socioeconomic marginality in sentencing: The built-in bias in risk assessment tools and the reproduction of social inequality. *Punishment & Society, 19*(4), 463–481.

van Mastrigt, S. B., & Farrington, D. P. (2009). Co-offending, age, gender and crime type: Implications for criminal justice policy. *British Journal of Criminology, 49,* 552–573.

van Mastrigt, S. B., & Farrington, D. P. (2009). Co-offending, age, gender and crime type: Implications for criminal justice policy. *British Journal of Criminology, 49,* 552–573.

Van Ness, D. W., & Strong, K. H. (2014). *Restoring justice: An introduction to restorative justice* (5th ed.). New York: Routledge.

Van Zee, A. (2009). The promotion and marketing of OxyContin: Commercial triumph, public health tragedy. *American Journal of Public Health, 99,* 221–227.

Vásquez, B. E., Maddan, S., & Walker, J. T. (2008). The influence of sex offender registration and notification laws in the United States: A time-series analysis. *Crime & Delinquency, 54*(2), 175–192.

Vélez, M. B. (2001). The role of public social control in urban neighborhoods: A multilevel analysis of victimization risk. *Criminology, 39*(4), 837–864.

Vera Sanchez, C. G., & Gau, J. M. (2015). Racially neutral policing?: Puerto Rican and Mexican young adults' experiences with order maintenance policing. *Journal of Qualitative Criminology and Criminal Justice, 3*(2), 166–194.

Vining, R. L., Jr., Wilhelm, T., & Collens, J. D. (2015). A market-based model of state supreme court news: Lessons from capital cases. *State Politics & Policy Quarterly, 15*(1), 3–23.

Visher, C. A. (1986). The Rand inmate survey: A reanalysis. In A. Blumstein, J. Cohen, J. A. Roth, & C. A. Visher (Eds.), *Criminal careers and "career criminals"* (vol. 2; pp. 211–291). Washington, DC: National Academy Press.

Vizzard, W. J. (2015). The current and future state of gun policy in the United States. *The Journal of Criminal Law & Criminology, 104,* 879–904.

Volkow, N. D. (2014). America's addiction to opioids: Heroin and prescription drug abuse. Retrieved from https://www.drugabuse.gov/about-nida/legislative-activities/testimony-to-congress/2016/americas-addiction-to-opioids-heroin-prescription-drug-abuse (Accessed 6 December 2016).

von Hirsch, A. (1976). *Doing justice: The choice of punishments.* New York: Farrar, Strauss, and Giroux.

von Hirsch, A. (1982). Desert and white-collar criminality: A response to Dr. Braithwaite. *The Journal of Criminal Law and Criminology, 73*(3), 1164–1175.

von Hirsch, A. (1984). The ethics of selective incapacitation: Observations on the contemporary debate. *Crime & Delinquency, 30,* 175–194.

von Hirsch, A. (1986). *Past or future crimes: Deservedness and dangerousness in the sentencing of criminals.* Manchester, UK: Manchester University Press.

von Hirsch, A. (1998). Penal theories. In M. Tonry (Ed.), *The handbook of crime and punishment* (pp. 659–682). Oxford: Oxford University Press.

von Hirsch, A. (2011). Proportionate sentences: A desert perspective. In M. Tonry (Ed.), *Why punish? How much? A reader on punishment* (pp. 207–238). Oxford: Oxford University Press.

von Hirsch, A., & Ashworth, A. (2005). *Proportionate sentencing: Exploring the principles.* Oxford: Oxford University Press.

Wagner, F. A., & Anthony, J. C. (2002). From first drug use to drug dependence: developmental periods of risk for dependence upon marijuana, cocaine, and alcohol. *Neuropsychopharmacology, 26*(4), 479–488.

Wagner, P. (2014). *Tracking state prison growth in 50 states*. The Prison Policy Initiative. Available at https://www.prisonpolicy.org/reports/overtime.html (accessed 4 May 2017).

Wakefield, S., & Uggen, C. (2010). Incarceration and stratification. *Annual Review of Sociology, 36*, 387–406.

Walker, S. (1984). "Broken Windows" and fractured history: The use and misuse of history in recent police patrol analysis. *Justice Quarterly, 1*(1), 75–90.

Walker, S. (1993). *Taming the system: The control of discretion in criminal justice 1950–1990*. New York: Oxford University Press.

Walker, S. (2001). *Sense and nonsense about crime and drugs: A policy guide* (5th ed.). Australia: Wadsworth.

Wallace, C., Mullen, P. E., & Burgess, P. (2004). Criminal offending in schizophrenia over a 25-year period marked by deinstitutionalization and increasing prevalence of comorbid substance- use disorders. *American Journal of Psychiatry, 161*(4), 716–727.

Wallace, L. N. (2016). Baltimore's juvenile curfew: Evaluating effectiveness. *Criminal Justice Review.* DOI: 10.1177/0734016815626971

Wareham, J., Dembo, R., Poythress, N. G., Childs, K., & Schmeidler, J. (2009). A latent class factor approach to identifying subtypes of juvenile diversion youths based on psychopathic features. *Behavioral Sciences & the Law, 27*(1), 71–95.

Warner, B. D., & Rountree, P. W. (1997). Local social ties in a community and crime model: Questioning the systemic nature of informal social control. *Social Problems, 44*(4), 520–536.

Weatherburn, D., & Moffatt, S. (2011). The specific deterrent effect of higher fines on drink-driving offenders. *British Journal of Criminology, 51*(5), 789–803.

Weber, M. (1978). *Economy and society: An outline of interpretive sociology*. Berkeley, CA: University of California Press.

Weinrath, M., Donatelli, G., & Murchison, M. J. (2016). Mentorship: A missing piece to manage juvenile intensive supervision programs and youth gangs? *Canadian Journal of Criminology and Criminal Justice, 58*(3), 291–321.

Weisburd, D., & Braga, A. A. (2006). Introduction: Understanding police innovations. In D. Weisburd & A. A. Braga (Eds.), *Police innovation: Contrasting perspectives* (pp. 1–23). Cambridge, UK: Cambridge University Press.

Weisburd, D., & Eck, J. E. (2004). What can police do to reduce crime, disorder, and fear? The Annals of the American Academy of Political and Social Science, 593(1), 42–65. .

Weisburd, D., & Green, L. (1993). Policing drug hot spots: The Jersey City drug market analysis experiment. *Justice Quarterly, 12*(4), 711–735.

Weisburd, D., Mastrofski, S. D., Greenspan, R., & Willis, J. J. (2012). *Growth of Compstat in American policing*. Washington, DC: National Institute of Justice.

Weisburd, D., Mastrofski, S. D., McNally, A., Greenspan, R., & Willis, J. J. (2003). Reforming to preserve: Compstat and strategic problem solving in American policing. *Criminology & Public Policy, 2*(3), 421–456.

Weisburd, D., Telep, C. W., & Lawton, B. A. (2014). Could innovations in policing have contributed to the New York City crime drop even in a period of declining police strength?: The case of stop, question and frisk as a hot spots policing strategy. *Justice Quarterly, 31*(1), 129–153.

Weisburd, D., Telep, C. W., Hinkle, J. C., & Eck, J. E. (2010). Is problem-oriented policing effective in reducing crime and disorder? Findings from a Campbell systematic review. *Criminology & Public Policy, 9*(1), 139–172.

Weisburd, D., Waring, E., & Chayet, E. (1995). Specific deterrence in a sample of offenders convicted of white collar crimes. *Criminology, 33*(4), 587–607.

Weisburd, D., Waring, E., & Chayet, E. (2001). *White-collar crime and criminal careers*. Cambridge, UK: Cambridge University Press.

Weisburd, D., Wooditch, A., Weisburd, S., & Yang, S. M. (2016). Do stop, question, and frisk practices deter crime? *Criminology & Public Policy, 15*(1), 31–56.

Weisel, D. L., Painter, E., & Kusler, C. R. (1997). The police response to gangs: Case studies of five cities. Washington, D.C.: Police Executive Research Forum.

Weitzer, R. (2011). Sex trafficking and the sex industry: The need for evidence-based theory and legislation. *Journal of Criminal Law and Criminology, 101*(4), 1337–1369.

Weitzer, R. (2013). Rethinking human trafficking. *Dialectical Anthropology, 37*(2), 309–312.

Weitzer, R. (2014). New directions in research on human trafficking. *Annals of the American Academy of Political and Social Science, 653*, 6–24.

Weitzer, R. (2015). Human trafficking and contemporary slavery. *Annual Review of Sociology, 41*, 223–242.

Weitzer, R., & Tuch, S. A. (2002). Perceptions of racial profiling: Race, class, and personal experience. *Criminology, 40*(2), 435–456.

Weitzer, R., & Tuch, S. A. (2005). Racially biased policing: Determinants of citizen perceptions. *Social Forces, 83*(3), 1009–1030.

Wells, G. L., Small, M., Penrod, S., Malpass, R. S., Fulero, S. M., & Brimacombe, C. E. (1998). Eyewitness identification procedures: Recommendations for lineups and photospreads. *Law and Human behavior, 22*(6), 603.

Wenzel, M., Okimoto, T. G., Feather, N. T., & Platow, M. J. (2008). Retributive and restorative justice. *Law and Human Behavior, 32*(5), 375–389.

Werb, D., Rowell, G., Guyatt, G., Kerr, T., Montaner, J., & Wood, E. (2011). Effect of drug law enforcement on drug market violence: A systematic review. *International Journal of Drug Policy, 22*(2), 87–94.

Wessel, D. (2010). *In Fed we trust: Ben Bernanke's war on the great panic.* New York, NY: Crown Business.

West, E. M. (2010). *Court findings of ineffective assistance of counsel claims in post-conviction appeals among the first 255 DNA exoneration cases.* New York: The Innocence Project.

Western, B. (2002). The impact of incarceration on wage mobility and inequality. *American Sociological Review, 67*(4), 526–546.

White, D., & Pitts, M. (1998). Educating young people about drugs: a systematic review. *Addiction, 93*(10), 1475–1487.

Whyte, W. F. (1943). *Street corner society: The social structure of an Italian slum.* Chicago: The University of Chicago Press.

Wilde, L. L. (1992). Criminal choice, nonmonetary sanctions and marginal deterrence: A normative analysis. *International Review of Law and Economics, 12*(3), 333–344.

Williams, K. (2000). The Antiterrorism and Effective Death Penalty Act: What's wrong with it and how to fix it. *Connecticut Law Review, 33*, 919–944.

Williams, V. (2016). 1994 crime bill haunts Clinton and Sanders as criminal justice reform rises to top in Democratic contest. *The Washington Post* (12 February 2016). Available at https://www.washingtonpost.com/news/post-politics/wp/2016/02/12/1994-crime-bill-haunts-clinton-and-sanders-as-criminal-justice-reform-rises-to-top-in-democratic-contest/?utm_term=.27c4fea487b0 (accessed 5 May 2017).

Williams, M. R., Demuth, S., & Holcomb, J. E. (2007). Understanding the influence of victim gender in death penalty cases: The importance of victim race, sex-related victimization, and jury decision-making. *Criminology, 45*, 865–892.

Williams, M. R., & Holcomb, J. E. (2004). The interactive effects of victim race and gender on death sentence disparity findings. *Homicide Studies, 8*, 350–376.

Williams, H. & Murphy, P. V. (1990). *The evolving strategy of police: A minority view.* Washington, DC: U.S. Department of Justice.

Willingham, A. J., & Ellis, R. (2016). *8 controversial executions that sparked lethal injection debates.* CNN.com (9 December 2016). Available at http://www.cnn.com/2016/12/09/health/controversial-executions-us-trnd/ (accessed 15 March 2017).

Willis, J. J., Mastrofski, S. D., & Weisburd, D. (2007). Making sense of COMPSTAT: A theory-based analysis of organizational change in three police departments. *Law & Society Review, 41*(1), 147–188.

Wilson, J. Q. (1968). *Varieties of police behavior.* Cambridge, MA: Harvard University.

Wilson, J. Q. (1983). *Thinking about crime* (rev. ed.). New York: Vintage Books.

Wilson, W. J. (1987). *The truly disadvantaged: The inner city, the underclass, and public policy.* Chicag: University of Chicago Press.

Wilson, D. G. & Bennett, S. F. (1994). Officers' response to community policing: Variations on a theme. *Crime & Delinquency, 40*(3), 354–370.

Wilson, J. A., & Davis, R. C. (2006). Good intentions meet hard realities: An evaluation of the

Wilson, J. Q., & Kelling, G. L. (March 1982). The police and neighborhood safety: Broken windows. *Atlantic Monthly, 127*(2), 29–38.

Wilson, S. J., & Lipsey, M. W. (2007). School-based interventions for aggressive and disruptive behavior: Update of a meta-analysis. *American Journal of Preventive Medicine, 33*(2S), S130–S143.

Wilson, D. B., Bouffard, L. A., & MacKenzie, D. L. (2005). A quantitative review of structured, group-oriented, cognitive-behavioral programs for offenders. *Criminal Justice and Behavior, 32*(2), 172–204.

Wilson, H. A., & Hoge, R. D. (2013). The effect of youth diversion programs on recidivism: A meta-analytic review. *Criminal Justice and Behavior, 40*(5), 497–518.

Wilson, D. B., MacKenzie, D. L., & Mitchell, F. N. (2005). Effects of correctional boot camps on offending. *Campbell Systematic Reviews, 1*(6), 1–45.

Wilson, D. B., Mitchell, O., & MacKenzie, D. L. (2006). A systematic review of drug court effects on recidivism. *Journal of Experimental Criminology, 2*, 459–487.

Wilson, D. B., Olaghere, A., & Gill, C. (2016). Juvenile curfew effects on criminal behavior and victimization: A Campbell Collaboration systematic review. *Journal of Experimental Criminology, 12*(2), 167–186.

Wilson, K.M., Torok, M. R., Wei, B., Wang, L., Robinson, M., Sosnoff, C. S., & Blount, B. C. (2016). Detecting biomarkers of secondhand marijuana smoke in young children. *Pediatric Research.* DOI: 10.1038/pr.2016.261

Wintemute, G. J., Drake, C. M., Beaumont, J. J., Wright, M. A., & Parham, C. A. (1998). Prior misdemeanor convictions as a risk factor for later violent and firearm-related criminal activity among authorized purchasers of handguns. *JAMA, 280*(24), 2083–2087.

Wolf, C. R., & Rosen, J. A. (2015). Missing the mark: Gun control is not the cure for what ails the U.S. mental health system. *The Journal of Criminal Law & Criminology, 104*, 851–878.

Wood, J., Sorg, E. T., Groff, E. R., Ratcliffe, J. H., & Taylor, C. J. (2014). Cops as treatment providers: Realities and ironies of police work in a foot patrol experiment. *Policing and Society: An International Journal of Research and Policy, 24*(3), 36–379.

Wood, P. B. & Brunson, R. K. (2011). Geographies of resilient social networks: The role of African American barbershops. *Urban Geography, 32*(2), 228–243.

Wood, W. R. (2015). Soliciting community involvement and support for restorative justice through community service. *Criminal Justice Policy Review, 26*(2), 131–155.

Worrall, J. L. (2016). Smart policing in Frisco, Texas: Geographic and temporal displacement in a micro place. *Policing: An International Journal of Police Strategies & Management, 39*(1), 36–51.

Wortley, R. K., & Smallbone, S. (2006). Applying situational principles to sexual offending against children. In R. Wortley & S. Smallbone (Eds.), *Situational prevention of child sexual abuse* (pp. 7–35). Monsey, NY: Criminal Justice Press.

Wright, D. T., & Mays, G. L. (1998). Correctional boot camps, attitudes, and recidivism: The Oklahoma experience. *Journal of Offender Rehabilitation, 28*(1-2), 71–87.

Wright, K. A., Pratt, T. C., Lowenkamp, C. T., & Latessa, E. J. (2012). The importance of ecological context for correctional rehabilitation programs: Understanding the micro-and macro-level dimensions of successful offender treatment. *Justice Quarterly, 29*(6), 775–798.

Wright, M. A., Wintemute, G. J., & Rivara, F. P. (1999). Effectiveness of denial of handgun purchase to persons believed to be at high risk for firearm violence. *American Journal of Public Health, 89*(1), 88–90.

Wright, R. G. (2008). Sex offender post-incarceration sanctions: Are there any limits? *New England Journal on Criminal and Civil Confinement, 34*, 17–50.

Young, W. (1979). *Community service orders: The development and use of a new penal measure.* London: Heinemann.

Zalman, M. (2012). Qualitatively estimating the incidence of wrongful convictions. *Criminal Law Bulletin, 48*(2), 221–279.

Zandbergen, P. A., & Hart, T. C. (2006). Reducing housing options for convicted sex offenders: Investigating the impact of residency restriction laws using GIS. *Justice Research and Policy, 8*(2), 1–24.

Zandbergen, P. A., Levenson, J. S., & Hart, T. C. (2010). Residential proximity to schools and daycares: An empirical analysis of sex offense recidivism. *Criminal Justice and Behavior, 37*(5), 482–502.

Zane, S. N., Welsh, B. C., & Drakulich, K. M. (2016). Assessing the impact of race on the juvenile waiver decision: A systematic review and meta-analysis. *Journal of Criminal Justice, 46*, 106–117.

Zedlewski, E. (2010). *Alternatives to custodial supervision: The day fine.* Washington, DC: U.S. Department of Justice.

Zevitz, R. G. (2006). Sex offender community notification: Its role in recidivism and offender reintegration. *Criminal Justice Studies, 19*(2), 193–208.

Zgoba, K. M. (2011). Residence restriction buffer zones and the banishment of sex offenders: Have we gone one step too far? *Criminology & Public Policy, 10*(2), 391–399.

Zgoba, K. M., Levenson, J., & McKee, T. (2009). Examining the impact of sex offender residence restrictions on housing availability. *Criminal Justice Policy Review, 20*(1), 91–110.

Zhang, S. X. (2016). The United States. In *Migrant smuggling data and research: A global review of the emerging evidence base.* Geneva, Switzerland: International Organization for Migration.

Zhao, J., Scheider, M. C., & Thurman, Q. (2002). Funding community policing to reduce crime: Have COPS grants made a difference? *Criminology and Public Policy, 2*(1), 7–32.

Zimring, F. (2003). *The contradictions of American capital punishment.* Oxford, UK: Oxford University Press.

Zimring, F. E., & Hawkins, G. J. (1973). *Deterrence: The legal threat in crime control.* Chicago: University of Chicago Press.

INDEX

Page references for figures are indicated by *f* and for tables by *t*.

100:1 rule, 24–25
1996 Antiterrorism and Effective Death Penalty Act
    (AEDPA), 132–133
2008 financial crisis, 168
2010 Dodd-Frank Wall Street Reform and Consumer
    Protection Act, 173

absolute deterrence, 11, 122
actuarial justice, 87
Adam Walsh Child Protection and Safety Act, 41,
    43–44, 54
addiction, drug. *see also* drug policy; *specific drugs*
    chemical composition, 30
    correctional populations, 9
    criminal offenders, 225–226
    decriminalization and legalization, 26
    deterrence, 28–30
    hypodermic syringe, 19
    mass incarceration, 119
    mental illness, 226
    prescription drugs, 27–28
    treatment, 31–32, 232
adherence, treatment and rehabilitation, 236
adjudication, juvenile court, 80
adjudicatory hearing, juvenile court, 80
agencies, public, 2. *see also specific agencies*
alcohol
    criminalization, origins, 21
    Prohibition and Volstead Act, 22–23
    Temperance Movement, 22
analytical lens, 3–5
Anderson, L. H., 162
Anderson, S. H., 162
Andrews, D. A., 234
Anti-Drug Abuse Amendment Act of 1988, 100
Antiterrorism and Effective Death Penalty Act (AEDPA),
    132–133
Applebaum, P. S., 50
Arsenault, E., 160
assault rifles, 101

assault weapons
    bans
        Assault Weapons Ban of 1994, 105
        empirical status, 110
        policies, 101
        rationales, 105
    definition, 105
    label, 101
Atkins v. Virginia, 134

background checks, guns, 99, 100, 104, 108–109, 110
Bailey, W. C., 144
Baldus, D. C., 135–136
Baldus study, 135
Bales, W., 162
Barnes, G. C., 160
Beccaria, Cesare, 115, 130
Bekelman, A. B., 162
Bentham, Jeremy, 115
benzodiazepine abuse, 27
Berenson, J. A., 50
Biderman, A., 170, 174
Bonta, J., 229, 234, 235, 236
boot camps, 150
    empirical status, 161, 239
borderline personality disorder (BPD), 230
Boston's Operation Ceasefire, 64–65, 66, 72, 254–255
Bouffard, J. A., 162–163
bounded rationality perspective, sex offenders, 53–54
Bowles, R. A., 161
Boyle, D. J., 161–162
BP, *Deepwater Horizon* accident, 174
Brady Act of 1993, 100, 108–109
Brady Handgun Violence Prevention Act, 100, 108–109
Braga, A. A., 219
Breed v. Jones, 78
Brent, J. J., 161
broken-windows theory, 207, 215–216, 218, 247
Brown, Johnny St. Valentine, 24–25
brutalization hypothesis, 139

Burchfield, K. B., 50
Bureau of Alcohol, Tobacco, and Firearms (ATF),
99–101, 105
Burgess, Ernst, 227
Burrow, J., 91
Butler, H. D., 162
Buttars, A., 161
Bynum, T. S., 50

Campbell, C. M., 164
cannabis
decriminalization, federal *vs.* state, 18
history, 19
capital punishment. *see also* death penalty
federal courts, 145
legal development, in U.S., 133–134
public opinion, 142–143
racial and gender disparities, 135–136
Supreme Court, 145
in West, 131–132
Caputo, G. A., 149, 150, 159
Carr, J. B., 89
certainty, in deterrence, 10–11, 140
death penalty, 141
perceived, 12
Challenge Program, 231–232
CHINS (children in need of supervision), 85
civil abatement, gangs, 65, 69, 72–73
civil commitment
constitutionality, 41
sex offenders, 48, 51
civil gang injunctions (CGIs), 65, 69, 72–73
civil remedies, white-collar offending, 176
Clarke, R. V., 211
Clean Water Act, 173–174
cocaine, 18
100:1 crack rule, 24–25
criminalization, origins, 21
Fair Sentencing Act, 25
Harrison Act of 1914, 22
Pure Food and Drug Act of 1906, 21
coca leaves, 18
Cochran, J. K., 144
code of the street, 59–60, 61
cognitive-behavioral therapy (CBT)
Challenge Program, 231–232
empirical status, 159, 237, 238
for rehabilitation, 229–232
juveniles, 238
Cohen, M. I, 162
cohesion, 245, 249–250
social disorganization theory, 247
Coker v. Georgia, 133–134
collaboration. *see also specific types*
police–community, 250–252
unilateral sanctions *vs.* international collaboration,
196–197
collective-behavior model, gangs, 60
collective incapacitation, 13–14, 117, 124
diminishing returns, 14–15
lambda, 14
communism, perceived threat, 20–21
community-based crime control, 242–257

cohesion, informal control, and quality-of-life policing,
249–250
communities as places, 246–248
community courts, 248, 252
control, sources, 242
fear of crime, reducing, 248
ideological adjustments, public health, 255–256
local leaders, groups, and nonprofits, 254–255
police–community collaboration, 250–252
punishment-oriented system, failure, 243–244
restorative justice and victim-centered approaches, 248,
252–254
theoretical origins, 244–246
community-based control, 244–245
place-based crime prevention, 217, 245–246
community courts, 248, 252
community policing (CP), 211–212, 242
empirical status, 220–221
policy, 211–212
rationales, 218
community service, 152, 163–164
compliance, white-collar offending, 175–176
Comprehensive Crime Act of 1984, 25
Comprehensive Drug Abuse Prevention and Control Act
(CDAPCA), 23, 24
Comprehensive Gang Model, 63–64
Compstat, 213–214, 221
concealed carry laws (CCLs)
empirical status, 111–112
policies, 102–103
rationales, 107–108
Constitution, U .S.
civil commitment and, 41
gun policy and, 97–98
containment, sex offenders, 53–54, 55
control
community-based crime, 242–257 (*see also* community-
based crime control)
informal, 247, 249–250
local, policing, 206
self-control theories, gang membership, 58
social, neighborhood, 245
sources, 242
control-and-surveil approach, 243
Controlled Substances Act, 23
Convention on the Rights of the Child (UN), 200
*Convention on the Suppression of Trafficking in Persons and the
Exploitation of the Prostitution of Others* (UN), 191
co-offending, 15
Cook, P. J., 99
Correctional Program Assessment Inventory (CPAI),
237–238
correctional treatment and rehabilitation, 224–241. *see also*
treatment and rehabilitation, correctional
Costanza, S. E., 164
cost-effectiveness, intermediate sanctions, 155–156
courts
community, 248, 252
drug, 25–26, 34–35
law and policy, 1
specialized, 153
community courts, 252
empirical status, 164–165

Cox, S. M., 164
Cradock, A., 161
Crime and criminal-justice policy are driven by political, social, and economic factors, 5
crime-commission script model, sex offenders are "sick" hypothesis, 53, 54
crime mapping, 214
crime-pattern theory, 217
crime policy
    definition, 2
    political, social, and economic factors, 5
criminal justice. *see also specific topics*
    adult system, 75
    juvenile system, 75
    policy, defined, 2
criminal punishment. *see also* treatment and rehabilitation, correctional; *specific types*
    ethical justifications, 233–234
    white-collar offending, 178–179
curfews, juvenile justice
    empirical status, 89
    policies, 82
    as prevention, rationale, 86–87

data-driven policing, 212–214. *see also specific types*
    empirical status, 221–222
    policy, 212–214
Davis, R. C., 237, 238
Dawes, D., 160
day-reporting centers (DRCs), 150–151
    empirical status, 161–162
death penalty, 130–146
    Beccaria on, 130
    controversies, policy, 134–139
        brutalization hypothesis, 139
        documentation, racial, 135
        judicial elections, 138–139
        racial and gender disparities, 135–136
        warranted *vs.* unwarranted disparity, 135–136
        wrongful convictions, 136–138
    empirical status, 143–145
    executions, state *vs.* federal, 130
    history and origins, 131–135
        capital punishment, in West, 131–132
        capital punishment, U.S., legal development, 133–134
        death penalty, U.S., 132–133
        policy, controversies, 134–135
    morality, 130–131
    rationales, examining
        deterrence, 130, 139–141
        public opinion, 142–143
    retribution theory, 130
    states abolishing, 130
Decker, S., 122
decriminalization, drug, 26
    cannabis, 18, 26
Deepwater Horizon, 174
delinquency, juvenile, 79. *see also* juvenile justice
deterrence. *see also specific types*
    absolute, 11, 122
    antidrug laws, rationales, 28–30
    certainty, 10–12, 140, 141

on drug addiction, 28–30
    focused, pulling levers, 64–65, 68–69, 72
    marginal, 11, 122
    mass incarceration, 121–123
    offender-based, policing, 215
    perceptions, 12
    severity, 10–12
    swiftness, 10
    white-collar crime, 176–179
deterrence and incapacitation, 8–17
    assumptions and empirical tests, 10–16
        deterrence theory, 10–13
        incapacitation theory, 13–16
    policy and theory, 8
    policy implications, 16
    retribution and rehabilitation, 9–10
deterrence theory, 10–13
    assumptions and empirical tests, 10–13
    death penalty, 130, 139–141
    general deterrence, 10
    gun policy, 106
    limitations, 47
    mass incarceration, 121–123
    perception, 12, 139–140
    policy implications, 16
    rational-choice assumption, 121–122
    rational offenders, 43
    sex offenders, rationality, 43, 46–47
    specific (special) deterrence, 10
Dialectical-behavior therapy (DBT), 230–231
diminishing returns, collective incapacitation, 14–15
discretion
    beneficial use *vs.* misuse and abuse, 2
    street-level, 2
discretionary decision making, public agencies, 2
disparities. *see also* racial disparities; *specific types*
    gender, death penalty, 136
    racial
        death penalty, 135–136
        juvenile justice, 80–81
        mass incarceration, 118–120
    warranted *vs.* unwarranted, 135–136
disposition hearing, juvenile court, 80
disposition plan, juvenile court, 80
disproportionate minority contact, 80–81
District of Columbia v. Heller, 97, 102
diversion, juvenile justice
    empirical status, 89–90
    policies, 82–83
DNA evidence, wrongful convictions, 136–137
Dodd-Frank Wall Street Reform and Consumer Protection Act (2010), 173
Doleac, J. L., 89
drug abuse. *see also* addiction, drug; *specific laws*
    prescription drugs, 19, 27–28, 36
    prevention
        empirical status, 35–36
        rationales, 31
    treatment, 232
        drug courts, 25
        rationales, 31–32
Drug Abuse Control Amends of 1965, 23
Drug Abuse Control Amends of 1968, 23

Drug Abuse Resistance Education (D.A.R.E.), 31
drug addiction. *see* addiction, drug; drug policy
drug courts, 25–26
　empirical status, 34–35
Drug Enforcement Agency (DEA)
　origins, 23
　prescription drug abuse, 28
drug policy, 18–37
　cannabis decriminalization, 18, 26
　criminalization on drug use, 18
　empirical status, 32–36
　　drug courts, 34–35
　　prescription-pill abuse, reduction, 36
　　prevention programs, 35–36
　　war on drugs, 32–34
　federal, origins, 20–21
　laws and policies, 21–28
　　decriminalization and legalization, 26
　　drug courts, 25–26
　　early laws, 21–24
　　prescription drugs, 27–28
　　war on drugs, 24–25
　mass incarceration, 118 (*see also* mass incarceration)
　rationales, examining, 28–32
　　deterrence, 28–30
　　incapacitation, 30–31
　　prevention, 31
　　treatment, 31–32
　trends, brief history, 19
　use, U.S., 18
drugs
　gang operations, 62
　U.S. use, 18
Duwe, G., 161

Eck, J. E., 211, 219–220
educational attainment, incarceration risk, 119
effectiveness, mass incarceration, 126–127
　vs. efficiency, 114–115, 125–126
efficiency, mass incarceration, 127
Eighteenth Amendment, 22–23
election cycles, 4
electronic monitoring (EM), 151, 162
empirical evidence, 4. *see also specific topics*
　Empirical evidence is the best policy guide, 6
enhancement models, gangs, 60–61
Enmund v. Florida, 134, 140
enslavement, 186. *see also* human trafficking
Eterno, J., 249
ethical justifications, criminal punishment, 233–234
executions, state *vs.* federal, 130
expressive laws, 42

Fagan, J., 91
Fair Sentencing Act, 25
Farrell, A., 199, 201
fear of crime, reducing, 248
Federal Firearms Act (FFA) of 1938, 99
federal firearms license (FFL), 99, 100, 104
federalism, 5, 206
Feeley, M. M., 87
felony-murder convictions, 140–141
fidelity, program, correctional rehabilitation, 235, 237–238

fiduciary duty, white-collar offending, 170, 181
fines and fees, 151–152
　empirical status, 162–163
　on treatment and rehabilitation, 239
　white-collar offending, 173–174
FINS (families in need of supervision), 85, 92–93
firearm crime statistics, 96
Firearm Owners' Protection Act (FOPA) of 1986, 99, 101
firearm sentence enhancements (FSEs)
　empirical status, 110–111
　policies, 102
　rationales, 106–107
Floyd v. City of New York, 210
focused deterrence, pulling levers, 64–65, 68–69, 72
Food and Drugs Act, 172
foot patrol, 221, 248
forced labor, 187–188. *see also* human trafficking
Ford Motor Company, 167
Fornango, R., 219
foster care. *see* out-of-home placement, juvenile justice
Freud, Sigmund, 116, 227
Furman v. Georgia, 133

Gainey, R. R., 162
gang policy, 57–74
　empirical status, 70–73
　　Boston's Operation Ceasefire, 72
　　civil gang injunctions, 72–73
　　Gang Reduction Program, 71
　　G.R.E.A.T. program, 70–71
　　pulling levers, 72
　fear and street gangs, 57
　gang structures, organization, and rivalries, 62–63
　rationales, examining, 65–69
　　Boston's Operation Ceasefire, 66
　　civil gang injunctions, 69
　　Gang Reduction Program, 66–67
　　G.R.E.A.T. program, 65–66
　　intervention, 66–67
　　prevention, 65–66
　　pulling levers, 68–69
　　suppression, 68–69
　theoretical explanations, gang membership and activity, 58–61
　　enhancement, 60–61
　　individual-level predictors, 58–59
　　macrolevel and microlevel, 59–60
　U.S. overview, 63–65
　　Boston's Operation Ceasefire, 64–65, 254–255
　　civil gang injunctions, 65
　　Comprehensive Gang Model, 63–64
　　Gang Reduction Program, 64
　　G.R.E.A.T. program, 63
　　prevention, 63
　　pulling levers, 64–65
　violence and drugs, 61–62
Gang Reduction Program (GRP), 64, 66–67, 71
Gang Resistance Education and Training (G.R.E.A.T.) program, 63, 65–66, 70–71
gangsta-rap music, 61
Gault, Gerald, 78
gender disparities, death penalty, 136
general deterrence, 10

General Motors, 167
get-tough approach, 243. *see also* mass incarceration
   conservatives on, 121
   deterrence and incapacitation, 228
   history, 228
   juvenile, 79, 83, 86
   "nothing works," 78
   punishment-oriented system, 79
   sentence standardization, 157
   tough-on-crime politicians, 153
   Violent Crime Control and Law Enforcement Act, 120
   war on drugs, 24, 25, 120
Gies, S. V., 162
Glossip v. Gross, 134
Goldstein, H., 207, 219
Golub, A., 249
Gregg v. Georgia, 133
Grommon, E., 50
Gross, S. R., 137
Grossman, E. R., 89
gun buybacks
   empirical status, 111–112
   policies, 102–103
   rationales, 107–108
Gun Control Act (GCA) of 1968, 99, 100
gun policy, 96–112
   background checks, 99, 100, 104, 108–109, 110
   Constitution, 97–98
   controversy and debate, 96
   crime statistics
      firearm, 96
      handgun, 99
   empirical status, 108–112
      assault weapons bans, 110
      concealed carry and gun buybacks, 111–112
      firearm sentence enhancements, 110–111
      high-risk individuals, 108–109
   focus, high-profile incidents, 96
   markets, primary and secondary, 98
   rationales, examining, 103–108
      assault weapons bans, 105
      concealed carry and gun buybacks, 107–108
      firearm sentence enhancements, 106–107
      high-risk individuals, 103–105
   U.S. policies, 98–103
      assault weapons bans, 101
      concealed carry and gun buybacks, 102–103
      firearm sentence enhancements, 102
      high-risk individuals, 99–101
      single, lack of, 98
guns, in gangs, 61–62

habeas corpus, 132
halfway houses, 152, 164
hallucinogens, 23
Hall v. Florida, 134
Hamilton, Z. K., 164
handgun crime statistics, 99
Harmon, M. G., 127
harm-reduction model, 255–256
Harrison Act of 1914, 22
Hart, T. C., 50, 52
Healy, E., 162

heroin abuse
   prescription drug abuse on, 27
   Pure Food and Drug Act of 1906, 21
high-rate offending, correlates, 15
high-risk individuals, making guns unavailable to
   empirical status, 108–109
   policies, 99–101
   rationales, 103–105
hot-spots policing (HSP), 213, 221
house arrest, 151, 159
Huebner, B. M., 50
Hughes, L. A., 50
human-rights laws, 199–200
human trafficking, 186–203
   consent, role of, 188
   definition, 187–188
   empirical status, policies, 197–199
      domestic policies, U.S., 198–199
      international, TVPA and U.S. role, 198
      research overview, 197
   future directions, policies, 199–202
      economic sanctions, 201
      labor-migration and human-rights laws, 199–200
      law-enforcement activities, 201–202
   history, 186
   as organized crime, 189–190
   policies and origins, 190–193
      Convention on the Suppression of Trafficking in Persons and the Exploitation of the Prostitution of Others, 191
      criminal-justice *vs.* human-rights orientations, 190
      International Convention for the Suppression of the Traffic in Women, 191
      prostitution, regulation *vs.* abolition, 190–191
      Protocol to Prevent, Suppress and Punish Trafficking in Persons especially Women and Children, 191–192
      Trafficking Victims Protection Act, U.S., 192–193
      White Slave Traffic Act (1910), 191
   prevalence and victims, 188–189
   rationales, examining, 193–197
      criminal-justice response, 194–195
      human-rights response, 195–196
      unilateral sanctions *vs.* international collaboration, 196–197
Hurst v. Florida, 134
Hyatt, J. M., 160

Illinois v. Wardlow, 209
incapacitation, 8–17. *see also* deterrence and incapacitation; *specific types*
   collective, 13–15, 117, 124
   drug
      policy, 30–31
      rationales, 30–31
   mass incarceration, 123–124
   selective, 13, 15, 123–124
   sex offender policy, 48
   war on crime, 123
incapacitation theory, 13–16
   assumptions and empirical tests, 13–16
   co-offending, 15
   diminishing returns, 14–15
   offending rates, lambda, 14

policy implications, 16
replacement effects, 15
incarceration. *see also specific types*
 definition, 114
 mass, 114–129 (*see also* mass incarceration)
informal control, 249–250
information void, 3
innovation, 4
In re Gault, 78
In re Winship, 78
integrity, program, correctional rehabilitation, 235,
 237–238
intelligence-led policing (ILP)
 empirical status, 222
 policy, 213–214
intensive-supervision probation and parole (ISP), 150,
 160–161
interchangeability, 157
intermediate sanctions, 148–165
 empirical status, 158–165
 boot camps, 161
 cognitive-behavioral therapy, 159
 community service, 163–164
 day-reporting centers, 161–162
 electronic monitoring, 162
 fines and fees, 162–163
 halfway houses, 164
 intensive-supervision probation and parole, 160–161
 "nothing works," 159
 rehabilitation, 159
 RNR, 158–160
 specialized courts, 164–165
 framing, 149
 need, 148
 origins, 149–150
 politics and public opinion, 153–154
 prison *vs.* probation, 149
 rationales, examining, 154–158
 cost-effectiveness, 155–156
 interchangeability, 157
 rough equivalence, 157–158
 types, 150–153
 boot camps, 150
 community service, 152
 day-reporting centers, 150–151
 electronic monitoring, 151
 fines and fees, 151–152
 halfway houses, 152
 house arrest, 151
 intensive-supervision probation and parole, 150
 restitution, 152
 specialized courts, 153
 victim–offender mediation, 153
*International Convention for the Suppression of the Traffic
 in Women*, 191

Jacobs, J., 247
Jacob Wetterling Crimes against Children and Sexually
 Violent Offender Registration Act, 40
Jennings, W. G., 49–50
Jernigan, D. H., 89
Johnson, B. D., 91, 249
Jones v. Chappell, 140

Jordan, K. L., 91
judicial elections, death penalty and, 138–139
Jurek v. Texas, 133
just deserts, 9
 death penalty, 130, 143
justice system. *see also specific topics*
 decision-making power, 2
juvenile justice, 75–94
 delinquency, 79
 disproportionate minority contact, 80–81
 empirical status, 89–93
 curfews, 89
 diversion, 89–90
 out-of-home placement, 93
 status-offender programs, 92–93
 teen courts, 91–92
 waivers, 90–91
 history and origins, 76–79
 informality and decentralization, 75
 juvenile courts
 jurisdiction, 75
 procedures, 79–80
 policies, 81–86
 curfews, 82
 diversion, 82–83
 out-of-home placement, 85–86
 status-offender programs, 85
 teen courts, 84–85
 waivers, 83–84
 rationales, examining, 86–88
 curfews as prevention, 86–87
 status offenses as child saving, 88
 treatment and rehabilitation, 9, 87–88
 rehabilitation, 75
 status offending, 78

Kanaan, M., 161
Kansas v. Kendricks, 41
Kelling, G. L., 207, 209, 216
Kider, S. B., 161
Kilburn, J. C., 164
Kleck, G., 99, 112
Klein, M., 67, 73
Kline, P., 89
Koh, H. H., 201
Kovandzic, T., 126
Kras, K. R., 50
Kurlycheck, M. C., 91

labor migration, 188. *see also* human trafficking
 human rights laws, 199–200
laissez-faire capitalism, 175
lambda, 14
Latessa, E. J., 233, 234, 237, 238, 239
Lattimore, P. K., 160
lawmaking process, on policy–reality gap, 5
laws
 agency actors, 2
 courts, 1
 expressive, 42
 vs. policy, 1
 substantive, 3
 symbolic, 3, 97, 132–133

laws, drug, 21–28
    decriminalization and legalization, 26
    drug courts, 25–26
    early laws, 21–24
    federal, origins, 20–21
    prescription drugs, 27–28
    war on drugs, 24–25
Lawton, B. A., 219
leaders, local, enlisting, 254–255
legislation, 1. *see also specific types and topics*
Lehman Brothers, 179
Letourneau, E. J., 49
Level of Service Inventory–Revised (LSI–R), 236, 237
Levenson, J. S., 50–51
Levitt, S. D., 126
Liedka, R. V., 126
life-course theories, gang membership, 58
local leaders and groups, enlisting, 254–255
logic, policy analysis, 5
Logie, R., 122
long-term results, 4
Lowenkamp, C. T., 35, 233, 234, 235, 237, 238, 239
LSD, 23

machine guns, 101
MacKenzie, D. L., 160, 161
Maddan, S., 49
Madoff, Bernard, 167
marginal deterrence, 11, 122
Marihuana Tax Act of 1937, 23
marijuana
    decriminalization, 18, 26
    history, 18
Marshall, J. T., 49
Martinson, Robert, 77, 228–229
Martinson report, 77, 228
Marvell, T. B., 126
mass incarceration, 114–129, 244
    contemporary trends, 118–120
    definition, 114
    drug addiction, 119
    empirical status, 125–128
        effectiveness, 126–127
        effectiveness *vs.* efficiency, 114–115, 125–126
        efficiency, 127
        human costs and increased crime, 127–128
    historical trends, 115–118
    incarceration, defined, 114
    inherent logical flaws, 124
    mental illness, 119
    racial disparities, 118–120
    rationales, examining, 121–125
        deterrence, 121–123
        incapacitation, 123–125
        rehabilitation, 125
    U.S. rates, 114
    war on drugs, 118, 120
Maxson, C. L., 71
McBride, D., 161
McCleskey v. Kemp, 135
McCormick, A. E., 172
McDonald v. Chicago, 97, 102
McDougall, C., 161
McDowall, D., 89

McKay, Henry D., 227
McKee, T., 50
McKeiver v. Pennsylvania, 78
means over ends syndrome, 219–220
Mears, D. P., 90
Megan's Law, 40–41, 49
mens rea
    felony murder, 141
    white-collar offending, 177–178
Mental Health Step Down Unit program, 232
mental illness
    arrest rate, 225–226
    correctional populations, 9, 229
    criminal offenders, 225–226
    deinstitutionalization, 225–226
    drug addiction, 226
    homelessness, 226
    mass incarceration, 119
meta-analyses, 235–236
migration, 187. *see also* human trafficking
    assisted, 189
    labor, human rights laws, 199–200
    steps, 189
Miller, M., 49
Miller, N. A., 89
Minnesota v. Dickerson, 209
minority contact, disproportionate, 80–81
Mitchell, O., 35
Model Penal Code, 227
Models for Change Initiative, 92
Moffatt, S., 162
Moody Jr., C. E., 126
morality, death penalty, 130–131
Moral Reconation Therapy (MRT), 232, 237, 239
morphine, 18
Morris, N., 149, 157, 158, 163
Muftić, L. R., 162–163
Myers, D. L., 91

National Firearms Act (NFA) of 1934, 101
National Instant Check System (NICS), FBI, 100, 104, 108
National Labor Relations Act of 1935, 172
National Labor Relations Board, 172, 175
needle-exchange, 256
needs principle, correctional rehabilitation, 234–235
neighborhood-level disadvantage, 244–245
neighborhood watch, 250–251
Nichols v. United States, 41
Nobles, M. R., 50–51
nonprofits, local, enlisting, 255
Nonresidential Drug Abuse Program, 232
"nothing works," 77–78, 117, 159, 228

O'Connell, D. J., 161
offender-based deterrence, 215
offending rates, 14
Office of Substance Abuse Prevention, 24
Omnibus Anti-Drug Abuse Act of 1986, 24
100:1 rule, 24–25
Operation Ceasefire, Boston's, 64–65, 66, 72, 254–255
opinion, public. *see* public opinion
opioid abuse, surge in, 27

opium, 18
    criminalization of, origins, 21
    growth, Afghanistan, 28–29
    Harrison Act of 1914, 22
opportunity theories, policing, 217
order-maintenance policing (OMP), 209–210, 247
    empirical status, 219
    policy, 209–210
organized crime, 189–190
Ostermann, M., 161
O'Toole, M., 162
out-of-home placement, juvenile justice
    empirical status, 93
    policies, 85–86

Palermo Protocol, 191–192, 196–197
parens patriae, 76, 78
Park, Robert E., 227
partnerships, neighborhood, 247. *see also specific types*
    police–community collaboration, 250–252
Paternoster, R., 136
Payne, B. K., 162
peace, public, 246
Pearson, D. A., 161
penalty-based systems, white-collar offending, 177
penitentiary, history, 115
perception, deterrence theory, 12, 139–140
Perry v. Florida, 134
petition, juvenile court, 80
Piehl, A. M., 126
PINS (persons in need of supervision), 85
Piquero, A., 163
place-based crime prevention, 217, 245–246
place-based policing, 216–217, 221
Pleggenkuhle, B., 50
police–community collaboration, 250–252
police militarization, 207–208
police policy, 205–223
    aggressive policing, 243–244
    contemporary, and origins, 209–214
        community policing, 211–212, 242
        data-driven policing, 212–214
        intelligence-led policing, 213–214
        order-maintenance policing, 209–210
        problem-oriented policing, 210–211, 242
    decentralized model, 205–206
    empirical status, 218–222
        community policing, 220–221
        data-driven policing, 221–222
        intelligence-led policing, 222
        order-maintenance policing, 219
        problem-oriented policing, 219–220
    history of policing, U.S., 205–208
    local control and federalism, 206
    police militarization, 207–208
    rationales, examining, 215–218
        broken-windows thesis, 207, 215–216, 218
        citizen and community involvement, 218
        offender-based deterrence, 215
        place-based policing, 216–217
        problem-based prevention, 217
    Policies should be critically analyzed on the basis of logic
        and theory, 5–6
policing. *see specific types*

policy. *see also specific types*
    analysis, logic and theory, 5–6
    courts, 1
    definition, 1
    vs. law, 1
    theoretical foundation, 8
politics
    applications, 3
    Crime and criminal-justice policy are driven by
        political, social, and economic factors, 5
    crime policy, 5
    get-tough approach, 120, 121, 153 (*see also* get-tough
        approach)
    intermediate sanctions, 153–154
    white-collar offending, 181–182
Ponzi, Charles, 167
positivism, 116
Poynton, S., 162
premeditated crime, 10–11
premises
    Crime and criminal-justice policy are driven by
        political, social, and economic factors, 5
    Empirical evidence is the best policy guide, 6
    Policies should be critically analyzed on the basis of
        logic and theory, 5–6
prescription drug abuse
    laws and policies, 27–28
    problem, overlooked, 19
    reduction efforts, empirical status, 36
prescription drug monitoring programs (PDMPs), 27, 36
prison, 149. *see also* mass incarceration
    declining support for, 148
    history, 115
probation, 149
problem-based prevention, policing, 217
problem-oriented policing (POP), 210–211, 242
    empirical status, 219–220
    policy, 210–211
procedural-justice policing model, 251
process-based policing model, 251
Proffitt v. Florida, 133
Prohibition, 22–23
Project Safe Neighborhoods, 251–252, 255
proportionality principle, 9, 141
prostitution. *see also* human trafficking
    involuntary (*see also* human trafficking)
        prevalence and victims, 188–189
    regulation *vs.* abolition, 190–191
    voluntary, 188
*Protocol to Prevent, Suppress and Punish Trafficking in Persons
    especially Women and Children* (UN), 191–192
    unilateral sanctioning and pushback, 196–197
public health, 255–256
public opinion
    death penalty, 142–143
    intermediate sanctions, 153–154
    invoking, 3
public peace, 246
public policy. *see also specific policies*
    definition, 1
Pulaski, C., 135
pulling levers, 64–65
    empirical status, 72
    focused deterrence, 68–69

punishment, 10. *see also* deterrence theory
punishment, criminal. *see also* treatment and
    rehabilitation, correctional; *specific types*
  ethical justifications, 233–234
punishment-oriented system. *see also specific topics*
  failures and collateral consequences, 243–244
  get-tough approach, 79 (*see also* get-tough approach)
Pure Food and Drug Act of 1906, 21

quality-of-life policing, 249–250
quick fixes, short-term, 4

racial disparities
  death penalty, 135–136
  juvenile justice, 80–81
  mass incarceration, 118–120
Rasmussen, A., 92
rational-choice theory, 13, 217
Reasoning and Rehabilitation (R&R), 232, 237
recidivism
  general *vs.* offense-specific, 44
  prevalence, 224
  sex-offender, 39–40, 43–44, 49
Recommended Principles and Guidelines on Human Rights and
    Human Trafficking (UN), 200
refugees, 187, 200. *see also* human trafficking
registration and notification, sex offenders, 39–40, 46–47,
  49–50
rehabilitation, 9–10, 224–241. *see also* treatment and
    rehabilitation, correctional
  early history, 116–117
  empirical status, 159
  juvenile justice, 9, 75, 87–88
  mass incarceration, 125
  philosophy, 9–10
Reiss, Jr., A. J., 170, 174
Rengifo, A. F., 219
reoffending
  prevalence, 224 (*see also* recidivism)
  sex offenders, assumption, 43–44
replacement effects, 15
  drug crimes, 30
residency restrictions (RR), sex offenders
  empirical evaluations, 39–40
  empirical status, 50–51
  history, 41–42
  rationales, 47–48
Residential Drug Abuse Program, 232
Resolve Program, 232
responsivity, correctional rehabilitation, 234–235
restitution, 152
  on treatment and rehabilitation, 239
restorative justice, 248, 252–254
retribution, 9–10
  death penalty, 130
Reynolds, K. M., 89
risk prediction, offending, 15
risk principle, correctional rehabilitation, 234
RNR (risk, need, responsivity) model, 9
  empirical status, 158–160
  juveniles, 87
Roiper v. Simmons, 134
Romero, M. P., 111
Rosenfeld, R., 219

rough equivalence, 157–158
routine-activity approach, 217
Rydberg, J., 50

Salisbury, E. J., 127
Salt, J., 189
SARA model (scanning, analysis, response, assessment),
  211, 218, 220
Sarbanes-Oxley Act of 2002, 172–173
sawed-off shotguns, 101
Schedule I drugs, 23
Schedule II drugs, 23
Schedule III drugs, 23–24
Schedule IV drugs, 24
Schedule V drugs, 24
scholars, criminology and criminal-justice, 3–4
scientific evidence, 4
scientific positivism, 116
selection model, gangs, 60
selective incapacitation, 13, 15, 123–124
self-control theories, gang membership, 58
sentencing hearing, juvenile court, 80
setting, treatment and rehabilitation programs
  institutions *vs.* community, 238–239
  post-release, 239
severity, in deterrence, 10–11
  perceived, 12
sex offender policy, 39–55
  alternative
    bounded rationality, 53–54
    containment, 53–54, 55
    crime-commission script, 53, 54
    evidence-based practices, 54
    situational crime prevention, 53–54
  empirical status, 49–53
    civil commitment, 51
    collateral consequences, 52–53
    registration and notification, 49–50
    residency restrictions, 50–51
  history, 40–42
    Adam Walsh Child Protection and Safety Act, 41,
      43–44, 54
    Jacob Wetterling Crimes against Children and
      Sexually Violent Offender Registration
      Act, 40
    Megan's Law, 40–41, 49, 53
    Wetterling case, 39, 40, 53
  rationales, examining, 42–48
    geographic proximity, 47–48
    offender-centered, 42–43
    sex-offender label, 43, 44–46
    sex offenders are "sick," 43
    sex offenders will reoffend, 43–44
    shaming and deterrence, 46–47
    treatment and incapacitation (civil commitment), 48
  residency restrictions, 39–42, 47–48
  sex-offender recidivism, 39–40, 43–44
sex-offender registration and notification
    (SORN) laws
  empirical evaluations, 39–40
  history, 40
  rationale, 46–47
sex offenders are "sick" hypothesis, 43
sex offenders will reoffend assumption, 43–44

sex trafficking, female. *see also* human trafficking
    prevalence, 188–189
    risk, 187
Shapiro, S. P., 170
Shaw, Clifford, 227
Sherman Antitrust Act of 1890, 171–172
Simon, J., 87
simultaneity, 126
situational approaches, 13. *see also* community-based
        crime control
    place-based policing, 216–217, 221
    place-based prevention, 217, 245–246
    sex offenders, 53–54
slavery, 186. *see also* human trafficking
smuggling, 188. *see also* human trafficking
social control, neighborhood, 245
social disorganization theory, 245, 247
    gang membership, 59–60
specialized courts, 153
    community courts, 252
    empirical status, 164–165
specific (special) deterrence, 10
Spelman, W., 126, 211
Spergel Model, 63
status offender, juvenile justice, 78
status-offender programs, juvenile justice
    as child saving, rationale, 88
    empirical status, 92–93
    policies, 85
Stein, J., 189
Steiner, B., 91, 162
stigma, civil *vs.* criminal conviction, 176
Stockholm Syndrome, 194
stop and frisk, 210, 219, 243–244
street code, 59–60, 61
street-level discretion, 2
structural approaches, 13
submachine guns, 101
substance abuse. *see also* addiction, drug;
        drug abuse
    correctional populations, 9
    criminal offenders, 225–226
substantive laws, 3
Sundt, J., 127
"superpredator," 78
Supreme Court, United States
    capital punishment, 145
    increased size, Roosevelt's, 20
    interstate commerce regulation, 20
    on legislation, 1
surveillance, 243
Sutherland, E. H., 170, 181, 227
swiftness, in deterrence, 10
symbolic laws, 3, 97, 132–133

Taxman, F. S., 163
Taylor, A., 249
teen courts
    empirical status, 91–92
    policies, 84–85
Telep, C. W., 219
Temperance Movement, 22
Terry v. Ohio, 209
Tewksbury, R., 49–50

theory. *see also specific topics and types*
    policy analysis, 5–6
    policy grounding, 8
Therapeutic-community (TC) treatment, 231
Thinking for a Change (T4C), 232
third-party policing, 250
Tison v. Arizona, 134
Title II, Controlled Substances Act, 23
tommy guns, 101
Tonry, M., 149, 157, 158, 163
Torgerson, D. J., 161
trafficking
    drug, 31, 32
    human, 186–202 (*see also* human trafficking)
    sex, 187–189
Trafficking in Persons (TIP) reports, 193
Trafficking Victims Protection Act (TVPA), U.S., 192–193
    empirical status, 198
    T visas, 195
    unilateral sanctioning and pushback, 196–197
transfers, juvenile. *see* waivers, juvenile justice
treatment and rehabilitation, correctional, 224–241
    current trends, 228–229
    empirical status, 235–240
        adherence, 236
        boot camp, 239
        cognitive-behavioral therapy, 159, 237, 238
        Correctional Program Assessment Inventory, 237–238
        fines, fees, and restitution, 239
        implementation barriers, 239–240
        juveniles *vs.* adults, 238
        Level of Service Inventory–Revised, 236, 237
        low-risk *vs.* high-risk offenders, 234, 236–237
        meta-analyses, 235–236
        Moral Reconation Therapy, 237, 239
        program integrity, 235, 237–238
        Reasoning and Rehabilitation, 237
        risk, 236–237
        settings, 238–239
        supplementation, 237
        treatment modality, importance, 237
    history, 227–228
    implementation, 224
    inadequacies, 224–225
    mental illness and substance abuse, criminal offenders,
        225–226
    rationale, examining, 233–235
        juvenile justice, 9, 87–88
        principles, effective correctional rehabilitation,
          234–235
        rehabilitation and ethical justifications, 233–234
    reoffending, prevalence, 224
    techniques and programs, 229–233
        Challenge Program, 231–232
        cognitive-behavioral therapy, 229–232
        dialectical-behavior therapy, 230–231
        drug treatment, 232
        Mental Health Step Down Unit program, 232
        Moral Reconation Therapy, 232
        Reasoning and Rehabilitation, 232
        Resolve Program, 232
        therapeutic-community treatment, 231
        Thinking for a Change, 232
trial, juvenile court, 80

Tueller, S., 160
turf, gang, 60
T visas, 195
two-part system, 5
2010 Dodd-Frank Wall Street Reform and Consumer
    Protection Act, 173

United Nations
    Convention on the Rights of the Child, 200
    *Convention on the Suppression of Trafficking in Persons and
        the Exploitation of the Prostitution of Others*, 191
    *Protocol to Prevent, Suppress and Punish Trafficking in
        Persons especially Women and Children*, 191–192
    *Recommended Principles and Guidelines on Human Rights
        and Human Trafficking*, 200
    World Congress on the Environment (1972), 173
United States v. Comstock, 41
unwarranted disparity, 135–136
Useem, B., 126

VanderWaal, C., 161
victim-centered approaches, 252–254
victim–offender mediation, 153
Victims of Trafficking and Violence Protection Act (TVPA),
    U.S., 192–193
    empirical status, 192–193
    T visas, 195
    unilateral sanctioning and pushback, 196–197
Vieraitis, L. M., 126
violence
    gang, 60–62
    gun (*see* gun policy)
Violent Crime Control and Law Enforcement Act of
    1994, 101
Visher, C. A., 161
Volstead Act, 22–23
Voltaire, 115

waivers, juvenile justice
    empirical status, 90–91
    policies, 83–84
Walker, J. T., 49
Wallace, L. N., 89
Walsh Act, 41, 43–44, 54
war on crime, 117. *see also* mass incarceration
    incapacitation, 123
war on drugs
    Comprehensive Drug Abuse Prevention and Control
        Act, 24
    empirical status, 32–34
    failure, 18
    history, 117–118
    Latin America, as pretense, 21
    launch, 24
    laws and policies, 24–25
    mass incarceration, 118, 120
    on prison population, 25, 149
    on urban policing, 25
warranted disparity, 135
Weatherburn, D., 162
Weisburd, D., 219
Weisburd, S., 219

Wetterling, Jacob, 39, 40
Wetterling Act, 40
white-collar offending, 167–184
    2008 financial crisis, 168
    criminal prosecutions, few, 168–169
    definitions, 168, 169–170, 180–181
    fiduciary duty, 170, 181
    Ford Motor Company, 167
    General Motors, 167
    history, 167–168
    laws and policies, history, 170–174
        Clean Water Act, 173–174
        Dodd-Frank Wall Street Reform and Consumer
            Protection Act (2010), 173
        fines and damages, corporations, 173–174
        Food and Drugs Act, 172
        government and business connections, 171
        National Labor Relations Act of 1935, 172
        regulator agencies, 170–171
        Sarbanes-Oxley Act of 2002, 172–173
        Sherman Antitrust Act of 1890, 171–172
    laws and policies, theory implications,
        179–183
        criminal-law enforcement, 182
        definitions, criminal-law violations, 180–181, 182
        detection, 183
        education, business executives, 183
        opportunities, reducing, 182–183
        popular and political will, 181–182
        research, policy effectiveness, 179–180
        research, policy organizational and occupational
            offending, 180
    offender's social status, 170
    Ponzi and Madoff, 167
    rationales, examining, 174–179
        compliance, 175–176
        deterrence, 176–179
        proactive *vs.* reactive regulations, 174
White Slave Traffic Act (1910), 191
Wilson, D. B., 35, 161
Wilson, J. A., 237, 238
Wilson, J. Q., 117, 207, 209, 216
women, human (sex) trafficking
    prevalence, 188–189
    risk, 187 (*see also* human trafficking)
Wooditch, A., 219
Woodworth, G., 135
World Congress on the Environment, UN (1972), 173
Wright, E., 91
Wright, R., 122
wrongful convictions, death penalty and, 136–138

Yang, S. M., 219
Yeide, M., 162
Youstin, T. J., 50–51
youth courts. *see* teen courts

Zajac, G., 160
Zandbergen, P. A., 50, 52
zero-tolerance policies, school, 88
Zevitz, R. G., 49
Zgoba, K. M., 50